Ian Marcousé

AQA BUSINESS STUDIES for *A2* 2nd Edition

Andrew Gillespie

Malcolm Surridge

DYNAMIC LEARNING

HODDER EDUCATION
AN HACHETTE UK COMPANY

Acknowledgements

Every effort has been made to trace the copyright holders of material reproduced here, and to credit the sources used in research.

Crown copyright material is licensed under the Open Government Licence vl.0.

The authors and publishers would like to thank the following for permission to reproduce copyright illustrations:

Fig 2.1 © Rex Features; Fig 4.3 © Imagestate Media (John Foxx); Fig 7.1 © Lilyana Vynogradova – Fotolia; Fig 7.2 © ABACA/Press Association Images; Fig 10.2 © miles5 – Fotolia; Fig 11.1 © Martin Lee/Rex Features; Fig 12.1 © PA Archive/Press Association Images; Fig 13.2 © thefatcat – Fotolia; Fig 16.3 Courtesy H.J. Heinz Company Limited; Fig 17.2 © AP/Press Association Images; Fig 20.1 © Vittorio Zunino Celotto/Getty Images; Fig 23.1 © amana images inc./Alamy; Fig 25.3 © iphoto – Fotolia; Fig 26.1 © Daily Mail/Rex Features; Fig 26.2 © Design Pics Inc./Alamy; Fig 30.2 © Jonathan Hordle/Rex Features; Fig 31.3 © AP/Press Association Images; Fig 32.2 © stocker1970 – Fotolia; Fig 33.2 and 38.3 © PA Archive/Press Association Images; Fig 41.2 © lulù – Fotolia; Fig 43.1 © Alex Segre/Rex Features; Fig 45.2 © Photodisc/Getty Images; Fig 50.2 © Rex Features.

Orders: please contact Bookpoint Ltd, 130 Milton Park, Abingdon, Oxon OX14 4SB. Telephone: (44) 01235 827720. Fax: (44) 01235 400454. Lines are open from 9.00 to 5.00, Monday to Saturday, with a 24-hour message answering service. You can also order through our website www.hoddereducation.co.uk

If you have any comments to make about this, or any of our other titles, please send them to educationenquiries@hodder.co.uk

British Library Cataloguing in Publication Data
A catalogue record for this title is available from the British Library

ISBN: 978 1444 16818 1

First Edition Published 2009
This Edition Published 2012
Impression number   10 9 8 7 6 5 4 3 2 1
Year   2015, 2014, 2013, 2012

Hachette UK's policy is to use papers that are natural, renewable and recyclable products and made from wood grown in sustainable forests. The logging and manufacturing processes are expected to conform to the environmental regulations of the country of origin.

Cover photo © Lew Robertson/Corbis.
Typeset by Fakenham Prepress Solutions, Fakenham, Norfolk NR21 8NN
Printed in Italy for Hodder Education, An Hachette UK Company, 338 Euston Road, London NW1 3BH.

Contents

Section 5 Operations management

Section 6 External influences

Section 7 Managing change

Section 8 Exam technique

What's different about A2?

Definition

As you start your second year, you must ask yourself the question: 'What's different about A2?' Three key differences stand out:

1 A2 focus on objectives and strategy

2 The introduction of the external context

3 More challenging assessment objectives.

 ## Framing an answer – objectives and strategy

AS Business Studies looks at what managers *actually* do day by day; e.g. set budgets, hire staff and check on the quality of the firm's output. In effect, these are the jobs of middle managers in large organisations. A2 starts to look at what managers *should* do, especially those in more senior roles. In particular, it looks at how they should be thinking.

Junior managers ask: What must I do today? And perhaps have a checklist of things that must be done. More senior managers (especially company directors) should be asking themselves: Where are we heading? Where *should* we be heading? And what do we have to do to get there?

Some bosses have made huge impacts on the world by their amazingly bold ambitions. When, in 1999, a small new company talked of 'organising the world's information', it seemed crazily ambitious. Today Google's claim looks ever-more plausible. In most cases, directors set far more ordinary ambitions than this, but they still see it as essential to point out the goal on the horizon, and then set the path (the strategy) for getting there.

Your answers need to adopt that style. You need to see that the answer to every business question needs to bear in mind the objective and strategy being pursued. A core A2 topic is called 'investment appraisal', i.e. how to decide whether or not to spend money on an investment such as launching a new product. It is partly a number-crunching exercise, but will force you to decide, perhaps between two investment possibilities. Most students choose simply on the basis of which is estimated to be the more profitable. Most managers will choose on the basis of which fits in better with the firm's objectives. Top students consider both factors before making their recommendations.

In the coming weeks, you will look at the firm's overall objectives (goals) and then at the functional objectives, i.e. the goal for each of the business functions: marketing, finance, people and operations. Usually the objectives are set at a very senior level, and then more junior managers decide on a strategy (a plan) to achieve the objective.

From now on, before answering any question that carries 8 or more marks, always ask yourself the question: what are this firm's objectives? What are the functional objectives? And what strategies have been put in place to achieve them. Later in the term you should then be in a position to start questioning whether, for example, the objectives are sensible. In April 2011 Sony launched its first two tablet computers, in response to the hugely successful iPad2. It set itself the target of becoming the second biggest seller in the global market within a year. At least it hadn't said it would beat Apple, but it still seemed overly-ambitious given the strength of Samsung, HTC and HP within this market sector. Top students are willing to question firms' objectives and strategies.

The introduction of the external context

Doubtless your AS teacher talked last year about the economy and other factors outside the control of the business. But in fact they only appear on the A2 specification. Therefore, examiners will be especially comfortable about giving high marks to candidates showing a good grasp of this A2 subject matter.

Strictly speaking, this material is covered in Unit 4, not Unit 3. Therefore, you may not be taught the content of Unit 4 until after Christmas. Yet it is hard to see how a firm can set its objectives and strategy without thinking about the economy (ask Northern Rock shareholders). So a broad understanding of the economy will be helpful when answering Unit 3 questions about objectives and strategy.

To develop this understanding, reading *Business Review* magazine will help. Even better, though, is to look regularly at the Business section of the BBC's website www.bbc.co.uk. Don't bore yourself by trawling through loads of articles. Just choose one headline relating to the economy and read that one article. Ask your parents or teacher for explanation, by all means, but even if 20% is a mystery, you will benefit hugely from the 80% you can understand. Here are some ideas of typical article headings that would be really good to read:

- 'Unemployment up/down'
- 'Interest rate shock!'
- 'Pound up/down'
- 'Inflation up/down'
- 'Is Chinese growth slowing?'
- 'Recession/Boom'
- 'Government action...'
- 'Consumer spending boom/slump'.

When you start learning about the economy and other factors outside the control of the business in the classroom, you will find that you are far better able to understand the issues being raised. This, in turn, will make it much easier to understand some of the trickier concepts that exist within the economic aspects of business.

Exam answers and A2

It is important to note the differences in the way you are examined at A2. At AS, 60% of the marks come from showing 'Knowledge and understanding' and 'Application'. At A2 those skills account for just 40% of the marks. As you can see from Table 1.1, the bulk of A2 marks come from Analysis and Evaluation.

Table 1.1 Percentage of marks awarded at AS and A2

	AS	A2	Total
Knowledge and understanding	30%	20%	25%
Application	30%	20%	25%
Analysis	20%	30%	25%
Evaluation	20%	30%	25%
TOTAL	100%	100%	100%

Meaning of 'Analysis' and 'Evaluation' at A2

At A2, these two skills can be interpreted as follows.

- *A2 Analysis*: well-structured and well-developed arguments showing a clear sense of cause (Why did it happen?) and effect (What were the consequences?). The depth of argument is rooted in the ability to select and use appropriate business concepts or models. (Differences between 'Analysis' at AS and A2 are shown in Table 1.2.)

- *A2 Evaluation*: judgement shown throughout an answer, both when weighting an argument and when choosing the right words. The judgements made must be justified and should be appropriate to the specific business context and the specific question. Such judgements are helped by a broad understanding of the different problems of different businesses (large, small, manufacturing, etc.) and broad knowledge of the external context: the economy, the environment, social and ethical issues and the law. (Differences between 'Evaluation' at AS and A2 are shown in Table 1.3.)

Table 1.2 Differences between 'Analysis' at AS and A2

AS Analysis	A2 Analysis
The effect of the credit crunch on Tesco was not too bad. Its profits stopped rising as quickly and its decision to delay paying suppliers was probably a mistake. But while other firms were collapsing or needing to make staff redundant, Tesco did not need to take drastic action because people still needed their weekly shopping, so sales held up well.	Tesco was in a very strong position to survive the crunch because supermarkets provide essentials as well as luxuries, and Tesco's range went from 'Value' to 'Finest'. Its market dominance was also crucial, forcing suppliers to give Tesco the best promotional deals. It was able to set an aggressive strategy to meet a bold objective, whereas others just hoped for survival.

Table 1.3 Differences between 'Evaluation' at AS and A2

AS Evaluation	A2 Evaluation
The impact on Tesco was not too bad because it was fortunate enough to be operating in the supermarket sector. So the managers were never tested as sharply as those at the banks or house building firms. So the main single factor that helped them was luck.	Tesco had huge advantages over almost any other business in Britain. The fact that its management struggled at times shows how massive a shock came from the credit crunch and the recession. Fortunately for Tesco managers, continuing sales success stopped mistakes from becoming crises. No business is recession-proof, but Tesco is closer to this than any other British business.

In most of the above, the best single aid to improved performance is to read *Business Review*. Your teacher will know how to buy a subscription, but it is probably also available in your school/college library.

 ## Conclusion

A2 Business Studies is a significant step up from AS. The subject matter is tougher, the exam questions are tougher and your answers need to be more solidly based in theory. Nevertheless, there remain two key foundations. First, you must be able to define precisely the business terms you are using, i.e. accurate knowledge. Second, you must grasp the implications of the business context, i.e. be able to show the skill of application. Above all else, the more you read about business and the economy, the better able you'll be to distinguish between big issues and trivial ones. And that is virtually the definition of a top business student.

2

Corporate aims, mission and culture

> ### Definition
> Aims are a generalised statement of where you are heading, from which objectives can be set. A mission is a more fervent, passionate way of expressing an aim. Business culture is the ethos of the business – in other words, the ideas and attitudes that prevail among the workforce.

Introduction

Some children as young as 10 or 11 years of age seem very clear about what they want from life. They are determined to become a doctor or a vet. The clarity of their aim makes them work hard at school, choose science subjects and overcome any setbacks (a 'duff' maths teacher, perhaps). So whereas most GCSE/A-level students drift from one day to the next, these individuals are focused: they have their eyes on their prize. This is the potentially huge benefit that can stem from clear aims.

Indeed, you could say that some of these focused students are driven by a sense of mission. Their aim is not just to get the label of 'doctor' but also to make a contribution to making the world a better place. The drive shown by these students will be the most impressive of all.

For new small businesses there can also be a powerful sense of mission. A chef may open his/her own restaurant, driven largely by the desire to win a Michelin star (the *Michelin Guide* to restaurants is the world's most prestigious). In Gordon Ramsay style, the approach to achieving this may prove to be ruthless or even fanatical. Yet such a person is far more likely to achieve their aim than one who opens a restaurant thinking 'It would be nice to get a star; let's see whether it happens.'

In fiercely competitive marketplaces, passionate and determined businesses are always more likely to succeed than those that are drifting. This has been one of the secrets to the success of the *Sun* newspaper. Its owner and editors have always believed passionately that its mix of fun and sport works because it gives people what they want. Their view is that newspapers should not 'preach' to their readers. The *Mirror* used to be Britain's number one paper, but it has drifted back to number three, out-fought and out-thought by the *Sun*.

From the clear sense of mission at the *Sun* has come its workplace culture. This is cut-throat and ruthless, with the drive to get the best stories and the best scoops. It has also led to many headlines that are on the borderline between acceptable and disgraceful.

To switch examples, consider the position of the John Lewis Partnership. This employee-owned business (Waitrose and John Lewis stores) has a mission statement that reads: 'Our purpose is the happiness of all our members (employees) through their worthwhile, satisfying employment in a successful business.' By putting its staff first, John Lewis makes clear how different it is from

Figure 2.1 Gordon Ramsay

most businesses. The culture of the organisation fits in with this, as it is famously based on respect for each other, for customers, but above all for the institution that is John Lewis (one of the world's biggest employee-owned businesses).

To achieve a high grade at this subject, full understanding of this chapter is critical, because aims, mission and culture are fundamental to business success, and therefore exam success.

Aims

Aims are the generalised statement of where the business is heading. Possible examples include:

- 'to become a profitable business with a long-term future' (Zayka Indian restaurant, stated in January 2011)
- 'to become a football league club' (AFC Wimbledon, stated in 2008; achieved in 2011)
- 'to diversify away from dependence on Britain' (the implicit aim of Tesco in the past ten years).

One of the stated aims of the McDonald's fast food chain is to provide 'friendly service in a relaxed, safe and consistent restaurant environment'. The success of the organisation depends upon turning this aim into practice. In order for this to be achieved, employees must understand and share the aim. When a customer enters a McDonald's restaurant anywhere in the world they know what to expect. The organisation has the ability to reproduce the same 'relaxed, safe and consistent' atmosphere with different staff, in different locations. This has built the company's reputation. This corporate aim is effective because it recognises what lies at the heart of the organisation's success.

But do aims need to be written down? Many businesses do not write down their aims or even spend time trying to define them. This is particularly true of small organisations where employees know each other and understand their shared purpose. Even when an aim is unstated it may be possible to identify it by looking at the actions taken by a firm over time. Staff in a small firm may work together to achieve a common aim with a level of commitment that may not exist in a large firm that sets out its aims in writing.

Whether stated or unstated, corporate aims act as a basis upon which to form goals or objectives for the organisation (see Unit 3). These are the targets that must be achieved if the aims are to be realised. The success or failure of each individual decision within the firm can be judged by the extent to which it meets the business objectives. This allows the delegation of authority within the organisation, while at the same time maintaining coordination.

Mission statements

A **mission statement** is an attempt to put corporate aims into words that inspire. The mission statement

of Wal-Mart, the world's biggest retailer, is 'to give ordinary folk the chance to buy the same thing as

A-grade application

Examples of mission statements

- *Pret A Manger:* 'Pret creates handmade natural food avoiding the obscure chemical additives and preservatives common to so much of the prepared and "fast" food on the market today'
- *Twitter:* 'To instantly connect people everywhere to what's most important to them'
- *Body Shop:* 'Tirelessly work to narrow the gap between principle and practice, whilst making fun, passion and care part of our daily lives'
- *Coca-Cola:* 'To refresh the world – in body, mind and spirit'
- *James Dyson:* 'Long-term business success based on newly invented, innovatively designed products'
- *Nike:* 'To bring innovation and inspiration to every athlete* in the world' (*If you have a body you are an athlete)

rich people'. Shop floor staff are more likely to be motivated by a mission statement of this kind than by the desire to maximise profit.

It is hoped that, by summarising clearly the long-term direction of the organisation, a focus is provided that helps to inspire employees to greater effort and ensure the departments work together. Without this common purpose each area of a firm may have different aims and choose to move in conflicting directions.

It is also important to note that not every company has a written mission statement. The bosses of Innocent Drinks have always been clear that they and their staff 'live the mission' and therefore do not need to write it down. Marks & Spencer plc has stopped publicising a mission statement, perhaps because it has learnt that one statement cannot sum up the driving forces behind a whole, complex business.

For those that do use mission statements, the model shown in Figure 2.2 gives a clear sense of their purpose. To develop a strong mission statement it is necessary to link each of the four elements of the model so that they reinforce one another.

PURPOSE
Why the company exists

STRATEGY
The competitive position
of the company

VALUES
What the company
believes in

STANDARDS
AND
BEHAVIOURS
The policies and behaviour
patterns expected of
company employees

Figure 2.2 The mission model

In turn, each element suggests the following.

- *Purpose (i.e. the reason why the company exists).* This is clearly shown by the Nike **mission**, which emphasises the desire to provide innovative products for athletes. In fact a sceptic could point out that Nike builds much of its branding around advertising, imagery and visual design rather than product innovation. Nike's brilliance has been to keep everyone sure that the company cares about supporting athletes, rather than exploiting them.

- *Values (i.e. what the company believes in).* In the case of Pret A Manger, it is not just that it believes

in natural, fresh food, but also that the business has always:
  - used packaging that is made from recycled materials and can be recycled in future
  - taken care to source its products from suppliers that treat staff fairly
  - wanted to push customers to try new things, especially from sustainable sources.

The values of the business are a key part of its culture, and should also include the way staff are treated and other ethical considerations.

- *Standards and behaviours (i.e. the standards set by managers and the behaviour expected from staff).* Cambridge graduate Polly Courtney has told the *Observer* about her experiences as a highly paid banker in the City. The work culture meant that people would send emails at 2.00 in the morning to show how late they worked, and Polly found sexism rooted in a 'lads' culture in which nights out ended at the strip club. As the only woman in an office of 21, she was treated like a secretary and bypassed for the more important jobs. Polly wrote a book about her experiences, whereas others have successfully sued merchant banks on grounds of sex discrimination. Clearly the managements are wholly at fault in allowing such a situation to develop.

- *Strategy (i.e. the medium- to long-term plans adopted by the business to make the aims and mission achievable).* This is dealt with in Unit 4.

How valuable are mission statements?

As an example of the possible downsides of mission statements, it is interesting to look back at companies' former mission statements. For example, Coca-Cola used to say: 'Our mission is to get more people to drink Coke than water.' Today that seems quite a shocking idea. Clearly it would mean a dramatic worsening of the obesity problem that affects most of the developed world. Yet Coca-Cola had this as its mission statement up until ten years ago. The fact that it has dropped this statement in favour of the socially more acceptable 'to refresh the world' raises the question of whether mission statements are little more than public relations exercises.

Even more serious is the possibility that mission statements are a substitute for the real thing. They may be a bureaucratic management's attempt to provide a sense of purpose in a business that has none. If so, this would be the wrong way to approach the problem. If staff lack inspiration, the starting point is to find a real sense of purpose, probably through the staff themselves. For example, doctors and nurses used to be hugely proud to work for the NHS; now they are more likely to moan about its shortcomings. Writing a mission statement would be treated with derision by the staff. Far more important is to find out from staff what they dislike about the current management and discuss how to restore staff pride in the service.

Culture

Culture can be described as 'the way we do things round here'. In other words, it's the attitudes and behaviours shown within the workplace. This will be built up over many years as a result of:

● the aims or mission of the business: if the aim is to be innovative, this should affect the business culture

● the behaviour of the company directors and other senior staff: if they pay themselves huge bonuses and jump at chances to fly business class to questionable conferences, staff will pick up the idea that 'me, me, me' is at the heart of the business culture

● the attitude of senior management to enterprise and risk: if a failed new product launch leads to the dismissal of the manager leading the project, this will send out a message to all staff to beware of taking on responsibility, which could be very damaging in the long term

● the recruitment and training procedures: research has shown that dynamic companies have a mixture of different types of staff – some who are very organised, some who are creative but perhaps chaotic, some who are argumentative and so on; some HR departments use psychometric tests to recruit 'our type of person' and screen out potential 'troublemakers'; the culture could become quite passive – safe but dull – if new recruits are always the same type of efficient but uninspired people.

The culture of the business has many aspects that are fundamental to its success or failure. First are the business values. An organisation's mission statement provides an opportunity to shape this business culture. The challenge is to develop a set of values that employees can feel proud of. It should also motivate them to work towards the organisation's objectives. This may be difficult to achieve, particularly in large companies where each different department of the firm may have its own culture. In this case there may be no dominant corporate culture.

A-grade application

In 2011, two-and-a-half years after being taken over by Belgium's 'InBev' (for $52 billion), the US staff at the Budweiser brewery still hate the new culture. Budweiser was run as a huge family business, whereas InBev (brewers of Stella Artois and many more) is regarded at being 'about charts and sliderules'. Since the takeover profits have jumped ahead, but the US staff believe that poor staff morale has already hit market share, and so profits will suffer later. The company's internal research shows that its staff in Russia are happier than those in America.

The business culture will show through in many ways, including those described below.

● The team versus the individual: some organisations work in a 'dog-eat-dog' fashion, in which individuals are climbing up the career ladder partly through their ability to cut the rungs away from their rivals; in others, an individual's effectiveness when working with a team is especially highly prized.

● Attitude to hard work: in some businesses, as in some schools, the group norm is to laugh at those who work hard – they may be referred to as 'crawlers' (or worse). To survive, such a business must have a protected, perhaps monopoly, position. At the other extreme are organisations where working 12- to 15-hour days is regarded as a proper sign of commitment, such as in some City merchant banks. Perhaps the ideal is a boss who expects people to give their best throughout the day, but encourages everyone to go home at 5.30.

● Customer-centred or focused inwards? This is crucial, as many organisations allow staff to develop a 'them and us' attitude to customers. Customers can be viewed as the inconvenient people who disrupt the day-to-day life of the staff. One of Britain's main exam boards set up a call centre so that teachers could no longer phone staff directly, thereby 'distracting them from getting on with their jobs'. Yet what is an exam board for other than to serve its customers: teachers?

● **Attitude to risk:** as mentioned above, the key thing here is whether the business establishes an enterprising, risk-taking culture – as at Apple, Nintendo, Innocent and Toyota – or a bureaucratic culture in which risks are eliminated by layer after layer of managers who never seem to make

decisions. (Career advice: make sure to avoid working for such a frustrating business.)

● **Ethical stance:** the culture will help staff to know how to deal with difficult decisions, such as 'Should I accept this invite for a chat with our main competitor about prices?' or 'Should I accept this Christmas present from our main supplier?' In the best-run companies, staff will know that the business and all its employees are never to cut moral corners, even if profits are hit as a result.

A-grade application

Reckitt Benckiser

Reckitt Benckiser is the company behind Cillit Bang, Lemsip, Dettol, Strepsils and many other household brands. It's a big business, with annual profits of £1 billion, but it competes with two giants: Unilever and Procter & Gamble. Reckitt's chief executive, Bart Becht, says that the group's culture is 'the number one driver of success – no question. It is our only sustainable advantage. Everything else can be copied, but it's close to impossible to copy culture.'

A key target for Reckitt is that at least 40% of sales should come from products launched within the past three years. Therefore the business culture involves swift

decision making, innovation and risk-taking. Those joining the company can find the culture a bit of a shock, as it is fast-paced and quite aggressive. The low managerial labour turnover (10%), though, makes it clear that staff enjoy the achievement-focused culture. A recent recruit from rival Procter & Gamble describes the culture as 'much leaner, much more informal, much more individualistic' than that of his previous employer.

It is clear that Reckitt's 'strong' culture is needed for the number three business competing with two giants. It provides the strength, and the speed of thought and action that keeps the company successful.

Issues for analysis

In order to analyse the aims of an organisation there are a number of key issues that should be considered. These include the following.

● Are employees aware of what the organisation is trying to achieve? Is it necessary to write down these aims? Ideally, an understanding of the purpose of the business should be embedded so deeply in staff that it influences their actions without them realising it.

● If the aims are clear, is there really any need to repackage them as a mission statement? It may be that the process of devising a mission

statement is a worthwhile one, especially if all staff are involved. Yet the final text may be no more than a statement of the obvious, or may be so over the top that no one can take it seriously.

● Another key question for analysis is whether the aims of the organisation are reflected in its culture. For example, what is the underlying attitude towards risk-taking, sharing information and evenly distributing rewards in the firm? If the culture is strong and positive, it will not matter whether a new mission statement has been produced.

Corporate aims, mission and culture – an evaluation

Good evaluation is based upon a questioning approach to the subject matter. This should apply to the case material being looked at, and to the underlying theory. This section of the course provides huge scope for careful questioning; this should *not* be in the form of blanket cynicism ('all mission

statements are rubbish'), but by carefully considering the evidence. Is a new boss genuinely trying to improve the motivation and behaviour of staff for the benefit of customers and the business as a whole? If so, perhaps a mission statement is a valuable centrepiece to a whole process of culture change.

At other times, though, the case material may present a new mission statement as no more than a sticking plaster on a diseased wound. Genuine problems need genuine solutions, not slogans. You need to make judgements about which situation is which, then justify your views with evidence from the case and drawn from the theory set out in this unit.

A Revision questions (35 marks; 35 minutes)

1 Why do clear aims help people or businesses achieve their goals? (3)

2 Why may a formal statement of aims be unnecessary in a small business with a limited number of employees? (3)

3 Outline the difference between the workplace culture at the *Sun* and that of John Lewis. (3)

4 a What is the purpose of a mission statement? (3)

   b Identify the four elements that make up the 'mission model'. (4)

5 Explain why poor recruitment could lead to an ineffective business culture. (4)

6 Briefly explain whether you think *two* of the following businesses would be likely to have an entrepreneurial or a bureaucratic business culture (i.e. you choose two from four).

   a Marks & Spencer
   b Facebook
   c L'Oréal
   d Ryanair (6)

7 Look again at Coca-Cola's new mission statement compared with its old one (see page 6). Explain why it might be difficult to persuade staff to believe in a changed 'mission' such as this. (4)

8 Why are mission statements often criticised for being ineffective in practice? (5)

B1 Data response

Amazon aims

In 1994 a 30-year-old New Yorker called Jeff Bezos read about the internet. He moved to California and in a year had set up an internet bookshop. When orders came in, he packed and posted the books from his garage. By February 1999, Bezos employed 1600 people and his shares were worth $2500 million. In February 2010 there were more than 24,300 employees and sales of over $24,500 million. Jeff Bezos is the founder and 40% shareholder in Amazon. com, the world's biggest internet retailer.

What are the aims that helped guide him to become one of the first internet billionaires? His workforce mission is to 'Change the world in an important and fundamental way. Our motto is: Work hard, have fun, make history.' In the 2010 accounts Bezos included a copy of the letter he sent with the 1997 annual report, to show that the entrepreneurial culture of the business was unchanged: the aim in relation to customers is to 'provide the best customer experience … That means we have to have the biggest selection! The easiest to use website! The lowest prices! And the best purchase decision information!'

Asked about his huge wealth, Bezos replied: 'I don't think it matters much. The biggest change is that I don't have to look at menu prices any more.'

Questions *(40 marks; 50 minutes)*

1 Distinguish between aims and mission with reference to this case. (6)

2 a What is meant by an 'entrepreneurial culture'? (2)

   b Why may it be harder to maintain this culture in a large business than in a small one? (6)

3 What evidence is there in the text that business people are not motivated only by money? (6)

4 Outline four factors that might lead to a change in Amazon.com's aims in future. (8)

5 Discuss whether Mr Bezos was successful because of his aims or because his success allowed him to adopt such aims? Explain your answer. (12)

Case study

The John Lewis culture

Very few bosses of public limited companies rose to their position via a job in personnel or human resources. Most have had a career in finance, marketing or operations. The John Lewis boss, Andy Street, is an exception. It may be his background as Personnel Director that makes him so focused upon his staff. Or perhaps it is simply a result of the John Lewis **ethos**.

What makes John Lewis unusual is that, in 1929, its founder put all the company's shares into an employee-owned trust. In other words, the shares went to the staff instead of to Lewis's children. Today, nearly 72,000 John Lewis 'partners' work for a business that has no conventional shareholders. Nor does it have a profit motive, other than to provide an annual bonus to the staff and to provide the finance for the growth of the enterprise.

If anyone doubts whether this can work, take a look at the accounts at www.johnlewispartnership.co.uk. In 2010 the accounts showed a sales revenue of nearly £7.4 billion and an operating profit of £390 million. This profit margin is very similar to that of Tesco.

Andy Street visits his 29 John Lewis and 240 Waitrose stores regularly and says that he can tell within minutes if a store's culture is not right: 'It's about the extent to which we manage to bring that dream alive of having motivated partners giving excellent customer service.'

The John Lewis culture is especially strong because labour turnover is exceptionally low. Many staff have worked at John Lewis since school or university (including Andy Street). The other factor is the John Lewis mission, which emphasises the need to satisfy staff in order to satisfy customers. This, of course, is due to the partnership approach (i.e. that the owners of the business are its staff). The uniqueness can be seen in the way the business describes its culture on its website:

What unites all of us is our behaviour, which is based on our powerful and distinctive partnership culture. You can work in a company where you can be honest, give respect, recognise others, show enterprise, work together and achieve more, as well as being a co-owner.

Some other retailers like to refer to John Lewis as halfway to working for the civil service. But the partnership's success at building market share and profitability makes it seem more than just a big bureaucracy. On Boxing Day 2010, the first day of the John Lewis sale, Andy Street was at his local John Lewis branch to help serve the rush of customers. Being this down to earth should help him ensure that staff remain clear that, ultimately, it is the customer that matters.

Source: *The Observer*, www.johnlewispartnership.co.uk

Questions *(40 marks; 50 minutes)*

1 Outline two distinctive features of the business aims of the John Lewis Partnership. (6)

2 a Calculate the profit margin at John Lewis. (3)

   b Outline two actions the business could take to improve its profit margin. (8)

3 Based on the text, explain in your own words the workplace culture of John Lewis. (8)

4 On the basis of the evidence provided, discuss whether you would want to work for John Lewis. Explain your answer. (15)

Corporate objectives and strategy

Definition

Corporate objectives are the company-wide goals that need to be achieved to keep the business on track to achieve its aims. Ideally they should be SMART (i.e. Specific, Measurable, Ambitious, Realistic and Timebound). Corporate strategy would provide a medium- to long-term plan for meeting the objectives.

Introduction

The key to success in understanding business is to see that every business is different. Even among public limited companies, the personality of the boss and the circumstances of the business can divide firms that seem to be in very similar positions. In consumer electronics, the objectives of Apple are completely different from the objectives of Microsoft. Similarly the objectives of fast-growing, low-cost AirAsia are wholly different from those of long-established airlines such as Cathay Pacific or British Airways. Then come the other types of business, from sole traders and private limited companies through to social enterprises and employee cooperatives.

Broadly, there is a clear distinction to be drawn between public companies (plcs) and every other type of business organisation. This is because only plcs have shareholders who have no connection with the business other than that they own its shares. A 30-year-old who decides to buy £2000 worth of easyJet shares cares about only two things: the share price and the level of annual payments (dividends) paid out by the business. These are known as **shareholder value**. They are determined by two factors: the annual profits made by the business currently and investors' expectations of the business's future. If people think the growth prospects are terrific, the shares will be highly rated and therefore highly priced. A minority of share buyers may care about the social or environmental record of the business, but most care only about shareholder value.

A-grade application

Easy money?

Stelios, the multimillionaire founder of easyJet, resigned from its board on 14 May 2010. He planned to seek shareholder support for moves to force the management away from its objective of growth. Sir Stelios, who controls 38% of easyJet shares, believes that the budget carrier should stop spending money on new aircraft and seek to maximise profits and pay a dividend.

Sir Stelios and easyJet first clashed over strategy last year in a row that led to the departure of Sir Colin Chandler, the chairman. Sir Stelios reached a compromise with the board last year to cut growth from 15% a year to 7.5%, but he now wants to cut growth effectively to zero.

The latest phase of the disagreement over strategy erupted in the previous week when Sir Stelios described Andy Harrison, the outgoing chief executive, as overrated. However, easyJet's largest institutional shareholder yesterday backed the airline's management and its existing strategy. David Cumming, head of UK equities for Standard Life, which owns nearly 10% of the airline, said:

> We are happy with the management team, we are happy with the strategy, things are improving.

> They are doing a good job, given what is happening in the airline industry. To be honest, although we are, as a sort of act of courtesy, listening to what Sir Stelios's views are, we are not supportive of them at present.

As shown in the case of easyJet, the plc shareholders' desire for rising profits can put a huge amount of pressure on the directors. Therefore there will always be many plc managements that place profit at the centrepiece of their corporate objectives.

For organisations other than plcs, there are many possible alternative objectives. There will be fishing shops that open up because individuals with a love of the sport have it as a lifetime ambition. The profits may not be great, but the satisfaction may be terrific. There will also be companies that start up with the intention of running a social enterprise. One well-known example is Duncan Goose, who founded Global Ethics Ltd in order to channel profit from selling bottled water into digging water wells in Africa.

Corporate objectives for plcs

- *Maximising shareholder value* (see Figure 3.1) is increasingly presented by the board of directors of large companies as the modern equivalent of profit maximisation. Share prices reflect the present value of the dividends the company is expected to pay out in the future. As a result, this objective means taking actions that maximise the price of the organisation's shares on the stock market.

- *Growth* in the size of the firm: the managers of a business may choose to take decisions with the objective of making the organisation larger; the motivation behind this goal could be the natural desire to see the business achieve its full potential; it may also help defend the firm from hostile takeover bids. If your firm is the biggest, who could be big enough to take you over? Being number one in a marketplace is a version of the growth objective. It has been at the centre of the long-running battle between Nike and Adidas – both want to be the world's top provider of sportswear.

- *Diversification* in order to spread risk: in other words, to reduce dependence on one product or market. By 2000, Tesco boss Terry Leahy could see that there was little further growth to be gained in

A-grade application

In 2006 Adidas completed a £2 billion takeover of American sportswear rival Reebok. Herbert Hainer, boss of the German giant Adidas, said that the deal 'represents a major strategic milestone for our group'. The real purpose was to bring Adidas closer to its long-term goal of overtaking Nike as the world's biggest sportswear business. Mr Hainer went on to say, 'This is a once-in-a-lifetime opportunity to combine two of the most respected and well-known companies in the worldwide sporting goods industry.'

The Adidas versus Nike feud continued at the 2010 World Cup, especially when Nike was able to exploit the embarrassment of Adidas at the criticism of its new *Jabulani* football.

Britain, once Tesco's share of supermarket sales had gone beyond 25%. So he started on a huge overseas expansion, which led – by 2010 – to Tesco having 65% of its shop floor space outside the UK. Diversification would help Tesco keep growing, but would also reduce its dependence on the UK market. The severe recession in Britain in 2008/2009 proved difficult for Tesco, but it was helped by its profitable businesses worldwide. A

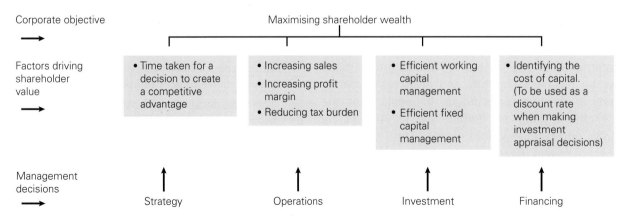

Figure 3.1 Measuring shareholder value

firm may also diversify if it has a key product in the decline phase of the product life cycle – for example, cigarette manufacturers.

● However, although diversification is one way of spreading risk and therefore reducing it, strategy expert Igor Ansoff has long warned how difficult it is to achieve successful diversification. In other words, diversifying is risky to do, yet reduces business risk if it can be achieved successfully. The risks involved in attempting to diversify come from two main sources.

1 First, the business will not understand the customers in a new market as well as in an existing one, such as Tesco attempting to succeed in America or China.

2 Second, the marketing strengths of an existing brand name and existing distribution channels may no longer apply. For instance, Heinz once decided to launch a vinegar-based household cleaning product. Consumers rejected this diversification because Heinz lacked credibility as a provider of anything other than food.

Conclusions on objectives for plcs

Some academics argue that plc bosses have two sets of objectives. The first is based on profit 'satisficing' – in other words, achieving 'enough' profit rather than the maximum amount. A chief executive may be able to see how to get profit up by 30% in the coming year, but may worry that short-term profit gains will hit the longer-term security of the business. Therefore the boss makes decisions that can boost profit by 15% (enough to keep the shareholders happy) leaving scope for more profit growth in the coming years. Having found a way to keep the shareholders quiet, the directors can then decide on other objectives, such as to diversify.

> ### A-grade application
>
> Why is Cadbury the master of the UK chocolate market, yet a bit player in UK biscuits and ice cream, and similarly small in the French, German and US chocolate markets? Within its core UK market, the name Cadbury means tradition, quality, social acceptability and a particular taste that most know and love. From Cadbury's point of view, the UK market is where it has virtually guaranteed high levels of distribution and in-store display, a full understanding of the different likes and dislikes of consumers, and a workforce steeped in market knowledge. There have been occasional strategic lapses, but in general Cadbury can feel secure in its core market expertise and strength.
>
> When straying from this market, however, different rules apply. In the ice cream market the Cadbury name means nothing other than reassurance about chocolate coating, and distribution becomes a weakness because it is virtually impossible to match Walls' promise to meet any retailer's order within 24 hours (even during a heatwave). Worst of all, though, is that Cadbury does not know whether to target Crunchie ice cream at adults or children, because it does not really understand the consumer.

Corporate objectives any business might adopt

Any business has certain objectives that may become fundamental to the operation. For new businesses, and for any that are struggling in the marketplace, the key one is survival. If things are going reasonably well, so that survival is not in doubt, a business might aim to increase its growth rate or its profitability. If these are also going well, the directors may look beyond the immediate financial needs to the 'market standing' of the business (see Figure 3.2).

Finally, there is the possibility of a business organisation that has no commercial drivers, other than to generate the funds to achieve a social objective. Such an approach is rare, because many of the firms proclaiming their social or 'green' credentials are simply cashing in on a consumer concern.

Even though non-profit motives are unusual, good answers show an understanding that businesses have many different objectives.

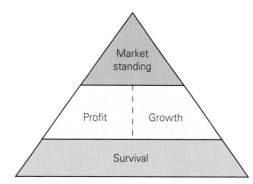

Figure 3.2 Pyramid of business objectives

13

Market standing

For firms that already have a profitable, growing business and reasonable insulation from operational risks, the final piece in the corporate jigsaw is to establish an image that helps add value to the product range, and gives the consumer the confidence to assume the best in the company, not the worst. When Barclays announced the closure of hundreds of rural bank branches, the media and the general public queued up to condemn the company's greed and its lack of concern for its social responsibilities. Yet Black & Decker was able to announce 1000 redundancies in north-east England with hardly a murmur from the national media.

To have high market standing, the public needs to believe that the business operates as a force for good, whether through its products, its employment practices or its positive approach to its social responsibilities. All these things can be managed, as long as the commitment and the resources are available. For instance, the voluntary use of social and environmental audits can be the basis for building a reputation for ethical trading.

To have *really* high market standing, though, more is needed than just clever management of public relations. Apple is a company that most people *believe* in. If a product such as the iPad is priced at £499, consumers assume that it costs around that amount to make and is therefore worth it. The brand embodies key images of the latest technology, the most creative designs and a business that is helping make life better for us all. Apple doesn't just have good management, it has an aura that makes it stand out.

Not-for-profit motives

Years ago people would have thought that social objectives imply charity work rather than business activity. Yet running a charity can be a bureaucratic nightmare, as the rules and regulations are highly restrictive. Therefore a quicker way to do some good in the world is to start a social enterprise (i.e. a business with a social rather than financial objective). In the case of One Water, its objective for 2010/2011 is 'to build one new Playpump per day'. This would require the business to generate about £2.5 million a year of net profit, which would be an incredible achievement for a business that started only in 2005.

Other businesses might see their task as to improve what people eat, to improve how children learn or to build better houses (Housing Associations are not-for-profit housing 'businesses').

 # Corporate strategy

The managers of a business should develop a medium- to long-term plan about how to achieve the objectives they have established. This is the organisation's corporate strategy (see Figure 3.3). It sets out the actions that will be taken in order to achieve the goals, and the implications for the firm's human, financial and production resources. The key to success when forming a strategy of this kind is relating the firm's strengths to the opportunities that exist in the marketplace.

This analysis can take place at each level of the business, allowing a series of strategies to be formed in order to achieve the goals already established. A hierarchy of strategies can be produced for the whole organisation in a similar manner to the approach adopted when setting objectives.

- Corporate strategy deals with the major issues such as what industry, or industries, the business should compete in, in order to achieve corporate objectives. Managers must identify industries where the long-term profit prospects are likely to be favourable. In 2007, for example, Whitbread decided to pull out of the health club market by selling its David Lloyd Leisure subsidiary. It used the money to pay off some debt and put the remainder behind its fast-growing Costa Coffee chain, in particular, setting up 200 Costa Coffees in China. By 2011 this strategy looked very clever,

Figure 3.3 Corporate strategy

as Whitbread's shares hit new highs, while David Lloyd Leisure struggled to survive the recession.

● Business unit (or divisional) strategy should address the issue of *how* the organisation will compete in the industry selected by corporate strategy. This will involve selecting a position in the marketplace to distinguish the firm from its competitors – in the case of Costa Coffee in China, how to differentiate the business from Starbucks.

● Functional (or department) strategy is developed in order to identify how best to achieve the objectives or targets set by the senior managers.

If a strategy is to achieve the objectives set, it must match the firm's strengths to its competitive environment (see Figure 3.4). Whitbread decided that the market for health clubs in the UK was getting saturated and fierce competition was forcing clubs to cut prices, so it would be better to put its money behind the rapidly growing Costa chain and David Lloyd had to go.

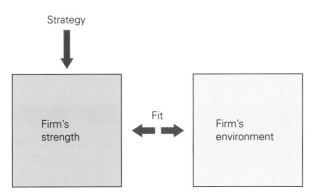

Figure 3.4 Achieving the objectives set: match the firm's strengths to its competitive environment

As a company develops over time its employees acquire knowledge and skills. This 'organisational learning' represents what the firm as a whole is good at doing, or its 'core capabilities'. The key products or services produced by the business will reflect these strengths. The 2011 launch of the iPad2 represented Apple's innovative abilities as a result of its research and development programme and design expertise.

Core capabilities need not be limited to a particular market. Marks & Spencer's move into financial services was based on a reputation for reliability and quality. This had built up over many years by its operation in the clothing and food markets. Corporate strategy can be shaped by identifying new opportunities to apply the existing strengths of the organisation.

Michael Porter, in his book *Competitive Advantage: Creating and Sustaining Superior Performance*, develops a method by which an organisation can analyse the competitive environment within which it operates in order to create strategic policy. He suggests that firms need to analyse five factors within an industry in order to understand the market-place (see Figure 3.5). This will help managers understand how fierce or how favourable the competitive environment is. Each of Porter's **'five forces'** provides information that can be used to help devise an appropriate business strategy.

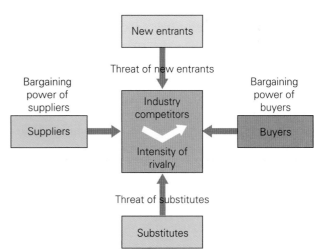

Figure 3.5 Porter's five forces framework

Porter believes that the overall strength or weakness of a firm's position depends on the following five factors.

1 *The intensity of rivalry with direct competitors.* In the ten-minute south London walk between South Wimbledon tube station and the Merton

Park Metro stop there are five men's hairdressers. None stands out, and all charge between £6 and £8 for a haircut. Elsewhere in London the price is more likely to be £15, but the intensity of rivalry here keeps prices down – and makes it impossible for any of the five to make a great living out of their business.

2 *The threat of new entrants.* In the case of the hairdressers, there is nothing to prevent someone else opening a sixth shop. The barriers to entry are very low, as all you need is perhaps £10,000 to decorate and equip an existing retail outlet. In other cases, the barrier to entry is huge. For example, who today could set up an internet bookshop to rival Amazon? The millions of pounds needed to build the infrastructure (depots, etc.) would need to be matched by a fortune in advertising to wean people away from the tried and trusted Amazon. So there is very little threat to Amazon, even though it is now a hugely profitable business.

3 *The threat of new substitutes.* In the 1870s margarine, invented in France, was launched into the American market as a cheap alternative to butter. Sales were poor until it was discovered that adding artificial yellow colourings made consumers far more likely to buy it (margarine is naturally white). Farmers found sales of milk hit hard (butter is just churned milk) so they protested against margarine. Today margarine has a large share of the 'butter' market round the world. New substitutes can be bad news for producers.

4 *Bargaining power with suppliers.* The buying manager responsible for buying all of Tesco's biscuits has power over the sales of 25–30% of all the biscuits made in the UK. Therefore Tesco has a huge amount of buying power. If a supplier wants to strike a special deal with Sainsbury's, perhaps only selling a new biscuit brand through Sainsbury's stores, Tesco will put a stop to that with one phone call. In contrast, a small corner shop has virtually no buying power (i.e. no leverage it can use to try to get a better deal for itself).

5 *Bargaining with customers.* When a small firm speaks to a big customer (e.g. the NHS, for medicines, or Hertz Rentals, for new cars), the minnow is likely to be very gentle. Only if the supplier is really huge would it be able to talk on level terms with the customer.

Porter's five forces help you to analyse whether a business is in a strong or weak position overall.

Issues for analysis

Does every business really need to write down its objectives and strategies? It may not be necessary, but it would always be useful. The fact is that running a large organisation is difficult, partly because staff who are one person among 80,000 (John Lewis) or 480,000 (Tesco) find it hard to be clear on what the business is trying to achieve overall. Writing down the objectives can help overcome this difficulty.

When analysing a business case study it is important to ask yourself the following questions.

● Do the objectives fit with the aims or mission of the business?

● Are the objectives clear and do they seem feasible (achievable)?

● Does everyone know and agree with these objectives (or are they a matter of dispute among staff or even among directors)?

● Are the strategies logical in relation to the objectives?

● Are the strategies achievable given the available resources (the right people; enough money; enough capacity)?

Armed with these questions it should be possible to analyse, and perhaps criticise, the corporate objectives and strategy.

Corporate objectives and strategy – an evaluation

The main judgements to be made are in relation to the analysis mentioned above (especially whether the strategy fits the objectives) plus the key issue of the external context. In other words, the corporate objectives and strategy must not only be right for the business, but also right for the year in question. If the economy is incredibly buoyant, as in 2006, ambitious corporate objectives might seem very wise. The exact same objectives in 2012 might be questionable, given widespread uncertainty over the strength of the British economy.

Judgements must always be subtle, so it is important to read with care about the external situation of the business. Examiners love to include phrases such as 'a fiercely competitive market' or 'a saturated market', and you need to pick up the messages. It is worth remembering that very few businesses can risk complacency about their market and their competition. A former chief executive of the giant computer business Intel, Andy Grove, once said 'only the paranoid survive'. Many other business leaders have loved to quote that to their own staff.

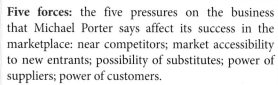

> **Key terms**
>
> **Five forces:** the five pressures on the business that Michael Porter says affect its success in the marketplace: near competitors; market accessibility to new entrants; possibility of substitutes; power of suppliers; power of customers.
>
> **Shareholder value:** the value to investors of owning a company's shares. This is a function of the share price (up or down) plus the level of dividend payouts. Both are a function of the firm's profits plus the expectations of the company's future prospects.

Further reading

Barfield, R. (1991) Shareholder value. *Accountancy*, October.

Porter, M.E. (1998) *Competitive Advantage: Creating and Sustaining Superior Performance*. Simon & Schuster.

A Revision questions *(40 marks; 40 minutes)*

1 a List four possible corporate objectives. (4)
  b Explain the extent to which each is focused on the short or long run. (8)

2 Explain why every leader of a public limited company must think hard about the objective of maximising shareholder value. (4)

3 Increasingly, chief executives gain huge rewards from bonus payments linked to the price of their company's shares. Outline how this might affect their approach to shareholder value. (5)

4 Explain the benefits Tesco is receiving from its corporate objective of diversification. (4)

5 What is meant by the term 'satisficing'? (2)

6 a List the five factors Porter suggests determine an industry's competitive environment. (5)
  b Explain why the price of a haircut is so cheap between South Wimbledon and Merton Park stations. (3)

7 Explain why it may be true to say that 'diversification is a risky way to reduce risk'. (5)

B1 Data response

Fizzy orange turns sour

In the three years to 2009 retail sales of Tango fell by 29%, from £38 million to £27 million. Tango, produced by the soft drinks producer Britvic, has a tough time competing with the Coca-Cola brand Fanta. In 2009, Fanta sales were £108 million.

Both brands have been suffering from the recent trend towards 'healthy' drinks. People see fizzy drinks as in some way less healthy than still ones; so even Fanta has struggled, with its 2009 sales down by 5% on the previous year. Orange fizz has also suffered from the growth of fresh orange juice, notably the powerful (Pepsi-owned) brand Tropicana. In the three years to 2009 Tropicana sales grew by 27% to £270 million.

Britvic products may also suffer from a struggle for credibility when in negotiation with the major retail chains. Now that the 'big four' supermarkets have a market share of around 65% of all grocery sales, it can be hard to get distribution for minor brands such as Tango. If the brand's sales continue to decline, it may become harder for Britvic to achieve the purchasing economies of scale necessary for a profitable brand.

Source: Britvic Soft Drinks Report 2007 and 2009; Nielsen data quoted in *The Grocer*, 19 December 2009

Questions *(20 marks; 25 minutes)*

1 Use Porter's five forces to analyse Britvic's position with its Tango brand. (10)

2 To what extent does the five forces approach seem to offer a fully rounded analysis of the competitive position of Tango? (10)

B2 Case study

Tesco in China

2010 saw major changes at the top of Tesco plc. Not only did long-standing boss Terry Leahy step down, but there were also striking shifts in corporate strategy. In 2004 Tesco bought a hypermarket chain in China called Hymall. Then, in 2005 it announced a plan to invest £1,250 million in building a chain of stores in America. China was put on the back-burner as the US plan got underway in 2007. By mid-2010 150 'Fresh 'n Easy' stores had been opened by Tesco in America. Yet in the 2009/2010 financial year the 150 US stores made an operating loss of £165 million on sales of £354 million.

By contrast, even though the Chinese economy was the world's fastest growing, Tesco China had made slow progress since 2004. In 2010 Tesco had 89 hypermarkets in China. By contrast its closest worldwide competitor (the French chain Carrefour) had 167 hypermarkets in China plus an extra 360 small discount stores.

Happily, early in 2010 the 'penny dropped' in Tesco's boardroom. Whereas in 2009/2010 Tesco allocated £100 million to capital investment in China (compared with £250 million in America), in 2010/2011 it will be providing £500 million for China. Indeed Tesco has said that by 2013 it will have more shop floorspace in China than in Britain. It is also showing its seriousness by setting up a dedicated Tesco China graduate training scheme in the UK.

For a long time Tesco's corporate objective had been growth. Yet its strategy of focusing on America rather than China seemed odd, unless it

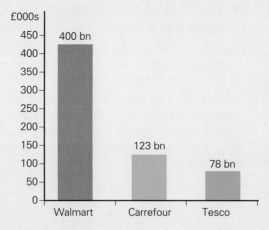

Figure 3.6 Worldwide sales turnover 2010: top three grocery retailers

was really trying to beat Walmart as the world's Number 1 (see Figure 3.6). By implication, it has now accepted the need to change its objectives and strategy. Six years after buying into China, Tesco is taking the country seriously.

Questions *(40 marks; 50 minutes)*

1 The three most common corporate objectives for plcs are maximising shareholder value, growth and diversification. Which of these seems to have been the most important to Tesco in recent years, based on the case material? Explain your answer. (12)

2 Use Porter's Five Forces framework to analyse Tesco's 2010 position within the world's grocery industry. (10)

3 It seems that Tesco made a mistake in focusing on America rather than China. Discuss how mistakes in corporate strategy might occur. (18)

 Essay questions *(40 marks each)*

1 Discuss whether 'corporate' objectives can mean much in a company as big and as complex as Tesco plc.

2 The management expert Peter Drucker believes that it is a mistake for a business to focus upon a single objective. To what extent do you support him in this view?

Functional objectives and strategy

 ## Introduction

Each of the four functional departments within a business (marketing, finance, operations and people) has its own objectives. Together, the four sets of objectives must match the organisation's own corporate objectives. Each of the four must fit together to make the overall targets reachable.

For example Tesco's corporate objective of opening 80 new superstores in China by 2016 (more than doubling its business in China) requires action by each of the four functions.

1 The marketing director might set objectives such as 'to boost Tesco brand recognition in China from 8% to 40% within three years'.

2 The finance director might set an objective of 'to finance £1,400 million of capital expenditure in China over the next three years'.

3 The operations director might set the objective of 'to increase the capacity of distribution warehousing in China from 2 million to 5 million sq ft by 2015'.

4 The personnel director might set the objective of: 'Switching our graduate recruitment focus so that 30% of our UK graduate intake speak Mandarin by 2014'.

If all four directors succeed in their own objectives, the business will be in a good position to achieve its overall goal.

 ## Corporate objectives

This topic is covered in Unit 3. For now, the key is to understand why and how different firms have different objectives. The mistake to avoid is the assumption that all businesses are driven by the desire for profit. Many are, but not all. Among many possible objectives, the following are the most common (see also Table 4.1).

Growth

The only explanation for Tesco's actions in the past 15 years has been that the business has been pursuing a growth objective. Originally this was to become Britain's number one, outstripping Sainsbury's (see Figure 4.1). After that was achieved, Tesco developed its business in Eastern Europe, South East Asia and

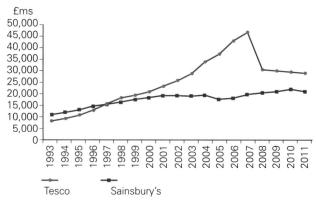

Figure 4.1 Annual sales: Tesco vs Sainsbury's

Source: www.fooddeserts.org

America – becoming the world's third biggest supermarket business. This is a wonderful objective for staff (lots of career openings), for managers and potentially shareholders, as long as profits improve as well. In fact, Tesco is also one of the world's most profitable supermarket chains.

Profit optimisation (i.e. making the 'right' amount of profit, not the maximum possible)

Most large firms want their profits to rise as smoothly as Tesco's sales line in Figure 4.1. So even if they know that a sudden rush for one of their brands could allow them to increase the price and make huge profits, few would be tempted. They do not want to risk alienating customers who may blog about being 'ripped off'; and they do not want profits to soar this year but slide next. Shareholders love to see steady profit growth.

Profit maximisation

This objective means making as much profit as possible, with the implication that it should be made in as short a time as possible. This is most likely to be the objective for a small to medium-sized business run by individuals with little regard for their customers or for the long-term reputation of their business. 'Cowboy' builders maximise their profit by charging high prices for shoddy work. They do not rely on repeat purchase, but on finding another unsuspecting customer victim. Few large plcs deliberately pursue profit maximisation, though executives with huge share options might take decisions that maximise profit this year at the possible expense of the future.

A not-for-profit motive

The owner of the One Water business, Duncan Goose, has a very unusual business objective. At present his charitable water business funds one new water well in Africa every eight to ten days. His objective is one a day. To achieve this he needs growth in the sales and in the profits made by selling bottles of One Water in the UK. Other businesses, such as John Lewis Partnership and the Co-op Bank, need profit to survive and to grow, but have not-for-profit objectives.

Table 4.1 Examples of different types of objectives

Type of objective	Example of objectives
Growth	• To become Britain's number one • To achieve a £1 billion turnover by 2015 • To double the customer base from 1.2 to 2.5 billion by 2019 (L'Oréal)
Profit optimisation	• To achieve profit growth of 10 to 12% a year for the next four years • To return profit margins to the 8% level achieved two years ago
Profit maximisation	• To drive profit up by at least 50% this year • To become Britain's most profitable window replacement business
Not-for-profit	• To become Britain's bank of choice for those concerned ethically about how their money is used (Co-op Bank) • To finance and build one water pump a day (One Water)

Functional objectives

Functional objectives are the targets of the individual business departments (functions). They will stem from the corporate objectives and are either set by the chief executive or may be the result of discussion between directors.

Having set the company's objectives, the key is to take care over each department's objectives. They must work separately and together, so that the overall goal can be achieved. For the 2012 London Olympics, the operations function had to get the stadia built on time, while the marketing department

had to sell the millions of tickets to fill the stadia to capacity. If one succeeded while the other failed, the London organisers would be laughed at by the world's media.

Success requires that the leaders within each department/function do the following.

● *Coordinate what they are doing:* what, when and how. Timing will be crucial, such as having the right amount of stock to cope with the demand expected on the launch day. So marketing, operations and personnel must be acting together, perhaps using **network analysis** software to make sure that the whole project is kept on track.

● *Make sure that all within their own department know the overall objective* as well as the functional one, and that all are motivated towards achieving it. In 2010 and 2011 British Airways cabin crew staff went on strike repeatedly in the face of the company's attempt to cut costs and restructure the business; the staff refused to believe management's suggestion that BA's survival was at stake

● *Work together to achieve a common goal:* this may seem obvious, but in many organisations managers and even directors are jostling for promotions or positions, not really working together. So the marketing director might be happy to see the operations director humiliated.

Functional strategies

A strategy is a medium- to long-term plan for meeting objectives. This should come about from a careful process of thought and discussion throughout the business, though key decisions will almost always be made at the top. To make the right decision about strategy, a useful approach is known as the 'scientific decision-making model' (Figure 4.2). It shows that strategy decisions must:

1 be based on clear objectives

2 be based on firm evidence of the market and the problem/opportunity, including as much factual, quantitative evidence as possible (e.g. trends in market size, data on costs, sales forecasts)

3 look for options (i.e. alternative theories – hypotheses – as to which would be the best approach); for example, to meet an objective of higher market share we could either launch a new product or put all our energies and cash behind our 'Rising Star' existing product

4 be based on as scientific a test of the alternatives as possible (e.g. a test market of the new product in the Bristol area, while doubling advertising spending on the Rising Star in the north-east – then comparing which approach provided the bigger market share gains)

5 control the approach decided upon – the final stage (e.g. if it's a new product launch, to manage the quality and timing of every aspect of

production, sales, advertising and delivery) – then review, to learn from any mistakes or unexpected successes before (the dotted line on the diagram) starting again with a new objective and a new strategy.

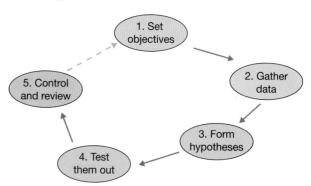

Figure 4.2 Scientific decision-making model

Within this process, the single most important thing is that the business should make sure that the functional strategies are all part of one overall strategy (and match the overall objective). For many years the objective of the Apple Corporation was to succeed by being more customer-friendly than its then only rival, Microsoft. The strategy for achieving this was to be one step ahead in design rather than technology. This strategy focus on design became the beginnings of a goldmine with the 2001 launch of the iPod. Table 4.2 describes what this meant for each functional area.

Table 4.2 Apple iPod strategy

Functional areas	Actual strategy in the early iPod years
Marketing strategy	Quirky poster advertisements emphasising street style rather than the product
Operations strategy	Design a great-looking product with distinctive headphones (the white wires) and a great interface
People strategy	Hire free-thinking people and give them the space and environment to be creative (don't over-manage or over-control them)
Financial strategy	Provide all the finance needed for product development, and don't over-control later decisions (e.g. the Nano launched while the original Shuffle model was still in its growth phase)

Issues for analysis

Top firms unite behind a single strategy based on clear objectives. Therefore, when analysing case material about any business, it is wise to ask the following questions.

- How clear is the overall company objective? Is it precisely stated, with a timescale, thereby making it easy to measure success or failure? This is often called a **SMART objective** (i.e. Specific, Measurable, Achievable, Realistic, Timebound).

- Having considered the overall objective, what are the functional objectives agreed by the directors? Is each one also SMART? Or does HR, for example, have only vague targets because the importance of the human element has been overlooked?

- Then comes the overall strategy, for which each of the functions should be contributing its own crucial part. In July 2010 LG had to admit that its inability to boost production of flat screens was holding back production of Apple's iPad. Between the April launch and July, more than 4.3 million iPads had been sold (more than $1 billion), but supply could not keep up with demand. Apple's superb marketing had been let down by mistakes in its operations (production) supply chain.

As with every aspect of business, success comes from working together towards a common goal.

Functional objectives and strategies – an evaluation

Having analysed the business situation, judgements have to be made. If a business hits problems, is one department (function) to blame (e.g. the marketing department let the side down because of a poor advertising campaign)? Are there specific staff who lack ability or motivation? Or was the problem more collective, due to poor communications within a department or (much more likely) between the functional areas?

Alternatively, it is sometimes the case that no one deserves blame (or praise for success). After more than ten years of sales and profit growth, Next and French Connection both struggled in the period 2006 to 2010. The rapid growth of Primark, Topshop and Zara meant the market became far tougher. For sales at Next to be falling by 2.5% a year was not necessarily a disgrace; just as, years earlier,

managers at Next did not really deserve the huge praise they received when sales were rising at 6% a year. They were largely benefiting from the period

Figure 4.3

when women lost confidence in the ability of Marks & Spencer to provide affordable, wearable clothes.

The key judgement, then, is whether a firm's success is entirely down to its own good management. A better explanation might be that external factors were largely the reason. In which case managers deserve credit for taking advantage of favourable circumstances; but they should beware of jumping to the conclusion that they have the magic touch.

A Revision questions *(25 marks; 25 minutes)*

1 What is meant by the term 'functional areas'? (2)

2 Why is it important that objectives should be:
   a measurable (2)
   b timebound? (2)

3 Are the following good or bad corporate objectives? Briefly explain your reasoning.
   a To boost our share of the fruit juice market from its current level of 22.3%. (4)
   b To become the best pizza restaurant business in Britain. (4)

4 What might be a successful overall objective for:
   a the charity Oxfam, which focuses on preventing and relieving famine (2)
   b the Conservative Party? (2)

5 Explain in your own words why it is important that the different business functions should work together to achieve the corporate (overall) objective. (4)

6 Explain the difference between an objective and a strategy. (3)

Data response

In August 2006 Claude and Claire Bosi put their Hibiscus restaurant up for sale. This was a surprise because it had two Michelin stars, making it one of Britain's top ten restaurants. The couple decided that, while still young, they must move from Ludlow in rural Shropshire to the challenges of opening in London. Could Claude Bosi's cooking stand out in London, when in competition with Gordon Ramsay, Jamie Oliver and many Michelin-starred restaurants?

They sold the restaurant for £250,000 and moved to London to look for a good site. Famously, business success in restaurants depends not only on great cooking but also on location, location, location. After several months they found a site in Mayfair that could be turned into a 60-seat restaurant, though the site, the building work and the equipment would cost 'around £1 million'. The finance would come from their own £250,000 plus share capital from a wealthy Ludlow customer and two of his friends.

The objective of the couple was to establish in London a restaurant as successful as the one in Ludlow. Clearly, London offers far greater potential, both financially and in terms of personal recognition. To recreate Hibiscus in London, Bosi persuaded most of his staff to move to London and has a menu that is largely made up of the dishes developed in Ludlow. He even buys many of his supplies from farms in Shropshire.

The restaurant opened in London in November 2007 and, as nearly 40% of new restaurants close within three years, its success is confirmed by the fact that it's still successful in November 2010 (and has won back its two Michelin stars). Apart from the quality of cooking, an important issue was pricing. The couple decided to charge the same price for three courses as they charged in Ludlow: £45. This may seem high, but is nothing like as expensive as restaurants such as Gordon Ramsay's, which are twice the price.

Questions *(20 marks; 35 minutes)*

1 Explain what you believe to be the business objectives being pursued by Claude and Claire Bosi. (5)

2 From the text, how SMART do the couple's objectives seem to be? (6)

3 Use Google to check on the progress of the business. You will find restaurant reviews and, at www.hibiscusrestaurant.co.uk, the restaurant's latest prices and marketing messages. Then comment on whether the couple seem to be succeeding in achieving their business objectives. (9)

Case study

L'Oréal: thinking ahead to 2019

L'Oréal is the world's No 1 cosmetics company. Not many French companies are leaders in their field, so this is remarkable. To stay No 1, L'Oréal has set the objective of doubling its customer base. As almost every woman in the west uses L'Oréal products (whether they know it or not, as brands such as Garnier, Maybelline, Giorgio Armani and Body Shop are actually L'Oréal) growth has to come from developing countries. In 2010 more than 33% of L'Oréal's €16.5 billion of sales came from developing countries. Ten years before, the figure was 16%; ten years before that it had been 8%.

The strategy for achieving this change is partly based on a re-focusing of the marketing efforts. In 2009, for instance, the cover of L'Oréal's annual report did not feature Cheryl Cole, but Freida Pinto – the beautiful young (Indian) star of the hit film *Slumdog Millionaire*. More importantly, though, the decision had been made to invest in Research and Development facilities in China and Brazil. In 2010 the Shanghai R&D centre

turned three years of work into a new haircare range. A careful study of Chinese hair, plus market research into local customs and tastes, led to the launch of a range of shampoos and haircare products suited to local hair types and cultural traditions, focusing on fragrance and gloss.

The value of L'Oréal's longstanding focus on developing countries was shown in the 2009 recession (see Figure 4.4).

Questions *(30 marks; 35 minutes)*

1 Outline L'Oréal's corporate objective and its strategy for achieving it. (6)

2 Explain why L'Oréal might have chosen this objective and strategy. (8)

3 To what extent does L'Oréal's strategy in relation to its marketing and operations functions seem likely to help it achieve its corporate objective? (16)

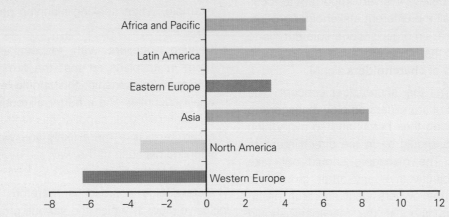

Figure 4.4 L'Oréal 2009 sales: percentage change from 2008

Responsibilities to stakeholders and society

> ## Definition
> A stakeholder is an individual or group that has an effect on and is affected by the activities of an organisation.

 ## Introduction

All firms come into contact on a daily basis with suppliers, customers, the local community and employees. Each of these groups has an impact on the firm's success and at the same time is likely to be affected by any change in its activities. If, for example, the managers decide to expand the business, this may lead to:

- overtime for employees
- more orders for suppliers
- a wider range of products for consumers
- more traffic for the local community.

Groups such as suppliers, employees and the community are known as the firm's **stakeholder** groups because of their links with the organisation. A stakeholder group both has an effect on and is affected by the decisions of the firm. Each stakeholder group will have its own objectives. The managers of a firm must decide on the extent to which they should change their behaviour to meet these objectives. Some managers believe it is very important to focus on the needs of all the different stakeholder groups. Others believe that an organisation's sole duty is to its investors (i.e. that decisions should be made in the best interests of **shareholders** alone).

This is known as the 'shareholder concept'. The logic is clear: the shareholders employ managers to run the company on their behalf and so everything the managers do should be in the direct interests of shareholders. The managers should not take the needs or objectives of any other group into consideration. If the owners want short-run profit, for example, this is what the managers should provide. If the owners want expansion, then this is what the managers should aim for. According to this view, the only consideration managers should have when making any decision is to meet their owners'

objectives. Generally, this means maximising **shareholder value** (e.g. increasing the share price and the dividends paid to shareholders).

The alternative view places emphasis on the need to meet the objectives of a wider group. This is known as 'the stakeholder concept' as opposed to 'the shareholder concept'. The stakeholder approach suggests that managers should take into account their responsibilities to other groups, not just to the owners, when making decisions. The belief is that a firm can benefit significantly from cooperating with its stakeholder groups and incorporating their needs into the decision-making process. Examples include:

- improving the working life of employees through more challenging work, better pay and greater responsibilities, so that the business benefits from a more motivated and committed workforce
- giving something back to the community to ensure greater cooperation from local inhabitants whenever the business needs their help – for example, when seeking planning permission for expansion
- treating suppliers with respect and involving them in its plans so that the firm builds up a long-term relationship; this should lead to better-quality supplies and a better all-round service; if, for example, your supplier has limited availability of an item, it is more likely you would still get supplied because of the way you have treated the supplier in the past.

The stakeholder approach is, therefore, based on an inclusive view in which the various groups that the firm affects are included in its decision making rather than ignored. This, it is argued, can lead to significant advantages for the firm.

What are the gains of the stakeholding approach?

There are numerous gains that might result from the stakeholding approach. For example, existing employees might be more willing to stay with the firm. It may also attract people to work for the organisation. Employees are increasingly concerned about the ethical behaviour of the organisation they work for. Firms that put the shareholders above all else may deter some people from applying for or accepting a job with them. The stakeholder approach is also increasingly popular with investors. There are a growing number of financial institutions that specifically seek to invest in organisations that follow the stakeholder approach, in the belief that it will lead to long-term rewards. A firm can also gain from better relations with the community, suppliers and distributors, and more favourable media coverage. By working with other groups rather than against them a firm is also less likely to be targeted by a **pressure group**.

However, while this approach may seem attractive in theory there are a number of problems in practice. First, the owners may insist that the managers serve their interests and no one else's. Many shareholders of public limited companies, for example, demand short-term rewards and may take some convincing that the firm should be paying attention to the needs of other groups. After all, it is their money that is invested in the business. Second, the managers may not be able to meet all their potential responsibilities to these various groups and may have to make some decisions regarding priorities. They may also have to decide between what they regard as their obligations to society and what is commercially viable.

Society's interest in the responsibilities of business seems to grow each year. This means people are expecting firms to take a much broader view of their activities than in the past. In spring 2011 the clothes retailer Gap was criticised for allegedly using suppliers who used child labour to make its clothes. Although Gap was not directly employing these children and had clear policies to try to ensure its suppliers did not do so either, it was still held responsible for the failings of others. It withdrew all the relevant garments from sale and burnt them!

Corporate social responsibility (CSR)

In recent years there has been a great deal of interest in corporate social responsibility (CSR). CSR refers to the extent to which a business accepts obligations to society over and above the legal requirements. This obviously refers to how it treats its stakeholder groups. Investors, customers, employees and the media regularly examine the way in which a business is treating various stakeholders. What is it doing to reduce its impact on the environment? To what extent is it protecting its employees and improving the quality of their working lives? How is it helping the local community?

When considering CSR, it is important to be cautious. Is it a reflection of a genuine concern by the business for its customers, staff and society? Or is it part of a public relations campaign to improve the firm's image? In January 2010 Nestlé's KitKat brand started to boast the Fairtrade logo. The company had agreed to source the cocoa beans from better-paid Fairtrade workers. No one would doubt the potential value of this, but why only KitKat? What about all the other Nestlé brands such as Aero, Smarties and Yorkie? The fact that it was using Fairtrade with just one brand made it seem that it was using CSR as an arm of marketing, not a meaningful commitment towards a fairer world.

Sainsbury's and social auditing

A number of companies now undertake a social audit. This means they have an external assessment of the impact of their activities on society. This is to help them understand the effect of their actions so that they can take appropriate steps and can be seen to be concerned about such issues. Supermarket chain Sainsbury's, for example, produces an annual social audit that examines its relationship with the four groups it believes are crucial to its success, namely:

1 customers

2 employees

3 suppliers

4 the community.

According to Sainsbury's, they plan to make substantial progress on the environment, focused on these commitments (to be measured each year in their Social Responsibility audit report):

> We will reduce our own-brand packaging weight relative to sales by 33% by 2015 against a 2009 baseline

> We will reduce our CO_2 emissions per square metre by 25% by 2012 against a 2005/2006 baseline

Are the stakeholder concept and CSR really new?

In recent years people have come to expect more from business organisations. In the past they were just expected to provide good-quality goods. Now many consumers want to know exactly how the goods are produced, what the company does for the environment and how it treats its employees. Stories about the exploitation of staff, the sale of goods to a military regime or the pollution of the environment can be very damaging to firms. This has probably resulted in more public companies adopting the stakeholder approach. However, there are a number of companies, such as the John Lewis Partnership, that pioneered this approach long before the term 'stakeholder' was even thought of. Many of the origins of this approach go back to the paternalistic style of companies such as Rowntree and Cadbury in the nineteenth century. These family companies were the major employers in an area, and built a reputation for treating customers, employees and suppliers with great respect.

Can a firm satisfy all stakeholder groups?

According to the shareholder concept a firm's responsibilities to other groups directly conflict with its responsibilities to shareholders. If the firm tried to help the local community, for example, this would take funds away from the shareholders. Similarly, more rewards for the owners would mean fewer resources for employees. In the shareholder view, all these different groups are competing for a fixed set of rewards. If one group has a larger slice of the profits it leaves less for others.

Under the stakeholder approach, however, it is believed that all groups can benefit at the same time. By working with its various stakeholder groups the firm can generate more profit. Imagine, for example, that more rewards are given to employees out of profits. In the short run this may reduce rewards for the shareholder, but in the long run it may generate more rewards for everyone. Better-quality work can lead to improved customer loyalty and therefore less marketing expenditure to achieve the same level of sales. Similarly, by building up better relations with suppliers the firm can produce better-quality goods leading to more orders and more business for both parties. However, at any moment managers are likely to have to decide which group(s) are most important. This will depend on the values of the owners and managers, the interests of different stakeholders and their power to bring about change. If, for example, stakeholders organise themselves into an effective pressure group they may be able to change a firm's behaviour through actions such as demonstrations and boycotts.

A-grade application

Stakeholders: American Apparel

Staff at American Apparel (AA) have long enjoyed some of the best terms and conditions in the US garment industry. Originally the company put 'sweatshop-free clothing' on every garment, but later changed it to 'vertically integrated'. In other words every part of every garment was made in American Apparel's Los Angeles factories. Even at a time when the US minimum wage was $5.25 an hour, AA workers earned at least $12 an hour. They also enjoyed subsidised lunches and free healthcare benefits (a huge issue in America). In 2008 the same workers received $25 million's worth of shares in the business.

AA's Chief Executive Dov Charney 'makes no bones' about why he does these things: 'not for moral reasons, it's just a better business strategy'. Certainly the booming sales of AA products in 2007 and 2008 made it clear that people loved to buy guilt-free, fashionable clothes.

Remarkably, though, Charney's individual dealings with staff have come under great scrutiny. Three women have filed sexual harassment suits against him, all of which have been settled before reaching trial. Then, in 2010, the share price collapsed as the company faced liquidation after admitting to 'material weaknesses' in its financial controls. The share price that had been $15 in 2008 fell to just 75 cents. Shareholders faced 'losing their shirts'.

Issues for analysis

When answering a case study or essay question it may be useful to consider the following points.

- An increasing number of firms claim to be adopting the stakeholder approach. They recognise their responsibilities to groups other than the shareholders and are taking their views into account when making decisions. Claims made by firms, though, may largely be for public relations reasons. Companies should be judged on what they do, not what they say.

- Even firms that genuinely mean to change will find many managers stuck in the previous culture of profit/shareholder first. Changing to more of a stakeholder culture will take many years.

- The stakeholder approach can lead to many benefits for organisations, such as attracting new customers, attracting and keeping employees, and building a strong long-term corporate image. However, the business may not be able to fulfil the objectives of all groups. Meeting the needs of one group may conflict with the needs of others.

- The stakeholder approach may prove to be a fad. When the profits of firms fall, for example, they sometimes decide that short-term profit is much more important than obligations to other groups. So a sharp recession would be likely to make every business more profit/shareholder focused.

Responsibilities to stakeholders and society – an evaluation

In recent years there has been much greater interest in the idea that firms should pay attention to their **social responsibilities**. Increasingly, firms are being asked to consider and justify their actions towards a wide range of groups rather than just their shareholders. Managers are expected to take into account the interests and opinions of numerous internal and external groups before they make a decision. This social responsibility often makes good business sense. If you ignore your stakeholder groups you are vulnerable to pressure group action and may well lose employees and investors. If, however, you build your social responsibility into your marketing this can create new customers and save you money through activities such as recycling.

It may not be possible to meet the needs of all interest groups, however. Firms must decide on the extent to which they take stakeholders into account. Given their limited resources and other obligations, managers must decide on their priorities. In difficult times it may well be that the need for short-term profit overcomes the demands of various stakeholder groups. It would be naive to ignore the fact that TV consumer programmes such as the BBC's *Watchdog* keep exposing business malpractice. Even if progress is being made in general, there are still many firms that persist in seeing short-term profit as the sole business objective.

Pressure group: a group of people with a common interest who try to further that interest (e.g. Greenpeace).

Shareholder: an owner of a company.

Shareholder value: a term widely used by company chairmen and chairwomen, which means little more than the attempt to maximise the company's share price.

Social responsibilities: duties towards stakeholder groups, which the firm may or may not accept.

Stakeholder: an individual or group that affects and is affected by an organisation.

A Revision questions (40 marks; 40 minutes)

1 What is meant by a 'stakeholder'? (2)

2 Distinguish between the 'shareholder concept' and the 'stakeholder concept'. (3)

3 Some people believe that an increasing number of firms are now trying to meet their social responsibilities. Explain why this might be the case. (3)

4 Outline two responsibilities a firm may have to:
   a   its employees (4)
   b   its customers (4)
   c   the local community. (4)

5 Explain how a firm might damage its profits in the pursuit of meeting its shareholder responsibilities. (4)

6 Explain why a firm's profit may fall by meeting its stakeholder responsibilities. (4)

7 Some managers reject the idea of stakeholding. They believe a company's duty is purely to its shareholders. Outline two points in favour and two points against this opinion. (8)

8 What factors are likely to determine whether a firm accepts its responsibilities to a particular stakeholder group? (4)

B1 Data response

Sandler plc produces a range of paints that are sold in the major DIY stores in the UK under the brand name Lifestyles. The company has had a very successful few years and expects demand to be much higher than capacity in the next few years. The company has considered two options:

1 extending capacity at its existing site, or

2 moving to a new purpose-built factory 60 miles away.

Although the second option is more expensive initially, building a completely new factory is estimated to be more profitable in the long run.

The problem is that the chosen site is close to an Area of Outstanding Natural Beauty (AONB) and the firm is concerned that protesters might object to it building there. Also, the closure of the existing factory at Headington will lead to serious job losses in the area. The company has been based at Headington for over 50 years and has worked well with the community. Telling the

workforce and local authorities will not be easy. On the other hand, it will be creating jobs at the new location, which is an area of high unemployment, whereas Headington is booming at the moment.

Questions (40 marks; 45 minutes)

1 Identify four stakeholder groups that may be affected if Sandler closes its Headington factory. Explain briefly how each would be affected. (8)

2 Should Sandler plc close its Headington factory? Fully justify your answer. (12)

3 If the firm decides to close its Headington factory, should it tell the employees immediately or wait until nearer the time? Explain your reasoning. (10)

4 Outline the difficulties Sandler might face with stakeholders other than the workforce if the decision is taken to move to the new site. (10)

Data response

Stakeholders vs shareholders

In a recent poll, 72% of UK business leaders said shareholders were served best if the company concentrated on customers, suppliers and other stakeholders. Only 17% thought focusing on shareholders was the only way to succeed. This represents a marked change from five years ago, when the stakeholding idea was widely ignored.

However, not everyone agrees with the stakeholder view. According to two UK writers, Shiv Mathur and Alfred Kenyon, the stakeholder view 'mistakes the essential nature of a business. A business is not a moral agent at all. It is an investment project ... Its *raison d'être* is financial.'

Others believe the stakeholder and shareholder views do not necessarily conflict with each other. For example, the US consultant James Knight writes:

Managing a company for value requires delivering maximum return to the investors while balancing the interests of the other important constituents, including customers and employees. Companies that consistently deliver value for investors have learned this lesson.

Source: adapted from the *Financial Times*.

Questions *(30 marks; 35 minutes)*

1 Distinguish between shareholders and stakeholders. (4)

2 Analyse the possible reasons for the growth in popularity of the stakeholder view in recent years. (8)

3 Examine the factors which might influence whether a firm adopts the stakeholder or the shareholder approach. (8)

4 Discuss the view that the interests of shareholders and stakeholders necessarily conflict. (10)

Case study

BP: shareholder or stakeholder approach?

On 21 April 2010, news emerged of an explosion on a rig on a BP oilfield in the Gulf of Mexico. Eleven people were killed and many others injured. At first BP said there was little chance of an oil spill, but within a few days it was clear that 200,000 gallons of oil were leaking per day. It was being talked about as perhaps the world's biggest ever oil spill. When media criticism began, BP boss Tony Hayward responded by pointing the finger at the oil rig operating company Transocean. This went down badly, as it implied that BP was trying to evade responsibility. It had outsourced the drilling job to Transocean, but was still legally and morally responsible.

Week by week the flow of oil, the disruption to the tourist and fishing industries and the gaffes of Tony Hayward made the situation worse. Worst of all was his crass statement in an interview that he 'wanted his life back'. This did not go down well with the families of the workers who had died in the explosion. The families were even more upset when they heard that problems on the exploration platform had been known about before the accident. It seemed that work had been rushed to save paying extra for the hire of the oil rig. Across America the same message seemed clear – BP was putting its shareholders' interests above that of its staff.

By 1 May analysts were speculating that the final bill for the accident and clean-up may reach $12 billion, of which BP would have to pay two-thirds. More important, though, would be this further reminder to the US motorist that BP is (a) not 'one of us' and (b) not a business to admire. Of course, anyone needing petrol will fill up at the first garage, but there are often competing petrol stations close by, in which case a brand name can matter.

President Barack Obama, 2 May 2010: 'Let me make it clear: BP is responsible for this leak. BP will be paying the bill.'

BP's ability to withstand criticism was fatally undermined by its track record in this area. In March 2005 a huge explosion at BP's Texas oil refinery had killed 15 people and injured more than 180. Most were BP's own staff. The year before, two workers had died at this same refinery when scalded by super-heated water that escaped from a high-pressure pipe.

In November 2006 an official US report made it clear that BP managers had known of 'significant safety problems' at the Texas refinery long before the deadly explosion. The US Chemical Safety Board (CSB) found numerous internal BP reports setting out maintenance backlogs and poor, ageing equipment. Late in October 2006 the CSB chairwoman blamed the explosion on 'ageing infrastructure, overzealous cost-cutting, inadequate design and risk blindness'.

She went on to say that 'BP implemented a 25% cut on fixed costs from 1998 to 2000 that adversely impacted maintenance expenditures at the refinery'. The report stated that 'BP's global management' (i.e. British head office) 'was aware of problems with maintenance spending and infrastructure well before March 2005' – yet they did nothing about it. The chairwoman delivered the final critique:

Every successful corporation must contain its costs. But at an ageing facility like Texas City, it is not responsible to cut budgets related to safety and maintenance without thoroughly examining the impact on the risk of a catastrophic accident.

BP confirmed that its own internal investigation had findings 'generally consistent with those of the CSB'.

Questions *(30 marks; 40 minutes)*

1 Explain two possible reasons why BP went wrong in its attitude to human and environmental safety in its US operations. (6)

2 Discuss whether BP was carrying out a 'shareholder' or a 'stakeholder' approach to its decision making during the period covered by the text. (12)

3 Is it time for stronger government controls on business activities? Justify your view. (12)

Essay questions *(40 marks each)*

1 'Meeting the objectives of different stakeholder groups may be desirable but it is rarely profitable.' Discuss.

2 Consider whether the objectives of the different stakeholder groups necessarily conflict.

3 'A manager's responsibility should be to the shareholders alone.' Critically assess this view.

6 Key AS financial issues

Definition

AQA's specification introduces A2 Financial Strategies and Accounts with the following:

This section examines the financial objectives of larger businesses, the ways in which financial performance might be measured and the strategies they may deploy. It builds upon AS Finance material.

So, what are the key things you still need from AS Finance in order to do well at A2?

 ## Profit

You'll remember that profit = revenue minus total costs. But can you still remember how to calculate total costs? It seems easy, but many A2 students can't quite remember the calculation, because they have forgotten about fixed and variable costs. Test yourself with this quick question (the answer is at the end of this short chapter; you'll check it in a moment).

Q. GG Ltd sells 1,200 units a week at £8 each. Variable costs are £3 per unit and the fixed costs are £4,000 a week.

a) What is GG's current profit?

b) What would its new profit be if a £1 price increase cut sales to 1,100 units?

Check your answers; if they are correct, you can move on to the next section in this unit.

If you found the GG Ltd question difficult, you need a quick reminder of fixed and variable costs.

AS reminder: costs and revenues

Variable costs are those that change as output changes. So the more you produce the more you have to spend. For a clothes shop, examples include the supplies of clothes, the cost of carrier bags and clothes hangers and any bonuses paid to staff, such as sales commission. To return to the GG Ltd example: in part (a) the variable costs would total 1,200 × £3 = £3,600; in part (b) the fall in sales cuts the variable costs total to 1,100 × £3 = £3,300.

Fixed costs do not change because of sales rising or falling. Examples include rent and salaries. Fixed costs can rise (rents can go up) or fall, but not because of changing levels of output.

Total costs come from adding total variable costs to fixed costs. In the CG Ltd example, part (a) above, total costs are £7,600 because you're adding £3,600 to £4,000.

Will you need to be able to do this at A2? Certainly; and take the total costs from total revenue to calculate profit.

Profit and cash flow

AS Finance focuses on profit, calculated as revenue minus costs. Probably the most important aspect of profit for A2 is to keep in mind the distinction between profit and cash flow. A whole paragraph of analysis can be undermined if you use 'profit' when the examiner knows that you mean cash. This has always been an important issue for examiners; the amazing events of the 2007 to 2009 credit crunch showed why. Profitable banks collapsed because they could no longer get enough cash to keep operating.

Example of cash flow versus profit

A specialist kitchen supplier receives a £345,000 order from Gordon Ramsay restaurants. A brand new kitchen must be built and equipped within eight weeks. The contract specifies a ten-week credit period for the customer. The kitchen supplier has worked out that the total costs for the job will be £300,000, giving a £45,000 profit. (See Figure 6.1.)

That's fine. £45,000 profit for an eight-week job sounds pretty good! But look carefully at the graph. For the first eight weeks the kitchen supplier is paying out £300,000 on materials, machinery and labour. After completing the work the firm waits ten weeks to be paid. Then the cheque for £345,000 arrives, transforming the cash flow position from −£300,000 to +£45,000. The profit and the cash flow both end up as +£45,000. But unless the firm had carried out a cash flow forecast, it would not have known the severe effect of the order on its cash flow forecast. If the kitchen firm's bank had not been willing to allow a £300,000 overdraft, the order could never have been completed.

So remember:

1 Cash flow and profit are different

2 Both must be calculated and considered with care before going ahead with a project

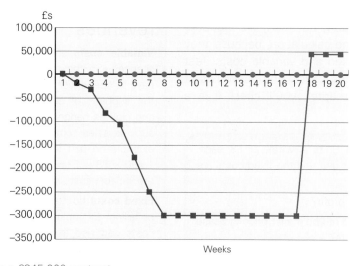

Figure 6.1 Cash flows on a £345,000 contract

Sources of finance

The material learnt at AS in invaluable. It is well worth rereading that material. At A2 it's important to be able to distinguish clearly between internal and external sources of finance, and between short- and long-term sources. The key to effective financial management is to match your liabilities to your assets. If your assets are fully tied up in the long

term (e.g. an investment in an organic farm that should start making profits in four years' time), you are at risk if your debts need to be repaid next week. Long-term assets need long-term financing; short-term assets need short-term financing.

So a business with a 25-year property investment should finance it by a long-term source such as share capital or a 25-year loan. A business needing finance for one week should use a short-term method such as an overdraft.

Budgeting and cost and profit centres

At AS you will have covered budgeting and variances. At A2 that is developed further by looking at cost and profit centres. It would be sensible to brush up on this material, as budgeting and cost centres require students to combine their understanding of finance with people aspects of the A2 course.

Key AS financial formulae for A2

Key financial formulae for A2 are given in Table 6.1.

Table 6.1 Key financial formulae for A2

profit	total revenue – (fixed costs + [variable costs × quantity sold])
contribution per unit	selling price – variable costs per unit
break-even point	$\dfrac{\text{fixed costs}}{\text{contribution per unit}}$
net cash flow	cash in – cash out

Test yourself

Test yourself on the following questions to find out whether you know enough AS Finance to provide a sound basis for the A2.

Knowledge questions (50 marks, 50 minutes)

1 Define fixed costs. (2)

2 What formula is used to calculate a firm's break-even output? (2)

3 What are the three key lines shown on a break-even chart? (3)

4 Define margin of safety and describe what it would look like on a break-even chart. (4)

5 State two reasons why a firm benefits from forecasting cash flows. (2)

6 How is a firm's net cash flow calculated each month? (2)

7 Outline one advantage and one disadvantage of using an overdraft as a source of finance. (4)

8 What is meant by the term 'venture capitalist'? (2)

9 Explain why profit and cash flow are different. (6)

10 Explain why delegating budgetary control may help to motivate middle managers. (4)

11 a Calculate Company X's profit if it makes and sells 2000 units at a selling price of £15 per unit. Variable costs are £7 per unit and fixed costs per month are £10,000. (4)

   b Calculate Company X's break-even point. (2)

   c What is Company X's margin of safety? (2)

12 Fill in the gaps on the cash flow forecast shown in Table 6.2. (11)

Table 6.2 Cash flow forecast

	January	February	March	April
Cash in	45	40		40
Cash out	40		36	42
Net cash flow		(3)	8	
Opening balance	15			
Closing balance				

7 Financial objectives and constraints

Definition

Financial objectives outline what the business wishes to achieve in financial terms during a certain period of time. Constraints are the internal and external factors that affect the firm's ability to achieve these objectives.

 ## Types of financial objective

It is generally assumed that all businesses operate in order to maximise profit. This is of course true to a certain extent – why would people invest in a business if not to make profit? However, within this there are many other considerations, as outlined below.

Ownership vs management

In a small business the management and the owners are often the same people. In large companies such as a **public limited company (plc)** the management (the directors) and the owners (the shareholders) are usually separate. The shareholders will want to see a healthy and immediate return on their investments, but the directors may have other aims: they may be looking for growth or diversification, or may be content to just keep the business ticking along (satisficing). An increasing trend is for the bonuses of company directors to be related to the achievement of the financial objectives. Directors may therefore have an interest in setting targets that are achievable rather than challenging.

Short term vs long term

Some business goals, such as growth or diversification, will need investment. This may mean a reduction in short-term profits with the hope of increasing returns in the future. If a business is in difficulty it will need to focus much more on survival, so increasing profitability will be a definite short-term goal.

Stakeholders vs shareholders

In some businesses the pursuit of profit may cause conflict between the different groups with an interest in the business, as in the following examples.

● The rise of interest in the environment has meant that costs have increased for many firms and therefore profit has been reduced. However, many firms have also discovered that they can make huge savings, such as by limiting waste.

● Some firms, most notably supermarket chains, are accused of driving the prices of their suppliers to the lowest possible level. Low supply costs increase profits. Businesses need to ensure that there is a balance between keeping costs low and maintaining the quality of the supplies. In the food chain, tough bargaining by supermarkets may cause unacceptable welfare conditions for animals such as chickens and piglets; this, in turn, may backfire on the retailer's reputation.

● Taxation may be a consideration. Large multinational companies may deliberately reduce profit in one country in order to pay less tax, and increase profit in another where profits are taxed at a lower level. They are able to do this by charging differential prices between subsidiaries in different countries.

● Public image: a firm may choose to spend money on charitable concerns or sponsorship; this as a cost will reduce profit. However, it may well get a return on its investment through creating a better brand image or good public relations.

A-grade application

Financial objectives of UK businesses

Company	Financial objectives
Valeo (French supplier to the car industry)	To achieve a return on capital employed (ROC) of 30% by 2013
Unilever plc (Multinational producer of foods and household brands)	'We will continue to focus on volume growth as the main driver of long-term value creation, while delivering steady and sustainable year-on-year improvement in operating margin and cashflow'
Orange (Telecommunications)	'Organic cash flow generation in 2010 and 2011' (i.e. generating enough positive cash flow from day-to-day operations to help repay loans)
WPP Advertising agency	(Objective for 2011): 'A 1% increase in operating profit margins'

Profit is a major objective

Whether it is long or short term it is safe to say that, for most businesses, high and rising profits are a major objective. However, just stating that the firm wants to increase profit is a very general objective. Most companies will be more specific in defining their financial objectives. They may look to increase gross or net profit. They may also use other measures, such as return on capital employed (ROCE). The measurements of profitability are inter-linked. Firms that have a high gross profit margin will find it easier to finance high spending on research and development, marketing or investing in assets. Firms that have better control of costs are going to be more profitable than other firms in their sector. Businesses that generate high profits are going to have contented shareholders.

Revenue targets

The directors may set an overall aim, such as to increase revenue by 10% or more. This approach will be especially important for a business in the early stages of a growth market. For example, in the early days of Innocent Drinks, the key thing for the business was to grow rapidly in order to gain market domination before rival PJ Smoothies (owned by the massive PepsiCo) could get fully established.

Cash flow targets

All businesses need to keep a healthy **cash flow**. The level of cash flow should be carefully managed. A company that is cash short will have difficulty with the day-to-day management of its liabilities. It may find it difficult to pay **creditors**. It may also miss

Figure 7.1 Innocent Smoothie

opportunities to develop the business. A new order may have to be refused if it has insufficient cash available. A business that has cash reserves that are too high will be missing out on opportunities to use that cash to generate additional business. The 'right' level of cash will depend on the nature of the business. The business may set itself a target of keeping cash at a percentage of turnover or as a stated amount.

Cost minimisation

A business may concentrate on minimising costs. Lowering costs will increase profitability. This may

A-grade application

Saab runs out of cash

In the dreadful recession of 2009 General Motors (GM), America's most famous manufacturing company, 'went under'. To bring the car maker back to life, the US government guaranteed more than $25 billion of loans. As part of the deal between GM and the government, it was agreed that the loss-making Saab car division must be sold off. In spring 2010 this was achieved when the tiny Dutch sports car manufacturer Spyker 'saved Saab'. Given that Saab had sold 80,000 cars a year before the recession, this was incredible. But as no one else wanted Saab, General Motors accepted the only offer they received.

To finance the takeover, Spyker was 'helped' by the European Union, by General Motors itself and by the Swedish government. In early 2011 things looked good when a contract was agreed between Spyker and a Chinese importer keen to get sole rights to import – then produce – a well-known European brand of luxury cars. Yet, by March 2011, cash flow was making it hard to pay the suppliers on time. Production was halted for several weeks, while Spyker worked through financial tools such as sale and leaseback deals on its property. But when it resumed in June, it was only a week until it stopped again. This time there was no cash to pay the wage bill. By mid-July 2011 it was hard to see how the company could survive. This would cost not only Saab's 3,800 staff their jobs, but also risk those at the original Spyker factory.

be a general overall aim, such as reducing fixed costs by 5%, or it may be more specific such as to reduce wastage in the factory and therefore reduce material costs by 4%. A strategy of cost minimisation may be necessary when times are hard (see Table 7.1).

Return on capital employed (ROCE)

This is a measure of how well the company is using its assets to create profit. It is calculated by taking net profit or operating profit as a percentage of capital employed. (See Unit 10 on ratio analysis.)

Capital employed is all the long-term finance used to operate the business. Although this is a measure of profitability it concentrates on the use the business is making of its assets. Obviously, the business will want the highest possible return. It is important that the business should achieve a ROCE of more than the rate of interest that it is paying on borrowed funds. The ROCE can be improved by reducing capital employed or by increasing net profit.

Shareholder returns

These can be expressed in terms of the dividend payments that will be given to shareholders or in terms of maintaining or adding value to the share price. Shareholders hope to gain from their investment in the business in two ways.

1 Any increase in the value of their shares will mean that they can sell their shares at a higher price than they were bought at. This is a capital return.

2 Shareholders receive income on their shares through the payment of dividends by the business. Yearly profit made by the business can either be kept in the business for development (retained profit) or distributed to shareholders as dividends. These dividends are the income that the shareholders receive as a return on their investment. If the company is making insufficient profit to satisfy shareholders then shareholders will sell their shares and invest elsewhere. This in turn will cause the share price to fall.

A business that is seen as a poor investment by shareholders will find it very difficult to attract investment. It is therefore important that the level of profit and the level of dividends are kept at a level that satisfies shareholders. This in turn keeps the value of the share price high. Balancing the retained profit and dividend distribution is a difficult decision. If the business wants to expand or diversify it may wish to retain more profit and therefore risk upsetting shareholders by paying low dividends.

Table 7.1 Cost-cutting strategies

To cut fixed costs	To cut variable costs
● Consider closing loss-making branches or factories ● Consider moving the head office or main factory to a lower-cost location ● Consider carefully whether a layer of management could be removed to reduce staffing costs	● Renegotiate with existing suppliers to try to agree lower prices ● Look for new suppliers, perhaps from a low-cost country such as China ● Redesign the goods to make them simpler and therefore quicker and cheaper to produce

A-grade application

Volcanic ash hits airline profits

Companies, especially travel companies, are used to external factors that affect their profits. But the disruption caused by the volcano in southern Iceland's Eyjafjallajokull glacier was totally unexpected and the severe travel disruption caused by the closure of European airspace during April and May 2010 had a massive impact on airline profits. Ryanair for example announced that the disruption had cost it £42 million.

This was an unpredictable external constraint on Ryanair's ability to meet its financial objectives.

Figure 7.2 Icelandic volcano erupting

How are financial objectives set?

Financial objectives are determined by taking into account the overall company aims. They express the financial aspects of the overall company plan. They will be decided like any other business objective, by taking into account the internal position of the business and the external business environment. The internal aspects of the business such as what the business is currently doing and what resources it has available, will determine what the business can achieve. This has to be put into the perspective of the external environment. The external environment will affect how easy it is to carry out the plans. An increase in sales is unlikely to be achieved in an economy that is going into recession.

What makes a good financial objective?

As with any other business objective, financial objectives should be SMART:

- *Specific* – they should be clearly defined so that all staff know and understand the aims
- *Measurable* – if the objective can be measured then it is possible to see if the target has been achieved
- *Achievable* – a good objective is challenging but it must be achievable; to set a target that is impossible is demoralising for staff – it could also create poor shareholder and public confidence if objectives are not met
- *Realistic* – any objective should make good business sense
- *Timebound* – financial targets usually relate to the company's financial year; they can also look further into the future.

Internal and external influences on financial objectives

There are many factors that will influence the way a firm sets its financial objectives. These can be categorised as internal and external constraints.

Internal constraints

Financial

Although it may seem strange to talk about internal finance as a constraint on financial objectives it can play an important part. The pursuit of higher profit

might be constrained by lack of cash flow, especially at a time of rising or even booming demand.

Labour force

Any business activity requires the cooperation of the workforce. It is also important that the business has the manpower with the necessary skills.

Type of business

New or young businesses may set themselves

financial objectives but because of inexperience or the difficulty in assessing a new market they may set unrealistic targets. Larger, more established businesses will find it easier to set and achieve their objectives because of the experience that they have. Plcs may be more constrained in their objectives, as they will have to satisfy the shareholders as well as the management.

Operational

A firm that is close to **full capacity** may find that it has fewer opportunities for improving the profit-ability of the business, unless it has the confidence and the resources to increase capacity, perhaps by moving to bigger premises.

External constraints

Competitive environment

The plans of almost every business can be affected by the behaviour and reaction of competitors. A plan to increase profit margins by increasing prices may be destroyed if competitors react by reducing prices or by advertising their lower prices.

Economic environment

The state of the economy plays a vital part in how well businesses can achieve their financial targets. A booming economy will help businesses to improve sales. However, high interest rates would reduce customers' disposable income and therefore spending, so financial targets may not be met. The effect will depend on the business. Supermarket own-brand producers may do better, whereas branded goods may suffer.

Government

A firm may find its financial objectives limited by regulatory or legislative activity. Consumer watchdogs such as the Office of Fair Trading (OFT) have powers to fine businesses that they believe are not acting in the best interests of consumers. Legislation may also be introduced that increases business costs. A recent European Union environmental policy has forced producers of goods such as refrigerators to pay for their disposal when consumers have finished with them.

Building in the constraints

Good business planning involves being aware of the possible constraints. The internal constraints are easier to evaluate. External constraints will always be subject to more uncertainty, as they are outside the power of the business. It is therefore important when setting financial objectives that the business includes a series of 'what if' scenarios.

A-grade application

Zara back in profit

Zara, the Spanish-owned high street fashion chain, has 4,700 stores in 77 countries. In August 2011 it posted the annual results for the UK branch of its international operation.

This showed that it had made a pre-tax profit of £15.8 million for the year to 31 January 2011, compared with a profit of £0.6 million for the previous year. This huge improvement was achieved due to improved cost control, plus the launch of an e-commerce website.

Anticipating tough conditions on British high streets, Zara's management had decided not to open any new stores in 2010 or 2011. Cutting back on investment helped boost profits, as did a sales uplift of 7% – largely due to the new website.

In spite of this improvement Zara warned that rising unemployment and the 'still difficult economic situation' meant consumer spending was expected to remain volatile throughout 2011.

Issues for analysis

When analysing financial objectives the key issues are as follows.

- How have the objectives been determined? Any consideration of the firm's objectives must be put into the context of the business and its external environment. Think about the type of business and who the objectives are aiming to please.

- You will need to have an understanding of the different measures used to define financial objectives. It is especially important to ask whether a firm is setting the 'right' objectives:

is it pursuing revenue growth when a focus on profit would be more appropriate?

- Are the objectives realistic? A challenging objective may look good in the annual report but is it achievable?

- When looking at why a business has failed to meet or has exceeded its financial objectives, you need to consider the part played by both the internal and the external constraints, and the extent to which these are important.

Financial objectives and constraints – an evaluation

There are advantages and disadvantages to setting tight financial objectives. Some people consider that objectives are vital to give direction to the business. A good set of objectives will enable plans for each sector of the business to be developed. Each individual within the organisation will then know the role that they are to play. Without objectives, the business may drift aimlessly.

Other people consider that objectives can stifle entrepreneurship and initiative. They feel that managers operate to satisfy the objectives but do not go beyond them. They also feel that they dampen risk-taking, which may prevent a business from taking the kind of leaps forward shown by Apple (iPhone, iPad) and Nintendo (Wii).

Key terms

Annual report: the annual financial statement showing the financial results for the business; for any limited company this is a statutory requirement.

Cash flow: the flow of cash into and out of the business.

Creditors: people who are owed money by the business.

Full capacity: when the business is fully utilising all its assets.

Public limited company (plc): a company with limited liability and shares that are available to the public. Its shares are quoted on the stock exchange.

Revision questions (40 marks; 40 minutes)

1   What is meant by financial objectives? (2)

2   Why is improving or maintaining profit likely to be the most important financial objective? (4)

3   Give two examples of how stakeholder interests might affect the setting of business objectives. (6)

4   What is meant by 'retained profit'? (2)

5   List two likely results for shareholders if profits fall? (4)

6   Explain the term 'return on capital employed'. (4)

7   List and explain two possible internal constraints on achieving financial objectives. (6)

8   Discuss two external constraints that should be taken into account when financial objectives are set by *one* of the following businesses.
    a   Innocent Drinks
    b   Game (software retailer)
    c   Versace clothing. (8)

9   What government activity might act as a constraint on businesses achieving their financial objectives? Give an example. (4)

Data response

What a difference a book makes!

Quercus Publishing plc is an independent publisher based in London. The company was founded by Mark Smith and Wayne Davies in May 2004. Both had previously worked for the Orion Group, one of the United Kingdom's leading publishing companies. In June 2010 they issued the following Press statement:

The Board of Directors at Quercus Publishing Plc, the award-winning independent publisher, are pleased to report on trading for the six months ended 30 June 2010. The Company's interim results are expected to be issued on 27 September 2010.

Sales across all sectors have continued to be well ahead of management forecasts and, as a result, the Company's performance for the year ending 31 December 2010 is now expected to significantly exceed market expectations.

As a result of this strong trading, unaudited management accounts for the six months ended 30 June 2010 show:

● Revenue of £15.0 million (compared with revenue of £5.55 million in the same period in 2009).

● Group operating profit for the period rising to £3.40 million (against a loss of £0.10 million in the same period in 2009).

● Improvement in Group margins, despite the continued decline in the UK book retail market and the wider economic and financial issues.

Mark Smith, Chief Executive of Quercus said: 'Our results continue to be driven by double-digit growth across the business and, most significantly, by the continued success of Stieg Larsson's Millennium Trilogy, for which we own the global English language rights. These books represent the three best selling fiction titles in the UK over the last six months, and Larsson is the first to have sold more than 1 million Kindle e-books through Amazon'.

Source: Quercus Publishing Plc.

Questions (40 marks; 40 minutes)

1 What was the percentage rise in revenue for the six-month period up to June 2010 compared to the same period in the previous year? (4)

2 Explain why the rise in pre-tax profits and the rise in revenue are not the same. (8)

3 What is meant by 'These figures show improvement in Group margins, despite the continued decline in the UK book retail market and the wider economic and financial issues'? (8)

4 What factors would the company have to take into account when setting financial objectives for the next financial year? (8)

5 Discuss whether it is sensible for a business such as a publisher to set financial objectives. (12)

Case study

Paper quality hits De La Rue

De La Rue was founded in 1821 as a printing business. It began printing in 1860 and in 2003 it took over the printing of bank notes for the Bank of England. It now prints bank notes for 150 governments, as well as making documents such as passports, driving licences and cheque books. It also prints holograms onto credit cards.

In March 2010 its annual report showed that in the year to 27 March 2010 its revenue was £561.1 million, up by 12% from the previous year, and profit before tax was £97.6 million, up by 13%.

In July 2010 the company announced that it had discovered quality problems at one of its factories that produce specialist paper. Until the problem was revealed the share price had been consistently high as investors were happy with the performance of the company and its high dividend payout. The shares lost around 20% of

their value in the weeks after the problem was announced. The chief executive took personal responsibility for the problem and resigned. The company said that it expected sales in 2010 and 2011 to be 'materially lower' after halting production at the paper factory where the quality problems had been detected.

Questions (30 marks; 35 minutes)

1 Why would shareholders be happy with a high dividend payout? (4)

2 Explain why the share price fell when the problems that the company faced were announced. (6)

3 Explain how the quality issue is likely to affect the company profits in future years. (8)

4 Examine the financial measures the company might have to take to recover from the quality problem. (12)

Essay questions (40 marks each)

1 Financial objectives are only there to please shareholders. Discuss.

2 Setting financial objectives is a waste of management time. Discuss.

3 Financial objectives are more important for large organisations. Discuss.

8 Income statements (profit and loss accounts)

> ### Definition
> An income statement is an accounting statement showing a firm's sales revenue over a trading period and all the relevant costs generated to earn that revenue. Public limited companies use the term income statements, whereas small firms refer to the profit and loss account (sometimes abbreviated to 'the P&L').

 ## Introduction

The function of accounting is to provide information to various stakeholder groups on how a particular business has performed during a given period. The groups include shareholders, managers and creditors. The period in question is usually one year. The key financial documents from which this information can be drawn are balance sheets and income statements. This unit focuses on the income statement; the balance sheet is covered in Unit 9.

The income statement records all a business's costs within a given trading period. Income statements constitute a vital piece of evidence for those with interests in a company. For many stakeholders, profit is a major criterion by which to judge the success of a business:

- shareholders are an obvious example of those assessing profitability
- government agencies such as the tax authorities require data on profits or losses in order to be able to calculate the liability of a business to **corporation tax**

- suppliers to a business also need to know the financial position of the companies they trade with in order to establish their reliability, stability and creditworthiness
- potential shareholders and bankers will also want to assess the financial position of the company before committing their funds to the business.

For all these groups the income statement provides important information.

Making a profit is one of the most significant objectives for business organisations. It is this profit motive that encourages many people to establish their own business or expand an existing one. Without the potential for making a profit, why should individuals and companies commit time and resources to what may be a risky venture? Even charities must seek to generate revenues to at least match their expenditure, otherwise they cannot survive. Therefore the income statement is as important to a charity as it is to a company.

 ## The uses of income statements

The data within an income statement can be used for a number of purposes:

- to measure the success of a business compared with previous years or other businesses
- to assess actual performance compared with expectations

- to help obtain loans from banks or other lending institutions (creditors want proof that the business is capable of repaying any loans)
- to enable owners and managers to plan ahead – for example, for future investment in the company.

Measuring profit

Profit is what remains from **revenue** once costs have been deducted. However, the word 'profit' on its own means little to an accountant. Profit is such an important indicator of company performance that it is broken down into different types. This enables more detailed comparisons and analyses to be made.

The main types of profit are described below.

Gross profit

This is the measure of the difference between income (sales revenue) and the cost of manufacturing or purchasing the products that have been sold. It measures the amount of profit made on trading activities alone (i.e. the amount of profit made on buying and selling activities).

gross profit = revenue − cost of goods sold

Gross profit is calculated without taking costs, which could be classified as expenses (administration, advertising) or overheads (rent, rates), into account. This is a useful measure as, if a company is making a lower level of gross profit than a competitor, it is clear that the company must look very closely at its trading position. It may be that the business should attempt to find a cheaper supplier, or may need to put its prices up.

Net profit

This is found by subtracting expenses and overheads from gross profit. It is often termed **operating profit**.

net profit = gross profit − (expenses + overheads)

Net (operating) profit is a more important measure than gross profit, because it takes into account all the operating costs including overheads. A business may find itself making a healthy gross profit but a very small net profit in comparison to competitors. The business may not be controlling costs such as salaries and distribution as effectively as it might. The calculation of both gross and net profit allows stakeholders to make a detailed and informed assessment of a business's performance.

Profit quality

It is not just the amount of profit that a business makes that is important, but also the likelihood of this profit source continuing for some time. If a profit has arisen as a result of a one-off circumstance (such as selling assets for more than their expected value), its quality is said to be low because it is unlikely to continue into the future. On the other hand, high-quality profit is trading profit that is expected to last for a number of years. For instance, the annual operating profit Arsenal makes through its turnstiles is high quality, whereas a transfer profit made by buying a player for £2 million and selling for £10 million is regarded as a low quality 'one-off'.

Determining profit

Businesses calculate their profit or loss at regular intervals during a trading period. This supplies managers with important information to assist in the running of the business. At the end of the trading period the final calculation is made, which will form a major element of the published accounts.

Since 2005 there have been significant changes to the way that public companies in the UK present their accounts. They must now comply with the International Financial Reporting Standards (IFRS). This requirement has not yet been extended to **private limited companies**. This move is intended to bring about greater similarities between the ways in which companies in different countries report on their performance. Differences still remain between European and American systems, but they will be brought into a single format in future. Consistent standards make it easier to compare the financial performances of companies in different countries, making it easier for companies (and individuals) to invest across national boundaries. This section considers income statements in a structure that meets international (IFRS) requirements; therefore, it matches the approach used by all Britain's public limited companies (plcs).

Figure 8.1 sets out the basic structure of an income statement. Although this is the format adopted by a large number of firms, there is some variation according to the type of business.

		£m
	Revenue	26.0
less	Cost of sales	(17.0)
gives	Gross profit	9.0
less	Overheads	(4.0)
gives	Operating profit	5.0
less	Financing costs	1.5*
gives	Profit before taxation	6.5
less	Tax	(2.0)
gives	Profit after taxation for the year	4.5

*In this case more interest was earned than paid out

Figure 8.1 Basic structure of an income statement

The income statement comprises four main stages, as outlined below.

1 First, 'gross profit' is calculated. This is the difference between the income (this can also be called sales revenue) and the cost of the goods that have been sold. The latter is normally expressed simply as 'cost of goods'.

2 Second, 'operating profit is calculated'. This is done by deducting the main types of overhead, such as distribution costs and administration costs.

3 Next, 'profit before taxation' is calculated, which is arrived at by the inclusion of interest received by the business and interest paid by it. These are normally shown together as a net figure labelled 'financing costs'.

4 The final stage of the income statement is to calculate 'profit after taxation'. This is arrived at by deducting the amount of tax payable for the year and shows the net amount that has been earned for the shareholders.

Calculating gross profit

This element of the income statement shows how much revenue has been earned from sales less the **cost of goods sold**. In other words, it calculates gross profit.

income (revenue) − cost of goods sold = gross profit

When calculating revenue, sales taxes such as VAT are excluded as they are paid directly to the tax authorities.

The next stage in calculating gross profit requires businesses to deduct cost of sales from the sales figure.

cost of goods sold = opening stock + purchases − closing stock

Cost of goods sold shows the expenses incurred in making or buying the products that have been sold in the current financial period. In most cases, companies will actually start a financial period selling stock that was made or bought in the previous financial period. The cost of these stocks is therefore brought into this period as this is when it is going to be sold. To this is added the purchase of goods made within the period.

Finally in the calculation of cost of sales, closing stock is deducted. These leftover stocks (closing stocks) need to be subtracted from the cost of goods sold, as they have not been sold. Their cost will be accounted for in the following trading period.

Logically, the closing stocks at the end of one financial period become opening stocks for the next period.

These calculations provide a value for the total cost of goods sold during the period in question. An example of a trading account is shown below.

H Baker Ltd: Gross profit for the period ended 30 May		
	£	£
Revenue		47,800
Less cost of goods sold		
Opening stocks	4,700	
add Purchases	24,000	
less Closing stocks	6,000	22,700
Gross profit		25,100

Figure 8.2 Example of a trading account

If cost of goods sold exceeds income, a loss is made.

Calculating operating profit

The next stage of the income statement sets out the net operating profit, or net operating loss, made by the business. The gross profit figure is necessary to calculate operating profit so this naturally follows on from calculating gross profit.

An important relationship to remember is that operating profit equals gross profit less expenses.

Expenses

Expenses are payments for something that is of immediate use to the business. These payments include cash expenditures on labour and fuel, as well as non-cash items such as depreciation.

Examples of overhead expenses include:

- wages and salaries
- rent and rates
- heating, lighting and insurance
- distribution costs.

Operating profit

Deducting expenses from gross profit leads to operating profit. Most firms regard this as the key test of their trading performance for the year. At the very least a firm would want operating profit to be:

- up by at least the rate of inflation compared with the previous year
- a higher percentage of the capital employed in the business than the cost of that capital (e.g. the interest rate)
- at least as high a percentage of capital employed as that achieved by rival companies
- high enough to ensure that shareholders can be paid a satisfactory dividend but still have money left to reinvest in the future of the business.

Financing costs

Financing costs can add to or subtract from the operating profit of a business. Most companies have relatively high borrowings and therefore can have to pay out a large proportion of their profit in interest charges. Japanese and German companies like to have substantial bank deposits earning interest, so this item can be a positive figure.

Profit before and after taxation

All businesses pay tax on their profits. Companies pay corporation tax on profits. Over the period 2011 to 2014 the rate of corporation tax paid by larger UK companies is being cut from 28% to 24%. Once tax has been deducted, the final figure on the income statement is profit after taxation for the year. This figure is also known as the company's 'earnings'.

Using profits

'Earnings' can be used in two main ways: it can either be distributed or retained. Usually businesses retain some profits and distribute the remainder. The balance between these two uses is influenced by a number of factors.

- *Distributed profit:* the company directors will decide on the amount to be paid out to shareholders in the form of dividends; if the shareholders are unhappy with the sum paid out, they can vote against the dividend at the Annual General Meeting.
- *Retained profit:* any prudent owner or manager of a business will use some of the profit made by the business to reinvest in the business for the future.

A complete income statement for a private limited company is shown in Figure 8.3.

H Baker Ltd: Income statement for the period ended 30 May

	£	£
Revenue		47,800
Less cost of goods sold		
Opening stocks	4,700	
add Purchases	24,000	
less Closing stocks	6,000	22,700
Gross profit		**25,100**
Less expenses		
Wages and salaries	8,100	
Distribution	1,850	
Advertising	2,300	
Rent and other bills	3,550	
Depreciation	1,200	17,000
Operating profit		**8,100**
Financing costs		500
Profit before taxation		**7,600**
Taxation		2,128
Profit after taxation for the year		**5,472**

Figure 8.3 Example of a complete income statement

Examining income statements

The first thing to do when studying a profit and loss account is to look at the title. The title will always give the following information:

- business name
- income statement for the year ended
- DD/MM/YYYY.

The title provides some important information. First, the business name shows whether the firm has unlimited or limited liability. If the latter, it shows whether it is a small private company (Ltd) or a larger public limited company (plc).

The year-end date is also an important factor to take into consideration when comparing company accounts. Many types of businesses and markets suffer from trends and fashions as well as seasonal fluctuations in demand. The dates of the financial year can affect what the accounts will show. If the income statement covers a period of less than one year's trading, it is worth noting whether it covers key selling periods such as December.

Most income statements record the appropriate information for at least two years' trading. This assists stakeholders in identifying trends. For example, it is possible to look at the increase, if any, in revenue, expenses or operating profit. This helps to make a judgement about the financial well-being of the business.

Public limited companies

Public limited companies (plcs) are required by law to publish their accounts. This means that they are available for scrutiny not only by the owners (share-holders), potential investors and bankers, but also by competitors.

When a company draws up its income statement for external publication it will include as little information as possible. Public limited companies usually supply no more detail than is required by law. This format is illustrated in Figure 8.4, for Tesco.

Income statements and the law

The legal requirements relating to income statements are set out in the Companies Act 2006. This legislation demands the production of financial statements including an income statement. It also specifies the information to be included in these accounts.

The income statement does not have to detail every expense incurred by the firm, but summarises the main items under standard headings. The Act sets out acceptable formats for presentation of the relevant data. A summarised form of one of these is shown in Figure 8.4, for Tesco.

The notes to the income statements must disclose details of:

- auditor's fees
- depreciation amounts
- the total of directors' pay and fringe benefits
- the average number of employees, together with details of cost of wages and salaries, together with National Insurance and pensions.

Summarised group income statement for Tesco plc
(year ended 27 February 2010)

	2010 (£m)	2009 (£m)
Revenue (sales excluding VAT)	56,910	53,898
Cost of sales	(52,303)	(49,713)
Gross profit	**4,607**	**4,185**
Administrative & other expenses	(1,527)	(1,252)
Profits arising from other ventures	410	346
Operating profit	**3,490**	**3,279**
Finance income	265	116
Finance costs	(579)	(478)
Profit before tax	**3,176**	**2,917**
Taxation	(840)	(779)
Profit for the year	**2,336**	**2,138**

Figure 8.4 Example of a summarised income statement

Companies must disclose the following information.

- *Exceptional items:* these are large (usually one-off) financial transactions arising from ordinary trading activities. However, they are so large as to risk distorting the company's trading account. An example of exceptional items took place when the high-street banks incurred unusually large bad debt charges.

- *Extraordinary items:* these are large transactions outside the normal trading activities of a company. As a result they are not expected to recur. A typical example is the closure of a factory or division of a business. Once a factory is closed down, the costs of closure cannot arise again in future years.

A-grade application

Redrow takes action following loss

In 2009 the UK housebuilder Redrow plc made an operating loss of £120 million on sales of just £300 million. The collapse in the UK housing market had devastated the business, leaving it with unsold houses and a landbank that had slumped in value. This awful operating performance pushed its debt level up to 70% of all the firm's capital (known as 'gearing', this is a well-known measure of a firm's ability to survive hard times).

Impressively, even though the UK housing market remained quiet, in September 2010 Redrow was able to announce an operating profit of £12 million. By cutting staff numbers and pushing hard on both sales volumes and prices, it had managed to boost revenue by over 25% while keeping operating costs largely unchanged. As a result, it was able to cut its debt level from 70% to 11%.

Issues for analysis

- The income statement provides an insight into the performance of a business. Identifying trends in revenue can provide evidence about the success of a company within the marketplace. Is revenue rising after allowing for inflation? If so, this could be a healthy sign. If Tesco's UK sales are rising by 6%, but Sainsbury's at 9%, Tesco's shareholders will want answers from the company's chief executive.

- The income statement also gives details of how well the company is controlling its costs. Analysing the trends in gross and operating profits can be of value. For example, a rising figure for gross profits alongside a falling operating profit figure suggests that a promising business is not controlling its expenses.

- The key to analysing an income statement is to look at the performance of the business over a number of years. This may involve comparing various elements of the income statement to gain a further insight into the business.

Income statements (profit and loss accounts) – an evaluation

Two evaluative themes can be considered in relation to income statements. It is easy to make the assumption that a rising level of operating profit is evidence of a company that is performing well. There are a number of factors that need to be considered when making such a judgement. Has a new management pushed up prices, boosting profit for a year or so, but at the cost of damaged market share in the future? Is a company that pollutes the environment, uses materials from unsustainable sources, but makes a large profit, a successful business? Is profit necessarily the best measure of the performance of a business?

Even if we assume current profits are a good indication of how a company is performing, a number of other factors need to be taken into account. Is the market growing or declining? Are new competitors coming onto the scene? To what extent is the business achieving its corporate objectives? Is the profit earned likely to be sustained into the future – that is, is the profit of good quality? Information such as this is vital if a meaningful judgement is to be made about business success.

Key terms

Corporation tax: a tax levied as a percentage of a company's profits (e.g. 25%).

Cost of goods sold: calculation of the direct costs involved in making the goods actually sold in that period.

Gross profit: revenue less cost of goods sold; profit made on trading activities.

Operating profit: gross profit minus expenses.

Private limited company: a business with limited liability whose shares are not available to the public.

Revenue: sales revenue (i.e. the value of sales made); also known as income.

Stock exchange: a market for stocks and shares; it supervises the issuing of shares by companies and is also a second-hand market for stocks and shares.

Revision questions (40 marks; 40 minutes)

1 Give two possible reasons why a firm's bank would want to see its income statement. (2)

2 Outline two ways in which employees might benefit from looking at the income statement of their employer. (4)

3 List the elements necessary to calculate cost of sales. (4)

4 Distinguish between gross and operating profit. (4)

5 Last year Bandex plc made an operating profit of £25 million. £20 million of this came from the sale of its London training centre. The previous year the business made a profit of £15 million. Use the concept of 'profit quality' to decide whether last year was successful or unsuccessful for the business. (6)

6 Explain why even a charity such as Oxfam might want to make a profit. (4)

7 Explain what might be included under the heading 'financing costs'. (4)

8 Give one example each of exceptional and extraordinary items that might appear on the income statement of a business. Briefly explain each one. (4)

9 Look at the Tesco income statement in Figure 8.4.
 a Calculate the percentage increase in its (i) 2010 income and (ii) profit before tax. (4)
 b Explain one conclusion that can be drawn from those findings. (4)

Data response

The chairman of Thurton plc has come under some pressure lately. Shareholders have complained about the firm's lacklustre performance. Today, though, he is creating favourable headlines. The *Sunday Press* has announced that 'Thurton drives forward'. In the *Financial Guardian* the chairman is quoted as saying: 'This is a great day for Thurton. Profit before tax is up by more than 50% and we have been able to double our dividends to shareholders. I am confident we will be able to maintain or increase this dividend next year.'

Income statement for Thurton plc

	This year (£m)	Last year (£m)
Revenue	24.5	25.8
Cost of sales	10.0	9.6
Expenses	12.4	11.1
Operating profit	?	?
Extraordinary item	6.4	—
Finance income	0.5	0.4
Finance expenses	0.9	0.9
Profit before taxation	?	?
Taxation	2.4	1.4
Profit after taxation for the year	5.7	3.2

Figure 8.5 Income statement for Thurton plc

Questions *(25 marks; 30 minutes)*

1 Calculate Thurton plc's operating profit and profit before taxation for this year and last. (4)

2 Analyse Thurton plc's profit performance this year, by comparing it with last year. Within your answer, consider the quality of the profit made by Thurton this year. (9)

3 Use your analysis to comment on the accuracy of the chairman's statement. (12)

 Data response

Reckitt Benckiser plc is one of the world's leading manufacturers of cleaning products, and a member of the FTSE 100 Index of the largest companies traded on the London **Stock Exchange**. The company was formed by a merger between Britain's Reckitt & Colman and the Dutch company Benckiser NV. Reckitt Benckiser has operations in more than 60 countries and exports to more than 200 countries. The company focuses on high-margin yet steady-selling products such as Cif and Cillit Bang cleaners. It has shown strong growth in profits in recent years.

Questions

(40 marks; 50 minutes)

1 a Calculate Reckitt Benckiser's cost of sales for both periods. (5)

 b Calculate each figure as a percentage of the company's revenue for the corresponding period. (4)

 c Comment on your findings. (6)

2 a Calculate the percentage increase Reckitt Benckiser achieved in 2010 compared with 2009 in:

   i revenue (3)

   ii operating profit. (3)

 b Analyse the data to suggest why the increase in operating profit was greater than the increase in turnover. (8)

3 Why may it be risky to judge a firm such as Reckitt Benckiser on its profit performance over a six-month period? (11)

Reckitt Benckiser group income statement (summarised)

	Six months to 30/06/2010 £m	Six months to 30/06/2009 £m
Revenue	4,064	3,783
Cost of sales	?	?
Gross profit	**2,437**	**2,234**
Operating expenses	(1,473)	(1,415)
Operating profit	**964**	**819**
Net finance income	7	(3)
Profit before taxation	**971**	**816**
Taxation	(243)	(203)
Profit after taxation for the year	**728**	**613**

Figure 8.6 Reckitt Benckiser plc Group income statement (summarised)

Source: Reckitt Benckiser Interim Report, 2010.

Balance sheets

> ## Definition
> The balance sheet is an accounting statement that shows an organisation's assets and liabilities at a precise point in time, usually the last day of the accounting year. Assets are resources owned by the organisation that have a monetary value. Liabilities are debts owed by the organisation to others.

 ## Introduction

Unit 8 explained how an income statement provides information on how a business has performed over a given period of time, such as a year. It is the business equivalent to the question: 'How much did you earn last year?'

This unit focuses on the balance sheet. This accounting document looks at a different question: 'How rich are you?' To find out how rich someone is, you would need to find out what they own and what they owe on a particular day. The balance sheet does this for a business, with the particular day being the last day of the financial year. Balance sheets provide the means whereby owners, managers, financiers and other stakeholders can obtain information about an organisation that is not available on the income statement.

Since 2005 UK plcs have had to comply with the International Financial Reporting Standards (IFRS), which, in truth, make accounts more complicated to read. This requirement does not apply to private limited companies. This unit will start by looking at private limited company balance sheets, before moving on to plc balance sheets.

The balance sheet shows where a business has obtained its finances – its liabilities. It also lists the assets purchased with these funds. Therefore the balance sheet shows what the business owns and what it owes. For many financiers this is of vital importance when deciding whether or not to:

● invest in a business

● lend it some money

● buy the organisation outright.

A balance sheet enables the various stakeholders to make decisions as to that company's stability, its ability to pay debts and its ability to expand. A balance sheet therefore shows how secure a business is and what the potential for profit may be. It shows the asset strength built up in a business over all its years of trading. In effect, therefore, it shows the wealth of the business at a point in time.

How a business is financed and the resources it owns are of vital importance when making business plans and decisions. For example, if an organisation wanted to buy an expensive piece of equipment, how should it do it?

● *Buy it outright using cash from its bank account?* Yes, if there are sufficient funds to do so. But may the business be left short of money to meet future needs like paying bills and wages, or buying new stock?

● *Get a loan from the bank?* Again, this is a reasonable method of finance provided the business does not already have a lot of loans. Existing debt levels are shown on the balance sheet and can be examined to avoid the firm becoming dangerously indebted.

● *Attract new investors?* An organisation can take a partner or attract new shareholders. With the new funds invested it can purchase the equipment outright, therefore incurring no monthly payments or interest. However, new investors will receive a share of company profits and may want a say in the running of the business.

There is no single correct answer to the above. It depends on many factors, including the individual company's current circumstances. Some organisations may have a very healthy bank balance, whereas others may be struggling. It is the balance sheet that shows the current circumstances of the

business. By analysing this information, decisions can be made to match the source of finance to the business needs.

The composition of the balance sheet

The balance sheet of a business is a 'snapshot' showing the position of a company at a given point in time. It shows only what the business owns and owes on the date the balance sheet was compiled – in other words, the balance sheet is a picture of an organisation's assets and liabilities at that date.

The main classifications that are used in balance sheets for most private limited companies are described below. We shall see later that similar categories are used for public limited companies, but that different terminology is used.

Assets
Fixed assets

Fixed assets are those items of a monetary value that have a long-term function and can be used repeatedly, such as vehicles or machinery. These are assets the business plans to hold for a year or more, and are not intended for immediate resale.

Current assets

These are items of a monetary value that are likely to be turned into cash before the next balance sheet date. These include stocks, debtors and cash. Debtors and cash are often called liquid assets.

Other assets

These are assets that do not fall into either of the above categories (e.g. investments in other businesses).

Liabilities
Owners' capital

Owners' capital includes money or resources invested by the owners; it is called 'capital' for sole traders or partnerships and 'share capital' for limited companies.

Long-term liabilities

This refers to money owed by the business that has to be paid in more than one year's time.

Current liabilities

This is money owed by the business that has to be paid in less than one year's time. Examples include overdrafts, trade **creditors** (suppliers) and unpaid tax.

The structure of the balance sheet

The vertical balance sheet is the one most widely used in business today. By law, all public limited companies must publish their accounts in this form. Therefore it is the format focused upon in this unit.

The foundations of the balance sheet (at the bottom) consist of the firm's capital. This may have come from shareholders, bankers or from reinvested profit. If Spark Ltd has £400,000 of capital invested, it follows that it must have £400,000 of assets. The top section shows the type of assets bought. Figure 9.1 shows a summarised and simplified version of this position.

Spark Ltd: Simplified vertical balance sheet

	£
Long-term (fixed) assets	300,000
Short-term (current) assets	100,000
Total assets	400,000
Total capital	400,000

Figure 9.1 Example of a simplified vertical balance sheet

Assets on the vertical balance sheet

Fixed assets are long-term assets, including the following.

Tangible assets:

- land and buildings – property owned by the business, either freehold or leasehold
- plant/machinery/equipment – anything from specialised machinery used in manufacturing to computers or even furniture
- vehicles – all types.

Intangible assets:

- goodwill – the prestige a business enjoys, which adds value over and above the value of its physical assets
- patents/copyright – exclusive rights to make or sell a particular invention.

Current assets include stock, debtors and cash. In balance sheets, these assets are treated differently from fixed assets. This is because they change on a daily basis as bills come in, stock is sold and cash comes into the shop tills. The sudden arrival of £20,000 of stock from a supplier adds to current assets. But if the company now owes £20,000 to that supplier, it is clearly no better off. Thus current liabilities such as this are deducted from current assets to give a total called net current assets (also known as **working capital**).

Spark Ltd: Fuller version of the firm's balance sheet

	£	£
Property	180,000	
Machinery and vehicles	120,000	300,000
Stock	80,000	
Debtors and cash	60,000	
Current liabilities	(40,000)	
Net current assets		100,000
Assets employed		400,000
Total capital		400,000

Figure 9.2 Example of a fuller version of a vertical balance sheet

Notes

- The two-column format allows individual items to be shown on the left, leaving the 'big picture' totals to be seen clearly on the right.
- Current liabilities of £40,000 have been deducted from the £140,000 of current assets to show net current assets (or working capital) of £100,000.

- Assets employed of £400,000 still balances with the capital employed (total capital).

Capital on the balance sheet

Companies have three main sources of long-term capital: shareholders (share capital), banks (loan capital) and reinvested profits (reserves). Loan capital carries interest charges that must be repaid, as must the loan itself. Share capital and reserves are both owed to the shareholders, but do not have to be repaid. Therefore they are treated separately. Share capital and reserves are known as share-holders' funds.

Assuming Spark Ltd's capital came from £50,000 of share capital, £250,000 of loan capital and £100,000 of accumulated, retained profits, the final version of the vertical balance sheet would look like this:

Spark Ltd: Balance sheet for 31 December last year

	£	£
Property	180,000	
Machinery and vehicles	120,000	300,000
Stock	80,000	
Debtors and cash	60,000	
Current liabilities	(40,000)	
Net current assets	100,000	
Total assets less current liabilities		400,000
Loan capital		(250,000)
Net assets		150,000
Share capital	50,000	
Reserves	100,000	
Shareholders' funds		150,000

Figure 9.3 Example of a final version of a vertical balance sheet

The concept of capital as a liability

It is hard to see why money invested by the owners should be treated as a **liability**. This is due to a concept in accounting called 'business entity'. This states that a business and its owners are two separate legal entities. From the point of view of the business, therefore, any money paid to it by the shareholders is a liability because the firm owes it back to them. In reality, capital invested by the owners is likely to be paid back only in the event of the business ceasing to trade.

More detail on balance sheet calculations

Working capital

Current liabilities need to be repaid in the near future, ideally using current assets. Taking the former away from the latter gives a figure called working capital. This shows an organisation's ability or inability to pay its short-term debts.

If current assets exceed current liabilities the business has enough short-term assets to pay short-term debts. It has positive working capital and should therefore have enough money for its day-to-day needs.

If current assets are less than current liabilities the business does not have enough short-term assets to pay short-term debts. Working capital is negative (e.g. current assets are £50,000 but current liabilities are £70,000, so working capital is –£20,000). This may mean a day-to-day struggle to pay the bills. In this case the figure on the balance sheet may be called net current liabilities.

The balance between current assets and liabilities is a very important figure. Suppliers and banks expect to be paid when debts are due. At the very least, the failure to pay on time will mean a worsening in relations. At worst, it may result in court action.

In Figure 9.4, Ted Baker plc has plenty of working capital, because its £32 million of short-term (current) liabilities are easily covered by its £70 million of current assets.

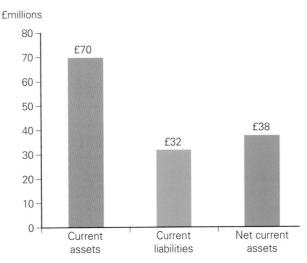

Figure 9.4 Ted Baker plc working capital, 2010

The effect of making a net loss on the balance sheet

In the event that a business makes a net loss rather than a net profit over a financial year, then the layout of the balance sheet remains completely unchanged. The only effect is that the loss reduces the reserves figure and therefore cuts the shareholders' funds. This will be balanced in the accounts by a reduction in the net current assets.

This reflects that if a business has made a loss over the financial period, expenses have exceeded revenues received. Therefore the overall value of the business will have fallen and so must the value of the owners' funds invested.

The published accounts of public limited companies

The implementation of International Financial Reporting Standards (IFRS) has required that listed public companies present their balance sheets in a format slightly different from that set out above. There are a number of differences in the terminology used on the IFRS balance sheet, as outlined below.

● Fixed assets are called non-current assets but continue to include tangible and non-tangible assets.

● There are two changes within the current assets section of the balance sheet: stocks are renamed as inventories and debtors are now termed 'trade and other receivables'.

● Under current liabilities creditors are referred to as 'trade and other payables'.

● Long-term liabilities are renamed 'non-current liabilities'.

● Reserves in the final section of the balance sheet are supplemented by 'retained earnings'. Retained earnings are profits that a company has generated that have not been paid out to shareholders.

● Shareholders' funds are termed 'total equity'.

The overall structure of the balance sheet is the same, even though the terminology varies. The two figures that balance are the net assets of the business (simply all its assets less its total liabilities) and the total equity figure (which is share capital invested plus reserves and retained earnings from past trading). The reason for balancing the figures in this way is to enable shareholders to see at a glance what the balance sheet suggests the business is 'worth' – that is, the bottom line of the balance sheet (total equity).

The implications of the changes introduced by IFRS rules are greater than just changes in terminology, but are not within the scope of this book. The main reason is to allow greater comparability between the performances of companies in different countries. It is hoped that this will increase investors' confidence and therefore encourage international investment flows.

Figure 9.5 is a summary of a recent balance sheet for the UK pub chain JD Wetherspoon. This follows the IFRS format for listed companies, though a few minor differences exist between the formats of balance sheets for different public companies. However, it is common for two years to be shown side by side. This is to help financial interpretation of the accounts and the analysis of trends.

Key conclusions to be drawn from JD Wetherspoon's balance sheets over the two years include:

- the company's long-term borrowing (non-current liabilities) has increased significantly between the two years

Balance sheet for JD Wetherspoon as at 25 July 2010

	2010	2009
	£m	£m
Non-current assets	845	797
Inventories	20	18
Receivables & cash	46	41
Total assets	911	856
Current liabilities	(177)	(258)
Non-current liabilities	(572)	(430)
Net assets	162	168
Share capital	145	145
Reserves & retained earnings	17	23
Total shareholders' equity	162	168

Figure 9.5 A summary of a balance sheet for the JD Wetherspoon pub chain

Source: adapted from annual accounts for JD Wetherspoon, 2010

- current liabilities outweigh current assets, causing net current assets to be strongly negative
- Reserves fell in 2010. This was a reflection of the very difficult trading period for pubs in recessionary Britain.

Window dressing accounts

'Window dressing' means presenting company accounts in such a manner as to flatter the financial position of the company.

Window dressing is a form of creative accounting that is concerned with making modest adjustments to sales, debtors and stock items when preparing end-of-year financial reports. There is a fine dividing line between flattery and fraud.

In many cases, window dressing is simply a matter of tidying up the accounts and is not misleading. Two important methods of window dressing are as follows.

1 Massaging profit figures: surprisingly, it is possible to 'adjust' a business's cost and revenue figures. At the end of a poor year, managers may be asked

to bring forward as many invoices and deliveries as possible. The intention is to inflate, as much as possible, the revenue earned by the business in the final month of trading.

2 Hiding a deteriorating **liquidity** position: this allows businesses to present balance sheets that look sound to potential investors. A business may execute a sale and leaseback deal just prior to accounts being published. This increases the amount of cash within the business and makes it look a more attractive proposition.

It is important to remember that, although window dressing happens, the overwhelming majority of companies present their accounts as fairly and straightforwardly as possible.

Issues for analysis

- The balance sheet is an important statement full of information for anyone with an interest in a business. Analysis of the balance sheet can provide the reader with an insight into the strengths and weaknesses of a business, its potential for growth, its stability and how it is financed.

- The balance sheet gives details as to where and how an organisation has obtained its finance, alongside information as to what this finance has been spent on. This allows judgements to be made about the financial performance of the business in question.

- Examining individual balance sheets can be interesting and provides the reader with a great deal of information. However, it must be remembered that a balance sheet is only a 'snapshot' of a business on one day out of 365, and that for a meaningful analysis to take place it must be compared to previous balance sheets, to see what changes or trends can be identified. The primary method of balance sheet analysis is through accounting ratios. These are explained in Unit 10.

Balance sheets – an evaluation

Several key areas can be considered with regard to balance sheets. The first is the assumption that just because a company possesses thousands or millions of pounds' worth of assets it is doing well. It is how the company has financed these assets that counts. A company could look to be in quite a stable position, but what would be the effect of a rise in interest rates if most of the company is financed by debt?

Similarly, equal importance must be placed on the short-term asset structure of the company. Many profitable companies close down or go into liquidation, not through lack of sales or customers but through poor short-term asset management (i.e. management of working capital).

As with all financial data and decisions, it is not sufficient just to consider the numerical information. External considerations such as the state of the market or economy must be taken into account. Comparisons with similar-sized organisations in the same industry must be used. Any worthwhile judgement requires an investigation into the non-financial aspects of the business. A company could have millions of pounds of assets, a healthy bank account, a good profit record and be financed mainly by share capital. However, all this means little if the workforce is about to go on strike for three months or its products are becoming obsolete.

> ## Key terms
>
> **Creditors:** those to whom a firm owes money (e.g. suppliers or bankers); these may also be called payables.
> **Fixed assets:** items of value the business plans to hold in the medium to long term, such as vehicles or property.
> **Liability:** a debt (i.e. a bill that has not been paid or a loan that has not been repaid).
> **Liquidity:** a measurement of a firm's ability to pay its short-term bills.
> **Working capital:** day-to-day finance for running the business (current assets – current liabilities).

A Revision questions (30 marks; 30 minutes)

1 Define the term 'balance sheet'. (2)

2 Distinguish between non-current and current assets. (4)

3 Explain why it is that the two parts of a balance sheet will always balance. (2)

4 What are the main reasons for presenting a balance sheet in vertical format? (3)

5 How would you calculate working capital? (2)

6 Why is it important for a supplier to check on the liquidity of a potential customer? (4)

7 Explain what is meant by the term 'window dressing'. (4)

8 Describe two ways in which a business might window dress its accounts. (4)

9 What is the difference between an intangible and a tangible non-current asset? (3)

10 State two items that may be listed as current liabilities. (2)

B1 Data response

Questions (20 marks; 25 minutes)

1 a Identify ten mistakes in the balance sheet in Figure 9.6. (10)

 b Draw up the balance sheet correctly. (10)

D Parton Ltd: Year ending 31 December 20XX	
	£000
Property	600
Stock	120
Machinery (at cost)*	240
Creditors	100
Cash	170
Reserves	350
less Debtors	280
Tax due	140
Assets employed	(200)
Net current assets	760
Overdraft	200
Share capital	500
Capital employed	760
*Book value: £120,000	

Figure 9.6 Balance sheet for D Parton Ltd

B2 Stimulus question

The balance sheet shown in Figure 9.7 is taken from Honda's 2010 annual report and accounts. Honda is one of the world's best-known and largest manufacturers of cars and motorbikes. In 2010 the company's sales turnover fell to $92 billion, from $102 billion in 2009. In the 2010 financial year the company's operating profit doubled to $3.9 billion.

Questions
(30 marks; 40 minutes)

1 Explain the meaning of the following terms:

 a balance sheet

 b net assets. (4)

2 Describe two external users of financial

information, and explain why they might analyse a balance sheet. (6)

3 a Identify three key trends in this data. (3)

   b Analyse the possible causes and implications of the trends you have identified. (6)

4 Evaluate the usefulness of this data to an investor considering purchasing shares in Honda. (11)

Honda balance sheet as at 31 March 2010	2010	2009
	$bn	$bn
Intangible non-current assets	7.0	6.5
Tangible non-current assets	68.4	66.8
Inventories	10.1	12.7
Receivables and cash	39.5	34.4
Current liabilities	(36.7)	(43.1)
Net current assets	12.9	4.0
Non-current liabilities	(40.3)	(35.1)
Net assets	**48.0**	**42.2**
Share capital	2.8	2.6
Reserves & retained earnings	45.2	39.6
Total equity	**48.0**	**42.2**

Figure 9.7 Honda balance sheet as at 31 March 2010

 Case study

Imperial Tobacco is the world's fourth-largest international tobacco company; it manufactures, markets and sells a comprehensive range of cigarettes, tobaccos and cigars. The company grew significantly during the 2006–2007 financial year, principally as a result of buying up other companies.

Questions

(40 marks; 50 minutes)

1 Distinguish between net current assets and net current liabilities. (3)

2 a Complete Imperial Tobacco's balance sheet by stating the missing figures. (3)

   b Explain one way in which Imperial Tobacco plc might have window dressed its accounts to make them look as favourable as possible. (4)

Balance sheet for Imperial Tobacco plc as at 30 September 2009	2009	2008
	£m	£m
Non-current assets	24,600	22,600
Inventories	2,900	2,800
Trade and other receivables	3,000	2,900
Cash & equivalents	1,300	800
Current liabilities	(11,400)	?
Net current assets/(liabilities)	?	(3,100)
Non-current liabilities	(13,900)	(13,200)
Net assets	6,500	6,300
Total equity	6,500	?

Figure 9.8 Balance sheet for Imperial Tobacco plc

3 Imperial Tobacco is expanding by buying other companies. Analyse whether its balance sheet is strong enough to encourage banks to lend it further capital to finance its plans. (12)

4 To what extent can you judge the performance of Imperial Tobacco plc over the period 2008–2009 from the information included in the company's balance sheet? (18)

 Essay questions *(40 marks each)*

1 'Balance sheets can only measure the financial worth of a business. The real worth depends upon far more.' In relation to any business with which you are familiar, discuss how important a balance sheet is, then, in judging whether a firm is well managed.

2 With reference to any business with which you are familiar, consider whether its balance sheet is more useful than its cash flow forecast, or vice versa.

3 'Balance sheet evaluation is the key to making successful long-term investment decisions.' With reference to any real-world business, consider the extent to which you believe this to be true.

10 Ratio analysis

Definition
Ratio analysis is an examination of accounting data by relating one figure to another. This approach allows more meaningful interpretation of the data and the identification of trends.

Introduction

The function of accounting is to provide information to stakeholders on how a business has performed over a given period. But how is performance to be judged? Is an annual profit of $1 million good or bad? Very good if the firm is a small family business; woeful if the business is KFC and annual sales exceed $10 billion. What is needed is to compare this information to something else. This can provide a way of judging a firm's financial performance in relation to its size and in relation to the performance of its competitors. The technique used to do this is called ratio analysis.

Financial accounts, such as the income statement and the balance sheet, are used for three main purposes:

1 financial control
2 planning
3 accountability.

Ratio analysis can assist in achieving these objectives. It can help the different users of financial information to answer some of the questions they are interested in. It may also raise several new questions, such as:

● Is this company/my job safe?
● Should I stop selling goods to this firm on credit?
● Should I invest in this business?

Interpreting final accounts: the investigation process

To analyse company accounts, a well-ordered and structured process needs to be followed. This should ensure that the analysis is relevant to the question being looked at. The seven-point approach shown in Figure 10.1 is helpful.

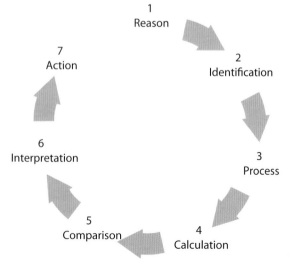

Figure 10.1 Seven-point approach to ratio analysis

Types of ratio

The main classifications of ratios are as follows.

- *Profitability ratios:* measure the relationship between gross/net profit and revenue, assets and capital employed. They are sometimes referred to as performance ratios.

- *Activity ratios:* these measure how efficiently an organisation uses its resources, such as inventories or total assets.

- *Liquidity ratios:* these investigate the short-term financial stability of a firm by examining whether there are sufficient short-term assets to meet the short-term liabilities (debts); the 2008 to 2010 credit squeeze showed that even banks can run out of the cash they need to keep operating.

- *Gearing:* examines the extent to which the business is dependent upon borrowed money; it is concerned with the long-term financial position of the company.

- *Shareholder ratios:* this group of ratios is concerned with analysing the returns for shareholders. They examine the relationship between the number of shares issued, dividend paid, value of the shares and company profits.

The following sections look at each classification of ratios in more detail.

Profitability ratios

For private businesses, a key objective is to make a profit. But how much profit? Consider the following example.

Example

Companies A and B operate in the same market. At the end of the year they report profits as follows:

	Company A	Company B
Profit	£100,000	£1 million

Which is the more successful company? Company B, surely. However, take into account the following additional information.

	Company A	Company B
Profit	£100,000	£1 million
Capital invested	£200,000	£10 million

This shows that Company A has done very well compared with the capital invested in the business. Much better, in fact, than Company B. Profitability ratios allow comparisons such as this to be made in detail. The figures can be compared in percentage terms. This makes comparison easier.

	Company A	Company B
Profit £	100,000	£1 million
Divided by	£200,000	£10 million
× 100 (to get a percentage)	50%	10%

Company A's success can now be seen much more clearly.

Unit 8 distinguished between various types of profit. Because of the different types of profit, there are a number of different profit ratios. The net profit margin was looked at within the AS course. There are two other profitability ratios to consider.

Gross profit margin

This ratio examines the relationship between the profit made before allowing for overhead costs (gross profit) and the level of revenue. It is given by the formula:

$$\text{gross profit margin} = \frac{\text{gross profit}}{\text{revenue}} \times 100$$

For example, a furniture shop buys sofas for £200 and sells them for £500 each, making a gross profit of £300 per sofa. In a week it sells ten, so its gross profit is £3000 and its revenue from sales is £5000. The gross profit margin is therefore:

$$= \frac{\text{gross profit}}{\text{revenue}} = \frac{\text{£3000}}{\text{£5000}} \times 100 = 60\%$$

Note that although this sounds a terrific profit margin, no allowance has yet been made for all the overhead costs of the business, such as rent, rates, staff costs, advertising and much more.

Interpretation

Obviously, the higher the profit margin a business makes the better. However, the level of gross profit margin will vary considerably between different markets. For example, the amount of gross profit percentage on clothes (especially fashion items) is far higher than on food. Any result gained must be looked at in the context of the industry in which the firm operates. It will always be possible to make comparisons with previous years' figures. This will establish whether or not the firm's trading position has become more or less profitable.

Altering the ratio

The gross profit margin can be improved by:

● raising sales revenue while keeping the cost of sales the same, or

● reducing the cost of sales made while maintaining the same level of sales revenue.

Return on capital employed (ROCE)

This is sometimes referred to as being the primary efficiency ratio and is perhaps the most important ratio of all. It measures the efficiency with which the firm generates profit from the funds invested in the business. It answers the key question anyone would ask before investing or saving: 'What annual percentage return will I get on my capital?'

$$\text{ROCE} = \frac{\text{operating profit}}{\text{capital employed}} \times 100$$

Operating profit is profit after all operating costs and overheads have been deducted. It is, however, profit before interest and taxation are paid. Capital employed is all the long-term finance of the business (debt plus equity).

Interpretation

The higher the value of this ratio the better it is. A high and rising ROCE suggests that resources are being used efficiently. ROCE measures profitability and no shareholder will complain at huge returns. The figure needs to be compared with previous years and that of other companies to determine whether this year's result is satisfactory or not.

A firm's ROCE can also be compared with the percentage return offered by interest-bearing accounts at banks and building societies. If bank interest rates are 6%, what is the point of a sole trader investing money in his or her business, working very hard all year and making a return on capital employed of 4%? He or she would be better off keeping the money in the bank, taking little risk and staying at home.

So what is the *right* level of ROCE? There is no clear answer, but most companies would regard a 20% ROCE as very satisfactory. The returns achieved by a selection of public companies in 2011 are shown in Table 10.1.

Altering the ratio

The return on capital employed can be improved by:

● increasing the level of profit generated by the same level of capital invested, or

● maintaining the level of profits generated but decreasing the amount of capital it takes to do so.

Table 10.1 The return on capital employed (ROCE) achieved by a selection of public limited companies in 2011

Company	Annual operating profit	Capital employed	ROCE
Apple Inc (electronics)	$33,000,000,000	$79,800,000,000	41.4%
Burberry (clothing)	£302,000,000	£830,000,000	36.4%
Tesco (retailing)	£3,811,000,000	£29,475,000,000	12.9%
Honda Motor*	$3,910,000,000	$88,241,000,000	4.4%

*2010 figure (2011 was hit hard by the tsunami, i.e. was even worse).

◗ Financial efficiency ratios

These four ratios are concerned with how well an organisation manages its resources. Three of them investigate how well the management controls the current situation of the firm. They consider stock, debtors and creditors. This area of ratios is linked, therefore, with the management of working capital. The fourth ratio looks at the position of the whole

business: how well it is generating sales income from the investment it has made in assets. This important ratio is called asset turnover.

Stock (or inventory) turnover

This ratio measures the number of times a year a business sells and replaces its stock – on plc balance sheets stock is termed 'inventories', but for the purpose of this ratio we will use the term stock. For example, if a market stall trader bought stock from wholesalers every morning and sold all the stock by the end of the afternoon, replacing the stock daily would mean a stock turnover of 365 times per year. The formula for stock turnover is:

$$\text{stock turnover} = \frac{\text{cost of goods sold}}{\text{stock}}$$

This is expressed as times per year.

Interpretation

This ratio can only really be interpreted with knowledge of the industry in which the firm operates. For example, we would expect a greengrocer to turn over stock virtually every day, as the goods have to be fresh. Therefore, we would expect to see a result for stock turnover of approximately 250 to 300 times per year. This allows for closures and holidays and the fact that some produce will last longer than one day. A second-hand car sales business might take an average of a month to sell the cars; therefore the stock turnover would be 12 times.

It is possible to convert this ratio from showing the number of times an organisation turns over stock to showing the average number of days that stock is held. It is given by the formula:

$$\frac{\text{stock turnover}}{\text{number of times}} = 365$$

This is expressed as days (e.g. 'the company holds 7 days' worth of stock').

Altering the ratio

The stock turnover ratio can be improved by:

- reducing the average level of stocks held, without losing sales, or
- increasing the rate of sales without raising the level of stocks.

Note that the stock turnover ratio has little meaning for service industries as they do not buy or sell stocks of goods.

Debtor days

This particular ratio is designed to show how long, on average, it takes the company to collect debts owed by customers. Customers who are granted credit are called debtors. On public companies' balance sheets they are called 'trade receivables', but we will use the term debtors for this ratio. The formula for this ratio is:

$$\text{debtor days} = \frac{\text{debtors}}{\text{annual income}} \times 365$$

This is expressed as days.

The accounts for the fashion clothing business Ted Baker plc make it possible to calculate the following debtor days' position (see Table 10.2).

Interpretation

In other words, the average Ted Baker customer took 44 days to pay in 2010 and 53 days to pay in 2011. By being slower collecting its money from customers, Ted Baker worsened its cash position. Better to have the cash than to be waiting for it.

Altering the ratio

The debtors' collection period can be improved by reducing the amount of time for which credit is offered (e.g. from 60 to 30 days), increasing the efficiency of the credit control department or by offering incentives for clients to pay on time e.g. cash discounts. A common approach is **aged debtors analysis**; this means sorting debtors into the age of their debts to you – oldest first. This helps to focus upon collecting debts from the slowest payers. It may also encourage a firm to refuse to supply a persistent slow payer in future.

Creditor days

This particular ratio is designed to show how many days, on average, it takes the company to pay its suppliers. Creditors are people and organisations that are owed money by the business. On public companies' balance sheets they are called 'trade payables', but we will use the term creditors for this ratio. The formula for this ratio is:

$$\text{creditor days} = \frac{\text{creditors}}{\text{cost of sales}} \times 365$$

The accounts for the fashion clothing business Ted Baker plc make it possible to calculate the following creditor days' position (Table 10.3).

Table 10.2 Information from the Ted Baker accounts: debtor position

	Annual income	Debtors	Debtor days
Year to 30 January 2010	£163.5m	£110.7m	44 days
Year to 29 January 2011	£187.7m	£27.3m	53 days

Table 10.3 Information from the Ted Baker accounts: creditor position

	Cost of sales £ million	Creditors £ million	Creditor days
Year to 30 January 2010	63.6	24.8	142 days
Year to 29 January 2011	71.9	34.9	177 days

Interpretation

In other words, the average Ted Baker supplier had to wait 142 days to be paid in 2010 and 177 days in 2011. Ted Baker is getting worse, and from a shockingly poor starting point. This would be important to know if your business was considering supplying Ted Baker for the first time (it's a long wait!). From Ted Baker's point of view, though, it's great to be able to hold onto the cash for ages before paying.

Altering the ratio

Creditor days can be reduced by paying bills more promptly. This might actually worsen a business's cash position but could improve its corporate image.

Asset turnover ratio

The asset turnover ratio measures how many pounds' worth of sales a company can generate from its net assets. Net assets are non-current assets plus net current assets less non-current liabilities. In other words, they equal total equity. Company directors often use the phrase 'make the assets sweat' – in other words, make the assets work hard. If there is a period in the year when a factory is quiet, an active company director might want to find a source of extra business. In this way the company could keep generating sales from its existing assets. This would push up the value of the asset turnover ratio.

$$\text{asset turnover} = \frac{\text{annual income}}{\text{assets employed}}$$

This is expressed as times per year.

Ted Baker had the asset turnover figures in 2010 and 2011 shown in Table 10.4.

Remarkably, Ted Baker's asset turnover remained constant year-on-year. Every pound's worth of investment in assets generated £2.42 of annual sales revenue. Businesses want this figure to move upwards over time as the business gets better at generating high customer demand. Although the stabilising of this figure might be disappointing, both figures represented a big increase in asset turnover compared with a few years earlier (it was 1.98 in 2005). A fair conclusion is that a pleasing long-term trend has stabilised in the short term.

Interpretation

Some companies pursue a policy of high profit margins, perhaps at the cost of high sales. An antiques shop in an expensive part of town may be beautifully laid out but never seem to have any customers. Its asset turnover will be low because it generates low sales from its high asset base. Fortunately for the firm, its profit margins may be so high that the occasional sale generates enough profit to keep the business going.

Other companies may follow a low-price, high-sales approach. Tesco used to call this 'pile them high, sell them cheap'. Here profit margins may be low, but the asset turnover so high that lots and lots of small profits add up to a healthy profit total. Asset turnover, then, should be looked at in relation to (net) profit margins. If net profit margins are multiplied by asset turnover, the result is the company's ROCE. So boosting asset turnover is as helpful to a firm as boosting its profit margins.

Altering the ratio

To increase asset turnover there are two options. Either work at increasing sales from the existing asset base (making the assets 'sweat'). Or sell off under-utilised assets, so that the sales figure is divided by a lower asset total. Either approach would then have the effect of boosting a company's ROCE.

Table 10.4 Information from Ted Baker accounts: asset turnover figures

Year	Sales revenue £ million	Assets employed £ million	Asset turnover
2010	163.6	67.5	2.42 times
2011	187.7	77.6	2.42 times

Liquidity ratios

These ratios are concerned with the short-term financial health of a business. They are concerned with the organisation's working capital and whether or not it is being managed effectively. Too little working capital and the company may not be able to pay all its debts. Too much and it may not be making the most efficient use of its financial resources.

Current ratio (also known as the liquidity ratio)

This ratio looks at the relationship between current assets and current liabilities. It examines the **liquidity** position of the firm. It is given by the formula:

$$\text{current ratio} = \frac{\text{current assets}}{\text{current liabilities}}$$

This is expressed as a ratio; for example, 2:1 or 3:1.

Example

Bannam Ltd has current assets of £30,000 and current liabilities of £10,000:

current ratio = current assets : current liabilities

= £30,000 : £10,000

= 3 : 1

current ratio = 3

Interpretation

The above worked example shows that Bannam Ltd has three times as many current assets as current liabilities. This means that, for every £1 of short-term debts owed, it has £3 of assets to pay them. This is a comfortable position.

Accountants suggest the 'ideal' current ratio should be approximately 1.5:1 (i.e. £1.50 of assets for every £1 of debt). Any higher than this and the organisation has too many resources tied up in unproductive assets; these could be invested more profitably (or the cash should be handed back to shareholders). A low current ratio means a business may not be able to pay its debts. It is possible that the result may well be something like 0.8:1. This shows the firm has only 80p of current assets to pay every £1 it owes.

The current ratios of a selection of public companies in 2011 are shown in Table 10.5. As this table shows, it would be wrong to panic about a liquidity ratio of less than 1. Some successful firms such as Tesco are able to operate in the long term with surprisingly low liquidity ratios.

Altering the ratio

If the ratio is so low that it is becoming hard to pay the bills, the company will have to try to bring more cash into the balance sheet. This could be done by:

- selling under-used fixed assets
- raising more share capital
- increasing long-term borrowings
- postponing planned investments.

Acid test ratio

This ratio is sometimes also called the quick ratio or even the liquid ratio. It examines the business's liquidity position by comparing current assets and liabilities, but it omits stock (or inventories) from the total of current assets. The reason for this is that stock is the most illiquid current asset (i.e. it is the hardest to turn into cash without a loss in its value). It can take a long time to convert stock into cash. Furthermore, stock may be old or obsolete and thus unsellable.

By omitting stock, the ratio directly relates cash and near cash (cash, bank and debtors – known as liquid assets) to short-term debts. This provides a tighter measure of a firm's liquidity. It is given by the formula:

Table 10.5 The current ratios of a selection of public companies in 2011

Company	Balance sheet date	Current assets	Current liabilities	Current ratio
Ted Baker plc	29/01/2011	£83,800,000	£39,200,000	2.14
Burberry plc	31/03/2011	£870,000,000	£534,300,000	1.63
Honda Motor	31/03/2011	$56,405,000,000	$42,913,000,000	1.31
Tesco plc	26/02/2011	£11,869,000,000	£17,731,000,000	0.67
JD Wetherspoon	23/01/2011	£70,181,000	£165,846,000	0.42

$$\text{acid test ratio} = \frac{(\text{current assets} - \text{stock})}{\text{current liabilities}}$$

Again, it is expressed in the form of a ratio, such as 2:1.

Interpretation

Accountants recommend that an 'ideal' result for this ratio should be approximately 1:1, thus showing that the organisation has £1 of short-term assets for every £1 of short-term debt. A result below this (e.g. 0.5:1) indicates that the firm may have difficulties meeting short-term payments. However, some businesses are able to operate with a very low level of liquidity – supermarkets, for example, who have much of their current assets tied up in stock.

The acid test ratios of a selection of public companies in 2011 are shown in Table 10.6.

Table 10.6 The acid test ratios of a selection of public companies in 2011

Company	Balance sheet date	Current assets – stock (inventories)	Current liabilities	Acid test ratio
Ted Baker plc	29/01/2011	£41,308,000	£39,200,000	1.05
Burberry plc	31/03/2011	£622,200,000	£534,300,000	1.16
Honda Motor	31/03/2011	$45,583,000,000	$42,913,000,000	1.06
Tesco plc	26/02/2011	£8,707,000,000	£17,731,000,000	0.49
JD Wetherspoon	23/01/2011	£50,693,000	£165,846,000	0.31

Gearing

Gearing is one of the main measures of the financial health of a business. Quite simply, it measures the firm's level of debt. This shines a light onto the long-term financial stability of an organisation.

Gearing measures long-term loans as a proportion of a firm's capital employed. It shows how reliant the firm is upon borrowed money. In turn, that indicates how vulnerable the firm is to financial setbacks. The Americans call gearing 'leverage'. In boom times, banks and investors find leverage (debt) very attractive; but high gearing always means high risk.

Highly geared companies can suffer badly in recessions, because even when times are hard they still have to keep paying high interest payments to the bank.

The formula for gearing is:

$$\text{gearing} = \frac{\text{long-term loans}}{\text{capital employed}} \times 100$$

This is expressed as a percentage.

Interpretation

The gearing ratio shows how risky an investment a company is. If loans represent more than 50% of capital employed, the company is said to be highly geared. Such a company has to pay substantial interest charges on its borrowings before it can pay dividends to shareholders or retain profits for reinvestment. The higher the gearing, the higher the degree of risk. Low-geared companies provide a lower-risk investment; therefore they can negotiate loans more easily and at lower cost than a highly geared company.

Table 10.7 The gearing ratios of a selection of companies in 2011

Company	Balance sheet date	Non-current liabilities (long-term loans)	Capital employed	Gearing
Ted Baker plc	29/01/2011	£1,550,000	£77,600,000	2.0%
Burberry plc	31/03/2011	£96,400,000	£830,100,000	11.6%
Honda Motor	31/03/2011	$41,127,000,000	$96,244,000,000	42.7%
Tesco plc	26/02/2011	£12,852,000,000	£29,475,000,000	43.6%
JD Wetherspoon	23/01/2011	£577,425,000	£768,046,000	75.2%

Carlyle Capital Corporation

During the credit crunch a US blogger with the fabulous name of Postman Patel warned that the Carlyle Capital Corporation (an American investment fund) was unable to pay its bills. Within a week it had collapsed, owing over \$16 billion. It emerged that Carlyle Capital had a gearing level of 97%. In other words, only 3% of the money it invested was its own money; all the rest was borrowed. When times were good its shares were worth \$20 each. Now they were worth nothing. High gearing means high risk. Ridiculously high gearing means ridiculously high risk.

Banks would be especially reluctant to lend to a firm with poor liquidity and high gearing. It is useful, therefore, to look at the gearing for the same firms whose liquidity was investigated earlier. This is shown in Table 10.7.

JD Wetherspoon (a chain of low-priced pubs) has a high gearing level. The company might experience difficulties if interest rates rose, or if it encountered a really poor period of trading. However, if its markets have growth potential, the company probably has the resources to benefit from it.

In contrast, Burberry, and especially Ted Baker, have very low gearing levels. This could be a weakness if the economy was expanding rapidly. Their management teams could be judged as timid, as the companies are not in a position to benefit from rapid growth. An investment in a firm with a low gearing could be regarded as safe, but dull.

Altering the ratio

The gearing ratio can be altered in several ways, depending on whether the organisation wishes to raise or lower its gearing figure.

Raising gearing	Reducing gearing
Buy back ordinary shares	Issue more ordinary shares
Issue more preference shares	Buy back debentures (redeeming)
Issue more debentures	Retain more profits
Obtain more loans	Repay loans

Shareholder ratios

Investing in shares provides two potential sources of financial return. The share price might rise, providing a capital gain. In addition, firms pay annual dividends to shareholders. The size of the dividends depends upon the level of profits made in the year. Shareholder ratios provide a way of judging whether the shares are expensive or inexpensive, and whether the dividends are high enough. They do, however, put some pressure on companies to achieve short-term profits and to pay out high dividends. This may damage the interests of the company's stakeholders in the long term.

Earnings per share (EPS)

This ratio measures the company's **earnings** (profit after tax) divided by the number of ordinary shares it has issued. This can be used to measure a company's profit performance over time. It is shown on the income statements of public limited companies. The EPS also shows the potential for paying out a dividend to shareholders. It is given by the formula:

$$\text{earnings per share} = \frac{\text{profit after tax}}{\text{number of ordinary shares}}$$

This is usually expressed in pence.

Interpretation

Earnings per share is relatively meaningless if analysed on its own, although the higher the result the better for shareholders. Meaning can only be established by comparisons with previous years' results. A rising EPS is likely to please shareholders.

Altering the ratio

This ratio can only really be improved by increasing the level of profits made. This may cause the pressure for short-term profits mentioned earlier.

Dividend per share (DPS)

This ratio is calculated by dividing the total dividend to be paid to the shareholders by the number of shares issued. Thus:

$$\text{dividend per share} = \frac{\text{total dividends}}{\text{shares issued}}$$

The result of this ratio is normally expressed in pence.

Interpretation

The result of this ratio does not provide much insight into the company's performance as it means little without comparison to the current share price for the company concerned. The ratio below (dividend yield) completes this calculation.

Altering the ratio

This can be done in two ways. The directors can announce that a larger proportion of the company's profits will be distributed to shareholders, as dividends or the number of shares that are issued by the company can be reduced through a buy-back scheme.

Dividend yield

This ratio directly relates the amount of dividend actually received to the market value of the share. It shows the shareholders' annual dividends as a percentage of the sum invested. It is given by the formula:

$$\text{dividend yield} = \frac{\text{ordinary share dividend}}{\text{market price (pence)}} \times 100$$

Interpretation

Again, the higher the result the better. However, it would need to be compared against previous years and the results of competitors.

Altering the ratio

As this ratio is based partly on the market price of ordinary shares, anything that affects this value will impact on the ratio. A higher result can be obtained by either making greater profits, or making a greater proportion of profit available for distribution as dividend.

Issues for analysis

- There are many more areas of ratio analysis than those outlined within this unit. Specialist ratios exist for all types of organisation, especially those in the public or voluntary sector where profits and capital are not so readily determined.

- Another aspect that needs discussion is that the analysis and interpretation of financial statements is really only the first step in a lengthy process. The data gathered from this exercise must be presented to and understood by those who will then go on to make decisions based upon it. Also consider the validity of making long-term decisions based upon findings from an income statement and balance sheet that may be several months out of date. As well as conducting ratio analysis, other information contained within the annual reports should also be used, such as the chairman's report.

- As a final point for further investigation, the accuracy of ratio analysis itself is often called into question. Factors such as the effect of inflation on accounts from one year to the next, differences in accounting policies and the effect of economic change may have a significant effect on the ratios.

Ratio analysis – an evaluation

Ratio analysis is a powerful tool in the interpretation of financial accounts. It can allow for **inter-firm comparisons**, appraisal of financial performance and the identification of trends. It can therefore be of great help in financial planning and decision making.

However, because of its usefulness and the range of possible applications, there is a tendency to attach too much importance to the results gained from this analysis. Other types of analysis exist, and there are sometimes more important issues at stake than just financial performance.

Many financial analysts are now using the concept of 'added value' to see if shareholder value has been increased. Consideration must also be given to the fact that often stakeholders are not fluent in financial and business terminology, and that the use of ratio analysis may be a case of 'blinding them with science'. Also, a changing society has seen a change in focus away from pure financial performance towards consideration of social and ethical factors. Although ratio analysis is useful, it is limited in the area it investigates.

Key terms

Aged debtors analysis: listing debtors in age order, to identify the slowest payers.

Earnings: for a company, earnings means profit after tax.

Inter-firm comparisons: comparisons of financial performance between firms; to be valuable, these comparisons should be with a firm of similar size within the same market.

Liquidity: the ability of a firm to meet its short-term debts; liquidity can also be understood as being the availability of cash or assets that can easily be converted into cash.

 A ## Revision questions *(40 marks; 40 minutes)*

1 List four groups of people who may be interested in the results of ratio analysis. (4)

2 State the key stages in conducting an analysis of company accounts using ratios. (7)

3 Briefly explain the difference between financial efficiency ratios and profitability ratios. (4)

4 Explain why the return on capital employed (ROCE) is regarded as one of the most important ratios. (3)

5 Why might the managers of a company be pleased if its stock (inventory) turnover ratio were falling? (4)

6 What might the figure for debtor days tell you about the way in which a business controls its finances? (4)

7 Outline the difference between the current ratio and the acid test ratio. (2)

8 Why might a small investor be particularly interested in the dividend yield ratio? (4)

9 Outline two problems a company might experience if its gearing ratio rose significantly. (4)

10 Explain one reason why investors might treat the results of ratio analysis with caution. (4)

 B1 ## Practice exercises *(73 marks; 90 minutes)*

1 J Orr Ltd makes garden gnomes. State and explain which three accounting ratios you think would be of most use to:

  a a firm wondering whether to supply J Orr with materials on credit (6)

  b the trade union representative of J Orr's workforce (6)

  c a pensioner, wondering whether J Orr will be a good investment (6)

  d the management of J Orr's main rival, Gnometastic Ltd (6)

  e J Orr's main customer, Blooms of Broadway garden centre. (6)

2 A garden furniture producer wants to buy a garden centre. It has identified two possible businesses and conducted some ratio analysis to help it decide which one to focus on. Look at the ratios for each business in Table 10.8, and decide which one you would recommend and why. (10)

Figure 10.2 Garden gnome

	£000
Fixed assets	860
Stock	85
Debtors	180
Cash	15
Current liabilities	(200)
Loans	(360)
Share capital	160
Reserves	420

Figure 10.3 Balance sheet for GrowMax Co as at 31 December

3 The balance sheet for GrowMax Co as at 31 December is shown in Figure 10.3.

  a Calculate the firm's net current assets and capital employed. (4)

b Last year's revenue was £1,460,000 and operating margin was 10%. Comment on the firm's profitability. (10)

c GrowMax's main rival offers its customers 30 days' credit.

  i How does this compare with GrowMax? (4)

  ii Outline two further questions the GrowMax management should want answered before deciding whether their customer credit policy should be revised. (6)

d Outline three difficulties with drawing firm conclusions from the ratios of two rival companies. (9)

Table 10.8 Ratio analyses for Blooms of Broadway and Cotswold Carnations

	Blooms of Broadway	**Cotswold Carnations**
Gross profit margin	60%	45%
Return on capital	15.2%	14.6%
Stock turnover	18 times	24 times
Gearing	52%	35%
Sales growth (last 3 years)	+3.5% per year	+4.8% per year

Data response

Since the beginning of the year, Phones4Kids has enjoyed rapid growth as a result of booming exports to America. Financing the increased production has required an extra £80,000 of working capital, and now the production manager has put in an urgent request for £240,000 of new capital investment.

The firm's managing director doubts that he can find the extra capital without giving up control of the business (he currently holds 54% of the shares). The finance director is more optimistic. He suggests that: 'Our balance sheet is in pretty good shape and the mobile phone business is booming. I'm confident we can get and afford a loan.' So it came as a huge blow to hear that Barclays had turned the company down. It wondered what it had done wrong ...

Questions (35 marks; 45 minutes)

1 Analyse why the bank manager might have turned the request down. (10)

2 Recommend how the expansion might be

Phones4Kids balance sheet as at 31 December

	£000	£000
Fixed assets[1]	420	420
Inventories	250	
Debtors[2] (receivables)	140	
Cash	130	520
Current liabilities		(380)
Non-current liabilities		(200)
Net assets		360
Share capital	50	
Reserves	310	
Total equity		360

1 Depreciated straight line over 10 years

2 Including a £15,000 debtors item 12 months overdue

Figure 10.4 Balance sheet for Phones4Kids as at 31 December

financed, showing the effect of your plan upon key indicators of the firm's financial health. (10)

3 Given your answers to 1 and 2, discuss whether the firm should proceed with its expansion plan. (15)

Data response

The Whitbread Group plc operates a range of brands in the hospitality industry. The company has interests in hotels, restaurants and coffee bars, including Premier Inn and Costa Coffee. Whitbread is listed on the London Stock Exchange and is a part of the FTSE 100 Index. The company was founded as a brewery in 1742 but no longer has any interests in brewing.

Questions (50 marks; 60 minutes)

1 State Whitbread plc's working capital in 2009 and 2010. (4)

2 Calculate Whitbread plc's:

  a 2010 cost of sales (2)

  b 2009 and 2010 gearing. (4)

3 a Assess the company's profitability in 2010 compared with 2009. (10)

  b What further information would be needed in order to make a full assessment of the effectiveness of the company's management at generating profit in 2010? (4)

4 a What are Whitbread plc's current ratios for 2009 and 2010? (4)

  b Briefly analyse the possible implications of these figures for the managers of the business. (6)

5 A major insurance company is considering buying a large number of shares in Whitbread plc as part of its investment portfolio. Assess the strengths and weaknesses for outsiders of using this company's accounts to decide on such a major decision. (16)

Whitbread plc: Extract from 2010 Interim (half year) Report and Accounts Summary Consolidated Income Statement

	2010 £m	2009 £m
Revenue	805.4	703.3
Gross profit	685.0	598.5
Expenses	(516.6)	(471.4)
Operating profit	168.4	127.1
Finance revenue	2.1	0.2
Finance costs	(19.5)	(21.3)
Profit before tax	151.0	106.0

Balance sheet, 2 September 2010

	2010 £m	2009 £m
Non-current assets	2,512	2,468
Inventories (stocks)	20	17
Trade & other receivables	98	86
Cash & cash equivalents	35	29
Current liabilities	(340)	(355)
Non-current liabilities	(1,201)	(1,201)
Net assets	1,124	1,044
Share capital	196	192
Reserves	928	852
Total equity	1,124	1,044

Figure 10.5 Summarised interim accounts, Whitbread plc
Source: adapted from Whitbread plc Interim Report 2010

Essay questions (40 marks each)

1 'Ratios are of little to no use to a person intending to make a small investment.' Comment on the accuracy of this statement.

2 'The ability to assess the long- and short-term financial stability of an organisation is vital to every stakeholder.' To what extent do you agree with this statement?

3 With the economy entering a recession, an investor wants to reassess her share portfolio. Examine which ratios she should focus upon, given the economic circumstances.

Limitations of accounts

> **Definition**
> 'True and fair view' is the phrase used by auditors when checking a firm's accounts, to confirm that they are accurate within the terms of the accounting practices used to draw them up.

 ## Introduction: giving a true and fair view?

The final accounts of a business are usually the first point of reference for anyone interested in analysing its value or performance over a period of time. For instance, the revenue and expenses generated over a period of time are reported in a firm's profit and loss account. The balance sheet gives us information needed to calculate its **book value** (i.e. the difference between its total assets and any liabilities it may have). Together these statements allow ratio analysis to be carried out. However, all this information gives an incomplete and possibly misleading view of what a business may actually be worth.

What accounts leave out

Focus on quantitative data

Money acts as the language of accounting, allowing business transactions to be measured, compared and added together. This means that accounts focus on items that can be given a financial value. Yet a successful business depends on a lot more than the price paid for property and equipment, or the size of its outstanding debt. For example, a firm's culture and its attitude to risk-taking will be at the heart of its performance. Similarly, a highly skilled, loyal and motivated workforce, a commitment to behaving in an ethical and environmentally friendly manner or a reputation for excellent customer service can increase a firm's ability to compete against rivals. These aspects of a business are likely to make it worth more, both to existing owners and potential buyers. However, such features are difficult to express in numerical terms and are, therefore, usually ignored by the main accounting statements.

Using profit as a performance indicator

Profit is generally regarded as one of the most important indicators of performance. Yet the long-term success of a business may depend on a firm's willingness to sacrifice profits, in the short term at least. It may be useful, therefore, to

Figure 11.1 A Reckitt Benckiser product

also consider other indicators, such as growth in revenue and market share or investment in research and development and new product success. For example, the massive Reckitt Benckiser plc (Cillit Bang, Air Wick fresheners, etc. – see the A-grade application) has a target that at least 35% of its sales should come from products launched in the past three years.

The state of the market

The nature of accounts means that they are historical (i.e. they reflect what has happened in the past, rather than commenting on the present or looking ahead to the future). No business can assume that the environment in which it operates will remain the same. The conditions that contributed to past performance, however recent, are bound to change at some point. For example, the number of competitors in a market may increase, or a healthy economy may suddenly descend into recession.

Although most large companies produce a chairman's statement, which may speculate on future prospects, this document is not, strictly speaking, part of the accounts and may be deliberately written to create an overly favourable impression.

Problems interpreting accounts

Although the purpose of a firm's accounts is to assign a value to the items contained within them, there are a number of reasons why such values should be treated with caution.

Land and buildings

The accounting convention of valuing assets at historic (or original) cost is likely to mean that any figures for land or property owned by a business are unlikely to reflect their current market value. Such fixed assets tend to appreciate in value over time, meaning they are effectively undervalued. This could mean that the business might struggle to raise loan finance, due to an apparent lack of collateral. Moreover, it could make it vulnerable to a hostile takeover from other firms keen to benefit from disposing of undervalued assets in order to generate funds.

Intangible assets

These include intellectual property such as patents, copyright and brand names. Such assets may well have a role in generating sales and profits for a business, especially for service-based firms that trade on image and reputation. However, estimating the monetary value of **intangible assets** can be very difficult. For example, the importance of even a well-known brand to a firm's success can quickly

diminish – perhaps as a result of negative publicity or a change in fashion. **Goodwill** is a concept that may arise when one business is bought by another. It refers to the value placed on the business by the buyer, over and above its book value, in recognition of its good reputation and established customer base. This may mean the business is worth more as a **going concern** than the value of its parts, but the buyer may end up overstating its value.

Debtors

Firms are usually content to sell goods on credit to customers in order to generate sales – any outstanding payments are recorded as a current asset on the balance sheet. However, this figure tells us very little about the nature of the debtors themselves. Does the overall debtors figure consist of regular customers who can be relied upon to pay on time, or long overdue amounts that are unlikely to ever be received? A high proportion of debtors made up of **bad debts** will result in an overvaluation of a firm's current assets on the balance sheet, increasing the chances of liquidity problems.

Stock

The value of stock at the end of a trading period affects both the value of the business due to its inclusion on the balance sheet (under current assets) and the value of profit (due to its effect on cost of goods sold in the trading account). But, given that stock is the least liquid of a firm's current assets, how reliable is the value attached to it? The value of stock can change rapidly, especially in industries subject to frequent changes in customer tastes. The traditional accounting practice is to value stock at cost or **net realisable value**, whichever is the lower. This means that the value of stock that will not sell is potentially zero!

Profit quality

The ability to generate profit is generally accepted as a key indicator of success. However, it is also worth checking the source of this profit in order to assess the likelihood of such profits continuing into the future. Selling off a piece of machinery at a price above its book value will generate a surplus, but this can only happen once and is, therefore, described as being of low **profit quality**. It is important that a firm's accounts separate 'one-off' low-quality profit from the high-quality profit that results from its normal trading activities.

Manipulating the published accounts

There are a number of reasons why a business may decide to manipulate its accounts in order to flatter its financial position at a particular point in time. Such practices, known as **window dressing** or creative accounting, do not necessarily mean that fraud has been committed, but may nevertheless result in the users of accounts being misled. There are a number of reasons why a firm might window dress its accounts – creating the impression that a business is financially stronger than it actually is can help to secure loans or support the sale of new shares. Common methods of window dressing include the following.

- *Sale and leaseback of fixed assets:* this allows a business to continue to use assets but disguise a poor or deteriorating liquidity position by generating a sudden injection of cash.

- *Bringing forward sales:* a sale is recognised (and included in profit calculations) when an order is made, rather than when payment is received. Encouraging customers to place orders earlier than usual will mean that they are included at the end of one financial period rather than at the start of the next, giving an apparent boost to revenue and profit.

- *A change in approach to depreciation:* for example, increasing the expected life of a fixed asset will reduce the annual depreciation charge, increasing the level of reported profit as well as increasing the asset value on the balance sheet. Presenting a more favourable set of accounts may attract more investment or help fight off a hostile takeover bid.

- *Writing off bad debts:* the decision to treat a customer's unpaid bill as a bad debt will mean that the figure has to be charged to the profit and loss account as an expense. This will reduce the firm's net profit figure, reducing the level of corporation tax paid.

The Companies Act 1985 places a legal obligation on companies to provide accounts that are audited and give a true and fair view of their financial position. In addition, the Accounting Standards Board has the responsibility of providing a regulatory framework in order to create greater uniformity in the way company accounts are drawn up. Despite this, the pressure on businesses to not only perform well but to be seen to do so is likely to mean that window dressing practices will persist.

Issues for analysis

Opportunities for analysis are likely to focus on the following areas:

- the problems of relying on financial data to analyse a firm's financial position and performance
- the difficulties of trying to get an accurate measure of the value of a business
- the consequences of failing to provide an accurate value of a business
- the reasons why a firm might attempt to window dress its financial position.

 Limitations of accounts – an evaluation

Accounting information plays a key role in assessing the value and performance of a business. However, using such information alone, and failing to consider other relevant factors will give an incomplete picture of a firm's current position and future potential.

The quality of the workforce, investment in new technology and the state of the market in which it operates may be difficult to quantify but may be more accurate indicators of a firm's long-term success than an impressive set of final accounts.

Key terms

Bad debts: when a firm decides that amounts outstanding as a result of credit sales are unlikely to be recovered, perhaps because the customer concerned has gone into liquidation.

Going concern: the accounting assumption that, in the absence of any evidence to the contrary, a business will continue to operate for the foreseeable future.

Goodwill: arises when a business is sold and the buyer pays more than its book value in recognition of the good reputation and customer base that is being obtained. This amount is shown as an intangible asset on the firm's balance sheet.

Intangible assets: these are assets that have no physical existence, such as plant and machinery, but contribute to sales and profits. Examples include patents, copyright, brand names and goodwill.

Net realisable value: this is the value given to an asset (usually stock) on the balance sheet if it is expected to be sold for less than its historic cost.

Profit quality: this assesses the likelihood of the source of the profit made by a business continuing in the future. High-quality profit is usually that which is generated by a firm's usual trading activities, whereas low-quality profit comes from a one-off source.

Window dressing: the practice of presenting a firm's accounts in a way that flatters its financial position (e.g. selling and leasing back assets in order to generate cash and disguise a poor liquidity position).

A Revision questions *(35 marks; 35 minutes)*

1 What is meant by the phrase 'a true and fair view' in the context of accounting? (3)

2 Identify three aspects of a business that may increase its value but are unlikely to be included in its accounts. (3)

3 Describe two problems that a firm might experience from understating the value of land or property that it might own. (6)

4 Analyse one reason for and one reason against attempting to include a value for a firm's intangible assets on its balance sheet. (6)

5 Explain the difference between a debtor and a bad debt. (4)

6 What is meant by the term 'window dressing'? (3)

7 Describe two reasons why a firm might window dress its accounts. (4)

8 Outline three ways in which a business might attempt to window dress its accounts. (6)

B1 Data response

Valuing global brands

Diageo is the world's leading producer of alcoholic drinks. Its portfolio includes a number of market-leading brands, including Guinness, Baileys, Smirnoff vodka, Johnnie Walker whisky and Tanqueray gin. Diageo's global sales (net of excise duty) for the year to the end of June 2010 increased from just over £9.3 billion to nearly £9.8 billion. The company's operating profits for the same period amounted to over £2.57 billion, up from nearly £2.42 million in 2009.

Like other breweries, Diageo faced a number of challenges during the year, including continuing recession in many economies and significant increases in the price of wheat and barley. However, according to Diageo's chief executive, Paul Walsh, the global diversity of the business and the strength and range of its brands would allow the company to continue to grow its operating profit. The firm experienced particularly strong growth in Asia, Latin America where it has a large Scotch business, and Africa where brands such as Tusker beer and Guinness are popular. Sales continued to grow in these markets throughout the global downturn and were responsible for around one-third of the company's annual earnings. Diageo is also building up a market in China, with brands such as Johnnie Walker.

Table 11.1 Extracts from Diageo's income statements 2008 to 2010 (as at 30 June)

	Year ending 30/06/2010 £ millions	Year ending 30/06/2009 £ millions	Year ending 30/06/2008 £ millions
Net sales	9,780	9,311	8,090
Gross profit	5,681	5,418	4,836
Operating profit	2,574	2,418	2,212

Table 11. 2 Extracts from Diageo's balance sheets 2008 to 2010 (as at 30 June)

	Year ending 30/06/2010 £ millions	Year ending 30/06/2009 £ millions	Year ending 30/06/2008 £ millions
Non-current assets	12,502	11,951	10,471
Current assets	6,952	6,067	5,521
Current liabilities	(3,944)	(3,986)	(4,707)
Non-current liabilities	(10,724)	(10,158)	(7,152)
Total equity	4,786	3,874	4,133

Table 11. 3 Diageo's global priority brands

Brand	Ranking	Annual sales volume (9 litre cases)
Smirnoff vodka	The world's leading premium spirit by volume	24.3 million
Johnnie Walker Scotch whisky	The world's leading premium spirit by value	14.3 million
Guinness	The world's leading stout	11.1 million
Bailey's	The world's leading liqueur	6.7 million
J&B	The number 4 Scotch whisky in the world	5.2 million
Captain Morgan	The number 2 rum in the world	9.4 million
José Cuervo	The world's leading tequila	4.5 million
Tanqueray	The leading imported gin into the United States	1.9 million

Questions *(25 marks; 35 minutes)*

1 Calculate the change in Diageo's gross and operating profit margins between 2008 and 2011. (5)

2 Analyse two possible influences on the value of Diageo's global priority brands. (10)

3 Examine the main arguments for and against Diageo including its brand names in the company's balance sheet. (10)

12 Financial strategies and accounts

 ## Introduction

In the period 2007 to 2008, banks throughout the world struggled to cope with wave after wave of 'restatements' of their financial position. Many that had been claiming to be highly profitable (and paying top staff huge bonuses) were having to admit huge 'write-offs'. In other words, their day-to-day accounting had failed to pick up huge potential losses, so these losses were suddenly being acknowledged. HSBC, for example, wrote off $12.7 billion of losses in the US mortgage market (the so-called 'sub-prime loans'). The resulting 'credit crunch' triggered a global economic downturn in 2008 to 2009, with many economies, including that of the UK, still struggling to return to economic growth in 2010.

Maintaining or improving the financial health of an organisation is vital if it is to continue to survive and develop in the long term. This requires not only profitable trading and careful cost controls, but also a sound financial structure. Financial health can be measured by a firm's gearing. An apparently profitable firm could be particularly vulnerable to changing economic conditions if the bulk of its capital comes from debt finance. In addition, the firm will need to maintain a healthy liquidity position to ensure that sufficient cash is available when it is needed.

Once established, some businesses may choose to continue to operate on a relatively small scale, perhaps in order to maintain an entrepreneurial culture. Most firms, however, see growth as a major objective. Operating on a larger scale offers a number of potential benefits to businesses, including the opportunity to benefit from economies of scale, and to spread risk by increasing product range or selling in new markets. Such growth will also need to be managed carefully in order to minimise risks and maximise the chances of success.

 ## Raising finance

The AS specification looked at the **external sources of finance** available to businesses at start-up. These – such as overdrafts, loans and venture capital – are also potential sources of finance for established businesses. There are also some additional ways for an established business to secure external finance. For example, suppliers may be prepared to offer generous trade credit arrangements in order to win the custom of growing firms with a proven track record of paying on time. Rapidly growing firms may also choose to ease cash-flow problems by **factoring** invoices. This involves selling them to a company that will pay a percentage of the invoice value in advance and then recover the outstanding amount, in exchange for a fee. Hire purchase and leasing offer firms a means of obtaining the use of assets without having to pay out large sums of money straight away. For limited companies, long-term finance can be obtained from equity or share capital, possibly via a **rights issue**, giving existing shareholders the opportunity to buy more shares at a price below the current market price, in order to raise finance relatively cheaply. Equity finance has the advantage of not having to be repaid. Unlike loan repayments, there are no interest charges and dividends to shareholders do not have to be paid if the company fails to make a profit.

Once a business has been operating for some time, it should also be able to rely on **internal sources of finance** (i.e. those generated from within the business itself). These will include those described below.

Retained profit

Trading profitably will create a source of funds that can be reinvested back into the business in order to buy new stock, replace worn out fixed assets or expand operations. This **retained profit** is an important source of long-term finance as it does not need to be paid back. The level of finance available from this source depends on the performance of the business and the rate of dividends expected by the firm's owners. Around 60% of all long-term capital comes from this source (which is also sometimes known as 'ploughed-back profits').

Sale of assets

Established firms own fixed assets, such as premises and machinery, which have been purchased to be used as part of its operations. Ideally, a firm can use redundant assets to do this (i.e. those that are no longer required as part of the production process). It may be possible to raise finance using assets that are still required, via **sale and leaseback**, by paying rent or a fee to the new owner.

Managing working capital more effectively

Established firms may grow complacent when it comes to managing **working capital**. Stocks may begin to build up and outstanding customer invoices may go unnoticed. Squeezing working capital (i.e. managing it more effectively) can create more finance for a firm's day-to-day activities, easing pressure on cash-flow. This could involve running down stocks or chasing up debtors. Relationships developed with suppliers over time may also mean that longer credit periods can be negotiated.

A-grade application

Innocent sells out to Coca-Cola

Global soft drinks giant, Coca-Cola, acquired a controlling stake of Innocent Drinks in April 2010, after investing an estimated £75 million in the company. The David and Goliath relationship between the two companies began in 2009 when Coca-Cola bought an 18% share of Innocent for £30 million. At the time, Innocent co-founder Richard Reed refused to confirm or deny whether future funds would be forthcoming, saying 'nothing is definite in the future but of course both sides hope the relationship will prosper'. The 2010 deal resulted largely from the disposal of shares by one of Innocent's original business angel investors. Reed claimed that Coca-Cola would continue to remain a passive investor but support Innocent's objective of further international expansion, by helping with issues such as distribution in new markets, such as Sweden. According to Reed, 'We remain in full operational control of the business and we should be able to proceed towards our goal of taking Innocent to every country in the world.'
Source: The *Guardian*

 ## Finance: is it adequate?

Adequate finance means having access to sufficient levels of funding to meet the firm's needs, as and when they occur. Established firms will need to pay workers, suppliers and other expenses on time, regardless of whether enough cash has been generated from sales to cover such expenses. They will also need to replace equipment and machinery when it wears out or becomes obsolete. Few businesses are faced with totally predictable demand. Therefore, adequate resources (including finance) should be available to respond successfully to a unexpected upsurge in orders, as well as allowing a firm to cope with an unexpected fall in sales.

Ensuring access to adequate funding is equally important for those firms looking to expand. Not only will such firms require capital for the purchase of new assets, but also to cover additional working capital requirements in the form of increased materials, wages and fuel. **Overtrading** refers to the situation where a business expands at a rate that cannot be sustained by its capital base. A sudden surge in orders may tempt firms to buy additional stocks on credit. However, a significant gap between having to pay for these stocks and receiving payment from customers could lead to liquidity problems. Inadequate funding is one of the most common reasons why apparently successful businesses with rapidly growing sales end up failing.

Finance: is it appropriate?

Appropriate finance means ensuring that the type of finance matches its intended use. An overdraft may provide a much-needed bridge between having to pay suppliers once month and being paid by customers the next. Yet it would be an expensive method of borrowing to finance asset purchase, unless it could be repaid quickly. There are a number of factors that will determine the most appropriate source(s) of finance for established businesses to use in any given situation. These include the following.

The type of business

Expanding businesses may decide to become limited companies in order to raise finance more easily and offer owners the protection of limited liability. However, private limited companies may still struggle to find sufficient shareholders as its shares are not openly available to the general public. Therefore the business may seek a public flotation on the stock market – opening up the possibility of ownership being spread widely among the public, as with a business such as Marks & Spencer plc, which has 250,000 different shareholders.

The level of success enjoyed by the business

It is often said that 'success breeds success', and this is usually the case with finance. Highly profitable firms are able to generate internal finance but are also likely to attract outside investors and creditors. Firms with low or falling profits may struggle to raise the finance needed to improve performance because they are seen as too risky. A well-worn business phrase is that 'banks don't deal with people who need them'.

The use of funds

A business looking to raise finance for working capital would normally use short-term finance (i.e. repaid within one year). On the other hand, capital expenditure on an expensive piece of machinery used within the business for a number of years is likely to require long-term finance (i.e. that required for much longer periods, usually over five years). See Table 12.1.

The attitude of the owners/ shareholders of the business

There are a number of reasons why the owners of a business may have an influence on the choice of finance. Some may prefer not to use loan finance, because of the risk of not being able to meet repayments on time. Others may avoid bringing in new shareholders or involving venture capitalists, in order to prevent their control of the business from being diluted (watered down). There may also be a conflict of interest between shareholders, who view profit as a source of dividend income, and managers, who would prefer to pay lower dividends in order to retain profits to finance expansion.

The state of the economy

Firms may be reluctant to borrow when economic conditions are deteriorating and sales are predicted to fall. A more buoyant economy may increase business confidence and encourage firms to take greater risks.

Table 12.1 Short-term vs long-term finance: some examples

	Short term	Long term
Internal	Squeezing working capital	Sale (and leaseback) of assets Retained profit
External	Trade credit Debt factoring Overdrafts	Bank loans Share (rights) issue Venture capital

A 2011 banking industry report has shown that only 8% of small and medium-sized enterprises (SMEs) actually applied for bank finance over the survey period. Many were put off by the economic climate and even more by fear of losing control of their business.

Even among the small number who applied for finance, significant proportions were turned down. 34% of loan applications were rejected, as were 15% of requests for overdrafts. The smaller the business, the more likely it was to be turned down.

If banks are, implicitly, channelling businesses towards overdrafts rather than loans, they are pushing firms into short-term borrowing. Many would prefer the greater stability implied by a long-term loan.

Allocating capital expenditure

Capital expenditure refers to money spent by a firm in order to support its long-term operations. The purchase of fixed assets, such as premises and machinery, is clearly an example of capital expenditure, as they are bought with the intention of using them over a number of years. Funds used to take over other businesses can also be regarded as capital expenditure, even if the assets acquired are subsequently sold off. It could be argued that firms should also regard spending on research and development as an item of capital expenditure, given that it is likely to provide benefits over a lengthy period of time.

The first issue to consider with capital expenditure is the amount needed to maintain a firm's operations in a healthy, efficient state. For example, Network Rail allocates about £2.5 billion a year to maintaining Britain's railway system. This includes replacing ageing trains with new ones, updating tired stations, and so forth. This expenditure can be regarded as essential. Without it, the business will start to go downhill. To switch examples, in 2010 the average age of British Airways' aircraft was ten years; contrast that with Singapore Airlines, which has an objective of having a fleet with an average age of three years.

Once enough capital is allocated to maintaining a healthy business, the key financial decision is how much to allocate to growth. During the 1990s, McDonald's poured billions of dollars into opening up more stores worldwide. Only in 2004/2005, when profits started to sag, did the business switch from quantity to quality. This change of strategy helped in the recent recession. By 2010 McDonalds was enjoying record profits while rival Burger King was struggling.

Any business, regardless of size, will have more potential uses of funds than the amount of finance available, so the allocation of capital expenditure will depend on corporate objectives and market conditions.

Implementing profit centres in a business

Profit centres are distinct sections within a business that can be regarded as self-contained, and therefore measured for their own profitability. In effect, a profit centre becomes a firm within a firm, which can help motivate the relatively small number of staff within the section. It is hard to feel important as one person among 450,000 other Tesco staff; but one person among 16 at an individual store can see the impact of their efforts.

The basis for establishing profit centres is very much dependent on the individual circumstances of the firm in question and may be based on:

● a person – individual employees within a business may be responsible for generating revenues and incurring costs

● a product – a multi-product business may be able to distinguish the separate revenues earned and costs incurred by individual product lines

● a department – areas within a business that perform certain functions may generate both costs and revenues

● a location – a business, such as a bank or retailer that is spread geographically, may choose to use each branch or division as a profit centre.

Establishing profit centres can provide valuable

information to a business to help it enhance its financial performance, perhaps enabling it to identify unprofitable areas that may need to be closed down. The responsibility delegated to managers of individual profit centres may also inject a degree of motivation. However, there are a number of potential problems in attempting to implement profit centres.

For example, it may prove difficult to choose an accurate method of allocating a firm's overheads to each profit centre. It may also lead to a situation where individual profit centres compete against each other, to the detriment of the business as a whole. See Table 12.2.

Table 12.2 Advantages and disadvantages of profit centres

Advantages of profit centres	Disadvantages of profit centres
<ul><li>The success – or otherwise – of individual areas of the business can be identified more easily</li><li>The delegation of control over local operations may increase motivation</li><li>Decision making will be localised, making it quicker and better suited to local conditions</li><li>When they work well, they are a perfect antidote to big-business bureaucracy that results in diseconomies of scale</li></ul>	<ul><li>Not all of the costs or revenues of a business can easily be associated with specific areas of operation</li><li>Areas of the business may end up competing against each other, damaging overall performance</li><li>The good or bad performance of one profit centre may be the result of external changes beyond its control (cutting the link between the performance of the group members and the results of the group activities)</li></ul>

Cost minimisation

One way that firms can achieve a competitive advantage over their rivals is by pursuing a strategy of cost minimisation. Firms operating in fiercely competitive markets may have little control over the prices they charge but can still make acceptable profits by pushing down unit costs as low as possible. In theory, cost minimisation is straightforward enough. For example, firms may be tempted to switch to the cheapest supplier or cut out staff training in order to offer the lowest prices possible. However, this is likely to lead to a loss of competitiveness in the longer term, as poor-quality and poorly trained employees result in customer dissatisfaction.

The key to implementing this strategy successfully is to charge prices that are close to but below the market average, to avoid arousing customer suspicions, and reduce average costs without compromising operations. Lower unit costs can be generated by producing standardised products in large volumes, in order to benefit from economies of scale, and finding ways of keeping overheads as low as possible. Examples of businesses that have been particularly successful at pursuing cost-minimisation strategies include Aldi, Ryanair, AirAsia and Primark. Focusing on price alone can lead to problems, however, if an even lower-cost competitor enters the market.

A-grade application

Ryanair: a model of cost minimisation

The establishment of Ryanair as Europe's leading low-fares scheduled passenger airline has been the result of a strategy of cost minimisation adopted in the early 1990s, following the appointment of chief executive Michael O'Leary. By targeting price-conscious leisure and business passengers, the airline has experienced phenomenal growth – from under a quarter of a million passengers in 1990 to over 67 million in the 12 months to April 2010. The company's success has largely been the result of its ability to contain costs and achieve a number

of operational efficiencies, without compromising customer service. These have included the following.

- *Frequent short-haul flights:* eliminating the need to provide passengers with 'frills' services, such as complimentary meals and drinks, which add to variable costs.
- *Using the internet for flight reservations:* the airline's system was upgraded in 2009 and accounted for over 97% of flight bookings in 2010, helping to keep labour costs down.

- *Favouring secondary routes:* e.g. flying to Girona rather than Barcelona in Spain. These less congested destinations mean faster turnaround times, fewer terminal delays and lower handling costs.
- *Minimising aircraft costs:* initially, this was achieved by the purchase of second-hand aeroplanes of a single type; however, in response to a recent shortage of such aircraft, the company has resorted to purchasing from a single supplier in order to limit training and maintenance costs, as well as the purchase and storage of spare parts.
- *Personnel productivity:* Ryanair controls its labour costs by paying highly competitive salaries to pilots and cabin crew but demanding much higher productivity levels than its competitors.

Figure 12.1 Ryanair

Issues for analysis

Opportunities for analysis are likely to focus on the following areas.

- The benefits and drawbacks of using different forms of finance in different circumstances (e.g. seeing that there are costs and risks involved in using an overdraft to finance long-term commitments).
- The need to think about financial strategy in relation to the overall strategy; for example, if the business has a bold, quite risky, marketing strategy (based, perhaps, on new product launches into short product life cycle markets) it is wise to have a cautious financial strategy (e.g. low gearing and high liquidity); this is the approach taken by firms such as Nintendo and L'Oréal.
- The advantages and disadvantages of adopting cost minimisation as a financial strategy and seeing its essentially close links with marketing, operational and personnel strategies. This is shown effectively in the A-grade application on Ryanair.

Financial strategies and accounts – an evaluation

Choosing an appropriate financial strategy is crucial to an organisation's continuing success, regardless of its size or its objectives. A business may need to raise finance for a variety of reasons – this finance will need to be both adequate and appropriate to its needs in order to be effective. Financial strategy is also very much concerned with how funds are used to support the development of the business. This involves making choices as to how expenditure is to be allocated between competing capital projects and controlling ongoing costs in order to ensure the firm's long-term financial health.

The most important judgements, though, are about getting the right balance between risk and safety. The 2008 collapse of Lehman Brothers was due to a faulty (foolish, even) financial strategy. Yet if managers are too cautious, they are likely to find their business left behind as rivals sweep past them. Greed is never good, but neither is it right to be *too* careful. Good chief executives find a way to be bold but sensible.

Key terms

Capital expenditure: spending on fixed assets (e.g. premises and machinery).

External sources of finance: funds generated from sources outside an organisation (e.g. bank loans, venture capital).

Factoring: passing a copy of a customer invoice to your bank, which then credits you with 80% of the invoiced sum within 24 hours, then collects the debt for you (for a fee of perhaps 4%).

Internal sources of finance: funds generated from an organisation's own resources (e.g. retained profit, sale of assets).

Overtrading: this refers to the liquidity problems experienced by a firm that expands without securing the finance required to support it – for example, to bridge the gap between paying suppliers and receiving payment from customers.

Profit centre: a part of a business for which a separate profit and loss account can be drawn up.

Retained profit: profit left over after all the deductions (and additions) have been made to sales revenue, including cost of sales, overheads, tax and dividends.

Rights issue: giving existing shareholders the right to buy extra shares in the business before allowing outsiders that right to buy; a rights issue usually offers the shares at a discount to the existing market price. It is likely to be cheaper to raise finance by this method than a full public issue.

Sale and leaseback: a method of raising finance by selling an asset but paying to continue to use it.

Working capital: the day-to-day finances needed to run a business – generally seen as the difference between the value of a firm's current assets and its current liabilities.

Revision questions (45 marks; 45 minutes)

1 State two reasons why an established firm might wish to raise finance. (2)

2 Describe two influences on a firm's choice of finance. (4)

3 Outline two ways in which a firm could raise finance to buy the additional stock needed to meet an unexpected order. (4)

4 Analyse two appropriate sources of finance available to a private limited company looking to set up a production facility in Poland. (6)

5 Use numerical examples to explain how a firm's gearing and liquidity position would affect its choice of finance. (6)

6 Explain why a rapidly expanding firm might suffer from overtrading. (4)

7 Using examples, briefly explain the difference between capital expenditure for maintenance and capital expenditure for growth. (4)

8 Explain what is meant by the term 'profit centre'. (3)

9 Analyse one benefit and one drawback for coffee retailer Starbucks from choosing to operate its outlets as individual profit centres. (6)

10 Examine one advantage and one disadvantage for a company such as Ryanair of adopting a strategy of cost minimisation. (6)

Data response

Financing growth at Mulberry

British handbag and leather ware designer and manufacturer, Mulberry, recorded its seventh consecutive year of sales growth in the 12 months to 31 March 2010. Despite trading in conditions that could hardly be described as supportive for luxury brands, Mulberry's revenue increased from £58.6 million in 2009 to £72.1 million in 2010. The company's pre-tax profits for 2010 were £5.1 million, up from £4.2 in the previous year.

Mulberry sells its products worldwide. In 2010, the company had 39 of its own 'full price' shops and department store concessions, as well as selling online via a recently redesigned website. Within the first ten weeks of the financial year beginning April 2010, like for like sales in shops and department stores had risen by 44%, with internet sales up by 99%.

The company's strong organic growth resulted of a significant rise in international sales, as well as increasing demand in the UK. The company's chairman confirmed that, 'A key objective of the management team has been the continued development of our business internationally. In particular, our business in Asia is growing rapidly. … It is clear that our best selling products in our home market have equal appeal internationally.' (See Table 12.3.)

The company intends to continue to finance its expansion in the UK and across the world from internal sources. According to Mulberry's chairman, 'These capital projects will absorb a significant amount of cash, as will the increased inventory that will be needed to meet the forecast demand for our products. We expect to be able to fund these investments from our existing cash resources and future cash flows.' (See Table 12.4.)

Questions *(40 marks; 45 minutes)*

1 Calculate the percentage change in Mulberry's profits between 2009 and 2010. (4)

2 Discuss the suitability of Mulberry's choice of finance for the continued expansion of the company. (18)

3 To what extent do you believe that an effective financial strategy is vital for companies like Mulberry in order to survive and develop in the long term? (18)

Table 12.3 Planned new Mulberry stores (2010 to 2011)

Own stores
● Relocation of New Bond Street store (London)
● Relocation of Manchester store to new Spinningfields mall
● New flagship store – New York

International partner stores
● Incheon Airport – South Korea
● Mall of the Emirates – Dubai
● Sydney – Australia
● Times Square – Hong Kong
● Kuala Lumpur – Malaysia
● Qatar

Source: www.mulberry.com

Table 12.4 Summary of Mulberry's results for the year ended 31 March 2010 – balance sheet

£000s	2009/2010	2008/2009
Non-current assets	10,760	11,694
Stock (inventories)	9,090	14,830
Receivables	8,263	6,032
Cash	12,171	3,710
Current and non-current liabilities	(13,819)	(11,882)
Total equity	26,465	24,384

Data response

Cost minimisation means success at Aldi

Privately owned German retailer Aldi opened its first UK store in 1990. The opening of the company's Exeter branch in April 2009 took its total number of supermarkets to 467, with a target of 500 by the end of the year. Although its share of the fiercely competitive UK grocery market was just over 3% at the end of 2009, its reputation as a quality discounter has led to a steady growth in popularity, particularly among the country's affluent middle-class. Indeed, this success led to supermarket giant Tesco launching a range of 300 'no frills' products, as well as a claim to match Aldi's prices on over 2,000 items.

According to Aldi, its success is down to its 'less is more' approach to retailing, with all decisions aimed at guaranteeing a 'low-cost shop' for its customers. Aldi's operations are designed around the key objective of minimising costs without compromising quality. This objective is achieved in a number of ways, as described below.

- Offering customers a limited range of its most frequently purchased own brand grocery and household products, rather than branded goods, allows the retailer to buy in bulk from suppliers. Only 1,000 products are stocked within its supermarkets, with hardly any duplication of lines, in order to remove the additional costs related to buying, supplying and product development. Many of these suppliers are well-known food manufacturers who are prepared to sell to Aldi at lower prices because of the large volumes involved.

(Although Aldi is small in Britain, it is huge in Germany and across Europe with around 7,500 stores.)

- Aldi has a no-frills in-store approach, where products are often sold straight from boxes rather than shelves and staff levels are kept to a minimum; this keeps overheads down. Music is not played in store to avoid the cost of having to purchase music licences. Customers have to pay for carrier bags and the use of a shopping trolley requires a £1 deposit, to encourage its return.

- One of the key reasons for Aldi's growth in popularity is its ability to combine low prices and standards of product quality that match those of leading brands. Despite its low prices, Aldi insists that it does not compromise when it comes to quality. The retailer has received a number of quality-related awards in recent years, including *Which?* and *Best Supermarket*, as well as *The Grocer's Grocer of the Year* and *Discounter of the Year* in June 2009.

Source: www.aldi.co.uk

Questions *(30 marks; 35 minutes)*

1 Analyse the main ways in which Aldi's operations are successful in minimising costs. (12)

2 To what extent do you believe that Aldi's financial strategy of cost minimisation will help it to increase its share of the UK grocery market further? (18)

Investment appraisal

 ## Introduction

Every day managers make decisions, such as how to deal with a furious customer or whether a cheeky worker needs a disciplinary chat. These decisions can be regarded as tactical (i.e. **tactical decisions**) because they are short-term responses to events. Investment appraisal applies to decisions that concern strategy rather than tactics (i.e. the medium–long term). As they are significant in the longer term, they are worth taking a bit of time over – ideally, by calculating whether or not the potential profits are high enough to justify the initial outlay (the sum invested).

Table 13.1 Tactical vs investment appraisal decisions

Tactical, day-to-day decisions	Decisions requiring investment appraisal
Should we open earlier on Saturdays?	Should we launch new product A or B?
We need to appoint one extra cashier	Should we make a takeover bid for Sainsbury's?
The production line must stop until we have found out why quality is poor today	Should we relocate our factory from London to Prague?
Stocks are high, shall we have a mid-season sale?	Shall we expand capacity by running a night shift?

To carry out a full investment appraisal might take a manager several weeks, even months. Not because the maths is so complex, but in order to find accurate data to analyse. For example, if trying to choose whether to launch new product A or B, a sales forecast will be essential. Carrying out primary market research might take several weeks until the results are received and analysed. Only then could the investment appraisal begin. Yet what is the alternative? To take an important decision without proper evidence and information? Table 13.2 gives an idea of the data required to take effective decisions using investment appraisal.

Table 13.2 The data required to take effective decisions using investment appraisal

Decisions requiring investment appraisal	Information needed to make the decision
Should we launch new product A or B?	Sales forecasts, pricing decisions, and data on fixed, variable and start-up costs
Should we make a takeover bid for Sainsbury's?	Forecast of future cash flows into and out of Sainsbury's; compare the results with the purchase price
Should we relocate our factory from London to Prague?	Estimate of fixed and variable costs there compared with here, plus the initial cost of the move
Shall we expand capacity by running a night shift?	Forecast of the extra costs compared with extra revenues

Quantitative methods of investment appraisal

Having gathered all the necessary facts and figures, a firm can analyse the data to answer two main questions.

1 How long will it take until we get our money back? If we invest £400,000, can we expect to get that money back within the first year, or could it take four years?

2 How profitable will the investment be? What profit will be generated per year by the investment?

To answer these two questions there are three methods that can be used:

1 payback period

2 average rate of return

3 discounted cash flows.

Two of these (methods 1 and 2) need to be used together; the third can answer both questions simultaneously. All three methods require the same starting point: a table showing the expected cash flows on the investment over time.

Table 13.3 Example cash flow table

	Cash in	Cash out	Net cash flow	Cumulative cash total
NOW*	–	£60,000	(£60,000)	(£60,000)
Year 1	£30,000	£10,000	£20,000	(£40,000)
Year 2	£30,000	£10,000	£20,000	(£20,000)
Year 3	£30,000	£10,000	£20,000	–
Year 4	£30,000	£10,000	£20,000	£20,000
Year 5	£30,000	£10,000	£20,000	£40,000

*NOW = the moment the £60,000 is spent; can also be called the initial outlay or the sum invested.

An example would be an investment of £60,000 in a machine that will cost £10,000 per year to run and should generate £30,000 a year of cash. The machine is expected to last for five years. The cash flow table would look like the one shown in Table 13.3.

Exam papers might present this information in the form of a graph. The graph in Figure 13.1 shows the **cumulative cash** total based on the above figures.

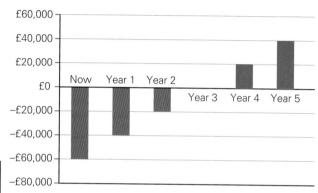

Figure 13.1 Cumulative cash flows on an investment of £60,000

These figures will be used to explain the workings of each of the three methods listed above, which we will now look at in more detail.

Payback period

Calculation

This method focuses on one issue alone: how long does it take to get your money back. In the above case, the £60,000 investment takes exactly three years to get back, as can be seen in the right-hand column: the cumulative cash total. All the £60,000 is recovered in three years because the business is generating £20,000 of cash per year.

If the annual net cash flows are constant over time, a formula can be used to calculate the payback period:

payback: $\dfrac{\text{sum invested}}{\text{net cash per time period}}$

e.g. $\dfrac{£60,000}{£20,000 \text{ a year}} = 3$ years

What if the cash flows aren't constant over time?

This can make it a little harder to work out a precise answer, though the principles are the same. For example, take the investment of £40,000 shown in Table 13.4.

Table 13.4 Example investment of £40,000

	Cash in	Cash out	Net cash flow	Cumulative cash total
NOW*	–	£40,000	(£40,000)	(£40,000)
Year 1	£20,000	£5,000	£15,000	(£25,000)
Year 2	£30,000	£10,000	£20,000	(£5,000)
Year 3	£36,000	£24,000	£12,000	£7,000

In this case, payback has not yet occurred by the end of Year 2 (there's still £5000 outstanding). Yet the end of Year 3 is well beyond the payback period. So payback occurred in two years and X months. To find how many months, the following formula will work:

$$\frac{\text{outlay outstanding}}{\text{monthly cash in year of payback}}$$

e.g. $\frac{£5000}{£12,000/12m} = 5$ months

In this case, then, the payback period was two years and five months.

Interpretation of payback period

The word investment suggests spending money now in the hope of making money later. Therefore every investment means putting money at risk while waiting for the profit. The payback period is the length of time the money is at risk. It follows that every business would like an investment to have as short a payback period as possible. Company directors may tell their managers to suggest an investment only if its payback is less than 18 months. This yardstick is known as a **criterion level**.

It is important to bear in mind the risks involved in investment. Even if well-researched sales estimates have led to well-considered cash flow forecasts, things can go wrong. For a new house-building business, an unexpected rise in interest rates may lead cash inflows to dry up, as buyers hesitate. Or a new 'AllFresh' restaurant may find that food wastage levels are much higher than expected, causing cash outflows to be disturbingly high. Getting beyond the payback period is therefore always a crucial phase.

Although managers like a quick payback, it is important to be beware of **short-termism**. If directors demand too short a payback period, it may be impossible for managers to plan effectively for the long-term future of the business. Quick paybacks imply easy decisions, such as for Primark to expand its store chain by opening its first store in Plymouth. A much tougher, longer-term decision would be whether Primark should open up stores in France. This might prove a clever move in the longer term, but the high costs of getting to grips with French retailing might lead to a minimum of a three-year payback.

The opposite of short-termism

In 2011 JCB, manufacturer of construction equipment, plans to start boosting its market position in China. It hopes to repeat its amazing success in India, where it is market leader with an astonishing 50% market share. Its achievements in India began 30 years before, in 1979, when it opened its first offices. Now it has three huge factories in India, one of which saw a doubling of capacity in 2010.

In its strongest market sector, for the 'backhoe loaders' seen on every construction site, JCB enjoyed a 40% world market share in 2010. Yet in China it has been an also-ran to giant rivals Caterpillar (USA) and Komatsu (Japan). Even if it takes 30 years to crack China, JCB seems up for the challenge.

Figure 13.2 JCB

Table 13.5 The advantages and disadvantages of payback

Advantages of payback	Disadvantages of payback
Easy to calculate and understand	Provides no insight into profitability
May be more accurate than other measures, because it ignores longer-term forecasts (the ones beyond the payback period)	Ignores what happens after the payback period
Takes into account the timing of cash flows	May encourage a short-termist attitude
Especially important for a business with weak cash flow; it may be willing to invest only in projects with a quick payback	Is not very useful on its own (because it ignores profit), therefore is used together with ARR or NPV (see below)

Average rate of return

This method compares the average annual profit generated by an investment with the amount of money invested in it. In this way, two or more potential projects can be compared to find out which has the 'best' return for the amount of money being put into it in the first place.

Calculation

Average rate of return (ARR) is calculated by the formula:

$$\frac{\text{average annual return}}{\text{initial outlay}} \times 100$$

There are three steps in calculating ARR, as follows.

1 Calculate the total profit over the lifetime of the investment (total net cash flows minus the investment outlay).

2 Divide by the number of years of the investment project, to give the average annual profit.

3 Apply the formula: average annual profit/initial outlay x 100.

For example, BJ Carpets is considering whether to invest £20,000 in a labour-saving wrapping machine. The company policy is to invest in projects only if they deliver a profit of 15%+ a year (see Table 13.6).

Table 13.6 Figures for BJ Carpets

Year	Net cash flow	Cumulative cash flow
0	(£20,000)	(£20,000)
1	+£5,000	(£15,000)
2	+£11,000	(£4,000)
3	+£10,000	+£6,000
4	+£10,000	+£16,000

Here, the £20,000 investment generates £36,000 of net cash flows in the four years. That represents a lifetime profit of £16,000 (see bottom right-hand corner of Table 13.6). To apply the three steps, then, proceed as indicated in Table 13.7.

Table 13.7 BJ Carpets: applying the three steps

Step 1	Identify lifetime profit	£16,000
Step 2	Divide by number of years (4)	£4,000
Step 3	Calculate annual profit as a percentage of initial outlay	$\frac{£4,000}{£20,000} \times 100 = 20\%$

BJ Carpets can therefore proceed with this investment, as the ARR of 20% is comfortably above its requirement of a minimum ARR criterion level of 15%.

Interpretation of ARR

The strength of ARR is that it is easy to interpret the result. Clearly firms want as high a rate of profit as possible, so the higher the ARR the better. This makes it easy to choose between two investment options, as long as profit is the key decision-making factor. (It might not be, because some firms are pursuing objectives such as growth or diversification.)

How do you interpret an ARR result, though, if there is only one investment to consider? For example is 12% a good rate of return? In this case the key is to analyse the **reward for risk**. This compares the ARR result with the only way to achieve a safe rate of return – by keeping your money on deposit at a bank.

Reward for risk

If an ARR result comes out at 12%, ask yourself what the current rate of interest is. If it is 5.75%, for example, a business could receive a 5.75% annual income at zero risk and by doing nothing. So, why invest? Well, in this case, the reward for investing would be the 12% ARR *minus* the 5.75% interest rate, meaning that the investment yields a 6.25% annual reward for taking a business risk. Clearly if the reward for risk was small, or even negative (5% ARR when interest rates are 5.75%) it would seem crazy to invest. Note that an implication here is that the higher the interest rate, the less attractive it becomes to invest. In an exam, the key is to interpret the ARR through the reward for risk, then make a judgement about how risky the investment seems. A 6.25% reward for risk, for example, would seem very low for a brand new restaurant, as 40% of new restaurants fold within three years of starting up. (See Figure 13.3.)

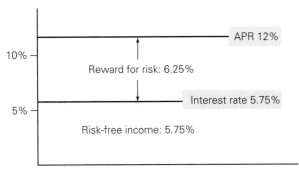

Figure 13.3 Reward for risk

The average rate of return (ARR) method takes account of all the cash flows throughout the life of a project, and focuses on the key decision-making factor: profitability. However, it ignores *when* the cash flows occur, which can have a significant bearing on the risks of a project. Look at the example of the *average* rate of return on two investments, both of £10,000, in Table 13.8.

Investments A and B come out with the same average profitability. Yet Investment A's quick, one-year payback makes it greatly preferable to Investment B. After all, it is much easier to forecast one year ahead than three years. So Investment B's crucial year 3 might prove much worse than expected, meaning the ARR proves much lower in reality than the 30% expected at the start.

Table 13.9 The advantages and disadvantages of average rate of return

Advantages of average rate of return	Disadvantages of average rate of return
Uses all the cash flows over the project's life …	… but, because later years are included, the results will not prove as accurate as payback
Focuses upon profitability	Ignores the timing of the cash flows
Easy to compare percentage returns on different investments, to help make a decision	Ignores the time value (opportunity cost) of the money invested

A-grade application

Estimating average rate of return

In January 2011 Alan Travis bought a flat in north London for £240,000. His plan was to let it out to tenants for a rental of £1200 a month (£14,400 a year). Although his mortgage payments would be slightly higher than this, he was sure that the property would enjoy a rise in value over the coming years. His forecasts enabled him to estimate a 7% average rate of return over a five-year period, and a possible 18% ARR if he holds on to the property for ten years. Of course, these figures depend entirely on his forecasts; are they too optimistic, given the weak position of the UK economy?

Table 13.8 Example of the average rate of return on two investments

Year	Investment A net cash flows	Investment B net cash flows
0	(£10,000)	(£10,000)
1	+£10,000	+£3,000
2	+£6,000	+£6,000
3	+£3,000	+£10,000
Average rate of return	30%	30%

Discounted cash flows

Useful though payback and ARR can be, they can work effectively only when used together. ARR provides information on average profitability, while payback tells you about the timing of the cash flows. Better, surely, to have one method that incorporates profits and time. This is the third method of investment appraisal, which is based on 'discounted cash flows'.

Discounted cash flow (DCF) is a method that is rooted in opportunity cost. If a firm invests £10,000 in computer software, it is important not only to ask 'What is the rate of return on my investment of £10,000?', but also 'What opportunities am I having to give up as a result of this investment?' At its simplest, £10,000 tied up in software prevents the firm from enjoying a 5.75% return on its money in the bank (when interest rates are 5.75%).

From the idea of opportunity cost, businesses want to know the implication of the timing of cash flows on different projects. If one investment generates +£40,000 in year 1, while another provides that inflow in year 4, the firm must consider what it is missing out on by waiting four years.

In short, it is always preferable to have money now than the promise of the same quantity of money in the future. This is because money held at the present time has a greater value than the same quantity of money received in the future. In other words, £100 received in a year's time is worth less to a firm than £100 in the bank today. How much less? Well, if interest rates are 10%, £100 in the bank for a year would become £110. So £100 in a year's time is worth 10% less than £100 today.

When considering potential capital investments on the basis of predicted future cash flows, it makes sense to ask, 'What will the money we receive in the future really be worth in today's terms?' These **present values** are calculated using a method called 'discounting'.

To discount a future cash flow, it is necessary to know:

- how many years into the future we are looking, since the greater the length of time involved, the smaller the present or discounted value of money will be
- what the prevailing rate of interest will be.

Once these have been determined, the relevant discount factor can be found. This can be done by calculation, or looked up in 'discount tables'. An extract from a discount table is given in Table 13.10.

The future cash flows are then multiplied by the appropriate discount factor to find the present value. For example, the present value of £100 received in five years' time, if the expected rate of interest is 10%, would be:

$$£100 \times 0.62 = £62$$

The higher the rate of interest expected, and the longer the time to wait for the money to come in, the less that money is actually worth in today's terms.

So how does a firm decide which discount factor to choose? There are two main ways.

1 The discount factor can be based on the current rate of interest, or the rate expected over the coming years.

2 A firm may base the factor on its own criteria, such as that it wants every investment to make at least 15%; therefore it expects future returns to be positive even with a 15% discount rate.

Table 13.10 Extract from a discount table

Table of selected discount factors						
Years ahead	4%	6%	8%	10%	12%	15%
0	1.00	1.00	1.00	1.00	1.00	1.00
1	0.96	0.94	0.93	0.91	0.89	0.87
2	0.92	0.89	0.86	0.83	0.80	0.76
3	0.89	0.84	0.79	0.75	0.71	0.66
4	0.85	0.79	0.74	0.68	0.64	0.57
5	0.82	0.75	0.68	0.62	0.57	0.50

This A Level includes just one technique of discounting future cash flows to find their present value; this is the net present value method.

Net present value (NPV)

Calculation

This method calculates the present values of all the money coming in from the project in the future, then sets these against the money being spent on the project today. The result is known as the net present value (NPV) of the project. It can be compared with other projects to find which has the highest return in real terms, and should therefore be chosen.

The technique can also be used to see if *any* of the projects are worth undertaking. All the investments might have a negative NPV. In other words, the present value of the money being spent is greater than the present value of the money being received. If so, the firm would be better off putting the money in the bank and earning the current rate of interest. Projects are only worth carrying out if the NPV is positive.

For example, a firm is faced with two alternative proposals for investment: Project Z and Project Y

(see Table 13.11). Both cost £250,000, but have different patterns of future cash flows over their projected lives. The rate of interest over the period is anticipated to average around 10%. The calculation would be as shown in the table.

Despite the fact that both projects have the same initial cost, and they bring in the same quantity of money over their lives, there is a large difference in their net present values. Project Y, with most of its income coming in the early years, gives a much greater present value than Project Z.

Interpretation

This method of appraising investment opportunities has an in-built advantage over the previous techniques. It pays close attention to the timing of cash flows and their values in relation to the value of money today. It is also relatively simple to use the technique as a form of 'what if?' scenario planning. Different calculations can be made to see what returns will be obtained at different interest rates or with different cash flows to reflect different expectations. The results, however, are not directly comparable between different projects when the initial investments differ.

Table 13.11 Project Z vs Project Y

| Year | Project Z | | | | Project Y | | |
	Cash flow	Discount factor	Present value (£s)		Cash flow	Discount factor	Present value (£s)
0	(£250,000)	1.00	(£250,000)		(£250,000)	1.00	(£250,000)
1	+£50,000	0.91	£45,500		+£200,000	0.91	+£182,000
2	+£100,000	0.83	£83,000		+£100,000	0.83	+£83,000
3	+£200,000	0.75	£150,000		+£50,000	0.75	+£37,500
		NPV =	+£28,500			NPV =	+£52,500

Table 13.12 The advantages and disadvantages of NPV

Advantages of NPV	Disadvantages of NPV
Takes the opportunity cost of money into account	Complex to calculate and communicate
A single measure that takes the amount and timing of cash flows into account	The meaning of the result is often misunderstood
Can consider different scenarios	Only comparable between projects if the initial investment is the same

Qualitative factors in investment appraisal

Once the numbers have been calculated there are decisions to be made. On the face of it, the numbers point to the answer, but they are only part of the decision-making process. For example, perhaps a board of directors can afford no more than £2 million for investment and must choose between the two alternatives shown in Table 13.13.

Table 13.13 Investment A vs Investment B

	Investment A	Investment B
Type of investment	New R&D laboratory	Relaunching an existing product with flagging sales
Investment outlay	£2 million	£2 million
Payback period	4.5 years	1 year
Average rate of return (over next five years)	8.2%	14.2%
Net present value	£32,000	£280,000

Investment B is clearly superior on all three quantitative methods of appraisal. Yet there may be reasons why the board may reject it. Some of these are outlined below.

- *Company objectives:* if the business is pursuing an objective of long-term growth, the directors might feel that a relaunch of a declining brand is too short-termist; they may prefer an investment that could keep boosting the business long beyond the next five years.

- *Company strategy:* if the business has been suffering from low-priced imported competition, it may seek higher value-added, differentiated products. Its goal may be to become more innovative and therefore the board may opt for Investment A.

- *Company finances:* if the £2 million investment capital is intended to be borrowed, the company's balance sheet is an important issue. If the business is highly geared, it may be reluctant to proceed with either of these investments, as neither generates an irresistible ARR.

- *Confidence in the data:* the directors will ask questions about how the forecasts were made, who made the forecasts and what was the evidence behind them. If the Investment B data came from the manager in charge of the product with flagging sales, may they be biased? (He or she may have been over-optimistic in interpreting the findings of small-scale market research.) Ideally, data used in investment appraisal should come from an independent source and be based on large enough sample sizes to be statistically valid.

- *Social responsibilities:* investing in recycling or energy-saving schemes may generate very low ARRs, but the firm may still wish to proceed for public relations reasons, to boost morale among staff or just because the directors think it is ethically right.

A-grade application

In 2010 Renault and Nissan opened a car factory in Chennai, India. It represented an investment of $990 million and provided the capacity to produce 400,000 cars per year. The new factory started up with a 1,500 workforce in May 2010. The first vehicle to be produced at the plant was the new Nissan Micra. The Nissan Micra is destined for the Indian market as well as for export to over 100 countries in Europe, the Middle East and Africa.

The investment took about four years from first idea to finished car output and received some financial support from the Indian government. Overwhelmingly, though, the numbers within the investment appraisal worked for three reasons:

- the Indian car market was projected to grow at 25% per year
- very low wage rates
- the low rates of interest charged by banks on two such powerful companies.

Issues for analysis

- Having mastered the mathematics of investment appraisal, the next key factor is to be able to interpret the results effectively. If the business has a payback criterion level of 18 months, is this holding it back in any way? Is there evidence that the firm is *too* focused on the short term? Of course, if the firm's cash flow or liquidity positions are weak, it is understandable if there is a great emphasis on speed of payback. Yet, in some cases, businesses are short-term focused for less acceptable reasons – for example, multi-million-pound short-term profit bonuses for directors may be leading them to ignore the long-term future of the business.

- Always ask yourself about the reliability of the data provided – how were they gathered; who gathered them; what variables were taken into account?

- Decisions should always be based on a mixture of quantitative and qualitative data. Beware of placing too great an emphasis on numbers on the basis that they are somehow more concrete and therefore more reliable. Qualitative factors may be more important, such as considering the environmental impact of a decision. Today's profits can turn into tomorrow's public relations disaster if stakeholders discover unacceptable side-effects of your approach to production.

Investment appraisal – an evaluation

Investment appraisal methods will often give conflicting advice to managers, who must be willing to make decisions based on a trade-off between risks and profit. This must be taken alongside the objectives of the business, which could well dictate which of the criteria involved is of most importance to the firm.

The size of the firm will also have an impact. Small firms will often have neither the time nor the resources to undertake a scientific approach to investment appraisal. They will often rely on past experience or the owner's hunches in making decisions such as these. In larger firms, however, the issue of accountability will often lead managers to rely heavily on the projected figures. In this way, should anything go wrong, they can prove they were making the best decision possible at the time, given the information available.

Key terms

Criterion level: a yardstick set by directors to enable managers to judge whether investment ideas are worth pursuing (e.g. ARR must be 15%+ or payback must be a maximum of 12 months).

Cumulative cash: the build-up of cash over several time periods; for example, if cash flow is +£20,000 for three years in a row, cumulative cash in year 3 is +£60,000.

Present values: the discounting of future cash flows to make them comparable with today's cash. This takes into account the opportunity cost of waiting for the cash to arrive.

Reward for risk: calculating the difference between the forecast ARR and the actual rate of interest, to help decide whether the ARR is high enough given the risks involved in the project.

Short-termism: making decisions on the basis of the immediate future and therefore ignoring the long-term future of the business.

Tactical decisions: those that are day-to-day events and therefore do not require a lengthy decision-making process.

A Revision questions *(40 marks; 40 minutes)*

1 Distinguish between qualitative and quantitative investment appraisal. (4)

2 Why should forecast cash flow figures be treated with caution? (4)

3 How useful is payback period as the sole method for making an investment decision? (3)

4 Briefly outline the circumstances in which:
   a payback period might be the most important appraisal method for a firm (4)
   b average rate of return might be more important than payback for a firm. (4)

5 How are criterion levels applied to investment appraisal? (3)

6 Explain the purpose of discounting cash flows. (4)

7 Using only qualitative analysis, would you prefer £100 now or £105 in one year's time, at an interest rate of 10%? (3)

8 Outline two possible drawbacks to setting a payback criterion level of 12 months. (4)

9 What qualitative issues might a firm take into account when deciding whether to invest in a new fleet of lorries? (4)

10 Why is it important to ask for the source before accepting investment appraisal data? (3)

B1 Data response

Investment appraisal

Questions *(30 marks; 30 minutes)*

1 Net annual cash flows on an investment are forecast to be as shown in Table 13.14.

Table 13.14 Forecast of net annual cash flows

	£000
NOW	(600)
End of year 1	100
End of year 2	400
End of year 3	400
End of year 4	180

Calculate the payback and the average rate of return. (6)

2 The board of Burford Ltd is meeting to decide whether to invest £500,000 in an automated packing machine or into a new customer service centre. The production manager has estimated the cash flows from the two investments to calculate the figures shown in Table 13.15.

Table 13.15 Comparison of two potential investments for Burford Ltd

	Packing machine	Service centre
Payback	1.75 years	3.5 years
NPV	+£28,500	+£25,600

a On purely quantitative grounds, which would you choose and why? (6)

b Outline three other factors the board should consider before making a final decision. (6)

3 The cash flows on two alternative projects are estimated to be as shown in Table 13.16.

Carry out a full investment appraisal to decide which (if either) of the projects should be undertaken. Interest rates are currently 8%. (12)

Table 13.16 Cash flows on two alternative projects

| | Project A | | Project B | |
	Cash in	Cash out	Cash in	Cash out
Year 0	–	£50,000	–	£50,000
Year 1	£60,000	£30,000	£10,000	£10,000
Year 2	£80,000	£40,000	£40,000	£20,000
Year 3	£40,000	£24,000	£60,000	£30,000
Year 4	£20,000	£20,000	£84,000	£40,000

Data response

Dowton's

Dowton's new finance director has decided that capital investments will be approved only if they meet the criteria given in Table 13.17.

Table 13.17 Criteria for approval of capital investments

Payback	30 months
Average rate of return	18%
Net present value	10% of the investment outlay

The assembly department has proposed the purchase of a £600,000 machine that will be more productive and produce to a higher-quality finish. The department estimates that the output gains should yield the cash flow benefits during the expected four-year life of the machine shown in Table 13.18.

Table 13.18 Estimates of cash flow benefits during four-year life of machine

Year 0	–£600,000
Year 1	+£130,000
Year 2	+£260,000
Year 3	+£360,000
Year 4	+£230,000

In addition:

1 the machine should have a resale value of £100,000 at the end of its life

2 the relevant discount factors are: end year 1 0.91; year 2 0.83; year 3 0.75; year 4 0.68.

Questions *(30 marks; 35 minutes)*

1 Conduct a full investment appraisal, then consider whether Dowton's should go ahead with the investment on the basis of the quantitative information provided. (16)

2 Outline any other information it might be useful to obtain before making a final decision. (8)

3 Explain two sources of finance that might be appropriate for an investment such as this. (6)

Case study

Green investment?

These days many businesses feel under pressure to show their green credentials. In the hotel business, the desire to become energy-efficient is also expressed by the finance director. Electricity and gas bills are huge, amounting to more than the cost of the cleaning staff who service the rooms. One London hotel, the Portman Square Radisson, has an annual electricity bill of £500,000.

In February 2011 a Peterborough hotel was offered a £50,000 deal to install a wireless technology system to analyse and control energy consumption throughout the hotel. The supplier made a promise that 'it would pay back within 24 months'. In other words, the energy saved would cut the electricity bills sufficiently to provide a 24-month pay-back period.

For the hotel manager, £50,000 is a lot to find in a very tough year for UK hotels – especially those outside London. But Angela loves new technology, and loves the idea of being able to boast to guests that hers is one of the first hotels in the country to install the system. Being able to boast an annual saving of 3 tonnes of CO_2 is also a big attraction.

Before signing the deal, she decides to turn the suppliers' figures into an investment appraisal table. She has been told that the system will need replacing every five years.

To help, the supplier company has also provided the data shown in Table 13.20.

Fill in the remainder of the cash flow table; then answer the following questions.

Questions *(40 marks; 50 minutes)*

1 a Complete the investment appraisal table, then calculate the Payback and Average rate of return on the basis of that data. (10)

b Comment on your results. (6)

2 Calculate the NPV on the investment. Explain which discount factor you are choosing and why. (8)

3 Discuss whether Angela should go ahead, based on quantitative and qualitative factors. (16)

Table 13.19 Cash flow

	Cash in	Cash out	Net cash	Cumulative cash
NOW		£50,000		
Year 1	£20,000	£2,000		
Year 2	£18,000	£2,000		
Year 3	£18,000	£2,000		
Year 4	£18,000	£2,000		

Table 13.20 Data provided by supplier

	2% discount factors	4% discount factors
Now	1.00	1.00
Year 1	0.98	0.96
Year 2	0.96	0.92
Year 3	0.94	0.89
Year 4	0.92	0.85

14 Integrated finance

 ## Finance – Introduction

The great thing about a finance question is that if you get it right you get full marks. With most written questions a right answer might only score 2 out of 6 or 3 out of 9. So revision on finance can be uniquely helpful in producing high grades.

Calculations in themselves, however, are only a means to an end. Businesses do financial calculations to help them to manage the business. In examinations you should treat the figures the same way. When answering questions on finance and, even when revising, ask yourself:

● What do they show?

● What do they not show?

● What other information would help to explain the situation?

Remember that the finance answer is only part of the information needed to make an assessment of the situation. Remember that in business, finance does not stand alone. It is always connected with other aspects of the business such as marketing or production. Controlling costs is not just important for profit. It also contributes to the marketing effort by enabling the company to charge lower, more competitive prices. Raising finance is linked to a firm's need to expand or invest in new facilities or equipment. This means that what may seem like a 'finance' question is in fact linked to operational issues such as capacity levels or automation.

 ## Why study finance?

All organisations have to raise finance in some way, decide how it should be spent and monitor and control its usage. Even if the overall performance of an organisation is not measured in financial terms (such as a football club) the effective management of its finances is extremely important. Studying and understanding finance is therefore very important and the financial function plays a critical role in the success of any organisation.

Financial measures and techniques show the following.

● How the business is performing. The income statement and the balance sheet are invaluable for this.

● How best to make an investment decision. Investment appraisal, break-even and contribution analyses are helpful for this.

● How to control the business. Key measures include cash flow forecasts, budgeting and cost accounting.

● How to judge the performance of your own business – probably through ratio analysis – either by comparing two firms side-by-side, or by analysing the business over time.

Who is concerned about finance?

Finance is very much an internal activity. Unlike marketing, there is no direct interaction with the consumer. Yet many groups are interested in, and affected by, the financial health of a business, including:

- workers who rely on the viability of the business to ensure that their jobs continue and their wages remain competitive

- customers, who will look to the business to provide good-quality products at reasonable prices. This means the business must control costs so that it can charge a reasonable price and still be profitable

- investors will be looking for a satisfactory return on their capital and will want to know that the business is being financially well managed

- the government, who will want the business to succeed, both as a source of employment and as a tax payer.

So a well-managed business will have a wide impact. Finance as a tool for good management will play its part. Financial decisions will impact on other aspects of the business and therefore are indirectly a part of the relationship with the customers and other external groups.

'A' grade finance

'A' grade finance relies on understanding, not just memory. Getting the calculations right is obviously one element of a top answer, but higher grades require more than doing calculations. Your knowledge of finance will generate 'A' grade marks only if you are able to place finance in a wider business context.

Another important consideration is to understand what is included in the figures and what is not. The figures may not tell the whole story. A top student will know that the figures may be only part of the picture and will look for other information. Two businesses may have identical sales this year but what about future prospects? One may be facing fierce competition from a new rival or experiencing problems with its staff. The other may have no threats and so faces a healthier outlook. 'A' grade students apply their answers to the circumstances of the specific business.

Top grade students are able to make recommendations and support them. Studying finance topics requires you to understand the current situation in order to see how to improve it, e.g. improving cash flow. A 'D' grade candidate might do little more than

outline the possible solutions: take out an overdraft or loan, use factoring or sell assets. To decide which of these options is right, an 'A' grade student will consider factors such as:

- What options are open in this specific case? A brand new firm would not have spare assets to sell; and a retailer would not be able to use factoring (as this only applies when businesses sell on credit to other businesses).

- What are the consequences of the different choices? If you decide to sell assets will you still be able to function? And if an entrepreneur takes out an overdraft, will the bank insist that he or she gives a personal guarantee to repay it if the business cannot do so? (This is quite likely.)

A good decision will be well supported and in context. A decision to cut price to boost profits may work if demand is price elastic but not if it is price inelastic. A decision to cut costs may work provided it can be done without much impact on quality but may be risky if it involves a sly cheapening of the product features.

Issues in finance

There are several recurrent themes in finance. Being able to discuss these will often help to give a deeper, more evaluative, answer, to a finance question.

Issue 1: the importance of profit

Profit is clearly important to a business. It is necessary for the business to continue and an essential requirement for growth. However, it does not have to be the overriding consideration and many businesses balance other objectives with the profit motive. For example, some small businesses may fulfil a personal need to survive financially with other personal needs such as enjoying work. Larger businesses may balance the profit made with the requirement to maintain good public relations, or to act in a socially responsible manner. Businesses may also forego immediate profit in order to put in place strategies for growth or survival or increased profit in the future.

Issue 2: profit v profitability

It is important to understand the difference between profit and profitability. Profit is an absolute number. If a particular business project earned a profit of £10,000 last year, is this good or bad? It needs to be related to another number such as the amount invested in it. If the £10,000 profit came from an investment of £20,000, this is a 50% return on your investment, which is good. If it required an investment of £100,000 to earn £10,000 profit, this is 10% which is not so impressive. Profitability measures profit is relation to some other figure and is measured in percentages. Terms such as 'profit margin' and 'profit' cannot be used interchangeably. 'A' grade students need to understand exactly what they mean and use them carefully.

Issue 3: the ethics of profitability

The media contains a great deal of discussion about the ethics of profitability, i.e. the moral dimension. Businesses need profit, but how much and at what cost?

What balance should be struck between profit and issues such as protecting the environment, exploiting workers or exploiting customers? Should producers of 'natural fruit smoothies' act as if they are the customer's friend if they are charging very high prices and making very high profits? Is this hypocrisy?

What about firms that produce or buy their products from developing countries where employees are paid very low wages. Is this acceptable? Or is it better that people in developing countries have some income rather than none?

Answering these questions will require a balancing of the various interests involved. When answering a question involving ethics it is important to look at all sides of the issue and to avoid becoming emotionally involved with one point of view. This may be very difficult if you have strong beliefs about an issue such as animal welfare, or the treatment of staff in developing countries compared to the UK. By all means express your views but remember to balance them with the other side of the case. When considering the rights and wrongs of profits, many people will be involved and it becomes important to look at issues from a variety of perspectives.

Issue 4: the importance of liquidity

Understanding this issue requires an understanding of the difference between liquidity and profit. Liquidity is about having access to enough cash on a day-to-day basis to meet the business's commitments. Even if the cash is not available within the business, all is not lost if it is able to generate the required cash from external sources. Poor liquidity is not just a short-term problem. Unless the business is properly funded the problem will keep returning. It is essential that the business has enough working capital to run the business effectively.

Issue 5: is financial management only for large businesses?

While larger companies have the resources to employ financial experts, good financial management is essential for all businesses. Many new businesses fail because of poor financial management; in fact it is one of the most common causes of early business failure. If anything, small businesses may need even tighter financial management than larger businesses. They will not have the resources to buffer the business if mistakes are made. They are also less likely to have access to outside funding to bail them out in difficult times. Small firms may have just one or two products, which means that financial risks are more concentrated.

However, as the business grows there will be a widening gap between ownership and control. The shareholders may not take an active role in the day-to-day affairs of the business. In this situation, financial management systems will be necessary to keep control of the business and ensure that the managers are pursuing the interests of the investors.

A Revision questions (60 marks; 60 minutes)

1 List three uses for company accounts. (3)

2 Why is profit important to a business? (2)

3 What is the difference between profit and cash flow? (2)

4 How can an understanding of contribution help a business? (2)

5 List two methods of investment appraisal. (2)

6 Describe the differences between the two methods. (4)

7 Name an accounting ratio that measures liquidity. (1)

8 Why is liquidity vital to a business? (4)

9 List two likely sources of finance for a new business. (2)

10 List and discuss two ways in which a business could finance expansion. (6)

11 What does a cash flow forecast show? (3)

12 How can cash flow forecasts help a business? (4)

13 Identify and discuss two ways in which a firm can deal with a predicted future cash flow shortage. (6)

14 What does break-even analysis show? (2)

15 Distinguish between fixed and variable costs. (2)

16 How do you calculate unit contribution? (2)

17 What is the purpose of budgeting? (2)

18 What is a cost centre? (2)

19 Why is window dressing a cause for concern? (3)

20 Explain two ways a firm could reduce its gearing level. (4)

B1 Data response

Massey Boots

Massey Boots produces boots for working men but has recently begun selling its boots for general wear. It has been surprised by the interest shown by teenagers and young adults. At the moment it produces three types of boot, but increased demand has placed considerable strain on the production facilities. The production manager believes that if the company produced only two types of boot, the production facilities could be used more efficiently. Then some of the problems it is facing at the moment could be reduced. It has decided to cut the range to two types and needs to decide which to continue producing. It is confident of selling all the boots it makes. The machinery and labour force can be used to manufacture any of the boots

without the need for additional expenditure. The maximum number of boots that can be produced is 300,000 pairs. The finance department has produced the figures shown in Table 14.1.

Total fixed costs are £600,000.

Questions (20 marks; 25 minutes)

1 Calculate the unit and total contribution for each type of boot. (6)

2 If the factory made only one type of boot calculate the break-even level of production for each of the three types. (6)

3 Using the calculations, comment on the production manager's suggestion. (8)

Table 14.1 Figures produced by the finance department

Type of boot:	Toughman	Roughneck	Cruncher
Sales per year	150,000	80,000	70,000
Selling price	£45	£40	£60
Costs			
Direct materials per boot	£12	£8	£18
Direct labour per boot	£13	£10	£12

Case study

Simon's gift shop

Five years ago Simon started a sole trader business. He was made redundant and used his redundancy payment, together with a loan of £30,000, to start up a gift shop in a suburb of Oldtown. Oldtown is a large town that used to be very prosperous but has suffered from the closure of a large factory in the last year. Simon's venture is doing well, however. His turnover has been rising steadily and last year he made a net profit of £42,000. Two years ago he took out another loan of £35,000 to expand and redecorate the shop. He has also ploughed back some of the profits in the business, and the total capital employed is now £130,000.

Simon feels that the time is right to start a second shop. Rents have fallen in the town, following the closure of the factory and there are premises available. He has identified three possibilities. These are:

1 a large shop in another suburb; this is fairly new, prosperous residential area

2 a shop in the centre of town close to the major chain stores; this is a busy area with plenty of passing trade but there are other gift shops in the area

3 a small shop in the redeveloped Docks area; this is some distance away but is a successful tourist area.

All three shops have five-year leases available.

Simon has estimated the costs and expected profit for each shop. These are shown in Table 14.2.

Simon will have to pay 10% interest on any borrowed money. The discount factors at 10% are:

- end year 1   0.91
- end year 2   0.83
- end year 3   0.75
- end year 4   0.68
- end year 5   0.62

Simon will need to go to the bank for a loan. The role play (see below) will involve preparing and presenting the case for the loan to the bank manager.

Preparation

1 Review each of the sites using investment appraisal techniques.

2 Evaluate the project.

3 Decide the course of action you think Simon should take.

Role play

Acting as Simon, make a presentation, suitable for a bank manager, applying for a loan to finance the investment.

Table 14.2 Costs and expected profits for shops located in three separate areas

	Suburb	Town centre	Docks area
Initial outlay	£80,000	£105,000	£116,000
Expected annual profit	£25,000	£35,000	£40,000

Case study

The Yummy Biscuit Company

The Yummy Biscuit Company has been operating for about ten years. It was started by two friends and was so successful that, eight years ago, the owners convinced friends and family to invest in the business. It converted to a private limited company. With the new expansion it was able to lease a factory on a new industrial estate and purchase new machinery. Business has been booming and it is now at full capacity. Production continues day and night, which is placing considerable strain on resources.

The company has now reached the point where the managers need to make some hard decisions. They feel there are two choices: to expand or to cut back sales to a slightly lower level. The latter option will take some of the pressure out of the system so that each machine breakdown does not cause a crisis. If the company is to expand it will need to raise about £200,000. This will pay for the new machinery, new premises and vehicles, and the recruitment and training of new staff as well as the cost of the move. Sales last year were £250,000 and overheads amounted to £150,000. Variable costs are 25% of turnover. If the company expands, the managers anticipate they can easily double sales and that overheads could be reduced to 50% of turnover.

The balance sheet at the end of the last financial year is shown in Table 14.3.

Table 14.3 Balance at financial year end for The Yummy Biscuit Company

	£
Fixed assets	265,000
Current assets	115,000
less Current liabilities	30,000
= Working capital	85,000
Assets employed	350,000
	£
Financed by:	
Loan	80,000
Share capital	250,000
Retained profit	20,000
Capital employed	350,000

Questions *(25 marks; 40 minutes)*

1 If the business decides to expand, discuss how it might raise the necessary funding. (6)

2 Calculate the actual profit for last year and the anticipated profit for next year, assuming that the company expands. (5)

3 In addition to the financial information, what else should the business consider before making the decision? (4)

4 Write a report to the company managers advising them whether or not to expand. (10)

15 Key AS marketing issues

> ### Definition
> The AQA specification for A2 Marketing states:
>
> This section considers the development of marketing strategies for larger businesses through a scientific approach to decision making. It builds upon AS Marketing materials.

The key issues raised at AS on which to build A2 marketing knowledge are outlined below.

Objectives, strategy and tactics

At A2, issues in marketing can all be fitted into the headings 'Objectives', 'Strategy' and 'Tactics'. Much of AS marketing was focused on tactical decisions such as price changes or promotional offers. At A2 the emphasis shifts to a bigger, longer-term view of marketing. The focus is on a broad-based strategic approach to marketing and an assessment of how marketing decisions are made.

The key to marketing objectives is that they are usually more ambitious than just 'increase sales'. They are usually based on a longer-term ambition such as clear product differentiation, e.g. to make Chanel the ultimate perfume (and therefore justify a startlingly high price).

From the AS, you will need to recall the marketing mix, but reappraise it in the light of the need to think longer term. Tesco has used the same slogan 'Every Little Helps' for more than 15 years, to its huge benefit. This has been a strategy and needs to be contrasted with 'Buy One Get One Free' (BOGOF) tactics. BOGOFs buy a quick boost to sales (but probably not profits). Successful strategy builds businesses.

Research and market analysis

A significant grounding in gathering and analysing marketing data is included at AS level. This helps to prepare for the section to be covered at A2 on scientific marketing decision making. Benefits can be gained from analysing the state of the markets in which a firm is operating or planning to operate, considering factors such as market growth, market size and market share. This allows a clear assessment of the attractiveness of that market to be made, suggesting entry or not, or even departure from an increasingly unattractive existing market. Good A2 marketing answers will be based on awareness of how well a firm understands its market. This, in turn, will depend on the accuracy of market research – and how well the findings have been interpreted.

Product differentiation and price elasticity

It could be argued that all marketing activity centres on attempts to differentiate a product from those of its rivals. Certainly product differentiation is a key concept at both AS and A2 levels. The critical benefit of successful differentiation is the flexibility to raise prices without demand falling too much. In other words, a highly differentiated product tends to have a relatively low price elasticity. Inelastic demand means that a firm facing rising costs will be able to pass on those increases to customers through higher prices, thus protecting their profit margins. Alternatively, a firm that is generating insufficient profit would be able to increase price on a price inelastic product and generate higher profit margins as a result. Given the strategic importance of this topic, careful revision of AS notes is necessary.

Portfolio management and product life cycles

AS level marketing introduced the concepts of the product life cycle and product portfolio management. The Boston Matrix is a strategic management tool and will therefore be useful when making strategic marketing decisions at A2 level. Firms such as Cadbury use this type of analysis not only to decide which brands to concentrate on, but also to make broader decisions such as whether to move more aggressively into the market for mint sweets or chewing gum. Decisions such as these are funda-mental to A2 work.

AS formulae for A2 marketing

You will need to know:

Market share: $\dfrac{\text{sales of one brand}}{\text{total sales in a market}} \times 100$

Market growth: $\dfrac{\text{change in sales since last year}}{\text{last year's sales}} \times 100$

Price elasticity: $\dfrac{\text{\% change in quantity sold}}{\text{\% change in price}}$

Revision questions (50 marks; 50 minutes)

1 Explain one benefit and one drawback of launching a product into a market that is growing rapidly. (4)

2 State the formula for calculating market share. (2)

3 State two methods of measuring market size. (2)

4 Briefly explain why a firm may benefit from segmenting its market. (4)
   a Distinguish between quantitative and qualitative market research (3)
   b Which would be more appropriate when assessing:
      i what price to charge for a new product
      ii why people prefer a rival product's packaging? (2)

5 Outline three possible causes of unreliable quantitative research results. (6)

6 Distinguish between strategy and tactics. (3)

7 Briefly explain two benefits of niche marketing. (4)

8 Briefly explain two benefits of mass marketing. (4)

9 Identify four possible ways of adding value. (4)

10 Outline how product differentiation reduces a product's price elasticity. (3)

11 State the formula for calculating price elasticity. (1)

12 Briefly explain what is happening to net cash flows during the different stages of the product life cycle. (3)

13 What is meant by the term 'distribution targets'? (3)

14 What are the two variables measured by the Boston Matrix? (2)

16 Understanding marketing objectives

Definition
Marketing objectives are the marketing targets that must be achieved in order for the company to achieve its overall goals, such as 'to boost sales from £25 million to £40 million within three years'.

How are marketing objectives set?

At a very senior level in the company

In most firms, marketing is central to board-level strategic decisions. Not marketing in the sense of price cuts and promotions, but marketing in the sense of analysing growth trends and the competitive struggle within the firm's existing markets, and decisions about which markets the firm wishes to develop in future. For example, the new chief executive of Asda announced in May 2010 the objective of overtaking Tesco as Britain's largest retailer of non-food items. As Asda's non-food sales were £6 billion compared with Tesco's £9.5 billion, this would be a huge challenge. Expect keen prices and a series of new product launches from Asda's 'George' clothing brand in the coming years.

Rooted in the company's vision of its future (its mission)

A **vision** is a company's projection of what it wants to achieve in the future. It should be ambitious, relevant, easy to communicate and capable of motivating staff – or even inspiring them. Google's original mission was 'to organise the world's information'. Today, that seems uninspiring, even obvious. In its day it seemed an incredibly ambitious idea.

A firm's marketing objectives need to reflect its long-term aims/mission. The American car company Chrysler's mission statement says: 'Our purpose is to produce cars and trucks that people will want to buy, will enjoy driving, and will want to buy again.' This sets the background for marketing objectives that focus on developing new, probably niche markets, exciting rather than ordinary cars, and promoting them in ways that emphasise fun rather than safety or family.

In his book *Even More Offensive Marketing*, Hugh Davidson suggests that there are six requirements for a successful company vision. These are listed in Table 16.1.

By striking a balance between what is achievable and what is challenging

Objectives work best when they are clear, achievable, challenging and – above all else – when staff believe in them. To fit all these criteria, the firm must root the objectives in market realities. In 2009 Pepsi launched a new, 'all-natural' product, Pepsi Raw, to the UK retail trade. This new product was priced significantly higher than traditional colas, but Pepsi hoped it would establish a new niche in its attempt to dent Coca-Cola's £1,000 million of UK retail sales. By 2011 Pepsi Raw had been withdrawn from the UK market.

Marketing objectives should not be set until the decision makers have a clear view of current customer behaviour and attitudes. This will probably require a lot of market research into customer usage and attitudes to the different products they buy and don't buy.

Once the marketplace and financial factors have been considered, objectives can be decided that stretch people, but do not make them snap. Cadbury has had a 30% share of the UK chocolate market for decades. Setting a target of 35% for two years' time would be implausible. After all, will Mars or Nestlé just sit and watch? A wise marketing director might accept the challenge of 32% in two years' time, but would warn everyone that it might be very difficult to achieve this. (Note: each 1% of the chocolate market represents over £20 million of sales, so these matters are not trivial.)

Table 16.1 Vision: six requirements for success

Requirement	Comment
1. Provides future direction	As shown in the above examples of Microsoft and Chrysler
2. Expresses a consumer benefit	e.g. Pret A Manger: 'Our mission is to sell handmade extremely fresh food ...'
3. Realistic	Realistic? Innocent Drinks 2010: 'To be the most talent-rich company in Europe'
4. Motivating	Body Shop: 'Tirelessly work to narrow the gap between principle and practice, whilst making fun, passion and care part of our daily lives'
5. Fully communicated	Easy to achieve if it's as simple as Kwik Fit's: 'To get customers back on the road speedily, achieving 100% customer delight'
6. Consistently followed in practice	A company might claim to be at the leading edge of technology; it will lose all credibility if it reacts to the next recession by cutting spending on research and development.

Source: Davidson (1997).

A-grade application

Marketing objectives can fail

In 2010 Toyota's new president (Akio Toyoda) scrapped an objective set years before by his predecessor. In 2002, when Toyota's share of the world car market was 10%, the then president set the objective of achieving a 15% share by 2010/2011. In the face of a storm of bad publicity about product quality, Toyoda placed the blame on this objective. He demanded that, in future, Toyota should focus on product quality and customers' needs, not on numerical targets.

Types of marketing objective

There are four main types of marketing objective:

1 increasing product differentiation
2 growth
3 continuity
4 innovation.

Increasing product differentiation

Product differentiation is the extent to which consumers see your product as different from the rest. It is the key to ensuring that customers buy you because they want you, not because you're the cheapest. It is a major influence on the value added and therefore profit margins achieved by the product.

To increase product differentiation requires a fully integrated marketing programme. Objectives must be set that separate your product from its rivals. These include:

● distinctive design and display

● unusual distribution channels – avoiding supermarkets, perhaps

● advertising based on image building, not sales boosting (e.g. television and cinema advertising rather than blockbuster sales promotions or competitions)

● an integrated marketing programme focused solely upon the relevant age group or type of person.

Growth

Some firms see growth as their main purpose and their main security blanket. They may reason that once they are number one, no one else will be able to catch them. So they set sales or market share targets that encourage staff to push hard for greater success.

This is understandable, but may prove self-defeating. A school or college pushing hard for rapid growth in student numbers would risk damaging its reputation. Class sizes would rise, hastily recruited new staff may be ineffective, middle management would be overstretched and quality standards would be at risk.

From a marketing point of view there is also the threat of 'cannibalisation'. This occurs when the sales of a newly launched product come largely from the company's existing products. This would have been the case when Cadbury launched a new 'Double Choc' version of its classic Dairy Milk bar. The bigger a firm builds its market share, the bigger the problem becomes. For example, if Wrigley launches a new chewing gum, sales will largely come from other Wrigley brands, as the company holds an astonishing 90% market share.

Cannibalisation has been a major problem in recent years for three giant businesses. In its pursuit of growth, McDonald's built up more than 100,000 stores worldwide before realising that its new stores were taking mainly from existing ones. Arguably Marks & Spencer has the same problem: every time it opens a Simply Food store at a railway station or motorway, it's robbing sales from existing large M&S stores.

Of course, the pursuit of growth may be essential. When social networking became the hottest property on the web, Facebook was right to rush to satisfy this demand. If it had not grown rapidly, others, such as Bebo, would have done so. Therefore the company's objective of rapid growth was very sensible. Too slow would have become too late.

Continuity for the long term

The companies that own major brands, such as Levi's, Bacardi or Cadbury, know that true success comes from taking a very long-term view. Unilever even tells its brand managers that their key role is to hand over a stronger brand to their successor. In other words, they must think ten years or so ahead.

Doubtless Bacardi could boost sales and profits this year by running price promotions with the major supermarkets and off-licences; or next year, by launching Bacardi iced lollies or bubble gum. But where would the brand's reputation be in a few years' time? Would it still be a classy drink to ask for at a bar?

Large firms think a great deal about their corporate image and the image of the brands they produce. They may try to stretch their brands a little, to attract new customers. Yet Cadbury must always mean chocolate, not just snack products. Levi's must always mean jeans, not just clothes. Only in this way can the brands continue to add value for the long term.

Innovation

In certain major sectors of the economy, a key to long-term competitive success is innovation – in other words, bringing new product or service ideas to the marketplace. Two main categories of business where innovation is likely to be crucial are fashion-related and technology-related, as shown in Table 16.2.

Table 16.2 Businesses where innovation is especially important

Business category	Business sector
Fashion-related	Music business Clothing and footwear Entertainment (e.g. eating out)
Technology-related	Consumer electronics and IT Cars and aircraft Medicines and cosmetics

There are two key elements to innovation: get it right and get in first. Which is the more important? This is not possible to answer, as past cases have given contradictory results. The originator of the

---

A-grade application

Market development and the Lynx effect

Unilever has a corporate objective of doubling sales volumes within the next five years. Its marketing objectives must match that. Broadly, it must then decide whether to set tough targets for successful new product development, or whether to boost sales of existing products. It has decided to focus on market development, based on such huge worldwide brands as Lynx*, which is the world's biggest male deodorant. It plans to achieve its growth targets by these three aspects of market development:

● more users (increasing market penetration)

● more usage (increasing 'consumption')

● more benefits (getting consumers to buy products with higher value added).

Whereas other companies might choose to 'milk' this top-selling brand, Unilever wants to push its sales as far as possible.

*Lynx is marketed as *Axe* outside the UK.

filled ice cream cone was Lyons Maid (now Nestlé), with a product called King Cone. Walls came into the market second with Cornetto. In this case, getting it right proved more important than getting in first. In many other cases, though, the firm in first proved dominant for ever. Coca-Cola ('the real thing'); Cadbury's chocolate (in Britain) or Hershey's (in the USA); even the humble Findus Crispy Pancake (with its 80% market share); all have built long-term success on the back of getting in first.

A-grade application

Although L'Oréal is brilliant at advertising its products, the heart of its success worldwide comes from innovation. For example it has recently achieved a breakthrough that allows ammonia (which smells) to be eliminated from hair colourants. This patented technique is one among hundreds L'Oréal achieves each year. Figure 16.1 shows that even in a very difficult year for L'Oréal – 2009 – it kept investing in R&D staff and in registering new patents.

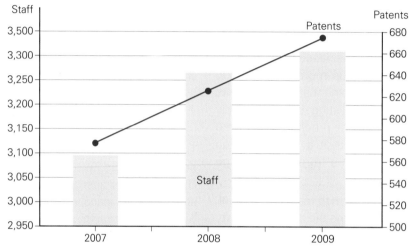

Figure 16.1 L'Oréal investment in innovation

Turning objectives into targets

The purpose of objectives is to set out exactly what the business wants to achieve. To ensure success, it is helpful to set more limited targets – staging posts en route to the destination. For example, a firm pursuing the objective of innovation may want at least 40% of sales to come from products launched within the past five years. If, at present, only 30% of sales come from this source, a jump to 40% will not be easy. The targets listed in Table 16.3 may help, especially if – as below – they are linked with the strategy for achieving them.

Targets such as these:

- ensure that all the marketing staff know what to aim for
- provide a sound basis for cooperation with

Table 16.3 Targets and strategies for meeting them

Timescale	Target (% of sales from products launched in past five years)	Strategy for meeting target
First year	32%	One national new product launch plus another in test market
Second year	35%	One national new product launch and two others in test market
Third year	40%	Two national new product launches

other departments (such as R&D and operations management)

- provide an early warning of when the strategy is failing to meet the objectives – should it be rethought? Or backed with more resources?
- help psychologically; just as an end-of-year exam can concentrate the mind of a student, so a target can motivate a manager to give of his or her best.

These benefits hinge on a key issue: have the targets been communicated effectively to the staff?

This is an obvious point, but vital nonetheless. If the entire marketing department is based in one large office, it would be astonishing if anyone was unaware of new objectives. But what if it is a retail business and there are 400 branches around the country? Then a head office initiative can fall down at the local level, when a local manager thinks he or she knows best. Expertly considered **marketing targets** may fail unless they are communicated effectively to all relevant staff.

Marketing objectives and the small firm

Do small firms set aside time to consider, set and write down objectives and targets? Very rarely. If you interviewed a dozen small business proprietors, you might find none who finds the time and several who would regard such time as wasted.

There are two issues here.

1 In a very small firm, with all business decisions taken by the proprietor, the marketing objectives may be clear in the mind of the boss, even though they are not written down. That may work satisfactorily. When the firm gets 15 or more staff, however, it may have to change.

2 The bosses of small firms often find themselves swamped by day-to-day detail. Customers expect to speak to them personally, staff check every decision and may wait around for their next 'orders'. Only if such bosses learn to delegate will

they find the time to think carefully about future objectives and strategy.

There are some bright, young entrepreneurs, however, who apply a more thoughtful approach. Julian Richer identified a gap in the hi-fi market for high-quality equipment sold by music enthusiasts at discount prices. This was intended to appeal to younger, more streetwise buyers. The target image was 'fun'. In the summer, customers at Richer Sounds receive free ice lollies; at Christmas, mince pies. The public face of Richer Sounds is that 'We have a laugh. We don't take ourselves seriously, but we do take our customers seriously.' Behind the scenes, though, careful target setting for stores and sales staff helped Richer Sounds achieve a *Guinness Book of Records* entry for the highest sales per square foot of any store in the UK.

Constraints on meeting marketing objectives

However well conceived, objectives do not automatically lead to success. Various factors may occur that restrict the chances of the objectives succeeding. These are known as **constraints**. They may occur within the firm (internal constraints) or may be outside its control (external constraints).

Internal influences

Finance

Financial influences affect virtually every aspect of every organisation. Even Manchester United has a budget for players, which the manager must keep within. A marketing objective might be set that is unrealistic given the firm's limited resources. That is an error of judgement. Or the firm may have the finance in place at the start, but setbacks to the firm

may cause budget cuts that make the objectives impossible to reach.

Personnel constraints

Personnel constraints may be important. The objective of diversifying may be appealing, but the firm may lack expertise in the new market. A recruitment campaign may fail to find the right person at a salary the business can afford. This may result in the project being delayed, scrapped or – worst of all – carried on by second-rate staff.

Market standing

The marketing objectives may be constrained most severely by the firm's own market position. The big growth sector in food retailing has been in chilled, prepared meals. So why has there been no activity from the food giant Heinz? The answer lies in its success at establishing itself as *the* producer of canned soup, and bottled salad cream and ketchup. The Heinz market image (its key marketing asset) constrains it from competing effectively in chilled foods.

External influences

Competition

Competition is usually the main constraint outside the firm's control. It is the factor that prevents the *Sun* from charging 50p a copy. It is also the factor that makes it so hard to plan ahead in business. You may set the objective of gaining an extra 1% market share, only to be hit by a price war launched by a rival.

Consumer taste

Consumer taste is also important. If fashion moves against you, there may be little or nothing you can do to stop it. A logical approach is to anticipate the problem by never seeking fashionability. When its FCUK logo was trendy, no clothing business was hotter than French Connection. When this joke wore thin, though, sales collapsed as customers steered clear of yesterday's brand.

The economy

The economy can also cause huge problems when setting medium- to long-term objectives. This year's economic boom becomes next year's recession. Sales targets have to be discarded and a move upmarket may seem very foolish.

Marketing decision making: the marketing model

Successful marketing is not just about thinking. It is about decisions and action. Marketing decisions are particularly hard to make, because there are so many uncertainties. The procedure shown in Figure 16.2 is one of the most effective ways of ensuring a decision is well thought through.

The intention is to ensure that the strategy decided upon is the most effective at achieving the marketing objectives. In this process, market research is likely to be very important. It is crucial for finding out the background data and again for testing the hypotheses. Test marketing may also be used. This is a way of checking whether the market research results are accurate, before finally committing the firm to an expensive national marketing campaign.

The **marketing model** is the way to decide how to turn a marketing objective into a strategy.

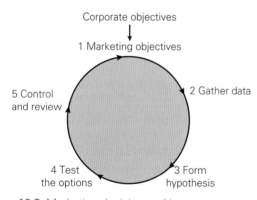

Figure16.2 Marketing decision making

Issues for analysis

- Marketing objectives are the basis for all marketing strategy. Therefore they will be central to almost every substantial exam question on marketing. For example, pricing decisions will depend upon the objectives. A firm pursuing growth might price a new product relatively cheaply, to ensure high market share and to discourage competition. Objectives will also affect the advertising approach: aimed at encouraging loyalty from existing users, or developing a new image/customer base.

- To understand objectives fully, it is vital to be

able to distinguish them from strategy. It is also important to remember that the setting of objectives cannot be done in isolation. The managers have to bear in mind the market situation, findings from market research, and the financial resources and personnel the firm has available. Warburton's objective of moving into the UK market for crisps foundered when it launched ChippidyDooDaa snacks in 2010. On paper the objective may have looked fine, but in practice it became a classic marketing failure.

Understanding marketing objectives – an evaluation

What career are you aiming for? If you have a definite answer to that question, you probably have a clear idea how to achieve it. You are also likely to be very well motivated towards the qualifications you need. Most A-level students have little idea of what they want to do. In other words, they have no objectives. As a result, they have no plan and may struggle to find the motivation to succeed at A-levels.

Marketing objectives are just as important. They allow a clear strategy to be devised, a plan to be set, and give the motivation to succeed. Therefore they are the most important element of marketing.

Further reading

Davidson, H. (1997) *Even More Offensive Marketing.* Penguin.

A   Revision questions (45 marks; 45 minutes)

1 Explain why it is important for a business to have clear marketing objectives. (3)

2 What do businesses mean by the term 'vision'? (3)

3 Why is it important that marketing objectives should be rooted in thorough market research? (4)

4 a   State the four main types of marketing objective. (4)
   b   Briefly explain which objective is most likely to be important for one of the following.
       a   Coca-Cola
       b   Twitter
       c   Subway. (3)

5 Why might a firm seek to increase the product differentiation of one of its brands? (3)

6 What problems might a firm face if it focuses solely upon short-term objectives? (5)

7 Is it essential that marketing objectives should be written down in detail? Explain your answer. (4)

8 Explain the meaning of the following terms.
   a   internal influences (3)
   b   external influences. (3)

9 Outline two external constraints that might affect car sales over the coming months. (4)

10 Identify and explain two problems a firm might face if it makes marketing decisions without using a decision-making framework such as the marketing model. (6)

Data response

Beanz meanz roublz?

Figure 16.3 A Russian Heinz tin

In spring 1997 Heinz made its first move into the Russian food market. Although the economy was growing at that time, average wage levels were still very low – typically under £25 per week. Yet Heinz chose to price its Baked Beans at around 50p per can – the equivalent of charging £5 in Britain.

Heinz had set its sights on the long-term objective of building a prestigious brand name. When the famous beans first came to Britain in 1901 they were sold by Fortnum & Mason for £1.50 per can. Now Heinz was aiming to pull off the same trick again – nearly 100 years later.

Its target sales figure for year 1 was 12 million cans in Russia. This compared with 450 million cans in the UK each year. If the company's strategy was successful, Heinz Beans might become trendy among Russia's growing middle classes. Even before the move by Heinz, its products were available on the black market, gaining it the status accorded to other western products such as Coca-Cola and Levi's.

Soon after launching in Russia, in August 1998, there was a virtual meltdown of the Russian economy that cut living standards sharply. To its credit, Heinz withstood this external constraint and persisted in this new market. In 2010 the Heinz annual report singled out Russia for its 'outstanding' growth. Will beanz mean more and more roublz? That remainz to be seen.

Questions *(30 marks; 35 minutes)*

1 Identify Heinz's marketing objective for its beans in Russia. (3)

2 State the target Heinz set as the test of whether its objective was met. (3)

3 a Explain the strategy Heinz chose to meet its objectives. (4)

   b Suggest and explain an alternative strategy it might have adopted. (6)

4 a Outline the external constraints faced by Heinz. (5)

   b Discuss how a business might react to changed external constraints, if it was determined to achieve its marketing objectives. (9)

Case study

Hoshil and Sunil's business started in rather dubious circumstances. While students they built up their capital by trading in 'second-hand' mobile phones. Now they were planning to open a nightclub aimed at young Asians. It would have two dance floors, one for Indian music and one for western pop music. One of the bars would be alcohol-free, have pool tables and music soft enough to allow people to chat. It would still be a nightclub, but with some of the benefits of a pub. The vision was clear: to provide a thriving social facility for young Asian men and women.

The investment outlay would be £150,000. Hoshil and Sunil put in £25,000 each and were fortunate that Hoshil's wealthy brother Satyam was able to put in the other £100,000. They would soon be ready to start.

Sunil and Satyam sat down to plan their marketing strategy. The objective was to maximise takings from day one – they needed to pay back their borrowings as soon as possible. After carrying out market research at their local community centre, the boys decided to focus on better-off 16 to 24 year olds. Prices would be kept relatively high, as there was no competition in the area. The location would be in the centre of Croydon, as the Tramlink service would bring people by public transport from a long way away.

Despite the agreement to focus on the better-off, when there was only a week until the opening night, Sunil panicked. Would there be enough people to create a good atmosphere? He printed 2000 leaflets saying 'Half Price Drinks For All The First Week!' and distributed them through the local newsagents. The opening night went very well and on the following Saturday it was impossible to move. By the second week, though, the numbers were dropping away. When research was carried out it showed that customers thought the drinks were expensive.

It took about six months to establish a really strong reputation as a top club. Large profits were being made and Hoshil's skills as a host were becoming well known. The national paper, the *Daily Jang*, ran a whole feature on him. He was very happy, while Sunil and Satyam were enjoying the large dividends on their investments.

Questions *(50 marks; 60 minutes)*

1 Outline the business importance of the following terms.

   a marketing strategy (5)

   b market research. (5)

2 How important to the success of the club was the clear vision and objectives? Explain your answer. (10)

3 Examine which of the four types of marketing objective were involved in this business success. (8)

4 How serious a risk did Sunil take by carrying out a marketing campaign that was at odds with the overall strategy? (10)

5 What do you consider to be the most important aspects of marketing for a small business? (12)

Analysing the market

Definition

When businesses refer to the market for their products, they mean the customers: how many there are, whether the number is rising or falling, what their purchasing habits are, and much else. Successful marketing relies on a complete understanding of 'the market'.

What market are we in?

This sounds a daft question, but the marketing guru Theodore Levitt considers it vital. Is Liverpool FC in the football business, the sports business or the leisure business? Some years ago Tottenham Hotspur nearly went into liquidation because of an unsuccessful diversification towards leisure clothing. The management thought it was in the leisure business, but its skills and the club's reputation stretched no further than football.

Long ago, Nintendo was Japan's number one producer of playing cards. It decided that its market was the broader games business and experimented with electronic games in the 1970s. Today it is a fabulously profitable producer of games consoles and software (its 2010 profit of £1.5 billion was much higher than the massive Sony Corporation). Sales of playing cards represent less than 1% of the modern Nintendo.

So Tottenham and Nintendo asked themselves the same question, came up with the same answer, but Nintendo made it work while Spurs flopped. Market analysis is never easy.

Figure 17.1

The purpose of market analysis

Managers tend to get caught up in the day-to-day needs of the business. A photo of Alexa Chan wearing a silk scarf might make sales leap ahead, forcing clothes store managers to focus 100% on how to find extra stocks of scarves. Market analysis should be a cooler, more thoughtful look at the market's longer-term trends. In 2010 Sony decided to focus the whole business on 3D. The company looked ahead at the market opportunity, realising that its strength in films, computer games and TVs put it in a great position to succeed with related technologies and products. It acted sensibly to position the business in the place where the consumer seemed to want to go.

Other clever pieces of market analysis include:

● Tesco spotting the opportunities in Hungary and Poland before other western retailers

● Danone seeing the opportunity for 'functional foods' (i.e. foods bought because they are believed to be good for you), such as Activia yoghurt, then putting more money behind its brands than anyone else; it showed huge confidence in its understanding of the market

- Harvey Nichols (classic London posh shop) seeing the opportunity for a branch in Leeds, in an era when there was plenty of money in the north; when it made the move, other retailers doubted whether Leeds would be posh enough – it was and it is.

All these examples have one thing in common: they are the result of careful analysis of trends within a market, backed by an ability to take bold decisions (and get them right).

Consumer usage and attitudes

Market analysis is rooted in a deep understanding of customers. Why do they buy Coca-Cola, not Pepsi? Yet they prefer Tropicana (made by Pepsi) to Minute Maid (made by Coke). And who are the key decision makers? Purchasers (perhaps parents buying a multipack in Tesco) or the users (perhaps young teenage children slumped in front of the television)? Is the brand decision a result of child pester power, or parental belief in the product's superiority? Knowledge of such subtleties is essential. Only then can the firm know whether to focus marketing effort on the parent or the child.

To acquire the necessary knowledge about usage and attitudes, firms adopt several approaches. The starting point is usually qualitative research such as group discussions. Run by psychologists, these informal discussions help pinpoint consumers' underlying motives and behaviour. For example, it is important to learn whether KitKat buyers enjoy nibbling the chocolate before eating the wafer biscuit – in other words, to discover whether playing with confectionery is an important part of the enjoyment. This type of information can influence future product development.

The major multinational Unilever has appointed a Head of Knowledge Management and Development (David Smith), to ensure that insights such as this can be spread around the business. As he says,

'The company's collective knowledge is potentially a great competitive advantage.' By encouraging improved communication and networking, Unilever believes it is benefiting from:

- improved decision making
- fewer mistakes
- reduced duplication
- converting new knowledge more quickly into added value to the business.

Among the other ways to gather information on customer usage and attitudes are quantitative research and obtaining feedback from staff who deal directly with customers. An example of the latter would be bank staff whose task is to sell services such as insurance. Customer doubts about a brochure or a product feature, if fed back to head office, might lead to important improvements.

Quantitative research is also used to monitor customer usage and attitudes. Many firms conduct surveys every month, to track any changes over time in brand awareness or image. This procedure may reveal that a TV commercial has had an unintended side-effect in making the brand image rather too upmarket, or that customers within a market are becoming more concerned about whether the packaging can be recycled.

Consumer profiles

Marketing decisions are very hard to make without a clear picture of your customers. Who are they? Young? Outgoing? Affluent? Or not. From product and packaging design, through to pricing, promotion and distribution – all these aspects of marketing hinge on knowing your **target market**.

A consumer profile is a statistical breakdown of the people who buy a particular product or brand (e.g. what percentage of consumers are women aged 16 to 25?). The main categories analysed within a

consumer profile are customers' age, gender, social class, income level and region. Profile information is used mainly for:

- setting quotas for research surveys
- segmenting a market
- deciding in which media to advertise (*Vogue* or the *Sun*?).

A large consumer goods firm will make sure to obtain a profile of consumers throughout the market as well as for its own brand(s). This may be very revealing. It may show that the age profile of its own customers is becoming older than for the market as a whole. This may force a complete rethink of the

marketing strategy. The company may have been trying to give the brand a classier image, but may end up attracting older customers.

Market mapping

Having analysed consumer attitudes and consumer profiles, it is possible to create a market map. This is done by selecting the key variables that differentiate the brands within a market, then plotting the position of each one. Usually this is done on a two-dimensional diagram as in Figure 17.2. Here, the image of shoe shops has been plotted against the key criteria of price (premium–budget) and purpose (aspirational–commodity). For example, Bally shoes are expensive and are bought to impress others. Church's are expensive but bought because their buyers believe they are a top-quality product.

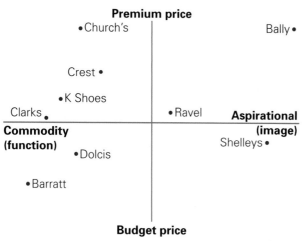

Figure 17.2 Market mapping

Market mapping enables a firm to identify any gaps or niches in the market that are unfilled. They also help monitor existing brands in a process known as **product positioning**. Is their image becoming too young and trendy? If so, booming sales in the short term might be followed by longer-term disappointment. By monitoring the position of their brands on the market map, firms can see more easily when a repositioning exercise is required. This may involve a relaunch with a slightly different product, a new pack design and a new advertising campaign.

A-grade application

The Jaguar XJ
Launched in 2010, the new Jaguar XJ was deliberately designed to restore the company's position within the luxury car sector. In the days when Jaguar was owned by Ford, the American car producer had pulled Jaguar's model range down towards the mass market. Its XF model, launched in 2009, was successful, but was perhaps too close to the mass market to truly reposition the company. The XJ, with prices from around £60,000, would emphasise that Jaguar should be seen alongside Mercedes and BMW, not Ford or Volkswagen.

The use of IT in analysing markets

Market analysis takes two main forms: looking from the outside at a market you'd like to enter; and looking from the inside at a market you're in. From the outside, the use of IT is limited to practical factors such as calculations and display of secondary or primary research. When you're within a market, though, there is huge scope for collecting data and learning how best to learn from it. For small firms, this can be overwhelming. For example, everyone with a website can easily find out how many 'hits' they have per day, and where the hits come from. They can find out how many people look at each page and how many abandon an attempt to

buy something. But is that information useful? Not necessarily.

A well-run business will try to collect data so that managers are better able to analyse their market and their position within that market. London's Hoxton Hotel targets younger, trendier travellers. It has a long-term strategy of building repeat business, i.e. it wants travellers to see the Hoxton as their London 'home'. As the bulk of Hoxton bookings are made online, the hotel can capture data on customers' age, sex, home town and how often they've stayed at the hotel. This data is used to monitor how well the business is achieving its objectives, and also to check on the Hoxton's positioning compared with secondary research data on the age of hotel-goers generally.

Issues for analysis

Among the main issues raised by this unit are the following.

- The importance to a firm of constantly measuring and rethinking its position in the market: this is why expenditure on market research needs to be regular; not just related to the latest new project.

- Given the importance of market knowledge, how can new firms break into a market? The answer is: with difficulty. Super-rich Microsoft launched Xbox in Britain in 2002, having to compete with the established Nintendo and Sony consoles. By 2011, despite the higher market share achieved by the Xbox 360, Microsoft was still many billions of dollars down on the Xbox experience.

- If all companies follow similar techniques for market analysis, why don't they all come up with the same answers? Fortunately, there remains huge scope for initiative and intuition. Two different managers reading the same market research report may come up with quite different conclusions. The Apple iPhone was the inspiration of a small group of developers at Apple (plus selected suppliers). The Wii was also a very individual achievement by a select few at Nintendo.

Analysing the market – an evaluation

Market analysis is at the heart of successful marketing. All the great marketing decisions are rooted in a deep understanding of what customers really want – from the marketing of Lady GaGa through to the sustained success of the (incredibly pricey) Chanel No. 5 perfume. The clever market stall trader acquires this understanding through daily contact with customers. Large companies need the help of market research to provide a comparable feel. Techniques such as market mapping then help clarify the picture.

Having learnt what the customer really wants from a product, perhaps helped by psychological insights from qualitative research, it is relatively easy to put the strategy into practice. If the marketing insight is powerful enough, the practical details of the marketing mix should not matter too much. The Nintendo Wii was a brilliant piece of marketing, but few commentators had anything good to say about the brand's advertising or packaging. The genius came earlier in the process.

Key terms

Product positioning: deciding on the image and target market you want for your own product or brand.

Target market: the type of customer your product or service is aimed at. For example the target market for KitKat Senses is 15- to 30-year-old women.

A Revision questions *(35 marks; 35 minutes)*

1 Reread 'What market are we in?' on page 116 and ask yourself 'What if Nintendo had not decided to define its market more widely? What would the business be like today?' (3)

2 Explain why Tesco's market analysis in Hungary and Poland can be described as 'clever'. (3)

3 Explain two reasons why it might be important to distinguish 'purchasers' from 'users'. (4)

4 Explain how qualitative research could be used helpfully when analysing a market. (4)

5 When *Look* magazine was launched in 2007 it announced that its target market was '24-year-old women'. Explain two ways it could make use of this very precise consumer profile. (4)

6 Explain how market mapping might be helpful to *two* of the following.
   a an entrepreneur looking at opening up a new driving school
   b the brand manager of Werther's Original sweets, worried about falling market share
   c a private school thinking of opening its first branch in China. (8)

7 Why does market research need to be carried out regularly, not just related to a new product? (3)

8 Explain the importance of market research in achieving effective market analysis. (6)

B1 Data response

What business is Cadbury in? For the first 100 years of the firm's life, the answer would have been chocolate. But in 1989 it bought the Trebor and Bassetts brands, to form a large sugar confectionery unit. With Wrigley enjoying uninterrupted growth in chewing gum, Cadbury then bought Adams – a major US gum producer (for £2.7 billion). It followed this up with purchases of other chewing gum producers, in countries such as Turkey.

In 2007, Cadbury launched the Trident gum brand in Britain. This was bold because Wrigley enjoyed a market share of more than 90% in the UK. By March 2008 Cadbury was able to announce that 'an astounding £38 million of extra sales value has been added to the gum category, with 75% of this growth delivered by Trident'. Cadbury's management confidently predicted five years of growth for Trident of as much as £20 million of sales per year.

By 2009, though, Trident was in sharp retreat, with sales falling to £19 million. Then Cadbury was submerged into the Kraft food business. So is Cadbury in the food business? The chocolate business? Or the confectionery business? It's hard to say.

Table 17.1 UK confectionery market 2009

Chocolate	£3,069m
Sugar confectionery	£1,007m
Chewing gum	£240m
Total market	£4,316m

Questions *(25 marks; 30 minutes)*

1 Explain why companies such as Cadbury need to ask themselves, 'What market am I in?'. (6)

2 a What is meant by the term 'market share'? (2)

   b Calculate Trident's share of the chewing gum market in 2009. (2)

   c Why might Cadbury have been worried about tackling a business with 'a market share of more than 90%'? (6)

3 Discuss what might have gone wrong with Cadbury's analysis of the chewing gum market. (9)

18 **Measuring and forecasting trends**

> **Definition**
> Forecasting involves estimating future values.

Introduction

It is very important for managers to look ahead. They need to think about what is likely to happen in their industry and prepare accordingly in all areas of the business. One of the most important forecasts that needs to be made is the **sales forecast**. This forms the basis of most of the other plans within the organisation. For example:

- the human resource plan will need to be based on the expected level of sales; a growth in sales may require more staff
- the cash flow forecast will depend on projected sales and the payment period
- the profit and loss forecasts will depend on the level of revenue predicted
- the production scheduling will depend on what output is required
- stock levels will depend on the likely production and demand over a period.

The sales forecast therefore drives many of the other plans within the business and is an essential element of effective management planning.

When a business starts up, it is extremely difficult to interpret its sales data. An ice cream parlour that starts up in April may find that sales double in May, again in June and again in July. Excited by the business success, the entrepreneurs may rush to open a second outlet. Yet a wet August may see sales knocked back followed by a sales slump in the autumn. The business may be overstretched and in liquidation by February.

As long as a business can survive the first year or two, managers can start to interpret its sales data. Above all else, managers want to understand the **trend** in product sales and compare it to trends in the market as a whole.

Moving averages

A useful way to show trends is by using a moving average. This is helpful in two main circumstances:

1 where there are strong seasonal influences on sales, such as in the ice cream parlour example

2 when sales are erratic for no obvious reason; wild ups and downs may make it hard to see the underlying situation.

Table 18.1 shows the 'raw data' for a small supermarket (i.e. monthly sales figures). As you can see, they jump around, forming no obvious pattern.

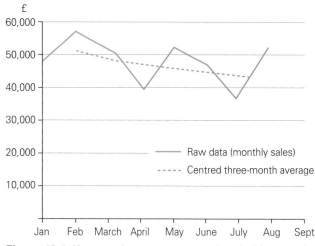

Figure 18.1 How moving averages reveal underlying trends

Table 18.1 Example of a moving average

	Raw data (monthly sales) (£)	Centred three-month total (£)	Centred three-month average (£)
January	48,000		
February	57,000		52,000
March	51,000	156,000	49,000
April	39,000	147,000	47,700
May	53,000	143,000	46,300
June	47,000	138,000	45,300
July	36,000	136,000	44,700
August	51,000	134,000	

To find the moving average of the data:

- the first step is to calculate a moving total, in this case a three-month total – in other words, the January–March figures are totalled, then the February–April figures, and so on.

- then, calculate the centred average (i.e. the January–March total of 156,000 is divided by 3 to make 52,000); this monthly average sales figure for January–March is centred to February, because that is the 'average' of January–March.

Note how well the three-month moving average clarifies the data, revealing the (awful) underlying trend. The graph (Figure 18.1) simply plots the raw data and the centred average to show the value of the technique.

Forecasting sales using extrapolation

The simplest way of predicting the future is to assume it will be just like the past. For the immediate future this may be realistic. It is unlikely (though not impossible) that the economy or demand will change dramatically tomorrow – an assumption that the pattern of sales will continue to follow recent trends may therefore be reasonable. If demand for your product has been rising over the past few months it may not be illogical to assume it will continue in the foreseeable future. The process of predicting based on what has happened before is known as extrapolation. Extrapolation can often be done by drawing a line by eye to extend the trend on a graph (see Figure 18.2).

Here a very steady upward trend over a long period may well continue and be predicted to continue. However, such stability and predictability are rare. The values of data plotted over time, called time-series analysis, can vary because of **seasonal variations**/influences and also because of genuinely random factors, which can never be predicted. For example, another outbreak of foot and mouth disease would lead to a sudden collapse in the sales of meat. Or a revaluation of the Chinese currency might lead to a huge wave of new tourists coming to London (1,300 million?). Despite the uncertainties, predicting sales based on extrapolated trends is the most widely used method.

As with every business technique, there is also a need for judgement. Look at Figure 18.3. Based upon the longer-term trend, you might believe that the recent downturn is temporary (as with UK house

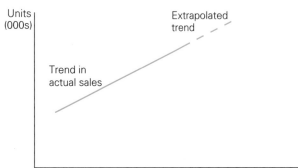

Figure 18.2 An extrapolated sales trend

prices, perhaps). Or it might be that you believe that the recent figures have established the likely trend for the future. It is never wise to simply use a calculator, a computer or graph paper without thinking carefully about what makes the most sense.

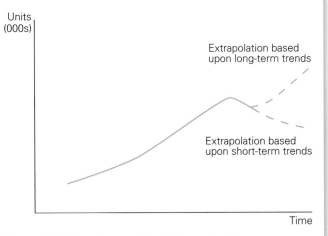

Figure 18.3 Requirement for judgement when extrapolating trends

Correlation

Businesses are always keen to learn about the effect on sales of marketing strategies such as TV advertising, sales promotion or direct mailshots. Often researchers will compare sales volume and advertising expenditure. A good way to do this is on a graph. In Figure 18.4 there is clearly a strong relationship, or correlation, between the two.

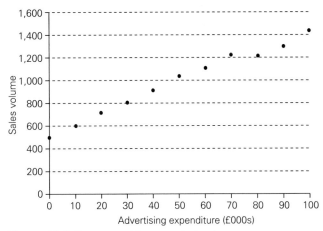

Figure 18.4 Strong positive correlation between advertising expenditure and sales

The correlation is positive: as one increases so does the other. It is important to realise that each point correlating the two variables represents one observation covering a period of time.

In Figure 18.5, however, there is not so much linkage as the diagram is little more than a collection of randomly dispersed points. In this case there is low correlation between advertising and sales, suggesting that the firm should stop wasting its money until it has found a way to make its advertising work more effectively.

What the researcher is looking for is cause and effect, namely evidence that the advertising has caused the increase in sales. Now correlation by itself does not indicate cause and effect. The rising of the sun in the morning may be strongly correlated with the delivery time of newspapers to letterboxes, but it does not cause them to be delivered. Strong correlation is evidence that cause and effect *may* be present. Further evidence is needed to know how the variables are affecting each other. Clearly, the purpose of advertising is to generate sales, so it is highly likely that cause and effect may be at work.

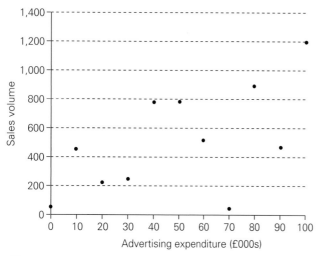

Figure 18.5 Loose correlation: are other variables important?

But managers know there are many variables at work all the time in markets. The sales of a product could rise because of cheaper credit terms, the disappearance of a competitor, or even unusual weather, and not just advertising. In cases like that presented in Figure 18.5, where there is weak correlation, researchers clearly should consider other variables as well as advertising.

Alternative methods of forecasting

The moving averages technique of forecasting has some limitations. The points calculated for the trend will always be less than the number of points in the actual raw data. This technique is most appropriate in stable circumstances when elements of the business environment, such as competition, are not expected to change very much. It is less useful in periods of change or instability.

Test markets

If a market or industry is undergoing major change or if you do not have past data to help you forecast sales then you may need to make use of experts' opinions or market research. By testing a product out in a small representative market, for example, you may be able to gather data from which you can estimate sales when you roll out the product on a bigger scale. Alternatively, you might ask experts who know the industry well to help you estimate likely sales.

The Delphi technique

One method of gathering expert opinion is known as the Delphi technique. This involves using experts who are asked for their opinions individually. Their comments are then summarised anonymously and circulated to the contributors, who are then invited to comment again in the light of the previous feedback. Each time the findings are circulated for a given number of times, or until a consensus is reached.

Scenario planning

Some businesses also use scenario planning. This process involves an analysis of particular scenarios in the future. Rather than simply estimating sales, for example, experts try to anticipate what market conditions will be and what will be happening in the market as a whole. For example, a business might try to consider the market in a position of fast growth or steady growth, and the impact of this on a range of business decisions.

The oil giant Shell is known for its use of scenario planning. For example, it will consider what the year 2015 might be like if oil prices had risen to $250 per barrel, or fallen to $50.

Other variables to consider when forecasting

When considering your sales forecast you will want to take into account any internal or external changes that you know are about to happen. External changes could include:

● new entrants into the market
● population changes
● climate changes or changes in weather conditions
● legal changes (e.g. limiting particular forms of promotion or increasing taxation)
● internal factors that you know may affect sales; this could include changes in the salesforce, changes in the amount of spending on promotion or the way that the money is being spent, or the launch of a new product.

In most cases the actual sales forecast will not be absolutely accurate. However, this does not make forecasting a waste of time – as long as it can provide an estimate that is approximately correct it will have helped the firm plan its staffing, funding and production. It is better to plan and be approximately right than not plan at all and be unprepared. However, it is always important to review your sales forecasts and compare this with what actually happened; this can help the firm to improve its forecasting techniques and provide better estimates in the future.

A-grade application

Retail sales in China

In 2006, Volkswagen China's Vice President for Strategy gave a presentation to analysts and investors. He forecast that the Chinese market for passenger cars would grow to between 4.5 and 5 million by 2010. In actual fact passenger car sales were more than 12 million in 2010! This huge underestimate forced Volkswagen to rush forward plans to boost factory capacity. Luckily for VW, construction projects in China are pushed forward much faster than anywhere else in the world, so the company could make up for its poor forecast.

Issues for analysis

● Forecasting is an important element of business planning.
● The sales forecast forms the foundation of many other of the business plans, such as cash flow and workforce planning.
● Sales forecasts are often based on past data, but must also take into account seasonal factors and changes in internal or external factors that are known about.

Measuring and forecasting trends – an evaluation

Sales forecasts can be very important to a business because so many other plans rely on them. They can determine how many people to employ, how much to produce and the likely dividends for investors. They may not always be accurate, but they can provide important guidelines for planning.

A badly run business will find itself in a crisis because its precisely forecast future turns out to be surprisingly different in reality. An intelligent manager tries hard to predict with precision, but thinks about the effect of sales being unexpectedly high or low. Nothing demoralises staff more than a sudden lurch by management (hiring one minute, firing the next). So the future needs thinking through carefully.

Key terms

Sales forecast: a method of predicting future sales using statistical methods.

Seasonal variation: change in the value of a variable (e.g. sales) that is related to the seasons.

Trend: the general path a series of values (e.g. sales) follows over time, disregarding variations or random fluctuations.

Revision questions (35 marks; 35 minutes)

1. What is a sales forecast? (2)

2. Explain how you can show the trend in a series of data. (4)

3. Explain how *two* of the following Heinz managers could be helped by two weeks' warning that sales are forecast to rise by 15%.
   a. the operations manager
   b. the marketing manager, Heinz Beans
   c. the personnel manager
   d. the chief accountant. (8)

4. What do you understanding by the term 'extrapolation'? How is it used to make a sales forecast? (5)

5. Explain how Coca-Cola might be helped by checking for correlations between the following factors:
   a. sales and the daily temperature
   b. staff absence levels and the leadership style of individual supervisors. (6)

6. Explain why it is risky to assume cause and effect when looking at factors that are correlated. (4)

7. What is the Delphi technique? (2)

8. Explain briefly how the 2012 Olympic Committee could make use of scenario planning. (4)

Data response

The US aircraft manufacturer, Boeing, has predicted an increase in demand from airlines for smaller aircraft, but large jumbo jet sales are expected to be lower than expected over the next 20 years. Boeing raised its projected sales of commercial jets by all manufacturers by $200 billion to $2.8 trillion (£1.4 trillion) in the next two decades. Regional, single-aisle and twin-aisle jets for non-stop routes would prove more popular than expected, it said. However, it reduced its forecast for jumbos carrying more than 400 people. Boeing now expects that the market will buy 960 of the bigger craft, down from the 990 it set out in last year's forecast.

20-year industry forecast:
- 17,650 single-aisle aeroplanes seating 90 to 240 passengers
- 6,290 twin-aisle jets seating 200 to 400 passengers
- 3,700 regional jets with no more than 90 seats, up from 3,450 forecast last year

- 960 jumbo jets seating more than 400 passengers.

According to Boeing, passenger numbers would rise by about 5% a year, while cargo traffic would increase by 6.1%. Emerging markets are crucial for future sales, with about one-third of the demand coming from the Asia-Pacific region. Boeing believes its success is secure, thanks to its relatively small 787 plane. It believes this will take sales from its rival Airbus. Twin-engined but with a long range, it will be able to fly direct to far more of the world's airports. This means that passengers will not need to make a connecting flight first to travel long distance.

Questions (30 marks; 35 minutes)

1. Analyse the ways in which Boeing might have produced its industry sales forecasts. (10)

2. Discuss the possible consequences for Boeing of the findings of its research. (20)

Case study

Forecasting and investment appraisal

'What's the fuss about? It's only a greasy spoon!'

That summed it up, thought Emma. Her accountant boyfriend Leon simply didn't understand her business. When she bought the Swan Café two years ago, it was so run down that the lease cost just £4,000. And it was now a thriving business. Close to the river in Oxford, it had a great trade from builders between 7.00 am and 9.00 am, from students from 9.00 am till 1.00 pm and from tourists between 1.00 pm and 4.30 pm. Then students drift back between 4.30 pm and 5.30 pm.

In the first week after opening her café, revenue was just £800. After costs, this left Emma with just £21 for herself. Today, weekly takings are as high as £5,600 and customers often queue to get in. Weekly profits are around £1,500 allowing a healthy cash nest-egg to build up at the bank.

Now Emma wants to buy the shop next door, available for £140,000 freehold. This would allow her to expand the seating area and also extend the size of the kitchen and the range of food offered. Her younger sister (Natalia) has carried out customer research at the cafe as part of her Business Studies coursework. It shows that customers love Emma's warm personality and the good food, but quite a few want more. The tourists are looking for freshly baked scones and cakes, while the University students would love a roast dinner in the early evening.

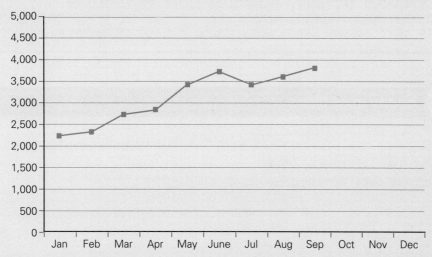

Figure 18.6 Number of customers per month in a year

Appendix A: Number of customers per month this year:		Appendix B: Estimated cash flows on the café extension (Yrs 1–4)		
			Cash inflows	**Cash outflows**
Jan	2,200		£000s	£000s
Feb	2,300			
Mar	2,700	Now		160
Apr	2,800	Year 1	160	130
May	3,400	Year 2	220	160
June	3,700	Year 3	270	200
Jul	3,400	Year 4	320	240
Aug	3,600			
Sep	3,800			

Natalia has promised to extrapolate recent monthly sales forward for the next few months, to provide Emma with an idea about how much profit the business should make (the figures from Appendix A form Figure 18.6).

Emma has asked Natalia to provide a further extrapolation to cover the next four years. She could then use it as a benchmark for judging sales after buying the shop next door. Would the investment of £140,000 be worthwhile? (In fact, the total investment would be £160,000, including the cost of decoration and equipment.)

While Natalia works on the sales figures, Emma is working on the costs. She knows she would need extra staff and perhaps some regular spending on advertising. Eventually the sisters are able to put together the data in Appendix B. They feel increasingly excited about the project, but Leon remains negative. His view is: 'I'm sorry, love, but I think it's just a small café. If you want to build a better business, open a restaurant. And I certainly wouldn't go ahead unless you can beat the standard industry criterion levels: two-year payback and a 15%

ARR. And where's the money coming from? Do you really want such a big loan around your neck?'

Questions *(40 marks; 50 minutes)*

1 From the information provided, do there seem good enough underlying reasons for Emma to expand the café? (6)

2 a Use Appendix A to calculate a three-month moving average of this year's customer numbers. (7)

   b Plot your results onto Figure 18.6. (Preferably with a red or blue pen) (3)

   c Extrapolate your trend line forward to make an estimate of the number of customers in December. Comment briefly on the result. (4)

3 a Use the information in Appendix B to calculate the payback and ARR on the café extension. Show your workings. (8)

   b Taking everything into account, discuss whether Emma should proceed or not with the investment. (12)

C Essay questions *(40 marks each)*

1 'Since we can never know the future, it is pointless trying to forecast it.' Discuss.

2 'Quantitative sales forecasting techniques have only limited use. Qualitative judgements are needed in a constantly changing world.' Evaluate this statement.

19 Selecting marketing strategies

Definition

Marketing strategies are carefully evaluated plans for future marketing activity that balance company objectives, available resources and market opportunities.

What are the keys to a successful marketing strategy?

A strategy is the plan of the medium- to long-term actions required to achieve the company goals or targets. Selecting the best marketing strategy means finding a fit between the company objectives, customer requirements and the activities of competitors.

The aim of this planning is to shape the company's activities and products to generate the best returns for the business. Marketing strategy is about adding value. It takes advantage of any unique selling points. It helps the business to identify the right mix between design, function, image and service.

Strategy is about the future

The term 'strategy' implies looking to the future. It is important not to look at what is working well now but at what future prospects are. Toyota recognised that there was a growing interest in environmental issues. It started to invest in the production of hybrid cars. Although requiring significant investment with no sure return, Toyota executives felt that this was the way forward. The move was highly successful, with demand for the Prius surprising everyone by outstripping supply.

Strategy must be achievable

Strategy is concerned with what is possible, not just desirable. It must take into account market potential and company resources. The company needs to recognise its own limitations and potential. It also needs to consider economic and social circumstances. If the world economy is weakening, firms will be much more cautious about entering new export markets. If the home market is stagnating, businesses may well concentrate on lower-priced 'value' products.

Strategy is company specific

Each company will have a different marketing strategy. The strategy selected will reflect the individual circumstances of the business. Different companies within the same industry may be pursuing different goals. The strategies that they select will reflect those different goals. Within the same industry, one company may be aiming to increase market share while another looks for cost reductions in order to compete on price. The tyre industry is a good example of this. The market leaders were faced with increasing price competition from developing countries. They had to develop new marketing strategies. Their responses differed: Goodyear reduced costs; Michelin put its effort into innovation and widened its product range; Pirelli decided to concentrate on the market for luxury and speed.

Marketing strategy is the marketing plan of action that:

- contributes to the achievement of company objectives
- finds the best fit between company objectives, available resources and market possibilities
- looks to the future
- is carefully thought out
- is realistic.

A-grade application

Krispy growth

Early in 2011 the US company Krispy Kreme announced a big expansion in Britain. The objective is to increase the number of UK stores from 47 in 2011 to 100 by 2016. Underpinning this growth objective is the sales success of KK doughnuts. UK sales in the year to January 2011 were £33.4 million, up from £29.7 million in the previous year. Given the apparently hostile external context (faltering economy plus ever-stronger public focus on body-shape), this 12.5% sales increase was a huge success.

In July 2011 the company outlined a new sales and promotional strategy to support this expansion. Krispy Kreme had always been famous for selling in boxes of 12, rather than single doughnuts. Now the company was to try to get the boxes into businesses. A sales team spent August 2011 giving away more than 78,000 doughnuts to office workers. High-profile business locations in

London, Birmingham, Portsmouth and Cardiff were singled out for treats. The sales teams' task was to identify an influential office worker, who could become the Krispy Kreme-buyer of the future – perhaps collecting the cash or organising birthday celebration boxes.

Katie de Souza, Krispy Kreme's Head of Marketing, said that 'Every workplace has an office hero – that person who can be relied on to bring in treats to brighten up a Monday or celebrate a birthday. We're working to engage this office audience and show them that a Krispy Kreme Dozen is a great choice'.

If Krispy Kreme can develop as the office treat of choice, the 100 KK shops should have a bright future. With the calorie count per Krispy Kreme doughnut ranging from 217 to 380, perhaps the Dozens should be limited to those who cycle to work.

Strategy versus tactics

Strategy is not the same as tactics (see Table 19.1). Strategy is an overall plan for the medium to long term. Tactics are individual responses to short-term opportunities or threats. The marketing strategy may be to increase sales by developing a new market segment. One of the tactics used may be to undercut a competitor on price in a price-sensitive segment of the market.

Table 19.1 Strategy vs tactics

Marketing strategies	Marketing tactics
• Keep the main message consistent over time (e.g. BMW – 'The ultimate driving machine') • Make sure that every message to the consumer shouts low prices – as Ryanair has done consistently for ten years	• Offer everyone who comes onto the Confused.com website a chance in a £1 million prize draw • Run a midweek special – 'All You Can Eat For a Tenner' during the winter months

Types of strategy

A useful way to look at marketing strategy is to follow the approach taken by Igor Ansoff, who developed 'Ansoff's matrix'. Before explaining this approach, it is helpful to look at Ansoff's view of 'strategy'. In his 1965 book *Corporate Strategy*, Ansoff described strategy as a decision of medium- to long-term significance that is made in 'conditions of partial ignorance'. This 'ignorance' stems partly from the timescale involved. If you look three years ahead there are huge risks that marketplace changes will make your plans and forecasts look foolish. Such

decisions are usually discussed and decided at board level.

Ansoff's matrix (Figure 19.1) is constructed to illustrate the risks involved in strategic decisions. These risks relate to the firm's level of knowledge and certainty about the market, the competition and customer behaviour – both now and in the future. The key issue is that risk becomes ever greater the further a firm strays from its core of existing products/existing customers (i.e. the top left-hand corner of the matrix).

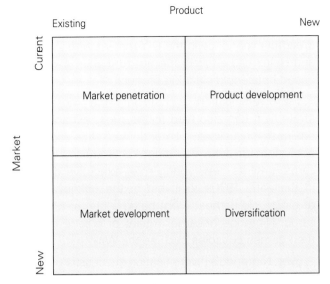

Figure 19.1 Ansoff's matrix

Ansoff identified four types of strategy within his matrix; these are described below.

Market penetration

This is about increasing market share by concentrating on existing products within the existing market. It is the most common and safest strategy because it does not stray from what the company knows best. If Tesco has opened 400 stores in towns all over Britain, and all are profitable, it is a simple matter of market penetration to open store 401 in a good-sized town that has not yet got its first Tesco.

Market penetration opportunities arise by:

● finding new customers – perhaps by widening the product's appeal to attract additional buyers

● taking customers from competitors – this may be achieved by aggressive pricing or by offering additional incentives to the customer

● persuading existing customers to increase usage – many food companies give recipes with their products to suggest additional ways of using the product; shampoo manufacturers introduced a frequent-wash shampoo to boost product usage.

Market development

This is about finding new markets for existing products. It is more risky because the company must step into the unknown. For Cadbury to start selling chocolate in Chile it would require a huge effort to learn to understand the Chilean consumer, yet it may still fail because customer psychology is complex and ever changing.

Market development can be carried out by the following means.

● **Repositioning** the product: this will target a different market segment. This could be done by broadening the product's appeal to a new customer base. Land Rover's traditional market was farming and military use; it has now repositioned the product to appeal to town dwellers.

● Moving into new markets: many British retailers have opened up outlets abroad. Some, such as Tesco and Laura Ashley, have opened up their own outlets. Others have entered into joint ventures or have taken over a similar operation in another country.

Burberry enjoyed huge success in 2010 and 2011 when it chose to open 100 new outlets in China. Yet the hugely successful sandwich chain Pret A Manger hit problems when opening up in New York and Japan. Even the mighty Gordon Ramsay had an embarrassment when he took a London restaurant concept to Glasgow, and it went bust.

Why the difficulty? Surely market research can reveal whether customers in Glasgow want the same things as those in London? Up to a point, perhaps. But the skill with market research is to know exactly what questions to ask and how to interpret the answers. This requires a degree of market knowledge that cannot always cross county boundaries, let alone national ones. This was why, over 80 years ago, the Ford Motor Company chose to set up a factory and offices in Britain, instead of relying on exporting from America. The rush of US firms that followed (e.g. Heinz, Gillette, General Motors/Vauxhall) was followed much later by Japanese companies such as Sony, Hitachi and Honda. All took huge risks at the start, but believed they would only succeed in the long term by getting a deep understanding of local habits and needs. Famously, Sony budgeted for a 15-year payback period when it started up in Britain.

Product development

Product development means launching new products into your existing market (e.g. L'Oréal launching a new haircare product). Hard though market development can be, it could be argued that product development is even harder. It is generally accepted that only one in five new products succeeds – and that is a figure derived from the large businesses that launch new products through advertising agencies. In other words, despite their huge resources and expertise, heavy spending on R&D and market research, plus huge launch advertising budgets, companies such as Birds Eye, Walls, L'Oréal and McVitie's suffer four flops for every success.

In highly competitive markets, companies use product development to keep one step ahead of the competition. Strategies may include those listed below.

● *Changing an existing product:* this may be to keep the products attractive. Washing powders and shampoos are good examples of this. The manufacturers are continually repackaging or offering some 'essential' new ingredient.

● *Developing new products:* the iPhone is a fantastic example of a new and successful product development, taking Apple from the computer business into the massive market for 'smartphones'.

Diversification

If it is accepted that market development and product development are both risky, how much more difficult is the ultimate challenge: a new product in a new market, or **diversification** in Ansoff's termi-nology. This is the ultimate business risk, as it forces a business to operate completely outside its

range of knowledge and experience. Virgin flopped totally with cosmetics and clothing, WH Smith had a dreadful experience in the DIY market with Do It All, and Heinz had a failed attempt to market a vinegar-based household cleaning product.

Yet diversification is not only the most risky strategy, it can also lead to the most extraordinary business successes. Nintendo was the Japanese equivalent of John Waddington, producing playing cards, until its new, young chief executive decided in the early 1970s to invest in the unknown idea of electronic games. From being a printer of paper cards, Nintendo became a giant of arcade games, then games consoles such as the Wii.

Even Nintendo's diversification success is dwarfed by that of Nokia, which once made car tyres and toilet rolls. Its transformation into the world's number one mobile phone maker would have been remarkable no matter what, but the fact that it came from tiny Finland makes it an incredible success. Ansoff emphasised the risks of diversification, but never intended to suggest that firms should fight shy of those risks. Risks are well worth taking as long as the potential rewards are high enough.

Marketing strategy in international markets

Entering into international markets carries the extra risk identified by Ansoff as market development. Naturally, the extent of the risk will depend on just how different the new market is from the firm's home country. For Green & Black's to start selling chocolate in France may not be too much of a stretch. French tastes are different and the

distribution systems are very different from those in Britain, but there are many similarities in climate and affluence. But what about selling organic chocolate to Saudi Arabia? Or China? Or Sierra Leone? Figure 19.2 shows the way Ansoff would indicate the increasing level of risk involved.

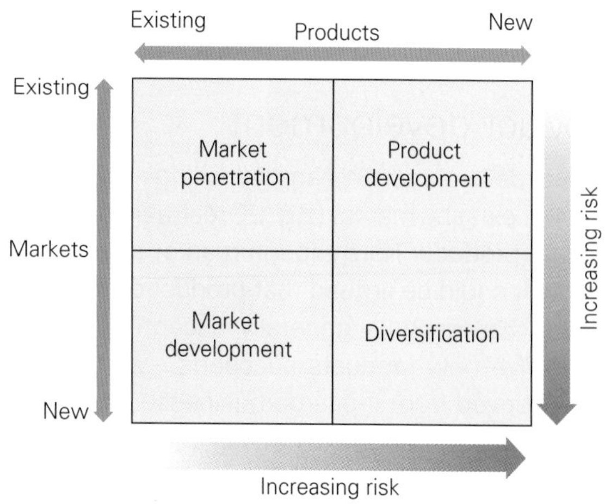

It is also possible that the product will need to be modified in order to be successful in the new market. International markets are littered with products and businesses that tried to shift their existing products and business models into overseas markets but failed. Even the best marketing strategies can fail. Some common causes of failure are:

● language/interpretation problems
● misunderstanding the culture
● mis-timing – this can be economic or even political.

All these can be minimised by careful research to ensure that there is a good understanding of the new market before the company attempts to do business.

Some of the most successful ventures into inter-national markets involve working in cooperation with existing firms in local markets.

Figure 19.2 Ansoff's matrix and risk

Low cost vs differentiation.

The business guru Michael Porter has long emphasised that marketing (and corporate) strategy is about choice. Directors must make a decision about where and how they want their products positioned – and stick by that decision. Bizarrely, in 2009 – as global recession hit Britain – Aldi's UK management decided to go 'upmarket'. Only when it abandoned that plan in 2011 did the company's share of the grocery market start booming again.

Porter says businesses must choose whether they are trying to be the lowest-cost operator in their sector (such as Ryanair in the airline market) or the most highly differentiated, such as Waitrose or Booth's in the grocery business. The worst place to be is the 'piggy in the middle' – trying to be classy and cheap at the same time.

These days, Porter's advice seems to work exceptionally well. Highly differentiated, expensive brands such as Burberry, Mulberry and Chanel are booming. At the other end of the price spectrum, clothing discounters such as Primark and Forever 21 are also doing really well. 'Piggies' such as Marks & Spencer struggle.

In exam case studies, situations are presented in which companies are often struggling to make up their minds on strategy; it often works well to cite Porter and then recommend decisive action to either attempt to be low-cost with low prices (Poundland, Primark, Ryanair) or to reposition the business as a highly differentiated operator (Mulberry, Booth's, Apple).

Marketing strategy: a continual process

Once the strategy has been developed, it needs to be constantly reviewed. An idea that looks good on paper will not necessarily work in reality. There may need to be some testing of strategies, especially if

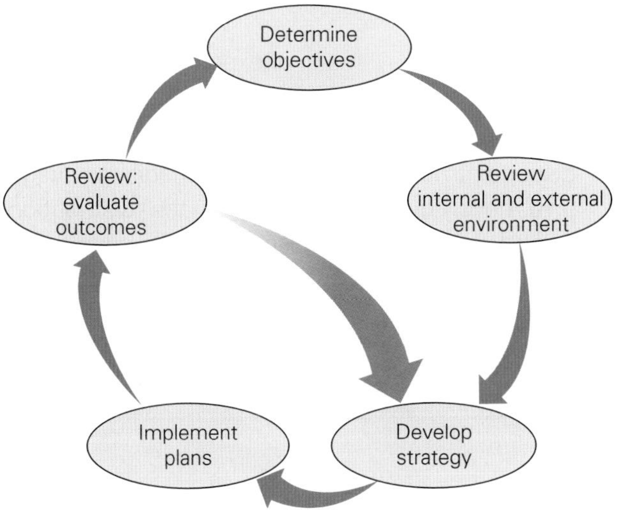

Figure 19.3 The strategic cycle

they are risky. Market research and monitoring are necessary to ensure that the actions are producing the desired results. Evaluation of results will feed back into the system and in turn contribute to the development of revised objectives and strategies. This ongoing cycle is known as the strategic cycle (see Figure 19.3).

A company's marketing strategy does not exist in a vacuum. It may provoke responses from competitors. Market opportunities will be changing constantly. If the company is to be successful, it needs to be responsive and to adjust the strategy to cope with any changes in the environment or within the company. For example, the giant Heinz company found that its approach to global marketing was ineffective – it shifted strategy to become more local. Only in Britain were baked beans an important seller, so the baked bean pizza was developed for the UK alone. In Korea, people love to pour ketchup on pizza, so a deal with Pizza Hut put a Heinz bottle on every table.

Assessing the effectiveness of marketing strategies

An effective marketing strategy achieves the marketing objectives; but is there more to it than that? Could a strategy be too successful? Perhaps yes, if a business is overwhelmed by demand it is unable to meet. In most cases, though, a marketing campaign that exceeds its targets is something to celebrate (see the A-grade application).

A-grade application

Meerkats do it for Comparethemarket.com

The Comparethemarket.com TV campaign proved a huge commercial success. Since launching the Meerkat campaign, CompareTheMarket has enjoyed a sales increase of over 75% and confusion among its rivals. Market leader MoneySupermarket has been forced to ditch one campaign after another (including one with Dragon Peter Jones) as it has tried to regain market share from Orlov the Meerkat. Marketing is rarely this simple.

More often, the issue will be how to judge a marketing strategy that has under-performed. It may have achieved certain targets, yet failed in the most important one: sales. When launching a completely new product, companies know that there are four stages consumers must go through before they purchase (known by the acronym **AIDA**):

- *Awareness:* in 2011 US fashion retailer Forever 21 spent more than £12 million opening its first shop in London; to get high sales it used online, viral media, and paid fashion blogger Bip Ling to promote the brand
- *Interest:* 'perhaps I'll have a look at the site'

- *Desire:* this might be conscious – 'If I can find that Kate Moss dress in my size I'm buying it' – or subconscious (i.e. you only realise you wanted that new Malteser chocolate bar when you find you've bought it when buying a magazine)
- *Action:* the actual moment of purchase; though it is important to remember that, for the advertiser, that is only the start; few products survive on single sales; success comes from repeat purchase and brand loyalty.

To assess the effectiveness of the marketing, it is sensible to measure performance at each of these stages. High brand awareness is useless if the brand image is too poor to create interest and then desire (at the time of writing, the Glade Flameless Candle has achieved this doubtful honour in the author's household). The single most important factor, however, is the 'conversion rate' from product trial to product loyalty. If that figure is low, the game is up and the marketing strategy has failed.

Possible reasons for a marketing strategy that fails to meet its sales objectives are:

- the objectives may have been unrealistic
- the budget (the total amount available to spend on the strategy) may have proved inadequate for the task
- competitors may react unexpectedly fiercely to your launch, making it very difficult to succeed
- one element of the mix may have proved a disappointment (e.g. promised media coverage (PR) never quite happened, or the distribution levels were lower than planned, or the advertising never had the impact that everyone expected).

As is clear, several of these are to do with poor performance by one or more members of the marketing team, but some are out of the company's control.

Issues for analysis

Issues that may need to be considered in response to case study or essay questions are:

- the relative importance of strategic market planning in different types of business – can small firms possibly devote the time, thought and resources to strategy that would be spent by firms such as Heinz?
- the added risk and uncertainty of moving into

international markets – firms need to ensure that the market is thoroughly researched; this can be difficult for all firms, but particularly for smaller enterprises

- the extent to which it is possible to develop clear strategies in a constantly changing marketplace
- the influence of individuals may be important – the degree of risk in a firm's strategy may depend

partly on the personality of the key decision maker; an entrepreneurial marketing director may achieve breakthroughs (or disasters) that a more cautious person would avoid

- how businesses find a balance between what is desirable and what is achievable – in some

firms, the balance is determined at the top (by directors who may not understand fully the market conditions); others adopt a more participative style, in which directors consult junior executives to get a clear idea of what can be achieved.

 ## Selecting marketing strategies – an evaluation

It would be nice to think that businesses carefully evaluate the marketing environment and then devise a strategy that fits in with overall company objectives. In reality, the strategy may be imposed by management, shareholders or even circumstances. In some instances, the only business objective may be survival. Strategy may then be reduced to crisis management. The other reality is that the business environment is not always clear and logical, so it may be very difficult to generate realistic and effective strategies.

Key terms

AIDA: a useful way to remember the stages in getting someone to try a new product – Awareness, Interest, Desire, Action.

Diversification: when a company expands its activities outside its normal range. This may be done to reduce risk or to expand possible markets.

Repositioning: changing the product or its promotion to appeal to a different market segment.

 ## Further reading

Ansoff, I. (1965) *Corporate Strategy*. New York: McGraw-Hill.

 ### A Revision questions (40 marks; 40 minutes)

1 What is 'marketing strategy'? (2)

2 What is a 'unique selling point'? Give two examples. (4)

3 What is meant by 'product differentiation'? (3)

4 What are the four steps in developing a marketing strategy? (4)

5 Why is it important for a firm to examine its internal resources before deciding on a strategy? (3)

6 What is the difference between 'market development' and 'product development'? (4)

7 How does marketing strategy relate to the objectives of a business? (4)

8 Why is market research an important part of marketing strategy? (4)

9 Why is market development more risky than market penetration? (4)

10 Apply the AIDA model to the recent launch of any new product or service. Explain how well the business has done at each stage. (8)

 ### B2 Data response

Apple's cash machine

The Apple iPod was launched in 2001, into a market dominated by Sony. For a company based on computers, the move into personal

music appeared risky. As the graph in Figure 19.4 shows, sales grew slowly; iTunes was launched in 2002 but only in late 2004 did iPod sales move

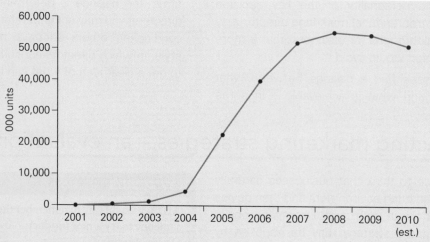

Figure 19.4 Worldwide iPod sales (3-monthly periods)

ahead dramatically. This was partly due to the launch of the iPod Mini, but also coincided with the start of the brilliant 'silhouette' advertising campaign. In fact, Apple has handled iPod's marketing strategy very cleverly.

iPod marketing mix

● *Product:* quick product development, from iPod 2001 to iPod Mini 2003, iPod Photo 2004 to iPod Shuffle 2005, and the iPod Touch in late 2007 and iPod Touch 4g in late 2010. As with all its competitors, the iPod is made (very cheaply) in China, so the key to its success is the stylish design, not high-quality manufacture.

● *Price:* always startlingly high; at launch, the iPod was over £200; even today the iPod Touch 3g is £189, whereas other MP3 players can cost as little as £20. Apple has managed the business dream of achieving market penetration at prices that skim the market.

● *Place:* nothing new here; Apple has distributed the iPod through the normal mixture of department stores, electrical shops and online retailers.

● *Promotion:* brilliant and lavish use of posters and TV, featuring one of the all-time great images, the 'silhouette'.

The key to the strategy has always been to achieve high credibility through brilliant design and a non-corporate image. Consumers have tended not to notice that the iPod is an amazing cash machine. In the year to June 2010, the revenues generated by iPod and iTunes exceeded $12,000 million.

Questions *(40 marks; 50 minutes)*

1 a What is meant by the term 'product life cycle'? (2)

   b Explain what Figure 19.4 shows about iPod's product life cycle in the period up to the middle of 2010. (5)

2 a Explain briefly how Ansoff would have interpreted Apple's move into the personal music market. (2)

   b Explain why Ansoff would have considered this move to be risky. (4)

3 Discuss which of the elements of iPod's marketing mix have been the most important in its sales success. (12)

4 Given the business's success with the iPod, iPhone and iPad, discuss whether Apple should now make a move towards the games console business, competing with Nintendo, Sony and Microsoft. (15)

 Data response

Greggs – getting the ingredients right

Kennedy McMeikan, the Chief Executive of Greggs, the High Street Bakers, made the following statement when announcing the half-year results for the company in August 2010.

We are making good progress with our strategy: making Greggs accessible to

more people through our shop opening programme, investing in our bakeries for greater efficiency and capacity for growth and realising the benefits of a strong, centrally run business.

Our accelerated shop opening and refit

programmes are progressing as planned, and delivering encouraging early results.

Results

Total group sales in the 26 weeks ended 3 July 2010 increased by 2.9% to £321 million (2009: £312 million). Like-for-like sales grew by 0.7%, in line with our expectations.

The cost environment in the first half remained in line with our expectations with increases in fuel and wage costs partly mitigated by deflation in energy prices.

Profit before taxation increased by 12.3% to £18.6 million.

Our shops

We opened 26 new shops during the first half and closed eight, giving us a total of 1,437 at the end of the half year. We are encouraged by the performance of our new shops, almost half of which are in locations such as industrial estates, business parks and transport hubs, improving our accessibility to customers and complementing our established presence on high streets.

We also completed 47 shop refurbishments during the half year. In London, we fitted eight shops based on the concept shop we trialled in 2009, making more space available to our customers to encourage browsing and self-selection in a contemporary shopping environment. These units have shown good sales increases. This reflects our learning from the initial concept shops, and we will refit a further 19 shops in the London area during the second half. If current performance trends are maintained, we will then roll the concept shop format out to other parts of the country as part of our normal store refurbishment programme.

Trading activity

With consumers now having less disposable income than a year ago, we have focused our promotional activity in the first half on ensuring that customers benefit from great value offers throughout the day.

In the first half we have sold more than two million meal deals, up 167% versus last year. Our current sandwich meal deal offers a freshly made roll with a choice of fillings, a 500ml soft drink and a packet of crisps. We have also had a good response to our seasonal promotion of two soft drinks for £1.80. We launched our breakfast rolls in February – bacon or sausage in a fresh, Greggs baked roll – and have now sold 4.5 million, helping to grow our sales in the traditionally quieter early morning period.

Our supply chain

Last year we undertook a review of our supply chain and announced plans to invest in our bakeries for significant shop growth and improved efficiencies. We are now beginning the first phase of this investment.

Outlook

The pressure on the trading environment looks likely to increase in the second half and we remain focused on managing costs tightly. We now expect an increase in ingredient cost inflation in the second half of the year, following the recent rise in wheat prices.

Despite the challenging trading environment, I believe that Greggs remains on track to deliver another year of progress.

Extracted from Greggs plc interim results for the 26 weeks ended 3 July 2010

Questions *(50 marks; 60 minutes)*

1 What is meant by 'like for like sales'? (2)

2 Why is it an important part of marketing strategy to 'manage costs tightly', especially in a business like Greggs? (8)

3 How may being a strong centrally run business help the marketing strategy? (6)

4 Why is the investment that Greggs is making in their bakeries an important part of the marketing strategy? (6)

5 Using the marketing mix, explain and evaluate Greggs' marketing strategy. (16)

6 How important is market research in determining marketing strategy for a firm like Greggs? (12)

 Essay questions *(40 marks each)*

1 How useful is Ansoff's matrix in evaluating the risk involved in new marketing strategies?

2 'Only large companies need and can afford to have a marketing strategy.' Discuss this statement.

3 'Marketing strategy can be successful only if a firm has set the right objectives.' Discuss.

4 'Marketing strategy is the key to business success.' Discuss.

Developing and implementing marketing plans

> ### Definition
> A marketing plan is a detailed statement of the company's marketing strategy. It explains how the strategy has been determined and how it will be carried out.

 ## The marketing plan

The marketing plan puts the company's marketing strategy into action. It explains the background to the planned marketing activity. It describes the marketing strategy and explains how it contributes to the overall corporate objectives. The marketing strategy is broken down into action plans. These are the individual activities that put the strategy into practice. In effect, the marketing plan shows how the marketing budget is to be spent.

The purpose of the marketing plan is to ensure that staff understand the actions that will be taken, the reasons behind the actions and the timing of the actions. For example, it is important that the production department knows when an advertising campaign will be run. It can ensure stocks are high enough to cover the boost to demand.

What does a marketing plan look like?

For smaller businesses the **marketing plan** may be an informal document. Larger companies will formalise the plans in report format. Typically, it will have the contents shown in Table 20.1.

Why is marketing planning important?

> If I had eight hours to chop down a tree I'd spend six sharpening my axe. *(Abraham Lincoln)*

A properly developed marketing plan is important because:

● it helps to ensure that marketing activity is properly focused and integrated

● it enables everyone in the organisation to know exactly what will happen, and when

Table 20.1 Typical contents of a marketing plan

Introduction	Gives an overview of the plan, and the economic and competitive background to it
Corporate and marketing objectives	States the overall business aims and the relevant marketing objectives
Marketing strategy	Outlines the strategy that will be used to achieve the objectives
Action plans	Details the individual marketing activities used to carry out the strategy, including above- and below-the-line activities, plus detailed timings
Detailed budgets	Breakdown of expected revenue and costs by product or department or marketing activity
Control tools	Details of how the budgets and plans will be monitored

- it enables the business to take advantage of market opportunities
- it helps to ensure that the business remains healthy by preparing for possible problems
- it puts the business in a better position to react to unexpected events.

How is the marketing plan determined?

Once the marketing strategy has been agreed it needs to be put into action. The strategy will have been determined taking into account all the internal and external issues that affect the business (see Unit 48). For example, if the strategy is to increase the market share of a product, the competitive situation will help decide whether to cut price or to launch a new product.

The plan must be realistic and take into account the internal situation of the business. It needs to consider, for instance, if there are enough staff with the right skills to carry out the plans.

The most important considerations are those listed below.

- *Finance:* the amount of finance that is available to spend on marketing will obviously be important. A business cannot plan a national advertising campaign if the finance available will only fund a local mail shot. However, even if funding is available, the plan should take into account the return on expenditure. The results of the marketing must be monitored to measure the effectiveness of the expenditure.

- *Operational issues:* the marketing plan should take into account whether the organisation can cope with the increased demand that may result from any marketing campaign. This may be in production or people terms. Boosting demand that cannot be satisfied by available stocks is a waste of time, effort and money. It may even backfire as ill will is created among retailers and consumers.

- *Competitors' actions:* any marketing effort is likely to promote a response from competitors. This needs to be considered at all stages of the planning process. A price reduction that produces a price war will do nothing except reduce margins for all concerned.

A-grade application

Nintendo Wii
When Nintendo ran out of Wii stock during its launch advertising campaign, analysts considered it to be a marketing planning failure. However, a similar tactic is proving to be successful for Apple. Analysts suggest that deliberately creating a shortage was a major part of Apple's marketing plan for its iPad2. When it was launched in the USA in 2011 customers seemed happy to queue to get their hands on the product. The launch in Europe was then delayed because of a shortage of the product. That in itself helped to fuel interest and demand. So perhaps the regular shortages of Nintendo products inspired Apple to use this approach as part of its marketing plan.

Once these three issues have been considered, the plans can be developed. The type of marketing activity that is used will be determined in different ways in different businesses. Some businesses will just continue to do what they did during the previous year: 'It seemed to work, so let's carry on.' Others will take a more sophisticated approach. This will involve analysis of what has worked well in the past. Which aspects of the marketing mix are more appropriate? Are there any areas that could be improved? What are the current issues that concern consumers? With the growth of environmental considerations many businesses are putting green issues at the heart of their marketing approach.

Marketing expenditure

The marketing department will have to work within the constraints of the allocated finance. One of the most difficult questions facing the marketing manager is how to spend the available resources. It is a common error to equate marketing expenditure with the cost of advertising. Many other costs are associated with marketing the product. Among the most important are the design and development of the packaging, thorough and independent market research and the achievement of good distribution.

How the available money is spent will depend on many factors. These include those listed below.

● *The likely return from the expenditure:* any marketing expenditure should produce a return. It should be evaluated in the same way as any investment in the business.

● *Type of product:* some products are supported by very high levels of spending while others are not. The level of spending may be related to how easy the product is to differentiate in the market. In markets where there is little difference between competing products, businesses will want to use marketing to give their product a competitive edge – to make it seem different. It is only possible to afford high marketing budgets, though, if the value added is high. Cosmetics, cars and washing powder are examples of this. Each is supported by high levels of promotional spending.

● *Product life cycle:* for most products the highest levels of expenditure will be in the launch and growth stages. From time to time the product may need to be supported with additional spending. This will happen when the product is given additional support as part of an extension strategy.

● *Type of customer:* companies selling consumer goods and services will tend to have higher levels of marketing expenditure than those supplying industrial customers.

Marketing budgets

A very important aspect of the marketing plan is the **marketing budget**. Once a plan has been developed it needs to be put into action. It is also important that the plan is monitored so that the business can see if the plan is being achieved and if it is being effective. A marketing budget must be set to both implement and control the firm's marketing expenditure.

In everyday language a budget is the amount available for spending. In business a budget is not only an expenditure target but also a target for achievement. The marketing budget is the quantified plan for the marketing department. It shows the marketing objectives in numerical terms, such as market share or distribution targets. It is usually produced as an annual budget, but for the purpose of control will often be broken down into monthly figures.

For example, the marketing objective may be to increase sales by 10%. The budget will give monthly sales targets that will deliver that annual figure.

Alongside the sales figures, targets for expenditure will be given. So if the additional sales are to be generated by a new advertising campaign, the budget will include expenditure targets for that advertising.

Measuring performance against budget

If performance is to be measured effectively then it is important that there is a range of data available. The management accounting system will produce some figures, such as sales and costs. It may need to be developed to produce other information to measure marketing effectiveness. Competitive information will be important. Car manufacturers look at market share figures based on new car registrations as a key measure of performance. If Ford's market share figures are slipping behind the targets, the company will step up its marketing effort (including price cutting) to regain its intended levels.

Sodastream comeback

In 2010 Sodastream launched a marketing campaign to try to revitalise its product. The machine, which was popular in the 1970s and 1980s, makes fizzy drinks at home. It is reusing the 'Get busy with the fizzy' tagline in a series of TV adverts – the first for nearly 20 years – in the hope of enticing a new generation to the product. The product has been redesigned to give it a more modern look and the range of drinks available has been increased to include diet and healthy versions. The whole marketing campaign is costing £3 million.

Only time will tell if this is money well spent.

Figure 20.1 Sodastream

Issues for analysis

There are several issues that are likely to be important when looking at marketing plans.

- Consideration should be given to the usefulness or otherwise of the plans. Do they really help the business to manage its marketing effort or does the process constrain real marketing initiatives? Quite often this will depend on other factors in the business, such as management style. Are staff encouraged to stick rigidly to the plan or is initiative rewarded?

- When considering how the plans are developed it is important to put the plans in the context of the business and its competitive environment. Consideration of how well a plan will work for this particular business must take these factors into account.

A key factor for businesses is setting the right level of marketing budget.

Developing and implementing marketing plans – an evaluation

The two most important aspects of marketing plans are getting the right level of marketing budget, then finding the right balance between a fixed plan and a flexible one. In a well-run business, the budget will be set after discussion between key managers and set at a level that takes into account the objectives and the difficulty in achieving them. If a new product is being launched into a fiercely competitive market, there should be no halfway house between setting a high budget or scrapping the whole idea. A compromise may be the worst of all worlds.

After the budget is set and decisions have been made about how and when to spend it, junior staff can put the plan into practice. TV commercials can be written and filmed; commercial breaks can be booked. If circumstances change within the year, though, it may be wise to make adjustments. A TV campaign planned for October might be brought forward to September if a rival is bringing out a new product. Every plan needs a degree of flexibility.

A — Revision questions (30 marks; 30 minutes)

Read the unit, then answer:

1 What is a marketing plan? (2)

2 List four topics that you would expect to be included in a marketing plan. (4)

3 Outline two reasons why firms prepare marketing plans. (4)

4 Why is company finance an important factor when preparing marketing plans? (5)

5 Why is it important that operational issues are taken into account when determining a marketing plan? (4)

6 How does the competitive environment influence marketing planning? (4)

7 What is a marketing budget? (2)

8 How can a marketing budget help to control marketing expenditure? (5)

B1 — Data response

Marketing plans show shift to internet marketing for business-to-business firms

A recent survey, undertaken by a business-to-business online magazine, discovered that, in spite of economic problems, businesses were planning to increase their levels of marketing expenditure. The survey also showed that online marketing expenditure would be the main focus of this increase. The survey, which was conducted online, had 250 responses; 60% of the respondents said that their firms planned to increase their marketing budgets, but 80% of them planned to increase their online marketing budgets. This was up from 70% in the previous year's survey. Only 10% of replies indicated that their marketing expenditure would be reduced; 70% of the businesses were planning to launch a new advertising campaign in the coming year and nearly half planned to increase the number of staff employed in marketing.

The main marketing goals identified by the survey were:

- getting new customers – 60%
- increasing brand awareness – 20%
- retaining customers – 15%.

Approximately a third of marketing budgets would be spent on online marketing. This is a 10% increase over last year's levels. This expenditure would be for:

- website development

- direct email marketing
- search engine marketing
- video webcasting
- sponsorship.

The other main results from the survey were:

- a large rise in the number of businesses planning to use event marketing
- a reduction in the amount of advertising in newspapers and magazines
- continuing growth in the use of direct mailing.

Questions (35 marks; 40 minutes)

1 What is meant by 'business to business'? (2)

2 Why might the results of this survey not give a true picture of marketing plans for all businesses? (8)

3 Why do you think there might be a trend for businesses to increase their marketing activity online? (5)

4 Why do you think that firms may be considering moving away from newspaper and magazine advertising and towards direct mailing? (8)

5 Discuss whether or not a business such as Marks & Spencer should spend a third of its marketing budget on online marketing. (12)

Case study

Ewans Motor Company

Ewans Motor Company is a car dealer based in the Midlands. It has two outlets. One has the franchise for a range of small family cars. The other offers larger luxury cars.

Business has been steady over the past few years, but has seen no real growth in total sales or profitability. The business is facing increased local competition from another garage offering a similar range of family cars. There is also the threat of an economic downturn in the area as one of the largest employers is threatening to cut staff as a result of lower export sales due to the stronger pound.

The owner, Peter Ewans, has brought in a new marketing manager with the hope that the business can cope with these challenges and hopefully increase profitability. The new marketing manager, Sharon Crisp, agreed to join the business providing the marketing budget was increased from its current 1% of turnover. She feels that in the highly competitive climate of the small car business, the budget needs to be slightly more than doubled. Sharon is sure that she can justify this additional expenditure by raising profitability. She also introduced the concept of a marketing budget that she feels is long overdue. Previously, expenditure has been

no targets set for sales or profitability. There has also been little or no monitoring of the results.

After analysing both the market situation and the figures for the business for the last few years, Sharon produced the marketing budget figures shown in Table 20.2.

Sharon felt that there was going to be a need to use some price discounting on the smaller cars to combat the increased competition in the area. Her plan was to allow the salespeople to discount the price by as much as they felt was necessary to ensure the sale. She allowed an average of £100 for each small car for this. To support the salespeople Sharon planned to double the mail shots. These would inform customers of special offers and also invite them to special family days. These days would be very child orientated, offering family entertainment and gifts for children; all the slightly increased promotional budget would be spent on this. She also planned to support the family days with additional advertising in the local press. The sponsorship of sporting activities in local schools fitted into the plan, so this would also be continued.

Industry reports suggested that the luxury car business would grow at about 6% in this year so

Table 20.2 Marketing budget

Budget	Last year	This year
Sales: small cars	1,600	2,000
Sales: luxury cars	800	950
Average selling price: small cars	£12,000	£11,900
Average selling price: luxury cars	£25,000	£25,000
Average contribution per small car	£840	£740
Average contribution per luxury car	£3,000	£3,000
Total marketing expenditure	£392,000	£800,000
Breakdown of marketing expenditure		
Price discounting	0	£200,000
Direct mailing	£100,000	£200,000
Advertising	£150,000	£250,000
Promotional offers	£92,000	£100,000
Sponsorship	£50,000	£50,000

Sharon decided to do very little except for mail shots to support this sector of the market.

At the end of the year the actual figures were as shown in Table 20.3.

Table 20.3 Actual figures at year end

	Actual
Sales: small cars	1,800
Sales: luxury cars	800
Average selling price: small cars	£11,800
Average selling price: luxury cars	£25,000
Average contribution per small car	£640
Average contribution per luxury car	£3,000
Total marketing expenditure	£960,000
Breakdown of marketing expenditure:	
Price discounting	£360,000
Direct mailing	£180,000
Advertising	£250,000
Promotional offers	£120,000
Sponsorship	£50,000

After analysing the results, Sharon feels that both the marketing plan and the budgeting exercise have been successful.

Questions *(50 marks; 60 minutes)*

1 Do you think that the marketing plan was appropriate for the business in its present circumstances? (10)

2 Why did Sharon Crisp feel that a marketing budget was long overdue? (4)

3 What advantages and disadvantages might there be for the business in introducing a marketing budgeting system? (8)

4 Calculate the variances between the budgeted and actual figures. (8)

5 Why do you think the more significant variances might have occurred? (8)

6 Using the figures and other information in the case study, comment on Sharon Crisp's assertion that the marketing plan and the budgeting exercise were successful. (12)

Essay questions *(40 marks each)*

1 Some businesses do not have formalised marketing plans. Discuss the arguments for and against a formal marketing planning system.

2 Discuss the advantages and disadvantages of a formalised budget for marketing.

3 Many firms are moving away from the 'last year plus a bit' approach to producing marketing budgets. Discuss two alternative approaches and explain why the firm might use these methods.

4 'Marketing budgets are the key to management and control of marketing activity.' Discuss.

Integrated marketing

 ## Marketing – an overview

Introduction

Which is more important to a firm – revenue or costs? You might say that they are equally important. Or you might say that a firm must have revenue; therefore, revenue is the key. Yet students revise costs (finance and accounting) far more thoroughly than revenue (marketing). This is partly because they feel weaker at finance and wish to improve; also, they underestimate the analytic demands (and importance) of marketing.

Firms can have many different objectives, but profit making is clearly a vital aspect of business activity. The most important formula in this subject is the one for profit.

$$\text{profit} = \text{total revenue} - \text{total costs}$$

or, to use the expanded form:

$$\text{profit} = (\text{price} \times \text{quantity}) - ([\text{variable cost} \times \text{quantity}] + \text{fixed costs})$$

Marketing decisions have a direct influence upon:

- the price and quantity of goods sold
- the variable cost per unit (as bulk-buying discounts are affected by sales volume)
- fixed costs, as they include marketing expenditures such as advertising and promotions.

In other words, marketing influences every aspect of the profit formula.

What is marketing?

- Is it about responding to consumers or persuading them?
- Is it about creating competition or attempting to avoid it?
- Is it ethical or unethical?

Every textbook has its own definition. A definition such as 'to fulfil consumer needs, profitably' suggests that marketing is about identifying and meeting needs, and is therefore serving the consumer's best interests. Is this true? Always? Do consumers *need* Snickers chocolate or a Smoothie?

Marketing today is seen as the all-embracing function that acts as the focal point of business activity. Top business consultant Richard Schonberger described the best modern firms as those that 'build a chain of customers'. In other words, marketing forms the link between the firm and its customers. It therefore determines the type and quantity of goods to be designed and produced.

'A' grade marketing

Marketing consists of a series of concepts and themes (such as the marketing mix). All good students know these; better ones can group them together and relate them to one another. They can be grouped as follows.

- An understanding of markets: the price mechanism, price elasticity, market segmentation, and competitive tactics.

- An understanding of consumer behaviour: psychological factors in product pricing and image, brand loyalty, consumer resistance.
- Product portfolio analysis: product life cycle, Boston Matrix.
- Marketing decision making: the marketing model, market and sales research and analysis, the need to anticipate, not just reflect consumer taste.

- Marketing strategy: both in theory and in practice through the marketing mix/four Ps. An understanding of risk through Ansoff's matrix.

- Marketing planning: how marketing plans are used and developed and the importance of marketing budgets in implementing and controlling the plans. The usefulness of budgets and variance analysis in reacting to changes in the marketing and business environment.

- 'A' grade marketing requires a grasp of big underlying issues such as those that follow. These are areas of discussion, which should lead you to make conclusions in answers or case studies. They represent ways of evaluating the wider significance of concepts such as the product life cycle.

Issue 1: is marketing an art or a science?

Is marketing about judgement and creativity, or scientific decision making? If it is a science, the numerate information provided by market research would lead to a 100% success rate with new products. The reality, of course, is different. Coca-Cola researched Vanilla Coke heavily – and spent millions advertising a flop. Yet Bailey's Irish Cream became a worldwide best-seller, even though research said women would not buy a whisky-based liqueur.

Marketing relies upon anticipating consumer behaviour. Research can help enormously, but the final decision on strategy is a judgement. Therefore individual flair and luck play an important part.

Issue 2: does marketing respond to needs or create wants?

It is easy to see the importance of marketing to the firm. But what are its effects upon the consumer/general public? Is it just a way of encouraging people to want things they do not need?

Health issues are important in this debate. You may be 'Lovin'' McDonald's, but is it what your stomach needs? And is it right that children should pester their parents for McCain Oven Chips when baked potatoes are cheaper and more nutritious? You must form some views on these questions. You may feel that the marketeers' pursuit of new products, flavours, trends and glitz makes life fun. Or you may feel that marketing can manipulate people, and that its most persuasive arm (TV advertising) needs to be controlled. The last (Labour) government banned fast food advertising during children's programmes, implying that they favoured control. The new coalition government is more inclined to leave these decisions in the hands of the companies themselves, i.e. to trust in the free market.

Issue 3: has market orientation gone too far in Britain?

The trend towards a market-led approach was good for companies, which produced the same products in the same way, year after year. Market orientation brought in new ideas and more attractive product design.

However, it also encouraged Ford to focus too much on the styling and imagery of their cars, while BMW and Honda concentrated upon their production quality and reliability and Toyota thought ahead with its new, greener technology. Money that had once been spent on research and development was now spent on market research. The number of engineering graduates declined as the numbers on marketing and accounting courses ballooned. Manufacturing industry depends upon high-quality engineers and a skilled workforce. Marketing alone is not enough.

A Revision questions *(50 marks; 60 minutes)*

1 Why is a reduction in price unlikely to benefit a firm whose products are price inelastic? (2)

2 Distinguish between primary and secondary research. (2)

3 Why might a firm's long-term pricing policy differ from its short-term one? (3)

4 Explain the term 'product differentiation'. (2)

5 Give two reasons why a firm may sell, for a limited period of time, part of its product range for a loss. (2)

6 List three factors a firm should consider when determining the price of a new product. (3)

7 Give two ways in which decisions made within the marketing department might affect activities in the personnel department. (2)

8 Distinguish between marketing objectives and marketing strategy. (3)

9 Identify three factors that are likely to influence the choice of distribution channel for a product. (3)

10 Give two examples of ethical dilemmas a marketing manager might face. (2)

11 Distinguish between product orientation and market orientation. (3)

12 A business decides to reduce the price elasticity of its product from £3.00 to £2.75. As a result, sales rise from 2,500 to 3,000 units. Calculate the price elasticity of demand for its product. (3)

13 Explain what is meant by 'negative income elasticity'. (2)

14 State two business objectives, other than profit maximisation, that will influence a firm's marketing strategies. (2)

15 The price of a good is 100p, of which 40p is the contribution. If the price is cut by 30%, how much extra must be sold to maintain the same total contribution? (3)

16 Only one in five new product launches is successful. Why? Give three reasons. (3)

17 State three ways of segmenting a market. (3)

18 What is a marketing budget? (2)

19 Suggest three possible extension strategies for a brand of bottled lager for which sales have levelled out. (3)

20 State two approaches a firm might take to defend itself if a price war broke out. (2)

B1 Data response

A manufacturer of footballs has sales of 100,000 units a month and fixed costs of £240,000 a month. Raw materials are £3.00 per unit and the pricing method is a 100% mark-up on variable costs. When it last increased its prices, price elasticity proved to be about 0.6. Now it is thinking of a further 10% price rise.

Questions *(15 marks; 15 minutes)*

1 Calculate the effect on profit of this 10% rise. State your assumptions. (8)

2 What factors may have caused the price elasticity to have changed since the time it was measured at 0.6? (7)

B2 Report writing

You are product development manager of a new tinned cat food called Leno. Its consumer USP (unique selling point) is 'a low-fat, high-fibre food for superfit cats'. Market research has convinced you that demand will be sizeable. Your marketing director wants to be satisfied on four key issues before giving the go-ahead to launch:

● that you have considered three pricing methods, and can now make a recommendation on a suitable pricing policy

● that you can explain the research you conducted and how it has helped you make your sales forecast

● that you can explain the method you will use to set an advertising budget

● that you have considered carefully three of the most likely responses by existing competitors to the launch of Leno.

Question (20 marks; 25 minutes)

1 Write a report to the marketing director covering these points.

C Essay questions (40 marks each)

1 'Marketing is the most important activity in the business.' Discuss this statement.

2 Do you agree that good-quality goods sell themselves?

3 Do you think that marketers ought to be concerned about encouraging people to spend money when it increases their debt?

Key issues from AS people management

It is clear from this that a thorough understanding of the AS content is crucial to this unit of work.

Motivation

You studied motivation theory and motivation in practice at AS level. You should ensure that you have good understanding of no more than two motivation theories as you prepare for any A2 examination (one should be either Herzberg or Maslow). These may well be helpful when analysing a question relating to staff morale and the performance of the workforce. Your AS work on 'motivation in practice' will help when you consider the A2 material covered in Unit 27 on employer/employee relations.

AS Reminder

Herzberg: his 'two-factor theory' suggested that people's needs at work break down into two:

● **Motivators** such as achievement and recognition for achievement, which can provide sustained job satisfaction (a passion for the job).

● **Hygiene factors** such as pay, status and working conditions, which are quickly taken for granted when they are satisfactory, but resented bitterly when unsatisfactory.

For Herzberg, **job enrichment** comes when people are responsible for a complete unit of work and trusted to get on with it; pay should be on a salary basis, with no distortions caused by bonus systems.

Maslow: his 'hierarchy of needs' suggested that everyone goes through stages of need, starting with the need for food (money), then progressing through the craving for safety (job security), for social contact, for status and – once all these other conditions are in place – a challenging, interesting job can allow for **self-actualisation**.

Structure

An organisation's structure will have a deep impact upon levels of efficiency, employee participation and effectiveness of internal communications. It is therefore important to consider any information relating to an organisation's structure carefully when assessing A2 case studies. Remember that in a business world in which many external factors cause problems, structure is something that senior managers can control. The effectiveness of the structure will have a big impact on employee participation (Unit 26) and employee relations (Unit 27).

Good A2 candidates are able to use with ease terms such as 'span of control', 'layers of hierarchy', 'delegation', 'consultation' and 'decentralisation'. To help you, the following definitions are taken from the *Complete A-Z Business Studies Handbook* 6th Edition, by Lines, Marcousé and Martin.

Definitions

Consultation: asking for the views of those who will be affected by a decision. These views should then be taken into account by the executive responsible for taking the decision.

Decentralisation: means devolving power from the head office to the local branches or divisions. This includes passing authority for decision making 'down the line', thereby accepting less uniformity in how things are done.

Delegation: means passing authority down the hierarchy.

Layers of hierarchy: means the number of ranks within the organisational structure, i.e. the number of different supervisory and management layers between the shop-floor and the chief executive.

Span of control: the number of subordinates answerable directly to a manager. It can be described as 'wide' if the manager has many direct subordinates or 'narrow' if there are few.

Measuring the effectiveness of the workforce

At AS level you learnt two widely used measurements of a firm's staff: labour productivity and labour turnover. Beware of confusing them (people do). Productivity is about efficiency, and is measured as output per worker (total output divided by the number of workers). Labour turnover refers to staff coming and going. So a high labour turnover means that staff join then leave quite quickly; this wastes the firm's spending on recruitment and induction training.

Key AS formulae for A2

Labour productivity: $\dfrac{\text{total output}}{\text{number of workers}}$

Labour turnover: $\dfrac{\text{staff leaving in the year}}{\text{average number employed}} \times 100$

Culture

The culture of the workplace is a massive issue at A2. At AS, the key theory was devised by Elton Mayo (this was optional at AS, so you may not have been taught it).

Both the role of the unofficial leader and the existence of group norms emphasise the importance of the culture of the workplace. In one workplace, staff will be enthusiastic in building the business; in another, the same types of people will be resentful and apparently lazy. Different classrooms show the same dramatic differences. Unofficial leaders can affect group norms and thereby establish the workplace culture.

AS reminder

Mayo: in the 1920s Mayo carried out a series of experiments at a factory in the town of Hawthorne, USA. These revealed the impact of **unofficial leaders** on workplace productivity and relations. For a manager to succeed with a suggested change to working practices, it would be necessary to persuade key individuals of the need for change. Important though the unofficial leaders are, an even more important issue is **group norms**, i.e. the ways of behaving considered acceptable by the majority of the workforce.

Mayo's research also uncovered the **Hawthorne effect** – the boost to morale and motivation that stems from managers taking an interest in the working lives of their staff.

Further reading

Complete A-Z Business Studies Handbook 6th Edition, by Lines, Marcousé and Martin. (Philip Allan, 2009)

Test yourself

What do you remember from AS People Management?

Questions *(50 marks)*

1 State the five levels of Maslow's hierarchy of needs. (5)

2 Identify three of Herzberg's:
   a motivators
   b hygiene factors. (6)

3 Explain what is meant by the term 'the Hawthorne Effect'. (2)

4 Briefly explain the benefits of using profit sharing as a financial incentive for staff. (3)

5 What is meant by the term 'span of control'? (2)

6 What is the effect on chains of command of delayering an organisation's structure? (2)

7 Identify the four main functions of HRM. (4)

8 Briefly explain why Herzberg felt that training was such an important factor in motivating staff. (4)

9 Identify three possible determinants of an organisation's culture. (3)

10 Briefly explain how effective HRM can improve productivity. (4)

11 Outline one argument for and one against the proposal that effective HRM will increase a firm's costs. (6)

12 Outline why changing an organisation's culture may prove difficult. (5)

13 Outline two reasons why a firm's labour turnover might increase sharply. (4)

23 Understanding HRM objectives and strategy

Introduction

People are a resource of the business. Like any other resource they have to be managed. In fact, many organisations claim their people are the most important of all their resources and that the management of them makes a significant difference to business success. In this unit we examine the activities involved in human resource management (HRM), typical HR objectives and different approaches to HRM.

The management of people

The management of people (otherwise known as human resource management) involves a wide range of activities. These begin with identifying the workforce requirements of the organisation in the future so that the appropriate plans can then be developed; for example, more staff may need to be recruited, existing staff may need training or redeployment, or in some cases redundancies may be needed. Planning ahead for these changes is known as **workforce planning**. Workforce planning involves an examination of the organisation's future needs, a consideration of the existing labour supply and then the development of plans to match the supply of people and skills to the demand.

Of course, people management is not just about the flow of people into and out of the organisation. It also involves managing people when they are part of the business.

This will involve activities such as those listed below.

- *Designing the jobs that people do:* this can have a big effect on their motivation and also their effectiveness; poor job design may be demotivating and fail to build on, or develop, individuals' skills.

- *Developing appropriate reward systems:* this will have a big impact on how employees behave. For example, a commission-based system is likely to push employees to make sales, but staff may be unwilling to do tasks that do not directly lead to a sale.

- *Developing appropriate training programmes:* these can serve a variety of purposes, such as informing employees of future developments within the business, developing employees' skills to do an existing job or helping them gain the skills needed to take on new tasks.

- *Developing effective communication systems:* these may include bulletins from managers, newsletters, systems of meetings or consultation with employee representatives. The communication systems will be designed to inform employees and at the same time achieve a desired level of consultation with staff.

The decisions taken by the human resource function will be linked to the overall business objectives and strategy. For example:

- if the business is growing the HRM function may need to recruit more staff; if it is expanding abroad it will recruit staff with language skills

- if the business is changing the nature of its operations the HRM function may need to invest more in training to ensure employees have the right skills; alternatively it may mean some jobs are lost and others are created

- if the business is trying to reduce its costs then the HR function will be looking for ways of helping to bring this about; for example, combining jobs, removing a layer of management or reducing the training budget.

The activities and objectives of the human resource function should, therefore, be integrated with the corporate plans and should contribute to the achievement of the corporate objectives.

At the same time, corporate planning needs to take account of a firm's human resource strengths and constraints. Expansion may not be possible in the short run, for example, if the firm does not have and cannot easily get the staff available. On the other hand, if employees have particular experience of and insight into a market sector this may make a business consider expanding into this segment.

A-grade application

Nursery nurse
kidsunlimited nurseries

We are looking for a qualified Nursery Nurse to join our team of dedicated care professionals to support and enhance the care and development of our children.

What can we offer you?

We believe that our staff are our greatest asset and therefore reward staff by offering an excellent employment package that includes:

- competitive salary
- 28 days' annual leave, increasing to 33 days
- flexible hours of work
- bespoke employee benefits package
- contributory pension
- discounted childcare
- comprehensive induction on commencement of employment
- range of further training and career opportunities to support your own development
- nationally recognised professional qualifications that include NVQs.

What can you offer us?

Applicants must be able to demonstrate the ability to provide and sustain an environment that is caring, welcoming and stimulating, and reflective of the kidsunlimited ethos and philosophy. Applicants must have minimum NVQ Level 2 or equivalent in Childcare and Early Years Education, and previous nursery experience is preferred.

Source: www.kidsunlimited.co.uk

Who is responsible for human resource management?

The responsibilities for human resource management may well lie with **line managers**. This means that the marketing manager may be responsible for managing her marketing team and dealing with all the 'people issues' that come with this. These might include recruitment, training and setting appropriate reward rates within an overall budget. Similarly, the operations manager may look after all the operations employees. This approach to HRM is quite common, particularly in smaller businesses where it may be felt that it is not financially viable (or indeed necessary) to employ a HR specialist.

However, in other organisations (often where there are more people to manage and therefore more people issues to resolve or plan for) there will be a specialist HRM department. People working within this department will act as advisers to the line managers, keeping them informed of the legal requirements affecting employing people, advising them on best practice and supporting them in HR issues. The final decisions are usually made by the line managers (after all, it is their team of staff), but the systems, procedures and approaches they use may well be developed by HR specialists.

HRM objectives

The overall aim of managing people is to maximise the contribution of employees on an individual and group level to the organisation's overall objectives. To do this, specific objectives need to be met. These HRM objectives, like all functional objectives, will be derived from the targets of the business as a whole.

An organisation's objectives for its people might focus on the aspects given below.

(Many of these specific areas of human resource management, such as workforce planning and employer–employee relations, are dealt with in more detail in later units.)

The desired level of staffing and skills

Organisations are continually changing in terms of the work being done and the way it is done. This reshaping requires changes in the human resource input. For example, it may require more people, greater flexibility or different skills. The human resource function is responsible for making sure the business has the right number of people at the right time, with the right skills and attitudes. This, of course, has a big impact on the ability of the business to meet its customer needs. A lack of appropriate staff can lead to delays for customers, rushed and poor-quality work, and an inability to accept some contracts.

By comparison, if the human resource requirements are met, a business may be able to provide a high-quality service and fulfil the expectations of customers. Achieving the right number of staff may be relatively easy if, for example, you can simply recruit more people when you need them. However, it can also be a very long-term process that involves enormous planning. In the case of the health service, for example, the training period for doctors and surgeons is several years. The NHS has to plan years in advance for the number of doctors it wants in relation to the number likely to be available.

Productivity

This measures the output per employee. This can be measured in many different ways, depending on the business. It could be the number of products made by each employee (or team), such as the cars produced per day. It could be the number of telephone calls answered in a call centre, the number of meals served in a fast-food restaurant or the number of claims processed in an insurance office. While the productivity of employees will depend on many factors, such as the level of investment in technology, it can be affected enormously by the way in which people are managed. Effective people management will lead to more motivated staff, a better organised workflow and employees who have the necessary skills.

By increasing productivity a business becomes more efficient. This is because if each employee produces more output the labour cost per unit is reduced. This can help to boost profit margins or enable the business to be more price competitive. Given that customers are continually looking for better value for money there is constant pressure on firms to increase their efficiency. This in turn puts pressure on businesses to increase their productivity, which is why this is a common HRM target.

Cost targets

Like all the functions, HRM must work within budgets. You cannot simply spend whatever you want because the money may not be there. All businesses work within constraints, and decisions must be made within these restrictions. However, this does not mean to say that all employees are paid the minimum wage or that staffing levels are always kept to the bare minimum; this all depends on the strategy being adopted. In the case of the budget airlines such as easyJet and Ryanair, for example, the focus is on tightly controlling costs; staff are expected to work a lot of hours for their money and undertake a wide range of tasks. Staffing levels are relatively low. However, in the case of Harrods, the upmarket department store, staffing levels are quite generous. In the case of investment banks such as Goldman Sachs, staff are paid very well to reflect the amount they earn for the business and the value of their skills. Organisations will therefore monitor their spending on human resources and set targets to ensure they get value for money in all aspects of the process (such as recruitment or training).

Employer/employee relations

The relations between managers and employees depend on the quality of communications and the trust between them. This in turn will depend on what communications mechanisms exist within the business, the extent to which employees are involved in making decisions and the way in which staff are treated. Are they listened to? And do they have the opportunity to influence the business policy? The nature of the relations between employers and employees will affect employees' commitment, their motivation and their readiness to work. You can tell when relations break down when employees and

managers fail to cooperate effectively; this can even result in a strike. The quality of these relationships will affect employees':

- – openness to change: the business environment is very dynamic, with internal and external change occurring all the time; employees' attitude to change and their willingness to cope with or embrace change will depend on the way they are managed and how well they get on with their managers

- – levels of motivation, their commitment to a job and willingness to provide a quality service: this is particularly important in the service sector, where the willingness of staff to help, to provide advice and to listen to customers can be an important differentiating factor

- – willingness to contribute ideas and innovate: if relations are good, employees will feel part of the business and strive harder to improve it.

Internal and external influences on HR objectives

As with all business functions, HR cannot operate independently of the operation as a whole. It can be affected by changes brought in by other functions or changes by the Board to the corporate objectives; in addition to these internal influences there may

be external factors, i.e. beyond the control of the organisation, such as changes to the economy. Table 23.1 sets out some key internal and external influences on HR objectives.

Table 23.1 Key internal and external influences on HR objectives

Internal influences on HR objectives	External influences on HR objectives
1. Corporate objectives, i.e. the overall goal will determine the HR goals and strategies	1. Market growth: if the business is in a growth market, HR objectives may focus on expanded recruitment, induction and management training
2. Corporate finance, i.e. the financial health of the business may determine whether the HR objectives are to be based on expansion or retrenchment	2. Changes in employment law: further big increases in minimum wage levels in China may make HR managers look instead to Vietnam or Sri Lanka
3. Operational objectives, e.g. if there is scope for factory automation it may be that redundancies or redeployments are inevitable	3. Ethical climate, e.g. if there were a genuine shift to ethically-based banking, some serious retraining would be needed throughout the sector
4. Marketing plans, e.g. if Innocent decide to launch their Smoothies in China, HR recruitment and training goals and strategies will have to change	4. Changes in competition: a new, fierce competitor may force a business to cut costs sharply in order to stay competitive; this will affect HR objectives and strategy

HR strategies: soft and hard HRM

Hard HRM

While all organisations undertake the various activities involved in managing human resources (such as recruitment, selection and training) the attitude and approach of managers towards employees can differ significantly. At one extreme we have what is called **hard HRM**. This basically regards employees as a necessary if unwelcome cost; people are an input that is required to get the job done, but it is believed that they add little to the overall value created by the business. With this approach managers see themselves as the 'thinkers'; they develop the best way of doing things and employees are expected to get on with it. This fits with the approach of F. W. Taylor, which you may have studied at AS level (see Unit 26 of the AS textbook).

Hard HRM usually adopts a top-down management style in which employees are directed and controlled. Employees are expected to fit in with the design of the organisation; managers and supervisors instruct them and then monitor their actions. Jobs tend to be broken down into relatively small units so that one person does not have much control over the process and a replacement can easily be recruited, selected and trained. This type of approach can often be seen in call centres, where the work of operatives is very closely monitored, or in highly controlled outlets such as McDonald's.

The hard approach to HRM has many benefits such as:

- the outcomes should be predictable because employees do as they are told
- employees should be easily replaceable
- managers retain control for decision making and so this reduces the risk of major errors being made.

However, the disadvantages of this approach include:

- a possible failure to build on the skills, experiences and insights of the employees; this can lead to dissatisfied employees and low morale
- a danger that the organisation as a whole is at risk because it relies so heavily on the senior managers; if they make mistakes the business as a whole could fail because there is no input from lower levels.

The hard HRM approach sees the business as a machine and employees are cogs within that machine. This may work well provided the machine is designed effectively and is fit for purpose, but the approach does not encourage change and flexibility. As the environment changes managers may not spot these developments at ground level and employees may not be able to cope with new demands being made on them.

Soft HRM

By comparison, the **soft HRM** approach takes the view that employees can add a great deal of value to an organisation, and the business should develop, enhance and build on their interests, skills and abilities. Under a soft approach managers see themselves more as facilitators. They are there to coach and help employees to do their job properly, perhaps by ensuring sufficient training is provided and that the employee can develop in his or her career. This approach fits with McGregor's Theory Y style of leadership (see box opposite).

The advantages of a soft approach to HRM are that:

- the organisation is building on the skills and experiences of their employees; this may enable the business to be more creative, more innovative and differentiated from the competition
- the organisation may be able to keep and develop highly skilled employees with expectations of a career with the business
- individuals throughout the business are encouraged to contribute, which may make the organisation more flexible and adaptable to changing market conditions.

The disadvantages of a soft HRM approach may be that:

- time is taken in discussion and consultation rather than 'getting the job' done
- employees may not have the ability or inclination to get involved; they may just want to be told what to do and be rewarded for it; in this case a soft approach to HRM may be inappropriate and ineffective.

Douglas McGregor's Theory X and Theory Y

McGregor's book, *The Human Side of Enterprise* (1960), popularised his view that managers can be grouped into two types: Theory X and Theory Y. McGregor had researched into the attitudes of managers towards their staff. He found that most managers assumed their employees were work-shy and motivated primarily by money; he termed this type of manager Theory X. The alternative view was from managers who thought that underperforming staff were victims of poor management. Theory Y managers think that as long as people are given the opportunity to show initiative and involvement, they will do so.

Which is the right strategy: hard or soft?

The attitude of managers towards their employees can be influenced by many different factors, such as those listed below.

- *Their own experience:* if you have taken an encouraging approach towards staff in the past and been let down then you may be reluctant to try this again.

- *The nature of the employees:* the skills, attitudes and expectations of employees will influence the way in which you manage them. If they are able, engaged and eager to progress then a soft approach is more likely.

- *The nature of the task:* if the task is simple, routine and repetitive then a hard approach is likely to be adopted. If there is little room for creativity or innovation because the task is standardised then the directive approach with clear instructions may well be the most efficient.

However, in general in the UK in recent years there has been a greater expectation by employees that they are involved in decision making and that managers take account of their welfare and skills development. The workforce is, on average, better educated than it was 20 years ago, employees are clearer about their rights (and there is more legal protection than before) and expects more in terms of their careers. Furthermore, we now have a 'knowledge economy', whereby many jobs require innovative thinking, independent decision making and the ability to 'think outside the box' (think of design work, software development, advertising, the music industry). As a result, a soft approach may be more suitable because it encourages individuals' contributions.

Figure 23.1 An employee with specialist skills

Issues for analysis

- There are two valuable lines of analysis built into this unit. The first is the question of who is responsible for the key HR decisions. The answer is often *not* the HR department. Most shop-floor workers are trained, managed and appraised by their supervisor. Similarly, most executives deal with their line manager, not their HR manager. In an accountancy department, then, it may be that the manager has little or no skill in people management; yet he or she may make all the most important decisions about the future of junior staff. HR departments can be little more than administration functions; all the key decisions about people are made elsewhere.

- The second issue is 'hard' versus 'soft' HR. This is also important, as it provides a useful analytic comparison. It encourages a view of HR that is questioning rather than flattering. In a world in which large companies worsen the pension rights of their own staff, it is right to be sceptical about whether modern HR methods are truly in the best interests of staff.

Understanding HRM objectives and strategy – an evaluation

Human resource management is one of the functions of a business. The overall approach to HRM (e.g. soft vs hard) and specific HRM decisions (e.g. to recruit or train) will be linked to the objectives and strategy of the business as a whole. A decision by a business to downsize or to expand abroad, for example, will have major implications for the HRM function. At the same time, the HRM resources of a business will influence the strategies a business adopts.

Key terms

Hard HRM: when managers treat the human resource in the same way they would treat any other resource (e.g. ordering more one week, and less the next); in such a climate, employee relations are likely to be strained and staff may see the need for trade union involvement.

Line managers: staff with responsibility for achieving specific business objectives, and with the resources to get things done.

Soft HRM: when managers treat the workforce as a special strength of the business and therefore make sure that staff welfare and motivation are always top priorities.

Workforce planning: checking on how future workforce needs compare with an audit of staff today, then planning how to turn the skills of today's employees into the skills required from tomorrow's staff.

 ## Further reading

McGregor, D. (1960) *The Human Side of Enterprise.* McGraw-Hill Higher Education.

Price, A. (2004) *Human Resource Management.* Thompson Learning.

 A **Revision questions** *(30 marks; 30 minutes)*

1 What might be the effects of managing human resources in the same way as all the other resources used by a business? (4)

2 Identify three important features of the job of a human resource manager. (3)

3 Some people think that schools should stop teaching French and instead teach Mandarin (Chinese). If a school decided to do this, outline two implications for its workforce planning. (4)

4 A fast-growing small business might not have a human resources manager. The tasks may be left to the line managers. Examine two reasons in favour of creating a human resources management post within such a business. (6)

5 Outline two ways in which a human resources manager might be able to help increase productivity at a clothes shop. (4)

6 Briefly discuss whether a Theory Y manager would ever adopt a 'hard HRM' approach. (9)

 B1 **Data response**

Extract from *Human Resource Management* (Price, 2004)

Storey (1989) has distinguished between hard and soft forms of HRM. 'Hard' HRM focuses on the resource side of human resources. It emphasises costs in the form of 'headcounts' and places control firmly in the hands of management. Their role is to manage numbers effectively, keeping the workforce closely matched with requirements in terms of both bodies and behaviour. 'Soft' HRM, on the other hand, stresses the 'human' aspects of HRM.

Its concerns are with communication and motivation. People are led rather than managed. They are involved in determining and realising strategic objectives.

Questions *(25 marks; 30 minutes)*

1 The passage explains that hard HRM emphasises 'headcounts' and managing numbers effectively. Outline one strength and one weakness of this type of approach to managing people. (6)

2 Explain what the author means by the phrase 'people are led rather than managed'. (8)

3 Discuss whether staff at a car factory such as Honda's plant in Swindon are likely to want to be 'involved in determining and realising strategic objectives'. (11)

 B2 ## Data response

BP was blamed by the public and Barack Obama for the 2010 Gulf Oil explosion and oil spill. But the defective oil rig was owned and operated by the US company Transocean. In September 2010 Britain's independent Health and Safety Executive (HSE) produced a hugely critical account of Transocean's activities in the North Sea. The company was accused of compromising safety by 'bullying, harassment and intimidation' of its staff. This was especially important because a separate HSE report had, in late August, shown that the combined fatality and major injury rate in the North Sea had nearly doubled in 2009/2010 compared with the previous year.

In 2009 the HSE visited four North Sea oil rigs operated by Transocean. Inspectors noted a common (and unusual) pattern that staff complained about the attitudes and behaviour of management. The *Guardian* newspaper stated that the (as yet unpublished) HSE report says that:

'"The company has not considered the human contribution to safety in a structured and systematic manner" and says the organisational culture is based on blame and intolerance.' (*Guardian* 9 September 2010). The HSE went on to comment that bullying, aggression, harassment, humiliation and intimidation were 'causing some individuals to exhibit symptoms of work-related stress, with potential safety implications'.

A regional organiser for the RMT union's offshore branch in Aberdeen was not surprised by the report, saying that 'I have dealt with three cases where workers were unfairly dismissed by Transocean and in each case I have been able to win compensation for them ... I know ... that other really serious accidents are not being reported because of widespread bullying and intimidation'.

Sometimes people assume that 'soft H.R.M.' is the modern way, with 'hard H.R.M.' a thing of the past. It is important to realise that shocking people management still exists today. It is rare to see it reported.

Source: adapted from an article in the *Guardian*, 5 September 2010.

Questions *(30 marks; 35 minutes)*

1 Explain the possible advantages to a company such as Transocean of adopting a 'hard HRM' strategy. (8)

2 Examine the possible advantages and disadvantages of trade union membership to employees on Transocean's North Sea oil rigs. (10)

3 Discuss the possible impact that Transocean's approach to its labour force might have on its workforce plans. (12)

 C ## Essay questions *(40 marks each)*

1 Discuss whether a 'hard HRM' approach is the right way to run a supermarket branch where 50% of the staff are part-time students.

2 Sainsbury announced recently that it planned to open a supermarket chain in China, the world's fastest-growing major economy. To what extent will Sainsbury's success or failure in China depend on a successful HR strategy?

Developing and implementing workforce plans

> ### Definition
> A workforce plan is developed to ensure a business always has the right number and skills of employees to meet the people requirements of the organisation.

 Introduction

Managing a firm's human resources is a key element of business success. This includes ensuring the business always has the number and skills of employees that it requires. The planning sequence is:

1 Find out the company's overall objectives and corporate strategy for the medium to long term

2 HR managers should then discuss with other functional managers the implications of the corporate strategy for future human resource needs

3 HR can then audit the current workforce to find out how well their skills match the skills needed in, say, three years' time

4 Then a workforce plan can be produced that anticipates the recruitment, training, retraining and perhaps redundancy levels implied by the mismatch between today's workforce and the workforce requirement in one or three years' time. See Table 24.1 for some possible examples.

Table 24.1 Relationship between corporate strategy and workforce plans

Corporate strategy	Implications for HR	Workforce plan
Poundland announces a move into Europe. In 2012/2013 it starts opening stores in Ireland – then may move into France	A new HR management team will be needed in Ireland, then France.	Plan now for the new HR structure in Ireland; start offering all ambitious staff free French lessons
Whitbread decides to run down its struggling restaurants division to focus more on booming Costa Coffee	The switch of focus may be tricky for staffing, with mismatches of skills (e.g. restaurant chefs would be wasted in a coffee bar) and perhaps a demoralised restaurant staff	Audit skills of current restaurant staff to see who can be retrained to work in the Costa division; prepare redundancy packages for other staff
Sainsbury's switches advertising slogan from 'Try something new today' (Jamie Oliver) to 'Live well for less'	A cutback on the range and variety of (expensive) fresh food, in a switch to 'Value' produce	Over three to five years reduce the number of skilled workers on deli and fresh fish sections (affecting recruitment and training)

Components of workforce plans

Recruitment and selection

The purpose of the recruitment and selection process is to acquire a suitable number of employees with the appropriate skills and attitudes. It is in the interests of the business to achieve this goal at a minimum cost in terms of both time and resources.

There are three stages to this process:

1 determining the human resource requirements of the organisation

2 attracting suitable candidates for the vacancy

3 selecting the most appropriate candidate.

Determining the human resource requirements of the organisation

Recruitment and **selection procedures** need to fit in with the overall workforce plan. **Workforce planning** starts by auditing the current employees. How many will retire over the next 18 months? What are their skills? And how many are prepared to take on new tasks or challenges? This information must be compared with an estimate of the future workforce needs, based on the firm's overall corporate strategy for the next year or two. A sales push into Europe, for example, might require more French or Spanish speakers; planned factory closures may require redundancies and redeployments. The workforce plan must then show how the business can move staff from where they are now, to where they need to be later on. With firms regularly reviewing their overall strategies their workforce plans need to be updated frequently as well.

Effective workforce planning requires managers to question the existing employment structure at every opportunity. Changes can occur when:

● an individual leaves the business because of retirement or finding alternative employment

● an employee is promoted within the business, creating a vacancy

● an increase in workload occurs

● the development of a new product, or an emerging technology, which means that the organisation requires employees with additional skills

● a change in the business strategy such as an expansion or downsizing, changing the overall people needs of the organisation.

Many businesses fill vacancies automatically with no analysis of alternative actions. However, it may be more effective to consider reorganisation of job responsibilities. For example, if someone has retired, you might consider whether the job should be redesigned. A good human resource manager will look ahead to the future needs of a department before just advertising for a replacement. Should the new job holder be able to speak a foreign language? Is a full-time employee needed? Should the business opt for increased flexibility by shifting to the use of part-time employees? Or should the tasks be contracted out to a specialist firm?

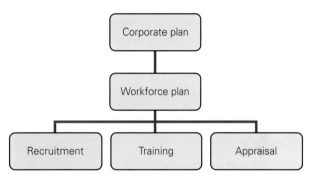

Figure 24.1 Origins of workforce planning

John Lewis
In May 2010 John Lewis announced an expansion in a customer service centre to be opened in Lanark, Scotland. An extra 200 jobs would take the total workforce to 450 in this new facility. John Lewis said that 80 new staff were being recruited straight away, to be part of the core team at the time the centre opens in late 2010 or early 2011. Some of the remaining staff will be transferred from among the 2,600 existing John Lewis staff in Scotland. The workforce plan envisages about 50% new recruits and 50% existing, experienced staff.

Attracting suitable candidates for a vacancy

Once the firm's human resource provision has been considered and the need for new recruits established, it is necessary to find a method of attracting suitable candidates.

The first step in this process is to develop a 'job description'. This will usually consist of:

● a job title

● a statement outlining how the job fits into the overall structure of the organisation

- details of the job's content, such as the tasks that must be performed and the responsibilities involved

- an indication of the working conditions the job holder can expect; this includes details of pay, hours of work and holiday entitlement.

Many firms will then choose to produce a person specification. This details the qualities of the ideal candidate, such as 'highly numerate', 'graduate' and 'good teamworker'. This should help to identify the criteria to use to shortlist and then select the best candidates from those who apply.

At this point the business must decide if the post will be filled from within the company or from outside it. 'Internal recruitment' (i.e. recruiting from within the business) ensures that the abilities of candidates will be known. In addition, other employees may be motivated by the evidence of promotion prospects within the firm. However, external recruitment will provide a wider pool of applicants from which to select. It can also introduce new thinking to the organisation.

The recruitment process can be expensive. It includes not only the cost of the advertising, but also the administration of, perhaps, hundreds of applications. Then there is the management time spent in the shortlisting and interviewing phases. The insurance giant Standard Life spends over £500,000 a year to recruit 50 management trainees. That's over £10,000 each!

The successful management of human resources demands that the effectiveness of recruitment advertising should be monitored. The most common method adopted is to calculate the cost of attracting each new employee. The appropriateness of recruits is also a concern. This can be judged by keeping a record of the proportion of candidates recruited by the firm who remain in employment six months and then one year, two years and even five years later. Standard Life is rightly proud that 99% of the graduate trainees it employs are still with the company two years later.

Selecting the right person for the job

The selection process involves assessing candidates against the criteria set out in the person specification. The most frequently employed selection process is to:

- shortlist a small number of applicants based on their application forms

- ask for a reference from their previous employers/ teachers

- call for interview those individuals whose references are favourable.

The choice of who will be offered the job is made by the interview panel, based on which candidate they feel most closely matches the person specification for the post. Research suggests that the use of interviews is not a very reliable indicator of how well an individual will perform in a job. This is largely because interviewers are too easily swayed by appearance, personal charm and the interview technique of applicants. A number of other selection techniques have therefore been developed to complement, or replace, the use of this selection procedure.

Testing

There are two types of test. Aptitude tests measure how good the applicant is at a particular skill, such as typing or arithmetic. Psychometric tests measure the personality, attitudes and character of an applicant. They can give an indication of whether the applicant will be a team player or a loner, passive or assertive, questioning or accepting, and so on. The firm can make a selection judgement on the appropriate type of person from experience, and from the specific requirements of the job. This approach is particularly common in management and graduate recruitment.

Many doubts have been raised about the accuracy and validity of psychometric tests. Do they give an unfair advantage to certain people? Certainly the questions must be checked to remove social, sex or racial bias. There is also concern about whether firms are right to want all their managers to have similar characteristics. A wide range of personalities may lead to a more interesting, sparky atmosphere with livelier debates and better decisions.

A-grade application

Shell seeks the right qualities

Dutch-owned oil giant, Shell, believes it knows the qualities required for management success. It has researched carefully among its own high-flyers and come up with a list. When recruiting management trainees it uses a variety of tests to see which applicant best matches the required qualities. These include the ability to explore problems about which they had little previous knowledge, to see long-term implications and to cope better with the unknown. The specific attributes Shell looks for include: problem analysis; creativity and judgement; drive, resilience and empathy (seeing other people's point of view); and the action qualities of organising and implementing.

Assessment centres

Assessment centres are a means of establishing the performance of job candidates in a range of circumstances. A group of similar applicants are invited to a centre, often for a number of days, for an in-depth assessment. They will be asked to perform tasks under scrutiny, such as role playing crisis situations. This is a good way to assess leadership qualities.

Research suggests this approach is the most effective selection technique for predicting successful job performance. Although the use of these centres is growing, they are expensive and time consuming. Only large firms can afford to use this recruitment strategy and it is appropriate only for individuals who will potentially fill senior positions within a firm in the future.

Whichever selection procedure is adopted, a growing number of organisations are encouraging line managers to become involved in the recruitment decision. The role of the human resource department is increasingly one of providing support to functional departments rather than driving the recruitment process itself. Line managers are more aware of the key requirements of a post because they see it being carried out from day to day.

A-grade application

Assessment centre inside track – from a 2010 blog

zinzen1234: 'I have recently been asked to attend the Asda Reality Assessment Centre in April. I have applied for the Ecommerce department. Has anyone previously been to the assessment centre there at Leeds?'

simstar88: 'I attended the Asda Assessment Centre and didn't get through due to lack of demonstrating a lead in the group. 1st Exercise was introduce yourself, say why you wanted to work for Asda and why Ecommerce. You then use your business ideas and talk about them amongst your team. Keep an eye on the time, this is very important. They ask you how Asda could be improved. Our group was slow and we discussed things for too long and didn't get enough done. Next was the role play, you have to persuade Ali that a green initiative is the right way to go. They are testing your reactions here (well that's what they said at the end of the day) to negative and positive responses from Ali. Then the business case, you need to present your ideas, you get 10 minutes to do this. I talked about loyalty cards (something they don't have) and also comparison sites, they didn't like that, they worried it would cause too much competition from Tesco.'

Source: http://tomcat4.prospects.ac.uk:8080/forum/viewtopic.php?t=5325

Training and development

Training is the process of instructing an individual about how to carry out tasks directly related to his or her current job.

Development involves helping an individual to realise his or her full potential. This concerns general growth, and is not related specifically to the employee's existing post.

An organisation that introduces a training and development programme does so in order to ensure the best possible return on its investment in people.

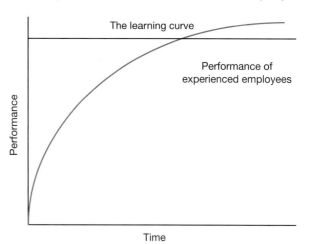

Figure 24.2 Objectives of induction training

The four key objectives of training and development are as follows.

1 To help a new employee reach the level of performance expected from an experienced worker. This initial preparation upon first taking up a post is known as 'induction' training. It often contains information dealing with the precise nature of the job, layout of the firm's operating facility, health and safety measures, and security systems. An attempt may also be made to introduce the individual to key employees and give an impression of the culture of the organisation. The firm's induction training should aim to drive each employee along their own personal learning curve as quickly as possible (see Figure 24.2).

2 To provide a wide pool of skills available to the organisation, both at present and in the future (see Figure 24.3).

Actual performance		Desired performance

Current level of skill — Required level of skill
Current level of knowledge — Required level of knowledge

Figure 24.3 The training gap

3 To develop a knowledgeable and committed workforce.

4 To deliver high-quality products or services.

The cost of not training

If an organisation chooses not to train its workforce it will be faced with additional recruitment costs. This is because when new skills are required existing employees will have to be made redundant and new people employed who have the right skills or experience.

Untrained staff will not be as productive, or as well motivated, as those who are trained. They will be unable to deal with change because their skills are specific only to the present situation. There may also be more accidents in the workplace if the workforce is unskilled. In addition, employees are less likely to know, and work towards achieving, the organisation's aims and objectives.

Training in practice

A wide range of research has indicated that organisations in the UK, both in the private and public sector, fail to invest appropriately in training and development. Many organisations view training only as a cost and therefore fail to consider the long-term benefits it can bring.

Rather than planning for the future by anticipating the firm's knowledge and skill requirements, many businesses develop training programmes only as an answer to existing problems. This is reactive rather than proactive. The UK government responded to the reactive nature of training by launching the Investors in People (IIP) campaign. This encourages firms to develop a more strategic view of training and development. An organisation can gain IIP accredited status if it analyses its training and development needs, plans and implements a programme in response, and evaluates the effectiveness of its provision.

A-grade application

Investors in People

Over ten years ago, business at the 62-bedroom Park Hotel in Liverpool was poor. Profit had fallen to £60,000 and the occupancy rate was only 30%. Ron Jones, general manager, decided that the fundamental problem was lack of repeat and recommended (word-of-mouth) business. The cause of this seemed to be the lukewarm efforts of staff.

He responded by bringing in an expert to retrain staff and build morale, and then went for the Investors in People (IIP) award. The first step was to devise a SWOT analysis in conjunction with staff. Then heads of department explained their objectives and the staff

skills required to achieve it. Every member of staff had a personal development plan drawn up and was given the training they required.

By the time of receiving the IIP award, the hotel had already gained in many ways. Labour turnover fell to 5% (compared with 35% for the industry nationally). Occupancy rose to 72% and the profit was in excess of £500,000 on turnover, which had doubled to £1.4 million.

The hotel's general manager, June Matthews, is certain that Investors in People stimulated higher participation and more positive attitudes among staff: 'Without a shadow of doubt it was worth it.'

Issues in implementing workforce plans

Inward migration

Businesses want to be able to recruit the best people at the lowest cost. In many cases they will be able to find the people they want from the UK workforce. But what about someone to clean the toilets in a London office block? What if no one is willing to do the job for less than, say £15 per hour? The employer would naturally like to find a worker from Eastern Europe willing to do it for the UK minimum wage rate.

Even more importantly, what if a world-leading UK software business such as ARM or Blinkx finds job applicants from India or America with better skills than are offered by British applicants? If no inward migration is allowed, the company has to make do with second-best skills; in time, that may affect the competitiveness of the business.

So government policy towards immigration may have a serious impact on workforce plans. Britain remains a hugely international economy, benefiting from considerable exports of manufactured goods and – especially – services such as finance, education and the creative arts. But to be a great place to run a business, British employers need to be able to recruit the best staff.

Cost-cutting

In some cases the corporate plan may involve restructuring and cost cutting. This may involve job losses as the scale or nature of the firm's operations change. Perhaps jobs are redesigned, offices are closed or operations are outsourced. In all these cases jobs may no longer exist and redundancies may have to be made. A redundancy occurs when there is a closure of all or part of the business. When they are made redundant employees are entitled to some financial payment (linked to the number of years they have worked at the business and their age); some firms will also work closely with employees to help them find alternative employment.

The labour market

The workforce plan is not only influenced by the firm's own strategy. It is affected by the state of the labour market. If there is a skills shortage in the UK, for example, the firm may have to look to recruit from overseas. Alternatively there may be a large supply of relatively cheap labour available that makes expansion easier or makes it viable to use more labour rather than invest in capital equipment. In recent years the UK has experienced a major inflow of labour from central and Eastern Europe (following the expansion of the EU in 2004). This has provided a relatively low-wage source of labour for many UK firms.

Changes in external labour markets, such as an increase in the minimum wage or a change in the age structure will influence a firm's workforce plan.

A-grade application

Migrant workers

The graph in Figure 24.4 shows the flow of Eastern European migrant workers in and out of the UK in the years following the enlargement of the EU. Figure 24.5 shows the sectors of the economy where they are now working.

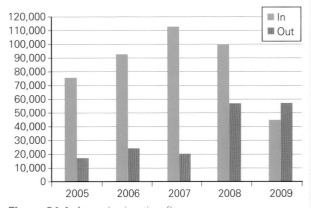

Figure 24.4 Annual migration flow

Source: National Statistics website: www.statistics.gov.uk

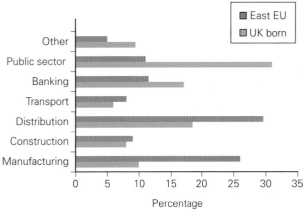

Figure 24.5 Are Eastern European migrants filling unpopular jobs?

Source: National Statistics website: www.statistics.gov.uk

Assessing internal and external influences on workforce plans

Workforce plans will be affected by various factors within the control of the business, and outside its control. The major factors are shown in Table 24.2.

For every business the effectiveness of their workforce plans will hinge on the HR teams' ability to cope with the interplay of these internal and external influences.

Table 24.2 Internal and external influences on workforce plans

Internal influences	External influences
1. The corporate objectives and strategy	1. Government legislation, such as immigration controls or laws relating to discrimination and diversity
2. The way in which the business functions decide (together) to implement the corporate strategy	2. Technological change, which might make automation hugely cheaper – and job cuts virtually inevitable
3. The financial health of the business and therefore the budget available for implementing the workforce plan	3. Competitive forces: if your rivals start a price war, you may be forced to put expansion plans on hold
4. The corporate image and ethos of the business (for example 'no-redundancies' may be part of the organisational culture)	4. The economy: in boom times it may be hard to recruit people of top quality (other than on huge wages); in recessions recruitment is easy

The value of using workforce plans

People play a vital role in the success of most business organisations. The creatives at the Saatchi & Saatchi advertising agency, the programmers at Google, the coaches and players at Chelsea are all essential to the organisation's success. Having the right people, with the right skills, is therefore critical to business planning. Without them you may not be able to expand, you may not be able to deliver the level of service offered and you may not make the profits you expect. Staffing shortages can mean you cannot meet customer orders; skills shortages may mean you lack the flexibility you need to compete effectively. Planning your human resource requirements and reviewing the workforce plan is therefore a major contributor to the overall performance of a business.

Nevertheless, in the wrong hands, any planning system can become a hindrance. It may become overly-bureaucratic, with power-hungry managers using their 'ownership' of the workforce plan to be too controlling. The football manager who spots a great young Turkish goalkeeper is told no, it's not on the plan – we're developing our own keepers through our youth academy. And the rapidly-growing store in Milton Keynes is told 'no more staff, as the plan says you have the maximum allowed'. Workforce planning is a necessary part of business, but needs to be used with intelligence, flexibility and with a clear sight of the needs of the whole business.

Issues for analysis

When analysing a firm's workforce plan be aware of the following aspects.

- Check that the workforce plan is closely linked to the overall corporate plan. Expansion is likely to mean recruitment; relocation may mean transfers or even redundancies. Effective human resource management means the business is planning ahead to identify its future workforce

requirements, rather than merely responding to short-term events and allowing these to shape human resource policy.

- Effective recruitment and selection usually involves preparing job descriptions and person specifications, in order to ensure the recruitment process selects individuals with the most appropriate skills for the vacant post.

- A business should try to use a range of selection techniques and be wary of relying on interviews alone.

- Training can help individuals have the skills and knowledge they need to perform to a better standard.

Workforce planning – an evaluation

Managing people effectively is the single most common factor that links successful organisations. This involves planning the human resource requirements very carefully as the business strategy or the external environment changes.

The success of a workforce plan will depend on how well it anticipated the demands for and supply of labour, and how well the corporate and workforce plan is implemented.

The importance of workforce planning has increased as the significance of employees in terms of a businesses competitiveness has been appreciated. Planning itself has become more difficult as the rate of change has increased.

Key terms

Selection procedure: the process by which organisations choose to differentiate between the applicants for a specific job in order to pick out the most appropriate candidate. The most commonly used technique is interview, but a range of different approaches (e.g. personality testing) are being used more frequently in order to complement traditional methods.

Workforce planning: the process of anticipating in advance the human resource requirements of the organisation, both in terms of the number of individuals required and the appropriate skill mix. Recruitment and training policies are devised with a long-term focus, in order to ensure the business is able to operate without being limited by a shortage of appropriate labour.

Revision questions (35 marks; 40 minutes)

1 Why is it important that an organisation challenges its existing employment structure each time an opportunity to do so emerges? (4)

2 Why do 'job descriptions' and 'person specifications' play an important part in the selection of appropriate personnel? (4)

3 What advantages does the process of internal recruitment offer to the business over the appointment of individuals from outside the organisation? (4)

4 Identify three benefits to a firm of using assessment centres in selecting key staff. (3)

5 What might be the costs of not training:
   a new supermarket checkout operators (4)
   b crowd stewards at Manchester United? (4)

6 What kinds of non-financial rewards might be offered to employees? (4)

7 What is the main purpose of 'induction' training? (4)

8 What benefits might a firm derive from achieving an Investors in People award? (4)

Case study

Human resource development at Prest Ltd

Three years ago Prest Ltd, manufacturer of electronic components, closed three factories and concentrated its operations on a single site. At the same time it reorganised the remaining plant to cut costs and improve product quality. Before modernisation, 50% of the machinery being used at the site had been over 15 years old. This was replaced with the latest equipment. The new production line was designed to run continuously, with operators being expected to take 'first level' decisions at the point of production to keep it functioning. As a result, tasks such as fault finding and machine maintenance became an important part of the job of each worker.

The modernisation of the plant signalled a shift to team working, in order to encourage employee flexibility. Multi-skilled operators were needed with a deeper understanding of the production system. The employees needed to know how the new machinery could best be used to ensure consistently high levels of production quality. These changes had clear implications for the human resource department at Prest. Recruitment would have to focus on a new type of employee, and existing employees would need to be retrained.

The human resource manager conducted a feasibility analysis in order to review the strengths and weaknesses of the company's existing workforce and its ability to handle the new situation. This concluded that both shop-floor supervision and the engineering section needed strengthening. In response, 15 new engineers were recruited and five staff redeployed to improve production supervision.

As an answer to the immediate need for greater skill levels, a comprehensive training programme in quality control was introduced for all staff. Machine operators were encouraged to mix with engineers during this exercise, helping to break down barriers between the two groups. For many individuals this was the first formal company training they had ever received. The development initiative was successful enough to stimulate requests for further learning opportunities. As a result, Prest created a link with a local technical college to provide more extensive instruction for those who wished to learn more about modern production techniques.

Although the benefits of the training were clear, three problems emerged that Prest had

not anticipated. The greater knowledge of the operators made them anxious to put their acquired skills into practice. After nine months the new production line had reached only 80% efficiency. Senior managers believed employees were losing interest when machinery was functioning normally. In addition, some workers felt the extensive training they had received was not reflected in enough increased responsibility. Their expectations of a more interesting job had been raised, but the reality seemed little different than before. Finally, 12 newly trained staff left the company because they could now apply for more highly paid posts at other firms in the area.

Prest also considered the long-term human resource implications of the move to a more sophisticated form of production. The workforce knew little about new production technology, so the firm's training school ran a course on robotics. The decision was also taken to provide a sponsorship scheme to encourage new recruits to study on an engineering degree course at university. The firm wished to ensure it did not face a shortage of talent in the long term.

Questions (40 marks; 40 minutes)

1 Analyse the possible implications for human resource managers following the introduction of new technology and different working practices at Prest Ltd. (8)

2 Discuss the human resource issues that might emerge as a result of the feasibility study conducted at Prest Ltd. (12)

3 Analyse the appropriateness of the development programme introduced by Prest Ltd in the light of the problems identified by the feasibility study. (8)

4 Consider whether the difficulties experienced after staff training at Prest Ltd suggest that employees can receive too much training. (12)

 Essay questions (40 marks each)

1 Johnson Engineering plc is suffering from a lack of skilled engineers. Consider how its human resource department might set about solving this problem.

2 In order to establish a competitive advantage, a business must make sure its selection,

development and reward of employees each 'fit' together in order to form a single human resource policy approach. Discuss how this might be achieved and the difficulties that may be encountered.

Flexibility and insecurity

Definition
Flexibility refers to the willingness and ability of a firm to adapt its operations in response to changing circumstances. This will require a workforce that is multi-skilled and a culture that accepts change. It may, however, lead to increased uncertainty and insecurity within the organisation.

The need for a more flexible approach

The dreadful Japanese earthquake and tsunami of 2011 wrecked a nuclear power plant, causing energy shortfalls throughout Japan. Electricity shortages caused factories to close down for several hours a day, until Japanese staff started to tackle energy usage voluntarily. People quickly found new ways to work and new ways to cut electricity overhead costs. Flexibility at work proved its value.

Today's businesses need a more flexible approach within their operations. The need has arisen for a number of reasons.

● Increasing competition means that the marketplace is subject to frequent and often rapid change. Firms need to be able to anticipate these changes and respond to them quickly in order to maintain a competitive edge.

● Many consumers want more customised goods and services (i.e. better tailored to smaller segments of the population); firms have to adapt the production process in order to meet demand, while still operating efficiently and keeping costs down.

● Increasing competition, especially from overseas firms, has forced businesses faced with fluctuating or seasonal demand to introduce greater operational flexibility, in order to eliminate any unnecessary costs.

To succeed in modern markets that are often fragmented into relatively small niches, and where customer tastes are ever changing, many firms have adopted lean production. This approach implies the use of machinery that can quickly be reprogrammed to carry out a range of tasks and the creation of a multi-skilled and flexible workforce that can quickly adapt – and be adapted – to meet a firm's changing requirements.

A-grade application

Benefits of flexible working
During the recent recession, a surprise to many was that unemployment stayed far lower than expected. Only in America did it shoot upwards. In Britain unemployment stayed low because of the willingness of staff to be flexible. In companies such as JCB and Honda UK, employees volunteered in 2009 to have cuts in their hours (and pay), to help their employers survive without needing to slash the workforce. Flexible working proved to be a benefit for both sides of industry.

Achieving greater flexibility within the workforce

There are a number of ways in which firms can attempt to increase the level of workforce flexibility, some of which are described below.

Functional flexibility

This occurs when workers become multi-skilled (i.e. they are given the scope and ability to carry out a variety of tasks (functions), rather than specialising in completion of one particular area). This can be encouraged through the use of job rotation, in which workers carry out an increased number of tasks at the same level of difficulty. In a hotel, for instance, the people who are usually on reception could spend time organising wedding receptions – giving them a wider understanding of the business. In Japan this is known as horizontal promotion, as it implies that the company has enough faith in the individual to invest time and money in training him/her for an extra job.

Increasing the level of functional flexibility should, in theory, mean that a firm's human resources can be used more effectively. Keeping workers fully occupied should lead to improved productivity. It should also mean that employees are equipped with the skills needed to cover for staff absences, minimising any disruption or loss of production that this may otherwise have caused. Individual workers may respond positively to the increased variety and new challenges provided, improving motivation and increasing productivity further. However, firms may be unwilling to bear the costs of additional training unless the benefits of adopting a new approach are obvious and immediate. See Table 25.1.

Table 25.1 Creating functional flexibility: benefits and drawbacks

Benefits	Drawbacks
Increases in productivity from greater utilisation of employees	Potential loss of production as workers switch between different tasks
Reduction in disruption to production caused by staff absence	Greater training requirements as individual workers need to acquire a wider range of skills, increasing costs
Greater employee motivation created by more varied and challenging tasks at work	Workers may be reluctant to acquire new skills, especially if there is no corresponding increase in pay

Numerical flexibility

All firms face the problem of having enough workers to respond to increases in customer demand, without having to bear the cost of employing unnecessary staff should sales decline temporarily. Increasing the level of numerical flexibility involves a firm using alternatives to the traditional approach of employing staff on permanent, full-time contracts. These alternatives include the use of temporary contracts, agency staff, and **subcontracting** or **outsourcing** certain operations to other firms. Flexible temporary staff enable firms to respond to a sudden rise in sales by increasing the workforce quickly – and then reducing its size just as quickly, should the sales increase prove to be temporary. However, while a reliance on temporary staff and external organisations may help to reduce costs and improve reaction to change, productivity may be harmed by a lack of expertise and worker loyalty to the firm.

Time flexibility

Greater flexibility can also be created by moving away from the traditional 9 to 5 working day and 38-hour working week in order to respond more effectively to customer demands. There are a number of methods used by firms to vary the pattern of working, including the use of part-time work, job sharing, annualised hours contracts and flexitime. For example, banks, insurance companies and mobile phone operators make extensive use of flexitime systems to provide 24-hour employee cover via the telephone and internet, in order to provide customers with greater convenience. Introducing greater time flexibility can also have a number of benefits for employees who may have family or other commitments during normal working hours. Providing staff with more flexible working arrangements can help to improve recruitment, increase motivation and reduce labour turnover, leading to reduced costs and boosts to productivity.

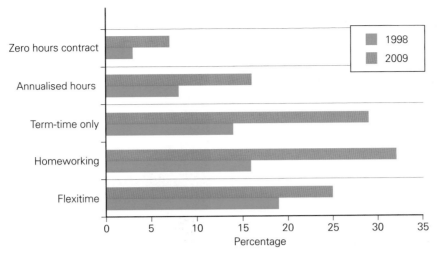

Figure 25.1 Changes in flexible working arrangements in the UK
Sources: DTI, CIPD and industry estimates.

A model of the flexible firm

The flexible firm is able to change its own structure in response to changing needs. This means creating a structure that allows quick changes to take place. In order to achieve this, firms have tended to identify a 'core', which forms the basis for all its operations, and a 'periphery', which consists of all the other tasks needed to run the firm but that are not central to the business.

For a firm producing household goods such as washing machines, **core workers** might comprise designers, the market research team and workers on the production line, among others. The canteen and cleaning staff, and even advertising campaign staff may be seen as being less central to the firm, and so may be employed on a part-time basis, or even brought in at specific times to undertake a specific task; these are known as **peripheral workers** (see Table 25.2).

Table 25.2 Core and peripheral workers

Core workers	Peripheral workers
Full-time employees	Part-time, temporary or self-employed
Do tasks central to the business	Perform less critical, or less permanent, tasks
Secure jobs	Insecure jobs
Committed to the firm's goals	Committed to self-interest

The benefit of being a flexible firm, of course, is that the periphery can be increased quickly when needed to meet a particular change in the marketplace.

In his book *The Age of Unreason*, Professor Charles Handy suggested that instead of firms comprising two elements, the core and periphery, there were actually three parts to modern firms; he called this idea the 'Shamrock Organisation', as illustrated in Figure 25.2. The first leaf of the shamrock represents the professional core, made up of qualified professionals, technicians and managers. The second leaf, called the contractual fringe, is for the work that has been contracted out to someone else because it is not central to the firm. Professor Handy notes that many firms that used to be manufacturers now do little more than assemble parts bought in from suppliers. As much as 80% of a firm's work may be done outside the business itself. The third and final leaf is the flexible labour force, made up of temporary and part-time workers. In effect, Handy has split the periphery into an internal periphery (the flexible labour force) and an external periphery (the contractual fringe).

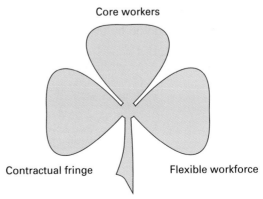

Figure 25.2 Handy's 'Shamrock Organisation'

171

A particular type of flexible worker is the homeworker. This is someone who works at home, probably on a laptop connected permanently to the main office. In some cases it can be that a full-time employee does two days a week at home – with fewer distractions from the phone, from meetings and from gossipy staff. In other cases, the business may want as few people as possible at head office, to keep overhead costs down, so they encourage staff to work at home, and perhaps occasionally come in and '**hot-desk**'.

Some really enjoy this arrangement, whereas it makes others feel insecure. Ideally, an employee would have this as an option; it would be much less satisfactory if it were forced upon the worker.

Figure 25.3 Working at home

A-grade application

Homeworking eases stress levels

Working from home reduces stress in office workers, but leads to fears about career progression, according to research. A survey of 749 staff in managerial or professional positions conducted by Durham Business School showed that homeworkers worried about missing out on 'water-cooler networking' – where potential opportunities for moving up the ladder are discussed informally in the office.

Despite these concerns, the study also found that working from home generally had a positive effect on an employee's work/life balance, giving them more time with the family, and leading to less stress and less chance of burnout.

Four in ten respondents who worked more than 20 hours per week at home reported feeling a great deal of stress because of their job compared with 65% of employees who worked solely in the office.

Source: *Personnel Today*, 20 March 2008 © Reed Business Information

Flexible operations and 'hard' HRM

Whether or not flexibility was necessary for a firm's success, 'hard HR' managers saw scope for increasing their control over staff. Full-time, permanent staff who were resistant to changes put forward by management might find themselves threatened with being 'outsourced'. Outsourcing is when a firm uses sources outside the business to undertake functions that used to be done internally by a section of the business itself. Tasks such as designing new products or undertaking market research can be bought in by the firm as and when needed. In effect, it turns what used to be a fixed cost (a staff salary) into a variable cost – a cost that need only be incurred when there is demand for it.

Although that may sound logical, it has some serious potential downsides. Outside contractors have no loyalty to the business and no reason to contribute anything that is not being paid for (such as an idea for doing things more efficiently). So firms that shrink their core workforce too much (see Figure 25.4) can find that the organisation is like a Polo – all outside and no heart.

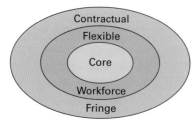

Large central core

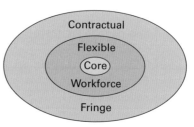

Small central core

Figure 25.4 The shrinking core

Insecurity

The increasing desire for firms to increase their flexibility has generated a number of concerns – in particular, in terms of loss of job security for workers. While those employees in core roles have continued to enjoy a great deal of job security, peripheral workers have experienced a growing sense of insecurity as the use of temporary contracts and the threat of insecurity has increased. An increasing number of workers have also had to overcome an instinctive resistance to change by having to repeatedly retrain in order to carry out new job roles. However, some would argue that demands for increasing flexibility within the workplace have created new opportunities and challenges, including opportunities to learn new skills and diversify into new career paths, rather than ending up 'stuck in a rut'.

 ## Issues for analysis

Opportunities for analysis may arise when asking the following questions.

- What is the pressure behind a change in production system from inflexible (mass) to flexible (lean)? If the reasons are positive, it may be easy to convince staff of the benefits. Unfortunately, the move to 'lean' can also be a move to 'mean' (i.e. increased flexibility may be at the cost of increased insecurity). Always, the question of trust is crucial. Does the workforce trust the management?

- What are the reasons behind a firm's decision to choose a more flexible approach to staffing? Is it to be more helpful to staff, perhaps especially those with small children? Or is it a way of maximising management control over staff, and minimising labour costs?

Flexibility and insecurity – an evaluation

The adoption of a more flexible workforce can, in principle, be an attractive prospect for any modern business, offering a number of benefits, including reduced costs and an increased ability to respond to changing customer demands. The separation of employees into a highly valued core and an easily dispensable periphery may allow a business to 'pick and mix' skills and obtain the exact combination required within the market at that particular moment in time.

However, it can also lead to a number of problems in the long term, especially if it creates insecurity among peripheral workers that leads to high levels of staff turnover. The ability to cut labour costs quickly and easily in the face of a downturn in the market has obvious attractions. However, in the long term, the establishment of a multi-skilled and loyal workforce, able to adapt and diversify into new markets, may lead to even greater success.

Key terms

Core workers: employees who are essential to the operations of a business, supporting whatever makes it distinctive or unique. Such workers are likely to receive attractive salaries and working conditions, and enjoy a high degree of job security.

Flexible approach: an approach to operations that implies a move away from mass production to batch production, the use of machinery that can be quickly reprogrammed to carry out a range of tasks, and the creation of a multi-skilled and flexible workforce that can quickly adapt to meet a firm's changing requirements.

Hot-desk: an approach that provides a temporary desk for homeworkers to use when they come to the main office; they are not allowed to leave any of their own possessions there.

Outsourcing: involves a firm finding an external business to carry out part of the production process, in order to cut costs or achieve a better level of service. For example, it might involve hiring cleaning or catering services from other businesses.

Peripheral workers: those workers who are not seen as being central to a firm's operations. They may carry out necessary tasks, but may be required only on a temporary basis and be easily replaced.

Subcontracting: where another business is used to perform or supply certain aspects of a firm's operations (see outsourcing).

Further reading

Handy, C. (1989) *The Age of Unreason*. Hutchinson.

A Revision questions *(40 marks; 40 minutes)*

1 Why might increased market change have an effect on the way people are employed today? (3)

2 Outline two reasons why firms may have chosen to adopt a more flexible approach to workforce arrangements. (4)

3 Briefly explain what is meant by the term lean production. (3)

4 Explain, using examples, what is meant by the term functional flexibility. (4)

5 Outline one advantage and one disadvantage for a small textiles manufacturer of trying to increase the degree of functional flexibility among its workforce. (6)

6 Explain what is meant by numerical flexibility in respect of a firm's workforce. (3)

7 State two ways in which a bank offering telephone and internet services to customers would benefit from introducing greater time flexibility. (4)

8 Explain the idea of the 'Shamrock Organisation'. (3)

9 Outline two reasons why a firm's employees might welcome the decision to move towards increased labour flexibility. (4)

10 Examine two reasons why the move towards greater flexibility might lead to increased insecurity within the workforce. (6)

Data response

Flexible working at First Direct

First Direct is one of the UK's leading commercial banks, providing a wide range of financial services via telephone and the internet to over 1.2 million customers. When First Direct began, high street banks opened only between 9.00 am and 3.00 pm, Monday to Friday. However, the company set out to create a different business model, based on the customer need for greater convenience. Since its establishment, First Direct's reputation has rested on the fact that it is the bank that never closes and ignores weekends and bank holidays. Operators in the company's call centres handle approximately 235,000 calls each week, more than 13,000 of which each day are outside normal working hours, and with more than 500 coming from overseas.

The company's operations have required it to develop a working culture that is very different from the traditional model. This has included longer shifts, a high proportion of part-time and home-based workers, and reliance on so-called 'mushrooming' – a term used to describe workers employed to work night-time shifts.

According to Jane Hanson, head of human resources at First Direct, 'It's about making life convenient … We have people phoning us while they're on holiday or in the middle of the night because they wake up worrying that they haven't paid their Visa bill.'

First Direct appears to have succeeded on a number of levels. The quality of its customer service has resulted in high rates of customer retention. Employees also appear to approve of the company's approach to flexible working – the company claims to have very good rates of staff retention, claiming, for example, that 90% of female staff return to their jobs after maternity leave.

Questions *(30 marks; 35 minutes)*

1 Identify two examples of flexible working practices used by First Direct. (2)

2 Analyse two possible benefits for a business such as First Direct of creating a more flexible workforce. (10)

3 To what extent is the creation of a more flexible workforce crucial to the continuing success of a company such as First Direct? (18)

Data response

Job insecurity leaves no time for lunch

Research suggests that only one in six workers in the UK take a regular lunch break and that the breaks are getting shorter as a result of increasing job insecurity. A survey carried out by human resources firm Chiumento discovered that only 16% of employees regularly take a 'proper' lunch break, defined as one of around an hour in length, away from their desk or work station at least three times a week. According to Andrew Hill, who helped to conduct the study:

> employees are struggling to keep on top of to-do lists and think the answer is to work harder, eating a sandwich at their desk as opposed to taking a full lunch break, and also not having sufficient breaks during the rest of the day … But these breaks are essential for staff to perform at their best and cope

with the daily pressures of work. Managers should be encouraging staff to take lunch breaks – their performance, and ultimately the business, may suffer otherwise.

The UK's average working week is amongst the highest in Europe, with three quarters of employees regularly working overtime but only one third being paid or given time off in return. One in six employees in the UK works more than 60 hours a week. Professor Cary Cooper, an occupational psychologist at the University of Lancaster, claims that, despite UK workers being considered the workaholics of Europe, productivity per capita in the UK remains lower than many other European countries. According to Professor Cooper, 'People feel as though they have to get to work early, stay late and not take lunch breaks' because of job insecurity and the desire to show commitment. However, in spite of these concerns, he believes that workers should still take proper lunch breaks two or three times a week because, ultimately, their managers will judge them on their output, not on their 'presenteeism'.

Source: *BBC News*

Questions *(30 marks; 35 minutes)*

1 Examine two possible causes of increasing job insecurity among UK workers. (10)

2 Discuss the key implications of the findings of the research into UK working practices contained in the case study for businesses. (20)

C Essay questions *(40 marks each)*

1 To what extent do you agree with the view that UK manufacturing firms can survive only by adopting 'hard HRM' methods?

2 Assess the possible impact of adopting more flexible working practices on the international competitiveness of a firm such as Cadbury.

26 Employee participation and team working

> ### Definition
> Employee participation refers to the extent to which employees are involved in the decision-making process. Team working means working in a group rather than in isolation, switching tasks as necessary and discussing ways of working more effectively.

Participation in practice

As early as 1918 Cadbury pioneered elected works councils in its Bourneville factory. Ten years later, Elton Mayo showed that morale and productivity can be boosted if staff feel involved and therefore respected. The main risk is that participation can become a three-monthly chore rather than part of the business culture. Effective participation is part of daily life, not postponed for a meeting. Nearly a century after Cadbury's initiative, employee participation remains patchy.

Figure 26.1 Working at Cadbury's Bourneville factory early in the twentieth century

Many managers realise that workers have a tremendous amount to offer in terms of ideas and insight into solving problems. Involving the people who do the work on a daily basis enables managers to learn how the job could be done more effectively. This reveals specific problems faced by the employees in a particular work area.

The importance of managers actually listening to their employees and paying attention to their social needs was highlighted in Mayo's study of the Hawthorne plant. When employees were asked for their opinions their productivity rose, simply because managers were paying them attention and showing that they were valued. Greater participation has been shown to have tangible results in many companies, such as higher motivation, more innovation and lower labour turnover. This means that developing more effective employee participation can be an important element of business success. It involves using one of your resources more effectively (and the human resource is the only one that can decide to walk out of the door and not return).

There are, of course, problems involved in participation. Involving more people may slow up decision making, although even this can be a good thing as it forces managers to discuss their ideas and listen to employees' comments. This may help to avoid hasty decisions, which are later regretted. However, there are some situations, such as a crisis, where a quick decision is important and where any delay may prove damaging. In this situation too much discussion could cause problems.

Participation can also prove frustrating. When people attend a meeting, for example, they often have very different ideas of what they are trying to get out of it. They may well hope to achieve one thing but become irritated when it becomes clear that others are trying to achieve something else. Managers may resent the fact that their ideas are being challenged by workers in meetings and may wish they did not have to discuss things at all.

Employees may also be unhappy because they may expect more power than they are actually given. Having become involved in decision making, they may well want more information or more control over issues than management is willing to allow.

Simply announcing that employees will be invited to participate more in decision making does not in itself necessarily improve the performance of the business. The process needs to be planned (e.g. who is to participate and how), employees need to be consulted so they understand the benefits and do not feel they are being exploited (i.e. being asked to give ideas in return for nothing) and the process managed (i.e. a regular review of what works and what does not).

A-grade application

Partnership

Everyone who works at John Lewis is an owner of the organisation and is called a 'partner'. The fact that partners have a stake in the business means that they have the right to expect managers to explain their decisions to them.

At store level, local managers meet with partners on a regular basis. They provide information on how their part of the business is doing and brief staff on issues concerning the organisation as a whole. Partners have the right to question any decision and receive an explanation. Managers in John Lewis are, therefore, far more accountable to staff than they are in most other organisations.

At the end of each financial year, a percentage of the profits is paid out to each partner. It may be as high as 20% of a partner's annual salary. John Lewis and its sister company, Waitrose, have been successful, growing businesses for many years. This demonstrates that employee participation has the potential to be a successful, profitable approach.

How do employees participate in decisions?

There are numerous mechanisms to increase the amount of employee participation within a firm. These occur at different levels within the organisation and deal with different types of issues. They include those described below.

Kaizen groups

Devised in Japan by firms such as Toyota and Nissan, these have become popular throughout the west. *Kaizen* means 'continuous improvement', so the idea is to meet regularly and keep coming up with ways to do things better (or to tackle niggling faults). For example, workers may meet to solve problems of high wastage levels in one part of the factory. Employees are usually paid for their time in meetings and are expected to present their findings to management.

Works councils

A **works council** is a committee of employer and employee representatives that meets to discuss company-wide issues. Works councils have worked well in some countries, such as Germany, but have not been so popular in the UK. A works council will usually discuss issues such as training, investment and working practices that affect the whole workforce. It will not cover issues such as pay, which are generally dealt with in discussions with trades union representatives.

Autonomous work groups

An autonomous work group consists of a team of people who are given a high level of responsibility for their own work. These responsibilities might include the scheduling of the work and decisions over the allocation of their tasks (they might choose to use job rotation). To be really effective, such teams should be invited to join recruitment panels for new staff and be given the capital budget necessary to buy new machinery when it is needed.

Employee shareholders

An increasingly common way to develop a common sense of purpose is to give employees shares in the business. For example, employees at Innocent Drinks and at Tesco have the opportunity to buy shares in the company. This should mean they become more interested in the overall performance of the firm, as well their own personal performance; if they can think of it as 'their' company rather than a company, job done.

In 2010 the oil company Total gave 25 of its shares to each of its 100,000 staff. As each share was worth more than 30 euros, this was a meaningful sum of money. In addition, 10,000 employees were offered share options, i.e. the right to buy shares at a discounted price.

Total explained that it 'wishes to develop employee shareholding and to allow the employees to understand better the basics of the company'. It continued to say that the share plan was 'intended to strengthen employees' sense of belonging to the Group and associate them with the Group's performance'.

Other methods

Other methods of encouraging employee participation include suggestion schemes and a more democratic style of management.

When deciding on how to improve participation in the business managers must therefore consider the options and decide which are most appropriate. The speed and method of introduction must also be considered to ensure that they are accepted and that employees value them as much as managers.

European directives

In most European countries the works council (which consists of elected representatives) is an integral part of employee participation within the firm. It is consulted whenever management plans to do anything that is likely to affect the majority of employees, such as changing employment terms and conditions or staffing levels. Up until recently, works councils have been very rare in the UK. However the EU's European Works Council directive is forcing some large UK firms to change their approach to employee participation and introduce works councils.

These works councils will have information and consultation rights in relation to company performance and strategic planning. In effect, there should be consultation and a dialogue on any proposed actions by the employer that could affect employees' jobs.

Consultation is defined in the regulations as 'the exchange of views and establishment of dialogue' between the employer and employees or employee representatives.

Teamwork

Many organisations now expect employees to undertake their work in teams. This is because they believe that **team working** leads to more efficient and effective production. People often respond positively to working with others because this satisfies their social needs (Mayo). The fact that managers are willing to delegate responsibility to teams also meets employees' ego and self-actualisation needs. Teams also allow individuals to gain from the strengths of others. There may be some areas in which you are relatively weak but someone else is strong, and vice versa. Imagine you are trying to solve a crossword, for example. It is usually much quicker and more fun sharing the task with others. Working in teams also allows individuals to change jobs, which can provide some variety at work.

Figure 26.2 Teamwork

However, some people do not particularly enjoy working in teams. This may be because of their personality or because they think their own performance would be better than that of the other members of the team – they are worried about being dragged down. Teamwork can also bring with it various problems: decision making can be slow and there may be serious disagreements between the members of the group.

Employee participation, team working and business success

Employees are an important resource of a business. They provide ideas for new products and new ways of doing things, they solve problems and they move the business forward. Utilising this resource effectively is therefore one of the many challenges of managers. As part of the process of human resource management managers must decide on the level and method of employee participation. They must weigh up some of the potential problems (such as the time and cost) with the benefits (such as more views and insights into problems).

It is not realistic, or even desirable, for everyone to participate in every decision. This would make for a very unwieldy organisation that is slow to react. So managers must decide who should be involved in various decisions. Teams and committees can help managers to cut across departments, divisions and products to improve communication and the sharing of information. They can provide a diversity of views, which is often essential in a business operating in global markets, and they can share a range of skills and talents. They also build employees' level of commitment and understanding of the firm's values and strategy, all of which makes participation (when done correctly) very important to business success. The benefits of participation can be seen in better decisions, fewer mistakes, higher levels of satisfaction and innovation, and greater effectiveness.

Issues for analysis

When analysing employee participation within an organisation you might find it useful to consider the following points.

- Approaches to participation are all rooted in the theories of Mayo, Maslow and Herzberg. Analysis can be enriched by making and explaining the connections between theory and practice.

- Greater participation by employees may provide the business with a competitive advantage. It may provide more ideas, greater motivation, greater efficiency and greater commitment from the workforce. This makes change easier, and – in the service sector – has a direct effect upon customer image.

- There is every reason to suppose that employees today need more opportunities for participation; nowadays employees are generally better educated and have a higher standard of living, and therefore want to be involved to a greater extent.

- Despite this, some researchers argue that many managers have become more authoritarian in recent years. Consequently, participation may have reduced in many organisations. This is especially true in the public sector, where staff in professions such as medicine or teaching find themselves less involved and less often consulted than in the past.

Employee participation and team working – an evaluation

Managed effectively, employees can provide better-quality and more innovative work at a lower cost and a faster rate. To achieve such improvements in performance employees must be involved. They must have the ability to contribute and feel they are listened to. Greater participation can help a firm to gain a competitive advantage. This is why managers in all kinds of successful organisations claim that their success is due to their people. However, despite the potential gains from participation this does not mean every manager has embraced the idea. After all, the more that employees participate in decisions, the more managers will have to explain their actions to them. Some managers find this change difficult to cope with.

Participation can also slow up the decision-making process and, if handled incorrectly, can lead to conflict. Greater participation must be part of a general movement involving greater trust and mutual respect between managers and workers. Employees cannot be expected to participate positively if, at the same time, their conditions and rewards are poor. Successful participation is part of an overall approach in which employees are given responsibility and treated fairly.

Managers must also consider the most effective method and the most appropriate degree of participation for their organisation. This will depend on the culture of the organisation, the pace of change, and the attitude and training of both managers and workers. Despite the growth of participation in the UK, employee representation is still relatively low – especially when compared with countries such as

Germany, where employees are often represented at a senior level. However, although this system appears to work well in Germany this does not necessarily mean it will work as effectively in the UK because of the two countries' different traditions and cultures.

Key terms

Industrial democracy: an industrial democracy occurs when employees have the opportunity to be involved in decision making. In its most extreme form each employee would have a vote. When examining a business you should consider the extent to which employees are involved in decision making.

Teamwork: individuals work in groups rather than being given highly specialised, individual jobs.

Works council: a committee of management and workers that meets to discuss company-wide issues such as training, investment and expansion.

Further reading

Herzberg, F. (1959) *The Motivation to Work*. Wiley International.

Maslow, A. H. (1987) *Motivation and Personality*. HarperCollins (1st Edn. 1954).

Mayo, E. (1975) *The Social Problems of Industrial Civilisation*. Routledge (1st Edn. 1949).

Revision questions (40 marks; 40 minutes)

1 Explain the possible benefits to a firm of greater employee participation. (5)

2 Why do some managers resist greater participation? (4)

3 Why do some workers resist greater participation? (4)

4 Examine two possible problems of involving employees more in decision making in a business such as Tesco plc. (6)

5 Consider the advantages and disadvantages to

a Europe-wide business such as Coca-Cola of having a works council covering staff from all its factories across Europe. (6)

6 Outline two benefits of teamwork. (4)

7 How would team working be viewed by a motivational theorist of your choice? (5)

8 Examine the possible impact on a firm's profit of a move towards the use of autonomous work groups in the workplace. (6)

Data response

John Lewis Partnership

John Lewis is one of the world's biggest employee-owned businesses. As all staff are 'partners' with a profit share and voting rights, it should have exceptionally impressive employee participation. In many ways it does. It has employee councils that meet regularly, to provide insights from the shop floor and to involve staff in decision making. And all staff can attend the Annual General Meeting.

As not everyone likes speaking in public, there is also a staff survey, answered by 93% of the 72,000 staff (in most businesses, a 40% response rate would be impressive). In 2009, the survey showed good results on the following four factors: 'be honest', 'show respect', 'recognise others' and 'work together'. Results were less impressive on two other criteria: 'show enterprise' and 'achieve more'. Now the key thing will be how senior managers respond to this information. Only if they can find ways to encourage staff to show more enterprise and gain more sense of achievement can the participation be said to be a success.

Questions *(25 marks; 30 minutes)*

1 a Identify two forms of **industrial democracy** used at John Lewis. (2)

  b Examine how one of the two might affect staff motivation. (4)

2 John Lewis provides the right structures for participation, but may fail to sufficiently encourage day-to-day consultation between managers and staff. Explain why that might undermine the effectiveness of its workplace democracy. (8)

3 Discuss how senior John Lewis managers might set about improving their staff's ability to 'show enterprise' at work. (11)

Case study

The Old Hen

'I don't know why I bother,' said Nina Burke, the manageress of the Old Hen pub in Oxford. She had just had one of the weekly staff meetings and all she had heard was one complaint after another. 'They want more money, they want shorter working hours, they want free food, they don't like the T-shirts they have to wear, and they don't like the shift arrangements. Honestly, I don't know why any of them even turns up to work, the amount they complain. They even seem to resent being asked for their ideas,' said Nina to her husband.

Nina began to wonder whether she was running these meetings effectively. The previous landlord had never really held staff meetings and had certainly not asked employees for their opinions. When she took over, he had said: 'Half of them will be moving on to new jobs anyway within a few weeks or are just doing this as a part-time job, so what's the point? Tell them what to do and then make sure they get on with it.' Nina began to think he may be right, although she had been very enthusiastic when she first had the idea of asking employees for their input.

She had noticed that staff in this pub seemed to leave very frequently and were generally pretty miserable. They seemed much less motivated than at her previous pub (where she was deputy manager). The money was not good but no worse than anywhere else. She decided it must be because they were not involved in decision making at all. In her last job everyone had felt able to give an opinion (even if their ideas were then ignored!) and were often asked what they thought about how the pub was run. It was a good atmosphere and Nina had enjoyed working there. She hoped she could recreate the same feeling here but was losing confidence that it would ever be possible.

Questions *(40 marks; 50 minutes)*

1 Consider whether Nina is right to try to introduce greater employee participation at the Old Hen. (10)

2 According to many motivational theorists, employees should respond positively to

greater participation. Discuss the possible reasons why Nina's schemes seem ineffective. (15)

3 An increasing number of managers claim to be encouraging employee participation. Consider why greater participation might be regarded as particularly valuable today. (15)

C Essay questions (40 marks each)

1 'Greater competitiveness and higher profits in the future will depend upon much more employee participation than in the past.' Critically assess this statement.

2 'Managers are appointed to make decisions. Workers are hired to do the job they are told.

Employee participation simply wastes time and money.' Critically assess this view.

3 'Teamwork brings with it more problems than benefits.' Discuss.

27 Effective employer/ employee relations

> ### Definition
> Are staff and management able to work together for the good of the business, or is there friction and inefficiency? Motivation can be undermined by poor employer/employee relations.

 ## Introduction

The relations between bosses and workers would be effective if communications were good and there was a sensible amount of give-and-take between them. They would be bad if there was a lack of trust, leading to restricted communication ('information is power') and the tendency to make demands rather than conduct conversations. In a perfect world, adults would behave in an adult manner towards each other. But just as no family is perfect, neither is any individual business organisation. The key is not to be perfect, but to be better than most.

There are three main areas to consider within the heading 'effective employer/employee relations':

1 good communications
2 methods of employee representation
3 the causes and solutions to industrial disputes.

A-grade application

ACAS
ACAS (the Advisory Conciliation and Arbitration Service) is Britain's most important, independent voice on the workplace. Over more than 30 years it has developed a view of what it thinks is the 'model workplace'. The ACAS model includes the following six themes:

1 ambitions, goals and plans that employees know about and understand
2 managers who genuinely listen to and consider their employees' views, so everyone is actively involved in making important decisions

3 people to feel valued so they can talk confidently about their work, and learn from both successes and mistakes
4 work organised so that it encourages initiative, innovation and working together
5 a good working relationship between management and employee representatives that in turn helps build trust throughout the business
6 formal procedures for dealing with disciplinary matters, grievances and disputes that managers and employees know about and use fairly.

Source: www.acas.org.uk

 ## Good communications

The importance of effective communication

Effective communication is essential for organisations. Without it, employees do not know what they are supposed to do, why they are supposed to do it, how to do it or when to do it by. Similarly, managers have little idea of how the business is performing, what people are actually doing or what their customers think. Communication links the activities of all the various parts of the organisation. It ensures that everyone is working towards a common goal and enables **feedback** on performance. Imagine studying for an exam if you were not told by the teacher what you were supposed to do and had no idea of your standard. Then you can appreciate how important good communication is. By communicating effectively the management is able to explain the objectives of the organisation and employees can have an input into the decisions that are made.

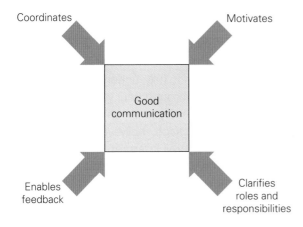

Figure 27.1 Good communication

Effective communication is also vital for successful decision making. To make good decisions managers need high-quality information. If they do not know what is happening in the market, for example, they are less likely to be successful. If, however, their market knowledge is good they are more likely to develop an appropriate marketing plan. Effective communication provides managers with the information they need, in a form they can use, when they need it.

Good-quality information should be:

● easily accessible

● up to date

● cost effective.

Good communication is also extremely important to motivate employees. People need to know how they are getting on, what they are doing right and in which areas they could improve. To work on your own without any kind of feedback at all is extremely difficult. It is much easier if someone is taking an interest and providing support. Interestingly, nearly all staff surveys reveal that employees do not feel that management communicate with them very effectively. So there is clearly a need for managers to improve in this area.

To ensure that communication is motivating, managers need to ensure that employees:

● understand the objectives of the organisation as a whole

● understand why their job is important and how it contributes to the overall success of the firm

● know how the job should be completed

● know how they are performing.

The importance of communication in employee/employer relations

In a well-run organisation with effective delegation and consultation, good communication will flow from the top and to the top. The overall business leader can do many things to help, as outlined below.

● Have a chat with every new member of staff; this may be impossible for the boss of Tesco's 480,000 employees, but is perfectly possible in most cases.

● Take regular initiatives to meet with staff; some retail bosses go out every Friday to two or three different stores to discuss problems with shop-floor staff; this is bound to encourage communication not only then, but also later, if an issue arises that an individual feels very strongly about, such as sex discrimination.

● Treat every piece of communication from staff as being as important as if it were from a friend or a big shareholder. If staff know their complaints or suggestions are being addressed, they will be happy to keep contributing their thoughts. Most staff want their workplace to be efficient, to allow them to do as good a job as possible; inefficiency is frustrating for all. Toyota reports that its Japanese staff alone make 500,000 suggestions a year for workplace improvement; this is perhaps because the company implements a high proportion of all the ideas put forward.

If the leader can get communications right, there is every chance that staff will do the same. Unfortunately there are some serious barriers to effective communication. The first is that middle managers may not want staff communicating over their heads to senior staff. If they insist that communications should filter up through the management layers, there is a chance at every stage that the message will be suppressed. Middle managers may not want their bosses to receive grumbles, complaints or suggestions. After all, they could be seen as criticism of the middle layers of management. Bosses have to make a special effort, therefore, to make sure that staff really do feel that they can communicate one to one with the business leader.

If communications are well managed, the impact on employer/employee relations can be huge. The many benefits to the business include those described below.

● Staff that understand the difficulties faced by the organisation, and therefore can seek to help management rather than criticise it. In 2009 the sharp recession meant that Honda UK had to shut its factories down for three months. Keeping staff aware of the problems helped encourage them to cooperate, even when job cuts were called for.

● If **vertical communications** are weak, frustrated staff may look for a trade union to represent their views to management. If the company is reluctant to recognise a union as the representative of staff, employer/employee relations may become very difficult. The Asda supermarket chain and the GMB union recently had a bitter dispute over union recognition for lorry drivers; a planned five-day strike was averted only when Asda backed down, granting recognition to the union.

● Ineffective communication, by comparison, leaves employees frustrated and dissatisfied. Poor communication makes people uncertain about their role or duties. They become unsure of what they are supposed to be doing. It can also lead to rumours going around the firm. This can cause problems if people get worried about things that are not actually true, or resent the fact that they have heard something before being officially told.

Communication and size

As a firm grows it tends to introduce more layers of hierarchy. This makes communication more difficult as vertical communications (from the top to the bottom) have to go through more people. This slows down decision making. It also introduces a greater risk that the message will get distorted. Instead of communicating directly to the person you want to talk to, you have to contact someone else, who then gets in touch with someone else, and so on. In the end your message can become rather confused.

Another problem is that as the number of people involved in an organisation increases, the use of written communication rises even faster. Instead of a quick conversation to sort something out, you can end up passing numerous messages backwards and forwards. This can lead to a tremendous amount of paperwork and is often far less effective than face-to-face communication. When you are actually talking to someone you can get immediate feedback and can see if they do not fully understand something. You can then talk it through until you are happy they have understood what you mean. When you send them a written message, however, you are never quite sure how they will interpret it. What you think you have said and what they think you have said can be very different.

Communication problems can also occur because of different business cultures within the firm. This is usually more of a problem in large firms than in small ones. If there are only a few people working in an office they tend to share the same approaches to work and the same values about what is and what is not acceptable business behaviour. If anyone new joins the group they soon learn the way that everyone else works and the newcomer will usually fit in quite quickly. In large organisations, however, it is much more difficult to develop a common approach. People tend to develop their own little groups within the firm so that the mood, attitudes and values of employees can vary tremendously in different parts of the firm. The marketing department, for example, may have a different view from the production department of what the business is trying to achieve and how it wants to conduct its business.

Methods of employee representation

Intelligent bosses realise that success depends on the full participation of as many staff as possible. Football managers typically use the club captain as the representative of the players. Small firms might have an informal group consisting of one person from each department; monthly meetings are used as a way to raise issues and problems, and discuss future plans. In larger firms, more formal methods are used to ensure that there is a structure to allow an element of workplace democracy. These include those listed below.

Works council

A works council is a committee of employer and employee representatives that meets to discuss company-wide issues. Although works councils have worked well in Germany they have not been so popular in the UK. However, under European Union legislation larger companies that operate in two or more EU countries must now set up a Europe-wide works council. Works councils will usually discuss issues such as training, investment and working practices. They will not cover issues such as pay, which are generally dealt with in discussions with trades union representatives.

Employee groups, organised by the business but with representatives elected by the staff

These may be little different from a works council, but the fact that they are purely the invention of the business (i.e. the management) may mean that they lack real credibility. Staff may know that management frown upon those who raise critical issues. They may be seen as little more than a talking shop that provides a veneer of democratic respectability. In a similar way, some school councils are vibrant and meaningful, while others are largely ignored by the school management.

Employee cooperatives

These range from huge organisations such as the John Lewis Partnership to the 150 staff at Suma (see below). Because all staff are part-owners of the business, all have a right to have their voices heard at every stage in the decision-making process. Inevitably, the board of directors includes representatives from ordinary shop-floor workers, ensuring that everyone's voice is heard.

A-grade application

Suma

Suma was born in 1975 when Reg Taylor started a whole-foods wholesaling cooperative in Leeds. Its purpose was to allow small independent health food shops to be able to buy together in bulk. Although Reg started it in his back bedroom, within a year a tiny two-storey warehouse had been bought in Leeds. Suma was one of the pioneers of organic foods, and has benefited greatly from the growing consumer interest in chemical-free food. This has caused its own pressures, as the cooperative has had to cope with employee growth from seven members in 1980 to over 150 today. All staff receive the same pay, no matter what their responsibilities may be, and all have an equal say in how the business should be run. The high level of staff motivation and participation has allowed Suma to become the number one organic foods wholesaler in the north of England.

For further information on Suma, go to www.suma.co.uk.

Trade unions

What is a trade union?

A trade union is an organisation that employees pay to join in order to gain greater power and security at work. The phrase 'unity is strength' is part of the trade union tradition. One individual worker has little or no power when discussing pay or pensions with his/her employer; union membership provides greater influence collectively in relations with employers than workers have as separate individuals.

Some people assume that union membership is only for people in low-status jobs. In fact, although trade unions are in decline in Britain some powerful groups of 'workers' remain committed to membership. For example, the PFA (Professional Footballers' Association) includes almost all Premiership players, and the airline pilots remain loyal to their union BALPA. Two years ago Hollywood script writers went on strike; they thought the film studios were being unfair in not sharing the revenues from sales of DVDs and computer games based on Hollywood films (they won huge concessions from the studios).

Traditionally, unions concerned themselves solely with obtaining satisfactory rates of pay for a fair amount of work in reasonable and safe working conditions. Today the most important aspect of the work of a trade union is protecting workers' rights under the law. Far more time is spent on health and safety, on discrimination and bullying, on unfair dismissal and other legal matters than on pay negotiations. One other important matter today is negotiations over pension rights. Recently, many companies have cut back on the pension benefits available to staff; the unions fight these cutbacks as hard as they can.

Traditionally, the key function of a union was 'collective bargaining'. This means that the union bargains with the employers on behalf of all the workers (e.g. that all nurses should get a 4% pay rise). The 2010/2011 industrial dispute between Virgin Atlantic and its cabin crew was a good example of this. Virgin staff wanted a substantial pay rise to match the wages earned by British Airways' staff. They pressed their union to threaten strike action to achieve their objectives.

Union recognition

'Recognition' is fundamental to the legal position of a trade union. In other words, management must recognise a union's right to bargain on behalf of its members. Without management recognition, any actions taken by a union are illegal. This would leave the union open to being sued. Until recently, even if all staff joined a union, the management did not have to recognise it. Why, then, would any company bother to recognise a union?

- Generally it can be helpful for managers to have a small representative group to consult and negotiate with. Collective bargaining removes the need to bargain with every employee individually.

- It may ease cases of possible difficulty, such as relocation or renegotiation of employment conditions and contracts. Trade union officials can be consulted at an early stage about causes, procedure and objectives. This may give the workforce the confidence that management are acting properly and thoughtfully. It also gives the opportunity for the trade union to offer advice or objection at an early stage. It promotes consultation rather than conflict.

- Trade unions provide a channel of upward communication that has not been filtered by middle managers. Senior managers can expect straight talking about worker opinions or grievances.

Today, UK employers with 21-plus staff members must give union recognition if more than 50% of the workforce vote for it in a secret ballot (and at least 40% of the workforce takes part in the vote). This government policy has helped unions to recruit more members at a time when membership is generally falling.

Methods of avoiding and resolving industrial disputes

It is only natural that there will be disagreements between management and staff. Clearly, staff want as high a pay rise as possible, whereas the bosses have a duty to their shareholders to keep costs down (and profits up). Usually, companies and unions are able to resolve their differences by compromising (i.e. give and take). Staff may 'demand' 8%, but only be offered 2%. After much wrangling, a compromise of 4% may be agreed. In some cases, though, a build-up of mistrust and hostility over time may mean that compromise is not seen as acceptable. Then an industrial dispute may occur, which may lead to industrial action, such as a strike.

When an industrial dispute occurs, it is up to the management and unions to resolve it. Sometimes, however, there seems to be no compromise that is acceptable to both sides. The result might be a strike – in other words, workers refusing to work and therefore giving up their pay. The inevitable conse-quence of a strike is that both the company and the employees lose money; therefore, there will soon be pressure for a way to resolve the dispute. Often, one or both sides will suggest bringing ACAS in to help. ACAS stands for the Advisory Conciliation and Arbitration Service; it is government-financed, but acts independently of government and politicians.

Founded in 1975, the mission statement of ACAS is:

to improve the performance and effectiveness of organisations by providing an independent and impartial service to prevent and resolve disputes and to build harmonious relationships at work.

ACAS seeks to:

- prevent and resolve employment disputes
- conciliate in actual or potential complaints to industrial tribunals
- provide information and advice
- promote good practice.

ACAS can be used by employers and employees to help them work together to resolve industrial relations disputes before they develop into confron-tation. Where there is a collective dispute between management and workforce, either or both may contact ACAS. Before acting, ACAS will want to see that union officials are involved and that the organisation's disputes procedure has been followed. ACAS can also be used to offer **conciliation** to the parties in a dispute, assuming their own procedures have been exhausted, to avoid damaging industrial action. Such conciliation is entirely voluntary and ACAS has no powers to impose a settlement.

If conciliation is unsuccessful, ACAS can offer **arbitration**, by providing an independent arbitrator who can examine the case for each side and then judge the right outcome to the dispute. If both sides agree in advance, the arbitrator's decision can be legally binding on both sides. Occasionally, ACAS is asked to provide a mediator who can act as an intermediary, suggesting the basis for further discussion.

A-grade application

In summer 2009 the management of the Post Office imposed new working conditions on its staff. In effect, the job of a postman would be casualised. Instead of specific, permanently-employed postmen having 'their round' to look after, workers on short-term contracts would be given different rounds on different days (flexible working). The postmen took unofficial, then official strike action against these changes. Their trade union,

Unite, repeatedly offered to take the dispute to ACAS, but Post Office management refused. Eventually, after many days of strikes, management and the union agreed a new deal in April 2010. There would be a minimum of 75% full-time, permanent staff, plus a 6.9% pay rise over the coming three years. Conciliation at ACAS could surely have achieved something similar six months before.

Issues for analysis

- When analysing employer/employee relations it is good to start with a clear understanding of the vision and objectives of the business. The vision at Innocent Drinks is 'to create a business we can be proud of'. As long as the company's decisions are in line with that vision, it is easy to see that it could be the basis of close cooperation between employees and their employers.

- Yet Virgin Atlantic boasts that 'our vision is to build a profitable airline where people love to fly and where people love to work'. This did nothing to prevent the 2008 and 2011 industrial disputes between cabin crew and management. So successful employer/employee relations is about much more than saying the right thing.

- When analysing a business situation, look beyond what managements say and see how they are actually treating their staff. Are they really showing respect by listening to what staff say and acting on their views. That, after all, is how Toyota became the world's number one car maker.

Effective employer/employee relations – an evaluation

Good relations are built on shared goals, on trust and on good communications. Yet they are always fragile. One instance of hypocrisy can ruin years of relationship-building. A boss may claim to be acting for the good of all the staff, yet switch production from Britain to Asia (James Dyson), or cut pension benefits to staff while keeping them intact for directors. In the long term, some firms really stick by the view that 'our people are our greatest asset', while others just pretend they believe that. Staff will learn which is which. Where they find they cannot trust their bosses, joining a trade union becomes a sensible way to get greater protection and greater negotiating power. Union representation will make the employer/employee relationship more formal, and occasionally more fractious. Yet, as Tesco has shown, trade union representation can help move a business forward. So it would be wrong to jump to the conclusion that unions are 'trouble'. Real trouble comes when employers and employees have no relationship at all.

Key terms

Arbitration: when an independent person listens to the case put by both sides, then makes a judgement about the correct outcome.

Conciliation: an independent person encourages both sides to a dispute to get together to talk through their differences. The conciliator helps the process but makes no judgements about the right outcome.

Feedback: obtaining a response to a communication, perhaps including an element of judgement (e.g. praise for a job well done).

Vertical communications: messages passing freely from the bottom to the top of the organisation, and from the top to the bottom.

A Revision questions (35 marks; 35 minutes)

1 Explain why good communications within a firm are important. (3)

2 Explain why feedback is important for successful communications. (3)

3 State three actions a firm could take in order to improve the effectiveness of communication. (3)

4 Identify three reasons why communications may be poorer in large firms than in small ones. (3)

5 Explain why good communication is an important part of motivating employees. (4)

6 How might a business benefit from a successful works council? (4)

7 Why might an employee cooperative have better employer/employee relations than a public company? (4)

8 Why is it so important to a union to gain recognition from employers? (4)

9 Outline the role of ACAS. (4)

10 Distinguish 'conciliation' from 'arbitration'. (3)

B1 Data response

Employee communication

Faced with intensifying competition and an accelerating pace of change, companies are seeing effective communication with employees as an ever more important part of organisational efficiency. It is also a constructive way to harness employees' commitment, enthusiasm and ideas. However, companies tend to place considerable emphasis on communicating big but vague messages about change and company performance. It is highly debatable whether such messages are relevant to employees or easily understood by them. Employee-attitude surveys consistently highlight communication as a major source of staff dissatisfaction.

While managers tend to use communication channels that send general messages downwards, employees place more importance on mechanisms that communicate immediate and applicable information. For example, around 40% of staff found one-to-one meetings with their manager very useful while less than 5%

gave business TV the same rating. Too many businesses try to tell staff too much, leading to communications overload. Successful communication methods involved discussion and feedback, whereas business TV or company newsletters provided purely one-way messages.

Questions (30 marks; 35 minutes)

1 Outline the possible value to staff of a 'one-to-one meeting with their manager'. (5)

2 Explain why communication is more than just 'the provision of information'. (5)

3 Explain why staff disliked business TV or company newsletters. (4)

4 Examine the importance of good communication within *either* a McDonald's restaurant *or* a supermarket. (7)

5 Discuss the problems that can occur when employees are dissatisfied. (9)

Case study

Honda China strike could spur broader worker demands

On Monday about 100 workers wearing white overalls and blue caps milled about the factory grounds of the Honda Lock plant, a supplier of locks to Honda's car-making operations in China, following action taken by many of the 1,500 workers on the previous Wednesday when they walked off the job. The standoff was relatively calm, in contrast to the previous week when hundreds gathered outside the gates and riot police briefly kept workers from leaving.

The strike became the latest in a series to hit factories around southern China's Pearl River Delta and a few other regions, by workers demanding a greater piece of China's growing economic pie. Commentator Liu Kaiming explained that:

> We've already seen a growing number of strikes in previous years, especially in 2007 and 2008, when the new labour contract law was introduced, and then there was a gap in 2009, but now we're seeing the trend resume.

> The Honda strike is an extension of that ... It also shows that there is a trend that is being driven by a new generation of migrant workers. They are more willing to speak out about their grievances, and are less tolerant of long hours and tough conditions than the older generation.

The strike at Honda Lock was the third to hit a Honda parts supplier in China in the last few weeks. The other two, at suppliers producing transmissions and exhausts, were settled after employees received wage increases.

Management at Honda Lock has offered a pay increase of 100 yuan ($15) in additional wages and another 100 yuan in allowances, but some employees at the plant said that is not enough.

'I'm more optimistic now we'll get more of a wage rise', said one worker leaving the factory on a bicycle on Monday. 'They urged us to resume work for the next few days and some assembly lines are working again.' Stories of employer intimidation have been balanced by rumours of sabotage of equipment by some employees.

Chang Kai, dean of the school of labour relations at Remin University in Beijing, said in an interview with the Chinese media that employers rarely considered how to link the development of businesses and of employees.

'What many of our businesses think about is how to cut costs, how to lower wages', he said. 'Collective negotiations are also not mature. There is no appropriate framework for them, nor are there means for applying pressure.'

Source: Adapted from Reuters, 14 June 2010.

Questions (35 marks; 40 minutes)

1 From the article, explain why the factory workers might benefit from belonging to a trade union. (8)

2 Examine the state of employer/employee relations at this Chinese supplier to Honda. (12)

3 At present, independent trade unions are banned in China. Discuss whether the progress of Chinese industry would be helped or hindered by allowing trade unions to represent workers, when both management and employees were happy to sign an agreement. (15)

Essay questions (40 marks each)

1 Consider the view that effective communications is at the heart of successful operations management.

2 'Greater competitiveness and higher profits in the future will depend upon much more employee participation than in the past.' Critically assess this statement.

3 'Good managers welcome trade unions as a way of improving workplace performance.' Discuss.

28 Integrated people in organisations

Human resources strategy: an overview

Some writers like to suggest that modern managers have a more enlightened view of staff than did their counterparts in the past. Sadly, there is little evidence of this. For every well-run firm with motivated staff there are businesses with staff who are frustrated or resentful. Good management of staff remains the single best way to succeed as a business. Yet it remains difficult.

As is clear from the Terminal 5 case study (see exercise B2 in the Workbook section below), the management of staff at British Airways has long been unsatisfactory. There has always been a 'them and us' culture that creates a barrier between management and the workforce. Many hospitals and colleges would say the same thing.

The underlying problem remains what Douglas McGregor (nearly 50 years ago) called Theory X and Y. Too many managers view their own staff with suspicion. This leads them to adopt 'hard HRM' practices such as incentive schemes, temporary contracts, and the regular setting and monitoring of targets. Most staff want to be trusted, involved, respected and paid a regular (and 'good') salary. Hard HR managers assume that everyone is motivated by money, and that without careful monitoring they may be too lazy to achieve anything.

Managing human resources successfully involves a delicate and continuous balancing between meeting the various needs and aspirations of employees and meeting the objectives of the business itself. Clearly, day-to-day personnel functions such as recruitment, training and appraisal still need to be carried out. However, any human resources strategy needs to be integrated into a firm's overall corporate planning if it is to develop and utilise its employees effectively. Firms also need to recognise that human resource strategies cannot be 'written in stone' but will be constantly evolving, shaped by events within the firm and also those in the external environment.

Issue 1: human resources holds the key to achieving competitive advantage

For most companies, long-term success relies not on screwing costs down to the last penny, but on constantly finding better ways to do things. Motivated marketing managers can find opportunities for new products, and can identify innovative ways to promote them. Operations staff who really care about what they are doing take pride in running trains on time or in delivering a truckload of biscuits on time to Asda. Better still, if you have a bright, enthusiastic staff, not only do your customers tend to notice (especially for service businesses) but also you find better and better people applying for jobs with you.

The better you can handle your people, the better able the firm will be to fight or beat the competition.

Issue 2: downsizing, delayering and outsourcing

Whenever the economy moves sideways or backwards instead of forwards, cost pressures can pile up. The drive to remain competitive increases the desire to create businesses that are as lean and flexible as possible. Suddenly firms start using terms such as 'downsizing' and 'delayering' as more elegant ways of saying that they are reducing staff numbers in order to cut costs. Downsizing means cutting staff throughout the business; delayering means cutting overhead costs by removing a complete management layer from the hierarchy. This would force senior staff to delegate more, as it will increase the span of control within which they have been working.

However, cost-cutting exercises produce one-off results that cannot be repeated year after year. Furthermore, firms may experience problems in meeting customer requirements due to skills shortages and quality shortfalls. This has led to a recognition that firms need to strike a balance between financial viability, on the one hand, and effective workforce planning on the other.

A Revision questions (80 marks; 80 minutes)

1 Explain what is meant by the term labour productivity. (3)

2 Outline two reasons why a firm would aim to increase labour productivity. (4)

3 Identify two possible human resource objectives for a mobile phone operator embarking on a programme of rapid expansion in order to keep up with increasing demand. (4)

4 Explain the difference between 'hard' and 'soft' human resources management. (5)

5 Identify three factors that might have an influence on the way a firm manages its human resources. (3)

6 Outline two benefits to a firm from developing a human resources strategy. (4)

7 What is the main purpose of workforce planning? (3)

8 Identify and briefly explain one internal and one external influence on the process of workforce planning. (4)

9 Explain what is meant by the term 'delayering'. (3)

10 Examine one advantage and one disadvantage to a firm from creating a flatter organisational structure. (6)

11 Briefly explain the meaning of the term 'centralised organisational structure'. (3)

12 Suggest two reasons why a business might adopt a centralised approach. (2)

13 Outline two implications for a firm moving from a centralised to a more decentralised structure. (4)

14 Briefly explain, using examples, what is meant by the term 'flexible workforce'. (3)

15 Analyse one potential benefit and one potential problem resulting from a firm attempting to create a more flexible workforce. (6)

16 Explain why maintaining effective communication with employees is important to a rapidly expanding business. (3)

17 Outline two benefits to a firm of increased employee participation in decision making. (4)

18 Outline three methods that a business could adopt to increase the level of employee participation. (6)

19 Examine one advantage and one disadvantage to an employer of collective bargaining. (6)

20 Describe two reasons why a car manufacturer such as PSA Peugeot Citroën would set up works councils. (4)

B1 Data response

Labour markets and regulation

The World Bank's 2011 report on 'Doing Business' includes some data about people at work. It implicitly assumes that 'ease of doing business' is always a good thing, even if it implies awful conditions for employees. Nevertheless, it provides an interesting insight into similarities and differences between China and India. This may serve to overcome the assumption that workers in China are more exploited than in India. The real situation is more nuanced. As shown in the data given in Table 28.1, there is even a case for saying that Chinese workers are better off – in some ways – than American workers.

Table 28.1 Comparison of labour markets in China, India, UK and the US

	China	India	UK	US
Monthly minimum wage for a 19-year-old (US$)	$160	$24	$1,805	$1,253
Maximum period allowed for fixed-term employment contracts	No limit	No limit	No limit	No limit
Minimum paid annual leave (days)	6 days	15 days	28 days	0 days
Government approval required if 9+ workers are to be dismissed	No	Yes	No	No
Notice period for redundancy	4.3 weeks	4.3 weeks	5.3 weeks	None
Severance pay for redundancy	23.1 weeks of salary	11.4 weeks of salary	2.6 weeks of salary	None

Source: World Bank, *Doing Business* 2011.

Questions *(30 marks; 35 minutes)*

1 Table 28.1 shows that the US labour market is liberalised and therefore employers have minimal regulations to restrict their actions.

   a Explain why employers may like having such a deregulated, flexible labour market. (6)

   b Explain why a deregulated, flexible labour market may not be in the interests of staff. (6)

2 Explain the significance to an employer of the figures for 'severance pay for redundancy'. (6)

3. The UK's new coalition government believes that the supply side of the economy can be improved by removing laws affecting employment. Discuss whether the UK's workforce would benefit in the long term from the removal of minimum wage legislation. (12)

Case study

BA's Terminal 5 fiasco

On the morning of 27 March 2008, every UK national newspaper carried articles on the wonderful new terminal opening at Heathrow that morning. BAA (the airport's operator) was proud that it had been finished on time and on budget. British Airways, with sole use of Terminal 5, looked forward to its huge advantage over every other airline – as they were all stuck in the scruffy, over-used Terminals 1–4. Everything was set for a public relations triumph.

But no one told the staff.

Baggage handlers from Terminals 1–3 arrived for their 4 o'clock shift to find insufficient parking, tough new security systems and huge changes to their working practices. The real chaos began when the new baggage-handling system started up. Many of the 400 British Airways' handlers were not only unable to find their workstations but were also unfamiliar with the new system:

'Only 50 or so of 400 baggage handlers had been fully trained when the terminal opened.'* Quickly overwhelmed, chaos struck as aircraft left without luggage and a baggage mountain of 25,000 items soon built up. Day after day of chaos followed, with flights being cancelled to allow the still fragile baggage systems to work.

How could this happen? After all, even a new system in an existing workplace can be hard to bed in. Here, three separate workforces were being uprooted and put into a brand new workplace, with brand new systems. Surely, with effective training and trialling, it should be possible?

When difficulties strike a business, the key thing is to have committed, involved staff with the power to make the necessary changes. At British Airways there has been a long history of suspicion between management and the workforce. The *Financial Times* reported that, 'While goodwill and staff flexibility are vital to any company experiencing the kind of minute-by-minute difficulties that have hit Terminal 5, they are often in short supply.'

On 5 April, the *Financial Times* ran an article reflecting on the chaos. It interviewed (anonymously) many senior managers at British Airways and BAA. Although there were elements of bad luck involved, the main message involved the culture of the workplace and the style of leadership. The paper said of British Airways:

Its failure to prepare staff for the move was compounded by a management culture that left them reluctant to raise concerns with the airline's abrasive boss, Willie Walsh ... A number of insiders said that he expected to be brought solutions rather than problems: 'He will have been told what he wanted to hear.'

* *Financial Times*, 5 April 2008, p. 5.

Questions *(30 marks; 35 minutes)*

1 Examine two key failures of human resource management in British Airways' move to Terminal 5. (8)

2 Outline two possible explanations of why 'only 50 or so of 400 baggage handlers had been fully trained' by British Airways. (4)

3 Explain the importance within a business of 'management culture'. (3)

4 To what extent should responsibility for a failure such as this be put at the door of chief executive Willie Walsh? (15)

29 Key AS issues in operations management

Definition

The AQA specification for A2 Marketing states:

This section considers the operational objectives and strategies that a business may use to achieve success in its particular market. It builds upon AS operations materials.

Introduction

In your study of operations management at AS level you will have come across three key ideas.

1 Effective operations: working with suppliers, for customers

2 Quality

3 Capacity utilisation.

It would be useful if you were to review these areas to gain a background for your A2 study of this part of the specification.

Effective operations

Customer service

From your AS studies it is useful to remember the importance of customer service from a very general perspective. Just as the best referees are unnoticed, so are the best waiters. And when ordering something online, no one wants to use the 'Customer Service Helpdesk'. People want to place their order with as few 'clicks' and as little fuss as possible. So great customer service is provided by clever design and planning.

Dealing with suppliers

It also helps to see a firm's relationship with its suppliers as a broad issue. It is not just a matter of good communications and efficient workings. There are also a series of ethical issues to consider: how honest and open is the relationship? Or are your suppliers a bit too generous with hospitality? And what of the conditions they impose (or allow) among *their* suppliers, perhaps working in Cambodia or Vietnam. Does your firm keep its mouth shut and eyes closed? Or does it press to understand more about working conditions?

Quality

Here, the key is to divide quality as an objective, manageable factor (e.g. my car's gearbox is built to last twice as long as yours) from quality as a matter of image and opinion. Within the AS syllabus the focus was on output quality, as achieved by quality control or quality assurance. This is important, but

starts to be really significant when image factors are also taken into account. Lexus cars regularly win awards for quality – and are seen by customers as worth paying extra for – because of their quality. In other words the key A2 skill is to mix quality in operations with quality as a marketing message or theme.

Capacity utilisation

All firms have a limit to the amount they can produce. It will be rare for a firm to be working at full capacity. In fact, it is probably unwise to work at full capacity, as this would imply the firm had no ability to increase output to meet any sudden surge in demand.

It would not help the firm, though, if it has too much capacity standing idle. The firm's fixed costs would be spread across a limited output, increasing the average cost of production, perhaps to a level where the firm would have difficulty in competing successfully in their market.

If a firm found itself with too much spare capacity, it has two choices:

1 reduce its capacity so that the amount being produced represents a high level of utilisation

2 increase its usage, perhaps by introducing a new product or carrying through an extension strategy on an existing one.

Most firms realise that demand for their products will never be stable enough to guarantee high capacity utilisation. Therefore they look for one of three main approaches. Two identified in the AS syllabus are: a flexible workforce or sub-contracting (see below). The third option is the one used by firms such as Innocent Drinks or Cobra Beer. They actually produce nothing themselves. Everything is outsourced, i.e. produced by a supplier, perhaps in a different, lower-cost country. This means they take on none of the risks involved in the production process; but, arguably, it means they lack full knowledge and understanding of the product itself.

AS reminder

Sub-contracting: this implies getting a supplier to take on part of a supply process for you. Often it is that you keep your own capacity at, say, 1,000 units a month, knowing that this figure is usually as low as it gets. Therefore you can keep your own factory working close to 100% capacity utilisation all the time. This keeps your **fixed costs per unit** as low as possible. When demand exceeds 1,000 units you get your sub-contractor to supply; the sub-contractor may charge a lot more per unit than it costs you to produce, yet you have the security of knowing that you can produce efficiently, even in hard times.

Flexible workforce: an alternative is to produce everything yourself, but using, in effect, different classes of worker. You employ the staff you need to produce 1,000 units a month. If demand rises above that level, you employ temporary or part-time staff to increase supply (perhaps on a night-shift). This might be needed for seasonal reasons, e.g. department stores hiring extra staff pre-Christmas. Your full-timers have a secure future; your flexible staff can be pushed aside when times are tough. Professor Charles Handy uses the terms **core** and **peripheral** workers to sum this situation up.

A Test yourself questions *(40 marks; 50 minutes)*

1 Honda produces its 'Jazz' car at its Swindon factory. It has decided to ask the Japanese supplier of the gearboxes to set up its own factory near to Swindon.
   a Outline two reasons why Honda wants a supplier it knows rather than a British gearbox-maker. (4)
   b Explain one reason why it might be helpful to have the supplier nearby instead of importing the gearboxes from Japan. (3)

2 For her birthday Claire went with a group of friends to a restaurant before going on to a night club. The restaurant waiting staff were friendly but made some mistakes. Claire's steak was rare instead of well done and Charli was handed the birthday cake by mistake. The dinner took far too long to serve, which irritated everyone.
   a Outline two pieces of poor customer service at the restaurant. (4)
   b Explain why the restaurant managers need to correct these faults. (4)
   c Explain how they might set about correcting the faults. (4)

3 Explain the difference between quality control and quality assurance. (4)

4 Explain why the adoption of Total Quality Management might have an impact on the culture within a business. (3)

5 A firm currently produces 6,000 units per week. It has a capacity of 9,000 units per week.
   a What is its capacity utilisation? (2)
   b State and explain two ways in which this firm's capacity utilisation could be improved. (6)

6 In 2011 there were 4.5 million seats available for plays at West End theatres in London; 3.15 million tickets were sold during the year.
   a What was the capacity utilisation? (2)
   b In the same year, capacity utilisation at ballet performances was 80%. Identify two benefits ballet companies will have enjoyed compared with those producing plays. (4)

30 Understanding operational objectives

Definition
Operational objectives are the specific, detailed production targets set by an organisation to ensure that its overall company goals are achieved.

Introduction

All organisations share common operational objectives, regardless of their size and the sector in which they operate. Ensuring that these objectives are met is vital in order to satisfy customer needs and compete effectively within the marketplace. All firms will attempt to produce goods and services that are 'fit for purpose', delivered quickly and on time. They will also aim to produce the right number of goods as cheaply as possible, bearing in mind the overall strategy.

If, like Ryanair, your target is to be the lowest-cost airline in Europe, every cost will be shaved to the minimum. If your business strategy is to be the highest-rated airline in the world (such as Singapore Airlines), you may accept costs that will seem high to other airlines. The crucial thing is that a firm's operational objectives must be fully in line with its objectives regarding marketing and its management of its people.

Finally, there needs to be enough flexibility within operations to allow activities to be varied or adapted quickly in order to accommodate changes in demand.

Key operational objectives

The key operational objectives are shown in Figure 30.1 and described below.

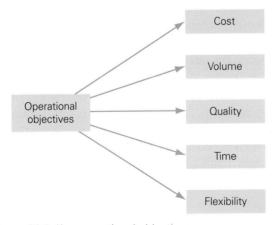

Figure 30.1 Key operational objectives

Cost

All firms are concerned with keeping costs down, particularly those that compete directly on price. Not only do costs determine what is charged to the customer – and, therefore, a firm's ability to compete – but also the profits that can be generated. During a period of economic downturn, a firm's ability to make further cost reductions can mean the difference between survival and failure. Costs are determined by the **efficiency** of a business. This can be measured in a number of ways – for example, wastage rates or the **productivity** of the workforce.

Cost cutting at Kingfisher pushes profits up

A programme of tight stock control and direct sourcing from manufacturers helped Kingfisher, the owner of DIY retailer B&Q, to increase its profits for the first half of 2010, despite tough trading conditions and disappointing sales figures. B&Q, which is responsible for 40% of Kingfisher's sales turnover, experienced a fall in like-for-like sales of 3.7% to £2.3 billion in the six months to July 2010. However, retail profit at B&Q increased by 15% to £171 million over the same period. Kingfisher has been sourcing its goods directly from manufacturers for two years. The direct sourcing plan relies on the company's combined group buying power to source common products that can be sold in its stores across the world.

Source: *Financial Times*, 16 September 2010

Volume

Ensuring that goods and services are made available in the right quantities may seem obvious but, in reality, this will require a firm to make decisions and commit resources now based on predictions of future demand. Overestimating the volume required is likely to lead to wasted goods, increased stock-holding costs and price cutting. On the other hand, underestimating the amount of products required will mean missed sales opportunities and customer dissatisfaction.

Quality

The exact meaning of quality for any individual organisation will depend to some extent on the nature of its operations. Put simply, quality is about getting things 'right' by meeting or beating customer expectations over and over again. Quality has a crucial role to play in guaranteeing customer satisfaction. Not only should firms aim to produce goods or services that are 'fit for purpose', they also need to create a sense of dependability by ensuring that products are ready when customers expect them. Failure to do so is likely to create customer dissatisfaction and encourage customers to switch to rival products. A high degree of quality and dependability

is also required within the organisation. Managers need to ensure that quality standards are being met. They also need to synchronise production so that products pass smoothly from one stage to the next. This will help to reduce production time and costs, meaning that goods are ready for dispatch to customers sooner.

Time

This factor is important in many ways, both to the consumer and the producer. Many consumers are 'money-rich, time-poor', as they rush from a well-paid job to pick up the kids, eat, then go out. So operations that can save time for the customer can be very successful (e.g. Tesco online grocery shopping, pizza delivery). Time-based management is also important to firms in product development. Stung by the success of the Toyota Prius, General Motors was desperate to get the first mass-market electric-only car out by 2010. By developing a successful pollution-free car before anyone else, the company was confident that it could regain its position as the world's number one car producer. At the time of writing, the company's first electric car, the Chevrolet Volt, was expected to be launched in the United States before the end of 2010. This will be followed by the launch of the Vauxhall Ampera, which is based on the same technology as the Colt, in European markets in 2011 and the UK in 2012.

The firm that is first to market is able to charge higher prices than its slower rivals. Speed is also important within the business. The faster items pass through the production process, the lower the costs of warehousing materials and work-in-progress.

Flexibility

Firms need to be able to vary the volume of production relatively easily, in order to respond effectively to unexpected increases or decreases in demand. The ability to adapt or modify a standard product range allows a firm to appear to be offering customised products that meet customer needs more precisely, but still benefit from high volume production, keeping costs down. This flexible approach to production is a form of **lean production** that has been used successfully by a number of companies, including computer manufacturer Dell.

Lean production reaches sportswear

Nike became the first sportswear manufacturer to embrace the concept of lean production when it established a new online design facility. Nike iD allows customers to create their own versions of a range of footwear and clothing. Customers follow a step-by-step customisation process, picking from a choice of colours and materials, and adding logos, names and personalised messages in order to create a 'unique' product. The customised goods are manufactured and delivered within four weeks of an order being placed. A 'teamlocker' version of the service also exists, offering the facility to sports teams and groups. The success of the concept has been followed up with the opening of a number of Nike iD Studios around the world, including London's Oxford Street. Each studio has a team of qualified design consultants on hand to help customers make their choices.

Source: www.nike.com

The importance of innovation

Innovation means more than merely inventing a new product or process – it involves turning a new idea into a commercial success. Innovation within operations is crucial to the long-term survival and growth of a firm, allowing it to keep ahead of the competition. New products will often require new production methods and machinery. New processes for producing existing goods or delivering services can help to reduce costs and improve the quality and speed of production.

In 2003, stung by the success of the European Airbus project, Boeing announced a new 'Dreamliner' plane that would fly 250 passengers longer distances non-stop than ever before. It would also be 20% more fuel-efficient than ever before because of a series of innovations. Up to 50% of the plane would be made from super-strong, but super-light 'composite' materials instead of traditional aluminium. And by getting suppliers to produce a one-piece fuselage (instead of the traditional two-pieces-then-weld) 1,500 aluminium sheets and 40,000–50,000 fasteners are eliminated from each plane. With 900 firm orders for this $150 million plane, it has become the most successful product launch in aviation history. (By the way, 900 × $150 million is $135,000 million!)

Figure 30.2 Boeing Dreamliner

The impact on operations of environmental objectives

The adoption of environmental policies by a firm will have a number of implications for its operations. For instance, it may mean that the business will need to change its supplies of materials to those that come from replenishable or recycled sources. It may need to adopt new processes that are more energy efficient, and produce less waste and pollution. Even the methods of transportation used to bring in materials and deliver goods to customers may need to be investigated in an attempt to reduce congestion. Furthermore, staff will need appropriate training in order to ensure that these policies achieve their objectives.

Influences on operational objectives

The nature of the product

The product is at the heart of any firm's operations, so its nature will obviously dictate operational objectives. For example, car manufacturers such as BMW and Mercedes have a long-established reputation for high standards of quality, which must be taken into account when developing new models.

Demand

The level and nature of demand will act as a major influence on operational objectives. A business must attempt to predict sales volumes and any likely fluctuations, in order to ensure that customer expectations are met in a cost-effective manner.

Availability of resources

A lack of availability of the right level and quality of resources, including human resources, can act as a major constraint in attempting to achieve operational objectives. For example, skills shortages in a number of industries in the UK, including healthcare, has led to a reliance on workers from abroad. Similarly, a shortage of financial resources will act as a constraint on the achievement of operational objectives.

Competitors' behaviour

Few firms have the luxury of operating alone in a market and no firm, however successful, can afford to become complacent. Rival firms will strive to increase their market share, and their activities are likely to have a major influence on operational objectives.

Issues for analysis

Opportunities for analysis are likely to focus on the following areas:

- considering the factors likely to permit or prevent a business from achieving its operational objectives
- examining the implications for a given business of repeatedly achieving key operations

- analysing the potential consequences for a business of failing to meet key operational objectives.

Understanding operational objectives – an evaluation

The effective management of operations is central to the success of any business, regardless of its size or the sector in which it operates. The key to this is a clear understanding of what the business is attempting to achieve. The establishment and communication of appropriate operational objectives is, therefore, vital in order to develop the strategies required to deliver this success.

> ### Key terms
>
> **Efficiency:** refers to how effectively a firm uses its resources. It can be measured in a number of ways, including labour productivity and wastage rates.
>
> **Innovation:** this means taking an idea for a new product or process and turning it into a commercial success.
>
> **Lean production:** instead of mass producing, it produces goods to order and therefore satisfies the customer while helping the firm avoid stockpiles of unsold stock.
>
> **Productivity:** measures how efficiently a firm turns inputs into the production process into output. The most commonly used measure is labour productivity, which looks at output per worker.

A Revision questions *(45 marks; 45 minutes)*

1 Explain what is meant by the term 'operational objectives'. (3)

2 Outline two reasons why it is important for a business to keep its costs as low as possible. (4)

3 Analyse the main consequences for a firm of failing to accurately forecast the volume of production required to meet demand. (6)

4 Briefly explain what is meant by 'quality' for a car manufacturer such as Mercedes. (4)

5 Choose *one* of the following businesses. Outline two possible ways in which it delivers quality to its customers.
   a Electronics manufacturer Sony

   b Luxury hotel chain Ritz-Carlton
   c Discount retailer, Aldi. (6)

6 Examine two key benefits for a firm that develops a reputation for quality. (6)

7 Give two reasons why a firm might aim to achieve a high degree of flexibility in its operations. (2)

8 Explain, using examples, what is meant by the term 'lean production'. (4)

9 Analyse two ways in which a business can benefit from a commitment to innovation. (6)

10 Outline one advantage and one disadvantage for a business from establishing environmental objectives. (4)

B1 Data response

New methods of reaching customers at Morrisons

Rising petrol prices, continued food price inflation and fears of falling consumer confidence and spending during 2010 served to further intensify pressure in the UK's already fiercely competitive grocery market. In response, Morrisons, the UK's fourth largest supermarket chain, revealed a range of initiatives designed to increase efficiencies and secure growth. The retailer announced its intention to enter the internet grocery market in the first half of 2011, joining rivals Tesco, Sainsbury's, Asda and Waitrose who all have established online ordering and delivery. Morrisons planned to trial the online service first, in order to gauge the likelihood of its success. According to the grocery industry group, IGD, the UK grocery home shopping market, currently worth £3 billion, is forecast to be worth around £7.5 billion by 2014.

Morrisons also revealed its decision to expand into the convenience sector of the grocery market by opening three stores of less than 3,000 square feet in the first half of 2011. By 2010, Tesco already had over 1,600 convenience stores, The Co-operative Group had around 2,000 and Sainsbury's had 335. Although Marks & Spencer and Waitrose also have a presence in the convenience market, the large chains only accounted for 6% of the 48,000 convenience stores in the UK. Other initiatives announced by Morrisons included an expansion of its own food production (the company owns 13 manufacturing sites), increasing the number of own-label goods on offer, trimming down ranges and streamlining its store supply line.

Source: *The Independent.*

Questions *(25 marks; 30 minutes)*

1 Analyse the key factors that are likely to have influenced Morrisons' decision to set up an online grocery shopping service. (10)

2 Re-read the section headed 'Key operational objectives' in this unit, then discuss Morrisons' likely operational objectives when entering the convenience sector of the grocery market. (15)

Case study

Renault targets the cheap mass market

2009 and 2010 saw a boom in Europe-wide sales of Dacia cars. When Renault bought Dacia in 1999, many commentators thought the French company had made a big mistake. Dacia's productivity was low and profits were non-existent. After a decade of hard work, Renault is enjoying a payback on its investment. Dacia's no-frills Logan saloon has a price tag of the equivalent of around £5,000, while the Logan estate sells for the equivalent of £6,000. Both models are targeted at customers who would normally opt to buy second-hand, rather than a brand new car.

The cars are made at Renault's Dacia plant in Romania. The Logan was originally intended to be sold in Romania only, but proved to be a huge success in both France and Germany, with waiting lists of customers eager to get hold of the car. Annual output at the plant was increased by the company from 200,000 in 2006 to 350,000 in 2008. Although workers at the Dacia plant are highly skilled, the production process is low-tech. However, the main reason behind the car's cheap price is low labour costs – a Romanian car worker gets paid an average of £170 per month, an eighth of the pay of equivalent workers in France.

Source: *BBC News*.

Questions *(20 marks; 25 minutes)*

1 Examine Renault's operational objectives in launching its Logan car range. (8)

2 To what extent do you agree that the other major car manufacturers will be forced to follow Renault and target the low-cost segment of the market? (12)

Operational strategies: economies and diseconomies of scale; optimum resource mix

> **Definition**
> Economies of scale are factors which cause average unit costs to fall as the scale of output increases in the long run. Diseconomies of scale are factors causing average costs to rise as the scale of output increases in the long run.

Two ways firms can grow

1 *Internal growth* occurs when a firm expands its own sales and output. Firms growing in this manner must invest in new machinery and usually take on extra labour too. Firms that are successful in achieving internal growth have to be competitive. Companies like Ryanair and Nike have grown rapidly by taking market share from their less efficient competitors.

2 *External growth* is created by takeover and merger activity. In October 2010 John W Henry, owner of the Boston Red Sox baseball team, bought Liverpool FC for just over £300 million. This meant a sudden increase in the scale of

Henry's business and gave him access to the global market represented by Premier League football.

There are many reasons why firms may wish to grow by takeover or merger. One of the most significant is that many managers believe growth will create cost savings for their firms. They anticipate benefiting from economies of scale. Unfortunately, this is not always true. Many mergers and takeovers actually reduce efficiency. Any economies of scale prove to be outweighed by diseconomies. Research has shown consistently that, on average, takeovers and mergers fail to improve efficiency.

Economies of scale

When a firm grows there are some things it can do more efficiently. The group term given to these factors is 'economies of scale'. When firms experience economies of scale their unit costs fall. For example, a pottery which could produce 100 vases at £5 each may be able to produce 1,000 vases at £4.50 per unit. The total cost rises (from £500 to £4,500) but the cost per unit falls. Assuming

the firm sells the vases for £6 each, the profit margin rises from £1 per vase to £1.50. Economies of scale are, in effect, the benefits of being big. Therefore, for small firms, they represent a threat. If a large-scale producer of televisions can sell them for £99 and still make a profit, there may be no chance for the small guy. There are five main economies of scale. These are discussed below.

Bulk-buying economies

As a firm grows larger it will have to order more raw materials and components. This is likely to mean an increase in the average order size the firm places with its suppliers. Large orders are more profitable to the supplier. Both the buyer and the potential suppliers are aware of this. Consequently, firms who can place large orders have significant market power. The larger the order the larger the opportunity cost of losing it. Therefore the supplier has a big incentive to offer a discount. Big multinational manufacturers like Volkswagen have been relentless in demanding larger discounts from their component suppliers. This has helped Volkswagen reduce its variable costs per car.

Technical economies of scale

When supplying a product or service there is usually more than one production method that could be used. As a firm grows it will usually have a greater desire and a greater ability to invest in new technology. Using more machinery and less labour will usually generate cost savings. Second, the new machinery may well be less wasteful. Reducing the quantity of raw materials being wasted will cut the firm's variable costs.

These cost savings may not be available to smaller firms. They may lack the financial resources required to purchase the machinery. Even if the firm did have the money it may still not invest. Technology only becomes viable to use if the firm has a long enough production run to spread out the fixed costs of the equipment. For example, a small company may wish to buy a new computer. As the firm is small it may end up using it for only two days a week. The total cost of the computer will be the same whether the firm uses it one day or five days per week. So the average cost of each job done will be high as the small firm is unable to make full use of its investment. Capital investment becomes more viable as a firm grows because capital costs per unit fall as usage rises.

Specialisation

When firms grow there is greater potential for managers to specialise in particular tasks. For instance, large firms will probably have enough financial work to warrant employing a full-time accountant. In many small firms the owner has to make numerous decisions, some of which he or she may have little knowledge of, for example accounting. This means the quality of decision making in large firms could be better than in small firms. If fewer mistakes are made, large firms should gain a cost advantage. See Figure 31.1.

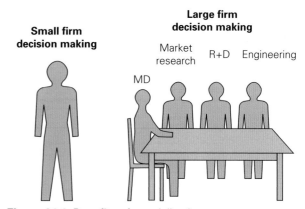

Small firm decision making

Large firm decision making

Market research   R+D   Engineering

MD

Figure 31.1 Benefits of specialisation

Financial economies of scale

Many small firms find it difficult to obtain finance. Even if banks are willing to lend, they will tend to charge very high rates of interest. This is because logic and experience shows that lending to small (especially new) firms is more risky. They are more likely to go into liquidation than large firms. There are two main reasons for this.

1 Successful small firms grow into large firms. Consequently, large firms tend to have more

established products and have experienced teams of managers.

2 Small firms are often over-reliant on one product or one customer; larger firms' risks are more widely spread.

The result of all this is that large firms find it far easier to find potential lenders. Second, they also pay lower rates of interest.

Marketing economies of scale

Every aspect of marketing is expensive. Probably the most expensive, though, is the sales force.

These are the people who visit wholesale and retail outlets to try to persuade them to stock the firm's goods. In order for a firm to cover the country, nothing less than six sales staff would be realistic. Yet that would cost a firm around £200,000 per year. For a small firm with sales of under £1 million a year, this would be a crippling cost. Larger firms can spread the costs over multi-million sales, cutting the costs per unit.

Other benefits of size

Apart from achieving cost-reducing economies of scale there are some other benefits attached to size.

Reduced risk

If a firm grows by diversifying into new markets it will become less dependent on one product. A recession might cause sales in one area of a business to fall. However, if the firm also manufactures products which sell strongly in recessions, the overall turnover of the organisation may change little. In recent years a high percentage of takeovers and mergers have involved firms operating in totally different industries. When Volvo bought out Procordia, a firm in the processed food business, Volvo was seeking a wider product base. This helps the company to avoid the risk inherent in 'having all your eggs in one basket'.

Increased capacity utilisation

Some firms may wish to grow in order to increase their **capacity utilisation**. This measures the firm's current output as a percentage of the maximum the firm can produce. Increasing capacity utilisation will spread the fixed costs over more units of output. This lowers the total cost per unit.

So if a fall in demand for chocolate meant that Cadbury's factories were under-utilised, it might be tempted to launch a new product to try to get better use of its factory space.

Diseconomies of scale

When firms grow, costs rise. But why should costs *per unit* rise? This is because growth can also create diseconomies of scale. Diseconomies of scale are factors that tend to push unit costs up. Large organisations face three main types of diseconomy of scale.

Poor employee motivation

When firms grow, staff may have less personal contact with management. In large organisations there is often a sense of alienation. If staff believe that their efforts are going unnoticed a sense of despondency may spread. A falling level of work effort will increase the firm's costs. Poor motivation

will make staff work less hard when they are actually at work. Absenteeism is also a consequence of poor motivation. This means that the firm may have to employ more staff to cover for the staff they expect to be absent on any given day. In both cases, output per worker will fall. As a result, labour costs per unit will rise.

Poor communication

Communication can be a significant problem when a firm grows. First, effective communication is dependent on high levels of motivation. Communication is only effective if the person being communicated with is willing to listen. If growth has left the workforce with a feeling of alienation, communication can deteriorate alongside productivity. A second reason for poor communication in large organisations is that the methods chosen to communicate may be less effective. As a firm grows it may become necessary to use written forms of communication more frequently. Unlike verbal communication, written communication is less personal and therefore less motivating. Written messages are easier to ignore and provide less feedback. Relying too much on written forms of communication could result in an increase in the number of expensive mistakes being made.

Poor managerial coordination

In a small firm coordination is easy. The boss decides what the goals are, and who is doing what. As firms grow, it becomes harder for the person at the top to control and coordinate effectively. The leader who refuses to **delegate** 'drowns' under the weight of work. The leader who delegates finds (later) that manager A is heading in a slightly different direction from manager B. Regular meetings are arranged to try to keep everyone focused on the same goals through the same strategy. But not only are such meetings expensive, they are also often poorly attended and lead to grumbles rather than insight. Coordination works well and cheaply in a small firm, but is expensive and often ineffective in large corporations.

Optimum resource mix

It is important to realise that growth normally creates both economies and diseconomies of scale. If growth creates more economies than diseconomies then unit costs will fall. On the other hand, if the growth creates more diseconomies, the opposite will happen (see Figure 31.2).

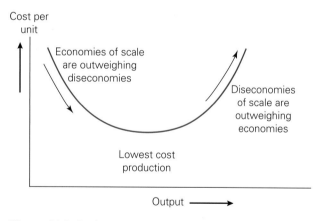

Figure 31.2 Optimum resource mix

Logically there is an ideal level of output at which the maximum economies of scale are not yet outweighed by diseconomies. This point is the 'optimum resource mix'; Figure 31.2 shows that this is the output level that yields the lowest unit (average) costs. For a manufacturer such as Renault,

this point might be the production of 1 million cars per year. For a small service business there may be few economies of scale. If so, the disadvantages of size soon outweigh the benefits. A small advertising agency may start to lose its teamwork and effectiveness beyond a staff level of 50 people and a sales revenue of £25 million a year.

This implies that every boss of every business should beware of growth for growth's sake. A firm that grows beyond its optimum resource mix risks being dragged down by inefficiency. The collapse of Woolworth's had many causes, but an underlying problem was being too big for its own good.

What can managers do about diseconomies of scale?

Diseconomies of scale are to a certain extent inevitable. However, this does not mean that managers should just accept them. With careful planning, many diseconomies may be minimised or avoided completely. They key point is that diseconomies are more likely to arise either when growth is unplanned, or when it is too rapid. When a firm embarks on a programme of growth it is vital that managers recognise the need to change and adapt. See Table 31.1.

Table 31.1 Action that may be taken by managers to rectify diseconomies of scale

Diseconomies of scale	Corrective action required
Poor motivation	Delegate decision-making power Job enrichment Split the business up by using the following: ● profit centres ● autonomous work groups
Poor communication	Improve employee motivation as above Send managers on attitudinal training courses Create new communication structures such as works councils
Poor coordination	Decentralise Empower employees Wider spans of control

 ## Issues for analysis

'Economies of scale' is a concept used frequently by students in examinations. When using it to analyse a business situation, the following points should be considered.

● In most business circumstances, a rise in demand cuts average costs because of improved capacity utilisation. In other words, if a half-used factory gets a big order, unit costs fall because the fixed overheads are spread over more output. This is great, but should not be referred to as an economy of scale. It is simply an increase in capacity utilisation. The term 'economies of scale' refers to increases in the scale of operation (e.g. when a firm moves to new, bigger premises).

● The cost advantages from bulk buying can be considerable, but are often exaggerated. A medium-sized builder can buy bricks at much the same cost per brick as a multinational construction company. It should also be remembered that materials and components form quite a low proportion of the total costs for many products. For cosmetics or pharmaceuticals, bought-in materials would usually cost less than one-tenth of the selling price of the product. So lively minds dreaming up new products will count for far more than minor savings from bulk buying.

● Traditionally, managers of growing or merging companies have tended to predict economies of scale with confidence, but to turn a blind eye to diseconomies. In the medium to long term, though, managerial problems of coping with huge organisations have tended to create more diseconomies than economies of scale.

 ## Economies and diseconomies of scale – an evaluation

Three important issues should be considered:

1 If diseconomies are all people problems, why can't they be better managed? Most diseconomies of scale are caused by an inability to manage people effectively. When firms grow managers must be willing to delegate power in an attempt to avoid the problems caused by alienation. Some types of manager might find it hard to accept the need for delegation. If the manager has strong status needs and has **Theory X** attitudes, he or she may find it difficult to cope.

Enriching jobs and running training courses are expensive in the short term. These costs are also easy to quantify financially. The benefits of job enrichment and training are more long term. Second, they are harder to quantify financially. This means that it can be quite hard for the managers of a company to push through the changes required to minimise the damage created by diseconomies of scale. Public limited companies may find this a particular problem. Their shares can be bought freely and sold on the stock market. This means that considerable pressure is put on the managers to achieve consistently good financial results. The penalty for investing too much in any one year could be a falling share price and an increased risk of takeover.

2 Do economies of scale make it impossible for small firms to survive? In highly competitive markets it is difficult for small firms to compete with large established businesses, especially if they try to compete with them in the mass market. In this situation the small firm will lose out nine times out of ten. The small firm will not be able to achieve the same economies of scale. As a result, its prices will have to be higher to compensate for its higher costs.

To a degree this view is correct. However, the fact that the majority of firms within the economy have less than 200 employees proves that small firms do find ways of surviving, despite the existence of economies of scale.

3 The importance of being unimportant. Many small firms do not need economies of scale to survive. They rely upon the fact that they do not compete head on with their larger competitors. Small firms often produce a highly specialised product. These products are well differentiated. This means the small firm can charge higher prices. So even though they have higher costs their profit margins can be healthy. The larger firms in the industry are frequently not interested in launching their own specialist products. They believe there is more money to be made from the much larger mass market. By operating in these smaller so-called niche markets, many small firms not only survive but often prosper. By being small and by operating in tiny market segments they are not seen as a threat to the larger firms. As a consequence, they are ignored because large firms see them as unimportant.

Key terms

Capacity utilisation: actual output as a proportion of maximum capacity.

Capital investment: expenditure on fixed assets such as machinery.

Delegate: hand power down the hierarchy to junior managers or workers.

Theory X: Douglas McGregor's category for managers who think of workers as lazy and money-focused.

 Revision questions (40 marks; 40 minutes)

1 Identify three managerial motives for growth. (3)

2 State two possible benefits of specialisation. (2)

3 Explain why large companies are frequently able to command larger discounts from their suppliers than are smaller firms. (4)

4 Outline two diseconomies of scale that might harm the profitability of a night club that opens a chain of 12 night clubs. (4)

5 Explain the likely consequences for a large firm of a failure to control and coordinate the business effectively. (4)

6 Many car manufacturers like Nissan are attempting to reduce the complexity of their designs by using fewer parts in different models. With reference to the concept of economies of scale, explain why this is happening. (4)

7 Give three reasons why employee morale can deteriorate as a consequence of growth. (3)

8 Outline three ways in which managers could tackle these morale problems. (6)

9 Explain how economies of scale could give a firm such as Ryanair a considerable marketing advantage. (5)

10 Explain 'the importance of being unimportant' to a small producer of luxury ice cream that competes locally with Ben & Jerry's (owned by the giant Unilever, which also owns Wall's). (5)

Data response

Geoff Horsfield and his sister Alex are worried about whether they can compete effectively with their big local competitor, Bracewell plc. Alex believes that Bracewell's economies of scale mean that Horsfield Trading cannot compete head-on. Therefore she wants to switch the company's marketing approach away from the mass market towards smaller niches.

Geoff is not sure about this. He knows that Bracewell has a more up-to-date manufacturing technique, but has heard of inefficiencies in the warehousing and office staff. He doubts that Bracewell is as efficient as Alex supposes. Therefore he argues that Horsfield Trading can still compete in the mass market.

Fortunately, the employment of an accountant from Bracewell plc has enabled direct comparisons to be made. These figures, shown in Table 31.2, should help Geoff and Alex to decide on Horsfield's future strategy.

Questions *(30 marks; 35 minutes)*

1 Calculate the capital investment per employee at each company. What do the figures tell you? (6)

2 Outline the probable reasons for Alex's wish to aim at smaller market niches. (5)

3 a What explanations may there be for the differences between the guarantee claims of each business? (8)

  b What may be the short- and long-term effects of these differences? (6)

4 Outline any other evidence in the case of diseconomies of scale at Bracewell plc. (5)

Table 31.2 Comparison of Horsfield Trading Ltd and Bracewell plc

	Horsfield Trading Ltd	Bracewell plc
Capital investment	£240,000	£880,000
Factory employees	28	49
Other employees	7	21
Guarantee claims per 100 sales	1.2	2.1
Output per employee (units per day)	21	23

Case study

Burgers – big or small

Despite concerns about obesity the UK market for fast food is still growing. The market leader in the UK is still McDonald's which has 1,225 UK outlets. The sheer scale of McDonald's UK operation creates significant economies of scale. For example, by rolling out the brand across the UK, McDonald's has managed to create substantial marketing economies of scale. Economies of scale enjoyed by large dominant companies can make life extremely tough for smaller companies, battling to make headway in the same market.

A new entrant to the UK fast-food market dominated by McDonald's is the Gourmet Burger Kitchen. The business was set up by three New Zealanders who spotted a gap in the UK market for premium quality gourmet burgers, freshly prepared to order. In addition to a standard burger and chips, the GBK menu also includes more esoteric items such as a chorizo spicy Spanish burger and a hot chicken satay sandwich. On average a burger at GBK costs from £8 to £10.

In 2010 GBK had just 54 restaurants in the UK, most of which were located in the Greater London area. The company has already won several 'Best burger' and 'Best eats' awards in the capital. The management of the Gourmet Burger Kitchen has set an objective of growth. In five years' time they want to have 350 restaurants in the UK.

Business analysts believe that GBK programme of growth could yield substantially more economies of scale than diseconomies of scale.

Questions *(35 marks; 40 minutes)*

1 What is meant by the term 'economies of scale?' (2)

2 Explain why economies of scale are important to companies such as McDonald's and GBK. (7)

3 a What are marketing economies of scale? (2)

   b Explain two reasons why McDonald's will be able to achieve more marketing economies of scale than GBK. (4)

4 Identify and explain two additional economies of scale that the GBK might be able to benefit from if they manage to achieve their objective of having 350 UK outlets. (6)

5 Explain two diseconomies of scale that could affect GBK if it manages to achieve its growth targets. (6)

6 Examine one strategy that a small company such as GBK could use to compete effectively against a larger firm, such as McDonald's. (8)

Case study

The Tata Nano: India's very own Model T Ford

Economies of scale are very important to car manufacturers. For example, manufacturers that produce in high volumes will tend to have lower bought-in component costs because these mass producers enjoy market power over component suppliers. Technical economies of scale are also important too. Niche market manufacturers will not have the sales volumes needed to dilute the high fixed costs of purchasing modern capital that has the potential to drive down average cost.

Over one hundred years ago, Henry Ford recognised the power of economies of scale in terms of their ability to create mass markets. Ford realised that price cuts were needed to make cars affordable for the average American family. Cost saving economies of scale made these price cuts possible, without any loss of profit margin. Additional sales created by lower prices created a bigger market. Production increased, creating more economies of scale, which made a second round of price cuts possible – a virtuous circle was created.

Price cuts → Rising sales → Economies of scale → Lower unit costs → Price cuts

Figure 31.4 The virtuous circle

By UK standards, India is still a poor country. In 2010 per capita income in India was less than $3,000 per year. With incomes this low one would expect car sales in India to be relatively low. However, they are not! In 2009 over 1 million new cars were sold in India. Furthermore,

Figure 31.3 The Tata Nano

the market is also growing very rapidly too. In 2010 the Indian car market is expected to grow by 50%.

The growth increase in demand for cars in India can be partially explained by macroeconomic factors. The 'global financial crisis' has not had much of an impact on the Indian economy, which is still expanding at over 8% per year, creating a gap in the market for a cheap family car for India's growing middle-class. This gap in the market was filled in 2008 by the Indian car maker, Tata, who launched the now world-famous Nano, which sells for the equivalent of just $2,000. The Nano is a simple no-frills car that is extremely cheap to mass produce. For example, the car's boot does not open, it does not have power-steering and only has one, rather than two windscreen wipers and wing-mirrors.

Car ownership in India is still very low, just 13 in every 1,000 Indians own a car. In Britain the corresponding figure is 450 cars. The Indian car market is far from being saturated, and the long-term growth prospects for this market look very good, especially if the Indian economy continues to grow at its current rate. A rapidly growing economy and car market will create the possibility for more economies of scale for the likes of Tata. The $2,000 Nano could get even cheaper. In short, Tata stands a very good chance of being able to replicate the virtuous circle achieved by Henry Ford over a century ago.

Questions *(30 marks; 35 minutes)*

1 Explain the meaning of the term 'economies of scale'. (3)

2 To equip the Nano, Tata buys windscreen wiper blades from the German supplier, Bosch. Explain why, over time, Tata might be able to impose cuts in the price it pays to Bosch. (6)

3 Explain how economies of scale can create a competitive advantage. (6)

4 Sales of the Tata have been growing rapidly in India. Discuss the implications of this trend for Tata's stakeholders (15)

C Essay questions *(40 marks each)*

1 Small firms are often said to have better internal communications than larger organisations. Does this mean that growth will always create communication problems? If so what can be done about these difficulties?

2 MHK plc is a large manufacturer of semiconductors. Discuss the opportunities and problems it may face if it decides on a strategy of growth through centralising production.

3 Given the existence of economies of scale, how do small firms manage to survive?

Research and development and innovation

Definition

Research and development (R&D) is scientific research and technical development. Innovation means using a new idea in the marketplace or the workplace.

 ## Introduction to innovation

New ideas and inventions are not the only job for the R&D department. The idea must be developed into a usable process or a marketable product. Not only will the R&D specialists need to be involved in this process, but also the other main functional areas of the business will need to help out too.

Innovation and finance

Invention, innovation and design all require significant amounts of long-term investment. Innovation takes time, and that time is spent by highly paid researchers. The result is that firms who are unwilling to accept long payback periods are unlikely to be innovators. Short-termist companies are far more likely to copy other firms' successes. In fact, much of the money spent by firms on invention and innovation provides no direct payback. Ideas are researched and developed before discovering that they will not succeed in the marketplace. The result is that innovation is something of a hit-and-miss process. There are no guaranteed rewards, but the possibility of a brand new, market-changing product. It is these successes that can radically alter the competitive conditions within a marketplace, allowing an innovative company to claim a dominant position.

Innovation and people

Inventors are sometimes caricatured as 'mad scientists' working alone in laboratories with bubbling test tubes. This is far from the truth. For many years, firms have realised that team working provides many of the most successful innovations. As a result, research teams are encouraged to share their breakthroughs on a regular basis in the hope that the team can put their ideas together to create a successful product. These research teams are often created by taking specialists in various different fields of operation, from different departments within an organisation. This means that a team may consist of several scientists, an accountant, a production specialist and someone from the marketing department. This blend of expertise will enable the team to identify cost-effective, marketable new ideas that can be produced by the company, without the need for the new idea to be passed around the different departments within an organisation.

Invention, innovation and production

As mentioned previously, invention and innovation are not limited to finished products. New production processes can be invented or developed. These can lead to more efficient, cheaper or higher-quality production. Furthermore, new products often need new machinery and processes to be developed for their manufacture. Design is also important in production. The process needs to be thought through clearly so that every machine and activity has a logical place in the production system.

Innovation and marketing

Many would argue that the most important element of the marketing mix is the product itself. Successful product development keeps a firm one step ahead of the competition. This usually means keeping one step ahead in pricing as well. Whether you are introducing a new drug such as Viagra or a new football management computer game, you have the opportunity to charge a premium price. Innovative new products are also very likely to get good distribution. Tesco is very reluctant to find space on its shelves for just another ('me-too') cola or toothpaste, but if the new product is truly innovative, the space will be found.

Research and development is carried out by companies in order to develop new products or improve existing products. Larger firms, particularly multinational companies, will tend to have separate research and development facilities. These will be staffed by highly trained scientists, usually working towards developing products to a specific brief.

Product-orientated firms are likely to focus on areas of scientific expertise and push their researchers to produce the most technically advanced product possible. For market-orientated firms, the research brief will largely be influenced by the needs of consumers and any gaps identified in the market. However, it is important to note that R&D is *not* market research.

As can be seen from Figure 32.1, some industries see particularly heavy R&D spending. One in particular is the pharmaceutical industry. These companies spend vast quantities of money, researching new drugs or cures for diseases. Developing a new product in this market can generate millions of pounds of revenue for many years.

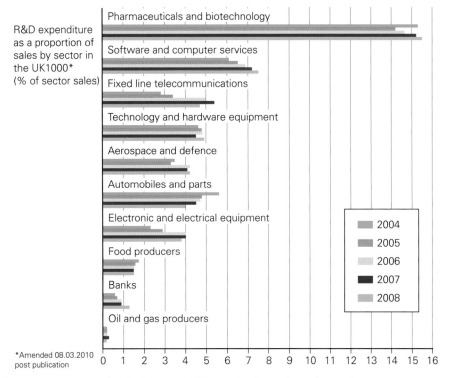

Figure 32.1 R&D as a percentage of sales in some UK manufacturing industry sectors

Source: Department for Business Innovation and Skills – R&D scoreboard www.innovation.gov.uk/rd_scoreboard/

Protecting new ideas

There are three main avenues open to firms whose R&D produces useful outcomes.

1 *Patents:* a patent is the exclusive right to use an invention. Patents can last for up to 20 years. Patents are a commodity that can be bought, sold, hired or licensed.

2 *Registered designs:* designs can be protected in two ways. Design right gives a weaker form of protection than a patent, but registered designs

can be used only by the firm or individual holding the registration. The registration can last for up to 25 years and, just like a patent, can be bought or sold.

3 *Trademarks:* a trademark allows a firm to differentiate itself, or its products, from its competitors. Most trademarks are words or symbols, or a combination, but sounds and smells can be registered as trademarks too. Registration of a trademark is denoted by the symbol ®.

Benefits of successful R&D

- *Monopoly:* successful innovation, assuming it is protected by a patent, creates a monopoly. Such a situation, in which there is only one supplier of a particular type or product, offers huge benefits to the successful innovator.

- *High price:* with no competition, the selling price can be set high to cream off revenue from customers who want the product. This pricing strategy of skimming the market allows the firm to reduce its prices as it anticipates competitors arriving, perhaps as a result of finding an

alternative way to make the product, or the expiry of the patent.

- *Reputation:* innovators tend to have a positive reputation in the minds of consumers. Sony's development of the first ever personal stereo occurred over 30 years ago, yet it has maintained the impetus that this innovation bought by continuing to develop 'cutting edge' products and kept the benefit of being seen as a pacesetter in the consumer electronics market.

A-grade application

Pharmaceutical giant Eli Lilly believes it has found an answer to the problem of financing the development of new wonder drugs. It is widely said that bringing a new heart or cancer drug to the market can cost upwards of $1.3 billion. And as it can take 8 years of trials to prove that the drug is safe, firms may have only 12 years of patent life in which to get their money back.

In February 2011 Eli Lilly announced successful trials of a financing system in which a venture capital company funds most of the development work. If it's a success, Lilly would then pay royalties to the financier. Lilly's head of research said this supports the firm's innovation strategy, which is based on 'molecule uniqueness, speed and cost efficiency'.

Unsuccessful R&D

The problem with spending huge amounts of money on research and development is that it carries no guaranteed return. New scientific developments may prove to be unusable in the market. Perhaps the idea is one that nobody actually wants or, alternatively, the firm may not be able to find a way to put its new idea into large-scale production at a viable cost. It is this problem that explains perhaps the major stumbling block to R&D budgets: very few firms are willing to invest when there is not a measurable return. The nature of R&D requires substantial sums to pay for the scientific expertise and equipment needed and, therefore, the only firms willing and able to invest in R&D are likely to be very large firms that also have a management team committed to long-term, rather than short-term, success.

R&D and international competitiveness

Innovation is a crucial factor in determining the international competitiveness of a country's businesses. A country whose companies invest heavily in R&D is likely to find its economy healthy as its firms find

Table 32.1 Selected countries' R&D as a percentage of GDP

Rank	Country	R&D as a % of GDP
1	Sweden	3.7
2=	Finland	3.5
2=	South Korea	3.5
4	Japan	3.4
5	Iceland	2.8
6	United States	2.7
7=	Denmark	2.6
7=	Germany	2.6
7=	Singapore	2.6
10	Austria	2.5
11	Canada	2.0
12	Belgium	1.9
13	United Kingdom	1.8
14	Slovenia	1.5

Source: World Bank, 2010.

success in export markets and have the innovative products needed to stave off import competition in their home market. It may therefore come as something of a worry to UK readers to see the UK in 13th place in the world league of R&D shown in Table 32.1. The implications of this are far reaching and serious for the UK. With higher costs of manufacturing than many countries, allied with a failure to innovate, the UK may struggle to find a genuine competitive advantage in the twenty-first century's global marketplace. This could spell economic stagnation.

Issues for analysis

- Invention should not be confused with innovation. The British have a proud record as inventors. Hovercraft, television, penicillin, Viagra and many more products were British inventions. In recent years, however, there has been less success in this country with innovation. The Japanese have been the great innovators in electronics, the Americans in computers and the Swiss in watches. British firms have failed to invest sufficiently to develop ranges of really innovative new products.

- Major innovation can completely change a firm's competitive environment. The market shares of leading companies may change little for years, then an innovation comes along that changes everything. The firm that has not prepared for such change can be swept aside. This has happened to music stores that have not established a major presence on the internet.

- Good management means looking ahead, not only to the next hill but the one after that. Anticipation makes change manageable. It may even ensure that your own firm becomes market leader due to the far-sightedness of your own innovation. In turn, that would ensure high product differentiation and allow relatively high prices to be charged.

- Innovation can happen in management procedures, attitudes and styles. A management that is progressive and adventurous might well find that an empowered workforce is generating the new ideas that seemed lacking before. It would not be wise to assume that invention and innovation is all about scientists and engineering. It is about people.

Figure 32.2 Hovercraft (British invention)

Innovation and research and development – an evaluation

The fundamental theme for evaluating any question involving invention and innovation is long- and short-term thinking. Invention and innovation are long-term activities. Companies whose objective is short-term profit maximisation are unlikely to spend heavily on innovation. However, a firm with objectives directly related to producing innovative products is likely to spend heavily on research. GlaxoSmithKline, Britain's highest spender on R&D (£3.96 billion in 2010), is an excellent example.

Most British companies do not have a particularly impressive record in invention and innovation. Table 32.1 shows that a comparison of international R&D spending places Britain outside the top ten. The conclusion must be that short-termism is a particular problem in Britain. An unhealthy focus on success in the short term does not fit in with a commitment to expensive R&D, designed to ensure long-term growth. As a result, British firms have a tendency to please their shareholders with high dividend payments, rather than retaining profits for investment in R&D.

Selling innovative products is not the only way to build a successful business. Many firms carve out a successful segment of their market based on selling copycat products at lower prices and their ability to cut costs to the bone, maintaining a satisfactory profit margin. However, these low-cost firms tend to be based in countries with lower labour costs than the UK. Other costs in the UK, such as property and business services, are also high relative to international rivals and, therefore, this low-cost strategy is unlikely to work for many UK firms trying to compete internationally. As a result, it seems likely that the continued survival of major UK multinationals is dependent on producing innovative products based on successful R&D.

A Revision questions (40 marks; 40 minutes)

1 Distinguish between product and process innovation. (3)

2 Why is it 'vital' to patent an invention? (3)

3 Explain why R&D has an opportunity cost. (2)

4 Briefly explain the role of each of the following departments in the process of successfully bringing a new product to market.
   a Marketing
   b Finance
   c HR. (12)

5 Why might product-orientated firms produce more inventions than market-orientated ones? (4)

6 How are the concepts of short-termism and innovation linked? (4)

7 What effect would a lack of innovation have on a company's product portfolio? (4)

8 Many businesses are concerned at the fall in the number of students taking science A-levels. How might this affect firms in the long term? (4)

9 Explain how a firm may try to market a brand new type of product developed from successful R&D. (4)

B1 Case study

Mach 3: at the cutting edge of technology

Gillette's UK research and development facility is located just outside Reading. Men in white coats test revolutionary shaving technologies – all searching for the perfect shaving experience. From its position of UK market dominance (57% market share), which has been based on innovation, including the launch in 1971 of the world's first twin-bladed razor, Gillette is pushing forward the frontiers of shaving technology. The newest model to have been developed by Gillette is the Mach 3. The new product has been described as the 'Porsche of the shaving world', with its sleek design, and its hefty price tag of £4.99 for the handle and two cartridges. The Mach 3 was advertised in America as the 'billion-dollar blade'. However, this was probably an underestimate of the costs incurred during the razor's seven-year development:

● $750 million (£440 million) on building the production system for the razor
● $300 million on the launch marketing
● $200 per year on research and development.

Gillette expects to sell 1.2 billion units of the Mach 3 per year.

The testing regime for Gillette's new products involves a product evaluation group of more than 3,000 men throughout the UK, who are supplied with Gillette products and provide feedback on the level of quality consistency, in addition to testing experimental products. Among these guinea pigs are the mysterious men who turn up at the research facility in Reading every morning – paid for the shaving risks they take there and performing the role of test pilots – sworn to secrecy on the new technology they are using.

The building, an old jam factory, is kitted out with the latest CAD technology. Research focuses on computer models of human skin – a substance that Gillette has found very tough to model accurately. However, its current modelling is the most accurate it has ever used and skin irritation is measured using the same laser technology as that employed in police radar guns. The jam factory was the birthplace of the Mach 3, a birth heralded by success in the long-running attempt to add a third blade without causing blood loss. With sales of the Mach 3 starting off at encouraging levels, the old jam factory appears to have turned out another winning idea.

Questions *(40 marks; 45 minutes)*

1 Using examples from the text, suggest what marketing advantages arise from successful innovation. (8)

2 Describe the pre-launch testing methods used by Gillette, and explain why these are so vital to success. (9)

3 Why might the research laboratories for a product as ordinary as a razor be shrouded in secrecy? (6)

4 Using examples from the Gillette story, explain why successful innovation requires input from all departments within a firm, not just the research and development department. (12)

5 Given the information in the text, how long will it take Gillette to recover the research, development and launch costs of the Mach 3, if running costs average out to £2.99 per unit? (5)

Case study

R&D in pottery

Josiah Wedgwood & Sons Ltd is part of the huge Waterford Wedgwood company formed by the takeover of ceramics firm Wedgwood by the Irish glass manufacturer Waterford Crystal. Despite a history dating back hundreds of years, Wedgwood still needs to carry out R&D to maintain its position in a hugely competitive global market. As is so common for many major British brands, Wedgwood can survive in the global market only by offering top-quality products at reasonable prices. In the push to bring costs down without sacrificing quality of design, Wedgwood has developed a brand new piece of machinery that is able to print intricate designs on non-flat surfaces (i.e. cups). Previously, patterns were applied to cups by hand as decals (stickers). New decals took around four weeks to produce, while the application of the decals pushed the lead time for a new design up to 16 weeks. The machine has enabled direct printing onto cups and therefore reduced lead times to just one week for new designs. In addition to far quicker delivery to customers, the machine has significantly reduced material and labour costs while maintaining high-quality products. Wedgwood identified three key factors in the success of the machine's development:

1 management commitment was critical to a potentially high-impact yet risky project in which each machine cost over €0.5 million

2 development engineers with the experience to develop radical new approaches and machinery

3 collaboration between technical, production and engineering departments.

Source: adapted from: www.manufacturing foundation.org.uk

Questions *(30 marks; 35 minutes)*

1 Analyse the financial benefits that Wedgwood will receive as a result of the new machine. (8)

2 Briefly explain how the new machines should provide marketing benefits. (4)

3 Analyse the likely reaction of staff to the development of the new machine. (6)

4 Consider how the case demonstrates the need for collaboration of different departments in successful R&D. (12)

Essay questions *(40 marks each)*

1 To what extent does an innovative product guarantee success?

2 'Any business has two, and only two, basic functions. Marketing and innovation.' Discuss whether there is value in this statement by Peter Drucker.

3 'Luck is the most important factor in successful innovation.' Discuss the validity of this statement.

4 'Spending on research and development is wasted money since many firms find success through copying other firms' products.' Discuss this statement.

Industrial and international location

> ### Definition
> The site(s) where a firm decides to carry out its operations.

The location decision

This unit looks at the expansion or relocation of a business, including decisions relating to international location.

The choice of location for a business is crucial to its success. Opting for the 'right' location can help keep costs of production low while generating higher revenue from sales than alternative sites. For instance, costs can be reduced by opting for cheaper premises, closer proximity to suppliers or locating in an area with effective transport links. High-street locations make retailers more visible to customers and are more likely to attract sales.

Once a firm is established, there are two main reasons why managers may be faced with making a location decision.

1 It may be the result, for example, of a decision to expand operations by operating as a multi-site organisation, acquiring additional factories, offices or outlets. This can help to increase capacity and sales, and it may also help the business to recognise and respond to local market conditions more effectively. However, the business may require a new structure in order to continue to perform effectively, and a duplication of certain functions and job roles – especially at management level – can lead to increased overheads.

2 It may also result from a decision to relocate operations to a new site – one that may be in a position to attract more customers, offer better opportunities for modernisation or lead to a reduction in operating costs. Before going ahead, however, the business needs to consider the costs of relocation as well as the benefits. For example, will existing employees accept the move or leave the firm, leading to increased recruitment costs and a loss of expertise?

Making the choice: quantitative methods

If Boeing wants to set up its first aircraft factory in Europe, it is clear that there are some key issues to do with numbers. It will need a massive site, which might have a cost ranging from £50 to £300 million, depending where it is. Then there are wages, which might range from £300 to £1500 per person per month, depending on whether the location is eastern Poland or western Germany.

Given its importance to the success of a business, it is vital that the location decision is based on accurate data. There are a number of quantitative decision-making techniques that can be used, including those discussed below.

Investment appraisal

This refers to a set of techniques that can be used to assess the viability of a project (i.e. will the expected returns from the relocation site meet or exceed corporate targets?). Alternatively, they can be used to help choose between two or more sites for expansion or relocation that are under consideration. For example:

- *payback* provides information on how quickly the investment costs of a project will be recovered from expected revenues or cost savings

- *average rate of return (ARR)* calculates the average annual profit generated by a project, expressed as a percentage of the sum invested.

Ideally, the results of any analysis using **investment appraisal** techniques would present a business

with the location that enjoyed the quickest payback period and highest ARR. This is unlikely in reality, so the choice will be based on the individual firm's circumstances. A firm faced with liquidity problems, for example, is likely to go for the option with the quickest payback. (See Unit 13 for more information on investment appraisal.)

Break-even analysis

Calculating the break-even point tells a firm how much it needs to produce and sell in order to avoid making a loss, given its current level of fixed costs and contribution per unit. Fixed costs will include rent on premises (or the interest charged on loans for land purchase), business rates and staff salaries, whereas the cost of raw materials and transportation may be regarded as variable. A prime location that improves image or the level of convenience offered may mean that products can be sold at higher prices. Clearly, differences in these costs between locations are likely to have a significant effect on a firm's break-even level of output and sales and, therefore, the overall profitability of a project.

Formula reminder:

$$\text{break-even point} = \frac{\text{fixed costs}}{\text{contribution per unit}}$$

Qualitative factors

There are a number of other factors that, although less easy to measure in terms of their impact on costs and profitability, can have an important influence on the eventual choice of location for a business. Many entrepreneurs may have chosen to locate near to where they live and remain there, despite the potential financial benefits of relocating elsewhere. Many borough councils and regional development agencies aim to tempt businesses into relocating by offering a better quality of life for owners and employees.

The reputation of a particular location and its association with a particular industry may continue to act as an incentive, encouraging new firms to locate there. This may continue even after the original reasons for doing so are no longer significant (known as **industrial inertia**). The concentration of an industry in a particular area may lead to a number of **external economies of scale**, including the availability of suitably skilled workers and locally based suppliers.

Making the optimal decision

Every manager faced with a decision hopes to make the best decision in the circumstances. With location, however, it is impossible to know what is the 'best'. In the 1990s Honda chose to establish a factory in Pakistan instead of India, believing that the Pakistan economy had better growth prospects. Only when its Pakistan factory was struggling in 2008 did Honda acknowledge that it should have focused on India.

All a manager can hope to do is make the most sensible decision in the circumstances, accepting that it might be five or twenty years before anyone really knows whether it was the right thing to do. This is known as an '**optimal** decision': striking a sensible balance between varying pressures. In Europe, for example, instead of choosing the lowest-cost location in eastern Romania, or the location with the highest availability of skilled staff (in Germany), the optimal decision may be to strike a balance, choosing a location in Portugal.

An optimal decision will bear in mind quantitative and qualitative factors, and probably be based on careful and detailed research, but also consultation with managers and workers.

A firm's location decision is likely to be influenced by several factors. Some can be quantified but many cannot. The factors may include:

- the cost and suitability of the site
- access to customers
- access to supplies
- access to workers – either highly skilled or low-cost, or some combination of the two
- quality of the area's infrastructure
- availability of government assistance.

A-grade application

In February 2011 Kosei Pharmaceutical of Japan opened offices in Slough, near Heathrow airport. Its initial staffing included 13 from west London, though the two 'bosses' were from Japan. Kosei spent nearly two years deciding where to locate, in its first move away from Japan. It looked at China and America, but decided on Europe and then on Britain. Critical was the openness of the UK market to both imports and exports (with Europe the planned trading partner). The final decision of Slough was influenced by the airport, but also by relatively low property rental costs, the quality of schools available nearby (for the families of the two senior Japanese staff) and on legal matters to do with immigration and business regulations.

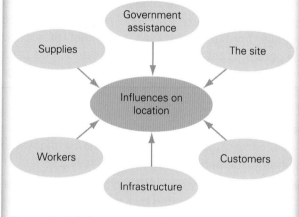

Figure 33.1 Influences on a firm's location

International location

A **multinational** organisation is a business with production facilities in a number of different countries. There are a number of ways in which a firm's operations may develop an international dimension. These include the following.

To exploit new markets

A firm operating in a slow-growth or saturated domestic market might decide to target foreign customers in order to generate new sales. Alternatively, developing a number of overseas markets should protect a business to some extent from recession and falling demand at home. Either way, locating closer to overseas customers will help firms to recognise and understand differing tastes and requirements.

To benefit from greater economies of scale

An increase in a firm's scale of production may lead to a reduction in unit costs, perhaps as a result of receiving discounts for buying larger quantities of raw materials. Lower average costs should lead to an improvement in competitiveness by allowing firms to lower prices or generate funds for new product development. However, the extent to which a firm may benefit from economies of scale depends on whether it can produce standardised products to meet demand across a range of markets, or whether differences in tastes require significant modifications.

To benefit from cheaper labour costs

Taking advantage of large pools of cheap, unskilled labour is a long-established practice of UK manufacturers relocating low-skill production processes to developing countries in order to reduce costs. However, the growing supply of young, well-educated workers in low-wage economies, especially in Asia, has stimulated the relocation of many industries in both the secondary and service sectors (see Table 33.1). Moreover, the latest expansions of the European Union have given UK firms access to relatively low-cost locations in Poland, Romania and the Czech Republic, with the additional protection of a common legal system.

To benefit from cheaper land and reduced transportation costs

Cheaper land and taxes (as well as fewer legal restrictions on issues such as health and safety and employment law) in other countries may permit a firm to reduce its fixed costs. These may be offered as an inducement to attract foreign investment by national governments. In addition, there may be further significant cost savings to be enjoyed by relocating overseas, in order to be closer to either suppliers or customers. The economies gained by being closer to key suppliers in the Far East and

Figure 33.2 Dyson factory, Wiltshire

new markets in Japan and Australia was one of the main reasons given by James Dyson for the relocation of his company's production activities from Malmesbury, Wiltshire, to Malaysia (see data response B1 on page 226).

To minimise the impact of exchange rate fluctuations

The revenue and costs of firms producing in the UK and exporting to or importing from overseas will be subject to exchange rate fluctuations. For example, an appreciation in the value of sterling against the euro is likely to lead to a loss of sales for UK exporters to markets within the eurozone. This is because the increased euro price will lead to a fall in demand. Alternatively, a cut in the euro price in order to maintain demand will lead to a reduction in revenue per unit sold. Moving production to a location within the eurozone would offer protection from such fluctuations.

To overcome trade barriers

National governments and international trading blocs use a number of measures to protect domestic industries and markets from competition from foreign firms. These may include **quotas**, **tariffs** or **non-tariff barriers**. For example, the European Union uses a range of protectionist measures against goods from outside the area that act to increase prices and reduce demand. Companies from non-member states can, however, overcome these trade barriers and gain free access to EU markets by locating production facilities within its boundaries.

Table 33.1 Comparative pay rates between India and the UK

Occupation	Salary in India	% of UK salary
Call centre operator	90p to £1.25 per hour	13–20%
Top law graduate	£4,700 per year	11–14%
Farm worker	£500 per year	5%

Source: various, October 2010.

Offshoring

In the past few years, the practice of **offshoring**, where firms transfer aspects of their operations from high-cost to low-cost countries, has become a controversial issue in the UK. In particular, concerns about the number of jobs lost from the domestic economy have generated a great deal of media coverage and trades union campaigning. The majority of the activities 'offshored' to date have included call centres and software development, as well as **business process outsourcing** (BPO) of tasks such as payroll processing. However, the trend is increasingly towards the transfer of higher-value jobs, such as those in research and development (R&D) and financial services. These activities are either carried out in company-owned facilities or outsourced to separate firms based in low-cost countries. Currently, the main offshore bases include India, China, Poland, Russia, South Africa and Brazil. India has proved to be a particularly attractive destination for UK businesses looking to offshore activities, producing over 2 million English-speaking graduates every year.

Potential problems of international location

Although expansion or relocation of operations into overseas markets can offer a number of benefits, firms must also be aware of the potential problems that can arise, including those described below.

Language and cultural differences

Given that barriers to communication can exist within firms employing workers that speak the same language, it is not difficult to imagine the potential problems and costs associated with managing an international, multilingual workforce. UK firms have benefited from the fact that English is commonly spoken around the world and remains the language of business. However, there are a number of differences in working practices between countries, including the length of the working week and number of public holidays, which can impact on performance and productivity.

Economic and political instability

The dynamic nature of the business environment means that firms need to be able to adjust to a certain level of change if they are to enjoy long-term success. However, rapid and unforeseen changes can pose serious challenges to survival. Because of this, firms are more likely to opt for international locations with a history of economic and political stability.

Impact on public image

A number of UK companies have attracted media attention over allegations of worker exploitation in low-cost economies, in order to keep costs down and offer cheap prices to consumers. A recent report published by War on Want claimed that workers from Bangladesh were paid less than 5p an hour (less than £80 per month) to produce clothes for UK retailers Tesco, Asda and Primark, despite all three companies being signed up to an initiative designed to provide such workers with an accepted living wage and improved living conditions.

A-grade application

UK taxes force big businesses to consider relocation

A report commissioned by HM Revenue and Customs in 2010 claimed that one in five large businesses operating in the UK were considering relocating abroad for tax reasons. The research also showed that 64% of those surveyed felt that the burden of red tape faced by large companies had also increased. At the time, the chief executives of a number of banks, including HSBC and Barclays, announced that they would seriously consider relocating their head office operations if the UK government adopted policies that were out of line with other countries.

Source: *The Daily Telegraph*.

Issues for analysis

Opportunities for analysis using this topic are likely to focus on the following areas:

- examining the advantages and disadvantages to a firm of relocating
- comparing quantitative and/or qualitative aspects of different location sites
- calculating and commenting upon the most profitable location for a firm
- analysing the factors that a business would take into account before establishing production facilities overseas.

Industrial and international location – an evaluation

Location is a key aspect of all business operations. Even in the most footloose of industries, firms cannot afford to ignore the need for sufficient quantities of appropriately skilled workers or effective transport and communications networks. The optimum location is the one that allows a business to keep costs down while maximising revenue opportunities. Once made, incorrect location decisions can be costly to put right, and can lead to customer inconvenience and dissatisfaction. However, in a dynamic and increasingly competitive environment, the pressure on firms' costs is relentless. Therefore, firms need to regularly assess the suitability of their location in order to ensure that their operational strategy continues to be effective.

Key terms

Business process outsourcing: moving administrative tasks, such as accounting and human resources management, to an external firm.

External economies of scale: cost advantages enjoyed by a firm as a result of the growth of the industry in which it is located (e.g. close proximity of a network of suppliers).

Industrial inertia: when firms continue to locate in a particular area or region even after the original advantages of doing so have disappeared.

Investment appraisal: a range of quantitative decision-making techniques used to assess investment projects, including payback, average rate of return and net present value.

Multinational: a business with productive bases – either manufacturing or assembly – in more than one country.

Non-tariff barriers: hidden barriers put in place by governments to restrict international trade without appearing to do so (e.g. insisting on technical standards that are difficult for foreign firms to meet).

Offshoring: the relocation of one or more business processes – either production or services – from one country to another.

Optimal: a decision based on the best available compromise between different objectives or factors.

Outsourcing: moving business functions from internal departments to external firms.

Quota: a trade barrier that places restrictions on the number of foreign goods that can be sold within a market in a given period of time.

Tariff: a tax placed on imports in order to increase their price and therefore discourage demand.

A Revision questions (40 marks; 40 minutes)

1 Outline two reasons why a business might choose to relocate its operations. (4)

2 Identify four factors that might influence a firm's location decision. (4)

3 Examine one advantage and one disadvantage for an estate agent that locates on a town's main high street. (6)

4 Briefly outline two quantitative methods that

could be used to help a business decide between two location sites. (4)

5 What is meant by the term industrial inertia? (2)

6 Describe one external economy of scale that might result from the concentration of an industry in a particular area. (3)

7 Recently, fashion group Burberry announced its decision to relocate production from its factory in Treorchy, Wales, to a site in Spain, Portugal, Poland or China. Examine two reasons why Burberry may have decided to relocate production overseas. (6)

8 Explain the difference between **outsourcing** and offshoring. (5)

9 Analyse two problems that a bank might experience as a result of relocating some of its business processes to the Philippines. (6)

 Data response

Dyson's Asian relocation creates UK jobs

Relocating the production of Dyson vacuums from Wiltshire to Malaysia in 2002 was seen at the time as a serious blow to UK manufacturing. The move, which was followed in 2003 by the transfer of washing machine manufacture to Malaysia by the company, resulted in the loss of 600 workers from Dyson's Malmesbury factory. Inventor and company owner, James Dyson, claimed that lower costs and proximity to both component suppliers and major markets in Japan and the United States were the key reasons for the move. The company had also been refused planning permission to expand the Malmesbury plant. According to Dyson, pre-tax profits per employee tripled within a year of the move. Between 2003 and 2005, Dyson's US sales turnover alone grew from £34 million to £100 million.

By early 2010, Dyson employed around 2,500 staff in 49 countries worldwide. The company's growth has meant that the size of its UK workforce has returned to where it had been before the relocation of production. In April 2010, it announced plans to increase the number of engineers and scientists employed at its Malmesbury headquarters from 350 to 700, taking the total number employed at the site to over 1,600. Dyson believes that investing in design and engineering is key to fighting competition from firms based in low-cost countries, such as China. According to him, '... We can never be cheaper. The only way to win is to keep ahead in terms of innovation.'

Source: The *Guardian*, This is Money, RCA website.

Questions *(25 marks; 30 minutes)*

1 Examine the key factors that were responsible for Dyson transferring the manufacture of vacuums and washing machines from the UK to Malaysia. (10)

2 To what extent do you agree with the view that UK manufacturers like Dyson have to locate production abroad in order to remain competitive? (15)

 Data response

Made in England – still!

Unlike many other UK textile firms, John Smedley continues to refuse to close down its factories and relocate its production abroad. Despite high costs and a seemingly unstoppable flow of cheap imports, the luxury knitwear manufacturer remains firmly rooted in the Derbyshire location where the business was first established over 225 years ago. According to the company, its heritage is an important part of the 'indefinable quality' of its products. The company's fine-knit wool and cotton sweaters and cardigans have long been popular with royalty and celebrities. Around 70% of its production is exported, mostly to Japan. Annual sales turnover for 2010 was around £17 million.

John Smedley's survival strategy is based on targeting a low-volume niche and competing on the grounds of quality, rather than price. The key ingredients in the manufacturing process are a highly-skilled workforce of around 450 employees, carefully sourced materials and a rigorous system of quality control. According to Dawne Stubbs, the company's creative director, the mineral springs located just behind the mill where production takes place are also responsible for the softness of the knitwear. Each garment produced has been washed in water taken from the springs since the business began in 1704.

Despite the continuing popularity of its products, John Smedley has faced a number of problems in recent years. The company continues to struggle with increasing raw materials and energy costs. A rise in the value of the pound against the yen at one point made the company's products 20% more expensive in Japanese markets. However, it rejected proposals to offshore production to China after discovering that this would result in a price reduction on average of £8 per garment.

Source: John Smedley, *BBC News*.

Questions *(18 marks; 20 minutes)*

1 To what extent do you agree with John Smedley's decision to keep production at its Derbyshire location? (18)

Case study

Relocating production at Blueberry Fashions Ltd

'It's the decision that no one wanted to face, but we have no choice.' The words of Blueberry Fashions managing director, Susanne Burrell, gradually sank into the other members of the board. Despite 12 months of a high-profile campaign that had included a number of local celebrities, the company had just announced its decision to go ahead with the closure of one of its three factories in the UK in a little over a year's time, resulting in the loss of over 350 jobs. Despite the firm's success in maintaining its reputation as one of the UK's most successful global brands in recent years, there was no escaping the fact that many of its designer items could be made at a higher quality and a significantly lower cost elsewhere in Europe. Sites in a number of locations were under consideration, but the board had yet to reach a decision.

Question *(20 marks; 25 minutes)*

1 On the basis of the evidence provided, evaluate the relocation options available to Blueberry Fashions. (20)

Appendix A Comparative figures, 2011

	Poland	Slovakia	Romania
Forecast cost of expansion (€m)	4.2	5.1	3.9
Unemployment rates %	12.8	8.6	4.1
Growth rates %	6.5	8.8	5.9

Essay questions *(40 marks each)*

1 Lord Sieff, former head of UK retailer Marks & Spencer, is reported to have once said, 'There are three important things in retailing: location, location, location.' To what extent do you agree with this view?

2 Discuss the implications for UK service-sector firms that have offshored IT or administrative functions to low-cost economies, such as India.

34 Planning operations (including CPA)

> ## Definition
> Planning how a project will be carried out to ensure that it is completed quickly, cost-efficiently and on time. A network diagram helps identify the critical path, which shows the activities that require the most careful management scrutiny.

 ## Operational planning

Operations management involves many considerations, including location, quality, stock control and information technology. Well-run firms will bring all these aspects into a single strategic plan. This should then be turned into a day-by-day plan to show supervisors and workers exactly what they should be doing. What, when and how. This kind of planning and control is fundamental to effective management. A useful model for planning an operational project is network analysis. It provides the basis for monitoring and controlling actual progress compared with the plan.

 ## Network analysis

Network analysis is a way of showing how a complex project can be completed in the shortest possible time. It identifies the activities that must be completed on time to avoid delaying the whole project (the 'critical path'). Management effort can be concentrated on ensuring that these key activities are completed on time. This leaves greater flexibility in timing the non-critical items. The objectives are to ensure customer satisfaction through good timekeeping and to minimise the wastage of resources, thereby boosting the profitability of the project.

Have you ever tried to put together some flatpack furniture? Piece of wood A has to be fitted into piece B and then screwed into C. Meanwhile, someone else can be gluing D and E together. Then ABC can be slotted into DE. (And on and on until worker/parent A is screaming at worker/parent B.) The manufacturer's instructions follow the exact logic of network analysis. This would work well, were it not that the instructions are usually set out poorly, and the 'workforce' is untrained. In business it is easier to make the technique work effectively.

A **network** shows:

- the order in which each task must be undertaken
- how long each stage should take
- the earliest date at which the later stages can start.

If a house-building firm can predict with confidence that it will be ready to put roof beams in place 80 days after the start of a project, a crane can be hired and the beams delivered for exactly that time. This minimises costs, as the crane need only be hired for the day it is needed, and improves cash flow by delaying the arrival of materials (and invoices) until they are really required.

A network consists of two components.

1 An 'activity' is part of a project that requires time and/or resources. Therefore waiting for delivery of parts is an 'activity', as is production. Activities are shown as arrows running from left to right. Their length has no significance.

2 A 'node' is the start or finish of an activity and is represented by a circle. All network diagrams start and end on a single node.

As an example, the flatpack furniture example given earlier would look as shown in Figure 34.1.

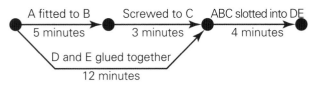

Figure 34.1 Flatpack network

How long should it take to complete this little project? Although A, B and C can be completed in 8 minutes, D and E take 12, so the final 4-minute activity can occur only after the 12th minute. Therefore the project duration is 16 minutes.

Rules for drawing networks

1 The network must start and end on a single node.

2 No lines should cross each other.

3 When drawing an activity, do not add the end node straight away; wait until you have checked which activity follows.

4 There must be no lines that are not activities.

5 Due to the need to write figures in the nodes, it is helpful to draw networks with large circles and short lines.

A-grade application

Delays can cost billions

The first commercial flight of Boeing's 780 'Dreamliner' plane took place in Autumn 2011. This was nearly eight years after the new plane was announced and more than two and a half years after the plane's first test flight. Nippon Airways had been expecting to fly its first Dreamliner in 2008, so it was kept waiting for three years!

The problem arose because of difficulties with the new lightweight materials being used in the plane. The most serious was a redesign announced in 2009 to 'reinforce an area within the side-of-body section' of the plane! The direct cost to Boeing has been estimated at more than £4 billion. The indirect effects are no less severe. Before Boeing admitted that its project was behind schedule, its European rival Airbus was struggling to sell its competitor A350 plane. In 2009 Virgin announced it was cancelling its Boeing order to buy Airbus planes. In 2010, Boeing received net orders for the Dreamliner of *minus* 4 planes, while Airbus enjoyed positive net orders for 78 A350s.

When the design problem became the critical one for Boeing, management failed to find a successful way of coping. In this case, poor critical path analysis cost Boeing billions of pounds.

Case example: the need for networks

A chocolate producer decides to run a '3p off' price promotion next February. Any need for network analysis? Surely not. What could be easier? Yet the risk of upsetting customers is massive with any promotion. What if a huge order from Tesco meant that Sainsbury's could not receive all the supplies it wanted?

Think for a moment about the activities needed to make this promotion work smoothly. It would be necessary to:

● tell the salesforce

● sell the stock into shops

● design the 'flash' packs

● estimate the sales volume for one month at 3p off

● get 'flash' packs printed

● order extra raw materials (e.g. a double order of cocoa)

● step up production

● arrange overtime for factory staff

● deliver promotional packs to shops . . .

. . . and much, much more.

An efficient manager thinks about all the activities needed, and puts them in the correct time sequence. Then a network can easily be drawn up (see Figure 34.2).

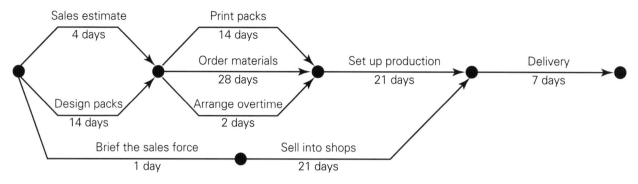

Figure 34.2 '3p off' network (1)

Once the manager has found how long each activity is likely to take, he or she can work backwards to find out when the work must start. Here, the work must start 70 days before 1 February. This is because the longest path through to the end of the project is 70 (14 + 28 + 21 + 7).

Having drawn a network, the next stage is to identify more precisely the times when particular activities can or must begin and end. To do this, it is helpful to number the nodes that connect the activities. It also makes it easier to follow if there is not too much writing on the activities. Figure 34.3 shows the 3p off example with the activities represented by letters and the nodes numbered.

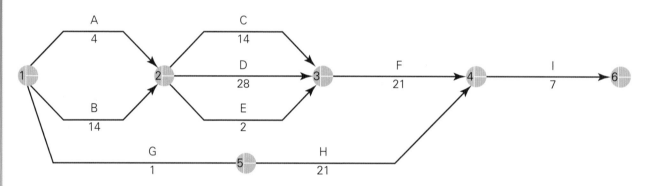

Figure 34.3 '3p off' network (2)

Earliest start times and latest finish times

Space has also been left in the nodes in Figure 34.3 for two more numbers: the earliest start time (EST) and the latest finish time (LFT). The EST shows the earliest time at which the following activities can be started. On Figure 34.3, activities C, D and E can begin only after 14 days. The reason for this is because, although A takes only four days, C, D and E need both A and B to be complete before they can

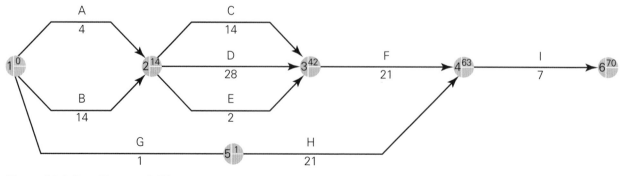

Figure 34.4 '3p off' network (3)

be started. So the EST at node 2 is the longest path through to that node (i.e. activity B's 14 days).

Figure 34.4 shows the complete network, including all the ESTs. Note that the start of a project is always taken as 0 rather than 1. Therefore activities C, D and E can start on day 0 + 14 = 14. Activity F can start on 0 + 14 + 28 = 42. And the earliest the project can be completed is by day 0 + 14 + 28 + 21 + 7 = 70.

Calculating the ESTs provides two key pieces of information:

1 the earliest date certain resources will be needed, such as skilled workers, raw materials or machinery; this avoids tying up working capital unnecessarily, for instance by buying stocks today that will not be used until next month at the earliest

2 the earliest completion date for the whole project (this is the EST on the final node).

The EST on the final node shows the earliest date at which the project can be completed. So when is the latest completion date that a manager would find acceptable? As time is money, and customers want deliveries as fast as possible, if next Wednesday is possible, the manager will set it as the latest acceptable date. This is known as the latest finish time (LFT).

The LFT shows the time by which an activity must be completed. These times are recorded in the bottom right-hand section of the nodes. The LFT shows the latest finish time of preceding activities. The number 42 in the bottom right-hand section of node 5 (Figure 34.5) shows that activity G must be finished by day 42 in order to give activities H and I time to be completed by day 70.

The LFTs on activities are calculated from right to left. In node 6 the LFT is 70, because that is the latest a manager would want the project to finish. Node 4 shows the LFT for activities F and H. Both must be finished by day 63, to leave seven days for activity I to be completed. Working back through the nodes:

- node 5 – LFT = 42, because 63 – 21 = 42; therefore activity G must be finished by day 42
- node 3 – LFT = 42, because 63 – 21 = 42; therefore activities C, D and E must be finished by day 42
- node 2 – LFT = 14, because unless A and B are finished by day 14, there will not be enough time for D to be completed by day 42; therefore to calculate the LFT at node 2 you must find the longest path back to that node (42 – 28 = 14)
- node 1 – LFT = 0 because the longest path back is 14 – 14 = 0.

Calculating the LFTs provides three main pieces of information.

1 It provides the deadlines that *must* be met in order for the project to be completed on time.

2 It helps to identify the activities that have 'float time' – in other words, some slack between the EST and the LFT; activity H can be started on day 1 and must be finished by day 63, but takes only 21 days to complete; so there is no rush to complete it.

3 It identifies the critical path.

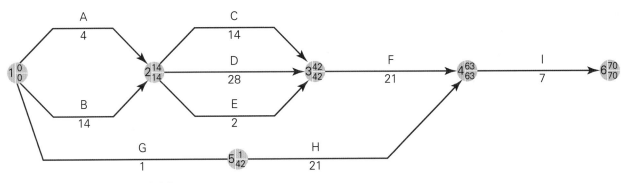

Figure 34.5 '3p off' network (4)

The critical path

The **critical path** comprises the activities that take longest to complete. They determine the length of the whole project. In this case it is activities B, D, F and I. These are the activities that must not be delayed by even one day, for then the whole project will be late. With C a delay would not matter. There are 28 days to complete a task that takes only 14. But D is on the critical path, so this 28-day activity must be completed in no more than 28 days.

Identifying the critical path allows managers to apply **management by exception** – in other words, focusing on exceptionally important tasks, rather than spreading their efforts thinly. Of the nine activities within the 3p off network, only the four critical ones need to absorb management time. The others need far less supervision.

If a supervisor sees a possibility that an activity on the critical path might overrun, he or she can consider shifting labour or machinery across from a non-critical task. In this way the project completion date can be kept intact.

To identify the critical path, the two key points are:

1 it will be on activities where the nodes show the EST and LFT to be the same

2 it is the longest path through those nodes.

When drawing a network, the critical path is identified by striking two short lines across the critical activities (see Figure 34.6).

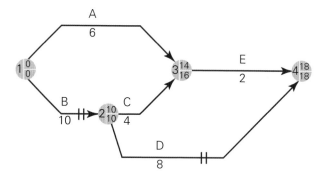

Figure 34.6 Indicating the critical path

Non-critical activities

Any activity that is not on the critical path is non-critical. Even if there is a delay to a non-critical activity, it may be that the project can be completed on time. A non-critical activity has some slack (e.g. it takes two days to complete, yet there are five days in the schedule between its earliest start time and its latest finish time); these three days of slack are known as 'float time'.

A firm might take the opportunity to get the job done straight away, then switch staff to other activities. Or the managers may give staff the extra time to give more thought to the activity. For example, designing a new logo may need only two days, but it may well be that a better logo could be designed in five.

Advantages and disadvantages of using network (critical path) analysis

Advantages

- It requires careful planning of the order in which events need to occur, and the length of time each one should take. This should improve the smooth operation of an important project such as a new product launch.

- By identifying events that can be carried out simultaneously, it shortens the length of time taken to complete a project. This is an important element in the modern business focus upon

time-based management. For example, if a law is passed that allows 14-year-olds to ride motorbikes with engines of less than 40cc, the first company to design and launch a suitable product would do extremely well.

- The resources needed for each activity can be ordered/hired no earlier than their scheduled EST. Just such a focus upon careful planning of when stocks are needed is the heart of just-in-time production systems. In this way cash outflows are postponed as long as possible, and the working capital tied up in the project is minimised.

- If the completion of an activity is delayed for some reason, the network diagram is a good starting point for working out the implications and deciding on appropriate courses of action.

Disadvantages

- A complex project (such as the construction of the Olympic village) entails so many activities that a drawing becomes unmanageable. Fortunately, computers can zoom in and out of drawings, enabling small parts of the network to be magnified and examined.
- Drawing a diagram does not, in itself, ensure the effective management of a project. Network analysis provides a plan, but can only be as successful as the staff's commitment to it. This suggests that staff should be consulted about the schedule and the likely duration of the activities.
- The value of the network diagram is reduced slightly because the activity lines are not in proportion to the duration of the activities.

Issues for analysis

Issues for analysis in relation to networks include the following.

- That critical path analysis (CPA) allows a business to translate strategies into plans of action – enabling each member of staff to know what has to be achieved by when; practical techniques such as this are needed to enable delegation to be effective.
- Drawing networks is a valuable skill, but at least as important is interpreting diagrams that have already been drawn; this can be made easier by asking 'What if?' questions about different scenarios. What if a critical activity is delayed? What if critical activity B can be bought in from an outside supplier who promises to take half the time?
- The need for a technique such as CPA to enable just-in-time to work in practice; care over timing and meticulous organisation are the essentials in both systems.
- Networks are a crucial way to organise resources so that working capital usage is minimised; this is especially important in long-term projects such as construction work or new product development.

Planning operations (including CPA) – an evaluation

The cliché 'time is money' has been around for years. Only recently, though, have systems such as just-in-time focused clearly on time-based management. Time is vital not only because it affects costs, but also because it can provide a crucial marketing edge. Forever 21's key advantage over Next is that it is much quicker at getting catwalk fashions into high-street shops. So time can add value. Careful production planning can also help to get a firm's new product to the market before the opposition.

Network analysis is a valuable practical tool for taking time seriously. It involves careful planning and can be used as a way of monitoring progress. If critical activities are falling behind schedule, action can be taken quickly. This serves as a reminder that successful business management is not just about clever strategic thinking. Ultimately, success depends upon what happens at the workplace or at the construction site. Network analysis is a helpful way to ensure that strategies become plans that can be carried through effectively. Nevertheless, they guarantee nothing. Ensuring that the paper network becomes reality will remain in the hands of the managers, supervisors and staff on the job. So effective personnel management and motivation will remain as important as ever.

Key terms

Critical path: the activities that must be completed on time for the project to finish on time. In other words, they have no float time at all.

Management by exception: the principle that because managers cannot supervise every activity within the organisation, they should focus their energies on the most important issues.

Network: a diagram showing all the activities needed to complete a project, the order in which they must be completed and the critical path.

Network analysis: breaking a project down into its component parts, to identify the sequence of activities involved.

A Revision questions (35 marks; 35 minutes)

1 Explain the business importance of operational planning. (3)

2 Identify two objectives of network analysis. (2)

3 Distinguish between an activity and a project. (3)

4 State three key rules for drawing networks. (3)

5 Explain how to calculate the earliest start time for an activity. (4)

6 Why is it important to calculate the latest finish time on an activity? (4)

7 What is meant by 'the critical path' and how do you identify it? (4)

8 Explain why it would be useful to know which activities have float times available. (3)

9 Analyse the value of network analysis for a small firm in financial difficulties. (4)

10 Explain how the use of critical path analysis could help a firm's time-based management. (5)

B1 Data response

Activity	Preceded by	Duration (weeks)
A	–	6
B	–	4
C	–	10
D	A & B	5
E	A & B	7
F	D	3

Questions (40 marks; 40 minutes)

1 a Construct a network from the above information. (6)

  b Number the nodes and put in the earliest start times. (4)

2 a Draw the following network:

  Activity A and B start the project. C and D follow A. E follows all other jobs. (6)

  b Work out the earliest start times of the

activities and put them in the nodes if, in the above question, A lasts 2 days, B = 9 days, C = 3, D = 4, E = 7. (4)

3 a Use the following information to construct a fully labelled network showing ESTs, LFTs and the critical path. (12)

Activity	Preceded by	Duration
A	–	3
B	–	9
C	–	2
D	A	5
E	C	3
F	B, D, E	5
G	C	9

  b If the firm was offered a £2,000 bonus for completing the project in 12 days, which activity should managers focus upon? Explain why. (8)

Case study

Every Friday needs managing

Last Friday had been a washout. Claire, Bren, Alliyah and Ruth had dithered over what to wear, where to go and how to get there, and ended up watching a rotten DVD in Bren's bedroom. This week was going to be different. Bren had just been taught critical path analysis and she was determined to use it to 'project manage' Friday night. As it was Bren's birthday on Friday, the others had to agree.

They sat down on Tuesday to agree all the activities needed for a great night out. They started by focusing on the activities:

Alliyah: We have the best nights when we start at Harry's Bar for a couple of hours, then on to the Orchid at about midnight.

Claire: I like Harry's but prefer RSVP; no argument, though, we should go to the Orchid.

After half an hour back and forth, the agreement was Harry's at 9.00 and Orchid at 12.00.

Then they realised that there was a lot more to it than that. It would take half an hour to get to Harry's and they'd have to get ready beforehand: bath, hair, nails, make-up. And what about the preceding activities? Shopping for a new top … and shoes … and earrings … and getting some highlights done.

They argued about which comes first, a top and then shoes and earrings to match? Or the other way round? It was time for Bren to set it all out (see table below).

Questions *(15 marks; 20 minutes)*

1 Draw up Bren's network, to help plan her birthday. (8)

2 How much float time is there on activities E and D? (2)

3 Explain why workers on a building site could benefit as much or more from critical path analysis as Bren and her friends. (5)

Activity		Preceded by	Duration
A	Booking a hair and nails appointment	–	1 minute
B	Clothes shopping	–	4 hours
C	Shopping for shoes	–	3 hours
D	Shopping for earrings	B, C	1 hour
E	Hair and nails appointment	A	2 hours
F	Bath	D, E	1 hour
G	Make-up and get dressed	F	1 hour
H	Constant phone conversations	–	24/7

Data response

Davey & Prior Building is a struggling partnership. Three of its last four jobs have been completed late and have therefore incurred cost penalties. Jim Davey blames the suppliers but Anne Prior is convinced that Jim's poor organisation is the real cause. Now Anne has persuaded Jim to plan the next project using a network analysis software program.

Questions *(25 marks; 30 minutes)*

1 Explain the circumstances in which network analysis is useful to firms such as Davey & Prior. (5)

2 Jim has broken the next project down into the following activities:

Activity	Preceded by	Duration (weeks)
A	–	6
B	A	2
C	A	4
D	–	8
E	B	12
F	B, C, D	6
G	B, C, D	9
H	D	10
J	F, G	5

a Draw the network, complete with full labelling. (10)

b Indicate and state the critical path. (4)

c If a machinery failure delays the completion of activity E by three weeks, what effects would this have on the project? What might Anne and Jim do about it? (6)

C Essay questions (40 marks each)

1 Your uncle is a builder who dislikes 'paperwork and planning'. You have heard that he is about to embark on his biggest ever project, building four two-storey houses. Attempt to persuade him to adopt network analysis to help him plan and control the work. Make sure your arguments are relevant to the building industry and are solid enough to persuade a doubter.

2 'Using network analysis to manage projects is as important to the finances and marketing of a business as it is to operations management.' Discuss.

35 Kaizen (continuous improvement)

Definition

Kaizen is a Japanese term meaning continuous improvement. Staff at firms such as Toyota generate thousands of new ideas each year – each aimed at improving productivity or quality. Over time, these small steps forward add up to significant improvements in competitiveness.

Introduction

'If a man has not been seen for three days his friends should take a good look at him to see what changes have befallen him.'

This ancient Japanese saying seems to sum up kaizen quite nicely. Continuous improvement or 'kaizen' is a philosophy of ongoing improvement based around small changes involving everyone – managers and workers alike. There are two key elements to kaizen:

1 Most kaizen improvements are based around people and their ideas rather than investment in new technology.

2 Each change on its own may be of little importance. However, if hundreds of small changes are made, the cumulative effects can be substantial.

In the 1990s, the term 'kaizen' was virtually unknown outside Japan. Research carried out in Britain in early 2010 showed that over 80% of private sector businesses say they use strategies for continuous improvement.

A-grade application

An example of a kaizen improvement comes from Barclaycard. In processing billions of pounds of credit card transactions per year, a major problem is fraud. An employee suggested a way of analysing bogus calls to the company's authorisation department. This has saved Barclaycard over £100,000 a year. The precise method is secret, but it works by blocking the credit card numbers of callers trying to buy goods fraudulently. It can also trace the callers, resulting in the arrest of the fraudsters involved.

The components of the kaizen philosophy

Describing kaizen as just 'continuous improvement' is simplistic. To work effectively kaizen requires a commitment from management to establish a special, positive culture within the organisation. This culture must be communicated and accepted by all those working at the company. It must permeate the whole organisation. What are the characteristics of this culture or philosophy?

One employee, two jobs

According to the Kaizen Institute the goal of any kaizen programme should be to convince all employees that they have two jobs to do – doing the job and then looking for ways of improving it. The kaizen culture is based on the belief that the production line worker is the real expert. The worker on the assembly line does the job day in day out. This means knowing more about the causes of problems and their solutions than the highly qualified engineer who sits in an office. The kaizen philosophy recognises the fact that any company's greatest resource is its staff.

Teamworking

To operate kaizen successfully employees cannot be allowed to work as isolated individuals. Teamworking is vital to the process of continuous improvement. These teams are composed of employees who work on the same section of the production line as a self-contained unit. Each team is often referred to as a 'cell'. The members of a cell are responsible for the quality of the work in their section. Over time the cell becomes expert about the processes within its section of the production line. Kaizen attempts to tap into this knowledge by organising each cell into a quality circle. The members of each cell meet regularly to discuss problems cropping up within their section. The circle then puts forward solutions and recommendations for the management to consider.

A-grade application

Tesco: 'Every Little Helps'

How would you react if Lidl or Aldi announced the intention of becoming Britain's number one, high quality grocery chain? The better you know these discount stores, the more you would laugh at the thought. Yet that was the position of Tesco when it decided to move upmarket in the early 1980s. It had been famous for being a cheap, low cost, low quality alternative to Sainsbury's. Over the following two decades it had a mountain to climb, yet stumbled upon the slogan 'Every Little Helps'. This not only became the clever advertising line when introducing initiatives such as Clubcard and 'Only One In the Q' (or we'll open another aisle). It also became vital behind the scenes, as staff started to realise that small steps forward were appreciated by management.

Using its 'Every Little Helps' approach has led Tesco to the situation in which, by 2010, its annual profit of £3,400 million dwarfs Sainsbury's £610 million.

Empowerment

Empowerment is essential to any kaizen programme. Empowerment involves giving employees the right to make decisions that affect the quality of their working lives. Empowerment enables good shop-floor ideas to be implemented quickly.

Once the necessary kaizen apparatus is in place good ideas and the resulting improvements should continue. The number of suggestions made each month should improve over time once employees see the effects of their own solutions. However, if quality circles and teamworking are to be truly effective employees must be given real decision-making power. If good ideas are constantly being ignored by management they will eventually dry up as the employees become disillusioned with the whole process.

A-grade application

Using teamworking to create kaizen customer service benefits

Julian Richer is a strong believer in the merits of teamworking and kaizen. Richer is the owner of a highly innovative and successful hi-fi retailing chain called Richer Sounds. Apart from offering excellent value for money, Richer has utilised the creative ideas of his staff to create customer service with a difference. For the benefit of every Richer Sounds customer each outlet is equipped with its own free coffee and mint dispensing machine. Each shop has its own mirror which says 'You are looking at the most important person in this shop' and a bell that customers can ring if they feel that they have received excellent service. Many of these innovations have come from Richer's own style of quality circle. Once a month, staff at each outlet are encouraged to talk to each other about new ideas. To lubricate this process, Mr Richer gives each of his staff £5. This is because at Richer Sounds they hold their kaizen discussions at the pub!

Potential problems of implementing a successful kaizen programme

Culture

In order for kaizen to really work, employees must be proud to contribute their ideas to the company. Japanese companies do not offer financial rewards in return for suggestions. Their attitude is that employees are told that kaizen is part of the company policy when they are recruited. For them, employee commitment to kaizen is gained via genuine staff motivation rather than by financial bonuses. Creating the right organisational culture is therefore vital for success. Resistance can come from two quarters:

1 Management resistance: managers with autocratic tendencies may be unwilling to pass decision-making power down the hierarchy.

2 Employee resistance: a history of poor industrial relations and a climate of mistrust can create resistance to change among the staff. Employees may see the 'new empowerment programme' as a cynical attempt to get more out of the staff for less. The result? Reluctant cooperation at best, but little in terms of real motivation.

Training costs

Mistakes made by managers in the past can have severe long-term effects. Changing an organisation's culture is difficult, as it involves changing attitudes. The training required to change attitudes tends to be expensive. It can also take a very long time to change attitudes. Consequently, the costs are likely to be great.

Justifying the cost of kaizen

The training cost and the opportunity cost of lost output is easy to quantify. It may be harder to identify and prove the financial benefits of a kaizen programme. Managers can quite easily produce financial estimates of the benefits of capital investment. It is much harder to assess programmes designed to develop the stock of human capital within the company. Consequently, in firms dominated by the accountant it can be very difficult to win budgets for kaizen programmes.

Famous quotes about continuous improvement

'Continuous improvement is better than delayed perfection.'
Mark Twain, famous American writer

'If there's a way to do it better … find it.'
Thomas Edison, inventor

'If you're not making progress all the time, you're slipping backwards.'
Sir John Harvey Jones, former chief of ICI

'I believe that there is hardly a single operation in the making of our car that is the same as when we made our first car of the present model. That is why we make them so cheaply.'
Henry Ford, legendary car maker

'Our company has, indeed, stumbled onto some of its new products. But never forget that you can only stumble if you're moving.'
Richard Carlton, former chief at American giant 3M

'Be not afraid of going slowly; be only afraid of standing still.'
Chinese proverb

Source: *The Ultimate Book of Business Quotations*, Stuart Crainer.

 ## The limitations of kaizen

Diminishing returns

Some managers argue that the improvements created through a kaizen programme will invariably fall as time goes on. The logic is that the organisation will seek ways of solving the most important problems first. So by implication, the problems that remain will become progressively less important.

If this is the case, it might prove to be difficult to maintain staff enthusiasm. However, supporters of kaizen would reject this criticism on the grounds that there is no such thing as a perfect system. According to them, even the best system is capable of being improved. A former chief executive of Cadbury Schweppes was asked which management theory was the most overrated. He replied 'If it ain't broke don't fix it. Everything can be improved.' This is a perfect statement in favour of kaizen.

Radical solutions

Sometimes radical solutions implemented quickly are necessary in order to tackle radical problems. Kaizen may not be appropriate in all situations. The solution might have to be more dramatic than yet another change to an old system. It may be time to throw out all of the old and replace it with something totally new. This is usually the case in industries facing radical changes brought on by a rapid surge in technology, or a change in competition.

In 2010 Cadbury closed its Keynsham, UK chocolate factory, switching a great deal of production to Poland. This was partly because of the lower wage levels in Poland but was also (so the company said) because the Keynsham factory was reaching the end of its useful life. It was too late to keep on patching up a fading factory. The new factory would make Cadbury better able to withstand increased competition within the European market for chocolate.

 ## Issues for analysis

1 Kaizen is not a process that can simply be imposed on reluctant staff. It has to be part of a workplace culture that is based upon respect for staff. Kaizen originated in Japanese car factories such as Toyota and Nissan, where staff would often be well-paid university graduates. If managers hire minimum wage staff and boss them around, it would be absurd to expect them to contribute positively to a kaizen programme.

2 Kaizen improvements to a product are more likely to be effective in the earlier stages of a product's life cycle. If the kaizen programme is started too late it may only slow down the rate of decline rather than reverse it.

 ## Kaizen (continuous improvement) – an evaluation

Does the kaizen approach encourage bureaucracy? In the global market of the twenty-first century, managers have come to realise that an ability to adapt and change is vital if the firm is to survive. However, many managers and many businesses have great problems with change management. The main issue is that many individuals are frightened of the uncertainty that usually goes hand in hand with change. Some managers seek security, stability and predictability in their own working lives.

In the circumstances, it is not surprising that those who are afraid of anything too radical choose kaizen. This is because each improvement is relatively small. In summary, when those with bureaucratic tendencies embrace kaizen the result can be very little in terms of meaningful change.

Are kaizen and radical change mutually exclusive? It is possible to use both approaches. Even in Japan kaizen is not used exclusively. The Japanese have their own word, 'kaikaku', which roughly translated means 'a radical redesign'. In practice, many Japanese firms use kaikaku as a source of a major breakthrough when one is required. They then follow this up with a kaizen programme, in order to perfect and then adapt this new system to suit new conditions as they emerge.

Key terms

Business culture: the attitudes prevailing within a business.
Kaizen: continuous improvement.
Suggestion scheme: a formal method of obtaining written employee suggestions about improvements in the workplace.

 ## Further reading

Stuart Crainer (1997), *The Ultimate Book of Business Quotations*, Capstone Publishing.

Revision questions (35 marks; 35 minutes)

1 Give three reasons why kaizen improvements can prove to be cheaper than improvements gained via business process re-engineering. (3)

2 State three limitations of the kaizen philosophy. (3)

3 Explain why a re-engineering programme can lead to a deterioration in employee morale within the organisation being re-engineered. (3)

4 Why might some managers find it harder to implement kaizen than others? (4)

5 Give three reasons why it is vital to involve both management and shop-floor staff in any programme of continuous improvement. (3)

6 To be truly effective why must kaizen programmes be ongoing? (3)

7 Why is it important to set and monitor performance targets when attempting to operate kaizen? (4)

8 Explain how kaizen can help to create a better motivated workforce. (4)

9 Why might some managers believe that kaizen brings diminishing returns over time? (4)

10 Explain how 'Every Little Helps' has helped turn Tesco into Britain's Number 1 retailer. (4)

 Data response

Hail the star

Julian Hails was once a star player in lower league football teams such as Southend. He believed in teamwork, in training and in continuous improvement. He joined Star Electronics as a sales manager, but became managing director after just three years – promoted over the head of the chairman's son, Richard Star. His enthusiasm was infectious, and his kaizen programme soon bore fruit. This was fortunate because a slump in Star's sector of the electronics market caused a decline in market size.

At the latest board meeting, Julian presented figures recording the impact of the company's kaizen programme (see Table 35.1). Young Richard Star took the opportunity to snipe at Julian's achievements, saying: 'So after this programme of continuous upheaval, I see our total costs per unit are higher than they were two years ago.'

Questions (30 marks; 35 minutes)

1 Explain the links between 'teamwork' and 'continuous improvement'. (4)

2 Analyse the data provided above to evaluate the key successes of Julian's policies. (12)

3 Explain what Richard Star meant by his use of the term 'continuous upheaval'. (6)

4 What further information is needed to assess the validity of Richard Star's claim? (8)

Table 35.1 Impact of the company's kaizen programme

	Two years ago	Last year	This year
Rejects per unit of output	7.8	6.8	6.2
Assembly time (minutes)	46	43	39
Stock value per unit of output	£145	£128	£111
Direct costs per unit	£42.50	£39	£36.50
Overhead costs per unit	£64	£67	£72

Case study

Kaizen 2.0: Frugal innovation

Thirty years ago Japan overtook America to become the world's leading car producer. American producers were taken aback – and they were even more shocked when they visited Japan to find out what was going on. They found that the secret of Japan's success did not lie in cheap labour or government subsidies (their preferred explanations) but in what was rapidly dubbed 'lean manufacturing'. Japan had transformed itself from a low-wage economy into a hotbed of employee-led shop-floor innovation. Soon every factory around the world was run in a lean way.

Emerging countries are no longer content to be sources of cheap hands and low-cost brains. Instead they too are concentrating on innovation, making breakthroughs in everything from telecoms to car making to health care. They are redesigning products to reduce costs not just by 10 per cent, but by up to 90 per cent. They are redesigning entire business processes to do things better and faster than their rivals in the West.

Even more striking is the emerging world's growing ability to make products for dramatically lower costs than their competitors: no-frills $3,000 cars and $300 laptops may not make headlines, but they promise to change far more people's lives than iPads will. This sort of advance – known as 'frugal innovation' – is not just a matter of exploiting cheap labour, though cheap labour helps. It is a matter of exploiting the resource of employee ideas to redesign products and processes and cut out unnecessary costs. In India, Tata created the world's cheapest car, the Nano, by combining dozens of cost-saving tricks.

Source: based on a special report in *The Economist*, 15 April 2010.

Questions (30 marks; 35 minutes)

1 Define the term kaizen. (2)

2 Explain two benefits of kaizen to companies. (6)

3 Explain how a company such as Tata might set about making kaizen improvements. (8)

4 Discuss the possible reasons that might explain why some firms embrace the kaizen philosophy, while others reject it. (14)

C Essay questions (40 marks each)

1 Two years ago the management team at Lynx Engineering commissioned a benchmarking survey to assess its relative position within the marketplace. To their horror the managers discovered that they were lagging behind their competition in terms of both cost and product quality. In an attempt to rectify the situation a massive £2 million re-engineering programme was announced. Two years later things have still not improved. Assess what could have gone wrong. What should the company do next?

2 How might a firm set about improving its efficiency? What factors are likely to affect the success of any strategy designed to achieve this goal?

'It has been proven time and time again that in order to survive firms must be willing to initiate change successfully within their own organisations. Firms that are afraid of change will fail because those that are more adventurous will always leave them behind.' To what extent do you agree or disagree with this statement?

36 Integrated operations management

Operations management

Operations involves the management and control of the processes within an organisation that convert inputs into output and then delivery. Traditionally this activity was called 'production'. Now, with more than 70% of all jobs in Britain based within the service sector, it seems wrong to use such an old-fashioned term. Operations management is as important within a service business as in manufacturing. In both cases, a satisfied customer is one that gets exactly what they want at the time they want it. Customers are likely to want this to be achieved with as little effort on their own part as possible (e.g. one click of a mouse button leads to an on-time delivery of piping-hot 12-inch pepperoni pizza).

In order to achieve that one-click magic, managements establish appropriate operational objectives and then design and implement strategies in order to achieve success. They need to consider:

- the purpose and implications of innovation: some managers take innovation to mean 'launching new or novel products', such as the ludicrous Lemon Yoghurt KitKat chocolate bar (which flopped); the important innovation may be to create the most user-friendly website.
- that because every business is unique, the factors influencing location are unique to that firm; one pizza place might need an expensive high-street location, whereas another will thrive in a cheaper side street (especially if online ordering forms part of its strategy)
- the positive and negative implications for a firm from implementing lean production techniques

- how businesses decide on their scale of production, the benefits of getting the decision right and the problems caused by getting the decision wrong.

In order to achieve a good A-level grade, it is vital to move beyond an understanding of the new terms and concepts introduced and to consider the possible implications for the business involved. Two of the key issues underpinning operations management are considered below.

Issue 1: the link between operations management and the other business functions

A firm's operations are central to the business: without a product there would be no business. However, successful operations management cannot be achieved independently of a firm's finance, human resources and marketing functions. Effective operations will depend on the existence of sufficient numbers of appropriately skilled and motivated employees, yet the techniques used within operations can make a significant contribution to the motivation (or otherwise) of the workforce. Similarly, investment in suitable machinery, and the development of innovative products and processes will be possible only if sufficient finance can be made available, while new products and increased productivity can improve a firm's financial position. In other words, changes in operations need to be considered in the wider context of the business as a whole.

Issue 2: the link between operations management and competitiveness

Efficient operations have always held the key to a firm's ability to continue to prosper in a competitive environment. If, on a sunny day, a trip to a sweetshop reveals an empty ice cream fridge, the customer will go elsewhere next time. In a world where there is a fine line between success and failure, this can be very important. The fine line can best be seen by taking a Wednesday-evening walk down a street full of restaurants. Some are empty and some are frantic. Rents are very high in such areas, so today's empty restaurant is tomorrow's business closure.

The importance of effective operations can only grow in importance as the degree of competition intensifies.

In 2011 the new coalition government responded to weak economic performance in Britain by declaring that 'The march of the makers' was the future of the UK economy. In other words, it was time to rebuild manufacturing (which had slipped to account for only 12% of GDP).

Fortunately, two factors were in favour of UK manufacturing competitiveness: the first was the 20 to 25% fall in the value of the pound between 2007 and 2011. This would make UK manufacturers 20 to 25% more price competitive compared with companies in America or the Far East. The second was the weak jobs position. With unemployment relatively high, brighter young people could be attracted to work in manufacturing. This would boost the position of some of Britain's brilliant exporters of manufactured goods (see Table 36.1).

Given the rise and rise of China as the world's biggest manufacturing country, it would be easy to say that Britain cannot compete. In fact, Germany has shown the way, with its world class companies such as BMW and VW. The successes in Table 36.1 show that Britain can manage the same success, as long as companies focus on high-value, highly differentiated items.

Figure 36.1 Britain's export of manufactured goods

UK company	Type of product	% of sales made overseas
JCB	Construction vehicles, diggers and so on (JCB has about 10% of the world market)	Over 75%
ARM	Microchips for portable devices (in every iPhone, iPad, PSP etc.)	Over 90%
Mulberry	Producers of leather goods, notably handbags	Sales in Asia up over 300% in 2011
Autonomy	World-leading provider of 'enterprise software', i.e. specialist software for businesses	Over 90%

A Revision questions *(80 marks; 80 minutes)*

1 What is meant by operations management? (2)

2 Using examples, briefly explain the difference between an operational objective and an operational strategy. (4)

3 Identify two possible operational objectives that a business might have. (2)

4 Outline two ways in which operations management can affect a firm's competitiveness. (4)

5 Explain why Terry, an A-level student, was wrong to write that 'economies of scale mean that production costs are falling'. (5)

6 Outline two economies of scale that might be enjoyed by an expanding sports shop business. (4)

7 Explain what is meant by the term diseconomies of scale. (3)

8 Why might the growth of a business from five staff to 400 lead to a loss in employee motivation? (4)

9 Analyse two consequences of deteriorating communications within a rapidly expanding business. (4)

10 Suggest two ways in which a firm could attempt to ensure coordination within the business as it grows. (4)

11 Outline one advantage and one disadvantage to a manufacturer of wool jackets when switching from a labour-intensive to a more capital-intensive system of production. (6)

12 Explain the difference between product and process innovation. (4)

13 Examine two possible consequences of a cut in expenditure on research and development at games console and software manufacturer Nintendo. (4)

14 Outline two factors that might affect the location of a call centre for an insurance company. (4)

15 Briefly explain two reasons why a UK manufacturer of electrical goods might choose to switch its operations to an overseas location. (6)

16 Analyse two ways in which a building firm operating in a period of falling property prices could benefit from the use of critical path analysis. (6)

17 Outline the main purpose of lean production. (3)

18 Identify three possible causes of waste for a car manufacturer. (3)

19 Describe one potential benefit and one potential drawback for a firm deciding to adopt a system of just-in-time production. (4)

20 Explain why worker empowerment is essential to the successful implementation of a *kaizen* programme. (4)

B1 Case study

Lean chocolate

A classic production problem for Cadbury is how to pack the ten types of chocolates that go into their Roses and Heroes brand boxes. It used to require a lot of manual labour and a buffer stock of 170,000 boxes! Beccy Smith, Cadbury's associate principal scientist, told Confectionerynews.com that after a huge amount of preparatory work, successfully introducing industrial robots had improved productivity and 'also reduced our cardboard usage and transport requirement enormously'.

As is typical of lean production, Cadbury worked for a long time to make this changeover a success. It bought-in simulation software called 'Witness' that 'visually represents real-world processes in a computer-generated model'. This allows 'What if?' scenarios to be tested, such as 'What if we used robots instead of people?' Cadbury also expects the software to be useful in addressing 'factors such as seasonal spikes in production'.

A representative from the software supplier explained that 'This level of insight (provided by the software) is crucial for food manufacturers if they are to preserve margins and remain competitive'.

Source: Confectionerynews.com (William Reed Media) 12 August 2011.

Questions *(35 marks; 40 minutes)*

1   a   Is the above case study an example of innovation by product or by process? (1)

    b   Explain why the distinction is important in a case such as this. (5)

2   Examine the impact of the 'Witness' software on the costs, benefits and risks of innovation. (8)

3   Explain the impact of these changes on the balance between labour intensive and capital intensive production at Cadbury. (6)

4   Discuss the degree of impact on Cadbury's competitiveness of lean management of resources such as cardboard, transport and people. (15)

Case study

Staffing at John Smedley

The luxury knitwear manufacturer, John Smedley, was introduced in a case study in Unit 33. You do not need to re-read that case study, as all the relevant material for the following questions is provided here.

It would be easy to sympathise with any UK textiles manufacturer, faced with a seemingly unstoppable flood of cheap imports from Asia, that decided to ring the factory bell for the last time and relocate abroad. However, John Smedley remains firmly rooted to the Derbyshire location where the business was established over 225 years ago. In fact, according to the company, its heritage is an important part of the 'indefinable quality' of its products. The company, whose fine-knit wool and cotton sweaters, tops and cardigans are favoured by celebrities such as Victoria Beckham and Madonna, has a workforce of 450 and generated sales of £17 million in 2010.

The company's survival strategy is based on targeting a low-volume niche, competing on grounds of quality rather than price. The average retail price of a John Smedley piece of knitwear is £100. Around 70% of the company's production is exported, mostly to Japan. A highly skilled workforce, carefully sourced materials and a rigorous system of quality control are vital ingredients in the manufacturing process.

The company has been faced with a number of challenges in the past. It was forced to close its spinning division, resulting in a significant number of redundancies, after making losses in 2002 and 2003, and continues to struggle with

the problems caused by rising raw material and energy costs. A rise in the value of the pound against the yen over the last few years has made the company's products 20% more expensive in Japanese markets. However, the company rejected proposals to offshore production to China after discovering that this would result in an average price reduction of only £8 per garment.

One of the main constraints facing John Smedley is a chronic shortage of suitably skilled workers. The company's staff receive between six months' and two years' training, and are paid between £300 and £400 per week. Many existing employees are close to retirement, as the firm has been unsuccessful in recruiting younger workers. In an attempt to deal with this, it has introduced a number of Japanese knitting machines, at a cost of £125,000 each, able to produce a whole garment in around one hour.

Source: John Smedley, BBC News.

Questions *(30 marks; 35 minutes)*

1   Examine the key influences on the operational objectives of John Smedley. (6)

2   Assess the main implications of the company's decision to move to a more capital-intensive method of production. (12)

3   To what extent do you agree with the company's decision to keep production at its Derbyshire factory? (12)

Case study

Efficient operations support expansion at BareFruit Juice

When BareFruit Juice was established by Col Marafko, its aim was to transform the negative image of fast food by establishing the first genuinely healthy juice bar chain in the UK. Since then the business has expanded rapidly nationwide and has ambitions to become a major international brand. According to Col, the company's market penetration has been achieved by offering 'a better product at more competitive prices' than rivals. The smoothies and juices on sale contain no colourings, preservatives, flavourings, sugar concentrates or pasteurised ingredients, and are prepared to order in front of customers.

The key operational objectives set by the firm focus on the provision of a quality service. For a 'fast food' chain, a quality service has to mean a speedy service; the company has a demanding three-minute service time target, and staff are trained to acknowledge customers and take their orders as quickly as possible. The taste experience is at the forefront of product development and depends on the sourcing of quality ingredients from reputable suppliers using traceable supply chains. Stocks have a very limited shelf life – one day in the case of fresh fruit and up to one week for frozen ingredients. Stock management is the responsibility of each store manager and an average of between three and four days' supply of frozen ingredients is held as a buffer. However, sales are heavily influenced by the weather and can fluctuate dramatically, emphasising the importance of good relationships with suppliers.

Visibility – the extent to which a firm's operations are exposed to customers – is an important part of customer service at BareFruit. The genuine and honest use of ingredients is a core principle for the business. Ingredients are freshly squeezed and blended to order, in front of customers. Visibility also has an important influence on the location of the juice bars. The firm's research suggests that 40% of people eat or drink something while out shopping, and a large number of customers buy on impulse.

Current BareFruit bars are all located in large covered shopping centres, such as Manchester's Arndale Centre and Merry Hill near Dudley in the West Midlands.

The company uses footfall data to choose units in the busiest areas, rather than within dedicated eating areas. Such locations mean that BareFruit's overheads are high – the cost of premises is the company's single biggest cost, with rents and business taxes accounting for nearly 45% of total costs. Keeping variable costs down is, therefore, crucially important and the control of waste is a key feature of the company's training programmes.

A culture of continuous improvement (*kaizen*) has been firmly established within the business, and all staff are encouraged to put forward ideas on how to improve service and enhance the customer experience. The core offer of a range of classic smoothies has been gradually extended to include sandwiches, soups and other healthy snacks. For an extra 50p, customers can upgrade their smoothie with the addition of a booster. BareFruit has also confirmed its commitment to the environment by ensuring that over 95% of the drinks' packaging used by the company is fully biodegradable.

Source: BareFruit Juice.

Questions *(40 marks; 50 minutes)*

1 Describe three ways in which BareFruit attempts to deliver a quality service to its customers. (6)

2 Examine the importance of quality to a company such as BareFruit. (8)

3 Identify the key influences on the location of BareFruit juice bars. (8)

4 Analyse two ways in which BareFruit might have benefited from establishing a culture of *kaizen* within the business. (6)

5 Discuss two changes that BareFruit could make in order to reduce operating costs. Explain which of the two you would recommend, and why. (12)

37 Introduction to external influences

Definition
An external influence is a factor beyond a firm's control that can affect its performance. Examples include: changes in consumer tastes, laws and regulations and economic factors such as the level of spending in the economy as a whole.

The impact of external influences on firms

Some external influences have a favourable effect on firms. SAGA holidays specialises in providing holidays targeted at the elderly. A good example of a beneficial external influence for SAGA holidays might be the rise in life expectancy. An ageing population will enlarge SAGA's target market, giving the company a good opportunity to increase its revenue and profit. As shown in Figure 37.1, the number of over-65s is set to boom over the coming years.

Other external influences can have adverse effects on firms. In autumn 2010 the UK government's Comprehensive Spending Review announced cutbacks on school-building work amounting to £1,000 million. For private sector building businesses, this was a direct hit on their revenue, profits and workforce. At the same time, sharp cuts in spending on the police may force businesses such as jewellers to spend more on private security guards.

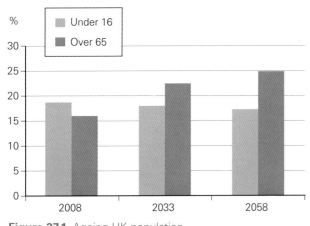

Figure 37.1 Ageing UK population

Source: National Statistics website: www.statistics.gov.uk

New laws and regulations
Changes in the law can have a dramatic effect on a business. A good example is the regulation changes to child car seats that came into effect in September 2006. They forced all motorists to provide 'seat restraints' for children sitting in the back of a car. For example, every child under 12 must not only wear a seat belt, but must also be sitting on a 'booster seat'. Younger children and babies must have their own special car seat.

Overnight this regulation created a huge boost for businesses such as Britax (car seat manufacturers) and Halfords, the main motor supplies retailer. From a business point of view, this is a marvellous type of external change, because the government announced the change in early 2005, giving the companies involved plenty of time to build production capacity and stock levels. In Halford's case the company's profit rose 44% between 2006 and 2011.

Demographic factors
Demography refers to changes to the size, growth and age distribution of the population. **Demographic** changes can create opportunities for some firms. However, for other firms the same demographic trend might create a threat.

In recent times one of the most important demographic changes to impact upon Britain is immigration. In 2004 the European Union expanded by admitting ten new member states: Poland, Czech Republic, Hungary, Slovakia, Slovenia, Estonia, Lithuania, Cyprus, Malta and Latvia. Britain, along with Sweden and Ireland, granted the citizens of the new EU 10 the immediate right to live and work in Britain. In 2004 wages in Eastern Europe were far below the wages offered to British workers. Between 2004 and 2008, more than 800,000 Eastern Europeans arrived and registered to work in the UK. Since then, job losses in the 2009 recession sent many home. but firms that have benefited overall from this external influence include JD Wetherspoon and property developers.

Immigration helps to keep wages in check. Pub chains like JD Wetherspoon have benefited from a plentiful supply provided by inward migration into the UK. Most migrants from Eastern Europe are hard working and have the skills to work behind a bar. JD Wetherspoon continues to expand. Without immigration JD Wetherspoon might have struggled to attract the additional labour required to expand, or been forced to pay higher wage rates. Wetherspoon's also saw the marketing opportunity, stocking a wide range of Polish bottled beers to help boost profit.

Most East European immigrants to Britain could not afford to buy property, so they rented instead. The increase in the number of renters encouraged property developers to buy to rent. Britain now has over a million landlords. The boom in Buy-To-Let property helped house prices double, creating capital gains for landlords. Without immigration from Eastern Europe it is unlikely that this opportunity for property development would have existed.

On the other hand, immigration from Eastern Europe has disadvantaged some UK businesses. For example, as a direct consequence of immigration many UK plumbing firms have been forced into cutting their prices. In the past there was an acute shortage of plumbers in the UK. Unsurprisingly, given the lack of competition, plumbers could charge customers pretty much whatever they liked. Today the situation is very different. The influx of Polish plumbers into Britain has forced prices down and standards up. This is good news for British homeowners with blocked sinks, but bad news for British plumbers who were able to enjoy high income levels until the competition arrived.

Technological factors

Technological change can also create opportunities and threats for firms. Before the advent of digital technology, ITV only had two competitors: the BBC and Channel 4. Today the situation is completely different. Technological advances mean that ITV has to compete against the hundreds of channels provided by Sky and cable TV providers such as Virgin. Advances in internet technology have opened up new entertainment possibilities (such as YouTube and Facebook) that compete head on with conventional TV. These technological advances threaten ITV's ability to generate revenue from selling advertising slots. On the other hand, these same technological advances have created opportunities for entrepreneurs with vision, such Larry Page and Sergey Brin, the founders of Google.

Commodity prices

Commodities are internationally traded goods such as oil, copper, wheat and cocoa. Commodities are normally bought by firms as a raw material. For example, as Figure 37.2 shows, the price of oil rocketed in 2008, then fell back in the recession before recovering in 2011.

The price of oil is an important external influence for most firms. Oil prices affect the cost of transportation because petrol, diesel and kerosene all come from crude oil.

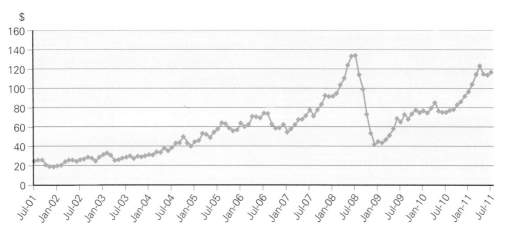

Figure 37.2 Oil prices

Source: IMF Primary Commodity Prices, 7 September 2011

Oil is also a very important raw material. Even companies such as Apple will be affected by rising oil prices because it will cost Apple more to buy in the plastic pellets needed to produce the casings for its laptop computers, iPods, iPads and iPhones. The price of oil is determined by the relative strength of the world supply and the world demand for oil. The world oil price is beyond the control of any single firm; making it an excellent example of an external influence.

Economic factors

Individual firms have no influence over economy-wide factors such as the rate of economic growth, the level of unemployment and the rate of inflation. However these factors will definitely affect firms. Firms will also be affected by government fiscal and monetary policy responses. For more details see Unit 40.

A-grade application

Companies such as the airline Ryanair will always suffer when oil prices soar, as fuel is their largest single operating cost. Ryanair operates on slender profit margins, so the 2008 oil price rise forced it into passing most of this cost increase on to customers by way of higher fares. Unfortunately, most of Ryanair's customers are likely to be quite price sensitive because most of Ryanair's customers travel for leisure, rather than for business reasons. If the price elasticity of demand for Ryanair flights is elastic the airline will lose revenue when fares are raised. Evidence arrived when Ryanair announced that its 2008 profits were 27% down on the year before.

Fortunately, the dramatic fall in the price of oil that occurred in late 2008 enabled Ryanair to cut its operating costs. By March 2010 Ryanair was back in the black, reporting a profit of £289m for the year.

What can firms do about external influences?

Make the most of favourable external influences while they last

Luck can play an important role in determining whether a business flourishes or not, especially in the short run. However, over time good and bad luck has a habit of evening out. The key to success then is to make the most of any favourable external influence whilst it lasts. For example, the debt-fuelled consumer spending boom between 1997 and 2007 greatly assisted those companies supplying luxury goods and services.

However, these firms should not have relied on this frothy boom for their success because it was a factor over which they had no control. They should have made the best of the situation while it lasted, but also asked themselves a series of **'what if' questions**. In this case, 'What if the banks withdraw cheap and easy credit? What would be the effect on consumer sales?'

Minimise the impact of unfavourable external influences

When faced with adverse external influences, successful firms make compensating internal changes to their business to offset the external constraint. Ryanair can do nothing about rising oil prices. However, Ryanair can attempt to cut other costs within the business to compensate for the rising oil price. If Ryanair can improve its internal efficiency the impact of the adverse external influence can be minimised. Successful businesses try as far as it is possible to internalise external constraints.

Issues for analysis

- Most firms, most of the time, have their fate in their own hands. Most have built up regular customers who keep coming back and therefore have reasonably predictable sales. Poor managers may drive some customers away, but it may take a long time before the cracks start to show. As long as the poor managers are replaced before too long, the business can be brought back on track. This situation has occurred with Marks & Spencer, Sainsbury's, Tottenham Hotspur FC and perhaps every other sports club.

● Just sometimes, though, a company's whole existence can be thrown into question by an external factor. In 2011 HMV struggled to survive in the face of dismal high street sales and the consumer shift to music downloading. Circumstances such as these are a huge test of the management. For other companies, changing technology, new competition or changes in the law may be every bit as significant. The good student spots the big issues and starts to think how to handle them.

Introduction to external influences – an evaluation

An important aspect of any evaluation of external factors is to distinguish between external change that is predictable and change that is not. For example, tourist businesses had five years to plan for the London Olympics in 2012. They can research into previous Olympic events and decide on their strategies. Contrast this with the complete unpredictability of events such as the 2011 earthquake and tsunami that wiped out the tourist trade in Japan, or the flooding that wrecked businesses in Missouri, America in May 2011.

Managers that fail to deal with predictable events are exceptionally weak. Those that succeed in unexpected situations are especially impressive.

Key terms

Demographic: factors relating to the population, such as changes in the number of older people or in the level of immigration.

'What if' questions: are hypothetical, i.e. they are used to test out different possibilities or theories.

A Revision questions (25 marks; 25 minutes)

1 What is an external influence? (2)

2 Explain how a company such as Cadbury might be affected by a decision made for Britain to withdraw from the European Union. (6)

3 Give examples of the type of firms that probably benefited from the invasion and military occupation of Iraq. (4)

4 In 2009 Scottish and Newcastle closed its huge brewery in Reading. Give examples of firms in and around Reading that might be adversely affected by this decision. (4)

5 Record companies find it increasingly difficult to generate revenue because of file sharing sites that enable music lovers to illegally download music. What actions should record companies take to minimise this external constraint? (4)

6 British Airways suffered a world-wide humiliation with its 'bag-mountain' at the launch of Terminal 5. Can the management put problems such as this down to bad luck? (5)

Data response

Britain's monster credit binge

At the beginning of 2008 Britain had not suffered from a recession for well over a decade. During that time interest rates were historically low. These low interest rates led to many consumers in Britain taking on steadily higher levels of debt. So what was the money spent on?

TV property shows such as *Location, Location, Location* encouraged many people to borrow huge sums of money to purchase property for investment purposes. Property was seen as a one-way bet. At the time many people believed that 'house prices only ever go up'. The result was a speculative bubble in UK property. Banks also helped to provide the fuel for rampant house price inflation by relaxing lending standards. As house prices rose many households took the opportunity to spend the profit locked up in their homes by re-mortgaging. The equity released was mostly spent on imported luxuries. Britain was living beyond its collective means. Famously, the TV presenter Kirstie Allsopp said she would 'eat my hat' if property prices fall. They did; she didn't.

The banking credit crunch finished off the boom. As the availability of credit dried up, house prices began to fall. Consumer confidence

nosedived and house prices fell sharply in 2009. Although there was then a slight recovery, by early 2011 house prices were falling again (if only slightly). See Figure 37.3.

The problem with debt is that it has to be paid back. At the start of the recession total UK personal debt stood at £1,421 billion, more than the entire country's GDP. After lots of effort to repay debts during the recession, the figure was little changed by April 2011. Taking out a loan is easy. Repaying it is much, much harder.

Questions *(35 marks; 40 minutes)*

1 What is a recession? (2)

2 Outline two broad conclusions you can draw from the graph of house prices. (6)

3 Explain three examples of firms that benefited from the UK's house price boom. (6)

4 a What is consumer confidence and why is it important to firms? (4)

   b How might falling UK house prices affect consumer confidence? (5)

5 Discuss the actions that a private school might take in order to prepare for a recession. (12)

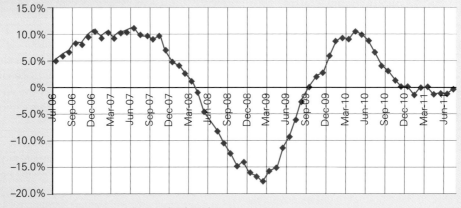

Figure 37.3 UK housing and annual price change

Case study

The power of external factors

Aggreko plc is a hugely successful supplier of temporary power and air conditioning supplies. Its 2010 turnover of more than £1 billion included contracts for supplying power to the World Cup and the Winter Olympics. Its 2010 annual report included 2,500 words on 'Principal risks and uncertainties'. The company focused mainly on economic conditions, but it acknowledged the political risks in operating in 100 countries including many in the Middle East and Africa. In 2010 no one could have forecast the political upheavals in the Middle East in 2011 (the 'Arab spring' and the civil war in Libya). This threatened Aggreko's sales to oil fields, and raised doubts about whether the business would be paid by governments whose existence was under threat.

The benefits of sales diversification emerged in spring 2011, when the dreadful earthquake and tsunami in Japan led to more than 20,000 deaths or disappearances. The tsunami, in turn, created a nuclear power disaster at the Fukushima power plant. Within a few weeks Aggreko beat international competitors to win a £60 million contract to provide temporary electricity to northern Japan. On its own that was worth more than the World Cup and Winter Olympic contracts combined. As Aggreko's 'International Local Business' division had total sales of £188 million, this single contract in Japan would boost the figures dramatically.

It was understandable that Aggreko had expected the world economy to be its biggest source of external shocks in 2011. In reality, the hit to profit in the Middle East was more than compensated for by the company's success in Japan. In late June 2011 the company announced that the full year's trading would be more than 20% up on 2010. Given the weakness of economic growth in the developed world, this was a terrific performance.

Questions *(25 marks; 30 minutes)*

1 What is an external constraint? (2)

2 Why were events in the Middle East an example of an external constraint? (4)

3 Explain 'the benefits of sales diversification' in the context of Aggreko plc. (5)

4 Discuss whether it is right, morally, to look for a profit in a situation such as that of northern Japan in 2011. (14)

Impact on firms of economic factors

Definition

'Economic factors' can sometimes be described as 'macro-economic factors', i.e. affecting the whole economy, such as a change in interest rates.

 ## Economic growth and the business cycle

What is economic growth and why does it matter?

Over time the economy tends to grow. This means that the output of goods and services produced by the country increases compared with the year before. Economic growth is caused by productivity advances, perhaps due to technological innovation. This means that more goods and services can be produced with the same population. Economic growth is important to a country because it improves the standard of living. If the UK economy produces more goods and services, there will be more goods and services for UK citizens to consume. Economic growth in Britain has tended to average 2.5% per year. This causes the average level of affluence to double every 25 to 30 years.

Economic growth is very important to firms. A growing economy creates more opportunities as consumers' tastes change. It is easier to set up or expand a business in a country that has a rapidly growing economy. New gaps emerge in the market, creating more opportunities for budding entrepreneurs.

The economic growth rate of other countries will also be a concern for British firms. For example, the rapid growth in China has led to rising demand for Rolls Royce cars. To cope with the extra orders, Rolls Royce might have to take on extra staff. The company will also have to buy in more components. This will benefit suppliers who will also have to increase output and perhaps employment. The UK is a small country with a domestic market that is also quite small. 90% of the cars Rolls Royce sell are for export. UK firms like Rolls Royce that want to grow depend, in part, on the economic growth rate in other countries.

The business (economic) cycle

Unfortunately, the economy does not grow at an even rate over time. History shows that the British economy has experienced periods when the economy has grown rapidly. These periods are called booms. Booms are usually followed by recessions; during a recession economic growth grinds to a halt. Technically, a recession is defined as 'two successive quarters of falling output', but even a slowdown can be called a 'growth recession'. If matters do not improve, the economy could end up in a slump. A slump is a sustained period of negative

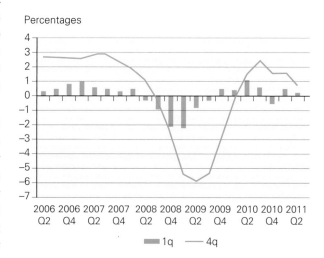

Figure 38.1 UK changes in GDP 2006 to 2011
Source: National Statistics website www.statistics.gov.uk

Table 38.1 The phases of the trade cycle

	Boom	Recession	Slump	Recovery
Consumer and business confidence	Optimistic	Doubts emerging	Pessimistic	Gradually returning
Consumer spending	High. Low levels of saving. Spending supplemented by credit	Falling. Spending financed by credit starts to fall	Falling. Consumers save to pay off debts built up during the boom	Rising. Debts have now been paid off
Economic growth	Strongly positive	GDP begins to fall	GDP growth might now be strongly negative	Weak, but slowly improving
Unemployment	Close to zero	Low, but starting to rise	High	High, but starting to fall
Inflation	High, and possibly accelerating	Still positive, but falling. Firms now start to think twice about raising prices	Stable prices, or even some deflation (falling prices) is possible	Price stability
Number of firms failing	Low	Low, but rising	High	Falling
Business investment	Firms are optimistic about the future. Investment takes place for both replacement and expansion purposes	Falling. Expansion programmes may be postponed	Close to zero. Even replacement investment may have to be postponed to conserve cash	Slowly rising. Replacement investment projects previously postponed might now get the green light

economic growth. The Japanese economy experienced this situation during the period 1990 to 2003.

The UK economy has recently suffered from a very severe recession, the deepest since the 1930s (see Figure 38.1). By the end of 2009 the recession had caused the output of the British economy to fall by 6%. The recession lasted for a year and a half. The UK economy was helped out of recession during the first half of 2010 by an unorthodox monetary policy measure known as quantitative easing. This added £200 billion of cash to the UK's money supply. By the first half of 2011, the new government's policy of sharp cuts in its spending raised the spectre of another economic slowdown. For the UK the only consolation was that this was a world recession, with similar economic problems experienced elsewhere in America and Europe. Only China and India went through this period unscathed. The phases of the trade cycle are shown in Table 38.1.

The impacts of the business cycle

The cycle affects firms in different ways, according to the type of good or service it sells. In general,

luxury goods businesses like Ferrari benefit most from economic booms. On the other hand, firms like Lidl may struggle during economic booms because consumers will probably respond to a boom by 'trading up' to more expensive alternatives such as Waitrose.

Managers must be expert at predicting the future state of the economy. It takes time to plan and introduce changes. Firms that react to economic changes once they have already happened usually struggle to compete.

What actions should a producer of luxury goods take today if it predicts a recession in the near future?

Business objectives

During a recession a producer of luxury goods might need to change its corporate objective from growth or profit maximisation to one of survival. During a recession revenue is bound to fall. The key to survival is to minimise losses, which can be achieved by introducing a package of cost-saving measures. Some of these changes might permanently damage the competitiveness of the business. For example, cutting back on expensive new product development may leave the product with an ageing product range in the future. However, if the firm does not cut costs now the business might not have a future to worry about! In a recession managers usually have to make difficult and unpopular decisions.

Marketing

Some businesses react to a recession by changing their marketing strategy to emphasise value for money in an attempt to hold up revenue at a time when the market might be shrinking. Some companies might consider reacting to a recession by cutting prices to help boost sales. However, this might be risky because a price cut might cheapen the brand's image resulting in a loss of sales once the economy recovers.

Production

Sales of luxury goods fall during a recession. To prepare, producers of luxury goods should aim to cut production sooner rather than later. Cutting production cannot be achieved over night. For example, suppliers of raw materials and components will probably have minimum notice periods written into their contracts. If the firm waits until sales start falling before cutting production, the result is likely to be a build-up of stock. Stock is expensive to store and it also ties up cash. During recessions expansion plans tend to be shelved because the extra capacity created by expansion will not be needed at a time when sales are expected to fall.

Human resource management

During a recession a manufacturer of luxury goods might not need as many staff because fewer are being sold. One way of slimming down a workforce is via compulsory redundancy. Getting rid of staff because they are not needed any more is expensive, may create negative publicity and is bad for staff morale. A better alternative may be to reduce the wage bill via **natural wastage**. This involves suspending recruitment. By not replacing employees who leave or retire, the workforce will fall naturally without the need for redundancies.

Some firms use the job insecurity created by a recession to force through changes in working practices that are designed to reduce costs. During a recession job opportunities elsewhere tend to

be scarce. Ruthless managers might use this to their advantage. They would argue that the whole business will be leaner and fitter as a result.

Finance

Firms fail when they run out of cash (creditors with unpaid bills take you to court). During recessions producers of luxury goods leak cash because of low demand. Logically, the best chance of survival is for those businesses that started the period of recession with healthy balance sheets, low borrowing levels and high liquidity. To conserve cash during an unprofitable period of trading, a business could do the following.

- Carry out a programme of zero budgeting throughout the organisation to trim any waste from departmental budgets.
- Restrict the credit given to customers and chase up debtors who currently owe the firm money.
- Rationalise: sell off any under-utilised fixed assets such as machinery and property. This will bring cash into the business.
- Attempt to refinance the business by taking on additional loan capital. Unfortunately, during recessions the availability of credit tends to dry up as banks re-assess their attitude towards risk. If a firm can persuade a bank to grant loan capital it will normally only be lent at a penalty rate of interest.

Evaluation: the impacts of recession

Recessions do not last for ever. Aim to survive so that you can benefit when the economy recovers. Not all firms suffer during a recession. Companies selling essentials may even gain ground. However, during a boom these same companies will probably have to take cost-cutting measures in order to survive.

Firms can do nothing about booms or recessions; they are external factors that are beyond the firm's control. However, managers need to make offsetting internal changes to the business, cutting costs for example, to minimise the worst effects of the recession. The challenge for management is to have a long-term strategy that can keep the business healthy in good times and bad.

What actions should a firm take in an economic boom?

But what if there is a boom? What should a firm do with the windfall profits it may be able to make? In the UK the threat of takeover might encourage public limited companies to increase their dividend payments to shareholders. Unfortunately, paying increased dividends will do nothing to improve the firm's long-term competitiveness. Managers running companies owned by long-termist shareholders will be able to use the profits made possible by an economic boom to increase their investment in new products and production methods that will make their business more competitive in the long run. Businesses owned or run by more conservative owners might decide to set aside some of the profits made by the boom as a cash reserve that will improve the firm's chances of surviving the next recession, when it arrives.

Most banks react to economic booms by relaxing their lending standards. As a result, firms that wish to expand will normally find that it is easier and cheaper to borrow the funds that they need to finance the expansion. Banks also tend to be more willing to lend to customers that want credit. A surge in the availability and the price of consumer credit will obviously help car manufacturers and other firms that produce expensive 'big ticket items' that consumers typically purchase using credit. Spread across the economy, theses actions can lead to rising **inflation**.

The effects of inflation on a firm's financial position

Introduction: what is inflation?

Inflation measures the percentage annual rise in the average price level. Inflation reduces the purchasing power of money within an economy. For consumers inflation increases the cost of living. At the same time, inflation usually leads to rising wages, so households are not necessarily any the worse off. Most people's **real wages** may be unchanged in value, so consumer spending in the shops need not be affected.

The impacts of inflation on a firm's finances are mixed.

Advantages of inflation to a business

Inflation makes real assets become worth more. For example, the value of any property or stock that the firm might own will increase if prices are going up. A firm with more valuable assets will have a more impressive balance sheet. As a result, the firm might find it easier to raise long-term finance from banks and shareholders because the business now looks more secure.

Firms with large loans also benefit from inflation because inflation erodes the real value of the money owed. Firms with high borrowings find that the fixed repayments on their long-term borrowings become more easily covered by rising income and profits. After, say, five years a £1 million loan may be worth only £0.75 million by the time the borrower repays the loan. In the same way, some householders have trivial mortgage payments because they took out the loan to help buy a house valued then at £40,000 (and perhaps worth £240,000 today).

Drawbacks of inflation

Inflation can damage profitability, especially for firms that have fixed-price contracts that take a long time to complete. For example, a local building company might agree a £5 million price for an extension to a local school, which is expected to take three years to finish. If inflation is higher than expected, profit might be wiped out by the unexpectedly high cost increases created by the inflation. Even if there were an agreement for the school to pay an inflation allowance on top of the price, the producer would have to fund the unexpectedly high cash outflows.

Inflation can also tend to damage cash flow because inflation will also push up the price of machinery. Consequently, inflation tends to penalise manufacturing companies like Ford, who need to replace their machinery regularly in order to stay internationally competitive.

Inflation can also damage industrial relations, i.e. the relationship between the business and its staff. When making pay claims for the year ahead, staff representatives (perhaps a trade union) will estimate what the inflation rate is likely to be in the future. This estimate may be higher than that expected by management. Differences in inflationary expectations have the potential to cause costly industrial disputes that may damage a firm's reputation.

Evaluation: the impacts of inflation

Inflation will impact upon different firms in different ways according to the type of product they sell, the production methods (and lead times) used and whether the firm has many loans or not. For example, inflation might benefit a hairdresser but severely damage a company engaged in heavy manufacturing such as the aeroplane-maker Airbus Industries.

Unemployment

Unemployment is created when the demand for labour has fallen relative to the available supply of labour. Rising unemployment tends to be associated with recessions. During economic booms unemployment usually falls. In addition to the demand for labour, unemployment can also be affected by factors such as emigration and immigration that affect the supply of labour. Unemployment can be measured as a total or as a rate (the percentage of those of working age who are not in work and who would like a job).

When the recession hit in 2008 some economists expected UK unemployment to rise and reach 3 million. Fortunately, the rise in unemployment was far less dramatic. By July 2011 UK unemployment, as measured by the Labour Force Survey, had 'only' reached 2.5 million. It seems likely that the rise in unemployment was stemmed by a combination of policy interventions, and by a preference on the part of British workers to accept part-time work rather than redundancies. The coalition government's decision to cut the UK's fiscal deficit sharply and quickly makes it possible that UK unemployment will start to rise again in the near future.

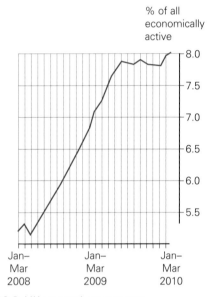

Figure 38.2 UK unemployment rate

Source: National Statistics website: www.statistics.gov.uk

Figure 38.2 shows the impact of the early period of the 2008 recession.

Table 38.2 Positive and negative impacts of unemployment

Benefits created by unemployment	Costs/problems created by unemployment
Tough managers might use the fear created by unemployment and the potential for redundancies to force through cost-saving changes in working practices.	Unemployment can create insecurity, which could sap morale within the business.
When unemployment is high most employees choose to stay where they are, as job vacancies begin to dry up. Labour turnover falls when unemployment is high. Low rates of labour turnover save the firm money on recruitment, selection and training.	Unemployment can affect consumer spending, which in turn can affect a firm's revenue and profit. For example, in 2011 Pfizer closed its huge R&D centre in Sandwich, Kent, leading to more than 2,000 job losses. This will hit hundreds of local service sector businesses, such as dry cleaners, pubs and sandwich shops.
Recruitment should become a lot easier. When unemployment is high the firm should receive plenty of applications for any vacant position. The quality of applications should also improve too. For example, during a period of high unemployment it may be possible to hire a graduate for a non-graduate post.	In areas where unemployment remains high in the long term, firms can be adversely affected by crime and other social problems created by unemployment. Structural unemployment (unemployment caused by a declining industry) can also result in a situation where the unemployed do not possess the 'right' skills.

The impacts of unemployment on firms

Unemployment can have both positive and negative impacts on firms (see Table 38.2).

Exchange rates

In Britain goods and services are sold in our currency, the pound. In America goods and services are sold in dollars. The exchange rate measures the quantity of foreign currency that can be bought with one unit of another currency, e.g. £1 buys $2. Movements in the exchange rate can dramatically affect profitability because the exchange rate affects both the price of imported and exported goods. Firms cannot influence the exchange rate. For example, the pound's rate of exchange against the US dollar is determined by the supply and demand for the pound on international currency markets. An individual firm is too small to affect the exchange rate; it is a good example of an external constraint that is beyond the control of any one manager. Exchange rates affect firms in different ways.

The impacts of a high exchange rate

Firms with large export markets

UK firms, such as Wedgwood pottery and Morgan cars, that sell a high proportion of their output overseas, will prefer a low exchange rate, i.e. a weak pound. Why is this so? The best way of explaining is via a numerical example.

America is an important export market for Morgan cars. Morgan charges its UK customers £25,000 for a basic 2 Seater Roadster.

To achieve the same profit margin in the USA, Morgan will have to charge a price in US dollars that will convert into £25,000. At the end of 2009 the exchange rate against the US dollar was £1:$1.40.

Figure 38.3 The Morgan Roadster

To obtain £25,000 per export, Morgan charged its American customers:

£25,000 × $1.40 = $35,000

By November 2010 the exchange rate had gone up to £1:$1.60. To generate the same £25,000 of export revenue per car sold, Morgan now had to charge its American consumers:

£25,000 × $1.60 = $40,000

In other words, the rise in the pound meant that Morgan needed to increase the US price of their cars by $5,000 to maintain the current profit per car. If Morgan reacts to a rising pound by putting prices up in the USA, demand for the 2 Seater Roadsters will almost certainly drop, causing Morgan's profitability to fall. On the other hand, if Morgan decides against raising its prices in the USA they will have to accept a lower profit on each car sold; either way Morgan loses out as a result of a higher pound.

Conclusion: exporters hate it when their currency rises in value; they like it to fall, not rise.

Firms that import most of their raw materials or stock

Retailers that import most of their stock prefer a high exchange rate. A high exchange rate reduces the cost of buying goods from abroad. For example, Jack Daniel's whiskey is a popular product with Tesco's British consumers. It has to be imported from the American firm that produces it. If the price of a case of Jack Daniel's is $70 the price paid by Tesco will be as follows:

If the exchange rate is £1: $1.40, the case will cost Tesco:

$70 / 1.40 = £50.00.

However, if the exchange rate goes up to £1: $1.60 the same case of Jack Daniel's will now cost Tesco:

$70 / 1.60 = £43.75.

A high exchange rate will benefit Tesco because they can buy imported goods more cheaply. They can then make more profit on each bottle of Jack Daniel's that they sell to UK customers.

The impacts of a low exchange rate

The impacts of a weak exchange rate are the reverse of those from a strong exchange rate. Firms such as Morgan that were damaged by a strong currency find life easier when the exchange rate falls. A weak pound makes their exports seem cheaper to foreign consumers, so Morgan should be able to sell more of its cars in America.

On the other hand, firms such as Tesco will be damaged by a low exchange rate because it will now cost Tesco more in pounds sterling to buy in its imported stock. If Tesco reacts to the falling exchange rate by raising its prices, the company could lose customers. If Tesco does nothing it will make less profit on each unit of imported stock sold.

A-grade application

One of Europe's most successful manufacturing businesses is Airbus Industrie. Ten years ago the American Boeing was the undisputed leader of aircraft manufacture worldwide. Nowadays Airbus and Boeing are neck and neck. A real problem for Airbus, though, was when the euro became very strong against the US dollar. Between 2005 and early 2008 the euro rose 50% against the dollar. This raised the possibility that Airbus planes would have to be priced far above its Boeing competitors.

The impact on Airbus was awful. It had to price its planes in dollars, but almost all its costs were in euros. This led, in March 2008, to a very unusual announcement: Airbus would insist on paying all its European suppliers in dollars in future. This would pass the exchange rate risks onto those suppliers. Before, a rise in the euro would make it harder to afford to pay the European suppliers. Now, a rise in the euro would be offset slightly by the cheaper prices for supplies. The suppliers (such as Britain's Rolls Royce engines) complained bitterly, but they had little choice but to accept.

More recently the euro has weakened slightly against the dollar, making it easier for Airbus to gain profitable orders. In 2010 Airbus achieved a 52% market share in new orders for 100+ seater aircraft. In 2011 it looks as if Airbus will do even better, as its order books are overflowing. This is important as more than 150,000 European jobs rely directly on Airbus. As Britain makes all the wings for Airbus planes, UK jobs are also secured when Airbus does well.

Evaluation: what can firms do about the economy and the exchange rate?

- A weak pound might benefit Morgan. However, it would be unwise to rely on a weak pound for its profitability because the exchange rate can change.

- Economic booms will also benefit Morgan because it sells luxury goods that have a positive income elasticity of demand that is well above one. Sales will tend to grow at a faster rate than the general economy. Unfortunately, despite politicians' assurances, economic booms are not permanent. So it would also be unwise for both Morgan and Tesco to rely on a favourable external business environment for their profitability.

- No one can reliably forecast economic trends, but successful firms are prepared for any possible circumstances. They will have asked 'What if?' a specific economic trend depresses profitability. Firms can do nothing about the exchange rate and the economy. However, they can make internal changes to their businesses that are designed to minimise the worst effects of a possible economic problem. For example, if Morgan believes that the pound will carry on rising against the American dollar the company could attempt to cut its costs by automating production. In short it could aim to internalise external constraints.

Issues for analysis

- There are two main ways to consider businesses and economic change.

- The more obvious is how a business should respond, e.g. to a rise in interest rates. It may anticipate a rise in customer demand and therefore increase production; it may rethink its marketing strategy.

- The second issue is tougher: what strategies should a firm carry out to protect itself from unknown economic changes in the future. By definition this will be difficult, as how can one anticipate the unknown? Yet, in the lead-up to the recent recession, was it so difficult for a bank or a house builder to anticipate the problems that might arise in future? The problem, often, is that directors of plcs have such huge financial incentives to achieve profit increases that they ignore actions to protect the business from possible downturns. In a family-run (Ltd) business there is a much greater reason to think about the next ten years rather than the next ten months.

Economic growth and the business cycle: an evaluation

Businesses are sometimes badly run, leaving them exposed to potential collapse if interest rates rise or a recession occurs. In other cases bad luck may be a factor, e.g. a well-run café has to close because the factory nearby closes down. In an ideal world, every business would anticipate every risk facing it, and devise a relevant survival strategy. This may not always be possible.

One of the best judgements a director can make is to ensure that a firm is always equipped financially for any future economic change. If the business keeps its borrowings relatively low and its liquidity relatively high, it will survive almost any problem. Toyota's ability to survive its 2010 quality problems and the 2011 tsunami shows the value of a strong balance sheet. Toyota had always been hugely liquid.

Key terms

Inflation: although often defined as the rate of rise in the average price level, inflation is better understood as a fall in the value of money.

Natural wastage: allowing staff levels to fall naturally, by not replacing staff who leave.

Real wages: changes in money wages minus the rate of change in prices (inflation), e.g. if your pay packet is up 6% but prices are up 4%, your real wage has risen by 2%.

A · Revision questions *(30 marks; 30 minutes)*

1 What is the business cycle? (2)

2 Explain why a business such as Chessington World of Adventures might be affected by a recession in America. (4)

3 Define the term 'the business cycle'. (2)

4 Explain two typical features of a recession. (4)

5 Give an example of a firm that might benefit from a recession in the UK. (1)

6 What is 'trading down' and why does it occur? (3)

7 Why might a firm respond to the threat of a recession by suspending recruitment, even before the recession actually arrives? (3)

8 What are inflationary expectations and why are they important? (4)

9 How might inflation benefit a small one-stop convenience store? (3)

10 Explain, giving two reasons why staff morale can plummet during a recession. (4)

Data response

New Look struggles

The first half of 2011 was a real struggle for the UK economy, with miserably slow growth and uncomfortably high inflation. With the RPI at 5% for June and July 2011, yet wages rising at no more than 2%, household disposable incomes were being squeezed.

For companies such as Marks & Spencer, this would inevitably mean tough times, but surely it would be good for a retailer of low-priced fashion clothes? Yet although Primark did quite well, UK sales at New Look fell by 9.7% in the first half of 2011 and the company's annual profits collapsed from £162.7 million in 2010 to £98 million in 2011.

New Look's problems stemmed from two bad decisions. First, the company misread the UK economy. It assumed that the recovery of 2010 would develop further in 2011, allowing the business to push its styles and prices up-market. Newly appointed chief executive Alistair McGeorge said 'We put together a range of products where the weighting of prices was too much at the higher end of where we'd normally expect it to be'. In future New Look will be returning to a clearer focus on the budget end of the market.

The second problem for the business came from internal disruption caused by the decision to relocate the group's buying, merchandising and design teams to London. This caused labour turnover to jump, and may have distracted staff from their job functions.

One bright spot for the business was that its website achieved a 40% increase in sales, making it the second most-visited women's clothing website. Perhaps that is an area to build on in the future.

Source: various newspaper reports.

Questions (30 marks; 35 minutes)

1. a What is 'the RPI'? (2)

   b Explain why the RPI might have an effect on household disposable incomes. (6)

2. It seems odd that shop sales fell 9.7%, yet online sales rose by 40%. Outline two factors that might explain this. (6)

3. To what extent were New Look's problems a result of economic factors? (16)

Case study

Antonia Dyball-Jamieson is worried. She is the founder and managing director of 'Emporium', an up-market chain of clothes shops located in prosperous market towns in Surrey such as Reigate and Guildford. Fashion Emporium stocks aspirational high fashion brands such as Jack Wills and Abercrombie and Fitch that sell at premium prices, e.g. £70 for a logoed T-shirt. The business serves a target market made up of privately educated teenagers, whose expenditure is largely funded by their high-income-earning parents who work, mostly, in financial services in the City of London. The high prices that Antonia is currently able to charge ensure that each of her stores operates with a low break-even point and a healthy safety margin.

Over the past seven years the business has

taken advantage of a favourable economic climate and has expanded steadily. On average, Antonia manages to open a new 'Emporium' branch every year and, on a like-for-like basis, Emporium has managed to increase their sales by 7% annually. During the boom years the business has found it relatively easy to raise the additional loan capital required to enlarge the business.

Over the past couple of months Antonia has become increasingly concerned about the state of the economy. Her favourite economic guru, Evan Davis, the BBC's Economics editor, recently predicted that economic growth could grind to a halt next year. Even more alarmingly, Vicky, Antonia's old friend from university, warned that investment banks, such as Goldman Sachs were planning large-scale redundancies.

Vicky also complained that she had been told by her boss that her bonus this year would be that she would be keeping her job; last year she received £120,000 in addition to her basic salary of £75,000. 'How will I cope without my bonus!' wailed Vicky.

In the next week Antonia has some big decisions to make. She has found an excellent potential location for her next branch of Emporium in prosperous Godalming, which will cost £5,000 a year to lease. In addition £20,000 will have to be spent fitting out the new site, and five new members of staff will have to be hired and trained. Antonia's father, Sebastian, believes that she should not postpone her expansion plans. According to him, David Smith, the Economics correspondent for *The Times*, believes that the economy will continue to grow because interest rates will stay low for the foreseeable future.

Questions *(40 marks; 45 minutes)*

1 Calculate the income elasticity of the products sold by Emporium assuming that, on average, incomes in Surrey have risen by approximately 2% per annum over the past seven years. (4)

2 Explain why businesses such as Emporium are particularly sensitive to movements in the trade cycle. (4)

3 Describe three actions that Antonia could take to help prepare her business for a down-turn in the trade cycle. (6)

4 Should Antonia go ahead with her plans to open a new Emporium store in Godalming? Discuss the arguments for and against. (10)

5 Using the case study as a starting point, discuss whether it is essential that managers, such as Antonia, have a good understanding of economic theory in order to make effective long-run decisions. (16)

Case study

British economy statistics

Year	Economic growth rate %	Inflation % (RPI)	Unemployment rate % (based on the claimant count measure of unemployment)
1980	−2.5	17.8	6.0
1981	−1.2	12	9.4
1982	1.6	8.6	10.9
1983	3.3	4.5	10.8
1984	2.6	5.0	11.0
1985	3.8	6.0	10.9
1986	4.3	3.4	11.2
1987	4.8	4.1	10.0
1988	5	4.9	8.1
1989	2.2	7.8	6.3
1990	0.4	9.5	5.9
1991	−2.2	5.9	8.1
1992	−0.5	3.7	9.9
1993	2.5	1.6	10.4
1994	4.3	2.5	9.2
1995	2.8	3.3	7.9
1996	3.4	2.9	7.2

Year	Economic growth rate %	Inflation % (RPI)	Unemployment rate % (based on the claimant count measure of unemployment)
1997	2.7	2.8	5.4
1998	2.7	3.3	4.6
1999	2.7	2.4	4.3
2000	3.0	3.0	3.6
2001	2.4	1.8	3.2
2002	1.8	1.7	3.1
2003	2.5	2.9	3.0
2004	3.2	3.0	2.7
2005	2.1	2.8	2.7
2006	2.6	3.2	3.0
2007	3.1	4.3	3.5
2008	−2.8	4	5.2
2009	−4.8	−0.5	7.2
2010	1.8	4.4	7.8

N.B. 2010 figures based on annualised data collected during September of that year

Source: National Statistics website: www.statistics.gov.uk/

Questions *(20 marks; 25 minutes)*

1 Plot the data shown in the table onto a graph designed to illustrate trends in the UK's economic growth rate, inflation rate and unemployment rate over the period 1980 to 2010. (6)

2 Can you identify any boom or slump years? (4)

3 Compare and contrast the characteristics of a boom with the characteristics of a recession. (8)

4 What is the main limitation of this data to managers? (2)

Globalisation and development

 ## Introduction

Globalisation is by no means a new force. In 1900 a quarter of the world's population lived under a British flag, bringing with it a 'culture' of tea, cricket and – from 1902 – Marmite. In the 1920s, American companies such as Ford and Coca-Cola started their moves to multinational status. By the 1960s Mickey Mouse, US films and British pop music were global forces. Yet the term 'globalisation' only really started to stick in the 1980s. It was in this period that the huge growth of McDonald's, Levi's jeans and Coca-Cola made people start to question whether the world was becoming a suburb of America. The 1990s growth of Microsoft and Starbucks brought the question further into focus. Figure 39.1 gives a sense of the extraordinary growth in world trade, but lends little support to any view that globalisation 'arrived in the 1990s'.

The term globalisation encompasses many issues. Some are based on cultural questions, such as whether a language such as French can survive the onslaught of (American) English. Some are based on ethical questions that seem much more stark when a rich western company is getting its supplies from Cambodian labour paid 30p an hour. Others are more focused on the economic question 'Are global giants wiping out national producers and restricting consumer choice?' Clearly these are all massive questions in a Business A-level course.

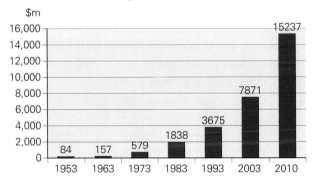

Figure 39.1 Growth in world exports, 1953 to 2010
Source: World Trade Organization, www.wto.org

 ## Government efforts to increase world trade

Trade between countries had been growing for centuries until the 1929 Wall Street crash led to increasing **protectionism** worldwide. The political changes in Germany and Japan in the 1930s (which led to the 50 million deaths in the Second World War) were partly due to these two countries' concern at being excluded from export markets. With the lessons learned from this, governments since 1945 have tried hard to make it easier for countries to do business with each other.

Following marathon negotiations lasting from 1986 to 1994, the World Trade Organization (WTO) was established in 1995. Overnight the value of tariff-free imports went from 20% to 44% of the worldwide total. Today it is over 50%. In other words, only in a minority of cases are taxes placed on imported goods. The development of the WTO was boosted further when China joined in 2001.

The WTO tries to ensure that there is **free trade** between countries, but that the trade is based upon common rules. For example, all WTO member countries should provide legal protection for the **intellectual property** of companies and individuals.

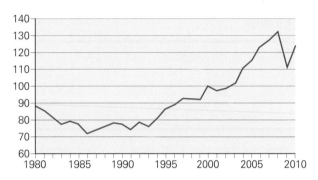

Figure 39.2 Ratio of world exports of goods and commercial services to GDP, 1980 to 2010 (2000 = 100)
Source: IMF for world GDP, WTO Secretariat for world trade in goods and commercial services.

Figure 39.2 shows the growth of exporting as a percentage of countries' GDP since the 1980s. It also shows the shock to the world economy of the 2009 recession.

Many people argue that WTO rules favour rich countries against poorer ones. There is a strong case for saying that free trade is the ideal form of trade for countries and companies at a similar stage of development (because it encourages competition). But less developed countries would surely benefit from protection of their **infant industries** until they have developed a scale of production that enables them to compete with multinational giants. In the early days of the motor industry in Japan and China, local car companies were protected by huge tariff barriers (import tax rates of around 40%). In both countries there is no longer any need for import tariffs as the industries are efficient and competitive.

Although the WTO can be criticised for the extent to which policy making is dominated by America and Europe, there is no doubt that global economic growth in recent decades has spread increased prosperity far and wide around the world. Very sadly, the child mortality figures for Nigeria (see Table 39.1) show there is still a long way to go.

The case for globalisation

Joseph Stiglitz, in his book *Globalization and its Discontents* (2002), became the world's most famous critic of globalisation. Yet he identifies many important benefits from increasingly open world trade. To him, the biggest step forward by far is the increase in the number of people in less developed countries whose lives have been improved. He mentions the opening up of the Jamaican milk market (allowing US competition in) as a huge benefit to poor children in Jamaica, even if it hurt the profits of the local farmers. It is also important to bear in mind that, however awful the figures may be for infant deaths before the age of 1, they are incomparably better than they were 20, 40 or 50 years ago. Globalisation of healthcare is as important here as the globalisation of the economy.

Among the main advantages of globalisation are:

- increased competition forces local producers to be efficient, thereby cutting prices and increasing standards of living (people's income goes further)

- providing the opportunity for the best ideas to be spread across the globe (e.g. AIDS medicines, water irrigation and mobile phones)

- if multinational companies open up within a country, this may provide opportunities for employment and training, and allow local entrepreneurs to learn from the experience of the more established businesses

- providing outlets for exports, which can allow a country to boost its standards of living by reducing dependence on subsistence farming (growing just enough to feed the family)

- it has provided the opportunity for a series of countries (e.g. Egypt, Mexico, China and India) to break away from poverty; for example, average living standards in China rose by 1,000% between 1990 and 2010; Table 39.1 shows the impact economic growth can have on infant mortality.

Table 39.1 Infant mortality (deaths of under-1s per 000)

	1990*	2011 (est)**
Egypt	67	25
Mexico	42	15
China	36	16.5
India	82	49
Nigeria	120	85
UK (for comparison)	8	4

Source: *Unicef statistics, August 2010 (www.childinfo.org); **CIA World Factbook August 2011

A-grade application

Bangladesh

In the 20 years until 1990, the annual growth rate in Bangladesh* was an extremely low 0.6%. This left its under-5 mortality rate at 149 per 1,000 in 1990. Each year, more under-5s died in Bangladesh than all the under-5s living in Britain. By 1990 Bangladesh was developing a clothing industry based upon very low-wage labour, targeting western companies. In the period 1990 to 2009 the growth rate rose to 3.3% per person, helping the infant mortality rate to fall from 149 to 52 per 1,000.

Bangladesh has by no means become a wealthy country. Many households have no access to clean water and, by 2009, only 22% of the population had a phone. But economic progress has made an impact, and should continue to do so.

* Bangladesh, with 160 million people, is the world's seventh most populated country

The case against globalisation

The economic case against

Critics suggest that globalisation has made it harder for local firms to create local opportunities. In 2002 virtually no overseas car producer had a factory in India; but, with the growth of the Indian economy, by 2011 Hyundai, Suzuki, BMW, Toyota, Nissan and Honda were present, with Peugeot and Ford announcing new factories by 2012. Although the local Tata Motors has announced the production of the world's cheapest new car (at £1,250 each), it may be that the middle of the car market will be captured by the big European and Far Eastern car producers.

There is also concern that new production in a country does not necessarily mean new wealth. Some multinational firms establish a factory locally, but use it in a way that could be called exploitation. In India there are many clothing factories that supply companies such as Gap, Primark and Asda. Wage rates are extremely low by western standards, and working conditions are poor. Little of the value created by the sale of a £20 jumper in a London Gap outlet may seep back to India. If the clothing design, the branding and the packaging are all done in the West, all that is left is labour-intensive, low-paid factory work.

The social and cultural case against

In 2002, a French farmer made the headlines worldwide by bulldozing a McDonald's outlet. He was protesting about the Americanisation of France. Remarkably, even the French cosmetics powerhouse L'Oréal is inclined to show English-language television commercials in France. The increasing number of US outlets in French high streets was the farmer's main concern: KFC, McDonald's, Subway, Gap, Starbucks, and so on. Around the world, many agreed that their high streets were starting to look like those in America; they probably discussed it on their iPhone while also listening to Britney Spears on their iPod. Globalisation started to be criticised for making our lives less interesting by reducing the differences between countries and cities.

Among the main disadvantages of globalisation are:

● that everywhere starts to look like everywhere else

● that globalisation is built on exploitation – the strong exploiting the rich

● that it may make it hard for local producers to build and grow in a way that is suited to local needs.

Nigeria

There is probably no country in the world that has under-achieved as severely as Nigeria. In the 20 years to 1990 its economy *shrank* by an average of 1.4% a year. Its 1990 child mortality of 230 per 1,000 was among the world's worst. Since then, growth has averaged just 1.3% a year; this is despite the fact that Nigeria is oil rich. Over the past 20 years more than £75 billion of oil has been exported from the country. This has been good for BP and Shell, but the people of Nigeria have little benefit to show for all this wealth. Corruption has been an important problem, but many Nigerians would point to the oil multinationals as well as their own leaders. The benefits of globalisation have passed them by.

Globalisation and the British economy

Britain should probably have benefited more from the growth of world trade, given the country's 10% share of world exports in 1950. Since then, though, there has been a process of **deindustrialisation** in Britain, as industries such as textiles, ship building and car production wilted under foreign competition. Figure 39.3 shows Britain's dramatic decline in the years between 1953 and 1973. Since then there has been a further, steady reduction in Britain's share of 'merchandise exports'.

Fortunately for the economy, Britain has kept its strong position in sales of services to countries around the world. In 2010, Britain was second only to the United States in its share of the market for internationally traded services. Whereas the 2010 share of world trade in goods was 3.8%, Britain's share of 'invisible' exports was over 6%.

It is also important to remember that the increase in world trade of the past ten years has brought a significant increase in living standards in Britain. On average, those in work are very much better off than ten years ago, with items such as clothes, cars, furniture and household electronics down sharply in price. Cheap imports from China and Cambodia are not only enjoyable, but are also vital in keeping UK inflation low. Low prices help our money to go further, making us all better-off.

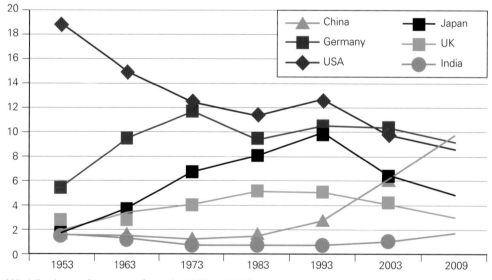

Figure 39.3 World's share of exports of goods 1953 to 2009

Source: World Trade Organization, www.wto.org.

Development

The most important thing is to realise that development happens. In 1981, 50% of the world's population lived on less than $1.25 a day (about 80p). By 2005 the figure had fallen to 21% (the figures are a true comparison, because changes in prices have been allowed for). By 2015, the World Bank estimates that the figure will have fallen to about 12%. Let's be clear, here, that 12% of a 7 billion world population means that nearly 1,000 million people will still be living on extremely low incomes. That, in itself, is a disgrace in a world where there is so much wealth. But it is wrong to treat the issue of development with a shrug of the shoulders. There are hopeful signs. Table 39.2 shows the economic performance of a selection of less developed countries. Despite the figures in the right-hand column, the two central columns show that improvements are definitely occurring.

In the period since 1981, the big development wins have been achieved in China, in South East Asia more generally, and in South America. Without exception, these gains have come about as a result of economic development. In other words, poverty has not been reduced because rich Chinese have given more to poor Chinese; this has come about because the Chinese economy has been able to produce more wealth for all.

Does economic aid have much to do with this relative success? Not really, as governments and charities rarely do enough to make much impact throughout a country. For countries such as China, India and Mexico, the key factors have been:

- greater willingness to accept inward investment from multinational or other big, wealthy companies from the West or Japan
- greater enterprise on the part of the local business population
- more stable government than before, especially in India and Mexico
- easier access for exports to countries such as Britain, America and the rest of Europe, partly thanks to the World Trade Organization.

Table 39.2 Economic performance of selected countries

	GDP at PPP 2010*	Average annual growth in GDP per head 1970–1990	Average annual growth in GDP per head 1990–2009	% of population below $1.25 a day 1994–2008
Bangladesh	$1,700	0.4	3.4	50%
Benin	$1,500	0.3	1.2	47%
China	$7,600	6.6	9.0	16%
India	$3,500	2.1	4.8	42%
Nicaragua	$3,000	–3.7	1.9	16%
Nigeria	$2,500	–1.4	1.7	64%

*Source: *CIA Factbook 2011* and *Unicef Statistics 2011* (www.childinfo.org).

Issues for analysis

Globalisation needs to be seen as a catch-all term that may mean different things to different people. It is assumed to be a very new thing (which is arguable) and is assumed by many to be a bad thing. When analysing issues to do with globalisation it helps to:

- be clear about the definition you are using and the limits you are placing on that definition (e.g. 'economic globalisation' but not 'cultural globalisation' – though you might later want to explore whether this separation is artificial)
- be calm, measured and balanced; whatever the strength of your views, push yourself to consider a different perspective – for instance, many people

feel strongly about 'sweatshop' work for low pay in countries such as Vietnam, but it may be that Vietnamese workers would prefer a factory job to a job in the fields; we cannot jump to conclusions about other people's lives

● avoid slipping into too small-scale a viewpoint; globalisation is at least as much about increasing competition between big western companies as it is between the west and the developing world; unarguably, Volkswagen versus Renault versus Toyota is global rivalry we all benefit from.

Globalisation and development – an evaluation

The judgements involved in this area need to be especially subtle. Beware of poorly justified judgements that may suggest intolerance towards others, or ignorance of the extreme disparities between incomes in rich and poor countries. The more you read about different countries' successes and failures, the better rooted your judgements will be.

It is also valuable to take a critical look at all the evidence provided, questioning whether the claims made by businesses about their motives is the truth or just public relations. The same sceptical approach should be taken to any other form of evidence, whether from pressure groups such as Greenpeace or from government ministers or officials. Globalisation is a topic in which opinions are often clearer than facts.

Key terms

Deindustrialisation: the steady decline in manufacturing output and employment that changed Britain from being an industrial powerhouse to a service-sector economy.

Free trade: imports and exports being allowed into different countries without taxation, limits or obstruction. This ensures that companies from different countries compete fairly with each other.

Infant industries: new, young industries in a developing country that may need extra, but temporary, protection until they have grown big and strong enough to compete with global giants (e.g. a new Zambian factory producing instant coffee, trying to compete with the global number one – Nestlé/Nescafé).

Intellectual property: legal protection for the rights of the originator of new written, visual or technical material (e.g. protected by copyright, trademarks or patents).

Protectionism: government actions to protect home producers from competition from overseas (e.g. by setting import taxes – 'tariffs' – or imposing import quotas that place a cap on the number of goods that can enter a country).

Further reading

Stiglitz, J. (2002) *Globalization and its Discontents.* Norton.

A Revision questions *(40 marks; 40 minutes)*

1 Re-read the definition of globalisation at the start of the unit. Outline one advantage and one disadvantage of the world 'becoming one market'. (4)

2 a Calculate the percentage increases in world exports in the following periods.

   a 1973 to 1983

   b 1983 to 1993

   c 1993 to 2003 (5)

  b How well do these figures support the idea that globalisation 'arrived in the 1990s'? (2)

3 Outline two reasons why consumers might suffer as a result of a government policy of import protectionism. (4)

4 Examine one reason why a new car factory in Nigeria might benefit if the Nigerian government used the infant industries argument to protect it. (4)

5 Outline two other factors that might affect a country's infant mortality, apart from economic development. (4)

6 Use Figure 39.3 to describe three major changes that have happened in the world economy between 1953 and 2009. (6)

7 Should wealthy countries increase the rates of tax on their own populations in order to finance greater help to people living on less than $1.25 a day? (5)

8 Outline three possible reasons that might explain why China's growth rate is so much higher than that of Nigeria or India. (6)

B1 Case study

Starbucks agrees to Ethiopian coffee branding

CSRwire.com reports that Starbucks and Ethiopia recently signed a distribution, marketing and licensing agreement that should help Ethiopian coffee farmers reap value from the intellectual property of their distinctive, deluxe coffees:

Eight months ago Oxfam began working to raise awareness of Ethiopians' efforts to gain control over their fine coffee brands. Today, Starbucks has honored its commitments to Ethiopian coffee farmers by becoming one of the first in the industry to join the innovative Ethiopian trademarking initiative.

We covered this story last winter, looking at how Oxfam threw the weight of its powerful nonprofit brand behind the cause of poor Ethiopian coffee farmers. At stake were the Sidamo, Harrar, and Yirgacheffe varietals, thought to be among the best in the world. Policy Innovations raises its mug to this multi-stakeholder cooperation.

Source: Fairer Globalization and *Policy Innovations*, 22 December 2007

Questions *25 marks; 30 minutes)*

1 Explain what 'intellectual property' there can be in Ethiopian coffee. (4)

2 Explain how Ethiopian farmers might benefit from this initiative. (6)

3 Discuss the possible reasons why Starbucks may have decided to sign this deal with the Ethiopian coffee producers. (10)

4 Explain what the author means by the phrase 'this multi-stakeholder cooperation'. (5)

Case study

Channel 4 cleared over Tesco child labour story

A Tesco complaint about a *Channel 4 News* item on child labour has been rejected by media regulator Ofcom. The *Channel 4 News* story alleged that child labour was being used by suppliers in Bangladesh in the production of clothes for Tesco stores.

Tesco complained that the report, which featured a 'little boy who looks no more than eight' and other allegedly underage workers, was unfair. The supermarket company, represented by solicitors Carter-Ruck, said the boy was in fact 12-years-old and claimed the 'child' workers featured were aged 18 or over. But Ofcom said the secretly filmed report – made by independent producer Evolve Television for *Channel 4 News* – was 'properly supported' and put in 'fair context'. Ofcom also said Tesco had been given an appropriate amount of time to respond to the allegations.

The media regulator, in its ruling published today, said *Channel 4 News* had not been unfair in its treatment of the supermarket. Ofcom added that the *Channel 4 News* report had 'questioned Tesco's ability to ensure its ethical standards are met throughout the supply chain'.*

'The report did not allege that Tesco was deliberately or knowingly using child labour to produce its clothing,' the regulator said. 'Rather, it showed that companies supplying Tesco were employing workers who were below the legal age limit in Bangladesh (i.e. aged under 14) and that some of these workers were producing clothes for Tesco.'

Tesco had claimed the boy who was described as looking 'no more than eight' was in fact 12. The company said he had no connection with the factory and was delivering lunch to his cousin. But *Channel 4 News*, in its response, said Tesco's claim was 'directly at odds' with what its film-makers had seen, 'namely that the boy was sewing creases into denim trousers as part of the production process'.

Channel 4 News editor, Jim Gray, added: '*Channel 4 News*'s reputation is founded upon its track record for delivering high-quality original journalism through thorough, rigorous and accurate investigation. This report possessed all of these qualities and investigative journalism remains at the heart of everything we do.'

Ofcom's Fairness Committee, its most senior decision-making body, made a provisional finding rejecting Tesco's complaint. The supermarket then requested a review of the provisional finding on the grounds that it was flawed. It was also not upheld.

*The supply chain is the network of suppliers that takes a product through all the stages from raw materials through to the retail store.

Source: John Plunkett, *Guardian*, 25 February 2008. Copyright Guardian News & Media Ltd 2008.

Questions *(30 marks; 35 minutes)*

1 Explain why it would be difficult for Tesco to 'ensure its ethical standards are met throughout the supply chain'. (8)

2 Discuss the probable reasons why Tesco decided to make this public complaint against Channel 4. (10)

3 Discuss whether Tesco should now withdraw all its clothing production from Bangladesh. (12)

Data response

Globalisation – it isn't easy!

In 1980 it wasn't obvious whether India or Pakistan had the better economic prospects. Yes, India's population was hugely bigger (685 million compared with 85 million for Pakistan) but Pakistan had a higher GDP per capita. Whatever the reasons, Honda opted for Pakistan. By 2005, even though India was the growth story, Honda's 50% share of Pakistan's car market was a big consolation. Honda Pakistan's position was very profitable, and its place was secured by owning Pakistan's only large car factory. For those growing up locally, the Honda Civic and Accord models epitomised luxury driving.

To keep its position strong, Honda embarked in 2005 on heavy investments in capacity expansion. The goal was to be able to produce 50,000 cars a year.

Then it all went wrong. From 2006 the market for passenger cars started to slide. Worse, competition from lower-priced cars from Korea, Malaysia and India chipped away at Honda's market share. In 2007, Honda sales were just 18,709 cars – from a factory capable of producing 50,000. Worse was to come, as sales slid further in the face of world recession and a collapse in security and consumer confidence. Healthy operating profits turned into severe losses.

Naturally enough, Honda's strategy had been to focus on 'the market' – largely companies or government departments buying prestigious cars for managerial staff. Yet from about 2005 the market moved more towards individuals buying cars for themselves. A Honda Civic was priced at about £11,000; a Suzuki Swift would cost half that figure. Honda's marketing strategy was facing the wrong way – looking backwards instead of forwards. In 2010 Honda's market share fell to 23%.

Questions (30 marks; 35 minutes)

1 Explain why a business might make a mistake when choosing which country to focus on. (6)

2 Honda's international strategy has been hugely successful; but not in this case. Examine why a successful international company such as Honda might fail within one country. (10)

3 Discuss two alternative strategies Honda might choose in the face of its current problems in Pakistan. Explain which you would recommend, and why. (14)

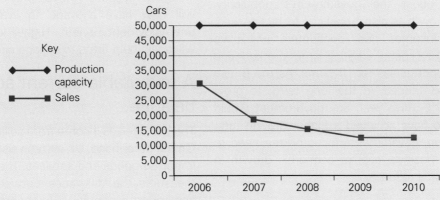

Figure 39.4 Capacity utilisation at Honda, Pakistan

Impact of government economic policy

> ### Definition
> Economic policy is the grouping of actions taken by the Chancellor of the Exchequer to try to achieve the government's economic objectives.

Government economic objectives

The most important goal of any politician is re-election. Electors make their voting choices partly on the competence of the government at managing the economy. Therefore any government will try hard to achieve its economic objectives, which typically include the following.

Economic growth

Economic growth occurs when the total value of all goods and services produced within the economy in a year increases. If the government can increase the rate of economic growth the material standard of living within the country will grow more rapidly, helping to boost the government's popularity. Economic growth is also beneficial to businesses. If average incomes rise, consumers will have more money to spend, creating larger markets and additional opportunities for UK firms. As the British economy has tended, in the long term, to grow at 2.25% to 2.5% a year, any government would be thrilled to have achieved a higher growth rate. In a recession, governments focus on the need to achieve any positive level of economic growth in order to signal a recovery.

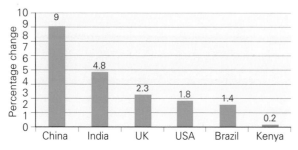

Figure 40.1 Long-run GDP per capita real growth rates, selected economies, 1990 to 2009
Source: Unicef, www.childinfo.org

Low inflation

Inflation is the percentage annual change in the average price level. Price stability will make it easier for UK firms to compete against their foreign rivals, both at home and abroad. The stability created by low inflation also encourages investment, leading to stronger economic growth.

Low unemployment

If the government can reduce the number of people in the country who are without work, the country's output should increase. Spending levels should also increase because those previously unemployed will now have a wage to live off, rather than unemployment benefit. Higher levels of spending will again help firms to expand and grow.

A favourable current account balance

The UK receives income from selling exports abroad. On the other hand, UK citizens also spend money on imported goods and services. The **current account** measures the difference between export income and import expenditure. In general, the government would like to avoid a current account deficit, a situation where import expenditure exceeds export income. Current account deficits are financed by a general increase in borrowing, or asset sales, across the economy, leading to a fall in society's collective net worth.

A stable exchange rate

The exchange rate measures the volume or amount of foreign currency that can be bought with one unit of domestic currency (e.g. £1:$1.60 means that one pound can buy one dollar sixty cents). A stable exchange rate helps firms to forecast how much profit, or loss, they stand to make from exporting or importing. If firms can forecast the future with greater confidence they will be more likely to go ahead and trade with foreign firms, boosting UK economic activity.

Government economic policies

The government uses economic policies to achieve its economic objectives. As a Business Studies student the key for you is to understand how these policies affect different types of business. The economic policies that you will need to know about are discussed below.

Fiscal policy

Fiscal policy refers to the government's budget. The budget concerns the government's tax and spending plans for the year ahead. The main forecast areas of government expenditure for 2010 to 2011 are as shown in Figure 40.2.

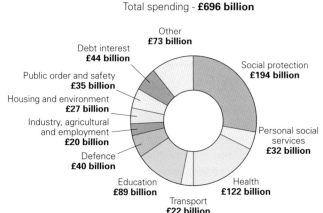

Total spending - **£696 billion**

Other **£73 billion**

Debt interest **£44 billion**

Public order and safety **£35 billion**

Housing and environment **£27 billion**

Industry, agricultural and employment **£20 billion**

Defence **£40 billion**

Education **£89 billion**

Transport **£22 billion**

Social protection **£194 billion**

Personal social services **£32 billion**

Health **£122 billion**

Figure 40.2 Government spending 2010 to 2011

Source: HM Treasury

How does government expenditure affect firms?

● In general, an increase in government spending will increase the total level of spending within the economy, causing most markets to grow. For example, if the government awards above-inflation pay rises for nurses, this could help businesses such as Asda or Ryanair that target ordinary working people. Nurses are likely to spend the bulk of any pay rise they receive (e.g. on a European holiday).

● About 40% of the UK economy revolves around government spending; firms such as construction companies (road and school building), publishers (textbooks) and computer suppliers are all hugely dependent upon government spending (see Figure 40.2). At the time of writing the UK government is planning cutbacks on public spending to get this figure down towards the lower end of the range shown in Figure 40.3.

Reduced spending on the NHS will cut the turnover of the construction companies that want contracts to build new hospitals. There will be multiplier effects too. For example, firms that supply the construction companies with the concrete, bricks and steel will suffer from government expenditure cutbacks. The same applies to drug manufacturers, and firms that produce medical equipment such as MRI scanners and hospital beds.

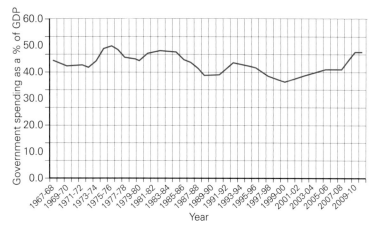

Figure 40.3 Government spending as a percentage of GDP

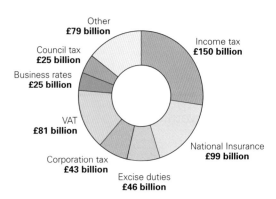

Government receipts
Total receipts - **£548 billion**

Other
£79 billion

Income tax
£150 billion

Council tax
£25 billion

Business rates
£25 billion

VAT
£81 billion

National Insurance
£99 billion

Corporation tax
£43 billion

Excise duties
£46 billion

Figure 40.4 Forecast government receipts, 2010 to 2011
Source: Office for Budget Responsibility

The main sources of tax income for 2010 to 2011 are as shown in Figure 40.4.

How does taxation affect firms?

- The largest component of the UK government's income comes from income tax. Income tax tends to reduce consumer spending because higher income tax rates widen the gap between gross (before tax) and net (after tax) pay. At times the government is forced into collecting more income tax in order to finance increases in public expenditure. This tends not to be a popular policy. Most firms do not benefit. If more money is collected through income tax, demand for products and services may shrink as consumer spending falls. The UK income tax system is mildly 'progressive'. This means that those earning lower incomes pay a smaller percentage of their income in tax than those earning higher salaries. Changes to the income tax system can affect some firms more than others. For example, an increase in the top rate of income tax from 40% to 50% would hit BMW car dealerships but might have no effect on sales of bicycles.

- Value added tax (VAT) is added to the retail price of a product. It is an example of an indirect tax (i.e. a tax levied on expenditure, rather than on income). In its first budget since coming to power, the UK's 2010 coalition government announced a target of boosting tax receipts by £8 billion per year by increasing the rate of VAT from 17.5% to 20%. VAT makes goods more expensive. Changes in VAT rules can affect businesses. If the government decided to extend VAT to newspapers the price of newspapers would be forced up, leading to a fall in the volume of newspapers bought and sold.

- Excise duties are indirect taxes levied, in addition to VAT, on a wide range of products including petrol, cigarettes and alcohol. The impact of excise duties on a market is very much influenced by consumer price sensitivity. For example, petrol retailers such as Shell tend not to be too badly affected by increases in petrol duty because the demand for petrol in the UK tends to be price inelastic. In other words, the price increase created by the increase in fuel duty has a minimal effect on the volume of petrol that Shell sells. Oil companies find it relatively easy to pass on any increase in petrol duty to the motorist by raising petrol prices. Increasing excise duty rates on a price-inelastic product also benefits the government because it will raise more in taxation from this market.

- Corporation tax is a tax levied on a company's profits. In the period 2011 to 2014 the UK government is to cut corporation tax steadily from 28% to 24%. A fall in the corporation tax rate gives firms an increased opportunity to invest because, all other things being equal, the less paid in corporation tax the greater the level of retained profit.

Types of fiscal policy

- *Expansionary fiscal policy:* the government runs an expansionary fiscal policy when planned government spending for the year ahead exceeds planned tax income. Expansionary fiscal policy tends to benefit most firms in the short run because the total level of spending in the economy will rise.

- *Contractionary fiscal policy:* the government runs a contractionary fiscal policy when planned expenditure is less than planned tax income. Contractionary fiscal policy tends to depress the total level of spending within the economy.

- *Neutral fiscal policy:* if planned tax income equals planned government spending the government's budget is said to be 'balanced'.

Monetary policy

Monetary policy concerns the availability and price of credit. In the UK, monetary policy is implemented by the Bank of England. The Bank of England's Monetary Policy Committee (MPC) meets every month to set the interest rate. The Bank of England's Base Interest rate since 1973 is shown in Figure 40.5.

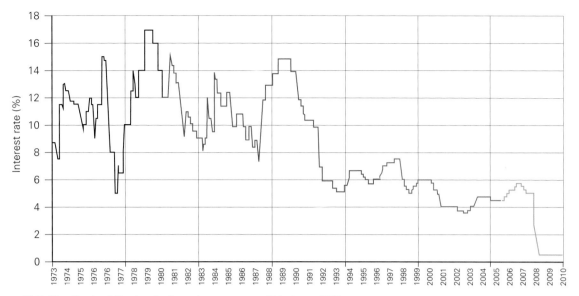

Figure 40.5 The Bank of England's Base Interest rate (%) since 1973

Source: Bank of England

The interest rate is the price of borrowed money. An increase in interest rates makes borrowing more expensive. On the other hand, saving becomes a more attractive proposition when interest rates rise. Interest rates are a powerful economic policy instrument because they can simultaneously affect a firm's revenue and costs.

Monetary policy can be tightened or slackened according to the economic circumstances. Recessions are caused by a lack of spending. If the economy is in recession the central bank will normally cut the interest rate because lower interest rates encourage people to spend more. Lower interest rates will encourage more borrowing and less saving.

On the other hand, during a boom demand is normally high and this can cause inflation. To reduce this threat the central bank normally reacts by 'tightening' monetary policy. This involves increasing interest rates. An increase in interest rates reduces borrowing and increases saving. As a result of the interest rate rise, total spending falls and the threat of inflation reduces.

The impact of interest rates on firms

The interest rate is a good example of an external constraint; it is a factor that is beyond the firm's control. However, changes in the rate of interest can affect a firm's costs and revenues.

Impact on business costs

Loan capital is an important source of finance for many businesses. The main benefit of a loan is

that, unlike retained profit, it can enable a firm to expand rapidly. However, unlike share capital, taking on additional loan capital does not compromise ownership. Highly geared firms, whose share capital is made up mostly of loan capital, can be highly vulnerable to interest rate changes, particularly if they have not borrowed at a fixed rate. A sudden increase in the interest rate will increase their fixed costs, leading to lower profits.

Impact on business revenue

Interest rates influence spending in a variety of different ways. During the 2009 recession, interest rates were cut to an all-time low of 0.5%. When the UK comes out of recession, the Bank of England is likely to begin gradually increasing interest rates to more normal levels such as 4%. Rising interest rates tend to depress consumer spending because they cut into disposable incomes. Disposable income measures the amount of income a person has to spend once taxes, pensions and other fixed outgoings have been subtracted from gross pay. There are several reasons why an increase in interest rates leads to lower disposable incomes:

Mortgage repayments

Most houses are bought using a mortgage – a loan that is secured against the value of the property. If interest rates go up the person owning the mortgage will now have to pay back more to the bank each month in interest, cutting into their disposable income.

Consumer credit

The UK is addicted to credit. According to the pressure group Credit Action, total UK personal debt at the end of July 2011 stood at **£1,451 billion**. If interest rates go up, those with large personal debts will find their monthly disposable incomes being cut sharply. If interest rates stay high, firms selling products bought on credit, such as cars and furniture, will probably suffer from falling sales.

Impact on investment

The rate of interest can affect investment decisions. If interest rates rise, the cost of funding an investment project will also increase if the project is financed using borrowed money. For firms with cash in the bank that do not need to borrow, the interest rate can still affect investment decision making because the interest rate also affects the opportunity cost of investing. Interest rates also affect the reward for risk – the difference between an investment's expected profitability (its ARR) and the prevailing interest rate – so the higher the rate of interest, the lower the level of investment spending by businesses.

Impacts on the exchange rate

A change in the interest rate tends to affect the exchange rate. If UK interest rates go up, wealthy foreign investors will be attracted to the pound: they will buy British pounds to take advantage of the high rates of interest that we offer. On the other hand, the reverse is also true. If the Bank of England decides to cut interest rates, the pound is likely to fall. The exchange rate is important for many businesses because it affects the price of imports and exports.

Evaluation; interest rates

Interest rates changes are mostly likely to affect:

- firms that want to expand quickly, but that lack the retained profit to fund the expansion internally
- highly geared firms that need to borrow heavily to invest in the latest technology in order to remain competitive
- businesses that sell luxury goods or discretionary items that are typically bought on credit.

A sudden rise in interest rates can be a disaster, especially for a company that has just borrowed heavily in order to expand. An increase in the interest rate causes costs to rise and revenues to fall simultaneously. Watch those profits fall! Many firms have been surprised by a sudden unanticipated rise in interest rates and have been forced into liquidation as a result.

Supply-side policies

The government uses supply-side policies to increase the economy's productive capacity. In other words, it is an attempt to make it easier for UK firms to supply UK customers with the goods and services they require. For example, opening up postal deliveries to private-sector business was intended to force the state-owned Post Office to become more efficient.

Types of supply-side policy

Privatisation

This is the selling off of state-owned organisations to private-sector owners. Firms in the private sector have to make a profit to survive. In order to make a profit in a competitive market firms must be efficient. Public-sector organisations do not have to make profit to survive. Instead, their role is to provide public services. If a public-sector organisation is inefficient its survival is not normally threatened. This lack of fear of closure due to inefficiency arguably leads to low productivity and inefficient management. **Laissez-faire** economists that favour the free market believe that the private sector will always be more efficient than the public sector. Unfortunately this could only be true in circumstances where there is effective competition. The privatisation of the railways, for example, simply established a series of railway monopolies that have been free to push rail fares to among the highest in the world. The privatisation of the Post Office may be equally ineffective.

Deregulation

Deregulation involves removing legal barriers to entering an industry. Deregulation therefore can make markets more competitive. An increase in competition should lead to an increase in efficiency. The greater rivalry between firms will force all firms to find ways of cutting costs so that they can survive by cutting prices. Until recently the air travel market between the UK and America was highly regulated. To operate on this route, airlines had to apply to the UK and the American governments for take-off and landing 'slots'. In the past, 'slots' were granted only to a limited number of American and British airlines. This acted as a barrier to entry, limiting competition on this route. Arguably, these regulations encouraged inefficiency and high prices. Recently the UK and the American governments deregulated this market in a so-called 'open skies agreement'. Today, any airline can now fly on this route.

Increase the incentive to work

Unemployment benefits and other social security benefits could be reduced. Benefit entitlement rules could also be tightened. For example, only those that are prepared to attend job interviews will receive their benefits. Income tax rates could also be cut. The personal tax allowance could be increased, which will increase the financial benefit of taking a low-paid job compared to remaining unemployed and living off benefits. An increased incentive to work will help firms that need extra labour to expand. Wage rates may also fall.

Flexible labour market legislation

A **flexible labour market** is a labour market that favours the employer rather than the employee. The labour market can be made more flexible by passing laws that do the following.

- Enable employers to dismiss workers with few legal formalities (e.g. the employee receives no compensation and is not entitled to notice of dismissal). It could be argued that this situation encourages employers to take on new staff when they wish to grow because the same staff can be released quickly and at little cost in a downturn.

- Reduce non-wage labour costs for the employer (e.g. in the UK employers pay minimal maternity pay for six months). In Sweden working mothers

receive two years' pay. It could be argued that low non-wage labour costs encourage UK firms to hire labour because it's cheaper to do so. The productive capacity of the economy should increase.

The UK labour market is a mixture of flexible and inflexible. The national minimum wage places an effective floor under wage rates. In America, the minimum wage is much lower than in Britain, providing lots of flexibility at the cost of lots of poverty.

Immigration

An influx of labour into a country will increase that country's labour supply, lifting the economy's productive capacity. Immigration can also help to ease skill shortages.

Education and training

If the government can increase the effectiveness of education and training within the economy, productivity (output per employee) should increase, which will help to lower costs. If the standard of education improves, the profitability of private-sector business investments should also increase. If it becomes more profitable for private businesses to invest they should respond, out of self-interest, by upping their investment levels. This will benefit the economy in general.

Transport infrastructure

If the government spends more money on upgrading Britain's road and rail networks, businesses should benefit. At present millions of pounds are lost each year because our roads are congested, and our railways are slow and antiquated. Like education, transport infrastructure is a form of complementary capital used by firms. If the quality of this infrastructure can be improved, the costs of operating a business in the UK will fall, increasing both the profitability and the desirability of investing in the UK.

▶ Coping with crisis

In normal times, government economic policy sets the long-term framework within which individual businesses can make decisions. Recent economic events are a reminder than not all times can be 'normal'. The period leading up to 2008 had seen a combination of risky lending and even riskier borrowing using new ways to bundle debts so that

no one quite knew what they were buying. When property prices fell (see Figure 40.6) it was clear that many banks would be in trouble. In fear of bank collapse, people withdrew their cash and only governments had the ability and the will to step in to (try to) solve the free market crisis.

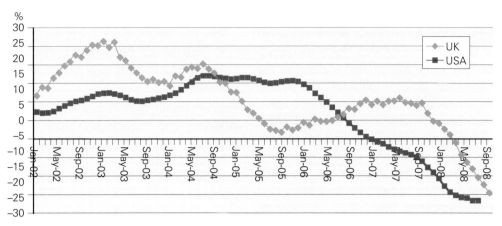

Figure 40.6 UK and US house prices

In Britain the government moved to help individual banks. The government also relaxed fiscal policy (cutting VAT, for example, to try to boost consumer demand). In America the government passed a bill providing a $700 billion rescue fund to buy up 'toxic assets'.

By 2011 these essential government actions caused their own problems. The government actions to bail out private sector banks had led to increases in public sector debt. Throughout the developed world governments responded by cutting their spending in order to balance their books. The resulting hit to economic growth threatened to cause still more crises in the years to come.

For businesses, tough times should mean tough decisions. Redundancies become more common-place and firms save cash rather than spend it on investment. Companies might be expected to understand that the poor economic conditions are a temporary problem. In fact, they often seize the opportunity to press government to make changes that favour business at the expense of workers or even consumers. In 2011 UK firms are pressing for widespread deregulation and for a freeze on the minimum wage. This moves beyond 'coping with crisis' towards exploiting it.

Issues for analysis

- It is important to have an idea about the impact the Chancellor's decisions can have on businesses, but high marks for analysis will come from the ability to use economics to explain the impact on business. The starting point will be to think with care about the business itself. Is it affected by exchange rates? (Topshop definitely is, but the *Sun* newspaper is hardly affected at all.)

- In this topic area, there is a close overlap between application and analysis. A sharp increase in National Insurance charges would have a fierce impact on a labour-intensive business, but not on a capital-intensive one. The analysis depends on the circumstances.

Impact of government economic policy – an evaluation

There is an age-old story about the boy who cried 'wolf' so often that no one believed him when a real wolf arrived. Business lobby groups are like this. Disgracefully, BP spent years warning that a move to lead-free petrol would be a serious mistake. Similarly, lobby groups warned of a huge rise in unemployment if the government brought in a minimum wage; this proved untrue. Exam papers often feature new

proposals by government – often opposed bitterly by business groups. No one should ever assume that business groups are unbiased in what they say. History shows that they argue their case fiercely, warning of dire consequences and then keep quiet when the change proves absolutely fine. Governments have to make decisions, and cannot always rely on businesses to be open and supportive of change.

Key terms

Current account: the country's accounts, when subtracting the value of imports from the total value of exports. If exports > imports, the account is in surplus.

Flexible labour market: a labour market with light regulation, making it easy for employers to pay what they want, and hire and fire as they see fit.

Laissez-faire: literally, 'let it be'. In economics it means leaving private-sector businesses to operate free from government intervention.

A Revision questions (40 marks; 40 minutes)

1 Distinguish between government economic objectives and economic policies. (4)

2 Explain why low inflation is an important government objective. (3)

3 Define the term 'fiscal policy'. (3)

4 Explain two examples of businesses that could benefit from increased UK government spending on pensions. (4)

5 Show two ways in which Tesco might be affected by an increase in the UK's rate of corporation tax. (4)

6 Define the term 'monetary policy'. (2)

7 Explain two reasons why the turnover of a posh French restaurant might be expected to fall following an increase in interest rates. (4)

8 Explain how a sharp increase in interest rates might affect a rapidly growing company such as Innocent Drinks. (6)

9 What are supply-side policies? (2)

10 Define the term 'privatisation'. (2)

11 What is 'deregulation'? (2)

12 Outline two reasons why the quality of education provided by the UK government might affect the profitability of Marks & Spencer. (4)

B1 Data response

Government cuts threaten construction jobs

Between 2011 and 2014 the Highways Agency plans to cut spending on Britain's road network by 44%. This will cut the government's capital expenditure from £1.6 billion in the year to March 2011 to £922 million by 2014. This may make sense for the government, which wants to save money to cut its fiscal deficit. However, the impact on private sector construction companies will be huge, because government is the biggest single customer for construction projects (with about 40% of total spending).

These cutbacks will affect construction companies (and their workers) plus key suppliers such as Aggregate Industries, which provides the cement and the 'aggregates' (stones for the foundations of roads or railway lines). Aggregate Industries' Swiss owners have already started reviewing capacity, staffing and production facilities given the forecast of demand declines as high as 40%.

The building industry's main trade organisation has described the Highways' Agency cutbacks as 'extremely disappointing considering the World Economic Forum has ranked the UK 35th in the world for quality of road infrastructure'. A further fall in this ranking could affect Britain's international competitiveness.

Questions (30 marks; 35 minutes)

1 Explain how the cut in road building could affect the government's fiscal deficit. (4)

2 Examine why the cut in spending may result in a rather lower improvement to the fiscal deficit than the government expects. (8)

3 The government believes that effective supply-side policies are the key to higher economic growth. How, then, can they possibly justify cutting investment in Britain's roads? Analyse and evaluate this question. (18)

Data response

Don't scrap the UK car industry

By early 2009, the UK's economy was nose-diving towards recession and one industry in particular were facing disaster head-on. New car sales are always hit hard by economic downturn, since consumers always have a cheaper alternative (buy a used car) or may be easily able to postpone their purchase until they can be more certain of their disposable income. With an estimated 800,000 UK jobs directly affected by the car industry (not just car factories, but suppliers and their suppliers, along with car dealerships), the case for special support for the industry from government was strong. The relief of the car industry is easily seen here in this press release from the car industry pressure group the SMMT (Society of Motor Manufacturers and Traders):

> Government has recognised the strategic national importance of the UK motor industry and taken positive steps to support it with the introduction of the Automotive Assistance Programme and the Scrappage Incentive Scheme. The market has seen some growth, leading to a cut in the rate of decline in production output, but industry remains fragile. It is vital that government continues to sustain and strengthen the economic recovery and build consumer confidence.

The scrappage scheme offered customers £2,000 towards the cost of a brand new car when they traded in a car that was 10 or more years old. Around 330,000 cars were sold under the scrappage scheme, while government estimates suggested that around 4,000 jobs were saved among manufacturers and suppliers

But looking at the graph in Figure 40.7, the effects of the policy are less clear cut.

The scrappage scheme finished in early 2010, roughly the same time as VAT went back up from 15% to 17.5%. Other support came in the form of promised government loans totalling around £750 million to help car manufacturers finance the building of new production facilities.

Questions *(40 marks; 50 minutes)*

1 To what extent does the graph prove that the scrappage scheme was vital to protecting the long-term future of the UK car industry? (12)

2 Calculate the effect of VAT increase in early 2010 on the price of a car that cost £20,000 before the increase. (4)

3 Analyse how the purchase of a brand new UK car has benefits to companies other than the car's manufacturer. (10)

4 Discuss whether the government was right to single out the car industry for specific support when the whole economy was suffering from a slump. (14)

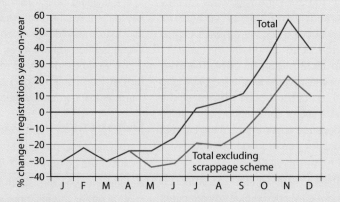

Figure 40.7 Change in monthly new car registrations in 2009

Government policies affecting business

The European Union

Britain is a member of the European Union. The European Union is a community of countries that form a single market as a result of laws centred on the free movement of people, goods, services and capital between all member countries.

The EU has undergone a series of expansions since starting with 6 founder members in the 1950s. At the time of writing there are 27 member countries, creating a market of nearly 500 million people generating over 30% of the world's economic activity. The map in Figure 41.1 shows the member countries, along with those countries hoping to join the EU at some point in the future.

EU expansion

British governments of recent years have tended to be broadly supportive of EU expansion. There are strong economic arguments for the UK to support an expansion of the single European market, based upon the following two major factors.

Increased size of market for UK exporters

EU enlargement means an increased size of market for UK exporters to other EU countries. Since a UK firm can sell its products in any other EU country without having to worry about paying import taxes or customs duties, membership of the EU provides UK firms with a 'home' market consisting not only of the 60 million or so who live in the UK, but the 500 million EU consumers. This can be contrasted with a similar situation for a US company with a home market of just over 300 million people. This larger 'home' market should give UK firms a competitive advantage over their US rivals.

Source of labour for British firms

Freedom of movement of people creates a source of cheap, often skilled labour for British firms, especially from newer EU members such as Poland and Romania. The issue of immigration is a controversial one, not just in the UK but in most other

Members
Hopeful future members
Non-members

Figure 41.1 European Union membership

western European countries. Extra workers put downward pressure on wage rates, which helps to prevent wage inflation. It also helps the economy to grow faster than its long-term trend growth rate. Unfortunately, the benefit to business and to shoppers is not shared by British workers, some of whom may have their pay pushed down to minimum wage rates by the competition for jobs.

A-grade application

UK immigration cap

In April 2011 the coalition government introduced a formal cap on the number of skilled worker immigrants allowed in from non-EU countries. A maximum of 20,700 would be allowed in per year. Typically, they would be earning over £40,000. For those earning £150,000+, no ceiling exists.

After conducting a study of its client companies, recruiting firm Poolia reported that many feel the cap on skilled migrants could cause severe problems for their business, but without generating much benefit in terms of UK unemployment figures. Even Conservative Boris Johnson has criticised the cap, saying it would 'put the economic recovery at risk by creating skills gaps'.

A single European currency

One political issue on which the UK has failed to join its European partners is that of the single currency, the euro. The UK government has no plans to adopt the euro as the UK's currency. Table 41.1 shows those EU members who use the euro. The central benefit is the ability to carry out international transactions without the need to worry about exchange rate fluctuations. At the time of writing (summer 2011) the pound had risen by around 10% against the euro within the past 12 months. This makes exporting harder for UK firms selling to countries using euros, as UK produced goods seem more expensive.

Successive UK governments have believed that the UK's economy is not suited to the euro. The concern is that any country that uses the euro has its monetary policy decided by the European Central Bank. It has to set one interest rate that is correct for all the economies that use the euro. If Germany needs high interest rates at a time when Britain needs low rates, will Britain's needs be taken fully into account? Especially after the Greek and Portuguese crises of 2011, it will be many years before a UK government starts the process of adopting the single currency. If and when this happens, many feel that the process should begin with a referendum of the UK electorate.

Table 41.1 EU members who use the single European currency (the euro)

Austria	Belgium	Cyprus
Finland	France	Germany
Greece	Ireland	Italy
Luxembourg	Malta	the Netherlands
Portugal	Slovakia	Slovenia
Spain		

Free trade

The World Trade Organization (WTO), is an international organisation that seeks to promote free trade between nations, by creating agreements governing the way in which global trading is conducted. The ultimate goal of free trade would mean an end to all import taxes (tariffs), and physical limits on the amount of goods that can be imported to any country (quotas).

Though not all countries in the world have signed all the WTO's agreements, all major economies are members, or are in the process of securing membership. The WTO also acts as a judge in disputes between countries where one feels another has broken free trade agreements. An example of this role is the WTO's investigation into the aircraft makers Airbus (Europe) and America's Boeing (both private-sector companies). The WTO is looking into whether each business has received illegal government subsidies to help them compete.

Free trade is a noble goal – the chance for the world economy to become truly efficient as those companies that do things best are able to offer their services globally. Unfortunately, it is not clear that free trade is always in the best interests of less developed economies. Japan, South Korea, China and India all began their periods of rapid economic modernisation with quite heavily 'managed' trading, i.e. they protected their still-immature companies and jobs until the businesses were big enough to stand on their own feet. Many economists still believe that protecting 'infant industries' can help long-term economic growth.

A government may be keen to protect jobs in its own country, by using trade barriers to discourage foreign competitors from entering the home market. For example, before the European Union, France 'protected' its wine makers from competition from Spain by placing an import tax on Spanish wines. Protectionist measures such as this give home producers a cost advantage. Governments may be keen to provide this protection to encourage the development of an industry that is new to a country. Other governments may be keen to protect certain industries to avoid job losses that might lead to an election defeat.

In every presidential election in America the candidates make speeches about 'protecting American jobs'. The World Trade Organization's job is to stop an election promise in America leading to job losses in Sheffield or Cairo.

A-grade application

The EU and USA at war

Despite generally cordial relations in many fields, there has long been a rather uneasy trading relationship between the EU and the USA. One recent row arose when the EU banned imports of US beef due to the overuse of growth hormone in 90% of US beef production. The USA countered this threat by announcing that it was considering imposing 100% tariffs (effectively doubling the selling price) on a range of EU products, including Danish ham, French truffles and Belgian chocolates. At the same time, the two powers were still fighting a trade war based around bananas, with the USA claiming that the EU had provided unfair subsidies to non-US banana producers. The USA, in retaliation, had imposed quotas (physical limits on the volume of imports) on EU products including Scottish cashmere sweaters and French handbags. Eventually the storm was sorted out at the WTO. In the short term, though, things were very uncomfortable for the companies that produce the goods in the firing line.

Figure 41.2 European cashmere goods that were under dispute by the USA

Legislation

UK businesses are subject to laws (legislation) passed by both the UK parliament and also the European parliament. Since both UK and EU law are passed by parliaments, housing members of political parties, laws are affected by party politics.

Traditionally, it has been safe to assume that Conservative governments try to interfere as little as possible with the workings of business. In other words, the tendency is to take a laissez-faire approach. This means trusting businesses to do their best for their customers and employees; in other words, let the market regulate business activities.

Labour governments are more likely to be suspicious that businesses may act in their shareholders' interests, not those of their customers. Therefore there is a greater temptation to bring in laws to regulate business activity. Before the Labour government established the National Minimum Wage in 1999, employers could, and did, pay as little as £3 an hour. The 2012 rate of £6.08 per hour is not riches, but provides some protection for the lower paid.

There are four main areas in which the law affects businesses:

1 employment
2 consumer protection
3 environmental protection
4 health and safety.

Employment legislation

Employment law sets out, and aims to protect, the rights of employees at work. These rights include the right to fair pay, sick leave, maternity and paternity leave, employment contracts being honoured, relationships with trades unions, the ability of employers to shed staff and the responsibilities of employers who make staff redundant. The implications of employment legislation are set out in Table 41.2.

As a general rule, businesses like to have minimal legal constraints on their activities. A business craves flexibility in the way it deals with its staff; legislation tends to impose certain restrictions on how staff are dealt with. UK business leaders argue that more employment legislation makes them uncompetitive relative to their international rivals. Yet UK employment legislation is not as tight as that in major rivals such as France and Germany.

Consumer protection legislation

Consumer protection law is designed to ensure that consumers are treated fairly by the companies from which they buy. This area of the law covers issues such as whether a product does what it claims to do, whether products are correctly labelled and measured out, levels of safety required from products, and the rights of the consumers after purchase for refunds or exchanges of faulty goods. Consumer protection legislation should ensure that no firms can gain an unfair competitive advantage by taking short-cuts in how their products are made. If all products and services must meet a minimum legal standard, this ensures against unscrupulous companies using unsafe and cheaper materials to gain a competitive edge.

Environmental protection legislation

Laws governing the impact of business on the environment are a key area today, given the increased acceptance of the need to legislate to protect the environment. A wide range of laws governs issues as diverse as the materials that firms must use for certain products, the processes firms are allowed to use in manufacturing and the extent to which firms must ensure their products are recyclable at the end of their lives. Environmental protection laws,

Table 41.2 Implications of employment legislation

Key area of employment law	Possible implications for firms
Minimum wage	Increased labour costs, which may lead to increased automation in the longer term and increased unemployment; on the plus side, employees may be more motivated by a fair wage satisfying basic needs
Right to a contract of employment	Meets employees' security needs but can reduce employers' flexibility in how they use their staff
Increased right to sick, maternity and paternity leave	Increased cost of paying for cover for these staff; however, staff may feel more valued as they feel well treated by employers, reducing staff turnover levels, which saves the costs of recruiting new staff
Redundancy	Reducing capacity becomes expensive due to statutory payments to staff made redundant; this can mean that closing a factory or office has a negative impact on cash flow in the short term
Trades union rights	Employers can be forced to deal with a trades union if enough staff are members; this does bring benefits as well as drawbacks

perhaps more than any others, seem to most firms to be a source of additional cost without much of an upside. Firms in the UK are also subject to EU laws; this is an area in which several EU directives have led to increased expectations of businesses in terms of the ability to recycle their products at the end of their lives (see below). Of course, all these firms feel a sense of injustice that they are competing against firms in other countries with less stringent environmental laws, feeling that their inter-national rivals have an unfair advantage when not having to meet the extra costs involved in abiding by environmental protection laws.

Health and safety legislation

Health and safety legislation is designed to ensure the safety of employees and customers within the workplace. The Health & Safety at Work Act 1974 places the major burden on employers. They have to provide a safe working environment for their staff. The main areas covered by the legislation include the physical conditions in which staff are required to work, precautions that firms are required to take when planning their work and the way in which hazardous substances must be treated in the workplace.

Despite the tight laws in Britain, there are still a worrying number of deaths at work, as shown in Table 41.3. Even more striking is that there are as many as 200,000 workplace injuries a year. Health and safety cannot be taken for granted.

A-grade application

Recycling 8 million cars

The EU End-of-Life Vehicles (ELV) Directive became operational in 2002, stating that all car manufacturers are responsible for the disposal of any new vehicles sold after that time. Britain's Society of Motor Manufacturers and Traders (SMMT) estimated the cost to the UK car industry alone as £300 million per year.

Figures provided by Friends of the Earth show the scale of the issue. With over 8 million vehicles scrapped every year within Europe, cars are a major source of waste. Of the 8 million tons or so of waste generated, three-quarters is already recycled; however, 2 million tons is still an awfully large hole in the ground to try to dig every year.

By 2009, the UK was struggling to cope with the demands of the directive, with only around one-third of scrapped vehicle owners completing the correct proce-dures for ensuring that the disposal of their vehicle adheres to the ELV Directive. Media commentators were blaming the UK government for failing to establish an effective system for enforcing the directive.

Table 41.3 Deaths at work, 2009 to 2010

Industry sector	Number of workers killed
Agriculture, forestry and fishing	38
Manufacturing	20
Construction	36
Service industries	91
Extractive and utility supply	7
Overall	192

Source: Public sector information published by the Health & Safety Executive.

Issues for analysis

- One major argument relating to government policies revolves around the UK's possible future adoption of the single European currency (the euro). A vast array of arguments has been put forward both in favour of and against the UK adopting the euro. Many arguments are economic, while others tend to be more overtly political, relating to issues of political sovereignty and loss of independence as a nation. The arguments that will concern you will be those that have a direct impact on UK businesses, such as the stability of the exchange rate. As more than half of Britain's exports are to EU countries, joining the euro would remove a significant source of uncertainty for British firms.

● Many exam questions debate the need for laws to govern the activities of businesses – in other words, laissez-faire versus government intervention. It will be helpful to have thought about the extent to which businesses can be trusted to look after the best interests of their customers and employees.

Government policies affecting business – an evaluation

There is a danger of making an unchallenged assumption that all trade is good, so free trade is a must. This assumption can – and indeed should – be challenged in several ways. Nevertheless, the British have grown wealthy on an economic system that seems to work, so it is understandable that we urge other countries to follow our approach. This allows large businesses to be allowed to do many good things, but also many less good ones. Worst, perhaps, is the avoidance of tax. This robs the country of the income required to improve public services.

Legislation seeks to ensure that all firms compete on a 'level playing field'. This is a noble goal, yet with increased international trade, there are circumstances where one country's tough legislation is the reason why a company from that country fails

to gain an international contract that is won by a company producing in a country with fewer laws affecting the cost they can offer the customer. The ultimate level playing field for businesses is one in which all countries have identical laws governing how businesses operate – and this is not going to happen in your lifetime.

For those who argue that laws are unnecessary because market forces will drive unscrupulous firms out of business, there is a disappointing lack of evidence to suggest that this argument holds water. Though plenty of businesses are convicted of breaking the law, it is a real challenge to find just one example of a firm that has been forced to close as a result of doing so. Is the incentive to avoid prosecution strong enough?

A Revision questions (25 marks; 25 minutes)

1   What is the name of the international organisation that seeks to regulate trade between nations? (1)

2   Explain the benefits that businesses gain from being based in an EU country. (5)

3   Briefly describe the main aims of the following legislation:
    a   employment laws
    b   consumer protection law
    c   environmental protection law
    d   health and safety law. (8)

4   Explain two possible consequences of a tightening of environmental protection laws for one of the following:
    a   a supermarket
    b   a chemical manufacturer
    c   a bank. (6)

5   Briefly explain why many firms would welcome a relaxation of employment laws affecting the rights of part-time staff. (5)

Case study

Cheapotels

The success of Cheapotels had caught analysts by surprise. There had seemed to be little demand in the UK for really cheap hotel accommodation until charismatic entrepreneur Rob Doyle launched the first five Cheapotels on an unsuspecting UK market three years ago. Since then, Rob has barely been out of the tabloids, pulling off all manner of publicity stunts to keep the brand in the public eye. He has also managed to open in another 13 locations across the UK.

Based on what Rob describes as a hardcore version of the 'no frills' philosophy that brought easyGroup success in the 1990s airline market, Cheapotel buys up cheap property in poor parts of major UK cities and offers a bare room with a bed and washbasin at a flat cost of £20 per room per night. Targeting young consumers has allowed Cheapotel to build a customer base around nightclubbers, stag and hen parties, and students coming out of late-night gigs.

Much of the firm's success has been attributed to Rob's marketing wizardry; however, deeper below the surface lies a clever extension of a well-known fact about the UK hotel market: a vast proportion of UK hotel workers are from other EU countries, working in the UK at minimum wage level. A total of 95% of Rob's staff are from Eastern European EU countries and Rob himself admits that wages are low. In addition, staffing levels are tiny relative to other hotels, with a minimal cleaning staff and just one receptionist/manager on duty in each location at any one time.

Contrary to all expectations, Cheapotel is profitable after just three years' trading, and despite very low profit margins, Rob is confident that this profitability can continue. He is confident enough to be planning to open in another 20 locations within the next 18 months, including Cheapotels in Prague, Krakow, Budapest and Bucharest.

Questions *(30 marks; 35 minutes)*

1 Analyse the reasons why Rob Doyle is likely to support further EU expansion. (8)

2 Explain why the case of Cheapotel can be used to illustrate the need for employment protection law. (6)

3 The front page of today's *Sun* features photos of a Cheapotel corridor with three rats running through it. Use the case study to discuss whether consumer protection law is necessary or whether market forces can be relied upon to ensure that customers receive a decent service. (16)

Case study

Forbes Bricks Ltd

Maintaining a legal factory is a lot harder than you might expect – just ask Dave Maisey, managing director of Forbes Bricks Ltd. Forbes is one of a handful of brick makers that can tailor-make any shape, size, colour or material of brick. This feature explains its continuing popularity among those restoring or maintaining older properties. A medium-sized firm, Forbes owns a single factory, in Kent, with a loyal workforce of skilled and semi-skilled staff. Dave, however, has the look of a tired man. Charged with managing most aspects of the business, Dave is also ultimately responsible for the firm's compliance with the legislation affecting the business. His biggest headache, he says, is health and safety legislation: 'They just don't seem to understand that making bricks is a dusty business. You can't make bricks without dust, and the inspector we had round the other week was measuring dust levels all round the shop floor, tutting as she went.'

The inspector from the HSE (Health & Safety Executive) was at the plant to measure the level of dust particles in the air and to assess the measures taken by the firm to ensure that staff suffered no long-term breathing damage from the dusty working conditions.

Dave continued: 'I'd only just finished a full risk assessment on the new kiln we've bought, so luckily I managed to impress her with that.

The inspector went over the accident record book, and our whole Health & Safety manual. I spent the whole day with her, time I could have spent out on the road finding new business, or working with the boys in the materials in section to find a better solution to some of the stock-holding issues we've had recently.'

Two weeks after the inspector's visit, Dave called a meeting of the firm's directors to discuss the recommendation from the HSE: to spend an extra £105,000 on extractor units to reduce the dust levels in the air to standards acceptable under UK and EU law. Dave was also worried about Purchasing Director Andy Hemmings recent visit to China. He feared that Andy may have found a factory with poor working conditions, paying well below Forbes' rates to staff and offering similar bricks at half the price.

Questions *(35 marks; 40 minutes)*

1 Analyse three reasons why Dave seems unhappy about the legislation affecting Forbes Bricks Ltd. (9)

2 Outline Dave's general responsibilities to his staff, according to UK Health & Safety law. (6)

3 To what extent does the case study illustrate the problems of different countries adopting different legal standards in a world encouraging free trade? (20)

Essay questions *(40 marks each)*

1 'Businesses will continue to infringe the law until the penalties they face are strong enough to hurt the individuals running those businesses.' To what extent is this statement accurate?

2 'Further expansion of the EU represents a great opportunity for large UK companies wishing to become global players.' Discuss why this may or may not be the case.

How firms respond to potential and actual changes

> ## Definition
> Potential changes are those that may be needed in future; actual changes are those that have really happened.

What changes need to be addressed?

Operating in a changing environment is an inescapable reality for businesses. Business success depends on how firms respond to both potential and actual changes. The list of changes below suggests the major external causes of changes to which firms will need to find a response. All the changes are covered elsewhere in this book, so the rest of this unit will focus on the following responses to these external changes.

Economic factors and trends in economic variables are covered in Unit 38, which deals with the impact on firms of the major economic variables:

- the business cycle and economic growth
- interest rates
- exchange rates
- unemployment
- inflation.

Globalisation of markets is covered in Unit 39.

Responses to change

Responses to change will vary from short-term actions to major changes in the firm's long-term plans. Short-term changes are known as tactical responses, while a long-term change to the firm's overall plans is considered to be a strategic change.

The rest of this unit will consider strategic changes, rather than tactical measures.

Marketing strategy

Product portfolio

Changes to the products made by the firm may represent a sensible response to external change. The basic choice is likely to be between expansion or reduction of the product portfolio. Should the firm launch new products to exploit a newly created opportunity? A firm expecting an economic downturn may consider the option of producing a low-cost version of a best-selling product that is likely to appeal in times when money is tighter. Alternatively, the chance to break into a new market, offered by political change, may result in the need to add a brand new product to the portfolio, specifically designed to cater to the needs of that market. For instance, in 2011 India still refused to allow large foreign retail companies to operate in the country. Tesco and others would love to have a presence in the world's second most populous country (1,180 million and rising). As yet they cannot. If and when the Indian government changes its mind, there will be a mad rush to be the first supermarket chain into India. The clever ones have already got their plans in place.

Reduction of the product portfolio may also make sense in some cases. External change may make some existing products poor sellers overnight, in which case a firm may decide to drop these immediately.

Image shift

Some external changes may prompt a shift in corporate image. A UK company suffering from increased global competition may find that it can gain a competitive advantage by pushing the 'Britishness' of the brand. Not only could this boost UK sales, but other markets may be keen to buy into a brand that plays on its Britishness, such as Burberry or Aston Martin.

Financial strategy

Sources of finance

Responding to changes usually requires cash. Whether a firm is launching a new product or laying off staff, some cash outlay will be involved. Therefore financially a firm needs to consider carefully the sources of finance it uses. Increased interest rates make borrowing more expensive and therefore less attractive as a means of raising capital. On the other hand, a booming stock market would mean that expected dividend payments may make share capital more expensive than loan capital. Careful assessment of the gearing ratio in the light of the external change will be the major analysis that needs to be conducted prior to deciding on an appropriate source of finance.

Returning cash to shareholders

At times, external changes lead to rationalisation, ranging from the sale of fixed assets to the sale of an entire subsidiary company. This will generate cash for the business. In some cases, firms may seek to protect their return on capital by buying back shares or returning cash to shareholders. This takes the cash off their balance sheet and therefore out of their capital employed. The result is that, without increasing operating profit, the firm's ROCE will be boosted.

Operations strategy

Update facilities

External change may be the stimulus behind a firm's decisions to upgrade its production facilities. Upgrading should boost efficiency and mean that the firm either gains a competitive edge, or simply keeps up with competitors who are taking advantage of the same opportunity.

Consider a new location

Changes that are likely to lead to increased demand may well prompt the construction of new facilities. This will allow the firm to increase its capacity in anticipation of increased levels of sales. It is important to consider how long it will take to make these new facilities operational. Major new construction projects – perhaps a new, state-of-the-art factory for a manufacturer – may well take in excess of a year. If the firm needs to react more quickly, there is another option available: subcontracting.

Subcontracting

Contracting another firm to carry out work for you is a far quicker way of increasing overall capacity. In the case of sudden change, this may be a useful alternative to building brand new facilities. Firms such as Nike and Gap tend to use subcontracting for most if not all of their production, since it offers greater flexibility. However, the experience of these firms, most notably criticism for poor treatment of workers in their subcontractors' plants, reveals a major problem. The business is losing control over the day-to-day operational side of its own production. This may lead to quality control problems or raise doubts on the part of customers.

Close facilities

Firms that decide demand is falling in the long term may decide to close some of their facilities permanently. These decisions, taken at the very highest level of the organisation, will be expensive, with redundancy payments and decommissioning costs to cover. However, in the long run they will allow a firm to reduce its fixed cost base to a level that makes break-even easier to achieve. In some cases, closure may in fact be a relocation – with a firm closing an operation in one country in order to shift operations to another, usually in search of lower costs.

A-grade application

Ford

Ford US was suffering from problems of overcapacity as Honda, Toyota and Volkswagen chipped away at its market share. It tried but failed to find marketing solutions to rebuild its market share. Faced with losses measured in billions of dollars, Ford decided to start a programme of factory closures, beginning in 2008; 16 plants were closed, with 30,000 jobs lost. Although the short-term impact was awful, by 2010 the company had returned to profitability. In the third quarter of 2010 it made $1.7 billion of operating profit.

HR strategy

Workforce planning is designed to incorporate the changes the firm expects into management of its people. Really good workforce planning will anticipate change and will already have started to respond to the implications of the change in ensuring that the firm has the right number of staff, with the right skills in the right places within the organisation. This will be achieved through a mix of a long-term approach to recruiting staff, using training to equip staff with the skills needed following the change, and perhaps also carefully shedding staff who will no longer be required. This is far less painful if achieved over the long run, through natural wastage, than a quick hit of redundancies.

Retraining

Firms that value the loyalty and experience of their staff may be able to adapt to change by retraining their existing staff. This would be a major undertaking for the HR department and would be likely to require a substantial investment. However, in return, the firm would maintain the flexibility that people offer over machinery, while it would also hope to

A-grade application

Workforce planning at John Lewis

In July 2011 John Lewis announced that it would be opening 10 'mini' department stores in the next five years. This will create 3,000 jobs. The scaled-down stores will be established in towns without the population levels for a full department store, such as Exeter, Guildford and York.

Although it is not announcing it yet, the company has a clear schedule for which store will open when. Therefore it can carefully plan its recruitment and training programmes, making sure that each store opens with an enthusiastic, expert sales force.

benefit from continued high levels of motivation within a workforce that feels valued.

Flexibility

In itself, creating a more flexible workforce may be an appropriate response to a change, or indeed

Table 42.1 Summary of common responses to change

Marketing	Finance	Operations	HR
New products	Raise extra finance	Update facilities	Workforce planning
Ditch existing products	Return cash to shareholders	Close facilities	Recruit
Image shift	When change is rapid, check variance against budget	Subcontract	Shed staff
Use Boston Matrix to appraise portfolio	Consider actions to lower fixed costs and therefore break even	Build new plants or consider relocation	Retraining to increase flexibility

an increasing rate of change. Workforce flexibility can be achieved through two fundamental routes. Building a staff that possess adaptable skills and are keen to embrace changes can allow a firm to maintain the agility needed to cope with change. Alternatively, a firm may choose to follow a model suggested by management thinker Charles Handy. He suggests keeping a small permanent ('core') staff whose major role is to coordinate specialist contractors hired on fixed-term contracts to fit the particular need faced by the firm at the time. The latter are the 'peripheral' workers.

Issues for analysis

- A crucial analytical question is suggested by this unit's title. Potential and actual changes will provoke differing responses from different firms. Those whose culture is more accepting of change are more likely to think about, discuss and plan for potential change. Other businesses are more likely to hope that change does not happen. Of course, anticipating changes might look foolish if the expected changes do not occur. On the other hand, slower-moving firms, with bureaucratic cultures, are unlikely to respond to change until after it has occurred. Though seemingly safer, such an approach may lead to failure in the long term as the firm ends up falling far behind its more flexible rivals.

- Responses to change will also offer the opportunity to consider several options. Breaking down a firm's choices, and assessing the pros and cons of each choice of action is exactly the analytical approach that Business Studies seeks to promote. Rest assured that any large firm considering how it should respond to change will go through a process similar to that which you should expect to demonstrate in an exam.

How firms respond to potential and actual changes – an evaluation

Judging the correct response to potential or actual changes is an area where evaluation is likely to be needed. Straightforward judgements as to the best possible response to change will be enhanced if they are clearly rooted in the context being considered. A firm with limited finances, operating on a national scale and seeking merely to survive, will probably respond in a very different way to a successful multinational firm. Answers showing an awareness of the impact of a firm's current position on its response to change will be better rewarded.

However, it is worth reflecting carefully on any changes to which a response is required. Some firms may actually be better off not responding, or at least waiting to see what happens. Several retailers struggled in early 2011 because they had anticipated economic recovery; instead there was stagnation. On the other hand, external changes could be the right time to make bold strategic moves such as a switch to an entirely different market. Above all else, though, be aware of the possibilities of failing to effectively 'read' the effects of the change appropriately. No business can forecast exactly how the future will turn out, and those that respond with flexibility may be better equipped to deal with the unexpected.

Revision questions *(40 marks; 40 minutes)*

1 a Identify three recent changes that may have affected major oil companies such as Shell and BP. (3)

 b Explain how *one* of those changes may have affected Shell or BP. (4)

 c Analyse the likely response of the oil company to the change explained in part b. (5)

2 Analyse two ways in which a confectionery manufacturer might respond to a tightening of the laws governing the advertising of unhealthy foods. (8)

3 Explain why workforce planning should help firms to respond effectively to *one* of the following potential changes:

 a the opening up of India's retail market to western supermarkets

 b a severe US recession that is hitting consumer confidence in Britain. (6)

4 Analyse two possible responses by British Airways to the arrival of competition from budget airlines on the profitable London–New York route. (6)

5 Analyse two possible marketing responses by a UK manufacturer of premium ice cream to a general worsening of the state of the UK's economy. (8)

Case study

G & A McInnes Ltd

G & A McInnes Ltd is a major manufacturer of mobile phone accessories. Though well established in the mobile phone market, it has only been around for 15 years. It has enjoyed a spectacular rise from market stall to UK's number one supplier of mobile accessories. The company's growth has been very hard to manage for brothers Gary and Adam. However, through a mixture of clever management and a heavy dose of luck, the firm evolved from a Glasgow market stall into a company employing 248 head office and sales staff. New designs are created at head office, sent to trusted Chinese manufacturers and shipped back to regional distribution centres in Europe. From these, the firm delivers direct to the retailers that stock the low-priced product range. Having started out in the UK, the company now sells in every EU market. The firm currently sells only in European markets.

As the New Year dawned, Gary and Adam talked over the changes facing the firm. A summary of the major issues is shown below:

● changes in economic growth rates in both the UK and EU (see Table 42.2)

● increased flak from pressure groups over the plastics used to manufacture the products, many of which are perceived by consumers as disposable

● handset manufacturers are broadening their own ranges of accessories, and adding more to the original phone bundles.

Gary had gathered a variety of numerical data that he considered relevant to the decision-making process they faced. Adam was particularly keen on breaking away from the firm's reliance on the European market. He felt that the time was right to expand geographically. He wanted to look into the possibilities offered by the rapidly developing Brazilian economy. He had brought his own data to the meeting to help to convince Gary that the firm's immediate future lay in South America. The weakening pound suggested to Adam that the firm may be better off operating from its existing facilities in Europe and simply exporting to Brazil. He did not, however, rule out the possibility of building a distribution centre in Brazil that could accept deliveries straight from its Far Eastern suppliers. (See Table 42.3.)

The brothers had plenty to discuss. Gary was unconvinced of the need for further expansion. He was concerned that the firm's growth had been too rapid and that they had allowed costs to spiral out of control. Perhaps they should spend the next few years consolidating the firm's position and boosting profitability by seeking to reduce cost levels without any focus on boosting turnover.

Table 42.2 Slowdown in EU markets

	This year	Next year	2 years' time	3 years' time
UK GDP growth (%)	1.1	2.0	2.2	2.7
EU GDP growth (%)	1.4	1.5	1.5	1.4
World GDP growth (%)	3.2	2.5	2.9	3.6

Table 42.3 Data for Brazil

	This year	Next year	2 years' time	3 years' time
GDP growth (%)	5.3	5.0	5.1	5.4
Mobile phones per 1,000 people	636	662	686	695
% houses with broadband	2.3	4.6	7.2	9.3

Strategic options:

1 consolidation – stay put, boost profits by cutting costs

2 export to Brazil – products still delivered to EU distribution centres, then sent directly to Brazilian retailers

3 build facilities in Brazil – construct a new distribution centre in Brazil that can accept products directly from China.

Questions (70 marks; 80 minutes)

1 Analyse the possible implications for the firm of the following changes in the case study.

a The forecast changes in economic growth in both the UK and EU. (10)

b Increased criticism from pressure groups over the plastics used to manufacture the products, many of which are perceived by consumers as disposable. (10)

c Handset manufacturers are broadening their own ranges of accessories, and adding more to the original phone bundles. (10)

2 Make a fully justified recommendation to the firm on which of the three strategic options to pursue. (40)

Case study

Three-way fight in China and India

Nestlé chocolate products recorded double-digit growth in emerging markets, driven partly by the performance of the lowest priced products in its portfolio, said the group as it posted gains of 7.5% in net profit for the first six months of 2010. The company noted strong performances for the group in the South Asia region, including India, Vietnam and Thailand, in Indonesia and China as well as gains in the Central/West Africa region. But growth in Europe and Japan was flat.

A market analyst told ConfectioneryNews. com that the Swiss multinational's growth figures are unsurprising, given the recognised buoyancy of the chocolate markets in certain markets within the developing world:

'The Indian market has been growing by up to 18% per annum in recent years, while growth of up to 12% is being observed in China.'

Cadbury reigns in India

Nestlé still trails Cadbury by some margin in India; Cadbury remains the market leader with a 70% share. The industry analyst said that Cadbury's Indian business has grown by around 20% per annum in recent years, and this remains one of its key growth markets – a situation, he maintains, that is likely to remain following its acquisition by Kraft.

And the confectioner with the leading position in the developing Chinese chocolate market is Mars, continued Thomas, which has a share of 15%.

'The company remains strong as a result of

the success of its Dove (Galaxy) brand, although some feel the sugar content should be lowered to adapt to the local palate. Other multinationals – such as Hershey – have been less successful in China,' he added.

The road ahead

A senior research analyst at US-based Bernstein Research said that expectations were for another financially strong quarter for Nestlé. Its KitKat brand remained a success at the core of its European and American chocolate business. This would lead to excellent year-end financial results for the company, and he said the Swiss group again showed 'its ability to deliver strong and balanced operating performance'.

Source: adapted from www.confectionerynews.com, 12 August 2010.

Questions *(45 marks; 50 minutes)*

1 Nearly ten years ago, Mars chose to focus on China while Cadbury chose India. Examine why Cadbury might have chosen to develop its business in India. (8)

2 Analyse the positive and negative factors in the bar chart shown in Figure 42.1 from the perspective of a marketing manager at Nestlé. (10)

3 Discuss the advantages and disadvantages to Mars of 'glocalising' its Dove (Galaxy) chocolate to suit local tastes in China. (12)

4 Nestlé may decide to set up a new factory in India, partly to enjoy the benefits of factory wage rates that are as low as 25p per hour. To what extent could this be said to be unethical? (15)

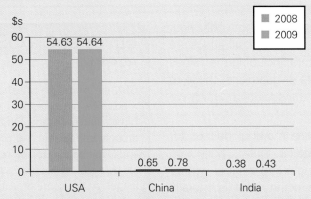

Figure 42.1 Market size and potential: chocolate spend per head
Source: Euromonitor, 2010

Essay questions *(40 marks each)*

1 To what extent is the ability to respond effectively to external changes the key to success in the modern global marketplace?

2 Discuss the possible strategic responses available to a UK high-street music retailer faced with a steady increase in the amount

of music and film downloads from online retailers.

3 'There is a danger in responding too rapidly to potential changes.' Discuss the truth of this statement in the context of a car manufacturer.

Business ethics

Definition
Ethics are the moral principles that should underpin decision making. A decision made on ethical grounds might reject the most profitable solution in favour of one of greater benefit to society as well as the firm.

What are business ethics?

Ethics can be defined as a code of behaviour considered morally correct. Our individual ethics are shaped by a number of factors, including the values and behaviour of our parents or guardians, those of our religion, our peers, and the society in which we live and work.

Business ethics can provide moral guidelines for the conduct of business affairs. This is based on some assertion of what is right and what is wrong. An ethical decision means doing what is morally right. It is not a matter of scientifically calculating costs, benefit and profit. Most actions and activities in the business world have an ethical dimension. This has been highlighted recently in relation to whole industries (such as the alcohol industry) and to businesses that use cheap labour in less developed countries.

Among the important ethical considerations in business are:

- dealing honestly and fairly with customers, i.e. the opposite of 'cowboy builders'
- protecting the environment through actions such as the use of sustainable sources of raw materials
- dealing with bullying, harassment and discrimination within the organisation
- the provision of accurate financial and other numerical information
- anti-competitive practices
- testing products on animals and similar production issues
- whistleblowing on unethical practices within the business.

Ethics at GlaxoSmithKline (GSK)

GSK is a major British producer of prescription medicines, vaccines and consumer brands such as Ribena and Lucozade. On 28 October 2010 its website proudly stated that the company had: 'a challenging and inspiring mission to improve the quality of human life by enabling people to do more, feel better and live longer.' At the same time it proclaimed that 'corporate responsibility is at the heart of our business'.

On the same day the Guardian newspaper reported that an American court had just awarded a world record payout of $96 million to a 'whistleblower' GSK employee. Her 10 months of warnings of contamination problems at a GSK factory were ignored, even though she was the quality control manager. She escalated the issue by alerting ever-more senior employees within GSK (such as the vice president of manufacturing and supply for North America) but was sidelined and later made redundant.

The Guardian reported that 'Legal papers show that GSK ... employees lied to US Food and Drug Administration (FDA) inspectors'. After the whistleblower (Diane Sevigny) took her story to the FDA, their investigation led to GSK agreeing in October 2010 to pay $750 million to achieve a criminal and civil settlement with the US authorities.

Ethics is not about what companies say; it's about what they do.

Source: *The Guardian*, 28 October 2010, p. 3.

Two major influences shape the moral behaviour of businesses. First, an organisation is composed of individuals, who all have their own moral codes, values and principles. Naturally, they bring these to bear on the decisions that they make as part of their working lives. Second, businesses have cultures that shape corporate ethical standards. The approach taken by the leaders of the business can have a big effect on both of these factors.

The article about GlaxoSmithKline (see box) illustrates a situation in which individuals and the corporate culture proved important.

Business ethics and business objectives

A useful starting point may be to consider business objectives in relation to ethical behaviour. We can pose the question 'Why do businesses exist?' For many businesses the answer would be 'to make the maximum profit possible in order to satisfy the owners of the business'.

Some notable academics support this view. Milton Friedman, a famous American economist, held the view that all businesses should use the resources available to them as efficiently as possible.

Friedman argued that making the highest possible profit creates the maximum possible wealth, to the benefit of the whole society.

Friedman's view, however, ignores the fact that the interests of the stakeholders may differ. Most people would consider it unethical to make staff redundant if the motive was purely to add to the bonuses earned by directors and dividends paid to shareholders.

The developing ethical environment

Every era witnesses a series of ethical crises for companies – individually or collectively. BP disgraced itself in its operations in America in 2005 and 2010. Virtually the entire banking sector has been an ethical no-go area as the pursuit of career progress and huge bonuses led to reckless speculation and a series of products that exploited consumers' naivety about finance.

Yet the picture isn't entirely bleak. In 2009 Cadbury became the world's first major chocolate company to convert all sourcing of a major brand to Fairtrade, when bars of Dairy Milk started to show a new logo. Nestlé soon copied by converting its huge KitKat brand to Fairtrade. This means that both companies promise to pay cocoa and sugar suppliers a generous minimum price to ensure better working conditions for farm workers.

Other companies have tried to operate on ethical principles since their inception. The extract below, taken from Innocent Drink's website, summarises its position.

Our ethics

We sure aren't perfect, but we're trying to do the right thing

It might make us sound a bit like a Miss World contestant, but we want to leave things a little bit better than we find them. We strive to do business in a more enlightened way, where we take responsibility for the impact of our business on society and the environment, and move these impacts from negative to neutral, or better still, positive. It's part of our quest to become a truly sustainable business, where we have a net positive effect on the wonderful world around us.

Source: Innocent Drinks website (www.innocentdrinks.co.uk/us/ethics)

One of the most significant developments in corporate ethical behaviour in recent years has been the move towards sustainability. Sustainable production means that a business seeks to supply its products in such a way as not to compromise the lives of future generations by, for example, damaging the environment or depleting non-renewable resources. A common feature of this aspect of ethical behaviour is the desire to reduce the company's 'carbon footprint' or even to become a carbon-neutral business. Some businesses find this an easier stance to adopt than others. Nike, the world's biggest sportswear business, has announced that it will become carbon neutral by 2011. Other businesses have found it more difficult to reduce or eliminate their carbon footprints, especially those in the manufacturing sector. However, a wide range of businesses in the UK have recognised the marketing benefits of taking this kind of ethical stance. The Eurostar story in the A-grade application illustrates the importance of sustainability in the transport industry. It also shows how Eurostar can use it as a competitive weapon against rivals such as easyJet and other budget airlines.

A-grade application

Eurostar goes carbon neutral

All Eurostar journeys from the new St Pancras International Station are carbon neutral thanks to offsetting, recycling – and fuller carriages. This makes Eurostar the world's first footprint-free method of mass transport. The impact of rail travel between London and Paris or Brussels had always been at least ten times lighter than the equivalent journey by plane, a traveller generating 11 kilograms of carbon dioxide compared with 122 by his or her counterpart on the plane. It is, the company says, the difference between enough CO_2 to fill a Mini and the amount needed to fill a double-decker bus.

Figure 43.1 Eurostar

But by making a raft of new changes across the business – from installing energy meters on all trains to tightening up on recycling and making 'train capacity efficiencies' (filling every seat, in other words) – the operator is lightening its environmental load. In addition, it has set itself a new target of reducing its carbon dioxide emissions per passenger by a quarter by 2012.

Source: *Daily Telegraph*, 14 November 2007 © Telegraph Media Group Limited 2007

Ethical codes of practice

An example of an ethical code of practice is:

> To meaningfully contribute to local, national and international communities in which we trade, by adopting a code of conduct that ensures care, honesty, fairness and respect.

As a response to consumer expectations and competitive pressures, businesses have introduced **ethical codes** of practice. These are intended to improve the behaviour and image of a business. The information about the Institute of Business Ethics (IBE) (see box) highlights the extent to which UK businesses have appreciated the importance of being seen to behave ethically. Furthermore, the very existence of the IBE is evidence of the growing importance of this aspect of business behaviour.

An ethical code of practice is a document setting out the way a business believes its employees should respond to situations that challenge their integrity or social responsibility.

The precise focus of the code will depend on the business concerned. Banks may concentrate on honesty, and chemical firms on pollution control. It has proved difficult to produce meaningful, comprehensive codes. The National Westminster Bank, for example, took two years to produce its ten-page document. A typical code might include sections on:

● personal integrity – in dealings with suppliers and in handling the firm's resources

● corporate integrity – such as forbidding collusion with competitors and forbidding predatory pricing

● **environmental responsibility** – highlighting a duty to minimise pollution emissions and maximise recycling

● social responsibility – to provide products of genuine value that are promoted with honesty and dignity.

A common feature of ethical codes of practice is that companies publicise them. This is because they believe that being seen to behave ethically is an important element of the marketing strategy of many businesses.

The Institute of Business Ethics (IBE)

The IBE was established to encourage high standards of business behaviour based on ethical values. Its vision: 'To lead the dissemination of knowledge and good practice in business ethics.'

The IBE raises public awareness of the importance of doing business ethically, and collaborates with other UK and international organisations with interests and expertise in business ethics.

It helps businesses to strengthen their ethics culture and encourage high standards of business behaviour based on ethical values. It assists in the development, implementation and embedding of effective and relevant ethics and corporate responsibility policies and programmes. It helps organisations to provide guidance to staff and build relationships of trust with their principal stakeholders.

IBE research

IBE research has found that companies with a code of ethics financially outperform those without. Now, most firms (85 of the FTSE100) have codes of ethics and so having a code is no longer a clear sign of being 'more ethical'; it is not sufficient to act as a unique selling point (USP). A commitment to embedding ethical values into business practice through a training programme differentiates companies from those that simply declare a commitment to ethical values.

The results of the IBE's research reveal that companies with a demonstrable ethics programme benefit from the confidence that is instilled in their stakeholders. This helps to build the company's reputation, enhances relations with bankers and investors, assists firms in attracting better employees, increases goodwill, leaves the firms better prepared for external changes, turbulence and crisis, and generally helps the firm run better.

Source: Institute of Business Ethics (www.ibe.org.uk)

Critics of ethical codes believe them to be public relations exercises rather than genuine attempts to change business behaviour. What is not in doubt is that the proof of their effectiveness can be measured only by how firms actually behave, not by what they write or say.

Pressure groups and ethics

The activities of **pressure groups** affect all types of businesses and most aspects of their behaviour. Most of the high-profile pressure groups are multi-cause and operate internationally. Greenpeace is one of the best-known pressure groups; it lobbies businesses to restrict behaviour that might adversely affect the environment. Other single-cause pressure groups exist to control the

A-grade application

Supermarket giant makes huge commitment to chicken welfare

Sainsbury's has made a commitment to improve the lives of 70 million chickens a year by moving away from selling the most intensively farmed chickens in a decision that is heralded as a 'huge step forward' by leading farm animal welfare charity, Compassion in World Farming.

The supermarket giant has announced a move away from stocking poor-welfare factory-farmed chickens across all the chicken it sells and will instead adopt the Freedom Food standard, or equivalent, as the minimum.

Dr Lesley Lambert, Director of Food Policy, welcomed the move, saying, 'This will dramatically improve the lives of 70 million chickens every year and is one of the most significant moves in farm animal welfare in the UK.'

Freedom Food or equivalent standards ensure more space, slower-growing birds with fewer welfare problems, and environmental enrichment such as straw bales, which allow for more natural behaviour.

'By reaching the equivalent of Freedom Food standards, Sainsbury's is leading the way among the big four supermarkets on chicken welfare, joining M&S and Waitrose as pioneers in this area. This is a huge step forward. We urge consumers to support higher welfare for chickens through the power of their purse and preferably choose free range,' continued Dr Lambert.

Source: Compassion in World Farming press release, (www.ciwf.org.uk)

activities of businesses in one particular sphere of operations.

- Action on Smoking and Health (ASH) is an international organisation established to oppose the production and smoking of tobacco. It publicises actions of tobacco companies that may be considered to be unethical. ASH frequently focuses on the long-term effects of tobacco on consumers of the product.

- Compassion in World Farming is a UK-based pressure group campaigning specifically for an end to the factory farming of animals. The group engages in political lobbying and high-profile publicity campaigns in an attempt to end the suffering endured by many farm animals.

The ethical balance sheet

Advantages of ethical behaviour

Companies receive many benefits from behaving, or being seen to behave, in an ethical manner. These are discussed below.

Marketing advantages

Many modern consumers expect to purchase goods and services from organisations that operate in ways that they consider morally correct. Some consumers are unwilling to buy products from businesses that behave in any other way. This trend has been accelerated by the rise of consumerism. This has meant that consumers have become increasingly well informed and are prepared to think carefully before spending their money.

Some companies have developed their ethical behaviour into a unique selling point (USP). They base their marketing campaigns on these perceived differences. An example of a high-profile company adopting this strategy is the Body Shop International.

A key point is that not only does the company seek to support relatively poor communities in the less developed world, but it publicises these actions. By creating a caring image through its marketing, the Body Shop hopes to gain increased sales.

Public relations advantages

Companies also gain considerable public relations advantages from ethical behaviour. Once again this can help enhance the image of the business, with positive implications for sales and profits.

In 2010, the Co-op Bank announced a 21% increase in operating profits to £177 million, while confirming the maintenance of its ethical principles. In the previous year it had enjoyed a 36% increase in current account holders. It put this down to confidence in the bank's security and to its strong ethical stance. The Co-op consistently says it will not lend to any company involved in the arms trade; and the whole Co-op movement is a strong supporter of Fairtrade products.

Positive effects on the workforce

Firms that adopt ethical practices may experience benefits in relation to their workforce. They may be able to recruit staff who are better qualified and motivated, because larger numbers of high-quality staff apply. Innocent Drinks has had an unusually low labour turnover rate since its creation in 1999. This cuts the employment costs associated with recruitment, selection and training. Creating an ethical culture within a business can also improve employee motivation. This may be part of a wider policy towards employee empowerment.

A-grade application

Cafédirect under pressure

Cafédirect plc, the UK's largest and longest-running Fairtrade hot drinks company, suffered in 2009 with a halving of profits and a sales decline of 13%. This was partly because so many rivals now claim to be Fairtrade or backed by the Rainforest Alliance.

Financial returns are only part of Cafédirect's impact, however. The company works directly with 39 grower organisations across 13 developing countries, directly benefiting the lives of 1.4 million people. In the same financial year, the amount paid to coffee, tea and cocoa growers over and above the market price totalled nearly £1 million, bringing the total for the past three years to more than £4 million.

Source: adapted from Cafédirect press release and annual accounts.

Disadvantages of ethical behaviour

Inevitably, a number of disadvantages can result from businesses adopting ethical policies.

Reduced profitability

It is likely that any business adopting an ethical policy will face higher costs. It may also be that the company has to turn down the opportunity to invest in projects offering potentially high returns.

Exploiting cheap labour in less developed countries may be immoral, but it can be very profitable. Equally, Cafédirect's commitment to purchasing supplies from sustainable Fairtrade sources means that it incurs higher costs than if it purchased raw materials without regard to the environment.

If a business wants to operate ethically, it must accept that principle has to override profit; this may be much easier to do in a family-run business than in a public limited company, with its distant, profit-focused shareholders.

 ## Ethical behaviour: future developments

It has been suggested that most of the interest in business ethics and its development has been in universities and colleges. However, there is increasing evidence available to suggest that ethical awareness is becoming more firmly rooted in business practice. A number of arguments can be set out to support the view that ethics will be of increasing importance to businesses throughout the world.

The adoption of ethical practices

Recent studies show that over 80% of the major businesses in the UK have implemented an ethical code of practice. Over 70% of chief executives see ethical practices and behaviour as their responsibility. Although everyone in a business needs to conform to an ethical code of practice, it is only senior managers who have the power to bring about the necessary changes in corporate culture.

The commercial success of high-profile 'ethical' companies

Companies that are seen to have high ethical standards have enjoyed considerable commercial success over recent years. Innocent Drinks was a stunning financial success until a stumble forced it into the arms of Coca-Cola in 2008/2009. Similarly, Toyota has benefited financially from its commitment to sustainable methods of production. The company's environmentally friendly hybrid car, the Prius, has been highly successful in global markets.

With its £177 million of operating profit in 2010, Britain's Co-op Bank shows that ethical principles can be highly attractive to customers. If a business consciously adopts 'ethical marketing' as a strategy – that's business, not ethics. But it's important to remember that 'good businesses' such as the Co-op Bank can make good profits. Principles can prove profitable; but the goal should be principle, not profit.

 ## Issues for analysis

- Sceptics might argue that many businesses may adopt so-called ethical practices simply to project a good public image. Such organisations would produce an ethical code of practice and derive positive publicity from a small number of 'token' ethical actions, while their underlying **business culture** remains unchanged. Such businesses, it is argued, would not alter the way in which the majority of their employees behave, and decisions would continue to be taken with profits (rather than morality) in mind.

- This may be a realistic scenario for a number of businesses. But it is also a dangerous strategy in a society where increasing numbers of people have access to information. The traditional and online media look to publicise any breaches in a business's ethical code of practice. Being revealed as hypocritical is always a difficult position to defend.

- Among the key issues for analysis are the following.
  - What is the underlying intent? If a decision

has been made on the basis of profit, it is not truly ethical. An ethical decision is made on the basis of what is morally correct.

- What are the circumstances? A profit-focused decision that might be considered questionable in good times might be justifiable when times are hard. For example, a firm threatened with closure would be more justified in spending the minimum possible on pollution controls.

- What are the trade-offs? In many cases the key ethical question is profit versus morality. In others, though, the trade-offs are more complex. Making a coal mine close to 100% safe for the workers would be so expensive as to make the mine uneconomic, thereby costing the miners their jobs.

Business ethics – an evaluation

Evaluation involves making some sort of informed judgement. Businesses are required to make a judgement about the benefits of ethical behaviour. Their key question may well be whether ethics are profitable or not.

In this unit, convincing arguments have been put together as to why this might be the case. For example, ethical behaviour can give a clear competitive advantage on which marketing activities can be based. However, disadvantages may lurk behind an ethical approach. The policy can be the cause of conflict and may be expected to reduce profits.

Operating an ethical policy gives a USP if none of your competitors has taken the plunge. Being first may result in gaining market share before others catch up. In these circumstances, an ethical code may enhance profitability. It can also be an attractive option in a market where businesses and products are virtually indistinguishable. In these circumstances a USP can be most valuable.

Ethical policies may add to profits if additional costs are relatively small. Thus for a financial institution to adopt an ethical policy it may be less costly than for a chemical manufacturer. Clearly companies need to weigh increased costs against the marketing (and revenue) benefits that might result.

Ethical policies are more likely to be profitable if consumers are informed and concerned about ethical issues. It may be that businesses can develop new niche markets as a result of an ethical stance.

Key terms

Business culture: the culture of an organisation is the (perhaps unwritten) code that affects the attitudes, decision making and management style of its staff.

Environmental responsibility: this involves businesses choosing to adopt processes and procedures that minimise harmful effects on the environment – for example, placing filters on coal-fired power stations to reduce emissions.

Ethical code: document setting out the way a company believes its employees should respond to situations that challenge their integrity or social responsibility.

Pressure groups: groups of people with common interests who act together to further that interest.

Stakeholder interests: stakeholders are groups such as shareholders and consumers who have a direct interest in a business. These interests frequently cause conflict – for example, shareholders may want higher profits while consumers want environmentally friendly products, which are more costly.

Voluntary codes of practice: methods of working recommended by appropriate committees and approved by the government. They have no legal authority – for example, much advertising is controlled by voluntary codes of practice.

Revision questions (35 marks; 35 minutes)

1 Define the term 'business ethics'. (2)

2 State two factors that may shape the moral behaviour of businesses. (2)

3 Outline one circumstance in which a company might face an ethical dilemma. (3)

4 Explain the difference between a business behaving legally and a business behaving ethically. (4)

5 Why might decisions made upon the basis of a moral code (ethics) conflict with profit? (4)

6 Look at each of the following business actions and decide whether they were motivated by ethical considerations. Briefly explain your reasoning each time.
   a an advertising agency refusing to accept business from cigarette producers (2)
   b a private hospital refusing to accept an ill elderly person whose only income is the state pension (2)
   c a small baker refusing to accept supplies of genetically modified flour (2)
   d a small baker refusing to deliver to a restaurant known locally as a racist employer. (2)

7 Why might a policy of delegation make it more difficult for a business to behave ethically? (4)

8 Give two reasons why a business might introduce an ethical code of practice. (2)

9 Why might a business agree to abide by a **voluntary code of practice**, when the code has no legal authority? (3)

10 Outline the positive effects the adoption of an ethical policy may have on a business's workforce. (3)

Stimulus questions

Saudi Arabia has agreed to buy 72 Eurofighter Typhoon jets from BAE Systems. The deal is worth about £4,400 million but contracts for maintenance and training are expected to take the bill to £20,000 million. In addition to the price paid for the planes, there is also expected to be a lucrative deal for the munitions that go with them.

BAE Systems is Britain's largest exporter of defence equipment and has publicly adopted a more ethical approach to its operations in recent years. BAE Systems said it welcomed 'this important milestone in its strategy to continue to develop Saudi Arabia as a key home market with substantial employment and investment in future in-Kingdom industrial capability'.

The negotiations had been overshadowed by a UK inquiry into allegations that Saudi Arabia took bribes from BAE under a military-plane deal struck between the two nations two decades ago. Britain's Serious Fraud Office last year investigated BAE Systems' £43 billion Al-Yamamah deal, which provided Hawk and Tornado jets plus other military equipment to Saudi Arabia. However, the investigation was pulled by the British government in December 2006 in a move supported by the then Prime Minister Tony Blair amid statements about the UK's national interests.

Questions (30 marks; 35 minutes)

1 Explain the phrase 'a more ethical approach'. (3)

2 Explain the ethical dilemma that BAE Systems might face in exporting fighter aircraft to Saudi Arabia. (6)

3 BAE Systems presents itself as a very moral company. Analyse the factors that might shape a moral business culture. (9)

4 Some business analysts have observed that the company's ethical policy will make it less profitable. Discuss whether this is likely to be true. (12)

B2 Case study

Vivien's bank under fire

Vivien's appointment as chief executive was front-page news. She was the first woman to lead one of Britain's 'big four' banks. Her predecessor, Malcolm Stanton, had been fired due to the bank's poor profit performance. The board made it clear to Vivien that a significant profit improvement was needed within 18 months.

Vivien's approach to management was broadly Theory Y. She trusted that people would give their best as long as the goals were clear. The manager of the bank's overseas section was delighted to be told there would no longer be a monthly review of performance; in future, an annual meeting with Vivien would be sufficient. The target of a 40% profit increase was more of a shock, but after discussion Vivien relaxed it to 33%.

At the half-year stage, Vivien was delighted to see that overseas profits were up by more than 30%. Her delegation programme had worked. The first sign that anything was going wrong came from an article in *Private Eye* magazine. Its headline, 'Vivien's bank under fire!' was followed by an article suggesting that the bank was the main financier of the arms trade in war-torn Central America. Within a fortnight the national papers had dredged up more scandal. The bank was accused of involvement with an environmental disaster in Brazil and a corruption case in the Far East.

Interviewed on BBC Radio 4's *Today* programme, Vivien defended herself by assuring the audience that 'Neither I nor any board member has any knowledge of any of these cases. I have put in hand a thorough inquiry that will look into every aspect of these rumours. This bank has an ethical code that we take very seriously. I am confident that these stories will prove to be just that. Stories.'

Questions *(50 marks; 60 minutes)*

1 Analyse the business benefits Vivien would have been expecting to gain from her policy of delegation. (10)

2 Why might her approach to delegation have created a situation in which unethical practices were adopted by the overseas section of the bank? (12)

3 Consider why the bank's ethical code may have been ineffective in this case. (12)

4 Business ethics are strongly influenced by the culture of the workplace.

   a What is meant by the term 'culture'? (3)

   b Discuss the approaches Vivien might take to influence the ethical culture of the bank in future. (13)

C Essay questions *(40 marks each)*

1 'A modern, democratically led company with an empowered workforce would be the type of organisation that would be expected to operate an ethical policy.' To what extent do you agree with this statement?

2 Discuss the view that few businesses take truly moral decisions and that most implement ethical policies to gain a competitive advantage.

Business and the environment

Definition

Environmental issues are those relating to pollution, global warming, sustainable development and other elements of the 'green' agenda. Businesses today are making more effort to measure and publicise their performance, as the environment is a concern to many stakeholders.

 ## Introduction

This is not a unit on the mechanics of the environment. You do not need a scientific understanding of the processes involved in climate change. Business students must be able to outline the ways in which the environment can act as an external constraint on the operation of business. Successful businesses need to consider the effects of their activities on the environment, whether positive or negative.

Many companies, especially large public limited companies, already have environmental policies. These may be designed to minimise any damage their activities may cause to the environment; or they may be to minimise the chances of damage to the reputation of the business. These policies usually cover production and operations and may be used as a positive message within marketing activities. Recently, the importance of the environment as a business issue has grown in virtually every developed and developing country. However, environmental legislation remains imperfect in the UK and elsewhere.

 ## The environmental issues affecting business

Pollution

As societies become wealthier, consumers start to think less about money and more about their quality of life. Factory smoke becomes unacceptable, as does the inconvenience and pollution caused by traffic jams. Voters put pressure on government to pass stronger laws. Firms find that 'fish die in river pollution disaster' is front-page news and can damage sales, so most of them try to prevent bad publicity by looking carefully at their noise, air and water emissions. Some firms even go so far as to pursue zero emissions.

Recycling

From Brazilian rainforests to South African gold mines, the extraction of natural resources is expensive and often environmentally damaging. Higher levels of **recycling** can reduce the need to extract more raw materials. It also reduces the amount of waste material that needs to be dumped or incinerated. Firms today are proud to display the recycling logo that tells the customer that they are trying to minimise their use of primary materials.

A-grade application

Latest English statistics show that 40.1% of household waste was sent for recycling between July 2009 and June 2010 – an increase on the previous year's figure of 39.7%. A waste campaigner for Friends of the Earth, said: 'The spectacular growth in recycling over the last ten years has helped Britain save cash, tackle climate change and create thousands of new jobs.'

Total household waste collected has continued to fall, with a 0.3% reduction to 23.6 million tonnes generated across England. The quantity of waste sent to landfill dropped some 2.32% from 12.4 million tonnes the previous financial year to 12.2 million tonnes for April 2009 to March 2010.

Sustainable development

Key building blocks of modern life include oil, coal and wood. If modern economies use these commodities excessively there must be a threat that, in the long term, the resources will run out. This has already started to happen with stocks of cod (and coincidentally, oil) in Britain's North Sea. Many businesses now try to ensure that they use replaceable natural resources. It can be to find greetings cards that are *not* made from paper from sustainable forests.

Global warming or climate change

Excessive production of carbon dioxide is believed to be a primary cause of climate change. This largely comes from burning fossil fuels such as coal and oil in order to produce electricity. Firms able to help counter climate change could expect excellent publicity. A recent development has been increased use of the term 'carbon footprint'. A carbon footprint is a term used to describe the amount of carbon dioxide produced by the operations of a person, business or process. The size of a company's carbon footprint can be reduced by using energy-saving measures along with taking steps to positively take carbon dioxide out of the environment (offsetting) – for example, planting extra forests.

A-grade application

Cheese and onion carbon footprints

Walkers was one of the first firms in the UK to add a carbon footprint label to its packaging. Figure 44.1 shows the breakdown of the 75g of carbon dioxide created in making a packet of crisps.

Coca-Cola, Boots, Cadbury and Innocent Drinks are also promising to introduce carbon footprint labelling.

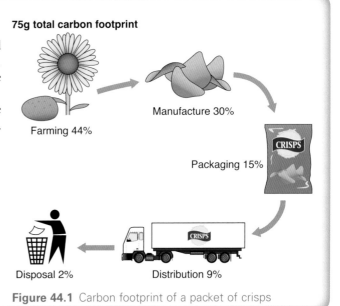

75g total carbon footprint

Farming 44%

Manufacture 30%

Packaging 15%

Distribution 9%

Disposal 2%

Figure 44.1 Carbon footprint of a packet of crisps

▶ International environmental standards

In 1997, 176 of the world's governments gathered in the Japanese city of Kyoto to agree targets for reducing emissions of harmful gasses. The major weakness of the agreement was that the world's largest polluter, the USA, failed to sign up. The US government rejected the Kyoto Protocol because it excluded fast-growing developing countries such as China. The December 2009 Copenhagen Accord failed to impose new mandatory targets to follow up Kyoto, but certain things were accomplished:

● The US finally accepted the importance of global warming and ratified Kyoto

- China set itself the target of reducing its carbon intensity* by 55% to 60% by 2020 (India targeted a 75% reduction); *carbon intensity means CO_2 emissions per unit of GDP.

In the same way that quality standards exist to certify excellence in quality control, there are similar certifications to highlight good environmental practice. The International Standards Organization (ISO) has an environmental certification (ISO 14001) that is mainly applicable to the manufacturing industry.

Environmental auditing

An **environmental audit** is an independent check on the pollution emission levels, wastage levels and recycling practices of a firm. If the results are published annually, there is a clear incentive for the business to try to do better. After all, if its wastage levels rise, newspapers will inevitably point this out to their readers. Therefore firms that carry out (and publish) environmental audits annually should be more willing to invest in ways to improve their environmental practices. BP, Shell and IBM have all published annual environmental audits for a number of years; however, there is no legal obligation to do so. As a result, firms who perform poorly in this area are unlikely to publish the results of any audit. Quite often, it is the firms that publish an environmental audit that have a poor image on green issues. In other words, they are trying to correct a weakness. The interesting question is whether the managers are trying to correct the real weakness, or the public's perception of a weakness? It can be hard to know.

The environment and marketing

There are a number of environmental issues that may have a bearing on the marketing decisions taken by firms. Many firms actively use environmental friendliness as a marketing tool. A good reputation can act as a positive encouragement to certain consumers to choose one brand over another. So firms have spent time and money building up a 'green' image as an integral part of their marketing strategy. Examples include the Co-operative Bank and (until the 2010 oil spill) BP.

If a firm is successful in creating a green image, a number of advantages may follow. In addition to increased sales and possibly stronger brand loyalty, a 'green' firm may well be in a position to charge a price premium for its products. Many different products, from shampoos to banks, trade on the environment as a unique selling point. This trend may continue until a 'green' image is no longer unique, but a requirement for all products.

A positive image in relation to the environment can help a firm's marketing activities. It is important to remember, however, that there is an opposite – and often much stronger – reaction to those who damage the environment. Bad publicity for firms who cause damage to the environment can result in significant marketing problems.

The environment and production

There are three stages of production in which environmental issues may have an important effect. These are illustrated in Figure 44.2.

1 The materials used to manufacture a product may be finite or replenishable. Materials such as oil or coal, once used up, cannot be replaced. These are materials of which the earth has a limited supply. Other materials may be replaceable, such as wood. If trees are planted to replace those cut down, the supply of wood can continue indefinitely. Therefore it is 'sustainable'. In some circumstances, firms may be able to choose whether to use finite or renewable resources to manufacture their products, e.g. plastic versus wood. Often the finite resource (plastic) is cheaper. The firm then faces a straight choice: cheap or environmentally sound.

2 The processes used to manufacture products may be more or less harmful to the environment. The key issue here is energy. Some processes

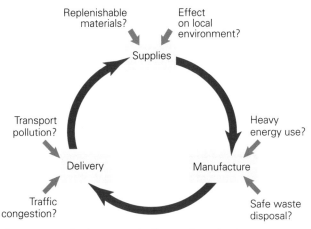

Figure 44.2 Environmental effects of production

require more energy than others and energy is a problem. The main sources of energy generation on earth are oil and coal – both finite resources. Furthermore, burning coal and oil to generate energy produces harmful emissions that damage the environment. There are more environmentally friendly energy sources, such as wind power, but energy generated in this way tends to be more expensive. Again, firms are faced with the choice: cheap or environmentally friendly?

3 Directly harmful pollution emissions can also cause immediate environmental damage. These may be the result of an accident, such as the Buncefield disaster discussed below.

A-grade application

Five years after the disaster, five companies were finally ordered in summer 2010 to pay a total of £9.5 million for their part in a massive explosion at an oil storage facility in Hertfordshire, which registered 2.4 on the Richter (earthquake) scale. Five years after the event, the environmental impact is still significant, as a result of oil and fire-fighting chemicals finding their way into the local groundwater, contaminating the local water supply. The fines imposed were partly for safety breaches and partly for the pollution caused.

 Issues for analysis

● The main issue for analysis is to consider whether the motives of organisations are strong enough to achieve actual environmental improvements rather than pretend ones. Today almost every piece of packaging has an environmentally based claim (e.g. recyclable, from renewable sources or made from recycled paper). But is it any different from before, or have the producers simply found a label they can attach without needing to change anything? In 2000, BP started proclaiming itself to be 'Beyond Petroleum'. It portrayed itself as the greenest of the oil companies. In fact, pollution disasters and industrial accidents at BP in 2005, 2006 and 2010 revealed that this was just 'hot air'. Nor are consumers much better than companies. Many talk about recycling and fuel savings, then drive off to the airport in their gas-guzzling cars.

● Another factor when analysing questions on this subject is to be sure to consider both costs and benefits. A course of action with environmental benefits may also have other social costs, such as unemployment. Is it right to make 200 workers redundant because the factory they work in is polluting the environment? It is important to consider all sides of every argument.

Business and the environment – an evaluation

Judgement can often be shown by looking for the underlying cause of a problem; in this context, the root cause of the environmental problems faced or caused by business. Although production activities may damage the environment, the bulk of environmental harm is actually caused by the consumption of products. Many firms are actually quite good at producing in an environmentally friendly way. However, their products may cause more harm to the environment when they have been consumed. This may be the result of the need to dispose of the consumed product or its packaging, or because the product is designed to be used only once, thus encouraging further consumption and therefore production.

Many environmentalists believe that the most

important step that business and consumers need to take is to move away from the so-called 'disposable society'. This is where products are used once and then thrown away. There may be a need to return to a more traditional situation where products are designed to last for a long time, in order to avoid the need to replace them frequently. This, however, might threaten to reduce levels of production, and presumably profit. This is therefore unlikely to happen as a result of decisions taken by businesses. Perhaps the only way is for consumers to act on what they say they believe about the environment. If people refuse to fly on holiday, airlines will cut flights and therefore cut pollution. Without real action, it is unfair to blame firms for carrying on largely as normal.

Key terms

Environmental audit: an independent check on the pollution emission levels, wastage levels and recycling practices of a firm.

Recycling: dismantling and/or sorting products so that they can be collected and reused. This reduces the need for fresh raw materials to be used.

Sustainable: a production process that can be continued indefinitely because it uses resources that are not depleting, e.g. wood.

A Revision questions (20 marks; 20 minutes)

1 What aspects of a firm's activities will be covered by an environmental policy? (3)

2 What is meant by the term 'sustainable development'? (3)

3 What marketing advantages may come from an 'environmentally friendly' image? (4)

4 'Environmentally friendly' firms may find various aspects of people management easier as a result of their image. Why might this be so? (4)

5 How can recycling lead to cost reductions? (4)

6 Why would longer-lasting products cause less harm to the environment? (2)

B1 Case study

Surprised by green success

The Toyota Prius is undoubtedly the standard bearer for green motoring. The Prius is a hybrid car, powered by an electric motor, backed up by a traditional petrol engine. The car's success followed its adoption by a number of environmentally conscious Hollywood stars, including Leonardo DiCaprio. The initial level of success took Toyota by surprise, so it could not keep up with demand. Since then, production capacity has been increased to cope with steadily rising global demand.

Toyota's competitors were caught without rival hybrid models, which became especially important when petrol prices jumped up in the period 2006 to 2008. For several years Toyota enjoyed its 'first-mover advantage' in the hybrid car market. As environmentally friendly cars take years to develop, the period with no competition allowed the Japanese company to further develop both the product and the Prius brand. In October 2010 Toyota announced that it had sold 2 million Prius cars, saving (it claimed) a total of 11 million tonnes of CO_2.

Questions (25 marks; 30 minutes)

1 Briefly explain the benefits to Toyota of gaining first-mover advantage. (4)

2 Analyse the possible problems that Toyota may have experienced as a result of failing to keep up with demand for the Prius. (8)

3 Discuss the view that the secret of environmentally friendly business is huge investment in research and development. (13)

Case study

World's biggest firms cause $2.2 trillion of environmental damage per year

A report commissioned by the United Nations for publication in late 2010 suggests that the world's 3,000 biggest firms cause $2.2 trillion of environmental damage per year. This is equivalent to roughly a third of their annual profits. The report seeks to quantify the environmental effects of huge multinational corporations, accounting for damage such as carbon emissions, local air pollution along with the damage caused by pollution and over-use of water.

'Externalities of this scale and nature pose a major risk to the global economy and markets are not fully aware of these risks, nor do they know how to deal with them', said Richard Mattison, leader of the report team for environmental consultants Trucost.

The final report may come up with an even higher figure since the $2.2 trillion does not include the effects of household and government consumption of these companies' products.

The debate over whether companies should be held fully financially liable for the environmental costs of their operations will be reignited, leading to further debate on how the world of business should get to grips with environmental change. The issue is already hotly debated, while there are a growing number of examples of businesses that have folded due to the disappearance of the natural resources they need to use – notably the loss of many agricultural businesses in California, caused by water shortages.

Source: *Guardian*

Questions *(50 marks; 60 minutes)*

1 Calculate the average cost to the environment caused by the operation of one of the 300 largest firms. (3)

2 Sectors such as power companies and aluminium producers, along with food and drink manufacturers, are said to be the main culprits. Analyse why such companies have such a significant environmental impact. (7)

3 Some argue that businesses should be forced to pay for the full environmental impact of their operating activities, including the environmental damage caused by consumer use after the business has sold the product. To what extent do you agree with this argument? (40)

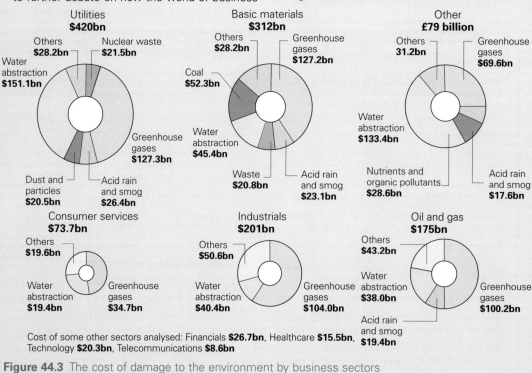

Figure 44.3 The cost of damage to the environment by business sectors

Source: *Guardian*, 18 February 2010. Copyright Guardian News & Media Ltd.

45 Business and the technological environment

Introduction

Technology is changing at an extremely fast rate. New products and new processes are being developed all the time. In markets such as computers and mobile phones hundreds of new products are being launched every month. The minute you buy the latest Blu-ray player, MP3 or phone you know it is about to be outdated. Firms face similar problems. The welding robot bought last month is already less efficient than the model announced for next month, probably at a lower price. Whatever you buy, whatever technology you use, the chances are someone somewhere is working on an improved version.

This rate of change is getting ever faster. Product development times are getting quicker and, consequently, more products are getting to the market in less time. The result is that the typical product life cycle is getting shorter. Naturally this creates serious problems for firms. With more and more products being developed, the chances of any one product succeeding are reduced. For many years research showed that only one in five new products succeeds in the marketplace. Today the figure is one in seven – in other words, six out of seven fail. Even if a new product succeeds, its life cycle is likely to be relatively short. Given the ever higher quality demanded by customers, firms are having to spend more on developing products but have less time to recoup their investment.

One of the main reasons for the rapid growth of technology is actually technology itself. The development of **computer-aided design (CAD)** and **computer-aided manufacture (CAM)** has enabled even faster development of new products and processes. Technology feeds off itself and generates even more ideas and innovations. This rapid rate of change creates both threats and opportunities for firms. The threats are clear:

- firms that do not adopt competitive technology will struggle to keep their unit costs down …

- … or provide goods or services of sufficient quality relative to their competitors.

Technology can certainly make life a great deal easier for firms. Just think of how slow it would be to work out all of a large company's accounts

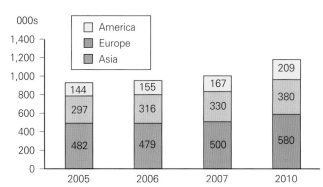

Figure 45.1 The growth in industrial robots

Figure 45.2 An industrial robot at work

by hand instead of using a computer spreadsheet. If one company avoids the latest technology while its rivals adopt it, it is likely to suffer real problems with competitiveness. The rivals may be able to offer lower prices or substantially better or faster service standards.

GM to take on Toyota

After a slow start following the introduction of its Prius model to the US market, Toyota has been selling over 100,000 of the vehicles a year, taking 50% of all hybrid sales. It took ten years for General Motors to react to this new technology. GM has now launched its electric car 'Chevy Volt' with an eight-year, 100,000-mile warranty on the battery. GM built 10,000 Volts in 2010 and 30,000 in 2011. The company claims that its technology is 'far ahead' of the competition. Experts, however, warn that the technology is still very new and for a few years it will be difficult to judge how readily the technology will be accepted. Unfortunately for the manufacturers, they need high sales to provide the economies of scale to bring the price of the car down and so attract more buyers.

Assessing the effects of technological change

Unfortunately, because of the costs involved, it is not always possible for a firm to acquire the technology it wants. New technology can represent a significant investment for a firm and cannot always be undertaken as and when the managers feel like it. This is particularly true when technology is changing at such a rate that any investment may be out of date very rapidly. The difficulty is knowing when to buy. Buy too late and you may well have lost the competitive advantage – your rivals will already be producing better-quality, more cost-competitive work.

As mentioned above, Toyota's high-tech, environmentally friendly Prius has made General Motors (GM) suffer. When GM decided not to invest in greener technology, it made itself over-reliant on gas-guzzling cars and vans. As oil prices soared, Toyota boosted market share from 10% to 16%, leaving GM trailing badly (see Figure 45.3).

A key technological change is the arrival of internet-driven services such as online shopping. In November 2006 internet sales in the UK were 3% of all retail sales; by June 2011 the figure had risen to 9%. In 2008, online grocery shopping accounted for 3% of the £120 billion grocery market. By 2012 it is expected that 12% of grocery sales will be online, making sales worth more than £14 billion. This will be a bonanza for a specialist online grocer such as Ocado, but will start to take a serious chunk out of the sales of the traditional stores. Any grocery business planning ahead needs to build-in the expectation that high-street sales will soon leak away to the internet.

In other sectors the situation is even more serious. Electronic delivery of music has brought many record shops to their knees; books and travel are also switching away from retail sales. Ten years ago, almost all British Airways' sales were made through travel agents; today the great majority of bookings are made online through the BA website.

To assess the effects of these changes, a business needs first to rethink its own position in the marketplace. For example, if standard, heavy grocery items such as potatoes, milk and washing powder are increasingly likely to be bought online, grocery stores must rethink what they are offering. They will need to increase the number of in-store tastings and make their displays more interesting. Good marketing will be a matter of finding reasons to get the shopper into the store.

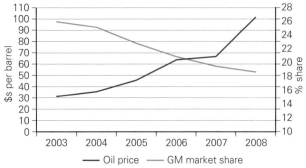

Figure 45.3 The effect of rising oil prices on General Motors

A-grade application

Early 2011 was a rotten time for discount fashion retailer New Look. Its UK shop sales fell by 9.7% compared with the previous year. A 'chink of light' for the firm came from its online sales. These rose by 41% compared with 2010, and made New Look the UK's second-most-visited women's clothing website. Faced with competition from Primark, Topshop and ASOS, this was a fine achievement. It also reassured the management that there was nothing wrong with the range of clothing, simply a problem with the prices and service levels within their stores.

The existence of online competition should make all tertiary businesses (such as shops) think even harder about successful customer service. Customers have always hated finding that a shop is out of stock of the exact product they wanted to buy; with the growth of the internet, this will become increasingly unacceptable. An unhappy shopper will not return; they may simply switch to Ocado's online retail supply.

There is also the possibility of unhappiness within the business, if staff come to feel that technological change is taking place too abruptly. The calamitous opening of Heathrow's Terminal 5 showed the potential pitfalls of introducing new technology among unhappy, untrained staff. In many cases, however, people object to change because they are scared by it or do not understand why it is needed. The management of technological change, therefore, needs careful handling. The process must be done at the right pace and employees must be involved wherever possible.

Resistance to change will come from:

- people who do not understand why it is necessary
- people who will be worse off (e.g. they no longer have the right skills)
- people who are worried unnecessarily about its effects
- people who disagree with it (i.e. they understand it, but are convinced it is a bad idea).

The response of businesses to technological change

Technological change can provide enormous opportunities for firms. There is a tendency to think of technology as a potential problem for businesses (e.g. something that may lead to unemployment). In fact, it is an aid to us all. Imagine what life would be like without televisions, phones, cashpoints or credit cards, for example. Similarly, technology makes working life considerably easier: routine jobs can be replaced, work can generally be speeded up and problem solving made easier. Just think what it would be like solving some of your business problems without a calculator.

Technology also creates new markets. Telephone banking, computer games and email are all relatively recent developments that we now take for granted. These markets create great opportunities for firms

A-grade application

Keeping the customer 'Appy

British Airways is keeping its customers 'Appy with a new App that allows customers to save time and check-in on their smartphones.

Executive Club iPhone users can use the new App to display new Mobile Boarding Passes on their phones, which can be scanned at check-in to speed up and enhance the boarding process. In addition, customers using Android and Blackberry devices will now be able to benefit from a version of the British Airways App.

The App's easy-to-use and stylish new interface also gives customers instant access to their Executive Club details and updates on flights.

Chris Davies, head of digital marketing, said:

Mobility and convenience is key for our customers, so that no matter where they are, they can turn to their mobile phones to find the very latest information about flights, check-in times and even access boarding passes allowing them to stay one step ahead.

It's all about improving the customer experience. We're committed to putting our customers in charge, making the British Airways' travel experience even easier.

British Airways was the first airline to develop an App for customers for the launch of the iPhone in the UK. Since then, over half a million customers have downloaded it from iTunes.

Source: British Airways press release, 19 July 2010.

able to exploit them and for employees with skills that are in demand.

As with any change, technological developments create potential gains and potential threats. Whether a particular firm wins or loses depends on its ability to predict this change and its ability to react. When it launched Vista in 2007, Microsoft was convinced it was a winner. Yet its new-technology features failed to catch on. Not all new technology is commercial magic. Therefore it is hard to anticipate the impact of changes in technology.

Issues for analysis

When answering questions about new technology, bear in mind that:

- technology creates both opportunities and threats; it both destroys and creates new markets; it can provide a firm with a competitive advantage or make its product or service obsolete
- it is helpful to distinguish between technology that changes markets, such as the launch of the iPad, and technology that changes processes, such as the introduction of robots into the production of Cadbury's Roses chocolates; in the former case, jobs may be created, but in the latter, jobs can be put at risk
- the introduction of technology needs to be carefully managed; managers have to consider issues such as the compatibility of the technology, the financial implications and how best to introduce it
- new technology can place additional stress on employees who might be worried about their ability to cope.

Business and the technological environment – an evaluation

Whether new technology provides an opportunity or a threat for an organisation depends on the technology itself, the resources of the firm and the management's attitude to change. Used effectively, new technology can reduce costs, increase flexibility and speed up the firm's response time. In all areas of the firm, from marketing to operations, technology can increase productivity, reduce wastage, and lead to better-quality goods and services.

However, it may not always be possible for a firm to adopt the most appropriate technology (perhaps because it does not have the necessary finance). Even if it does adopt new technology, the firm needs to ensure that the change is managed effectively. People are often suspicious or worried by new technology, and managers must think carefully about the speed of the change and the method of introduction. Organisations must also monitor the technology of their competitors. If they fail to keep up they may find they cannot match their competitors' quality standards. However, they may be limited by their ability to afford the technology. Typically, managers will be faced with an almost constant set of demands for new technology from employees. Nearly everyone can think of some machine or gadget they would like in an ideal world. Managers must decide on priorities, given their limited resources, and also look for the gains that can be achieved with existing equipment. As the *kaizen* approach shows, success sometimes comes from gradual improvements rather than dramatic technological change.

Key terms

Computer-aided design (CAD): uses a software package to help draw and store new designs in digital form.

Computer-aided manufacture (CAM): uses software to specify speeds, accuracy and quantity to an automated production system.

Revision questions (35 marks; 40 minutes)

1. What is meant by the term 'technology'? (3)
2. Explain how improved technology can improve a firm's performance. (4)
3. What benefits might a firm derive from linking CAD to CAM? (3)
4. Examine three possible problems of introducing new technology. (6)
5. Explain how technological change has helped in the following areas:
   a. retailing (3)
   b. stock control (3)
   c. car production. (3)
6. Outline two factors that might explain why there are relatively few robots in the UK. (4)
7. Why may technology be an important factor in a firm's international competitiveness? (3)
8. How may staff benefit from the introduction of new technology? (3)

Case study

Rising commodity prices put pressure on bakery manufacturers

Bakery and breakfast cereal manufacturer General Mills recently announced its intention to increase its prices to reflect the impact of higher commodity costs. General Mills has a global presence, but its profile in emerging markets is rather limited. The company's main market is breakfast cereal sales in North America. These account for around 75% of its global retail value sales, which reached US$12.2 billion in 2009.

Global wheat prices have risen by 37% over the last year (October 2009 to September 2010). Moreover, they have been steadily rising since August 2010 when widespread fires in Russia prompted a self-imposed ban on wheat exports from that country. The move sent shock waves through global commodity markets, with traders fearing scarcity of supply, and resulted in an immediate escalation in commodity prices.

Corn prices, which historically tend to be fairly stable, have not escaped the current food commodity inflation trend either. Monthly average prices rose by 23% over the October 2009 to September 2010 period, according to FAO official statistics. As with soybeans, corn prices are steadily increasing as a result of strong demand for animal feed in countries like China. This trend is, according to most industry sources, likely to continue on the back of stronger demand for milk and fresh meat in rapidly growing Asian economies.

Although used primarily to feed livestock, corn is a versatile grain with a diversity of uses. It is also processed into a multitude of food and industrial products, including starches, sweeteners, corn oil, beverage and industrial alcohol and fuel ethanol. Thousands of foods and other everyday items – from toothpaste and cosmetics to adhesives and shoe polish – contain corn derivatives.

Research suggests that there will be increased demand for corn for biofuel manufacturing over the short and medium term, driven by demand for renewable energy sources in developed markets. This trend will not only put pressure on global corn commodity prices but will also divert existing land stock from food to fuel production.

One key market expected to see an increase in demand for biofuel is the USA. The Energy Independence and Security Act was introduced in 2007 and aims to increase the production of clean renewable fuels. The Act establishes new standards and grants for promoting efficiency in government and public institutions. According to the Act, new and renovated federal buildings must reduce fossil fuel use by 55% (from 2003 levels) by 2010, and 80% by 2020. All new federal buildings must be carbon neutral by 2030. Corn, used for the production of ethanol-based fuels, is a commodity likely to be fully affected by current pressures to increase renewable energy output not only in the USA but also across most developed markets.

There are concerns in the industry about the medium-term capacity of food producers to meet the needs created by future population growth. Between 2009 and 2014 alone, the global population is projected to grow by around 400 million, according to the United Nations' estimates. Most of this growth will take place in meat-, wheat- and corn-hungry emerging economies in Asia-Pacific, North Africa and Latin America. By 2050, according to the same UN projections, the world population could reach the 9 billion mark, an increase of around 2.5 billion over 2009. This is the reason why wheat and corn commodity prices are predicted to remain under pressure over the medium to long term.

Source: Euromonitor International, 2 November 2010.

Questions *(35 marks; 40 minutes)*

1 America hopes that technological advances might help achieve targets such as the 55% reduction in fossil fuel usage. Explain how such advances might come about. (10)

2 The price of corn is expected to rise and rise, so it would be attractive to find a substitute. Discuss the possible difficulties in attempting to do this. (15)

3 Explain the possible impact of America's Energy Independence and Security Act on the economic survival of poorer people in emerging economies. (10)

Case study

Brooks

Last Monday the management of Brooks plc announced the purchase of new equipment that would radically improve productivity levels. The investment would lead to some job losses, the management explained, but there was no doubt it was in the best interests of the company as a whole. Employees had not been consulted because management felt they had more than enough information to make the decision. Consultation would simply slow up the process. In the long run, the new equipment should increase the firm's competitiveness and the purchase was an expensive necessity. Working practices would, of course, have to be altered and employees would certainly have to learn new skills. The managers promised to provide the necessary training although they could not guarantee everyone a job if they could not adapt successfully.

Following the announcement, the employees were furious and considered taking industrial action. Hearing the rumours of possible strikes the management admitted that it might not have handled the issue in the best way possible but would not reconsider the decision.

Questions *(40 marks; 45 minutes)*

1 What factors may have made the management of Brooks plc decide to invest in new technology? (8)

2 Do you think the employees at Brooks plc would be justified in taking industrial action? Explain your answer. (10)

3 Analyse the factors that the managers at Brooks plc might have taken into account before acquiring the new equipment. (10)

4 The management of Brooks plc admitted that they may not have handled the issue in the best possible way. In your opinion, how should they have handled it? Justify your answer. (12)

Essay questions *(40 marks each)*

1 'Technology is something to be feared rather than welcomed.' Consider this view.

2 To what extent should a firm make introducing new technology a priority?

3 'The key to better performance is better management not more technology.' Critically assess this view.

Impact of competitive and market structure

> ## Definition
> Competitiveness measures a firm's ability to compete, i.e. compares its consumer offer to the offers made by its rivals.

What is a competitive market?

In the past markets were physical places where buyers and sellers met in person to exchange goods. Street markets are still like that. In modern online markets, such as E-bay, buyers and sellers are unlikely to meet.

Some markets are more competitive than others. In general, a competitive market could be described as one where there is intense rivalry between producers of a similar good or service. The number of firms operating within a market influences the intensity of competition; the more firms there are the greater the level of competition. However, the respective size of the firms operating in the market should also be taken into account. A market consisting of 50 firms may not be particularly competitive, if one of the firms holds a 60% market share and the 40% is shared between the other 49.

Similarly, a market composed of just four firms could be quite competitive if they are of a similar size.

Consumers enjoy competitive markets. However, the reverse is true for the firms themselves. In competitive markets prices and profit margins tend to be squeezed. As a result, firms operating in competitive markets try hard to minimise competition, perhaps by creating a Unique Selling Point (**USP**) or using **predatory pricing**.

It could be argued that marketing is vital no matter what the level of competition is. Firms that fail to produce goods and services that satisfy the needs of their target consumers will find it hard to succeed in the long term. Ultimately, consumers will not waste their hard earned cash on products that fail to meet their needs.

The degree of competition within a market

One dominant business

Some markets are dominated by one large business. Economists use the word 'monopoly' to describe a market where there is a single supplier, and therefore no competition. In practice pure textbook monopolies rarely exist; even Microsoft does not have a 100% share of the office software market (though it does have a 90% share). The UK government's definition of a monopoly is somewhat looser. According to the Competition Commission, a monopoly is a firm that has a market share of 25% and above.

Monopolies are bad for consumers. They restrict choice, and tend to drive prices upwards. For that reason, most governments regulate against monopolies and near monopolies that exploit consumers by abusing their dominant market position.

Deciding whether a firm has, or has not, a monopoly is far from being a straightforward task. First of all the market itself has to be accurately defined. For example, Camelot has been granted a monopoly to run the National Lottery. However, it could be argued that Camelot does not have a dominant market position because there are other forms of gambling, such as horse racing and the football pools available to consumers in the UK. Second, national market share figures should not be used in isolation, because some firms enjoy local monopolies. A good example of a dominant local market position was the airport operator BAA. The company used to own three out of four London's airports. Acting on complaints made by airlines, the Competition Commission forced BAA to sell off Gatwick airport in December 2009. The commission hopes that additional competition will reduce the fees charged by airports to airlines for use of their facilities, leading to lower fares for passengers.

Firms implement their marketing strategy through the marketing mix. In markets dominated by a single large business, firms do not need to spend heavily on promotion because consumers are, to a degree, captive. Prices can be pushed upwards and the product element of the marketing mix is focused on, creating innovations that make it harder for new entrants to break into the market. Apple spends millions of dollars on research and development in order to produce cutting-edge products such as the iPad. Apple's 10-year-old iPod is still the market leader in MP3s with a 60%+ share of the massive US market. To ensure that Apple maintains its dominant market position new product launches are patented to prevent me-too imitations from being launched by the competition.

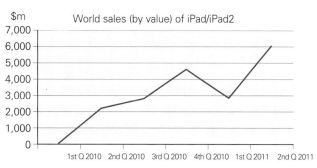

Figure 46.1 iPad Sales

Source: Apple published accounts; the quarters are adjusted from Apple financial year to calendar quarters, i.e. 4th Q = October–December.

Competition amongst a few giants

The UK supermarket industry is a good example of a market that is dominated by a handful of very large companies. Economists call markets like this **oligopolistic**. The rivalry that exists within such markets can be very intense. Firms know that any gains in market share will be at the expense of their rivals. The actions taken by one firm affect the profits made by the other firms that compete within the same market.

In markets made up of a few giants, firms tend to focus on **non-price competition** when designing the marketing mix. Firms in these markets are reluctant to compete by cutting price. They fear that the other firms in the industry will respond by cutting their prices too, creating a costly price war where no firm wins.

The fiercely competitive market

Fiercely competitive markets tend to be fragmented; made up of hundreds of relatively small firms who each compete actively against the others. In some of these markets competition is amplified by the fact that firms sell near-identical products called commodities. Commodities are products such as flour, sugar or blank DVDs that are hard to differentiate. Rivalry in commodity markets tends to be intense. In markets such as this, firms have to manage their production costs very carefully because the retail price is the most important factor in determining whether the firm's product sells or not. If a firm cannot cut its costs, it will not be able to cut its prices without cutting into profit margins. Without price cuts, market share is likely to be lost.

In fiercely competitive markets, firms will try, where possible, to create product differentiation. For example, the restaurant market in Croydon, Surrey, is extremely competitive. There are over 70 outlets within a two-mile radius of the town centre. To survive without having to compete solely on price, firms in markets like this must find new innovations regularly because points of differentiation are quickly copied.

Market saturation

The pattern of growth shown in Table 46.1 gives an idea of how competition can transform the way businesses operate. In 1970 there would only have been one Indian restaurant in any town or district. By 1990 there would often be two or three. Therefore, to be successful, there had to either be competition on price, or a move to more differentiation of menu and cooking style. Today, in a saturated market, a new Indian restaurant will have to offer something very special to get established.

Table 46.1 Number of Indian restaurants in UK

Year	No. of restaurants	Market growth rate
1960	500	
1970	1,200	140%
1980	3,000	150%
1990	5,100	70%
2000	7,940	56%
2004	8,750	10%
2009	8,750	0%

Changes in competitive structure

New competitors

The number of firms operating within a market can change over time. If new competitors enter, a market will become more competitive. New entrants are usually attracted into a new market by the high profits or the rapid growth achieved by the existing firms. After the Europe-wide success of airlines such as easyJet and Ryanair, a huge number of imitators came into the airline business, such as Air Berlin, Wizz and AirAsia. Although most of these have struggled to be profitable, they have unquestionably benefited the traveller, as they have kept prices fairly low.

In markets that are suffering from low or negative profitability, firms tend to exit, leaving the market less competitive than it was. In 2011 several UK retail markets suffered from business failures. These included the clothing sector, with the collapse of Jane Norman, and the homeware sector, with the failure of Habitat and Home Form.

2011 also saw a powerful new competitive presence in London's fashion retailing scene, as Forever 21 arrived from America to challenge Primark, New Look and TopShop.

The emergence of dominant businesses

A dominant business is one that has a high market share. Markets that are dominated by a single or a small number of businesses tend to be less competitive than markets that are less concentrated. Businesses that dominate their respective markets often possess the ability to set prices for all other smaller firms that operate within the same market. For example, the UK chocolate market is dominated by three companies: Cadbury, Nestlé and Mars. If a smaller firm, such as Finland's Fazer, wanted to try and enter the UK market it would probably set its prices below the big three in order to stimulate trial purchase.

Dominant businesses can emerge naturally over a long period of time due to organic growth. Organic growth occurs when a firm grows bigger because it has increased production and/or opened up new factories or branches. In the long-run, organic growth usually reflects a change in consumer preferences in favour of the firm that has achieved the growth. It requires customer support. Firms that sell products that consumers like will tend to grow naturally over time. For many years Tesco was No. 2 in the grocery market, behind its main rival, Sainsbury's. Gradually, Tesco managed to grow its market share by offering UK consumers lower prices and better quality than their main rivals. In 2011 Tesco dominated the UK supermarket industry, holding a market share of 30.7%. Asda, Tesco's closest rival, had a market share of about half that figure.

Dominant businesses can also emerge via takeover or merger. If two firms in the same industry and at the same stage of production integrate, the result will be an increase in market concentration and a corresponding fall in competition. In 2011 the media giant News Corporation (*The Sun*, *The Times*) tried to buy out BSkyB (Sky TV). The proposed takeover would have given News Corp a dominant position in the provision of news and entertainment to the UK public. Fortunately, the public fiasco over phone hacking forced the coalition government to put a stop to this bid.

Changes in the buying power of customers

Changes in the state of the economy can affect consumer spending levels, and with it the level of competition within most markets. For example, during recessions when national income is falling and unemployment is rising many consumers opt to spend less. The markets for luxury goods and services are likely to contract. When the American economy was under pressure in early 2010, sales of the iconic (and very expensive) Harley-Davidson motorbikes fell by 12%. As the market shrinks, rivalry increases because the same number of firms now has to fight for a falling number of customers. To maintain its sales in a shrinking market, each motorbike manufacturer wants to increase its market share. This usually means price cutting and may lead to a price war.

On the other hand, if consumer buying power is increasing markets tend to grow quite rapidly, especially for luxury goods that have an income elastic demand. During economic booms when incomes are growing rapidly most markets normally become less competitive, especially in the short-run. In the longer term the additional profits created by additional consumer spending power tend to attract new entrants into a market, making the market concerned more competitive again.

Changes in the selling power of suppliers

In addition to demand, the level of competition within a market is also determined by market supply. If market supply decreases but market demand does not, competition will increase. One factor that affects the selling power of suppliers is raw material costs. In recent times the price of oil has rocketed. Oil is a very important raw material. For example, even companies such as Apple will be affected by the price of oil. Plastic is made from oil. If the price of oil increases, Apple will need to pay more for the plastic pellets needed to produce casings for

its iPods, iPads, iPhones and iMacs. If the price of raw materials goes up, firms will tend to supply less because the profit generated from each unit supplied will fall. The selling power of suppliers also depends upon other factors such as wage rates and taxes. Wages are a day-to-day expense that consumes working capital. If wages go up, firms may be forced to cut output because they lack the working capital needed to maintain their current output level.

On the other hand, if profits are soaring and firms have plenty of working capital, supply is likely to grow.

Market sharing agreements

The level of competition within a market can change over time if established firms elect to set up a cartel. A cartel is a group of companies that operate in the same market that decide to cooperate, rather than compete, with each other. The members of the cartel collectively restrict market supply by agreeing to production quotas. Cartels lead to a less competitive market. A market with several firms apparently competing against each other may effectively be a monopoly.

A-grade application

Two years ago the Office of Fair Trading announced a probe into 112 construction companies. They were accused of '**collusion**', meaning getting together to agree who would win contracts in supposedly competitive situations. For example, an NHS hospital might ask five builders to bid for a £40 million contract to build a new hospital ward. Instead of putting forward an honest 'best price', the five would get together and agree to four falsely high bids, leaving one to get the business. Next time around, a different one of the five would get the contract.

Even though 40 of the building firms admitted to price fixing, the industry association claimed that no one had been overcharged. The Office of Fair Trading disagreed, stating that: 'Cartel activity of the type alleged today harms the economy by distorting competition and keeping prices artificially high.'

Responses of businesses to a changing competitive environment

In a market that has become more competitive firms might be forced into the following actions in order to defend market share.

Price cutting

Many firms attempt to fight off a competitor by cutting price. If the competition can be under-cut, consumers will hopefully remain loyal to the company that has cut its prices. Firms that use price cutting as a way of fighting off the competition will normally try to cut their costs in line with the price cut, in an attempt to preserve profit margins. If profit margins are already tight and costs have already been cut to the bone, it probably will not be possible to respond to a new competitor by cutting prices.

Increase product differentiation

Product differentiation is the degree to which consumers perceive a brand to be different, and in some way superior to, other brands of the same type of product. Some firms might be apprehensive about responding to a competitive threat by cutting price, because the long-term result could be a deteriorating brand image that could hinder, rather than help, sales. Many consumers still associate price with product quality. If product differentiation can be increased, consumers will be less likely to switch to products supplied by the competition. To a degree, differentiation helps a firm to insulate itself from competitive pressure. Firms that want to increase differentiation can do so by the means set out below.

Design

An eye-catching design that is aesthetically pleasing can help a firm to survive in a competitive market. By using design as a unique selling point British manufacturers can compete on quality rather than on price, making them less vulnerable to competition from China and India. Good-looking design can add value to a product. For example, the BMW Mini relies upon its retro 1960s styling to command its price premium within the small car market.

Brand image

Many products rely very heavily on their brand image to sell. When products such as Jack Wills clothes and BMW 4x4 cars are purchased, the consumer hopes to share some of the brand's personality. The consumer believes that some of the brand's image will rub off on them. They also hope that others will notice too. Public consumption of a brand tells others something about you. Purchasing famous brands, which are then publicly consumed, effectively amounts to purchasing elements of personal identity. In many markets brand image is crucial. A strong brand image can help a firm to fight off its competitors without having to resort to price cuts.

Unique product features

In markets that are highly competitive some firms react by redesigning their products to ensure that they possess the latest must-have feature. For example, in car market Toyota's hybrid drive technology has appealed to consumers that are interested in buying an environmentally friendly car with very low emissions.

Superior quality

Some firms try to fight off new competition by improving the quality of the products that they sell. If product quality can be improved consumers should stay loyal. A good example of a firm that has reacted to competition by improving product quality is Rolls Royce. Rolls Royce hopes to fight off its competitors by offering consumers a bespoke service for their new Phantom model. Consumers can choose special features, such as a 24-carat gold Spirit of Ecstasy, or the customer's initials embroidered into the seat headrests.

Find new markets

If a market suddenly becomes more competitive because new firms have entered the market some firms react by trying to find new markets overseas that are less competitive. Even companies such as Tesco find it easier to build sales by opening superstores in Eastern Europe, rather than trying to grow sales by taking yet more market share away from its UK rivals.

Takeover

Some large dominant firms react to a new successful competitor by trying to take them over. Among many examples are the purchase of Cadbury by the US giant Kraft and the purchase by Google of YouTube (Google paid $1.65 billion for a business that was only 20 months old). Although governments are supposed to stop takeovers that crush competition, their record is not impressive.

Predatory pricing

If it is not possible to reduce competition by taking over a competitor some firms might be tempted to use predatory pricing. Predatory pricing occurs when a firm cuts its prices in a deliberate attempt to under-cut a rival so that they go out of business. The prices charged are very low – so losses are made. Predatory pricing tends to be used by large dominant companies against smaller new entrants. These smaller firms tend not to have as much cash as the firm that started the price war. As a result, the smaller firm will be forced to close down way before the large firm runs out of money. Predatory pricing is illegal. However, it is still very common because the potential rewards that come from using predatory pricing greatly outweigh any fines imposed by the Competition Commission.

Issues for analysis

- Business guru Michael Porter has suggested that there are five forces that determine a firm's ability to compete effectively. These are the number of direct substitutes; the ability of new firms to enter the market; the bargaining power of buyers (e.g. Tesco buying over 30% of all Britain's groceries); the bargaining power of suppliers (e.g. a sweetshop buying chewing gum from Wrigley's, with its 90% market share) and the policies and actions of competitors.

- Any firm's competitive position can be analysed in this way. For example China protested loudly when the world's biggest mining company (BHP Billiton) offered nearly $150 billion to buy the world's Number 3, Rio Tinto Zinc. China was worried that the huge size of this supplier of minerals such as iron and copper would put the company in too strong a position when negotiating with buyers such as China. Changes in the buying power of customers or suppliers can affect a company, or perhaps even a country.

Impact of competitive and market structure – an evaluation

As has always been the case, the best way a business can ensure its survival in a competitive world is to find something it is good at, and stick with it. Cadbury is great when it concentrates on making chocolate; Heinz is brilliant at making and marketing baked beans. Even if the massive Hershey Corporation brings its chocolate from America, Cadbury need not fear. Similarly, the launch of Branston's Beans made little impact on Heinz.

Sometimes, though, big judgements have to be considered, such as to risk launching a new product in a new country. When Tesco did this in 2007, launching Fresh 'n' Easy stores in America, the questions were (a) did they need to? And (b) were they looking in the right direction? (Wouldn't China or India have made more sense?) In 2010 they finally admitted their mistake by increasingly massively their investment into China. All too often, business leaders take actions that seem more to do with ego than logic. Models such as Porter's 5 Forces are based on an assumption that business is about reacting to pressures, whereas a great deal of business decision making is about choices and judgements.

Key terms

Collusion: when managers from different firms get together to discuss ways to work together to restrict supply and/or raise prices. (See the Adam Smith quotation earlier in this unit)

Predatory pricing: when a financially strong company prices its products so low that it threatens to force weaker competitors out of business.

A Revision questions *(40 marks; 40 minutes)*

1 What is a monopoly? (2)

2 Explain two reasons why monopolies exist. (4)

3 How might an increase in competition within the UK banking market affect shareholders of banks such as Nat West and HSBC? (3)

4 Analyse two factors which could decrease the level of competition within the car market. (6)

5 Which stakeholder group benefits most from new entrants joining a market? (2)

6 Explain why some companies decide not to respond to additional competition by cutting price. (4)

7 Outline two reasons why a supermarket such as Waitrose might be concerned if Mars and Cadbury merged into one business. (6)

8 How might product differentiation help a firm to adjust to a more competitive market? (3)

9 Explain why many large firms prefer to buy out smaller rivals, rather than competing against them head-to-head. (4)

10 Discuss whether it is right for some firms to use tactics such as predatory pricing to influence market structure. (6)

B1 Data response

BA bosses accused of price-fixing by Virgin 'whistleblowers'

In 1993 British Airways found itself in court accused of using anti-competitive tactics in an attempt to force a much smaller new airline called, Virgin Atlantic, out of business. The so-called 'dirty tricks' used by BA included spreading malicious rumours about Virgin's solvency in order to deprive the company of credit. After a bitter legal battle in the High Court, BA apologised and agreed to pay Virgin over £600,000 in compensation.

How times change. Today, nearly 20 years later the same two companies stand accused of collusion. In April 2010 BA managers were summoned to appear in court to answer allegations that they had met with their rivals at Virgin to agree on a common fuel duty surcharge to impose on both BA and Virgin consumers. Over a period of a year and a half both airlines increased the fuel surcharges paid by passengers on long-haul routes from £5 to £60.

In the UK the Competition Commission is responsible for investigating alleged cases of anti-competitive behaviour. Unfortunately, anti-competitive behaviour, such as price-fixing, is still very common in the UK, despite the fact that it is illegal. One of the main problems faced by the Competition Commission is the difficulty faced by the Commission in acquiring the necessary evidence needed to prove in a court of law that anti-competitive behaviour has taken place. The commission now offers so-called 'whistleblowers' immunity from prosecution in exchange for information that enables a prosecution to take place. In this case, the evidence used to convict BA came from their co-conspirators. Virgin's Chief executive, stood as the main witness for the prosecution!

Questions *(30 marks; 35 minutes)*

1 What is a fuel surcharge and why do airlines impose them? (4)

2 Why is anti-competitive behaviour such as price-fixing illegal? (3)

3 Explain three reasons that might explain why anti-competitive behaviour persists despite the fact that it is illegal (9)

4 Discuss whether the Competition Commission was right to offer Virgin immunity from prosecution. (14)

Case study

Tesco's £9 toaster

The prices of consumer electronics, such as toasters, satellite TV set-top boxes and MP3 players, have tumbled in recent years. Supermarket chains such as Tesco now sell DVD players for less than £10 that previously cost hundreds of pounds. So, why have the prices of these goods fallen? In part, the price falls reflect the falling price of the components that go into consumer electronics. Low prices also reflect the fact that there is now more competition in the market. In the past, consumers typically bought items such as TVs and computers from specialist retailers such as Currys and Comet. Today, the situation is somewhat different; in addition to these specialist retailers consumers can now buy electrical goods over the internet and from supermarkets. Some industry analysts also believe that some of the supermarket chains are using set-top boxes and DVD players as loss leaders.

In today's ultra-competitive environment, manufacturers of consumer electronics face intense pressure from retailers to cut costs so that retail prices can be cut without any loss of profit margin. To cut prices without compromising product quality, manufacturers such as the Dutch giant Phillips have transferred production from Holland to low-cost locations such as China.

Questions (40 marks; 45 minutes)

1 Describe three characteristics of a highly competitive market. (6)

2 Explain why the market for consumer electronics has become more competitive. (5)

3 Examine three factors that would affect the competitiveness of a manufacturer of MP3 players. (9)

4 a Use a dictionary or A-Z to find out the meaning of the term 'loss leader'. (3)

  b Why do supermarkets use this tactic? (3)

5 Discuss whether, in today's competitive market for consumer electronics, firms must constantly cut costs and prices if they are to survive. (14)

47 Changes in ownership and competitive structure

> ## Definition
> Growth can occur as a result of naturally increasing sales levels. This is called organic, or internal, growth. Growth may also be the result of changes in business ownership – mergers and takeovers. Takeovers occur when one firm buys a majority of the shares in another and therefore has full management control.

 ## Organic growth

Organic growth is a safer, but slower method of growth than takeover. Its safety comes from the avoidance of the culture clashes involved in mergers or takeovers. Steady growth also avoids the need to add debt to a company's balance sheet, since finance is more likely to come from retained profits. However, a reliance on organic growth could lead firms to miss out on surges of growth in their industry if they fail to develop sufficient capacity to cope with the potential demand. For example, when Cadbury saw the increasing consumer interest in organic chocolate, it chose to buy up Green & Black's instead of developing its own organic brand.

Despite the appeal of takeovers to achieve rapid growth, the low success rate of takeovers and mergers encourages some businesses to aim for rapid organic growth. This is challenging, but can be achieved. In its first ten years of life, Innocent Drinks' turnover grew from £0.4 million to £130 million, entirely organically, i.e. without buying up other companies. That's a total growth of 32,400%!

A-grade application

Rapid organic growth
In the three months to June 2011 top-end UK fashion business Burberry continued its rapid growth. In China its sales grew by 20% on a like-for-like basis (i.e. in direct comparison with last year); in the rest of the world the comparable figure was 15% up. When the impact of new store openings was added in, total sales for the company rose by 34%. All this expansion was organic, i.e. achieved from within the business, not by buying up competitors.

 ## Mergers and takeovers: an introduction

Every time a company's shares are bought or sold on the stock exchange, there is a change in the ownership of that company. However, the significant changes occur when a majority of shares is bought by an individual or company. Any individual or organisation that owns 51% of a company's shares has effective control over that company. To successfully take over a company, a firm (or individual) must therefore buy 51% of the shares. In America, this process is called mergers and acquisitions (M&A), acquisitions being another word for purchasing.

Why do firms merge with or take over other companies?

See Table 47.1 for examples and reasons for takeovers.

Growth

The fastest way for any firm to achieve significant growth is to merge with, or take over, another company. The motives behind the objective of growth may be based on any of the reasons outlined below. However, as a basic motive behind mergers and takeovers, growth is often the overriding factor.

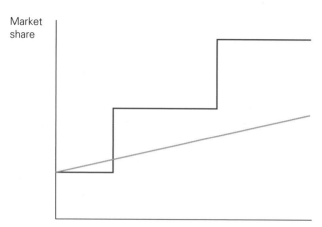

Market share

Figure 47.1 Organic (blue) vs external (red) growth

Cost synergies

Cost savings are often used as a primary argument for corporate integration. It is suggested that **economies of scale** will arise from operating on a larger scale. If two businesses merge, output will increase. As a result, they are more likely to benefit from economies of scale, such as cheaper bulk purchasing of supplies. Synergies are the benefits from two things coming together. In this context, it is that the two firms together will have lower costs (and higher profits) than the two firms separately. In effect, **synergy** means that 2 + 2 = 5.

Diversification

This means entering different markets in order to reduce dependence upon current products and customers. Diversification is a way of reducing the risk faced by a company. Selling a range of different products to different groups of consumers will mean that, if any one product fails, sales of the other products should keep the business healthy. The simplest way to diversify is to merge with or take over another company. This saves time and money spent developing new products for markets in which the firm may have no expertise.

Market power

When two competitors in the same market merge, the combined business will have an increased level of power in the market. It may be possible that this increased power can be used to reduce the overall competitiveness within the market. If prices can be increased a little, then margins will increase and the market will become more profitable.

Table 47.1 Reasons for takeovers, and some examples

Reasons for takeovers	Examples
Growth	• Royal Bank of Scotland beats Barclays to buy ABN Amro (Dutch) bank for £49 billion in October 2007 • Kraft's takeover of Cadbury in 2010
Cost synergies	• The British Airways merger with Iberia is estimated (by the firm itself) to generate some £350 million in cost savings over five years • Co-op taking over Somerfield (paying £1.7 billion)
Diversification	• Hewlett-Packard (HP) buys the UK's hugely successful Autonomy software group for £7 billion in 2011 • Chip manufacturer Intel's 2010 purchase of computer security software maker McAfee
Market power	• Indian car producer Tata (producers of the world's cheapest new car) buys Jaguar and Land Rover • B&Q's purchase of 31 Focus DIY stores boosted its UK market share in 2011

Types of business integration

There are four main types of merger or takeover (see Figure 47.2), as discussed below.

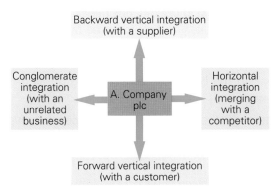

Figure 47.2 Vertical and horizontal integration

Vertical integration

Vertical integration occurs when one firm takes over or merges with another at a different stage in the production process, but within the same industry.

Backward vertical integration occurs when a firm buys out a supplier. In March 2008 Boeing announced the purchase of a key supplier to its 787 aeroplane. Boeing said it hoped this would enable it to overcome production problems that had delayed the delivery of the plane to British Airways and Virgin. The key benefit of a backward vertical takeover is security of supply.

Forward vertical integration means buying out a customer, such as the purchase of retailer Body Shop by cosmetics producer L'Oréal. This shows the major benefit of forward vertical integration – guaranteed outlets for your products.

Table 47.2 explains the major advantages and disadvantages of backward and forward vertical integration for three important stakeholders: the company (and its shareholders), the workforce and the customers.

Horizontal integration

Horizontal integration occurs when one firm buys out another in the same industry at the same stage of the supply chain. In effect, this means buying a competitor. In the UK, if the market share of the combined companies is greater than 25%, the Competition Commission is likely to investigate before the integration will be allowed. A recent example was the takeover by the Co-op of the Somerfield supermarket chain. The extra Somerfield stores increased Co-op's share of the UK grocery market from 6.2% in July 2010 to 6.9% in July 2011. Understandably, the Competition Commission showed no interest in the takeover.

Of the four types of takeover, the most common by far is horizontal integration with a competitor. Typical examples include:

● Adidas buying Reebok

● B&Q buying 31 Focus DIY stores.

For the purchaser, there are three major attractions:

1 huge scope for cost cutting by eliminating duplication of salesforce, distribution and marketing overheads, and by improved capacity utilisation

2 opportunities for major economies of scale

3 a reduction in competition should enable prices to be pushed up.

Of course, no purchaser states publicly that the plan is to push prices up. But if you owned four consecutive motorway service stations covering over 190 km of driving, would you not be tempted to charge a bit more?

A-grade application

Blu-ray triumphs

When video recorders were first available, Sony was horrified to find that its high-quality Betamax player was swept aside by the inferior VHS system. Toshiba, the originator of the VHS, had persuaded Hollywood film studios to use the VHS system for the film rental market. Sony decided: never again. The Japanese company chose (in the face of great hostility from America) to buy its way into the Hollywood studios. It bought Columbia Pictures and several other studios. At first it lost billions of dollars, as Sony struggled to manage a Hollywood studio effectively.

The huge reward came in early 2008. In an exact parallel of the earlier video wars, Sony had pitched its Blu-ray HD disk against Toshiba (and Microsoft's) preferred HD DVD. Using its power in Hollywood plus the strength of its Playstation franchise, Sony persuaded key businesses such as Disney to go for the Blu-ray format. Nowadays, high-definition DVD means buying Blu-ray from Sony.

As horizontal mergers have particular implications for competition, they are likely to be looked at by the Office of Fair Trading. If there is believed to be a threat to competition, the Competition Commission will be asked to investigate. The Competition Commission has the power to recommend that the Office of Fair Trading refuse to allow the integration, or recommend changes before it can go through. For example, if Unilever (which produces Walls ice cream and much else) made a bid for Mars, the Competition Commission would probably let the takeover through, on the condition that the Mars ice cream business was sold off.

Conglomerate integration

Conglomerate integration occurs when one firm buys out another with no clear connection to its own line of business. An example was the purchase by the household goods giant Procter & Gamble of the Gillette shaving products business. Conglomerate integration is likely to be prompted by the desire to diversify or to achieve rapid growth. It might also be for purely financial motives such as asset stripping (breaking the business up and selling off all its key assets).

Although the achievement of successful diversification helps to spread risk, research shows that

Table 47.2 The advantages and disadvantages of backward vertical integration and forward vertical integration

	Backward vertical integration	Forward vertical integration
Advantages to the company	• Closer links with suppliers aid new product development and give more control over the quality and timing of supplies • Absorbing the suppliers' profit margins may cut supply costs	• Control of competition in own retail outlets; prominent display of own brands • Firm put in direct contact with end users/consumers
Disadvantages to the company	• Supplier division may become complacent if there is no need to compete for customers • Costs might rise, therefore, and delivery and quality become slack	• Consumers may resent the dominance of one firm's products in retail outlets, causing sales to decline • Worries about image may obstruct the outlet, e.g. Levi stores rarely offer discounted prices
Advantages to the workforce	• Secure customer for the suppliers may increase job security • Larger scale of the combined organisation may lead to enhanced benefits such as pension or career opportunities	• Increased control over the market may increase job security • Designers can now influence not only how the products look, but also how they are displayed
Disadvantages to the workforce	• Becoming part of a large firm may affect the sense of team morale built up at the supplier • Job losses may result from attempts to cut out duplication of support roles such as in personnel and accounting	• Staff in retail outlets may find themselves deskilled. Owner may dictate exactly what products to stock and how to display them. This would be demotivating
Advantages to the consumer	• Better coordination between company and supplier may lead to more innovative new product ideas • Ownership of the whole supply process may make the business more conscious of product and service quality	• With luxury products, customers like to see perfect displays and be served by expert staff, e.g. at perfume counters in department stores • Prices may fall if a large retail margin is absorbed by the supplier
Disdvantages to the consumer	• The firm's control over one supplier may in fact reduce the variety of goods available • Supplier complacency may lead to rising costs, passed on to customers as higher prices	• Increased power within the market could lead to price rises • If the outlet only supplies the parent company's products, consumer choice will be hit, as in brewery-owned clubs or pubs

conglomerate mergers are those least likely to succeed. This is largely because the managers of the purchasing company have, by definition, little knowledge of the marketplace of the company that has been bought.

Retrenchment and demergers

Sometimes firms will decide that they have grown too large to be controlled effectively. This is likely to be the case when diseconomies of scale are causing huge reductions in efficiency. In such cases, directors may pursue a policy of **retrenchment** – deliberately shrinking in size. Reducing overall capacity in order to boost capacity utilisation seems logical. However, in reality retrenchment brings its own problems. Redundancies will lead to an initial hunk of cash outflows, while other effects may linger. Staff who have seen colleagues laid off may well retain a fear for their own jobs – will we be laid off in the next round of redundancies? Maintaining staff morale during and after retrenchment is a great management challenge – retrenchment poses a huge change management challenge.

Meanwhile, there has been growing scepticism about the benefits of mergers and takeovers.

Recent research has shown that the majority of takeovers are unsuccessful, as measured by criteria such as profits, market share or the share price. This has resulted in a growing trend in the past few years towards the **demerger**. This occurs when a company is split into two or more parts, either by selling off separate divisions or by floating them separately on the stock exchange. Demergers are often the result of unsuccessful takeovers. Once a firm has seen that the economies of scale it expected are not happening, it will seek to sell off the business it originally bought.

Another common situation leading to demergers is the desire of a company to reduce interest payments in times of economic downturn. Since many takeovers are financed heavily by borrowed capital, selling off recently acquired businesses will generate cash to pay back those loans.

Some firms, however, may simply decide to concentrate on core activities due to a change in their overall strategy. This might be caused by a change in economic circumstances or just because a new chief executive has been appointed. Having identified the core activities they will sell off others, even if they are profitable.

A-grade application

In 1998, Mercedes of Germany bought the US Chrysler car business for $38 billion. What followed was one of the most disastrous takeovers of all time. Not only did Chrysler lose billions of dollars in operating losses, but the German leadership's focus on America led to a downturn at Mercedes. Engineering and quality standards dropped alarmingly in 2003–2005, and Mercedes' reputation for quality took time to recover. In 2007, Mercedes finally accepted its failure and sold Chrysler for $7 billion. By early 2008 the demerger was completed. Some analysts have suggested that the total losses to Mercedes from its ten-year US nightmare might be as high as $100 billion. The 'spun-off' Chrysler was declared bankrupt on 30 April 2009 and later that year, the remnants of the business were bought by Fiat. By 2011, Chrysler sales in the US were up significantly – perhaps the Italians handled this takeover better than the Germans.

Private equity and gearing

Takeovers have always taken place between trading companies – for example, BP buying the US oil giant Amoco. However, a major new force has emerged in takeovers. Half the money spent on takeovers in the UK comes from 'private equity', not from 'ordinary' companies. Private equity snapped up Travelex, the Tussauds Group and Kwik-Fit. By 2007 private equity deals for firms as huge as Boots were going through (for £11 billion).

Private equity is a management group backed by sufficient bank finance to make a takeover – usually

of a public limited company. Usually the financing of these takeovers is hugely reliant upon bank loans. In other words, the gearing can be as high as 90%. If the business is doing well (perhaps because the economy is in an upturn), the high gearing can boost the profits made by the investors. Unfortunately, if there is an economic downturn, trading losses will quickly eat away the small shareholders' funds within the business, pushing it into liquidation.

Private equity is the latest term for what were once known as leveraged buy-outs (LBOs) in America and

management buy-outs (MBOs) in Britain. All share a common characteristic – extremely high gearing. This creates a situation of highly questionable business ethics – broadly 'heads I win, tails you lose'. If all goes well, the few private equity shareholders can make fabulous profits. If it goes wrong they can make staff redundant to cut costs and, if things continue to go wrong, pay themselves off before closing the business down. A 2008 report presented to the Davos forum of world leaders showed that private equity businesses cut 7% of staff within two years and have a significantly higher failure rate than ordinary businesses.

Debenhams store group has been a classic example of private equity. Taken private in 2004, the stores were re-floated on the stock market in 2006, creating enormous personal profits for the key directors. Since the 2006 flotation, the stores have lost market share and the shares have lost more than two-thirds of their value. From 200p in November 2006 the Debenhams share price was 58p in August 2011.

A serious criticism of a business such as Boots 'going private' is that it no longer has to provide the accounting information demanded from a public company. The people who felt like stakeholders in the old public company (staff, customers and, of course, shareholders) no longer have access to the accounts. Nor can they question the directors personally, as you can at a plc's **annual general meeting**.

Takeover decisions and Ansoff's matrix

A useful way to analyse the risks and rewards from a takeover is to apply Ansoff's matrix. This considers the extent to which a business is keeping close to its core business (and knowledge/experience) or whether it is moving into new territory. For example, in 2011 the US retail giant Wal-Mart paid $2.4 billion to buy an African supermarket business called Massmart. Does Wal-Mart know enough about African grocery shopping to make a success of this takeover? Only time will tell. On Ansoff's matrix, this radical move into a new market would be represented as a major, high-risk move. If Wal-Mart bought a store chain in Canada (or Britain, where it owns Asda), it would be much safer.

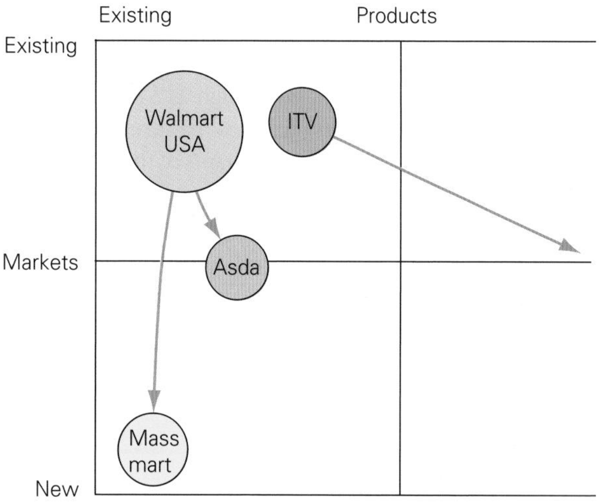

The same type of analysis could work for considering the risks involved in ITV's 2006 £175 million purchase of the social network (for oldies) site, Friends Reunited. What did a television channel understand about running a website? Not a lot, which may explain why this takeover flopped (ITV sold the business for £25 million in 2009, losing a cool £150 million). It could be debated whether this takeover was an example of product development or diversification. Either way it pushed ITV's management too far away from its area of expertise. It is a tough job running any business; it is often only arrogance that leads business leaders to believe they can run two different businesses at the same time.

Figure 47.3 Ansoff's matrix applied to takeovers

Issues for analysis

● The key theme for analysis when considering any question on mergers and takeovers is the identification of advantages and disadvantages. These are outlined briefly above, for each type of transaction. It is important to consider which advantages and disadvantages are likely to be relevant in the particular situation being considered. For example, a sugar producer that buys a soft drink manufacturer will not have any significant degree of control over the way its

- products are sold by retailers. In this case, one of the most significant advantages of forward integration disappears.

- Never forget that a merger or takeover will bring disadvantages as well as advantages. Research in America and Britain has shown consistently that the majority of takeovers fail to improve business performance. This is largely because managers anticipate the economies of scale from integration.

However, they overlook the diseconomies from problems such as communication and coordination.

- Another important analytical theme is the differing effects upon different stakeholder groups. Many questions will offer marks for analysing the effects on consumers, or the workforce, rather than simply focusing on the effects on the firm as a whole.

Changes in ownership and competitive structure – an evaluation

A key judgement that is required is to see through the public relations 'hype' that surrounds takeover bids. Company leader A makes a bid for Company B, claiming that 'synergies will lead to better service and lower prices to our customers'. Really? Or will it mean factory closures, the elimination of small niche brands and – later – higher prices for all? Similarly, the leader may claim that the reason for a takeover is very businesslike, such as 'creating a world-leading company'. Yet the high failure rate of takeovers must imply that many claimed business benefits are a fig leaf. The real reason for many takeovers is arrogance, and perhaps greed, on the part of the executives concerned.

An explanation for the problems firms may encounter after a merger or takeover is resistance to change. This will be especially true if the business cultures are widely different at the two companies. One may be go-getting and entrepreneurial; the other may be cautious and bureaucratic. Judgement is again required to consider whether a takeover is especially vulnerable to a clash of culture when the firms come together.

The other key issue raised in this unit is that of diversification. Traditionally, diversification was perceived as a good thing. Theorists such as Ansoff, Tom Peters and Bob Waterman have raised serious doubts. The management of the original company may know little about the industry within

which the new business operates. This means that those making major strategic decisions may be doing so from a position of ignorance. The advice in recent years has been to 'stick to the knitting' – in other words, concentrate on doing what you do best.

Key terms

Annual general meeting: the once-yearly meeting at which shareholders have the opportunity to question the chairperson and to vote new directors to the board.

Demerger: this occurs when a firm is split into two or more different companies.

Economies of scale: the factors that cause average costs to be lower in large-scale operations than small ones.

Management buy-out (MBO): a specialised form of takeover where the managers of a business buy out the shareholders, thereby buying ownership and control of the firm.

Organic: growth from within the business (e.g. getting better sales from existing brands, or launching new ones).

Retrenchment: a deliberate policy of cutbacks, perhaps to lower a firm's break-even point.

Synergy: this occurs when the whole is greater than the sum of the parts (2 + 2 = 5). It is often the reason given for mergers or takeovers occurring.

A — Revision questions *(30 marks; 30 minutes)*

1 What is horizontal integration? *(2)*

2 For what reasons might a manufacturer take over one of its suppliers? *(4)*

3 Outline two reasons for each why Nokia might like to make a takeover of:
   a Motorola *(4)*
   b Vodafone. *(4)*

4 Why might a firm decide to carry out a demerger? *(3)*

5 Why may takeovers be riskier when financed by 'private equity'? *(3)*

6 Why might diversification be a bad idea for a growing firm? *(3)*

7 Explain the meaning of the word 'synergy'. *(3)*

8 Explain why businesses should consider Ansoff's matrix before making a takeover bid. *(4)*

B1 — Data response

Body Shop: because you're worth it

When French cosmetics giant L'Oréal bought BodyShop there was a great deal of controversy. Body Shop shareholders and customers were concerned that L'Oréal would fail to maintain Body Shop's unique culture of socially responsible business. However, Body Shop was eventually sold for around £500 million, enabling L'Oréal to add another brand to its portfolio of products including Ambre Solaire, Lancôme, Elvive, Maybelline and Plenitude. L'Oréal's plan was to run Body Shop as a self-contained business, in an attempt to retain the firm's quirky, socially-concerned image. This, after all, has been a major selling point among a loyal band of customers who have given Body Shop a significant niche within the beauty market.

Questions *(35 marks; 40 minutes)*

1 Explain the possible motives behind L'Oréal's purchase of Body Shop. *(6)*

2 Analyse the possible difficulties that L'Oréal may encounter within Body Shop following the takeover. *(8)*

3 Explain why Body Shop will add to L'Oréal's product portfolio, without cannibalising existing brands. *(6)*

4 To what extent is L'Oréal's plan to run Body Shop as a separate business a sensible choice? *(15)*

B1 — Data response

The 30%/70% rule

On 15 May 2007, a £9 billion merger was concluded between the publisher Thomson and the news service Reuters. During this period of merger-mania, most corporate bosses have hardly bothered to justify the strategic logic behind the bid. Even though research shows that most mergers fail, rising share prices point to the love stock market investors currently have for takeovers.

The Thomson–Reuters merger took place in a week when Daimler (Mercedes) sold off the American business Chrysler after suffering losses of more than £20 billion since buying Chrysler in 1998. If Mercedes can't run a car company, what hope is there for any takeover bidder?

After announcing the merger, senior executives from Reuters and Thomson were interviewed by the *Financial Times*. They acknowledged that academics estimate that 70% of mergers fail, but chief executive Tom Glocer argued that Thomson–Reuters should be 'firmly in the 30% camp'. He continued: 'It's important to look at why they fail. A lot comes down to culture. This has been an unusually warm and close transaction.'

The senior executives seem to assume that, because they can work together, all the staff will get along with each other. This remains to be seen. Tom Glocer is right to identify culture as a critical issue, but naive to think it is easy to manage.

When talking about the merger in practice, Glocer outlined the £250 million of cost-saving 'synergies' they hoped to benefit from. He emphasised, though, that staff should not be concerned. Another executive pointed out that: 'The hardest integrations are when you are consolidating. We're not consolidating, we're growing.' (Consolidating means the same as rationalising – that is, usually it amounts to cutbacks in jobs and in the variety of product ranges.)

The big hope is that the merger will boost revenues rather than cut costs. The new chairman said that: 'The strategic fit is about as compelling as can be. Reuters is strong in Europe and Asia and Thomson in North America'.

In 1998 the claims made about Daimler and Chrysler were equally optimistic. The strategy was Mercedes in Europe and Asia, Chrysler in the USA. The failure of that 'merger' was all down to problems in management, notably the inability to create a new common culture. In five years or so it will be clear whether Tom Glocer was right to put Thomson–Reuters 'firmly in the 30% camp'.

Questions *(30 marks; 35 minutes)*

1 Explain the meaning of the following terms:

   a synergies (3)

   b strategic fit. (3)

2 Discuss whether Tom Glocer is wise to assume that this merger should be 'firmly in the 30% camp'. (12)

3 Examine why it can be hard to motivate middle managers within a newly merged business such as Thomson–Reuters. (12)

Case study

Intel secures the future

August 2010 saw market leading computer chip manufacturer Intel complete a $7.68 billion takeover of McAfee – a firm that designs and manufactures technology security products, notably anti-virus software. The deal marks a move away from Intel's specialisation in purely making the chips that go into PCs and mobile phones. However, the subtlety of the deal is that it will allow Intel access to the expertise of McAfee's workforce. Security expertise will allow Intel to build security features into their microprocessors used in laptops and mobiles. Industry analysts suggest that as computing becomes increasingly mobile, security for devices such as mobile phones must be stepped up to avoid the myriad internet security problems

from hacked bank accounts to computer viruses.

Intel's move also makes sense as it seeks to strengthen a relatively weak position in the mobile market – its core areas of success being desktop and laptop chips.

Questions *(50 marks; 55 minutes)*

1 Analyse Intel's purchase of McAfee using Ansoff's matrix. (6)

2 Discuss the possible problems that Intel may face in gaining the greatest benefit from their purchase of McAfee. (20)

3 To what extent does the case illustrate the benefits of being a market leader when trying to secure your long-term future? (24)

Table 47.3 Intel and McAfee

	Intel	McAfee
Founded	1968	1987
2009 revenue	$35bn	$2bn
2009 operating profit	$4.4bn	$173m
Number of employees	80,400	6,100

C **Essay questions** *(40 marks each)*

1 Discuss the people management problems that may arise within a firm that has been taken over.

2 'The high level of takeover activity in the UK leads to short-termism.' Explain why this is so and discuss the implications for UK firms.

3 Synergy is often quoted as the reason for mergers and takeovers.
a What is synergy?
b To what extent is synergy a myth?

Introduction

Most of the time, businesses can be successful by focusing on themselves, for example Mars concentrating on making consistently smooth Galaxy chocolate. This can lead to complacency if businesses stop 'looking over their shoulders' at their rivals, or stop looking at changes in the wider world. McDonalds ran into a 'firestorm' when it ignored rising criticism about its menu and its advertising focus on children. And while McDonalds was finding a way to 'put out the fire', Subway crept ahead to become the World's Number 1 fast-food chain.

Long-term business success is achieved when management is able to delegate short-term issues to middle-managers who understand the long-term plan. Then the senior managers can focus on the changing external influences on the business, from competition through consumer tastes to economic changes. The airline easyJet started as a low-cost rival to Ryanair. In recent years, though, it saw the opportunity to reposition itself. It is no longer the discount airline, it's the everyday airline: better value than British Airways and better service than Ryanair.

Some businesses are naturally insulated from external difficulties. Supermarkets such as Sainsbury's can increase their range of posh products when the economy is booming, and boost their 'value' ranges during recessions. Others, such as Topps Tiles, can't avoid the grip of the economy. In mid-2011 Topps Tiles sales fell by more than 10%; management couldn't be blamed, but needed to have prepared for the possibility of this happening. Every business is unique in its sensitivity to a range of external factors. Every generalisation is a mistake.

A useful way to look at each firm's sensitivity to external factors is to conduct a PEST analysis. This means looking at the company's vulnerability to Political, Economic, Social and Technological factors. A PEST analysis is a way of assessing changes in the major external influences on a business in the present and the future.

PEST analysis

Purpose

When a firm is considering its future, it will want a full assessment of its current and future situation. In addition to assessing the internal strengths and weaknesses of the company, the planners will need to assess the external environment within which the firm operates. The PEST framework offers a checklist of the major factors. Current and expected future factors can be listed under the appropriate heading in an attempt to ensure that all foreseeable events are considered in the strategic planning process. These factors are likely to fall into one of two categories – threats or opportunities. Threats represent possible or actual constraints on a firm's ability to achieve its objectives. An opportunity is a positive external chance for development that a firm may decide to pursue.

Political factors

Government policies can affect businesses both

directly and indirectly. The effects may be direct, such as tax incentives designed to encourage R&D expenditure. Or they may be indirect, such as sales of car audio equipment being hit by new environmental laws designed to reduce car use. See Table 48.1.

Political factors in overseas markets can also have an impact on business strategy. Installation of governments unfriendly to 'the West' may make it harder to trade with those countries. Meanwhile, rapidly growing markets such as China open up export opportunities as internal political change encourages international trade. Within Europe, the enlargement of the EU has provided sales and production opportunities. Cadbury, for example, produces much of its chocolate in Poland and has enjoyed booming demand for its products in Eastern Europe.

Economic factors

Variations in the overall level of consumer demand in an economy, perhaps caused by the trade cycle, affect some firms more than others. Well-run businesses have a good idea of how their sales respond to economic change. Sales of jewellery can easily fall by 10% if the economy dips by 2%. Careful planning ahead is vital in a business where stocks are so expensive to finance and to insure.

Individual economic variables, such as interest rates, inflation and exchange rates, will have an impact on many firms, but the trouble with assessing economic changes is that they are easy with hindsight but difficult to forecast! The hardest variable to forecast is the exchange rate. In just two weeks in August 2011 the Swiss franc rose 30% against the pound. British manufacturers that had bought Swiss industrial robots suddenly had to pay 30% more than they expected.

The key for businesses is to be prepared for all possibilities. They should look ahead and wonder: what if the pound rises by 10% or even 20%? And what if it falls by the same amount? The skill in strategic analysis comes in interpreting the likely effects on the business of the possible scenarios. This is called **scenario planning** by oil giant Shell, and is the company's favoured way to plan ahead.

Table 48.1 Effects of government policies on businesses

Possible government policies	Effects on firm
Laws on environment	Reduced sales or increased costs for some, while opportunities may arise for others
Health and Safety law	Increased costs to comply with the laws, e.g. spending on training and equipment
Employment law	Possibly less workforce flexibility, though this might force firms to behave more responsibly towards their staff
Competition policy	Constraint on possible merger or takeover strategy
Smoking ban	Businesses fought hard to stop the regulation banning smoking in public places; now most would wonder why they bothered
Foreign policy (e.g. war in Afghanistan)	Britain is the world's 2nd largest exporter of arms; war means higher demand for guns, bombs and bullets
Sanctions against certain countries	May remove possible export markets

A-grade application

In July 2011 the government announced that a £1.4 billion contract for trains would go to Siemens of Germany. This led Bombardier, UK's train business, to announce a threat to 1,400 jobs at its Derby manufacturing base. The government blamed the decision on its predecessor's commitment to competition; the terms of the contract forced the government to accept the lowest price (even if it meant jobs going overseas). Such was the strength of feeling about this in Derby that the government spent much of the summer trying to find a way to wriggle out of its award to Siemens.

In the first half of 2011 real incomes fell as prices rose by 5%, but average earnings rose by just 2%. With consumers feeling squeezed, the 'like-for-like' sales changes at some well-known store chains were as shown in Figure 48.1.

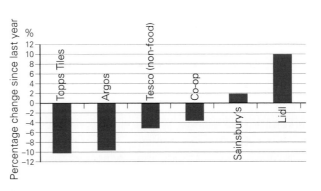

Figure 48.1 Like-for-like sales at some major retailers, 2011

Social factors

Changes in society can have a profound effect on a business. Businesses such as Nike, Danone and Innocent have benefited from the western fascination with healthy lifestyles. Coca-Cola, McDonalds and Walkers have had to battle against the same social pressure to avoid being hit hard. Table 48.2 shows a few current issues within the UK and their possible impact on the strategic planning of a business:

Technological (and environmental) factors

As scientific research allows the development of new technologies, the external environment in which firms operate will shift. The rate of technological change represents a major external factor affecting business strategy. Technological change is likely to have two major impacts on businesses:

1 *Production methods and materials can be enhanced*, offering major cost advantages through increasingly efficient methods of production. Such a cost advantage may provide a major

Table 48.2 Current issues within the UK and their possible impact on the strategic planning of a business

Social change	Explanation	Possible impact
Ageing UK population	Lower birth rates and longer life expectancy in the UK are contributing to a population which consists of a growing proportion of pensioners	Increased focus on niche markets catering to older consumers – anything from holidays to car insurance (and, of course, stairlifts)
Increased power of the 'pink pound'	Increasing acceptance of homosexuality has led to the growth of niches in many markets aimed specifically at the pink pound	Another opportunity to exploit a clearly definable niche market, leading to the creation of new brands, shops and clubs aimed squarely at the pink pound
Childhood obesity	Growing social concern over levels of childhood obesity, caused by a mix of poor diet and lack of exercise	Need to adjust product portfolio, introducing healthier children's food and accept government pressure to stop advertising fatty foods in children's TV programmes
Healthy lifestyles	Increased awareness of the need to lead a healthy lifestyle in order to live longer has changed spending patterns	Need to adjust product element of the marketing mix, perhaps using only organic ingredients. Health clubs move into the mass market away from the traditional, young adult niche

Clicks not bricks

As late as 2010, supermarket chain Morrisons refused to sell groceries online. It couldn't see a way to make an order-and-delivery business profitable. In 2011 it changed its mind, not really because it could see a new way to make profit, but because it was increasingly worried about the impact of online sales upon its retail chain. Web-based technology ('clicks') was pushing aside traditional shops ('bricks')

marketplace advantage with the ability to cut selling prices without accepting a loss of margin. Meanwhile, new methods may bring increased product quality, which may become a key feature of a company's marketing. Those firms that fail to take advantage of any technological advances in production methods are likely to struggle in a competitive market.

2 *Products may become obsolete as a result of technological change*. Smartphones may make the iPod an irrelevance, and downloading may mean that DVDs go the way of CDs. Such examples mean that PEST analysis plays a vital role in identifying as early as possible any technological changes that will damage the sales of existing products. Of course, such changes can also represent an opportunity to those firms who are able to produce brand new products that rely on new technologies. Such opportunities can bring high margins, market leadership and a strong reputation as an innovator for years to come, if the potential use for the technological change can be spotted early enough.

Increasingly, technological change is becoming interwoven with environmental issues. Having seen the rise and rise of the Toyota hybrid Prius, global car makers are desperate to be first with the next great step forward in greener motoring: the electric car. Nissan and General Motors both introduced new electric cars in 2011, but neither has been engineered successfully enough to make them affordable. This is a reminder that technology only affects markets when it is intelligently attuned to customers' needs and pockets.

Weaknesses

There are of course weaknesses to this type of formal analysis. The external environment is, by its very nature, unpredictable. PEST analysis is, therefore, to a certain extent a mixture of guesswork, experience and hunch. Not only will some external events catch firms by surprise, but also, the effects of external factors may be hard to figure out in advance. Something that had seemed an opportunity may in fact turn out to be a threat.

In 2006 the business author Nicholas Taleb wrote a book called *The Black Swan*. The point of the title is that everyone in Europe thought swans could only be white, until the first travellers to Australia told of **black swans**. Taleb's point was that people's ideas are fixed, based on their experience to date. Taleb warned of the likelihood that the economic, financial and housing boom would implode unexpectedly. As the book was published the markets duly collapsed. PEST analysis should always include some thought about how well the business could cope with a completely unexpected disaster.

Issues for analysis

- Breaking down the external factors facing a firm into the PEST categories can help to separate key from peripheral issues. Then a consideration of the implications of each external factor allows the construction of analytical chains of cause and effect. This is especially important because some factors may only have an indirect influence on an organisation

- Another issue to consider is the timeframe of a PEST analysis. How far into the future is the analysis trying to examine? Predicting external changes over the next year or two may be relatively straightforward in some industries, but in others, external changes can turn a market on its head within days – just consider the impact of the credit crunch on the banking and building industries – and on the finances of governments.

Integrated external issues (including PEST) – an evaluation

Judgement may come in the form of deciding which issues are most likely to occur and which are likely to have the most impact on the firm, then weighing them up to prioritise which issues need to come to the top of the strategic agenda following a PEST analysis. This is indeed the kind of risk assessment-based approach that many firms take when allocating resources to deal with PEST factors. Most resources go to dealing with those issues that are most likely to happen, and have the greatest potential impact on the company.

Successful interpretation of a PEST analysis is more likely to be achieved by those with a gift for interpreting market data and the experience required to really understand what the analysis means for a particular firm.

A final point to note is that effective management relies on an awareness of what is not foreseeable. Those who stick rigidly to the strategies constructed on the basis of a one-off PEST analysis are likely to be slow in reacting to unforeseeable changes.

Key terms

Black swan: an event that could not be forecast because it is outside past experience. Explored in more detail in Taleb, N., *The Black Swan* (Allen Lane, 2007).

Scenario planning: thinking of a range of possible future outcomes, both economic and social, then considering how the business should respond to those situations.

Further reading

Taleb, N. (2007) *The Black Swan*, Allen Lane.

A Revision questions (25 marks; 25 minutes)

1 Briefly explain why a firm needs to consider the external environment when planning its future strategy. (5)

2 Analyse the possible positive effects of an economic upturn on a manufacturer of luxury goods. (5)

3 Identify three possible products that could benefit from a trend towards increased use of the internet to provide home entertainment. (3)

4 PEST factors tend to provide both opportunities and threats to a business. If a strategy is to address both, explain how it might include:
  a opportunities
  b threats. (6)

5 Briefly explain two possible weaknesses of using PEST analysis. (6)

B1 Case study

Yeo Valley

Yeo Valley is a family-owned, West Country farming business that has specialised in organic dairy products for more than 20 years. It also acts as a farming coop, encouraging other local farmers to produce organic milk and cream that Yeo will buy and process into its yoghurts and ice creams.

Until the recent recession, things were going brilliantly for Yeo. Organic sales were booming, and its annual sales of over £180 million allowed the business to employ more than 1,000 people. Although Yeo's sales split was 40% organic and 60% non-organic, the brand's image was associated with its position as Britain's Number 1 supplier of organic dairy products.

When recession hit, though, organic products proved a big loser. From a market size peak of £1.1 billion in 2008, sales of all organic products fell by 25% to £850 million by 2011. This was largely because consumers knew that organic products cost more in the shops, yet they weren't really sure what health benefits were gained in return. One successful dairy brand, Rachel's Organic, responded by changing its brand name to Rachel's, i.e. it dropped the Organic reference. Yeo Valley suffered a sharp drop in sales in late 2008 and in 2009.

After a lot of heart-searching, Yeo came up with a strategic response in 2010. It decided to spend £5 million on a TV advertising campaign (the 'rapping farmers') that would re-establish the Yeo Valley brand as young, relevant and as an authentic British dairy business. Cleverly, the two-minute-long commercials were placed nationally in seven weeks of ITV's hit family show, the X-Factor. This created huge spin-offs such as the rapping farmers becoming a World Number 1 Youtube download.

Publically, Yeo has only said that its sales benefited by £3.5 million in the three months following the start of the campaign. This would be a very disappointing result of spending £5 million! Nevertheless it may be that Yeo will gain a long-term benefit from its greater brand awareness. In the year to May 2011 sales of organic products fell by 28.5% in Marks & Spencer. In such a harsh trading environment, it would be reassuring to know that your brand is much-loved and admired.

Now Yeo has to decide whether the social trend towards organic foods will return to growth once the UK economy recovers fully. After all, Fairtrade products are relatively expensive, yet sales boomed between 2008 and 2011. So has the term 'organic' lost its appeal permanently? Fortunately Yeo's 40/60 output mix shows that the business can, if necessary, switch from organic to non-organic products. With its strong brand name, people will trust Yeo Valley yoghurt whether or not it says organic on the pack.

Questions (30 marks; 35 minutes)

1 Summarise the above case in relation to the relevant elements within PEST analysis. (6)

2 Analyse the possible impact on Yeo Valley if sales of organic products fail to recover when the UK economy recovers. (10)

3 Write a report to Yeo Valley's directors explaining, with examples from the case, how a PEST analysis could help them develop a strategy for the next five years. (14)

Case study

Brompton Bicycle

Brompton Bicycle is Britain's biggest remaining manufacturer of bicycles. It produces its distinctive, foldable bikes in West London, providing skilled work in an area that has few remaining manufacturing jobs.

Over the past 15 years Brompton has more than quadrupled its output, from 7,000 to more than 28,000 bikes a year (each sells for £600 to £1,000, so this generates a substantial turnover).

Brompton has benefited greatly from two key factors. The first is the boom in cycling to work, especially in London. This was sparked by a 1999 government initiative that gave tax incentives for employers to get their staff to 'Cycle To Work'. Further government spending on cycle lanes in London kept the growth going. Of course, rising concerns about health and body image have also played a key role in this.

The second factor has been the fall in the value of the pound between 2007 and 2011. This has made Brompton bikes more affordable to European and American buyers, leading to a boom in export sales.

Now, in 2011, Brompton is working on its first new technology product for many years. In June 2012 it will launch its first electric bike, giving power-assistance for up to ten miles' riding, e.g. for getting up hills. It has worked on this project for several years, and the company is confident that the technology will match customer expectations and demands.

Questions *(30 marks; 35 minutes)*

1 Outline the key elements of this case within the framework of PEST analysis. (8)

2 Discuss which of the four PEST factors has been the most important in the case of Brompton Bicycle. (14)

3 Examine two factors you believe will be important in whether the electric bike proves a success. (8)

Causes of and planning for change

Internal and external causes of change

Change arises as a result of various internal and external causes. The internal ones (such as a change in objectives) should at least be planned for. External causes may be unexpected, which makes them far harder to manage. Table 49.1 sets out some possible internal and external causes of change.

Of all the issues relating to change, none is more crucial than when a business has to cope with a period of rapid growth. For example, the clothing brand Jack Wills took on 32% more staff between 2010 and 2011. This took the staff total to 1,700. This growth always threatens to take a business from its roots towards a bureaucracy.

Table 49.1 Examples of internal and external causes of change

Internal causes	External causes
● New growth objectives set by management ● New boss is appointed ● Decision to open up new export markets ● A decision to increase the shareholders' dividend makes it difficult to find the capital to invest in the business	● Rising consumer demand/the product becomes fashionable ● Economic boom benefits a luxury product ● Closure/fire/strike hits competitor, boosting your sales ● New laws favour your product (e.g. new safety laws boost sales of first aid kits)

Business effects of forecast rapid growth

In certain circumstances managers can anticipate a period of rapid **organic growth**. This may be temporary (such as the effect of a change in the law) or may seem likely to be permanent (such as the growth in demand for a hot website). The most successful firms will be those that devise a plan that is detailed enough to help in a practical way, but flexible enough to allow for the differences between forecasts and reality.

When rapid growth has been forecast, firms can:

● compare the sales estimate with the available production capacity

● budget for any necessary increases in capacity and staffing

● produce a cash flow forecast to anticipate any short-term financing shortfall

● discuss how to raise any extra capital needed.

Timescales remain important, though. The forecast may cover the next three months, but increasing capacity may involve building a factory extension, which will take eight months. In which case there may be five months of excess demand to cope with (perhaps by subcontracting).

Smooth though all this sounds, there remains a lot of scope for error. The starting point is the increased workload on staff. Extra sales may put pressure on the accounting system, the warehouse manager and the delivery drivers. With everyone being kept busy, things can occasionally start to go wrong. Invoices are sent out a little later, unpaid bills are not chased as quickly and stock deliveries are not checked as carefully. Suddenly the cash flow position worsens and costs start to rise. A strong, effective manager could retrieve this, but many are weak and woolly. Once they start to go wrong, plans are hard to sort out.

 ## Management reorganisation during growth

Problem of adjustment from boss to leader/manager

The typical creator of a successful new business is lively, energetic, creative, often impatient and always a risk-taker. Such a person will have a strong personality, and quite possibly an autocratic though charismatic leadership style. When the business started, their own speed of decision making, attention to detail and hard work were fundamental to the firm's success.

With success comes a problem. How to cope with the additional workload? At first the boss works ever harder; then he or she takes on more junior staff. Then comes the crunch. Is he or she willing to appoint a senior manager with real decision-making power? Or will a weak manager be appointed who always has to check decisions with the boss?

Staff will always find it hard to accept a new manager because everyone will know that it is really the boss's business. It is said that ten years after Walt Disney died, managers were still rejecting ideas on the basis that 'Walt wouldn't have done it that way.' How much harder if the founder is still there: James Dyson at Dyson and Larry Page and Sergey Brin at Google.

The boss must make the break, however. No longer should he or she attend every key meeting or demand regular reports on day-to-day matters. Delegation is necessary. In other words, authority should be passed down the hierarchy to middle managers without interference from above. And instead of looking for the next great opportunity, the boss may have to focus on getting the right management structure to ensure a smooth-running business.

Even if the founder of the company *is* able to adjust to managing a large organisation, there remains the problem of motivation. Will the new staff be as 'hungry' as the small team that built the business? Usually the answer is no. The drinks giant Diageo thinks it has a solution, though. It is a business with annual profits of over £2,000 million, based on brands such as Smirnoff, Baileys and Guinness. To keep staff hungry, the chief executive gives managers a 'HAT': a Hairy Audacious Target. In other words, he gives them a bold, challenging goal. Achieving these HATs will give each manager the chance to make huge bonuses. The chief executive believes HATs can stretch 'our people's imaginations to achieve these aggressive targets'.

Change in management structure/hierarchy

As a business grows, the management structure has not only to grow too, but also to change. New layers of management may be needed and completely new departments may be founded, such as personnel or public relations. And all the time, as the business grows, new staff are being recruited, inducted and trained. So there is constant change in personnel and their responsibilities. This can be disconcerting for customers and suppliers. Strong relationships are hard to build, making customer loyalty tough to achieve.

Even more important, though, is the internal effect of these personnel changes. With new staff appearing frequently, and managerial changes occurring regularly, team spirit may be hard to achieve. Junior and middle managers may spend too much of their time looking upwards to the promotion prospects instead of concentrating on their own departments. The potential for inefficiency, or even chaos, is clear. Too many new staff may mean too many mistakes. If customer relations are relatively weak, the result could easily be loss of business.

These unpleasant possibilities can largely be set aside if a good example is set from the top. If the founder of the business continues to be involved – especially on customer service – all may still be well. The leader needs to make sure staff keep sight of the qualities that brought the business its success in the first place. If new management structures threaten to create communications barriers, the leader should set an example by visiting staff, chatting to them and acting on their advice. The leader must fight against being cut off from the grassroots – the staff and the customers.

Risk of loss of direction and control

Each year, Templeton College Oxford produces data on what it calls the Fast Track 100. These are the fastest-growing 100 small companies in Britain. The December 2010 survey showed that, despite the recession, the top 10 of these firms enjoyed three-year growth rates of:

● sales turnover 85% + per year

● employees 65% + per year.

The typical Fast Track 100 firm had gone from 22 staff to 100 staff in the past three years. No wonder, then, that the key challenges faced by these companies were managing the growth in staff and infrastructure (source: www.fasttrack.co.uk).

The **entrepreneurs** who get swamped by the success of the business are those whose firms will fail to sustain their growth. They may become side-tracked by the attractions of expense account living. Or – the other extreme – they become so excited by their own success that they start opening up several different businesses. They assume that their 'golden touch' will ensure success in whatever they do. Instead, just as their core business becomes harder to handle, they are looking at a different venture altogether. Problems may then hit from several directions at once.

The key message is, therefore: focus on what you are good at.

Problems of transition in size

From private to public

At certain points in a firm's life there will be critical decisions to be made regarding growth. Few are more fundamental than the decision to 'go public'. A private limited company is a family business, often dominated by the shareholdings of one person – probably the founder. Although its accounts must be published, it is still able to maintain a substantial veil over its activities. Its private status minimises the pressures upon the management. A year of poor trading may disappoint the family, but there is no publicly quoted share price to embarrass the firm or to threaten it with a hostile takeover. This protection from outside pressures enables private companies to take a long-term view of what they want to achieve and how.

Switching from private to public company status is not, in itself, a difficult or expensive process. The big change comes when a firm floats its shares on the stock market. Only public companies are

allowed to do this. From the protected world of the private company, the firm will enter the glare of public scrutiny. Before floating, the firm must issue a **prospectus** that sets out every detail of the firm's business, its financial record, its expectations and its key personnel. Newspapers and analysts will scrutinise this fully, and carry on writing about the firm when every set of financial results comes out.

The purpose of going public is usually to achieve a substantial increase in share capital. This can enable a highly geared private firm to achieve a more balanced capital structure, as shown in Table 49.2.

In the case of Sharps plc, the addition of 50% more capital (from £8 million to £12 million) will give a huge opportunity for major expansion. Indeed, if the management act slowly, the purchasers of the £4 million extra shares may get restless. So the managers will be inclined to make a big move. Perhaps they will make a takeover bid. Or perhaps a diversification, by launching a new product range. Either way, the risks are substantial. Does this

Table 49.2 Cutting gearing by going public

Sharps Ltd (before going public)		Sharps plc (after raising £4m on the stock market)	
Loan capital	£4m	Loan capital	£4m
Share capital	£1m	Share capital	£5m
Reserves	£3m	Reserves	£3m
Capital employed	**£8m**	**Capital employed**	**£12m**
Gearing level:	50%	Gearing level:	33%

business have the expertise to succeed with either approach? What it needs is the confidence to keep focused upon what the management is good at. But the public pressure to make a big step forward may encourage the management to take a step too far.

Retrenchment

Just as big steps forward can lead to problems, so can steps backward. Yet few firms will keep growing without the occasional sharp setback. Retrenchment means cutting back. This may be achieved through a general reduction in staffing, or perhaps only a halt on recruitment. Most often, though, it will imply

a **rationalisation** in which there are significant changes to the organisational structure and/or to the capacity level of the business.

In 2011, there were major worldwide rationalisations by giants such as HSBC, British Airways and Toyota. In all cases, the key factor is to ensure that retrenchment does not cause lasting damage to morale, relationships and trust. Therefore it is vital to be honest, open, fair and as generous as possible to anyone who is losing a job.

When forced to cut back, firms have many options, as outlined in Table 49.3.

Table 49.3 The benefits and drawbacks of different types of retrenchment

Type of retrenchment	Advantages	Disadvantages
Freeze on recruitment and/or offering voluntary redundancy	• not threatening; should not cause problems of job insecurity • viewed by staff as fair	• no chance to reshape the business • good people are always leaving, so they need to be replaced
Delayering (i.e. removing a whole management layer)	• should not affect direct operations (such as staff on the shop floor) • may empower/enrich remaining jobs	• may over-intensify the work of other managers, causing stress • risk of losing a generation of managers • loss of promotion prospects for those who remain
Closure of a division or factory, or a number of loss-making outlets	• sharp reduction in fixed overhead costs will reduce break-even point • capacity utilisation may rise in the firm's other factories	• once closed, the capacity is unlikely to be available for the next economic upturn • loss of many good staff
Targeted cutbacks and redundancies in divisions throughout the business	• can reshape the business to meet future needs (e.g. no cutbacks among IT staff) • by keeping good staff, their average quality level may rise	• huge problems of perceived fairness (unless there is a high degree of trust) • job security may be hit ('Will it be me next?')

 # Planning for change

For managers who can foresee significant change, a strategic plan is needed. This should help in managing the change process, ensuring that the business has the personnel and the financial resources to cope. The strategic planning process is undertaken by an organisation's senior managers. The first decision they face is: 'How do we turn this change to our own advantage?'

Having established the strategic direction the organisation will adopt, the senior managers must next set the boundaries within which middle and junior management will take day-to-day decisions. A series of integrated actions must be set out. These

will have the purpose of moving the organisation forward in the identified strategic direction. This plan will be introduced over a period of time known as a 'planning horizon'. This will commonly be between one and three years, but may vary depending on how stable the organisation's competitive environment is. The greater the stability, the longer the planning horizon will be.

Strategic planning is only necessary because firms operate in a changing environment. If this was not the case then a single strategy, once designed, would bring success to the business on a permanent basis. However, changes in key

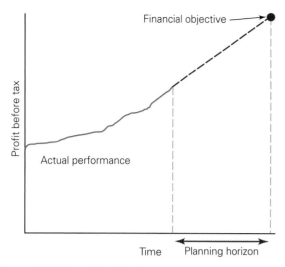

Figure 49.1 Financial objectives

variables such as technology, consumer tastes and communications make planning strategy increasingly important. The pace of change is intensifying, creating shorter product life cycles and encouraging increased competition. It is change that creates the '**strategic gap**' that must be closed by the second phase of the planning process.

Organisations that seek to achieve objectives such as the maximisation of long-term profits will set themselves financial targets. These will be influenced by shareholders' expectations and the personal and business ambitions of the company

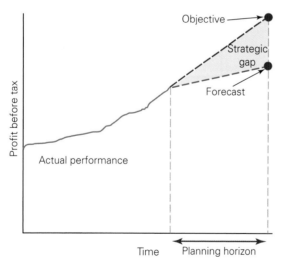

Figure 49.2 A strategic gap

directors. These expectations will determine the financial objectives of the organisation over the forthcoming planning period.

The difference between the profit objective and the forecast performance of the business, is known as a strategic gap (see Figure 49.2).

Closing a strategic gap

Once a strategic gap has been identified it is necessary to devise a series of strategies to close it.

It may be possible to achieve this to some extent by performing existing operations more efficiently, in order to reduce costs and boost profit. However, this is unlikely to solve the whole problem. Only careful strategic planning can develop the means by which the organisation can increase its effectiveness in order to meet its financial objective.

The analysis of the strategic gap should reveal how difficult it will be to cope with the change. The future may look bright, such as for an organic farmer in a period of change towards more care and thought over healthy eating. Or it may look bleak, such as for a house-building business in the wake of sharp falls in house prices. Whether the gap is upwards or downwards (forcing the business to retrench), a careful planning process should make the transition easier.

Contingency planning

A strategic plan should outline the critical assumptions that have been made about the future competitive environment. If the success of the project depends on these judgements a 'fallback' position, or **contingency plan**, should be developed in case they prove wrong. As part of the planning process, 'What if?' questions should be asked. For example, a manufacturer of bicycles, thrilled about the sales boom from 2006 to 2011 should ask the question: 'What if a slowdown in China forces oil prices back down again?' Lower oil prices would get people back into their cars, forcing demand down for sales of new bicycles. Contingency planning allows the firm to consider what action it will take if particular opportunities or threats emerge as a strategy is implemented.

Assessing the value of corporate plans

To achieve an ambitious target within a large, complex organisation requires a plan – a good one. Yet for every long-term triumph (Tesco overturning Sainsbury's to become Britain's Number 1 grocer or Whitbread switching from pubs to coffee bars) there are plenty of flops. Marks & Spencer has not been short of corporate plans in the past 20 years – but it has been short of successful ones.

So 'doing' a plan may be a necessary part of corporate success, but it is not sufficient. It needs to be the right plan, with the right, long-term horizons, backed by the right resources and with the right amount of luck. Tesco's success was partly down to Sainsbury's managerial weaknesses at the time – which was good fortune.

Table 49.4 shows the key factors that will determine the outcome of a corporate plan.

Table 49.4 Key factors that determine the outcome of a corporate plan

Success factors in corporate plans	Fail factors in corporate plans
1. The plan must be based on an ambitious but realistic objective	1. The corporate objectives may be flawed, e.g. Aldi trying to go 'upmarket' during the 2009 recession
2. The plan must be given time to work (for Tesco, 'Every Little Helps' took more than three years to make an impact)	2. Panicky shareholders may declare a new plan a flop because short-term company profits have fallen
3. The right resources must be found to back the plan, i.e. the right leaders, the right budget and the right 'route to market', e.g. distribution system	3. A corporate plan may be given too little backing by the Board, e.g. Next plc deciding to open up in China, but being too half-hearted to invest enough cash to achieve long-term success
4. The 'right leaders' must make the right decisions when real-world changes force the business to choose whether to stick rigidly to the plan, or to adapt it to new circumstances	4. When the plan isn't working, some businesses plough on regardless (which may be a mistake); others chop and change too quickly, which is even more likely to be a mistake
5. Factors outside the control of the business will always be important, so luck is a critical success factor. No one should assume that a plan succeeded because the leaders were clever; they may just have been lucky	5. Bad luck can be crushing, both to performance and morale. Good managers will keep staff going by assuring them that luck will change; but a good plan may be wrecked by bad luck; business is risky!

Issues for analysis

When tackling questions about the causes of – and plans for – change, the following lines of analysis are helpful.

- If the business faces rapid growth, is it planned (internal) or unplanned (external)?
- Is the business leader's management style capable of changing as the business develops?
- Does the firm have the financial resources to cope with the need for capital during a time of change?
- How well does the firm cope with growth shocks, such as a stock market flotation? Can the management keep focused upon the strategy and the strengths of the business?
- Would managers who have handled growth well be equally good at handling retrenchment? Only if they have and deserve the trust of the staff.

Causes of and planning for change – an evaluation

Change is normal, not abnormal. Therefore firms need to be alert to causes of change and quick to devise a strategic plan for coping. Many successful businesses do not have a formal strategic planning process. This does not mean that the issues raised here are not relevant to these organisations. The same problems must be dealt with when strategy emerges over time as when it is planned more systematically. The advantage of explicitly setting aside time for strategic planning is that managers' minds are concentrated on the key questions facing the firm in the future. Then the actions decided upon can be more closely integrated.

Key terms

Contingency plan: a Plan B in case Plan A goes wrong.

Entrepreneur: an individual with a flair for business opportunities and risk-taking. The term is often used to describe a person with the entrepreneurial spirit to set up a new business.

Organic growth: growth from within the business (e.g. sales growing rapidly because a product is riding a wave of consumer popularity).

Prospectus: a document that companies have to produce when they go public (i.e. are quoted on the stock exchange); it gives details about the company's activities and anticipated future profits.

Rationalisation: reorganising to increase efficiency. The term is mainly used when cutbacks in overhead costs are needed in order to reduce an organisation's break-even point.

Strategic gap: the difference between where the business is and where it plans to be.

Revision questions (50 marks; 50 minutes)

1 Explain why rapid growth can cause problems for a company's:
   a cash flow (2)
   b management control. (2)

2 Distinguish between internal and external causes of growth, using examples. (5)

3 Why may there be a problem in adjusting from 'boss' to 'leader/manager'? (4)

4 Identify three problems for a fast-growing firm caused by changes in the management structure. (3)

5 Outline two strengths and two potential weaknesses of stock market flotation for a rapidly growing business. (8)

6 Explain the possible problems (and benefits) to a small computer software firm of changing status from private to public limited company. (4)

7 Explain in your own words the idea of the planning horizon. (4)

8 Explain why it might be hard for young, inexperienced managers of a successful business start-up to cope effectively with an unexpected, dramatic change. (5)

9 a Explain the meaning of the term 'retrenchment'. (3)
   b Outline two suitable methods of retrenchment for an airline that is losing market share. (4)

10 Explain why it may be hard for a struggling jewellery business to fill the strategic gap. (6)

Data response

Lush profits

In 2010 the cosmetics producer/retailer 'Lush' won an award for being one of Britain's fastest-growing international businesses. From its base in the sleepy seaside town Poole, Lush achieved an overseas sales growth rate of 48% a year between 2007 and 2009. In 2009 70% of the company's sales were overseas. This helped support over 4,000 jobs.

When it was founded, in 1990, Body Shop was the store to beat. Now, with 672 stores in 42 countries, Lush's indulgent, attractive – but modestly priced – cosmetics are starting to overshadow Body Shop. Lush also benefits from the enthusiasm of its staff for the company's backing for ethical causes such as banning foxhunting, or demanding legal representation for the Guantanamo Bay detainees. Even in the savage 2009 recession, Lush managed to push revenue up from £153 million to £215 million, though profits fell from £19.4 million in 2008 to £13.9 million.

Growing from £0 to £215 million in less than 15 years inevitably involves problems. When it had grown to £50 million of sales the manufacturing staff noticed that products made from essential oils (that can cost £3,000 a kilo) were 'behaving' wrongly. After some weeks of panic Lush decided to get a chemist to analyse the oils. It emerged that suppliers had been adulterating the oils with as much as 70% synthetic chemicals. This problem led to the establishment of a professional buying team, together with a quality control manager.

Questions *(30 marks; 35 minutes)*

1 a Explain why Lush is likely to have had a significant increase in the number of layers of hierarchy within its business over recent years. (10)

   b Examine two ways in which an increase in the layers of hierarchy might harm operational performance at Lush. (8)

2 If Lush appointed a new chief executive, discuss the possible difficulties that might arise from a retrenchment plan in order to boost profits. (12)

B2 Data response

From Google to Facebook

Sheryl Sandberg wants to bring to Facebook what she brought to Google: discipline and inventiveness to foster rapid growth. Two weeks into her job as Facebook's chief operating officer (COO), the 38-year-old executive, second in command to 23-year-old CEO Mark Zuckerberg, is rolling out new management and operations procedures. Among these are guidelines for employee performance reviews, processes for identifying and recruiting new employees, and management-training programmes.

Ms Sandberg's experience of expanding operations and building talent is just what the social networking site may need as it aims for a big expansion. 'Facebook is a different space than Google, with tremendous potential to connect people, but it needs scale, it needs systems and processes to have impact, and I can do that,' she says.

The social networking site, which allows users to create personal profiles to share with friends, had more than 100 million visitors in January, a fourfold increase from the year-earlier period. But it's still burning up more cash than it is generating in revenues, according to people familiar with the company's finances.

At Facebook, which is privately held, Ms Sandberg is in charge of sales, business development, public policy and communications. One immediate focus is on international growth. Until a few months ago, Facebook was only for English speakers. Now it's available in French, German and Spanish, and within the next few months the site will be translated into 21 additional languages.

Meanwhile, Ms Sandberg must rally Facebook's 550 employees, who work at several offices in downtown Palo Alto, to embrace change. Many are recent college graduates who wear flip-flops and jeans to work, and scrawl graffiti on the office walls. At a company meeting two weeks ago, she addressed the concern among some employees that Facebook's close-knit culture will disappear as it grows.

'Scaling up is hard and it's not as much fun not to know everyone you work with,' she told employees. 'But if we get to work on things that affect hundreds of millions of people instead of tens of millions, that's a trade-off worth making.'

Mr Zuckerberg had been looking for a COO who could create a new business model, build a management team, ramp up operations and expand internationally – all of which Ms Sandberg had done at Google. She joined Google in 2001 without knowing exactly what her job would be. Over the following six years, she built Google's global online sales unit into the company's biggest revenue producer and expanded her staff from four to four thousand.

She developed a reputation for being a charismatic executive. She describes herself as a 'tough-love leader', who aims to 'mentor and demand at the same time, and make it safe to make mistakes,' she says.

Carol Hymowitz. Reprinted by permission of *Wall Street Journal*. Copyright © 2008 Dow Jones & Company, Inc. All Rights Reserved Worldwide.

Questions *(30 marks; 35 minutes)*

1 Outline two problems that might arise when a 38-year-old is appointed as number two to a 23-year-old. (6)

2 Discuss whether Ms Sandberg's speech to Facebook's employees is likely to have overcome staff concerns about whether 'Facebook's close-knit culture will disappear as it grows'. (10)

3 From the extract as a whole, discuss whether Ms Sandberg's ideas are likely to help or hinder Facebook in the dramatic growth that is forcing huge changes on the business. (14)

C Essay questions *(40 marks each)*

1 Dell Computers grew at a rate of 50% per year for nearly a decade. Outline the problems this might have caused. Evaluate the most effective ways for management to tackle them.

2 Discuss whether corporate plans are an effective way of dealing with unexpected changes such as a sudden collapse in confidence in the housing market.

50 Leadership and change

> ## Definition
> Leadership means taking the initiative to set clear objectives and to motivate or guide staff towards their achievement.

The meaning of leadership

Poor Christiano Ronaldo. He has to get by on £200,000 a week, while Britain's best paid boss received £90 million in remuneration in 2009 (£1,800,000 a week). Bart Becht, chief executive of Reckitt Benckiser, was Britain's highest paid business leader (he retired in 2011). He had presided over a hugely successful run since an Anglo-Dutch merger created Reckitt Benckiser (suppliers of Cillit Bang, Air Wick and Dettol) in 1999. Yet the business had its critics, especially after it was fined £10.2 million in 2010 for anti-competitive tactics relating to its Gaviscon brand. The main criticism of Becht, though, was being paid 3,000 times as much as the average Reckitt employee. Is leadership ever worth that much?

In recent years business leadership has become an industry in itself. Typically, business sections in bookshops have a couple of books on motivation, but dozens on leadership. At the same time leaders have gone from earning 40 times the salary of the lowest paid in an organisation to 120+

times more. Following behind has been the UK government, setting up special training schools such as the National Leadership College for future Head Teachers. It is assumed that dynamic success comes from dynamic, charismatic leaders. By implication, therefore, these fabulous people are worth fabulous sums of money.

Sometimes, this is unarguably true. What has Sir Alex Ferguson been 'worth' to Manchester United? And what was Sir Ken Morrison worth, in building his small supermarket business into a national chain between 1967 and 2008? Lots, undeniably lots. Great leaders exist, and they are worth big financial rewards. Unfortunately, there are many examples of ordinary leaders with ordinary achievements also being paid huge sums. Even though the amount paid may be relatively trivial for a big business, the implications are very significant: the media may be over-emphasising the importance of 'the great leader', making it harder for intelligent, but modest, bosses to be given time to succeed.

A-grade application

Fifty British business leaders descended on the European Parliament in November 2010 to lobby against proposals that would give pregnant women 20 weeks' maternity leave at full pay. Current UK rules mean that employers have to pay only six weeks' maternity pay at 90% of the mother's salary. Women then receive a further 33 weeks' statutory maternity pay, funded by the taxpayer, at £124.88 a week.

But the EU proposals, which were due to be voted on by the European Council in the following week, would cost British businesses £2.5 billion a year, according to the

British Chambers of Commerce. The business group said UK companies would bear the brunt of the costs at a time when many were still struggling after the recession.

The previous month, Britain's bosses had been accused of greed and ignoring economic reality after boardroom pay leapt by 55% over the previous year. FTSE 100 directors saw their total earnings soar in the 12 months to June 2010, thanks to sharp rises in bonuses and performance-related pay. The average FTSE 100 chief executive earns £4.9 million a year, or almost 200 times the average wage.

Before examining this topic further, it is useful to reflect on a key management issue: the difference between a leader and a manager. Management guru Peter Drucker once said that: 'Managers do things right; leaders do the right thing'.

In other words, an effective manager is someone who can put an idea or policy into action, and get the details right. By contrast, the leader is good at identifying the key issues facing the business, setting new objectives, then deciding what should be done, by when, and by whom. It is also sometimes argued that a leader needs to inspire staff. This is often confused with 'charismatic leadership', i.e. when the personal charisma of the leader inspires staff to give something extra or work a bit harder. Although some successful leaders such as Ghandi, Churchill and Mandela had charisma, many others had success despite quite dull personalities. The great British Prime Minister Clement Attlee 'had a lot to be modest about', according to Churchill. Business stars such as Leahy (Tesco) and Bamford (JCB) have also shunned the limelight. If a leader can get the big decisions right, personality becomes irrelevant. Liverpool FC's period as Britain's top club began with the charismatic Bill Shankly; yet the huge haul of trophies came later, under the leadership of the shy, slightly bumbling Bob Paisley.

The range of leadership styles

There are four main styles of leadership: **autocratic, paternalistic, democratic and laissez faire**. When handling change, different leaders are likely to handle the process of change as given in Table 50.1.

Table 50.1 Styles of leadership and change

	Autocratic	Paternalistic	Democratic	Laissez-faire
Understand the scope of the change needed	Leader hires a management consultant who reports directly to him/herself	Leader carries out an extensive consultation exercise among staff based on the known issues/ problems	Discussion and consultation will be delegated to middle managers, taking care to include shopfloor staff	A laissez-faire organisation may have been ahead of the external change, or may only react very late
Construct a clear vision	The management consultant writes a Vision Statement	This, again, will be done after consultation, though the leader will make the final decision	This should emerge, perhaps from suggestions from the shopfloor	A laissez-faire leader may expect staff to grasp the vision as things emerge
Appoint change managers	May, again, be management consultants; any internal appointees are used to doing what the boss wants	These will be appointed from among known 'team players', i.e. those who buy into the vision decided by the leader	These will be selected from the brightest and best throughout the organisation	This is unlikely to happen; it will be expected that everyone will change over time
Keep going through short-term problems	Any internal critics may be sidelined or 'made redundant'	When things get tough, the leader will draw upon tough, family love and the need to stick together	If everyone shares the vision and has agreed the strategy, this stage should not be a real problem	Because the change will be less controlled and therefore slower and more organic, this problem may not occur

The role of leadership in managing change

Like families, most organisations get set in their ways. So change is neither welcome nor easy. The job of a leader is to:

- Ensure that the pressures for change are understood – first among board members (the parents?) and then throughout the organisation/ family

- Construct a clear vision about what the new future will look like and a narrative that explains the steps in getting from here to there. This should only be done after a process of consultation that clarifies what the staff/family members want. If the vision is contrary to the views of staff, the leader should make sure that everyone understands his or her reasons for change

- Appoint the right managers to handle each aspect of the change, ensuring that everyone knows that the leader has delegated full authority to them (and therefore anyone who gets in their way is getting in the way of the boss); then support them with necessary resources plus your involvement and backing

- Keep going, even during the difficult short-term period in which the disruptions caused by change seem to outweigh any possible long-term gains. In this phase, the appointed change managers will need full and public support from the leader.

If that sounds hard, it actually is an understatement of the difficulties. These arise when, in the middle of the change, senior managers realise that their original analysis of the problem was not 100% right, i.e. a change is needed to the change! Quite commonly this arises because junior staff or even the customers were not listened to in advance. Then the leader must decide whether to carry on as if nothing has happened ('it'll be better than it was') or to halt the process, rethink, and then change direction midstream.

Assessing internal and external factors influencing leadership style

Some businesses are likely to be led by an autocrat, i.e. someone who keeps all the key decisions at the top. This is because of the nature of the business, e.g. McDonalds is likely to employ young people for relatively short periods of time, thereby undermining the purpose of delegation. By contrast a business such as Facebook, which needs constantly to be finding new features and services to re-excite users, should naturally be democratic. The leader needs super-bright software geniuses who will stay for as long as they're making an impact. Therefore the boss must make them know that their voices really count for something.

Among the many external factors influencing leadership style are:

- The market: is it static and slow-moving or dynamic, with short product life cycles?

- How fierce and competent are the competitors?

- Are major new opportunities opening up internationally, e.g. Burberry in China or Sainsbury's in India?

Among the internal factors influencing leadership style are:

- the culture and history of the organisation

- the quality of past recruitment, determining whether the leader can place full trust in the quality and commitment of staff.

- the resources available to the organisation; for example if finances are weak, delayering and then autocratic leadership may be necessary to get things happening.

As with every aspect of business, the key to successful analysis and evaluation is to think long and hard about the individual circumstances of each business in turn. In 2011 Britain's most admired business was John Lewis, a business led by a managing director that few have heard of – Andy Street. What people admire most about John Lewis is its commercial success despite an ownership structure that gives all power to its staff, not to outside shareholders. Excellent though Andy Street's performance may have been, the key feature of the business was laid down more than 80 years before, when the John Lewis cooperative structure was founded.

Assessing the importance of leadership

Big businesses can have huge impacts – on jobs, on communities and on people's satisfaction with life. Seeing people queuing for hours for the latest 'Call of Duty' software or Apple iPad is a reminder that some companies help people to enjoy their lives. Yet that can be contrasted with the ghastly 'achievement' of a trader called Trafigura, responsible for dumping a polluted chemical cocktail on Abijan, a huge African city. The point is simple: business matters and therefore business leadership matters. From the leader can come:

- the framework of ethics that affects the way staff act and react to pressures and temptations within their working life

- an attitude to business that might be entrepreneurial or may be cautious, even bureaucratic, e.g. the spectrum from Apple to Marks & Spencer; the message that comes from the leaders actions and decisions will affect the whole organisation

- the spread of an autocratic or a consultative approach that may affect the management of people throughout the business

- the big strategic decisions that shape the next three to ten years of the business, e.g. Kraft deciding to buy Cadbury, or if (when?) Facebook decides to start pushing advertising in the way that Google has; leaders are judged on their big decisions.

A-grade application

When new Marks & Spencer boss Marc Bolland was appointed, he wisely announced that he would spend six months on a strategic review. On 8 November 2010 he met the press to announce his findings. He planned on:

- evolution not revolution
- (another) redesign of the UK stores
- fresh expansion overseas
- reversing the move into stocking branded foods

- building a new website for the food side of the business, though (oddly) not one that could provide a full online service.

The conclusion reached by the press was that this was cautious, dull and rather negative. Many of the ideas were reversals of those of the previous M&S leader. Staff could not be inspired towards this visionless future.

Issues for analysis

Big businesses are like huge ships, sailing straight ahead. Turning them left or right takes a lot of effort and a lot of time. In many cases, the big decisions are made by committees of senior managers – and the result is rubber-stamped by the leader. A business such as Toyota employs hundreds of thousands of people in dozens of different countries. How can one person really know so much about

everything that he or she can make all the big decisions alone, and make them correctly? And in many cases the organisational culture precedes the new leader and remains unchanged by the time the leader has retired or been sacked. So it is important to analyse the evidence about the actual leader of the actual business in question.

Leadership and change – an evaluation

The business writer Robert Townsend suggested that many newly appointed leaders 'disappear behind the mahogany curtain', and are rarely seen again by staff. He thought that 'finally getting to the top' made many leaders focus more on corporate luxuries (Which jet shall we buy?) than on hard work.

Yet he knew that great leaders can make a huge difference to long-term business performance. He advocated a leadership model based on extensive delegation within tight, agreed budgets. Many follow that model today.

Ultimately, judging a leader takes time. The media

may find a new darling – perhaps someone who looks and sounds great on TV. That person's achievements may be praised hugely, and they may win 'Business Leader of the Year' awards. Yet it will be several years before anyone outside the business can appraise their performance. In most businesses it is easy to boost short-term profit: you push prices up here, and make redundancies there. This persuades the media and the shareholders that you are a fine leader. The real question, though, is whether your decisions will push the business forwards or backwards over the coming years. In an exam, therefore, hold back from rushing to praise (or condemn) a boss on the basis of short-term performance. Big business is a long game. Ninety minutes is a long time in football; a week is a long time in politics; five years is a long time in business.

Key terms

Autocratic leadership: is when the boss keeps all key decisions to him or herself, and gives orders rather than power to subordinates.

Democratic leadership: implies empowering people, i.e. delegating full power over the design and execution of substantial tasks.

Laissez-faire leadership: means allowing people to get on with things themselves, but without the coordination and control implicit within democratic leadership.

Paternalistic leadership: means 'fatherly', i.e. the boss treats staff as part of the family. Typically, this shows through as consultation, but with decision making remaining at the top (Dad decides).

Revision questions (30 marks; 30 minutes)

1 Why should a business with an ethical culture never engage in 'anti-competitive activities'? (4)

2 How might a paternalistic leader set about generating a clear vision for a business? (4)

3 In your own words, explain what Peter Drucker meant by saying: 'Managers do things right; leaders do the right thing'. (4)

4 Outline two external factors that maybe creating pressures for change within:
   a McDonalds (4)
   b Toyota. (4)

5 Outline one advantage and one disadvantage to a business of having as leader who has just won an award as 'Business Leader of the Year'. (4)

6 Freedom Foods produces organic, packaged foods such as sweets. A fall in sales has left the business operating at a small loss. It has 140 staff, of which 35 are employed in administrative jobs. Explain how an autocratic leader might attempt to get the business back into profit. (6)

Data response

Curry karma

Bangalore Balti (BB) started as a small curry house in Leicester. Word of its fresh, fiery food spread rapidly, creating the opportunity for expansion. By 2007 BB had 12 outlets across the Midlands, each run by a member of the owner's family. With plenty of cash in the bank, owner Safiq bought another chain of 16 Indian restaurants and converted them to the Bangalore Balti concept. This pushed the business into needing bank loans, which became a burden during the credit crunch recession of 2008 to 2009.

While Safiq was focusing on the financial pressures, things were slipping operationally. In particular, the managers of the 16 new restaurants showed less respect for the BB menu and seemed much less able to keep costs down and therefore profit margins up. It was also noticeable that labour turnover was higher in the new restaurants than in the original ones.

As the business entered 2011, its profits were below those of four years earlier. It was getting hard to pay the interest bills on the loans.

Something had to change.

Table 50.2 Bangalore Balti: figures for 2007 and 2011

	2007	2011
Labour turnover in the previous 12 months	8.4%	19.5%
% of staff with cooking skills	46.5%	28.%
Operating profit margin in the latest 6 months	12.8%	4.7%
Corporate overheads per £ of sales	8.4%	22.3%

Questions *(40 marks; 45 minutes)*

1 Outline one internal pressure and one external pressure for change at Bangalore Balti. (4)

2 a Discuss how Safiq might set about deciding how to change the business in 2011. (16)

b Analyse the text and Table 50.2, then recommend to Safiq the main changes she should make to her Bangalore Balti business. (20)

Case study

Change at Mulberry

When recession hit in 2008, what were the survival prospects for a 40-year-old producer of not-very-fashionable, expensive handbags? That is, bags costing £500 to £1,500 each? In the three years prior, even though sales of luxury products were booming, Mulberry had been 'going nowhere'.

The collapse in consumer confidence in Autumn 2008 caused immediate, dramatic effects. Although Mulberry's Somerset factory is its flagship, 70% of its bags (the more labour-intensive, fiddly ones) are made in China, Spain and Turkey. This forces the business to place orders for Autumn/pre-Christmas quite early in the year. Therefore, when demand slumped in October to December 2008, supplies continued to arrive. The company's stocks (inventories) doubled between March 2008 and March 2009. The effect of this on the balance sheet can be seen in Table 50.3.

The bar chart shown in Figure 50.1 gives a clear idea of how the increase in stock stripped the balance sheet of its cash in 2009. For Mulberry, as with every other business,

Table 50.3 Balance sheets for Mulberry in 2008 and 2009 as at 31 March

Mulberry balance sheets Correct as at 31 March	2009 £000s	2008 £000s
Non-current (fixed) assets	11,694	10,791
Inventories (stock)	14,830	7,785
Trade receivables (debtors)	6,032	5,548
Cash	3,710	10,237
Current liabilities	(11,750)	(11,821)
Non-current liabilities	(132)	(21)
Net assets	24,384	22,519
Share capital	9,878	9,878
Reserves	14,506	12,641
Total equity	24,384	22,519

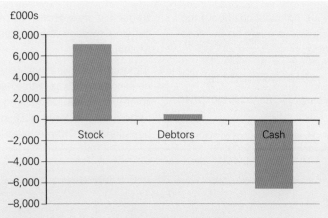

Figure 50.1 Change in current assets at Mulberry, 2009

stock management is critical to working capital management – and therefore both to cash flow and to liquidity.

Even though the recession was still in full flow, the period April to September 2009 saw a remarkable recovery by Mulberry. At the end of 2009 the company chairman reflected that 'sales for the six months to 30 September 2009 were significantly ahead of our expectations'. Remarkably, UK sales at Mulberry shops were 41% ahead of the previous year. This enabled the excessive stock level to be brought under control.

The explanation was simple. Mulberry had become fashionable. Chief executive Godfrey Davis had seen the changes to the luxury goods market and started to think of the incredible opportunities in China. He hired a creative director (Emma Hill) who saw handbags as fashion items for the younger market, instead of 'classics' for mums and grandmothers. Some middle managers at Mulberry were very critical of a switch from 'tried and tested classics' to the ups and downs of the latest trends. They worried about the ability of their factories to switch production quickly to new designs and

doubted their flexibility to increase output to match fashion-related demand spikes. This resistance to change was to prove unnecessary, as customers proved willing to wait to get their hands on the latest Mulberry bags.

The repositioning of the brand was complemented by a redesign of the online store. This change was also criticised internally because Mulberry owns some of its own retail outlets. Fortunately the 80% increase in sales through the website did not seem to dent shop sales.

In January 2010 Emma Hill launched an even bolder attempt at young, fashion-conscious consumers: the Alexa bag: named after style icon Alexa Chung. A wave of public relations-based articles appeared in publications from *Vogue* to *OK*. The £800 price tag proved no barrier to sales, as the first batch sold out in three weeks.

The 2010 annual results showed that Mulberry sales were 23% up on 2009 and operating profit 49% higher. In the midst of the biggest recession for several generations, Mulberry turned an important corner. In the past it had thought that only middle-aged women could afford posh handbags. Now it believes that young women will find a way to get the bags they want – even if it takes months of waiting. In his report to shareholders in June 2010, Godfrey Davis said they expected sales to China to rise by more than 100% in the coming year.

All this leaves the shareholders happy, but what about the other stakeholders? The Somerset factory now employs 195 staff, up from 110 four years ago. Chief executive Godfrey Davis admits that some customers complain when they realise that their bag is made in China or Spain, but insists that everything is made with high quality Italian leather. Therefore the quality

Figure 50.2 The Mulberry 'Alexa' bag

is assured and there are no questions about the animal welfare standards – as might be the case with leather from China.

Questions *(40 marks; 50 minutes)*

1 Examine the pressures for change that affected Godfrey Davis. (10)

2 Assume that Mr Davis has a paternalistic leadership style. How may he have set about carrying through the process of change at Mulberry? (15)

3 Although Mr Davis is well-rewarded financially, he is nothing like as highly paid as many other chief executives. Discuss how he might have performed if offered a £5 million bonus for boosting the 2010 profits at Mulberry. (15)

51 Organisational culture

Definition

Organisational culture sums up the spirit, the attitudes, the behaviours and the ethos of 'the organisation'. It is embodied in the people who work within the organisation, often via traditions that have built up over time.

Introduction

Unit 2 covered the key elements of business culture, such as:

- entrepreneurial versus **bureaucratic**
- purposeful versus purposeless
- ethical versus profit-driven
- focused on customers versus focused inwards.

In this unit the issues of business culture are developed in three main ways:

1 looking at Professor Charles Handy's famous analysis of types of culture
2 considering how to change an organisation's culture
3 assessing the importance of culture.

Handy's four types of culture

In his book *Gods of Management,* Charles Handy developed four ways of classifying business culture. These are discussed below and can be used to analyse business culture in more depth.

Power cultures

Power cultures are found in organisations in which there is one or a small group of power holders. Pleasing the boss can become the driving force behind the daily actions of staff. There are likely to be few rules or procedures and most communication will be by personal contact. This encourages flexibility among employees. Decision making is not limited by any code of practice. This can result in questionable, perhaps unethical, actions being taken in an attempt to please the boss. The leadership style in such a situation is clearly autocratic, and has been displayed in recent times by leaders such as Sir Alex Ferguson of Manchester United and Sir Alan Sugar (the central character in BBC TV's *The Apprentice*).

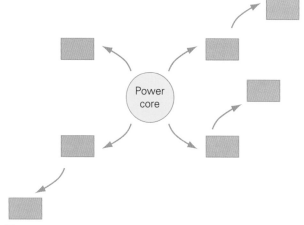

Figure 51.1 Power culture

Role culture

Role cultures are found in established organisations that have developed a lot of formal rules as they have grown. Power depends on the position an individual holds in the business, rather than the qualities of the person themselves. All employees are expected to conform to rules and procedures, and promotion follows a predictable pattern. This culture is bureaucratic, cautious and focused on the avoidance of mistakes. It may be appropriate when the competitive environment is stable – for example, in industries with long product life cycles. However, if the pace of change becomes more rapid, staff will struggle to adapt to new market conditions. This is the approach taken in businesses such as Microsoft, where the key thing is to preserve its huge share of the software market. The leadership style could be autocratic or paternalistic.

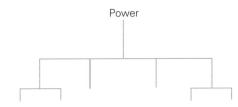

Figure 51.2 Role culture

Task cultures

Task cultures have no single power source. Senior managers allocate projects to teams of employees made up of representatives from different functional departments. Each group is formed for the purpose of a single undertaking and is then disbanded. Power within the team lies in the expertise of each individual and is not dependent upon status or role. This culture can be effective in dealing with rapidly changing competitive environments because it is flexible – for example, in markets with short product life cycles. However, project teams may develop their own objectives independent of the firm. The approach to leadership in such organisations is a mixture of paternalistic and democratic.

Person cultures

Person cultures are developed when individuals with similar training and backgrounds form groups to enhance their expertise and share knowledge. This type of culture is most often found within

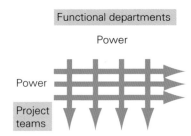

Figure 51.3 Task culture

functional departments of large, complex organisations, or among professionals such as lawyers or accountants. It is largely associated with democratic leadership.

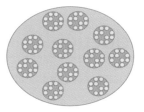

Figure 51.4 Person culture

A-grade application

David Cameron's coalition government has a distinctive culture. Individual ministers are given a great deal of freedom to develop radical policies. When these policies are first debated, they are backed fully by the Prime Minister, who seems happy to allow individual ministers the power to make major strategic decisions. In several cases, though, the policies are later scrapped or watered-down if there is sufficient public or media disquiet. This happened with the privatisation of English woodlands, the detailed reforms of the NHS and in the plan to halve the sentencing of criminals.

The culture within the government has none of the bureaucracy of role culture, or the teamworking of task culture. It is an unusual meshing of power and person cultures.

Changing the culture

When a new chief executive joins a business, his or her first impressions will be of the culture. Is the customer embraced by the business, or kept at arm's length by voicemail and answerphone messages? Do staff enjoy Monday morning or only Friday afternoon?

If the new chief executive is unhappy about the culture, achieving change is unlikely to come easily. After all, some staff may have been working at the same place for 15 years, and will find it very difficult to change. Even more problematic is that staff collectively have a set of attitudes that may be tough to overcome. A manufacturing business may be dominated by middle-aged engineers who are sure they know best how to make a car or a caramel. Switching to a more market-orientated business may be very difficult.

The key to success in this process will be to ensure that all staff believe that the change is genuinely going to happen (and, preferably, that the change is the right one). There will be middle managers who are crucial to making things happen (e.g. human resource managers or the finance staff who supervise the budget-setting process). If these people believe that the change is only skin-deep, they will hold back from supporting it. The engineers are likely to resist the change and perhaps they will prove right. Perhaps the new chief executive will be pushed aside by a board of directors who start to worry about whether a mistake is being made.

The key to cultural change, then, is to have a clear, consistent message. If everyone believes that the change is to be pushed through, they are far more likely to support it.

 ## Assessing the importance of culture

In recent years banks turned their backs on tradition and turned themselves into casinos. For centuries, a culture of caution had been at the heart of banking. The successful banker was one who went through a career without making any awful mistakes. Now this approach was considered old-fashioned. The focus was no longer on building a career; it was on building a bonus. As that bonus might be from £100,000 to £10,000,000 (a year!), who would look any further ahead than the coming months?

Nor was it difficult to make the profits required to get the bonuses. With plentiful cheap money (low interest rates) the clever thing was to borrow lots and lend it out as fast as possible. Why check on whether 'sub-prime' borrowers were likely to default in a year or two, if this year's bonus could be boosted to £500,000?

The collapse of this house of cards in 2008 and 2009 led to a predictable collapse into huge losses (estimated by the World Bank at $1 trillion). The culture of recklessness and greed had been created by a crazy bonus system that gave people (non-returnable) rewards based on the short term. In the longer term, the shareholders, the bank customers and governments had to pay the bills.

This example shows that culture is at the heart (or *is* the heart) of every organisation. Unusually, the banking example shows that culture can be transformed quite quickly, in certain circumstances. More often, businesses find that 'the way we do things round here' is very resistant to change. In 2007 Newcastle United FC appointed the hugely successful Bolton manager Sam Allardyce to transform its underperforming stars. He brought his own results-orientated approach to St James's Park and soon found himself swamped by the supporters' fury at his boring football. The 'Newcastle way' (the culture) is for bright, attacking, flair football. Big Sam did not last long.

Every organisation has its own culture. One school will have a staff room that is buzzing 40 minutes before the start of the day; another's staff car park will still be almost empty. One clothes shop will have staff who take their time helping customers, while another's staff play and joke with each other. And one charity will be focused entirely on the people it is set up to help, while another will behave as if the charity itself is more important than its 'customers'.

Distinguishing between healthy and unhealthy cultures is not difficult. It can be summed up in the following:

● focus on the customer versus focus on the staff (though senior management should appreciate that only a well-motivated staff will serve customers effectively)

A-grade application

In June 2010 half the top medical staff at Great Ormond Street hospital signed a letter of no confidence in its chief executive, Jane Collins. Consultant Dr Kim Holt told the *Daily Telegraph*: 'Medical staff have growing concerns over patient care. They feel that Great Ormond Street is not really living up to its reputation.' Another consultant said: 'They (management) are completely unwilling to listen. Anyone who complains is treated as a troublemaker and bullied out.'

Dr Holt went on to report other consultants' view of a 'culture of fear and intimidation' within the hospital. In effect, there was a culture clash between the consultants' traditional view of patient care and the chief executive's desire for change.

- an attitude of 'can-do' rather than of 'must we?'
- a real feeling for the organisation as 'us', as a long-term commitment
- a conviction among staff that the organisation is a force for good (i.e. not just a money-making machine).

Is change always better?

Not all cultural changes prove a success. Sometimes new leaders assume that a change in culture is essential, because they do not take the time to understand the strengths of the existing one. The Conservative governments of the 1990s swept away the tradition of NHS hospital wards being run by an all-powerful 'matron'. A failure to clean the ward properly would have meant risking the wrath of matron; cleaners cleaned. The new approach was to award contracts to outside cleaning companies, then check that agreed targets had been met. The matrons were pushed aside in favour of professional, 'can-do' managers. The managers were supportive of the new cleaning businesses; unfortunately, the cleaners were not so committed to cleaning. The later wave of MRSA-bug bacterial problems in hospitals can be put down to a management change based on inadequate understanding.

Issues for analysis

- Professor Charles Handy's four types of culture are quite hard to understand, but that can make them especially impressive as a tool to use within an analysis of a firm's culture. The analysis becomes all the more effective if you can relate the types of culture to the leadership style shown within the organisation.
- Yet culture goes far beyond Handy's approach, involving as it does the ethics of the organisation and the staff within it. In 2010, BP was not only humiliated for its huge spill in the Gulf of Mexico, but it was also given a record fine of $52 million for safety breaches at its Texas oil refinery. BP's US operation seemed to have a culture of putting profit before safety. To be able to identify ethical problems as an issue of culture is a vital skill. Analysis requires arguments that can show how one thing relates to another.

Organisational culture – an evaluation

Business leaders make many claims about the culture among their staff. They enjoy using words such as 'positive', 'can-do' and 'entrepreneurial'. Does the fact that the leader says these things mean that they are true? Clearly not. The leader cannot admit in public that the culture is 'lazy', 'negative' or 'bureaucratic'.

A well-judged answer to a question about culture will look beyond claims and public relations, and look for the evidence. Is there evidence that staff suggestions are welcomed and that they make an important contribution to the business? Is there evidence that mistakes are treated as learning experiences, rather than as reasons to be fired. And, perhaps most important of all, is there evidence that staff love their jobs and look forward to coming to work? All these things are tests of an organisation's culture.

Key terms

Bureaucratic: an organisation in which initiative is stifled by paperwork and excessive checking and rechecking of decisions and actions.

Person culture: where power comes from groups of people with the professional expertise to dominate and therefore create the culture, e.g. a group of professors dominating a university, enabling each, as individuals, to have influence but also independence.

Power culture: where the dominance of the leader (and his/her immediate circle of friends or advisers) overrides systems and conventional hierarchy. (This was the exact culture of Nazi Germany, where relatively junior staff could have power if they had access to Hitler.)

Role culture: where each individual has a tightly defined role that must be stuck to. Such an organisation will be bureaucratic and therefore highly frustrating for an individual with initiative. The culture will be dominated by the avoidance of risks.

Task culture: where groups of employees are delegated the power and resources to tackle tasks and projects, probably in a cross-functional way (so-called 'matrix management'). This is highly motivating, such as for the Nintendo development team that came up with the Wii.

Further reading

Handy, C. (1995) *Gods of Management*. Arrow.

A Revision questions *(30 marks; 30 minutes)*

1 Explain why it is unlikely that a task culture could exist in a business with an authoritarian leadership. (4)

2 Explain why a role culture would be inappropriate for a new software company seeking to be more innovative than Google. (4)

3 Sir Alex Ferguson has been manager of Manchester United for 25 years. When he retires, the new manager must either fit in with the culture created by Ferguson, or must change it. Examine two problems in changing the culture at an organisation dominated by one person, as at Manchester United. (8)

4 To what extent does the example of the UK banking sector in the lead-up to the credit crunch suggest that an entrepreneurial culture is not always a good thing? (6)

5 Recently a former quantity surveyor told the BBC that he had left the construction industry because he was so disillusioned by the problem of price fixing. Discuss how a new leader of a construction firm might try to change the culture to one of honest dealing. (8)

B1 Data response

The top job advertisement

Company: Topshop/Topman

Post: Area Trainer

Location: Oxford Circus, West London, Middlesex

Salary: circa £21—23K + excellent benefits

Working for Topshop and Topman is not like working for other fashion retailers. The size of the business, the culture of the company, the quality of training and direction of the business all combine to offer exciting and challenging careers. We currently have an exciting opportunity to join us an Area Trainer within our London flagship store, the world's largest fashion store. With over 1000 employees on site, you will be responsible for the delivery of leading training solutions that directly support the key business objectives.

Source: Myjobsearch.com website

Questions (30 marks; 35 minutes)

1 Examine two ways in which the culture of Topshop might be different from that of other clothing retailers. (6)

2 This particular job is at 'the world's largest fashion store' (the Oxford Circus branch of Topshop). Use Handy's four types of culture to discuss how the culture might differ in this Topshop outlet compared with a small Topshop branch employing perhaps 12 people. (12)

3 Discuss whether or not this job as Area Trainer would be one that you would like to get within the next five years. (12)

B2 Case study

Bakery culture

Gianni Falcone had built his Italian bakery up over a 40-year period in Britain. He came to escape a life dominated in the 1960s by the Sicilian Mafia, and started a bakery in south London. For the first ten years his life had been hard and very poor. Baking just white rolls and white bread, he had to keep his prices low to compete with local supermarkets. He would get up at 1.30am every day to get the bread prepared then baked, and his working day would end 12 hours later. With a young family of four, he could not get to bed until 8.30 in the evening. Five hours later he would be back to work.

Eventually he started to see ways of adding value to his dough. A half kilo loaf of bread with 30p of ingredients would sell for 80p, but roll it flat, smear tomato, cheese and herbs on it (cost: 25p) and it became a £3 pizza. A series of value-added initiatives came through, which added both to the popularity of the shop and to its profitability. By 2000 the queues on a Saturday morning were legendary. Gianni was

able to finance houses for all his family and he was starting to dream of owning a Ferrari.

By 2007 the business employed all the family members plus six extra staff. All worked the Gianni way. All knew the principles behind the business: ingredients should be as natural as possible and of as high a quality as possible. The customer is not always right (rowdy schoolchildren will be thrown out if necessary) but the customer must always be treated with respect. A slightly over-baked loaf will be sold at half price and day-old currant buns are given away to regular customers. Above all else, Gianni wanted to be honest with customers; they knew that all the baked goods were baked freshly on the premises.

Then, in 2010, Gianni was taken ill. The problem was with his lungs; quite simply, 40 years of flour in the bakery air had taken its toll. He had to retire. As none of his family wanted to take on the commitment to the awful working hours, he had to sell up. The only person with the inclination and the money to buy was an experienced baker from Malta, Trevi Malone. He bought the business for £250,000. Gianni was able to retire to the substantial home he had built in Sicily (now relatively Mafia-free).

From the start, Malone's approach was dramatically different. While Gianni had been ill, all the baking had been done by his bakery assistant Carol. She had worked miracles by herself, so that the shelves were full every morning. Now, from the first morning, Malone showed his distaste for her ways of working. Why did she use organic yeast when there were perfectly good, cheaper ones? Why did she 'knead' the dough in batches of 5 kilos when it would be better to do it by machine in 20-kilo quantities? And when she suggested that it would be good to start making hot cross buns, Malone snapped: 'This crazy place already makes too many different lines; just concentrate on what you're doing.' In the past, Carol's ideas had led to successful new products such as a top-selling apricot doughnut. Now she was to be silenced.

In the shop, Malone's approach was also quite different. Instead of casual clothes, everyone would wear uniforms; customers would be addressed as 'Sir' or 'Madam', and every order must be followed by an 'upselling' suggestion. The person who bought only a loaf of bread should be asked 'Would you like any doughnuts or cakes today?' The sales staff thought this was a daft idea, because – with so many regular customers – people would soon tire of being asked to spend more money. But they had quickly picked up the idea that Malone was not interested in discussion – he knew best.

Over the coming weeks things were changed steadily. The ham used on the meat pizza was changed from 'Italian baked ham' at £10 a kilo to a much cheaper Danish one (with 20% added water). As Malone said to Carol, 'Our customers don't see the ingredients label, so who's to know?' Malone noticed that doughnuts took longer to prepare than was justified by their 60p price tag, so he started to buy them in from a wholesale baker. Outsourcing was the sensible approach.

Within two months Carol was looking for a new job. She found it in another bakery, but soon left that as well, and went to college to retrain for a new career. Other staff steadily left, including all of Gianni's family. The newly recruited staff were accepting of Malone's rules, but none seemed particularly keen on the work. Perhaps that was fortunate, because sales started to slip after two months, and then fell at an increasingly rapid pace. Staff who left were not replaced, as they were no longer needed. Even more fortunate was that Gianni was not well enough to travel back to England. He never knew how quickly 40 years of work fell apart.

Questions (40 marks; 50 minutes)

1 Use the example of Gianni's bakery to discuss whether it is right to say that value added is at the heart of all business activity. (15)

2 Examine why outsourcing the doughnuts may not have been 'a sensible approach' for Malone. (10)

3 Malone paid £250,000 for a business that steadily went downhill. To what extent was the problem due to the change in culture within the workplace? (15)

Making strategic decisions

Definition

A strategic decision is one that is made in a situation of uncertainty and has medium- to long-term significance for the business. Once it's made, a strategic decision cannot easily be reversed.

Introduction

The word 'strategy' means a plan for meeting your objectives. It is therefore subordinate to objectives. Typically, directors set objectives and managers carry out the strategy. Yet the term 'strategic' means a lot more than this. Businesses refer to it in two ways: strategic thinking and strategic decisions.

Strategic thinking involves visualising what you hope to achieve within coming years (given consumer tastes and lifestyles, plus the competition you face), assessing the strengths of your business in relation to those aims, then identifying an approach that can enable you to get there. This process should be carried out with a wide range of senior – and, ideally, some junior – staff, in order to get a wide range of views and a real consensus. After this process of strategic thinking takes place, new objectives can be identified and a new strategic plan put into action.

Strategic decisions, then, are the result of strategic thinking. In 1990 the chairman of car tyre maker Nokia decided to stake the future of the business on a then still trivial business – the mobile phone. In the period 2001 to 2007 the directors of Northern Rock decided to change from being a sleepy building society based in the English north-east to become a major national bank. Both were hugely important **strategic decisions** and these two examples highlight that big decisions are not necessarily correct ones. Table 52.1 shows some examples of strategic decisions, contrasting them with smaller-scale day-to-day **tactical decisions** faced by managers.

Table 52.1 Examples of strategic and tactical decisions

Strategic decisions	Tactical decisions
• Should we relocate our factory from Slough to Sri Lanka? • Should we close down our out-of-town stores and concentrate more on online sales? • Should we focus all our investment capital for the next two years on building a sizeable operation in India? • Should we move from Anfield to a new, multi-million-pound, bigger stadium nearby?	• Should we replace our CCTV system as our current pictures are too fuzzy? • Should we mark down the prices on this Christmas stock today (23 December), rather than wait until the January sales? • Our labour turnover has been rising steadily, so should we conduct a staff questionnaire to find out what's wrong? • Should we switch our Sunday opening from 11.00–5.00 to 12.00–6.00?

Important influences on strategic decision making

Relative power of stakeholders

The 1990s had been very kind to Arsenal FC, as trophies kept coming and the club rivalled Manchester United as Britain's top football team. The supporters loved the club, the manager and the ground – Highbury – and felt sure the good times would keep coming. Arsenal's directors were not so sure. Highbury could hold only 38,000 people, while Old Trafford was steadily being expanded to take twice that number. If the Manchester club could generate twice the income, how could Arsenal continue to compete in the long term? So the directors took a £400 million gamble on moving the club to the 60,000-seater Emirates stadium. As the shares in the football club were held by a few wealthy people, this gamble was possible. If the shares had been held by the general public, there would have been much less willingness to such a chance. Directors can take bold strategic decisions only if they are supported by the shareholders. This may be easier in a business that is not a public limited company.

Available resources

Arsenal's £400 million gamble was very difficult to finance, but it proved possible. In other cases, a business may have a brilliant idea that has huge potential, yet it may be unable to secure the necessary finance. The business may lack the internal finance and find it impossible to persuade outsiders of the attractions of the proposal. In some years banks seem willing to offer finance to very unattractive propositions; in other years they refuse to finance rock-solid ideas.

Top companies try to make sure that they always have enough cash to be able to put strategic decisions into practice. On 25 June 2011, Apple had $76 billion of cash and cash investments on its balance sheet – to provide the liquidity to take advantage of any opportunity. Tesco plc also has a hugely strong financial position, allowing it to declare a massive store-building programme in China up until 2013.

Ethical position

In the 1990s the term business ethics meant little. Today it is a significant part of boardroom discussion in plcs and other businesses. The question remains, however, 'Are the discussions about how to operate ethically, or are they about how to be thought to be operating ethically?' In others words, is it genuine or is it for show? In fact, company directors can be forgiven for being quite cynical about ethics, because consumers are often as hypocritical as companies. People talk about animal welfare, but can't resist two chickens for a fiver; and they talk about global warming as they're driving down to the shops.

There is no doubt, though, that if consumers believe a business is a force for good, there can be financial benefits. Innocent Drinks did relatively little to deserve its reputation as an ethical business. Its high prices hardly implied a social desire to promote healthy living. Yet people accepted its story that it is a pure little company with a big heart. Even after Coca-Cola took a majority stake in the business, the Innocent logo suggested 'healthy' to consumers – whereas the Coke logo shouted 'unhealthy'. Innocent's image adds value to the brand.

Different approaches to strategic decisions

There are always two alternative methods to making a decision: evidence-based (scientific) or hunch. It is important to realise that either method may be successful, or unsuccessful. There is no evidence that one is better than the other.

In 2007 senior management at Whitbread plc went through a detailed analysis of the four operating divisions of its business. It decided that it had two 'rising stars', one 'dog' and one 'cash cow'. It decided that the correct strategy would be to sell the latter two divisions in order to generate

more cash to finance the growth of the two stars. Understandably, the 'dog' (the restaurants division, including Beefeater) was difficult to sell, but 'cash cow' David Lloyd Leisure was sold for £925 million. In this case, the strategic decision was based on evidence of the financial performance of the different parts of the business. Therefore it was logical – scientific even. By 2011 it was clear that the strategic decision had been a brilliant one. Both of the stars (Costa Coffee and Premier Inn) were booming.

In 2010, Apple made a significant strategic shift. Partly, perhaps, because of its focus on new product development, it had rather ignored China. Remarkably, in July 2010, the head of the Chinese computer giant Lenovo said: 'We are lucky that Steve Jobs (boss of Apple) doesn't care about China. If Apple were to spend the same effort on the Chinese consumer as we do, we would be in trouble.' That same month Apple opened a huge, modern store in Shanghai. The company announced that it would be the first of 20 new flagship stores throughout China. The reason for Apple's change of strategy was probably because the first half of 2010 saw Apple's sales revenues double in China. In 2011 they trebled again!

The significance of information management

The bosses of most plcs make their decisions on the basis of data, not hunch. Therefore information management is crucial. The first critical issue is to have full knowledge of your own business. This might seem obvious, but in January 2008 a major French bank found that one of its own employees had been gambling with €50 billion of the bank's money. Sorting out the mess cost more than £3.7 billion. A huge bank that, one week, was considering plans for its long-term future was in the next week fighting for its short-term survival.

Few businesses have such problems, but there are others that find out only much too late that their sales have been worse than expected. Good companies have good, up-to-date information about themselves. This requires IT systems that show instantly how the business is doing, so that the senior directors can think quickly about whether current strategies are working. If they are not, it may be time for a radical rethink.

A-grade application

Connaught Housing

On 23 June 2010 shares in the housing firm Connaught plc were 323p, valuing the business at £500 million. Then a series of blows made the share price crash by 95% within six weeks! On 10 August the shares were priced at 15p.

At the heart of the problem was that new management had announced that it was investigating the firm's accounting practices. As the firm had debts of £260 million, operating losses revealed by reworking the firm's income statement showed that the business could not keep up its interest payments.

The line between success and failure can be a fine one.

Issues for analysis

These days chief executives of plcs are paid huge sums (literally, millions of pounds) to run large businesses on behalf of the shareholders. The only reason to pay such high sums is to attract people who can get the key strategic decisions right. Before he stood down as Tesco's boss at the start of 2011, Sir Terry Leahy had successfully steered the company into Eastern Europe and the Far East. Yet he made a huge mistake spending £1,250 million moving Tesco into America. Although Sir Terry would have gathered as much information about the US grocery market as possible, ultimately the decision was made as much on the basis of hunch (backed by huge experience) as on scientific evidence. But in 14 successful years, Leahy was bound to make one strategic error. Weak leaders postpone decisions until it's too late. Far better to be decisive, even if the occasional decision proves a mistake.

When studying a business situation – perhaps in the exam room – these are the key questions:

- Has the business done all it reasonably can to gather data such as primary research?
- Has the business made effective use of relevant assets (including the expertise within its staff)?
- Does the leadership have the experience, the enthusiasm and the wisdom to make a sound judgement – and then ensure that the new approach is carried through effectively?
- Has the business the financial and human resources to turn the right idea into the right strategy?

Making strategic decisions – an evaluation

Strategic thinking should be radical, innovative and free from internal constraints such as 'that's not how we do things round here'. The traditions and culture of an organisation should always be taken into account, but cannot be allowed to act as an absolute constraint. Careful discussion with a wide range of staff should help bring insight to the process and assist in the process of communicating the need for a new approach.

If the strategic thinking is right, the strategic decisions should also be right. Sometimes, though, the pressures upon the decision makers lead to mistaken compromises. Shareholders who are unhappy about short-term profitability may not be willing to back a strategic decision that has a

five-year timeframe. Short-term cost-cutting may be the only language the shareholders understand. It is the job of the highly paid chief executives to find the right balance between what is right and what is acceptable.

Key terms

Strategic decision: one that is made in circumstances of uncertainty and where the outcome will have a major impact on the medium- to long-term future of the organisation.

Tactical decision: deciding what to do in circumstances that are immediate (short term) and where a mistake is unlikely to have a major impact on the business.

A Revision questions *(35 marks; 35 minutes)*

1 Explain the difference between 'strategy' and 'strategic'. (4)

2 Outline two qualities you would want in a manager who has to take strategic decisions. (4)

3 Look at Table 52.1. Explain why relocation from Slough to Sri Lanka would be regarded as a strategic, not a tactical, decision. (5)

4 Apart from shareholders, explain why two other stakeholder groups might be interested in the strategic decision to 'close down our out-of-town stores and concentrate more on online sales'. (6)

5 Briefly consider how well each of the following businesses could cope with a strategic decision that would require a major capital investment.
   a Business A has a current ratio of 0.95 and a gearing ratio of 55% (5)
   b Business B has an acid test ratio of 1.05 and would need to increase staffing levels by 12% to be able to produce the extra goods required by the strategy. (5)

6 Should business ethics ever be a matter of tactics, or should they always be part of the strategic thinking behind strategic decisions? (6)

B1 Data response

Strategic decisions in the ice cream market

Table 52.2 Markets for ice cream in selected countries

	Spending per capita US$	Population	Market size	Market growth pa (2007–2010 ave)
India	0.33	1,180m	$389.4m	16%
China	3.12	1,330m	?	18%
Russia	14.88	142m	?	3%
UK	43.66	62m	?	0%
USA	48.74	308m	$15,012m	0.3%

Anglo-Dutch Unilever is the UK ice cream market leader with its Walls ice cream brand. It is looking at whether to expand into China, India, Russia or America. The US ice cream market is mature and is dominated by large, well-regarded brands. China and India are both under-developed markets; until recently relatively few in the population had any discretionary spending for ice cream. Russians love ice cream, which is locally-made, cheap and very good.
Source: Euromonitor 2010.

Questions (25 marks; 30 minutes)

1 a Calculate the ice cream market size for China, Russia and the UK. (3)

   b If the ice cream market grows in 2011 at the average shown in the right column, what growth (in US$) will there be in the Chinese, Indian and US markets? (6)

2 Use all the above information to decide which of the four countries would be the best for Walls to launch into. Justify your answer. (16)

B2 Case study

Strategic decision for AirAsia

In 2009 and 2010 the award for the World's Best Low Cost Airline went to AirAsia. The company's story began in 2001, when Dr Tony Fernandes and three colleagues bought loss-making AirAsia and turned it into a low-cost carrier. At first they had 2 ageing Boeing 737 planes, 5 destinations and 250 staff. By early 2010 they had 90 new planes, 60 destinations and 7,500 staff.

AirAsia's operational strategy largely mimics that of Ryanair and easyJet: no frills, high aircraft utilisation (rapid turnaround); online booking and a single-aircraft fleet (to minimise staff training and engineering maintenance costs). A significant difference, though, is the desire to offer a friendly, comfortable service (hence the awards).

The biggest strategic difference is that AirAsia has set up a sister company AirAsia X that operates long-haul. From its London–Kuala Lumpur route, 40% of travellers fly onto their local destinations via AirAsia. But this approach has operational risks attached to it, because low-

Table 52.3 Key features of the Airbus A380 and Airbus A330

Feature	Airbus A380 'Superjumbo'	Airbus A330
List price per plane	$346 million	$212 million
Maximum passenger capacity	650 (with economy plus 'premium' class) 850 (if all economy class)	340 (with economy plus 'premium' class) 440 (if all economy class)
Special characteristics	Exceptionally quiet for passengers (and residents near airports)	More than 1,000 in service worldwide, so easy to get experienced pilots and engineers
Customer approval	Very high; airlines flying the A380 now (such as Emirates) can get a price premium of 10–20%	Nothing special

Table 52.4 Passenger numbers for AirAsiaX

2007	15,000
2008	270,000
2009	1,034,000
2012 (est)	3,000,000
2015 (est)	6,000,000

cost flying may be fine for short journeys, but sounds grim for 12- to 14-hour transcontinental flights.

AirAsiaX started flying in 2007 and had 8 aircraft by the end of 2009. Whereas AirAsia follows easyJet in having a fleet of Airbus A320 planes, AirAsia X flies the much bigger A330. In 2009 the business managed to buy 5 A330 planes through 'financing raised on its own balance sheet strength, and cashflow' (AirAsia annual accounts 2009).

Now, however, the firm needs to make a big strategic decision. It has been planning to go from 8 A330 planes to 25 by 2015. But should it switch to the bigger, better, but more expensive A380 plane? Long haul rivals such as Emirates, Singapore Airways, Qantas and British Airways have all bought the A380 'Superjumbo'. Instead of buying 17 new A330s, some in the boardroom suggest they should buy 15 A380s. As planes are made to order, it usually takes 2 to 3 years to receive the finished planes. So AirAsia will have to live with whichever decision is made.

£million

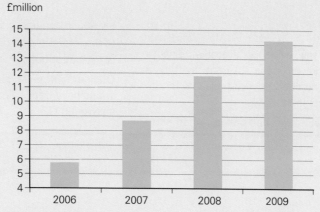

Figure 52.1 AirAsia passenger numbers
Source: AirAsia accounts

Table 52.5 AirAsia balance sheets (extracts) for 2008 and 2009

As at 31 December	2009 £million	2008 £million
Non-current (fixed) assets	1,835	1,500
Inventories (stock)	4	4
Trade receivables (debtors)	211	206
Cash	230	170
Total current assets	445	380
Current liabilities	(340)	(345)
Net current assets	105	35
Non-current liabilities	(1,415)	(1,215)
Net assets	525	320
Share capital	295	195
Reserves	230	125
Total equity	525	320

Source: AirAsia accounts; all figures converted from Malaysian currency at 5 per £.

Table 52.6 AirAsia income statements for 2008 and 2009

Year to 31 December	2009 £million	2008 £million
Revenue	627	571
Operating costs	(444)	(641)
Operating profit	183	(70)
Net financing costs	(58)	(104)
Profit before taxation	125	(174)

Source: AirAsia accounts; all figures converted from Malaysian currency at 5 per £.

Questions *(40 marks; 60 minutes)*

1 Based on the evidence available, discuss whether the business is right to buy a significant number of extra planes for its AirAsiaX operation. (14)

2 A second strategic decision is whether to acquire 15 A380s or 17 A330s. On the basis of the information provided in the case, which is the better option? Justify your view. (18)

3 Outline four extra pieces of information it would have been valuable to have had before answering Q2. (8)

Implementing and managing change

> ### Definition
> Change management involves controlling the activities required to move an organisation from its current position to a new one.

Identifying the need for change

Change is an unavoidable part of life, both for individuals and organisations. Existing markets decline and new products are developed. Experienced workers retire or leave, and are replaced by new employees with fresh ideas. According to recent research published by the Chartered Institute of Personnel Development (CIPD), organisations undergo major change once every three years on average, with smaller changes taking place almost continually.

The need for change can result from influences within and outside the business. Change is an inevitable part of business growth. For a firm that grows organically, this change may be relatively slow and steady, occurring over a prolonged period of time. However, managers will still need to have the skills and expertise required to anticipate and manage this change effectively. Change resulting from merger or takeover will be more sudden, and may be followed by a painful period of adjustment, even if careful planning has taken place beforehand.

Change may be anticipated, such as the introduction of a new marketing strategy, or unanticipated – for example, the collapse of an important supplier or a sudden deterioration in customer satisfaction. Changes may be beyond the control of individual businesses, such as the introduction of a national minimum wage or a ban on advertising during children's television programmes. A successful firm will see change as an opportunity to re-examine its operations and market conditions or, better still, anticipate changes before they occur and develop a competitive advantage over rivals.

Figure 53.1 Causes of organisational change

Organisational barriers to successful change

No matter how much time and how many resources are put into the planning stage, a number of organisational issues may arise that have a negative impact on the implementation of change within a business. These include the following.

- *A lack of effective leadership and project management:* the failure to coordinate projects effectively can lead to missed deadlines and wasted resources, affecting a firm's performance.

- *A lack of effective training:* a business must ensure that all those involved in implementing change initiatives have the expertise required to do so, including project management and leadership skills.

- *Poor communication:* effective two-way communication must be established between all the individuals and groups affected.

Resistance to change

Resistance to change may be defined as 'an individual or group engaging in acts to block or disrupt an attempt to introduce change' (CIPD). Workers within an organisation may resist change for a number of reasons. For example, people may be concerned about a loss of control or status, feel vulnerable to the threat of redundancy or resent the break-up of social groups within the workplace. Resistance may be directed at the change itself, perhaps because it seems to go against the prevailing culture, such as introducing an extra management layer to a business with an entrepreneurial culture.

Resistance can also come in different forms. Active resistance occurs when opposition is clearly stated, such as when workers decide to take industrial action. Passive resistance might include failing to attend meetings or respond to messages. Although more subtle, passive resistance can be just as (if not more) effective in blocking change, especially as its existence is less likely to be detected.

Dealing with negative responses and resistance to change requires a great deal of skill by managers. Such responses may result from rational and reasonable concerns and therefore need to be handled calmly and sympathetically. Then it should be possible to find a way forward and avoid a situation of stalemate.

To overcome resistance, key factors will be as follows.

- Objectives that are clear to all, and are accepted as necessary or desirable by the great majority of staff.
- Adequate resources for senior management to effect the change efficiently; these include financial resources, human resources, and the right operational and technological back-up.
- An effective training programme: this can be expensive, but not as expensive as the alternative – not training. Unmotivated or sceptical staff can be very critical of what they see as second-rate training. Poorly run training sessions can set the change process back; training must be excellent to be adequate. Therefore it needs to be planned and carried out by an important figure within the change process, such as the **project champion** (see below).

A-grade application

In October 2010 London's firefighters threatened to go on strike on 5 November, Britain's Firework (Bonfire) night. This night is the busiest of the year for firefighters, so the threat was both serious and extremely unpopular. The firefighters were protesting about a change in their shift patterns. For many years they had been working for two 9-hour day shifts followed by a 15 hour nightshift, followed by 4 days off. The employers were demanding a change to 11 hours per dayshift and 13 hours at night. The firefighters say this will leave them with less family time, while leaving London with less night cover. On the face of it, the differences between both sides seem quite small, so it should be easy to negotiate and resolve. The dispute became serious because the firefighters disliked the way the management tried to force the change through.

A-grade application

No project champion for Terminal 5

The new British Airways Heathrow Terminal 5 opened after 19 years of planning. The new terminal was trumpeted as a customer service breakthrough, with its high-tech new systems, such as that for baggage handling. Yet its opening proved a humiliating fiasco. The key problem was with the baggage-handling systems, leading to chaos as bags piled up.

It later emerged that staff who had been working at Terminals 1, 2 and 3 had received far less training than had been planned on the new technology system. Only 50 of the 400 baggage handlers had received the planned four days of training at Terminal 5. BA chief executive Willie Walsh had not delegated effectively to a project champion who could make sure that this big change worked effectively.

Implementing change successfully

Despite the individual circumstances and the particular changes faced by any given business, there are a number of key factors that should be considered in order to develop a programme that will incorporate change and overcome any resistance effectively. These factors include those listed below.

- *Ensuring that the objectives and details of any changes are communicated as clearly and as quickly as possible to employees:* leaving staff in the dark can lead to rumours and speculation about the changes that, once established, can be difficult to challenge. Far better to keep everyone informed of the objective and the plans.

- *Appointing a project champion:* it is easy for new ideas to be stifled by the bureaucracy within middle management; a project champion should have the power and the passion to push the change through and to persuade staff that the new methods will be more successful than the old.

- *Involving staff rather than imposing change:* unless there is a need for confidentiality, involving staff in the change process can lead to a number of benefits. Consulting staff regularly or setting up **project groups**, taking members from different functional departments, to work on particular areas should help to generate a wider range of ideas, but also help to combat anxieties and increase commitment by creating a sense of ownership.

- *Ensuring appropriate leadership:* no particular leadership style is most effective at dealing with change. The most appropriate style will depend on the circumstances of the particular organisation and the nature of the changes it faces. However, all leaders will need to provide their subordinates with the vision and rationale for change required to make the process a success.

- *Creating a culture for change:* a 'learning organisation' is one where change-orientated thinking has been embodied in all employees, so that change is seen as an opportunity rather than a threat. Such organisations are likely to be more receptive and to adapt more quickly to changes, even those that are unexpected. Over the years the England football team has been very resistant to any change in tactics; this can be contrasted with the huge fluidity of a team such as Manchester United, who accept the manager's decisions without a quibble.

Managing change

Once the process of change has been implemented, it needs to be managed effectively. This involves two stages.

1 *Control:* this involves taking steps to ensure that the final outcome of the change process is as close as possible to the objectives identified at the planning stage. Regular checks will allow the firm to detect problems quickly and deal with them promptly, in order to avoid delays and wasting resources. This will only be possible if the business has set measurable goals (i.e. quantifiable targets against which performance can be compared). However, even the SMARTest objectives are subject to influences beyond the control of the organisations that set them. **Contingency planning** encourages firms to attempt to identify what might go wrong and develop strategies to deal with these problems in order to get back on course. For example, training may prove to be inadequate – in which case, new courses need to be made available to remedy the situation quickly.

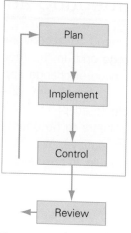

Figure 53.2 The process of managing change

2 *Review:* once change has been implemented and objectives achieved, the organisation needs to consider the 'What next?' scenario. This may seem strange, given the upheaval created by attempting to adjust to recent changes. However, the nature of business is to keep in touch with its marketplace. Increased competition, changes in technology and customer requirements mean that no business can afford to stand still for long.

Radical vs continuous change

Business process re-engineering (BPR) is an approach requiring an organisation to totally rethink its approach to its current operations. BPR focuses on the processes undertaken within the organisation, rather than its structure. This requires a clear idea of the specific roles of workers within the organisation and how they relate to customers. Once the aims and objectives have been established, the organisation is completely redesigned from scratch.

A key advantage of BPR is that it considers the efficiency of the organisation as a whole, in terms of meeting customer requirements, rather than simply focusing on individual parts. However, an organisation is unlikely to undergo such radical change unless it is faced with a crisis threatening its very survival, given the upheaval that it is likely to create. In most situations, businesses are more likely to prefer a kaizen approach (i.e. a process of continuous improvement).

Issues for analysis

Opportunities for analysis may arise in the following areas.

- A consideration of the benefits and problems of introducing a programme of change; this should take into account the crucial question of whether 'do nothing' is an acceptable alternative. The fiasco of British Airways' change to Heathrow Terminal 5 does not mean that it did the wrong thing; it just did it in the wrong way.
- Many management teams see change as an operational issue. For example, many government departments have wasted billions of pounds in trying to establish new IT systems that proved unusable. They saw the change as a technical, operational issue, driven forward by independent management consultants. Later investigations showed that the mistake was ignoring the importance of staff and the knowledge they have of how the systems really work. There is huge scope for analysing whether the correct way forward is via staff or via operations management (the ideal is an effective combination of the two).
- An analysis of the consequences of resistance to change within an organisation.

Implementing and managing change – an evaluation

All organisations need to accept and face up to the need for change and, in the modern business environment, the pace of change appears to show no signs of slowing down. Any business that is unwilling or unable to adapt to the ever-increasing pace of change appears to be doomed to become less and less competitive. Yet there are always exceptions to every rule. In business, every generalisation proves a mistake. For every nine businesses that need change to survive, there will be one that thrives on remaining unchanged, from a traditional private school to a producer of handcrafted British sports cars (such as Morgan) or handmade wedding dresses.

It is easy for managers to neglect existing customers or suppliers in an attempt to demonstrate their change management skills, but the resulting damage may cancel out the benefits of change. However, change requires the support of the employees within an organisation – without the support of employees, change is unlikely to succeed. The ability to establish trust between management and workers in the face of change appears to be the way forward in managing the process of change successfully.

Key terms

Business process re-engineering (BPR): a radical approach to changing an organisation, in which it is completely designed in order to meet the needs of customers more effectively.

Contingency planning: preparing for unlikely and unwanted possibilities, such as the onset of recession, or the collapse of a major supplier or customer.

Kaizen: the Japanese term for continuous improvement.

Project champion: an individual appointed from within an organisation to support the process of change.

Project group: where members of different departments within an organisation are put together (temporarily) to generate ideas, to put the plan into practice and maintain good communications between departments.

 Revision questions *(40 marks; 40 minutes)*

1 Outline two causes of change that might be generated from within a business. (4)

2 Describe two causes of change that are likely to be outside a firm's control. (4)

3 Examine the main consequences to a fashion clothing business of failing to identify and respond to changes in the external environment. (6)

4 Identify two reasons why a firm might encounter resistance to change from within the workforce. (2)

5 Use examples to explain the difference between active and passive resistance. (4)

6 Examine one way in which a business could attempt to successfully tackle resistance to change. (4)

7 Briefly explain the importance to effective change of a 'project champion'. (4)

8 Analyse one benefit of creating a culture of change within an organisation. (4)

9 Examine one potential benefit and one potential drawback to a business from adopting a programme of business process engineering. (4)

10 Outline the role that human resources managers can play in the change management process. (4)

 Data response

Bookstore restructuring leads to success

Foyles is one of the UK's oldest and best known bookstores. However, when Christopher Foyle was appointed chairman of the independent bookseller in 1999, the company was in a mess. Christopher took charge of the business following the death of his aunt, Christina Foyle, who had run the company for 54 years. Under Christina, the store's layout was based on a confusing categorisation of books by publisher, rather than by author or subject. Customers were forced to queue three times to buy books – the first to obtain a handwritten chit, the second to pay and a third to obtain their purchases. Foyle's reputation was such that one rival bookseller used the advertising slogan, 'Foyled again? Try Dillons'. The business suffered from a lack of financial management and the accounts were still being written up manually into ledgers. The market was getting increasingly competitive, with high street chains such as Waterstones and WH Smith, supermarkets and Amazon online selling cheap blockbusters. Sales turnover had fallen to £9.5 million and was falling at 20% a year. Christina refused to issue the staff with contracts and would dismiss them on a whim.

Christopher began a programme of modernisation, installing a new management team, introducing a proper accounting system and investing £4 million on refurbishing the main company's flagship store on the Charing Cross Road in London's West End. Staff were issued with contracts and the store layout was redesigned to be more customer friendly and stock more popular titles. A Foyles website was set up, which now accounts for over 10% of the company's sales, and new stores were opened near the Royal Festival Hall, at St Pancras International station and the Westfield shopping centre in London.

In 2008, Sam Husain was appointed as the company's chief executive. He has a background of accountancy and financial and management consultancy and is only the second non-family member to run the company since it was established in 1903. Christopher remains in the role of company chairman, conducting board meetings by videophone from his home in Monaco.

In September 2010, Foyles reported an impressive increase in operating profits, up from £80,625 in 2009 to £434,588 in the 12 months to June 2010. Sales turnover was up by 1.9% to £25.1 million and like-for-like sales grew by 9.7% in a book market where sales fell by 5.6%. According to chief executive, Husain, the success has come from working hard to provide a 'proper service' to book lovers, rather than the heavy discounting used by rivals. He said, 'We've really concentrated on aspects that make a bookseller a destination, so you look at a service, at quality of staff, at training, and all of these make each of our bookshops a special place to come and visit.'

Source: *The Financial Times*, *Independent*.

Questions *(20 marks; 25 minutes)*

1 Examine the key reasons why change was necessary at Foyles. (10)

2 Analyse the possible factors that led to change being implemented successfully at the bookseller. (10)

 Essay questions *(40 marks each)*

1 'The problem of change is people.' Discuss.

2 After 20 years as a full-service Italian restaurant, Luigi Ristorante is to change to a self-service format. Discuss the key aspects of change that Luigi should tackle to ensure that this new plan proves a success.

Introduction: change in the current business environment

Most business commentators agree that the greatest challenge facing managers currently is how to deal effectively with change. They are probably right in this, but underestimate the extent to which this has always been true (and always will be). There is not one single change today that compares with the arrival of steam power (and therefore the railways and electricity) or the arrival of motor transport. In every aspect of Business Studies, a broad perspective is essential.

Despite this plea for perspective, it is true to say that the pace of change appears to be speeding up. An increasingly competitive environment and the globalisation of markets have required firms to adopt a more innovative approach to their products and their production processes. Changes in economic conditions beyond the influence of individual organisations, such as exchange rate fluctuations or a reduction in the availability of credit, can force a complete strategic rethink.

The need for change may also come from within an organisation, perhaps as a result of the development of new products. The changes required may be structural, requiring a business to reorganise its activities and resources, or it may be cultural, altering established attitudes and norms. Change may be incremental or evolutionary, over a relatively long period of time, or revolutionary, such as the decision to transfer a firm's entire operations overseas. Finally, while some change can be anticipated and planned for, unforeseen events will still need to be managed effected if any negative consequences are to be minimised. Ultimately, while ignoring change or its significance to an organisation may be tempting for managers, the long-term consequences of doing so can be very costly indeed.

Change is a key concept within Business Studies. Students need to have an awareness of the variety of influences that might create a need for change, including economic, social, political, legal and technical factors, as well as the competitive structure of the markets in which firms operate. More important, though, will be to understand the managerial and cultural issues involved in making change an opportunity rather than a threat.

While the impact of and response to change need to be considered on an individual business basis, there are a number of common issues that underpin the successful management of change.

Three key issues in dealing effectively with change

Issue 1: planning change effectively

In order to succeed, programmes of change need detailed and thorough planning. An essential part of the planning process is to formulate clear objectives for change (i.e. the corporate aims that set out where the business wants to be). However, the business will also need to carry out an honest assessment of its current situation – 'where it is now' – in order to establish the 'strategic gap' in terms of the changes that are needed and the capabilities and resources required to achieve them. The planning process may also involve the need to prioritise. Too many changes introduced in short succession can lead to 'change overload' among staff, leading to increased stress and demotivation. Managers may, therefore, be required to make important choices regarding the areas where change is most urgently required.

Issue 2: managing change requires effective leadership

Leaders and managers have a critical role to play in managing the change process within an organisation. Although the stimulus for change can come from a variety of sources, managers are required to act as 'change agents'. They must provide clear vision, develop and monitor policies, and mobilise those involved by communicating and justifying the need for change. Failure to do so could lead to mistakes, delays and even resistance to change, reducing the effectiveness of the change initiative.

Issue 3: coping with change requires a suitable culture

The creation of a 'culture for change' would appear to be the most effective way of coping successfully with the demands of the modern business environment. An organisation where change-orientated thinking is an approach adopted by all individuals, rather than just senior management, is likely to be better equipped to react to even radical change more effectively. Furthermore, a firm that develops a positive approach is more likely to be able to anticipate and manage changes more effectively than a firm that sees every change as a crisis.

A Revision questions (80 marks; 80 minutes)

1 Identify two characteristics of a power culture. (2)

2 Analyse one benefit and one drawback for a business adopting a role culture. (6)

3 Explain why a task culture might be most appropriate for a company designing games software. (5)

4 Examine two problems that managers might face in attempting to move from a role culture to a task culture within the business. (6)

5 Explain the difference between a tactical and a strategic decision. (4)

6 Outline three possible effects on Walkers of a decision by government to ban the advertising of potato crisps and other fatty snack foods. (6)

7 Examine one external change that might have a serious effect on British Airways. (4)

8 Using examples, explain why the 'correct' management style is dependent on an organisation's individual circumstances. (4)

9 State the four phases involved in managing change. (4)

10 Explain what is meant by scientific decision making. (3)

11 Identify one benefit and one drawback of adopting a scientific approach to decision making. (4)

12 Briefly explain what is meant by a corporate plan. (3)

13 Outline two factors that could influence a firm's corporate plan. (4)

14 Outline two possible reasons why brands such as Marmite are able to last for more than 100 years with very little change in the product. (4)

15 State two possible internal causes and two external causes of change within an organisation. (4)

16 Outline the role of leadership in the process of managing change. (3)

17 Outline two changes that a company might consider making after merging with a competitor. (4)

18 Identify the key stages involved in the process of managing change. (3)

19 Explain what is meant by contingency planning. (3)

20 Examine one advantage and one disadvantage for a firm that adopts a *kaizen* approach to implementing change. (4)

Case study

HMV's black hole

HMV has blundered its way into a strategic black hole. Its mainstay products such as CDs and DVDs have collapsing total markets – plus a dramatic switch from retail to online purchasing. In 2011 its website rightly proclaimed 'HMV is a world-renowned brand'; unfortunately, it is barely a business. In 2011 its profits fell 61% and its net margins were less than 2%.

One of its management's main achievements in 2011 was selling off Waterstone's bookshops for £53 million. Although this was a big plus for a business with £200 million of debt, in fact HMV originally paid £300 million for Waterstone's – Britain's biggest bookstore chain. Selling for £53 million meant a loss of £247 million. While under HMV's control Waterstone's had decided that online sales would never reach more than 10% of the UK market for books. It therefore handed over ('outsourced') its online operations to Amazon.com! Today online accounts for 35% + of UK book sales, with Amazon taking four-fifths of that online business. It is Amazon that pushed Waterstone's face into the sand.

Now, without Waterstone's, HMV can look after its own 250 stores. Its 2011 strategy is to shift the business away from commodity items such as CDs. Instead it will focus on 'technology': more personal hardware items such as headphones and iPod/iPad accessories. Very properly, the board has crystallised its plans into 'SMART' targets (see Table 54.1) based on its 2011 sales profile. The table shows the critical need to focus on the Technology category (quadrupling sales).

Table 54.1 HMV sales for 2011 and targets for 2014

	2011	Target 2014
Visual (DVD/Blu-ray)	44%	30%
Music	27%	15%
Games	17%	19%
Technology	8%	32%
Other	4%	4%
Total HMV sales:	100%	100%

Source: HMV website 24 August 2011.

The company trialled the new approach by redesigning six test stores with a big increase in the floor space devoted to technology. This boosted technology sales by 100% and overall store sales by more than 8%. Accordingly, 150 more stores were being converted to the new format before Christmas 2011.

Two constraints remain a concern. The first is a human resource issue. Nowhere in the company's plans is there a clear statement of a major retraining programme for staff. Selling technology is very different from selling music. The company seems to be assuming that the skills are little different. The second is harder to address: HMV's 30 April 2011 balance sheet shows its acid test ratio to be 0.18. So how was it supposed to find the cash to revamp 150 stores? The likelihood will be that the store revamps (like the staff training) will be done on a shoestring. Successful strategies require the finances to back them up. HMV will require creativity and real management skill to make this work. And if it doesn't …? HMV may not survive.

Questions *(35 marks; 40 minutes)*

1 Discuss whether HMV's problems were largely due to factors outside the company's control. (15)

2 Examine whether HMV's new strategy of boosting Technology sales should be seen as a tactical or as a strategic decision. (8)

3 To what extent has HMV's management planned effectively for its new strategy of boosting Technology sales? (12)

Case study

Creating an effective organisational culture at Carphone Warehouse

Since opening its first store in London in 1989, Carphone Warehouse (CPW) has enjoyed significant growth. The mobile phone retailer now has over 1,400 stores spread across the UK and nine other European countries, and has expanded into a number of related sectors. In 2003, CPW launched its fixed-line telecommunications brand, Talk Talk, followed by the introduction of a lifelong free broadband offer to customers in 2006. The buy-out of rival AOL in October 2006 increased the company's customer base to 2.7 million users, making it the third largest internet service provider (ISP) in the UK, behind BT and Virgin Media. By April 2008, rumours had begun to emerge that CPW was considering taking over fourth-placed Tiscali, a move that would make the company the UK's largest ISP.

In 2008, six companies controlled 95% of the UK's increasingly mature ISP market, making competition fierce between rivals. CPW recognised the importance of customer service in such an environment, and the vital role played here by the company's employees. According to Cristina Jauregui, head of compensation and benefits at CPW, despite offering a relatively low starting salary, the company's organisational culture and benefits package help it recruit and retain staff with the right skills. She describes CPW as still having a 'small company mentality' and being 'a fun place to work'. It has made a point of retaining a number of features introduced when the business was first established. These include the 'beer bust', when it pays for drinks for employees at all of its sites on the last Friday of every month, and the annual employee ball. The company also operates a number of financial incentive schemes, including share option plans, in order to motivate staff and create an element of competition between store managers. The performances of all shops are measured against one another and, at the end of the year, managers of the top 25% of stores receive an extra 50% of shares – the bottom 25% have the same amount taken away!

Questions *(30 marks; 35 minutes)*

1 Describe three features of an entrepreneurial culture. (6)

2 Analyse the key advantages and disadvantages of the organisational culture created at Carphone Warehouse. (10)

3 To what extent to you believe that CPW will be able to continue to maintain a 'small company mentality' as it continues to grow? (14)

A-level examiners love a candidate who understands how to get the marks – it makes their life easier! Getting those marks is, on the face of it, quite simple. All you have to do when answering a question is to:

- define any key terms (show that you know what you're talking about)
- use them to examine the specific business context (the case material you're dealing with)
- analyse the question using theory when necessary, and with reference to the case
- make a judgement when you're asked to do so – and justify it.

The truth is that it is not that easy. Many students are poor at showing these skills in a classroom. Add in the pressure of the exam room and many students' ability to think 'goes out of the window'. It's replaced by one thing alone: the ability to remember. In the exam room, the examiner is trying to tap into the student's brain (have a look around; decide whether it knows enough and is clever enough to be worth an A). But many students are pushing the examiner away ('No, I think you've asked me the wrong question, dear examiner; what you should have asked me is this – look, I prepared it especially for you ...').

To the examiner, the pyramid in Figure 55.1 is the basis of all exam marking. It forms a pyramid because at the base is the foundation of every good answer: knowledge. If the question is on opportunity cost and you don't know what that is, no amount of waffle will dig you out of the hole. What the pyramid also shows, though, is that no matter how much knowledge you have, you cannot get more than 30% of the marks available, and that is never enough for a pass. Therefore it is essential that you master the other skills too.

At AS-level, the key skills are knowledge and application. Between them they account for 60% of the marks and therefore can enable you to achieve a grade B. At A2, the keys are analysis and evaluation, though it is important to remember that analysis is dependent on knowledge, and evaluation relies on good application.

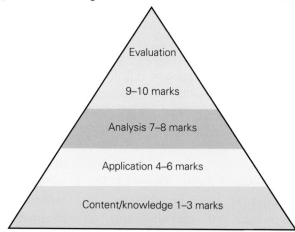

Figure 55.1 Pyramid of marks

Evaluation

9–10 marks

Analysis 7–8 marks

Application 4–6 marks

Content/knowledge 1–3 marks

Table 55.1 Assessment objectives for all A-level Business Studies specifications from 2008

Skills	AS	A2	A-level
Evaluation	20%	**30%**	25%
Analysis	20%	**30%**	25%
Application	**30%**	20%	25%
Knowledge	**30%**	20%	25%

Mastering each of the assessment objectives

Knowledge

Business Studies isn't Chemistry. In Chemistry you either know what happens when iodine is mixed with sulphuric acid or you don't. The same is true in some aspects of business. For example, do you know what happens when a business with cash flow problems turns to factoring? (Yes, it should improve the cash flow position.)

Yet in many other cases it is not obvious that technical knowledge is required. Many questions use words that anyone has access to, whether they have attended lessons or not. Here are a few examples:

1 Discuss how XYZ Ltd should improve the motivation of its workforce.

2 Examine the possible effects on XYZ Ltd of a rise in consumer spending.

3 Explain two ways in which XYZ Ltd could increase its profit.

In each of these three cases, a student with weak knowledge can write plenty and probably come out of the exam feeling great. Their result will be a great disappointment, however. This is because the examiner will see many of this candidate's answers as waffle.

Examiners are actually very generous – they want to give marks. But their great fear is giving a high mark to well-written waffle that, on a second reading, proves to be empty of business knowledge. So help them: start your answer with a precise definition that will convince them that you're a good student who attended lessons, did your homework and bothered to revise.

Your opening sentences in answer to the above three questions might be as follows.

1 Motivation, according to Professor Herzberg, is 'people doing something because they want to, not because they have to'.

2 Rising consumer spending will increase the sales of most products, boost sharply the sales of luxury products (and services), but cut the sales of 'inferior products' such as Tesco Value Beans.

3 Profit is revenue minus costs, therefore it can be increased by boosting revenue or cutting costs (fixed or variable).

Examiner tips on revising knowledge

1 Four weeks before the exam, make lists of all the key terms within the section of the specification being examined. Use the official exam board specification for this.

2 Write a definition for each of the terms, ideally based either on this book or classroom notes or the *Complete A–Z Business Studies Handbook* (6th edn, Philip Allan, 2009). Beware of Googled definitions, because most will be American and their business terminology is not quite the same as Britain's, and many will be aimed at university, not A-level, students.

3 Keep trying again to write the definitions from your own memory and from your understanding of the topic. For example, the explanation of profit given above is something that you would not memorise, but that you should 'know'.

4 Don't spend time trying to remember lots of advantages and disadvantages of things; this will distract you from the key matter: what is it (i.e. the definition).

Application

Application marks are given for your ability to think your way into the specific business situation facing you in the exam. This might be a context you know quite well (the launch of the Nintendo Wii) or might be one you have never heard of before (Tesco's unsuccessful first attempt at operating in America). In fact, it doesn't matter. The text will contain all you need to develop your answers to the questions.

To get OK marks at application, you need to use the material in the text effectively. Not just repeating the company name, but being able to incorporate factors such as Tesco's challenge in building up supply lines in America (i.e. making good deals with US suppliers).

To get full marks at application, you need not only to be able to use the context, but also to see its significance; for example, showing that you see the importance of Tesco deciding to halt its US expansion at 50 stores, when it had originally talked of building 200.

Every business is unique. It is also true to say that every year is unique for every business. The more you master the specific issues that relate to the specific company or industry, the better your marks at application.

Examiner tips on revising application

1 Throughout the course, take every opportunity to read *Business Review* articles, to read business stories in newspapers, to watch business TV (e.g. *The Apprentice*, *Dragons' Den*) and take note of relevant news items.

2 Three weeks before the exam, start working on the B1 and B2 exercises within this book. Read the text and write short notes on the key business aspects of that unique business. If possible, do this with a friend, so that you can swap ideas. It is helpful to debate which (of all the points you've identified) is the single most important feature of that business.

3 One week before the exam, start going through past papers. Identify the key features of that unique business and think about how they can be connected to the questions set.

Analysis

Analysis is shown in two main ways. The first is through the build-up of argument, in which you are showing an ever-deeper understanding of issues, causes and consequences. This can also be called 'sequences of logic'. In other words, 'if that happens, this will be the consequence'.

It is quite easy to practise sequences of logic using the 'analysis framework' shown in Figure 55.2.

Note that the key to analysis marks is not getting the initial points (cut its prices, hold prices, find a new niche), it's the ability to think each point through to its logical conclusion.

Examiner tips on revising analysis

1 Throughout the course, ask your tutor two questions: 'Why is that the case?' and 'What would be the effect of that?'

2 Two weeks before the exam, use the above model to think through any of the major topics in the specification (the ones on the left-hand side of the document).

3 One week before the exam, go through past papers, using the analysis framework on any question that carries more than 8 marks.

Evaluation

Evaluation means judgement. In other words, it's about you making a judgement and giving your reasons (i.e. justifying it). Each Friday, Messrs Ferguson and Wenger must make their decisions on team selection. They will talk through their judgements with their closest advisers, explaining their thoughts. The advisers (assistant manager and head coach) may argue or may agree. The managers' decision, of course, is final. In an exam, the ideal answer would give the judgement and explain it (in terms of tactics, the strength of the opposition, which players are on form, which are needed for next Tuesday's game against Barcelona, and so on).

In a business exam, you might be asked to recommend whether the firm should, or should not, launch a new product. You must decide on the basis of the evidence, then explain which aspects of the evidence pushed you towards your decision. You might also reflect on how confident you are of the decision. Is it a 'no-brainer'? Or is it finely balanced?

Other questions are more frustrating because they require you to invent your own evaluation (e.g. 'Discuss the advantages to XYZ Ltd of using the Boston Matrix'). This style of question gives you nothing real to evaluate, but needs you to seize any opportunities available to you. For instance, the accompanying text might tell you that XYZ Ltd's sales have been slipping a bit, recently. This might

1 What might be the effect on XYZ Ltd of a major new competitor arriving?

2 What might be the effect on XYZ Ltd of a rise in its labour turnover?

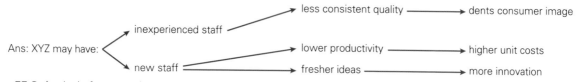

Figure 55.2 Analysis framework

enable you to suggest that, 'The most important benefit to XYZ would be the possibility that using the Boston Matrix will help the business identify and support one or more Rising Stars. This could enable the company to turn around its poor sales performance.'

Examiner tips on revising evaluation

1 Practise making judgements. For example, when you see a new restaurant opening up in your high street, do you think it will succeed? Do you think it will fail? Why do you think that? Then keep an eye on it to see how it's going.

2 Two to three weeks before the exam, start going through past exam papers, focusing on the judgements required.

3 On the day of the exam, make sure to leave yourself long enough to write a conclusion to any question that starts with trigger words such as 'Discuss', 'Evaluate' or 'To what extent'. Then, before starting to write the conclusion, ask yourself 'What do I really think about the answer to this question in this situation?' Then write your explanation for the judgement you have made.

How to revise for business exams

Studies have shown that good revision can add as much as two grades to a student's result at A-level. With increasing pressure for A and A* results, it is vital to appreciate what makes up a quality revision programme. This unit is intended to help.

Aims and objectives

A good revision programme should be aimed at achieving specific targets that will maximise your chances of success in the exam. How should these targets be set?

The basis for setting revision targets can be found in three places.

1 The specification (syllabus)
2 Past papers
3 Examiners' reports.

The specification

The content of the course will be outlined in some detail in the specification. Since the questions in the exam will be based closely on this document, you must ensure that you have sufficient knowledge of each area.

The specification will tell you what skills the examiner will be looking for. As well as basic factual recall as appropriate to the case being discussed, there will be a range of other skills you must demonstrate if you are to score highly.

Knowing what skills the examiner is looking for will help you to produce better-quality answers in an exam. However, like all skills these can only be developed through practice. So it is important to start your revision early and not leave it until the end. In fact, you should try and review your work every few weeks to make sure there are no gaps in your notes and that your files are well organised. This way it becomes easier to revise at the end of the course because everything is in place.

Definitions of higher academic skills

Analysis (breaking down)

● Identification of cause, effect and interrelationships.
● The appropriate use of theory or business cases/practice to investigate the question set.
● Breaking the material down to show underlying causes or problems.
● Use of appropriate techniques to analyse data.

Analysis involves a chain of argument linking ideas and concepts and showing the relationship between them. You might analyse why something happened or the consequence of something occurring.

Look back at previous answers you have written and try to find examples of how you could extend your responses. Were there any occasions when you could have used business theory such as elasticity, motivation or breakeven to strengthen your arguments and provided a higher level of analysis?

Synthesis (bringing together)

- Building the points/themes within the answer into a connected whole.
- Logical sequencing of argument.
- Clarity through summarising an argument.

This skill is particularly important when you have a piece of extended writing such as a report or an essay. In a good essay, for example, each paragraph will have a clear purpose. The arguments will be well organised and lead to a logical conclusion that builds on the earlier analysis. In some exams the synthesis marks may be awarded separately; in others they will be part of an overall mark for an answer.

Evaluation (judgement)

- Judgement shown in weighing up the relative importance of different points or sides of an argument, in order to reach a conclusion.
- Informed comment on the reliability of evidence.
- Distinguishing between fact and opinion.
- Judgement of the wider issues and implications.
- Conclusions drawn from the evidence presented.
- Selectivity – identifying the material that is most relevant to the question.

 # Past papers

Previous exam papers are also very important in helping you to prepare for your exam. They will show you exactly what sort of questions you will face and the number of marks available. They will also give you a feel for the type of words used in the question. It goes without saying that exam questions must be read carefully. However, there will be key words used in the questions that tell you how to answer them. There is, for example, a great difference in the answers expected for the following two questions.

1 Analyse the key elements of ABC plc's marketing strategy
2 Evaluate the key elements of ABC plc's marketing strategy.

Unless you know what is expected from these two questions, you are unlikely to know how much detail is required or how your answer ought to be structured.

 # Examiners' reports

These are available for each examination and can be found on the exam board's website (e.g. www.aqa.org.uk). They are written by the principal examiner of each exam and provide an insight into what he or she found worked well or was not so successful. By looking at these reports you will get a good sense of the weak areas of candidates and common issues they had when interpreting questions. This provides another useful input when it comes to revising and knowing where to focus your efforts.

 # Resources

The following list contains items which will be of enormous value in preparing for an exam. They should all be familiar to you before you begin revising, and should have played a constant part of your studies throughout the course.

- Class notes
- A copy of the specification
- Past exam papers, mark schemes and examiners' reports
- A revision plan
- Newspapers/cuttings files of relevant stories
- A good textbook
- Access to your teacher
- Other students.

Class notes

Since these are the product of your work and a record of your activities, they will form a vital part of your understanding of the subject. Hopefully, they will contain past work you have done on exam-style questions and model answers that will help prepare you for the exam. As you make notes try to make sure these will be legible and useful later on in your revision. Make sure you keep them in the right order as you go; having to sort them out later is much more of a challenge.

A copy of the specification

The specification tells you several important things:

- what knowledge you could be tested on
- what skills the examiner will be looking for
- how the marks will be allocated
- what you will be expected to do in each exam paper you will sit.

Past exam papers, mark schemes and examiners' reports

By working from past papers you will develop a feel for the type of question you will be asked and the sorts of responses you will be expected to give. The examiners' reports will give you an insight into what they thought worked well and what surprised them in terms of the responses. This in turn will give you some idea of how and what they want to assess in the future.

A revision plan

As described in the previous section. It will help keep you on target to achieve everything that you need to cover before the exam.

Newspapers/cuttings files

Since Business Studies is a real-life subject, the ability to bring in relevant examples will boost your answers and their grades. By studying what is happening in the business world you will be able to apply your answers much more effectively; this is because you will develop a better understanding of the key issues in different markets and industries. It will also help you to draw comparisons between different types of businesses which can lead to good evaluation. Keeping some form of 'business diary' where you track at least one story a week is a good way of keeping up to date with what is happening. When making notes about your story try to highlight the underlying business issues and relate it to theory rather than just describe it. This will help you to analyse cases and business situations.

A good textbook

One that will help clarify any points that you are still unsure about (this one we hope!).

Access to your teacher

Asking your teacher for help is vital. Your teacher is able to give you useful advice and insights, to quell sudden panics and to help review your progress by marking work done and suggest ways to improve your performance. Don't hold back – ask! Whenever you get a piece of work back where the mark is disappointing, make sure you know what you need to do differently next time. Read any comments on your work and try to improve in the specific areas mentioned in the next piece of work. Remember the journey to success is full of small improvements (this is, of course, the philosophy of kaizen).

Other students

Talk to other students to help discuss points and clarify ideas. Learning from each other is a very powerful way of revising. Studies often show that you remember something much more when you have to explain it to someone else. Why not agree as a group to revise some topics – study them individually then get together to test each other's understanding? This works very well. Remember you can all get A*s if you are good enough, so there is no problem helping others to improve their performance (as long as it is all their own work in the exam) and you will almost certainly benefit yourself from working with others.

 ## Learning the language of the subject

Clear definitions of business terms are essential for exam success. They count for much more than the odd two-mark question here or there. By showing the examiner that you understand what a term means you are reassuring him or her that your knowledge is sound; this is likely to help your marks for other skills as well. If the examiner is not convinced that you understand what a concept actually means then they are less likely to reward the other skills at a high level. Even on very high-mark questions it is important to define your terms.

When revising business definitions make use of:

- Definition cards
- Past papers
- Crosswords/word games
- Brainteasers

There are many possible sources of good definitions of business terms. In this book, key terms have been given clear and concise definitions. The definitions should be written without using the word in question. ('Market growth is the growth in the market' is not a very good definition, for example!)

It is important, then, that you can produce high-quality definitions in an exam. This can only be done through learning and practice. Possible ways to achieve this are as follows.

Definition cards

Take a pack of index cards or postcards, or similar-sized pieces of thick paper. On each one, write a particular term or phrase that you can find in the specification document. Remember to include things like motivation theories where a clear definition/description can give an excellent overview. It is extremely unlikely that you will be asked to know a precise definition for any term that is not in the specification.

On the back of each card write an appropriate definition. This could come from your class notes, a textbook or a dictionary such as *The Complete A–Z Business Studies Handbook*. Make sure that the definition you write is:

- concise
- clear

- does not use the word being defined in the definition.

Learn the definitions by continual repetition. Put a tick or cross on each card to show whether or not you came up with an acceptable effort. Over time, you should see the number of ticks growing.

Shuffle the cards occasionally so that you are not being given clues to some definitions because of the words or phrases preceding them.

Try the exercise backwards by looking at the definitions and applying the correct word or phrase.

Past papers

By using as many past papers as possible you can find out exactly what type of definition questions are asked. More importantly, you can see how many marks are available for them, which will tell you exactly how much detail you need to go into in your answer.

If possible, get hold of examiners' mark schemes. These will again give you a clear idea of what is being looked for from your answer.

Business crosswords and brainteasers

You will be able to find many examples of 'word games' in magazines such as *Business Review*. By completing these you are developing your business vocabulary and linking words with their meanings.

 # Numbers

All business courses contain aspects of number work which can be specifically tested in exams. It must be remembered, however, that there are two clear aspects to numbers:

1 calculation

2 interpretation.

The calculation aspects of business courses are one area where practice is by far the best advice. Each numerical element has its own techniques that you will be expected to be able to demonstrate. The techniques can be learnt, and by working through many examples they can become second nature.

Even if mathematics is not your strong point, the calculations ought not to cause problems to an A-level student. Something that at first sight appears complex, such as investment appraisal requires only simple techniques such as multiplying, adding and subtracting. Going through the workbook sections of this book will be invaluable. Ask your teacher for a photocopy of the answers available in the Teachers Guide.

Once calculated, all business numbers need to be used. It is all very well to calculate the accounting ratios, for example, but if the numbers are then unused the exercise has been wasted. You must attempt to follow each calculation by stating what the numbers are saying and their implications for the business.

 General tips for revision

1 Start early
2 Know the purpose of your revision
3 Work more on weaker areas
4 Use past papers as far as is possible
5 Keep a clear perspective.

And finally, do no more revision on the night before the exam – it won't help and can only cause you anxiety. Eat well and get a good night's sleep. This way you will be in good physical shape to perform your best in the exam.

 Further reading

Lines, Marcousé and Martin, *The Complete A–Z Business Studies Handbook,* 6th Edn (Philip Allan, 2009).

Business Review (Philip Allan, Market Place, Deddington, OX15 OSE).

How to write an essay

 Introduction

Some people believe that essays require a plan. Others favour spider diagrams. In fact, there is no evidence on exam papers that essay plans lead to better essays. Good essays are far more likely to come from practice.

So what are the skills that need practice? The single most important one is the ability to build an argument. Take this essay title question from a past A-level exam:

'A crisis has led to a dramatic loss of confidence among the customers of a medium sized company. Consider the effects this may have on the organisation and how it may respond.'

Many answers to a title such as this will include six, seven, perhaps twelve points. As a result, each point will be developed through no more than four or five lines of writing. In effect, a point will be made and then given a sentence or two of development. This approach can never develop the depth of analysis required for essay success. A far more successful approach is to tackle only two or three themes (not points), then develop each one into a lengthy (perhaps half page) paragraph. Acquiring the skill of writing developed prose proves equally important in case study work as well.

Having completed your analysis of key themes to answer the question, it is time to write a fully reasoned conclusion. This should be focused upon the question, making judgements on the issues you have analysed. A conclusion is usually worth about one-third of the marks for an essay, so it is worth devoting plenty of time to it. Certainly no less than ten minutes.

To help you write a good essay, ten golden rules you should follow are set out below.

 Ten golden rules

1. There is no such thing as an essay about a topic

An essay is a response to a specific title. At A-level, the title is usually worded so that it cannot be answered by repeating paragraphs from your notes. Hence there is no such thing as 'the communications essay', because every answer should depend upon the title, not the topic. A past A-level essay question read 'When selling a good, price is the single most important factor. Evaluate this statement.' This popular question was widely misinterpreted and yielded low marks to candidates. The reason was that few students focused upon the words 'single most important'. They chose, instead, to consider price in relation to the remainder of the marketing mix. Therefore they failed to weigh up the market, economic or corporate factors that could lead price to become the single most important factor (or not, as the case may be).

2. There is no such thing as a one-sided essay

If the title asks you to consider that 'Change is inevitable' (as on a past question), do not fall into the trap of assuming that the examiner just wants you to prove it. If there was only one side to an answer, the question would not be worth asking. The only questions A-level examiners set are those which can provoke differing viewpoints. Therefore, after developing a strong argument in one direction, write 'On

- Competitive organisational structures, including centralisation and decentralisation, delayering and flexible workforces (this section draws heavily from AS organisational structure)

- Effective employer/employee relations, including communications, employee representation and industrial disputes

What are the key features of a Unit 3 paper?

Unit 3 papers do **not** have exactly the same structure. There is variation in the way the text is written and presented, in the number of questions and the marks allocated to each question. However, there are a number of common features and knowing about these will help you to prepare for the examination.

- The examination paper is based on a case study of around 600 words. It comes with extensive appendices providing supporting numerical data or graphs. This data is vital to a full understanding of the issues involved.

- Some of the data provides critical background information, such as whether sales are rising or falling; other parts are needed to answer questions directly, such as forecast cash flows that can be used within an investment appraisal.

- The data could include information that stems from AS units, such as market share, labour turnover or profit.

- The Unit 3 examination comprises three to five questions, with mark-ranges varying between 8 and 36. A typical pattern is: Q1. 12 marks, Q2. 16 marks, Q3. 18 marks, Q4. 34 marks

- There are 80 marks on the paper; as the time allocation is 1 hour and 45 minutes, you are able to take 20 minutes to read the case and weigh up the numerical data. This gives plenty of time for some preliminary calculations, such as market

trends or rates of return on capital. After 20 minutes, you have a mark a minute, plus an extra 5 minutes 'float time'.

- Typically, the case is based upon a strategic decision the business must take; your job is to recommend which option to take, and explain your reasoning. Examples might include:

- Should a business relocate from Britain to India?

- Should a business go ahead with a massive expansion plan?

- Should a retail business close down all its loss-making branches?

- Should a restaurant chain switch from pizza to pasta?

AQA Unit 3: key features

- Based on a case study of a business facing an important decision

- The case material is half-text and half-numerical data

- Covers all of the Unit 3 specification, but also draws from AS Units 1 and 2

- Relatively few, high-mark questions

- 80 marks in total for this paper

- The time available is 1 hour and 45 minutes

How should I prepare for and tackle Unit 3?

Revision

On Unit 3 there are 16 marks (20% of the total) for knowledge. This does not sound a high proportion, but it is important to remember that success at the other skills (such as analysis) depends entirely on the precision of your knowledge of terms and formulae. So knowledge-based revision is important, and will bear a huge potential reward.

Your revision should also mean that you have mastered the relevant theory. For example, you

need to be able to explain why a technique such as Ansoff's Matrix is so important for firms facing big marketing decisions.

As part of your revision for this examination it is vital that you go through the Unit 3 specification and tick off all the subjects that you have studied. Make sure that you identify and take action over any gaps that remain. In addition, you need to read through a summary of the AS material. Fortunately, this is provided within this book, so remember to reread Units 6, 15, 22 and 29.

Practising sample papers

You must practise using past papers. Your teacher or lecturer will have copies of the sample papers that have been written, as well as several actual papers that have been issued. The lead author of this book has written some sample Unit 3 papers, so by all means email him at marcouse@btopenworld.com. You will also find past papers on the AQA website (www.aqa.org.uk).

Practising past papers will help you to develop the skills listed below.

Making effective use of the information in the case study

All of the exam questions relate directly to the case material. This means that you have to have relevant knowledge and apply it to the circumstances in the case study. Make sure to answer in relation to *the* specific business in the case study, and not just any business. Twenty-four (of the 80) marks on the paper are for applying your knowledge to the case study, i.e. 30% of the marks. You will find it easier to get high marks for application if you manage to relate the numbers in the appendices to the story given in the text.

This means that you must read the case study carefully – do not rush it as you should not be short of time. Identify the distinctive features of the case. These may include issues such as the type and/or uniqueness of the product idea, the organisation of the staff and operations and the quality of the

financial planning. Other important information could relate to competitors or market growth. Remember some of the most important information might be expressed in numerical terms.

Recognising the differing demands of questions

- **Analysis questions.** Some questions require you to write analytically, that is, to develop arguments. Such questions ask you to examine or analyse a business situation, problem or opportunity. An example would be: 'Analyse the case for Coffee Delight plc expanding further in the UK'. This means you have to **explain why** Coffee Delight would benefit from expansion. Ideally, you would identify one or two broad explanations, and develop an extended paragraph on each. This requires you to write several linked sentences to develop your ideas beyond 'making a point' towards constructing a real argument.

- **Evaluation questions.** These are tough, high-mark questions that ask you to make a judgement or a decision. You can recognise them by the use of words such as 'evaluate', 'discuss' or 'justify' or the phrase 'to what extent'. You are expected to construct alternative arguments (perhaps, strategies) and to reach and support a decision. An example of such a question could be: 'To what extent do you consider Coffee Delight plc's "hard" human resource strategy to have been a success?'

Unit 3 examination skills		
Skill	Marks/80	Percentage
Marks for knowledge	16	20
Marks for applying answers to case study	24	30
Marks for analysis	20	25
Marks for making judgements or decisions	20	25

59 Tackling AQA Unit 4

What subject matter does Unit 4 cover?

The Unit 4 exam asks questions rooted in Unit 4 of the AQA specification. However, A2 examiners are asked to write questions that also draw from the AS material, i.e. the knowledge you acquired last year. In addition, Unit 4 can draw from Unit 3 material (in a general way). Therefore your revision needs to bear the whole course in mind.

Unit 4 is called 'The Business Environment and Managing Change'.

The heart of this material is to understand:

● Corporate Mission, Aims, Objectives and Strategy. Much of this material will draw from Unit 3, but focusing on the whole business, not on individual functions such as marketing

● Changes in the external context of business, e.g. the national and international economy, government actions, legislation and the social, environmental and ethical environment

● How businesses manage change, whether caused by internal or external factors; this section includes leadership styles and approaches plus big strategic issues such as takeovers and mergers and contingency planning

Within Unit 4 are three main content sections. Each content section then has a series of topics that need to be learnt in order to tackle the exam with confidence. They are:

1 Corporate aims and objectives
  ● Mission statements
  ● Corporate aims, objectives and strategies
  ● Differing stakeholder perspectives

2 Assessing changes in the business environment
  ● Economic factors that need to be understood include: the business cycle, interest rates, exchange rates, inflation, unemployment and economic growth. These must be understood in relation to the UK economy, but also the international economy with a specific look at emerging markets; the key will be understanding the strategies firms might use in response to – or anticipation of – economic change

  ● Assessing the effects of political and governmental changes, including the impact of legislation and free trade; this should also include government economic policies: fiscal, monetary and supply-side

  ● Assessing the impact of social, ethical and technological changes upon business, including an evaluation of the ways firms respond to different pressures

  ● Assessing the impact on firms of changes in competition, market structure and the competitive environment

3 Managing change
  ● Internal causes of change, including decisions relating to changes in corporate size and structure, such as takeovers or retrenchment

  ● Planning for change, to include contingency planning

  ● Leadership styles and the role of leaders in the management of change

  ● Types of organisational culture, to include the categories set out by Professor Charles Handy: 'power culture, entrepreneurial culture and task culture'; then assess the problems and methods for changing organisational culture

  ● Making strategic decisions, incorporating the distinction between scientific decisions and those based on hunch

  ● Implementing and managing change, to see how (and if) change can be achieved successfully

What are the key features of a Unit 4 paper?

The structure of the Unit 4 paper is easily stated. You must answer two questions, each carrying 40 marks. The first is based on a pre-issued research task plus an additional, short text provided on the exam paper (about half a side of writing). The second is an essay out of a choice of three titles. Both questions test the same skill of extended, developed writing. The first also tests your ability to retain and use information from your own, real-world research.

Unit 4 papers share these features:

- Comfortably in advance of the exam, your teacher will tell you the research theme for the exam you are doing, for example 'globalisation'. Your teacher will also pass on the further detail provided by AQA, which usually amounts to six bullet points of quite detailed explanation, e.g. 'social, environmental and ethical issues resulting from organisations operating more globally'. This pre-released research theme will apply only to the questions in Section A. In Section B are essay titles that are completely separate from the research task.

- To prepare for Section A, you will be expected to research every aspect of the theme, perhaps starting with Google, then moving on to newspaper and magazine articles. The exam board has emphasised the need to 'study these issues in the context of business case studies'.

- In the exam room, Section A gives you a choice

between two different topics based on the theme. Each question will come with around 200 words of supporting text, to give you something extra to go on. You choose between the questions, each of which will be worth 40 marks. An example of a 40-mark question provided by AQA is 'With reference to Articles A and B **and** your own research, discuss the view that global expansion is inevitably unethical.' Clearly, the phrasing of this question is the same as an essay.

- Section B of the paper provides three essay titles. You choose one. It is marked out of 40 and is therefore worth the same as the Section A task. As emphasised above, these essays are not related to the research task. Each is likely to have its own unique context. Your answer must be applied to that unique context.

> **AQA Unit 4: key features**
> - Covers all of the Unit 4 specification, but also draws from Units 1, 2 and 3.
> - Section A is based on a pre-issued research theme
> - Section B is a standard essay paper; you answer one from a choice of three.
> - You must answer two 40-mark questions
> - 80 marks in total for this paper
> - The time available is 1 hour and 45 minutes

How should I prepare for and tackle Unit 4?

Revision

On Unit 4 there are 16 marks (20% of the total) for knowledge. This does not sound a high proportion, but it is important to remember that success at the other skills (such as analysis) depends on the precision of your knowledge of terms and concepts. So knowledge-based revision is important, and will bear a huge potential reward.

Your revision should also mean that you have mastered the relevant theory. For example you need to be able to explain why business culture is so important for firms facing major changes.

As part of your revision for this examination it is vital that you go through the Unit 4 specification and tick off all the subjects that you have studied.

Make sure that you identify and take action over any gaps that remain. In addition, you need to read through the summaries of the AS material provided in Units 6, 15, 22 and 29 of this book, and check through your Unit 3 notes to get a broad understanding of key topics such as company accounts, Ansoff's Matrix, HR planning and lean production.

Practising sample papers

You must practise using past papers. Your teacher or lecturer will have copies of the sample papers that have been written, as well as the actual papers that have been issued. The lead author of this book has written some sample papers, so by all means email him at marcouse@btopenworld.com. You will also find past papers on the AQA website (www.aqa.org.uk).

Practising past papers will help you to develop the skills listed below.

Making effective use of time for the research task

- **Googling.** Naturally, you would start by putting the key word into Google. It might be 'Corporate Social Responsibility' (but the topic will change every year, so ask your teacher). In January 2011 the phrase 'Corporate Social Responsibility' threw up 19,000,000 Google references. But just by pressing 'News' near the top of the screen, the number of references fell to 2,700. These are newspaper articles that can then be sorted in date order. Exams are set about 18 months before you sit them, so it would be interesting to read some articles written at the time the exam was written. It also makes sense to bring things up to date, so also do that.

- **Business Review.** This magazine tackles business from the point of view of an A-level student. Once the year's Unit 4 research task has been publicised, articles will be commissioned that cover the topic in some detail. The magazine may also have covered the topic before, so ask your librarian for help in tracing earlier material.

- **Books.** When 'globalisation' was the research task, there was one book that any examiner would have read. *Globalisation and its Discontents* by Joseph Stiglitz was a worldwide best-seller. Top students make sure they read relevant books – so do ask your teacher whether there are any key texts.

Recognising the differing demands of questions

Evaluation questions. In this exam there is only one type of question: evaluative. Each question is marked out of 40, and each has exactly the same marks awarded per skill. Knowledge and Application each carry 8 marks per question, with Analysis receiving 10 marks and evaluation 14 marks. In other words, your style of answer for Section A and Section B should be no different. In each case Application is an important skill. The only difference is that for Section A, the application will come from your research prior to the exam. For Section B you will only be able to rely on the information provided in the essay title.

Unit 4 examination skills		
Skill	Marks/80	Percentage
Marks for knowledge	16	20
Marks for applying answers to case study	16	20
Marks for analysis	20	25
Marks for making judgements or decisions	28	35

Index